A History of Christianity in Asia, Africa, and Latin America, 1450-1990

A History of Christianity in Asia, Africa, and Latin America, 1450-1990

A Documentary Sourcebook

Edited by

Klaus Koschorke, Frieder Ludwig *&* Mariano Delgado

In cooperation with Roland Spliesgart

William B. Eerdmans Publishing Company

Grand Rapids, Michigan / Cambridge, U.K.

Wm. B. Eerdmans Publishing Co.
2140 Oak Industrial Drive N.E., Grand Rapids, Michigan 49505 /
P.O. Box 163, Cambridge CB3 9PU U.K.
www.eerdmans.com

Printed in the United States of America

12 11 10 09 08 07   7 6 5 4 3 2 1

Library of Congress Cataloging-in-Publication Data

A History of Christianity in Asia, Africa, and Latin America, 1450-1990:
    a documentary sourcebook / edited by Klaus Koschorke, Frieder
    Ludwig & Mariano Delgado; in cooperation with Roland Spliesgart.
        p.   cm.
    Includes index.
    ISBN 978-0-8028-2889-7 (pbk.: alk. paper)
    1. Asia — Church history.   2. Africa — Church history.
    3. Latin America — Church history.   I. Koschorke, Klaus.
    II. Ludwig, Frieder, 1961-   III. Delgado, Mariano, 1955-
    IV. Spliesgart, Roland.

BR145.3.H57   2007
270 — dc22

                                                        2007021105

We would like to thank those authors and publishers who kindly gave permission for
copyright material to be used in this source book.

Contents

117934

Preface

The map of World Christianity has changed dramatically in the last century. While Europe and North America provided 82% of the Christian world population around 1900, the majority of Christians today (almost 60% in 2000) live in Africa, Asia and Latin America. The gravity of Christianity will continue to shift southwards in the next decades. This has significant implications for the global ecumenical discourse. During our life time, Christianity has become a world religion as never before in its history.

The present volume takes the changing ecumenical conditions into account. It documents the history of Christianity in Asia, Africa and Latin America in comparative perspective and enlarges the horizon of classical church historiography. Our text selection starts with the middle of the fifteenth century — the beginning of Iberian expansion — and concludes with the end of the cold war in the early 1990s. It is, of course, true that Christianity in Asia and Africa is much more ancient. Nevertheless the Iberian expansion marks a turning point, since only from that period onwards was Christianity present in the 'New World' and connections between the churches of the three continents developed.

In contrast to the prevailing Western perspectives on the history of Christianity in Africa, Asia and Latin America, this documentary history strives to give a voice to the multitude of local initiatives, specific experiences and varieties of Christianity in very diverse cultural contexts. This volume documents the voices of indigenous Christians who address such questions as the colonial conquest, slavery and the demand for ecclesiastical independence. It also gives expression to the denominational and contextual plurality of these "non-Western" churches. At the same time, however, the chapters of the book introduce overarching themes and relate the specific developments in Africa, Asia and Latin America to a general history of world Christianity.

The volume was written for the teaching and learning of church history in the first place. It may be also of interest for students and professors of mission studies, religious studies and general history. It can be used for lectures focusing on African, Asian and Latin American church history as well as for general lectures on epochs in church history such as reformation history or contemporary church history.

History of Christianity in Asia, Africa and Latin America is the result of a long and intense cooperation. Klaus Koschorke (Munich/Germany) was responsible for the section on Asia, Frieder Ludwig (St. Paul/USA) for the documents on Africa and Mariano Delgado (Fribourg/Switzerland) for the Latin American chapters. The texts regarding Protestantism in Latin America, as well as some other Latin American texts (documents 257-258, 276-281, 285-289, 296, 298-300, 310-315, 317), were selected and introduced by Roland Spliesgart (Munich). The book was first published in German (Neukirchener Verlag, 2004) and was initiated and coordinated by Klaus Koschorke. This English edition was coordinated by Frieder Ludwig.

The conceptual frame for this book was developed in close cooperation with Johannes Meier (Mainz). Numerous colleagues — in the field of Church History, Missiology, Religious Studies, and Global history — commented upon the successive drafts.

Brice Cantrell, Dr. Margaret Griesse, Dr. Suzanne Hequet, Dr. Daniel Jeyaraj, Dr. Elizabeth Koepping, Martha Matesich, Jessica Nipp and Dr. John Roxborough and Margaret D. Wilde helped to translate documents and introductions into English. The responsibility remains with the respective area editor. Dr. Elizabeth Koepping did a marvellous job by introducing these documents to her students at the Centre for the Study of Christianity in the Non-Western World (Edinburgh/UK) and commenting upon various drafts of the English version. The proof-reading was done by Roy Harrisville (St. Paul). Special thanks are due to Victoria Smith (Luther Seminary, St. Paul) who edited the manuscript.

The Münchener Universitätsgesellschaft, Luther Seminary (St. Paul), the University of Friburg (Switzerland), Misereor (Aachen) and the Thyssen Stiftung (Cologne) provided generous financial support without which this publication would not have been possible.

KLAUS KOSCHORKE • FRIEDER LUDWIG • MARIANO DELGADO

Standard Works and Literature Quoted in Abbreviations

D. B. Barrett/G. T. Kurian/T. M. Johnson (eds.), *World Christian Encyclopedia. A comparative survey of churches and religions in the modern world*. 2 vols. (Oxford, ²2001) (Abb.: *WCE*)

J.-P. Bastian, *Geschichte des Protestantismus in Lateinamerika* (Luzern, 1995) (Abb.: Bastian, *Protestantismus*)

P. Borges, *Historia de la Iglesia en Hispanoamérica y Filipinas (Siglos XV-XIX)*. 2 Vols. (Madrid, 1992) (Abb.: Borges, *Historia*)

M. D. David (ed.), *Asia and Christianity* (Bombay, 1985)

M. Delgado (ed.), *Gott in Lateinamerika: Texte aus 5 Jahrhunderten* (Düsseldorf, 1991) (Abb.: Delgado, *Gott*)

M. Delgado, *Abschied vom erobernden Gott* (Immensee, 1996) (Abb.: Delgado, *Abschied*)

E. Dussel, *A History of the Church in Latin America* (Grand Rapids, 1981)

E. Dussel, *The Church in Latin America 1492-1992* (Maryknoll, 1992) (Abb.: Dussel, *Church*)

J. England et al. (eds.), *Asian Christian Theologies. A Research Guide to Authors, Movements, Sources*. 3 vols (Delhi/Quezon City/Maryknoll, 2002-2004) (Abb.: England, *ACT*)

H.-W. Gensichen, *Missionsgeschichte der neueren Zeit* (Göttingen, "1976)

S. Gilley/B. Stanley (eds.), "World Christianities c. 1815–c. 1914" (*The Cambridge History of Christianity*, Vol. 8) (Cambridge, 2006) (Abb.: Gilley/Stanley, *World Christianities*)

H. Gründer, *Welteroberung und Christentum* (Gütersloh, 1992) (Abb.: Gründer, *Welteroberung*)

A. Hastings, *A History of African Christianity 1950-1975* (Cambridge, 1979) (Abb.: Hastings, *Christianity*)

A. Hastings, *The Church in Africa* (Oxford, 1994) (Abb.: Hastings, *Africa*)

E. Isichei, *A History of Christianity in Africa* (London, 1995)

O. U. Kalu (ed.), *African Christianity: An African Story* (University of Pretoria, 2005) (Abb.: Kalu, *African Christianity*)

K. Koschorke, Art. "Asia. History of Christianity," in: *RPP* 1 (2006)

K. Koschorke (ed.), *"Christen und Gewürze." Konfrontation und Interaktion kolonialer und indigener Christentumsvarianten* (Göttingen, 1998)

K. Koschorke (ed.), *Transcontinental Links in the History of Non-Western Christianity* (Wiesbaden, 2002)

K. Koschorke (ed.), *African Identities and World Christianity in the Twentieth Century*, in cooperation with J.-H. Schjoerring (Wiesbaden 2005)

M. K. Kuriakose (ed.), *History of Christianity in India: Source materials* (Madras, 1982) (Abb.: Kuriakose, *History*)

B. de Las Casas, *Werkauswahl* (Selected Works). 4 Vols. edited by M. Delgado (Paderborn, 1994-1997) (Abb.: Las Casas, *WA*)

A. Langley, *Ideologies of Liberation in Black Africa 1856-1970* (London, 1979)

K. S. Latourette, *A History of the Expansion of Christianity*. Vols. 1-7 (Grand Rapids, ^{N}1976)

F. Ludwig/A. Adogame, *European Traditions in the Study of Christianity in Africa* (Wiesbaden, 2004) (Abb.: Ludwig/Adogame, *European Traditions*)

S. H. Moffett, *A History of Christianity in Asia*. Vol. I: *Beginnings to 1500;* Vol. II: *1500-1900* (San Francisco etc., 1998/Maryknoll, 2005) (Abb. Moffett, *Asia*)

H. McLeod (ed.), "World Christianities c. 1914–c. 2000" (*The Cambridge History of Christianity*, Vol. 9) (Cambridge 2006) (Abb.: McLeod, *World Christianities*)

S. Neill, *A History of Christian Missions* (London 1990)

S. Neill, *History of Christianity in India*. 2 vols. (Cambridge 1984/85) (Abb.: Neill, *History*)

J.-M. Mayeur a.o. (eds.), *Geschichte des Christentums*. 14 vols. (Freiburg i.B. etc. 1991-2004) (Abb.: Mayeur, *Geschichte*)

H.-J. Prien, *Die Geschichte des Christentums in Lateinamerika* (Göttingen 1978) (Abb.: Prien, *Geschichte*)

W. Raupp (ed.), *Mission in Quellentexten. Geschichte der Deutschen Evangelischen Mission von der Reformation bis zur Weltmissionskonferenz Edinburg 1910* (Erlangen 1990) (Abb.: Raupp, *Mission*)

E. Schmitt (ed.), *Dokumente zur Geschichte der europäischen Expansion*. Vols 1-5 (München 1984ff.) (Abb.: Schmitt, *Dokumente*)

B. Sundkler/C. Steed, *A History of the Church in Africa* (Cambridge 2000) (Abb. Sundkler/Steed, *History*)

S. W. Sunquist a.o. (eds.), *A dictionary of Asian Christianity* (Grand Rapids 2001) (Abb. Sunquist, *Dictionary*)

T. K. Thomas (ed.), *Christianity in Asia. North-East Asia* (Singapore 1979)

Abbreviations and Omissions

[ ]   Square brackets within the documents indicate editorial comments.

[. . .]   Omissions within the documents which are longer than a sentence are indicated by square brackets and three points.

. . .   Omissions which are not longer than a sentence are indicated by three points.

TRE   Theologische Realenzyklopädie, 36 vols., Berlin 1976-2004

RGG⁴   Religion in Geschichte und Gegenwart, fourth edition, 8 vols., Tübingen 1998-2004

RPP   Religion in Past and Present. Encyclopedia of Theology & Religion, 10 vols., Leiden 2006-2011 (English version of the fourth edition of Religion in Geschichte und Gegenwart).

ASIA

I. ASIA 1450-1600

A. Christians in Asia before the Arrival of the Portuguese

1. St. Thomas Christians in India

The arrival of the Portuguese in Calicut in 1498 may have signified a new epoch of Asian Christian history. By no means, however, did it represent the beginning of a Christian presence on the continent whose origin can be traced back to early times. In India, reliable sources indicate the continual existence of Christian congregations from the third century CE to the present day. From the seventh century Indian congregations belonged to the network of the Nestorian "Church of the East," whose influence during the pinnacle of its expansion in the thirteenth and fourteenth centuries extended from Mesopotamia into Central Asia and China, and from Siberia to South India. In the Middle Ages, European sojourners such as Marco Polo and John of Monte Corvino repeatedly provide accounts of Christianity in India. One fifteenth century document is the testimony of the Venetian merchant Nicolò Conti, who traveled in India between 1415 and 1439 (a). Document b provides an early sixteenth century portrayal of conditions in India from the perspective of the Indian St. Thomas Christians. This is excerpted from a letter written in India in 1504 to the Patriarch of the Nestorian Church — Catholicos Mar Simeon — by a delegation of Indian clergy members after their return from Mesopotamia. They had visited the Patriarch in Mesopotamia and he had ordained them to the offices of priest or bishop.

a. Testimony of the Italian traveler Nicolò Conti (1415-1439)

Proceeding onwards the said Nicolò arrived at a maritime city, which is named Malepur [Mylapore, in Southeast India], situated in the second gulf beyond the Indus [Bay of Bengal]. Here the body of St. Thomas lies honourably buried in a very large and beautiful church. It is venerated by heretics, who are called Nestorians, and inhabit this city to the number of a thousand. These Nestorians are scattered all over India, in like manner as are the Jews among us. All this province is called Malabar.

b. A Syrian Document from c. 1504

Now we would inform thy love [Catholikos Mar Simeon] that by the assistance of God, and through thy accepted prayers, we arrived in the blessed country of India in good health. Thanks be to God, the Lord of all who does not confound those who trust in him! All the Christians of this side were greatly pleased with us, and our Father Mar John is still alive and hale and sends thee his greetings. There are here about thirty thousand families of Christians, our co-religionists, and they implore the Lord to grant thee a long life. They have begun to build new churches, are prosperous in every respect, and living in peace and security. . . . As to the monastery of St. Thomas the Apostle, some Christian men have gone into it, have inhabited it, and are now busy restoring it. . . . It is . . . in a town called Mylapore, in the country of Silan, one of the Indian countries. The countries of India are very numerous and powerful, . . . and our country in which the Christians are found is called Malabar [in present Kerala]. It has about twenty towns, out of which three are renowned and powerful: Karangol, Pallur and Kullam. . . . They contain Christians and churches, and are in the vicinity of the large and powerful city of Calicut, the inhabitants of which are idol-worshipping pagans.

Source: (a) R. H. Major (ed.), *India in the 15th Century. Being a Collection of Narratives of Voyages to India. The Travels of Nicolò Conti in the East, as related by Poggio Bracciolini* . . . (London, 1857), p. 7; (b) G. Schurhammer, *The Malabar Church and Rome during the Early Portuguese Period and Before* (Trichinopoly, 1934), pp. 1-10 (translated from: J. S. Assemani, *Bibliotheca Orientalis* . . . (Rome, 1758), 3/1, 589-599. — *Further Reading:* Neill, *History* 1, pp. 26-86; A. Mingana, *The Early Spread of Christianity in India* (Manchester, 1926), pp. 36-41; M. Mundadan, *The Arrival of the Portuguese in India and the Thomas Christians under Mar Jacob 1498-1552* (Bangalore, 1967). — *Further Reading, general:* J. C. England, *The Hidden History of Christianity in Asia: The Churches of the East before 1500* (Hong Kong, 1996); I. Gillman/H.-J. Klimkeit, *Christians in Asia before 1500* (Ann Arbor, 1999); S. H. Moffett, *A History of Christianity in Asia.* Vol. 1 (San Francisco, 1991); C. Baumer, *Frühes Christentum zwischen Euphrat und Jangtse* (Stuttgart, 2005) (An Illustrated History of the Eastern Churches); England, *ACT* I, 3-26.

2. Nestorians and Armenian Christians in Southern Asia (1508)

In the years 1503-1507 the Italian Ludovico di Varthema journeyed through Egypt, Arabia, Persia and India, and possibly further. Whether or not he continued his travels to the Malayan Peninsula, the Molucca Islands and Java, as described in his "Itinerario de Ludovico di Varthema Bolognese nello Egypto," published in Rome in 1510, is answered in various ways among scholars. He was a talented linguist and his detailed and accurate descriptions of these regions may simply stem from local oral traditions that he picked up. However his accounts provided Europe with new information about trade routes across the Indian Ocean. He also recorded the existence of scattered groups of Christians (Nestorians and Armenians) living in various regions of South Asia (India, Thailand, Burma) at the beginning of the sixteenth century.

And so we departed . . . and arrived at a city which is called Cacolon [Kâyankullam, in South India], distant from Calicut fifty leagues. The king of this city is a pagan and is not very rich. The manner of living, the dress, and the customs, are after the manner of Calicut. Many merchants arrived here, because a great deal of pepper grows in this country, and in perfection. In this city we found some [Nestorian] Christians of those of Saint Thomas, some of whom are merchants, and believe in Christ, as we do. These say that every three years a priest comes there to baptize them, and that he comes to them from Babylon [Mesopotamia]. [. . .] These Christians keep Lent longer than we do; but they keep Easter like ourselves, and they all observe the same solemnities that we do. But they say mass like the [Orthodox] Greeks [and revere four saints above all], that is to say: John, James, Matthew, and Thomas. The country, the air, and the situation, resemble those of Calicut.

[In Indian Bengal] we also found some Christian merchants. They said that they were from a city called Sarnau [Ayutthaya, capital of Thailand], and had brought for sale silken stuffs, and aloes-wood, and benzoin, and musk, These Christian said that in their country there were many lords also Christians, but they are subject to the great Khan [of] Cathay [China]. As to the dress of these Christians, they were clothed in a *xebec* [jerkin] made with folds, and the sleeves were quilted with cotton. And on their heads they wore a cap a palm and a half long, made of red cloth. These same men are as white as we are, and confess that they are Christians, and believe in the Trinity, and likewise in the Twelve Apostles, in the four Evangelists, and they also have baptism with water. But they write in the contrary way to us, that is, after the manner of *Armenia*. And they say that they keep the Nativity and the Passion of Christ, and observe our Lent and other vigils in the course of the year. These Christians do not wear shoes, but they wear a kind of breeches made of silk, similar to those worn by marines, which breeches are all full of jewels, and their heads are covered with jewels. . . . These people also said that they knew that on the confines of the *Rumi*, that is, of the Grand Turk, there are very great Christian kings. [. . .]

The city of Pego [Pegu, in present day Myanmar/Burma] is on the mainland, and is near to the sea. On the left hand of this, that is toward the east, there is a very beautiful river. . . . The king of this city is a pagan. Their faith, customs, manner of living and dress, are after the manner of Tarnassari; but with respect to their colour, they are somewhat more white. . . . This city is walled, and has good houses and palaces built of stone, with lime. The king is extremely powerful in men, both foot and horse, and has with him more than a thousand Christians of the country which has been above mentioned to you [Thailand]. And he gives to each, for pay, six golden *pardai* per month and his expenses. [. . .]

Source: J. W. Jones, G. P. Badger (eds.), *The Travels of Ludovico di Varthema in Egypt, Syria, Arabia . . . , Persia, India, and Ethiopia,* A.D. *1503 to 1510.* Translated from the Original Italian Edition of 1510 (London, 1863), pp. 79-181, 212-214, 215-218. Cf. also: L. D. Hammond (ed.), *Travelers in Disguise: Narrative of Eastern Travel* (Cambridge, 1963). — *Further Reading:* D. F. Lach, *Asia in the Making of Europe.* Vol. 1/2 (Chicago, 1965); Schmitt, *Dokumente 2,* pp. 227-230 (Bibliography).

3. Jews and Christians in China

After the fall of the Yuan Dynasty in 1368, Chinese and European reports on Nestorian communities in China virtually cease. However various accounts and archaeological findings document a continual Jewish presence (a) and the letters of Jesuit Matteo Ricci at the beginning of the seventeenth century also refer to the remnants of ancient Christian communities in China (b, c).

a. Jews in Kaifeng: The Stele of 1489

A stone inscription in front of the synagogue of Kaifeng gives evidence of its reconstruction in 1489 after having been flooded by the Yellow river:

Ai Ching and others presented a petition to the provincial Commissioner, requesting [and receiving] permission to reconstruct the synagogue according to the ancient synagogue of Chih-yüan [i.e., 1279].

b. Matteo Ricci on the Jews of Kaifeng (1605)

Some of us learned from a Jew that there are ten or twelve Jewish families in Kaifeng-fu, the capital of the Honan province, who have a beautiful synagogue that they have recently restored at the cost of 10,000 ducats. In the synagogue the Jews kept with much veneration the Pentateuch of Moses. . . . They number only a few families and, as far as we know, they have no synagogues elsewhere except in Kaifeng-fu, the capital of Honan province and in Hangchow-fu, the capital of Chekiang province. They lived there [in Kaifeng] for 500 or 600 years and many more families of their co-religionists with a synagogue stayed in Hangchow, the capital of Chekiang, and also in other parts, but [there] without a synagogue. However, they gradually vanished by dying out.

c. Matteo Ricci on the Remnants of Chinese Christianity (1605)

Letter from July 26, 1605:

A few days ago we learned that in the central region of China there lived for 500 years a considerable number of Christians and that there have remained important traces of them in many place. During the past three years I have written to you, Venerable Father [P. Claudio Acquaviva], that we have discovered a Christian community in territory conquered by China, but [they lived] outside of the Great North Wall. Until now, for the lack of a few ducats to undertake this trip, we have not sent anybody to investigate how many there are and where they came from. Now we know that in the central part of China, half a month's [travel] from here and equally far from Nanjing, there live five or six Christian families in Kaifeng-fu, the capital of Honan province. But, what little there existed of Christianity is almost entirely extinguished due to the fact that already several years ago their Church was changed into a temple of idols, called *Quanguam*. [. . .]

We learned [about the Christians in Kaifeng] through a Jew by profession of his faith [literally: "law"], nationality, and features, who came to visit me during the past days because he had heard of my reputation and because of the many printed books concerning our activities. He, therefore, understood that we were neither Moors nor gentiles and thought that we were of his faith. This man, whose surname was Ai, lived in the capital of Honan province. [. . .]

He said that they [the Chinese Jews] had preserved the tradition that many Moors, Christians and Jews had come with the king Tamerlane, when he conquered the whole of Persia and also China 800 years ago and that the Moors were predominant, while the Christians and Jews remained [only] a few. In the Honan region, however, there existed all of the three sects, although the Christian one was almost extinct.

Source: (a) D. D. Leslie, *The Survival of the Chinese Jews: The Jewish Community of Kaifeng* (Leiden, 1972), p. 29; (b) *Opere storiche del P. Matteo Ricci S.I.* Vol. 1: *I Commentari della Cina* (Macerata, 1911), pp. 469f; (c) R. Löwenthal, "The Early Jews in China . . ." (Folklore Studies 5, 1946, 353-398), 396f; cf. D. D. Leslie, *The Survival* . . . pp. 31f. — *Further Reading:* A. C. Moule, *Christians in China before the Year 1550* (New York, 1930), pp. 1-26; W. Ch. White, *Chinese Jews: A Compilation of Matters Relating to the Jews of K'ai-fêng Fu* (Toronto, 1966); R. Malek (ed.), *From Kaifeng to Shanghai: Jews in China* (Nettetal, 2000), pp. 30ff; Sunquist, *Dictionary*, pp. 139-146 (Art. China); England, *ACT* I, 10ff; N. Standaert (ed.), *Handbook of Christianity in China. Vol. I: 635-1800* (Leiden etc., 2001).

B. EARLY PORTUGUESE CONTACTS

4. Searching for "Christians and Spices" (1498)

On May 20, 1498, a Portuguese squadron under the command of Vasco da Gama landed in Southeast India near the trade center of Calicut. With this landing, the Portuguese, who had sailed around Africa (see document 115) and from East Africa across the Indian Ocean, achieved the elusive breakthrough of a direct sea route to Asia, for which Christopher Columbus' expeditions since 1492 (see document 218) utilizing the westward Atlantic route, had searched in vain. An account of Vasco da Gama's first trip to India in 1498 is available in the form of the *"Roteiro,"* an eyewitness account by an anonymous crew member. The following excerpt from this account reveals both the ideological and economic motives of the Portuguese who hoped to find "Christians and spices" in Asia, and the intercultural misunderstandings that were unavoidable.

And on Sunday we sailed past some mountains that tower over the city of Calicut, and we sailed so close to them that the ship's navigator recognized them and said this was the country we were trying to reach. And in the afternoon on that same day we dropped anchor, two leagues below the city of Calicut. [. . .]

And after we were anchored four rowboats came to us from shore. They came to find out who we were, and they showed us Calicut and told us its name. In the same way these rowboats came back to our ship on the other day, and the captain sent one of the exiles to Calicut and the people whom he accompanied brought him to a place where two Moors from Tunis lived, who could speak Castilian and Genoese, and the first thing they cried out to him was, "Go to hell! Who brought you here, anyway?"

They asked what we were looking for so far from home, and he answered, "We came to look for Christians and spices." They said to him, "Why hasn't the king of Castile sent anyone here, or the king of France, or the Signoria of Venice?" And he answered them that the King of Portugal would not tolerate that from the other countries, and they said that he would be well advised to do so.

Then they fed him wheat bread and honey, and after he ate he came back to the ships and one of the Moors came with him. And as the Moor came on board, his first words were, "Welcome, welcome! Many rubies, many emeralds! Get down on your knees and thank God that he brought you to this land of so many riches!" Hearing him speak we were very surprised and we could hardly believe that there was a man so far from Portugal who understood our language.

Source: A. Herculano/A. Castello de Paiva (eds.), *Roteiro da Viagem de Vasco da Gama em MCCCCXCVII.* (Lisboa², 1861), pp. 61-81. — *Further Reading:* C. R. Boxer, *The Portuguese Seaborne Empire 1415-1825* (Exeter, ^R1991); A. Disney/E. Booth (eds.), *Vasco da Gama and the Linking of Europe and Asia* (Oxford, etc., 2000); K. M. Panikkar, *Malabar and the Portuguese* (Bombay, 1929); F. M. Rogers, *The Quest for Eastern Christians: Travels and Rumors in the Age of Discovery* (Minneapolis, 1962); Neill, *History* I, pp. 87ff; K. Koschorke (ed.), *Christen und Gewürze* (Göttingen, 1998); G. J. Ames, *Vasco da Gama* (New York, etc., 2005).

5. Fictitious and Actual Contacts with the St. Thomas Christians

At first, the Portuguese considered everything non-Muslim to be Christian and celebrated their first worship service on Indian soil in a Hindu Temple by mistake (a). The gifts offered by the Europeans, who had grown used to African expectations, were found quite inadequate and were rejected by the Indian rulers (b). It was only later, on the second Portuguese expedition to Asia in 1500 under the command of Pedro Álvarez Cabral which led incidentally to the discovery of Brazil, that the Portuguese made contact with actual St. Thomas Christians. They also then realized that the king and inhabitants of Calicut were Hindus, not Christians (c).

a. Visiting a "Church" in Calicut (1498)

The city of Calicut is inhabited by Christians. . . . They are of tawny complexion. Some of them have big beards and long hair, whilst others clip their hair short or shave the head. [. . .] On the following morning, which was Monday, May 28th [1498], the captain-major [Vasco da Gama] set out to speak to the king, and took with him thirteen men, with me among them. We put on our best clothes for the occasion and we took bombards onto the boat with us and many trumpets and flags. On landing, the captain-major was received by the *alcaide*, with whom were many men, armed and unarmed. The reception was friendly, as if the people were pleased to see us [. . .].

They took us to a large church, and this was what we saw: The body of the church is as large as a monastery, all built of hewn bronze as high as a mast, on the top of which was perched a bird, apparently a cock. In addition to this, there was another pillar as high as a man, and very stout. In the center of the body of the church rose a chapel, all built of hewn stone, with a bronze door sufficiently wide for a man to pass, and stone steps leading up to it. Within this sanctuary stood a small image which they said represented Our Lady. Along the walls, by the main entrance, hung seven small bells. In this church the captain-major said his prayers, and we with him.

We did not go within the chapel, for it is the custom that only certain servants of the church, called *quafees*, should enter. These *quafees* wore some threads passing over the left shoulder and under the right arm, in the same manner as our deacons wear the stole. They threw holy water over us, and gave us some white earth, which the Christians of this country are in the habit of putting on their foreheads, breasts, around the neck, and on the forearms. They threw holy water upon the captain-major and gave him some of the earth, which he gave in charge to someone, giving them to understand that he would put it on later. Many other saints were painted on the walls of the church, wearing crowns. They were painted variously, with teeth protruding an inch from the mouth, and four or five arms. Below this church there was a large masonry tank, similar to many others which we had seen along the road.

b. Failure with the Samorin in Calicut (1498)

The king [the Samorin of Calicut], when he joined the captain-major [Vasco da Gama], threw himself upon another couch, covered with various stuffs embroidered in gold, and asked the captain-major what he wanted.

And the captain-major told him he was the ambassador of the King of Portugal, who was Lord of many countries and the possessor of great wealth of every description, exceeding that of any king of these parts; that for a period of sixty years his ancestors had annually sent out vessels to make discoveries in the direction of India, as they knew that there were Christian kings there like themselves. This, he said, was the reason which induced them to order this country to be discovered, not because they sought for gold or silver, for of this they had such abundance that they needed not what was to be found in this country. [. . .] In reply to this the king said that he was welcome; that, on his part, he held him as a friend and brother, and would send ambassadors with him to Portugal. [. . .]

On Tuesday [May 29], the captain-major got ready the following things to be sent to the king, viz., twelve pieces of lambel, four scarlet hoods, six hats, four strings of coral, a case containing six wash-hand basins, a case of sugar, two casks of oil, and two of honey. As it is the custom not to send anything to the king without the knowledge of the Moor, his factor, and of the Bayle, the captain-major informed them of his intention. They came, and when they saw the present they laughed at it, saying that it was not a thing to offer to a king, that the poorest merchant from Mecca, or any other part of India, gave more, and that if he wanted to make a present it should be in gold, as the king would not accept such things. [. . .]

It wounded our pride to be treated so shamefully by a king. [. . .] But we did not blame him overmuch, for we knew that we were a nuisance to the Moors who lived here. They were merchants from Mecca and from many other areas, and they knew us [and slandered us to the Samorin]. [. . .] On a Wednesday, the 29th [of August 1498], the captain-major decided to set sail, since he was of the opinion that we had already found that which we had sought — spices and jewels — and because we were not able to take our leave of the inhabitants of the land in peace and brotherhood, and so we set sail without delay and set out on our return journey to Portugal.

c. The Mission of Cabral (1500)

The city [Calicut] is large and has no wall around it [. . .]. The king is an idolater, although others [Vasco da Gama and his companions] have believed that they are Christians. These have not learned so much about their customs as we who have had considerable trade relations in Calicut. This king they call *Gnaffer*. Almost all his nobles and the people who serve him are men dark as Moors. And they are well-built men, and go nude above and below the waist. [. . .]

We were twelve or fifteen days . . . a distance from Cucchin [Cochin], at a place called Carangallo [Cranganore]. In this place there are Christians, Jews, Moors, and infidels [Zafaras]. Here we found a Jewess of Seville who came by way of Cairo and Mecca, and from there two other Christians came with us; they said that they wished to go to Rome and to Jerusalem. The captain had great pleasure with these two men. [. . .]

This lord of Cochin sent his ambassadors with these ships to this Most Serene King [of Portugal] and also two hostages, who returned in safety. On their return the Moors and people of Calicut made plans to capture them [the Portuguese] and armed more than one hundred and fifty small ships with more than fifteen thousand men. However, since they had cargoes, they did not wish to fight. Those could not attack them because these sailed with a side wind which they could not use.

In coming they reached an island where is the body of Saint Thomas, the Apostle. The lord of this treated them very kindly, and, having given them relics of the aforesaid saint, asked them to take spices from him on credit until the return voyage. They were laden and could not take more. They have been fourteen months on the voyage but only four on the return, and they say that in the future they can make it in eight months or ten at the most.

Source: (a) E. G. Ravenstein (ed.), *A Journal of the First Voyage of Vasco da Gama, 1497-1499* (London, 1898) (Reprint New York, ca. 1964), pp. 47-55; (b) ibid., pp. 58-76 (slightly altered); (c) *The Voyage of Pedro Alvares Cabral to Brazil and India.* Translated . . . by W. B. Greenlee (New Dehli/Madras, 1995), pp. 78f, 86, 121f. — *Further Reading:* A. Disney/H. Booth (eds.), *Vasco da Gama and the Linking of Europe and Asia* (Oxford, 2000); A. M. Mundadan, *History of Christianity in India I* (Bangalore, 1984), pp. 242ff, 255ff.

6. The Arrival of the Portuguese from an Arab Perspective

The Arab chronicler Kutb-ad-din at Nahrawali in the sixteenth century:

One of the astonishing and extraordinary events of the beginning of the tenth century after the Hedschra has been the arrival of the cursed Portuguese in India. They are a nation of the damnable Franks [i.e., Europeans]. One of their bands had put in at the strait of Ceuta, got as far as the [Sea of] Darkness and passed the Mountains of Al-Komr, where the Nile originates. [Before they reached the west coast of India, while they were still on the east coast of Africa,] they attempted to acquire information about this sea [the Indian Ocean]. They went on in this fashion until they appointed an experienced [Arab] sailor named Ahmad Ibn Malid as navigator. The leader of the Franks . . . had met him and the Portuguese admiral bewitched him. This sailor — he was drunken — revealed the route to the admiral. . . . In Goa, which is the name of a place on the coast of Decan currently in the hand of the Franks — they built a fort [. . .]. Further provisions from Portugal arrived without delay; they began to clash with the Muslims, took prisoners and plundered. They took every ship violently and inflicted great losses on the Muslims as well as all the other sea-folk.

Source: A. da Silva Rego/T. W. Baxter (eds.), *Documentos sobre os Portugueses em Moçambique e na Africa central 1497-1840.* Vol. I (Lisboa, 1962), pp. 32-35.

7. St. Thomas Christians on the Arrival of the Portuguese (1504)

Excerpt from a letter of St. Thomas Christian clerics to the Catholicos Mar Symeon, head of the Nestorian "Church of the East," from c. 1504:

Let it be also known to you, O Fathers, that the king of the Christians of the West, who are the Franks our brethren, sent to this country [India] powerful ships, and they were a whole year on the sea before they reached us. They came in a southerly direction on the other side of [the ocean from] the country of Ethiopia, that is to say, [from] Habash (Negroes), and they arrived at this country of India, where they bought pepper and other similar spices, and they returned to their country. Then they studied the way and learned it well. Thereupon the above-mentioned king, may God preserve his life, sent six large ships which reached the town of Calicut in six months because they had studied and learned the sea route. Now in the town of Calicut there are many Mohammedans, whom envy has enraged and maddened against Christians. They accused them before the pagan king, uttered lies concerning them, and said: 'These men have come from the West, and seen thy country and thy beautiful towns; they will return to their king and they will bring numerous armies on ships against thee; they will besiege thee, and take thy country from thee. [. . .]'

A lengthy account follows, describing the struggles between the Portuguese on the one side and the Muslims and the Samorin of Calicut on the other side, which ended with the defeat of the latter. It follows an account of the first contact of the delegation of St. Thomas Christians returning from Mesopotamia with the Portuguese:

There were about twenty men from them in the town of Cannanore, when we arrived from the town of Omruz to the Indian town of Cannanore; we went to them and told them that we were Christians, and narrated to them our story.

They were pleased with us, and gave us beautiful garments [as a gift]. . . . We remained with them two and a half months, and they ordered us one day to say mass. They have prepared for themselves a beautiful place, like a chapel, and their priests say their mass in it every day, as is their custom. On the Sunday, therefore, of Nusardail [the sixth Sunday after Trinity in the East Syrian Calendar], after their priest had finished his mass, we also went and said mass, at which they were greatly pleased with us. After that, we left them and went to our Christians, who were eight days distant from there.

Source: G. Schurhammer, *The Malabar Church and Rome during the Early Portuguese Period and Before* (Trichinopoly, 1934), pp. 2ff. — *Further Reading:* A. M. Mundadan, *The Arrival of the Portuguese in India and the Thomas Christians under Mar Jacob 1498-1552* (Bangalore, 1967), pp. 67, 70ff.

C. The Organization of Colonial Churches

8. Portuguese and Spanish Patronage in Mission

The division of the non-European world into Spanish and Portuguese spheres of influence, as decreed by Pope Alexander VI in the 1493 bull *Inter cetera* (see document 223a), and modified by the treaties of Tordesilla of 1494 and of Zaragoza in 1529, meant that the Philippine islands, effectively taken into possession 1565, became a Spanish colony, while the rest of Asia was allotted to the Portuguese. The two forms of colonial rule differed greatly. While the Portuguese were mainly interested in safeguarding their Asian trade monopoly, and never really got beyond a system of maritime bases with limited land possession, the Philippine Islands under Spanish rule experienced a far-reaching colonial presence. However the model of royal ecclesiastical patronage in mission was common to both Iberian powers. In return for a commitment to provide for the spreading of the Catholic faith in their territories, the colonial churches were subordinated to the control of the crown. This *patronate real* was anchored in a series of papal bulls that supported Portugal's claim to Asia and Africa (a), and described the rights and duties of the Spanish rulers in the Philippines and the Americas. The Spaniards interpreted their rights exclusively and sought to stop Rome's involvement whenever they could. In a statute from 16 March 1580, Philip II authorized his governor in the Philippines to immediately fill church positions as they became free (b). See also document 229.

a. The Papal Bull "Inter cetera" from Pope Calixtus III (1456)

Moreover by [our] aforementioned [papal] authority and with [our certain] knowledge, we determine, ordain, and appoint forever that ecclesiastical and all ordinary jurisdiction, lordship, and power in ecclesiastical matters only, in islands, villages, harbors, lands, and places acquired and to be acquired from [the

African] capes Bojador and Nam, through all of Guinea, and past that southern shore all the way to the [area of the] Indians, the position, number, nature, appellations, designations, boundaries, and localities of which we wish to be considered as expressed by this writing, shall belong and pertain to said knights and the [military] Order [of Christ] for all time. With these words we grant and give them [the Portuguese King Afonso, etc.] these [privileges] from now onwards, by the aforementioned [papal] authority and [certain] knowledge. [...]

Given in Rome in Saint Peter, in the year 1455 after the Incarnation of our Lord, on the third day before the Ides of March [13 March], in the first year of our pontificate.

b. The Exercise of Patronage in the Philippines (1580)

Due both to the great distance between the Kingdoms [of Spain] and the Philippines, and to the problems which may arise when a benefice lies vacant until we [Philipp II] present a successor to it, we hereby instruct the civil and military Governors of the named islands, whenever any Dignitaries, Cathedral Canons and Sinecure holders in the Metropolitan church are free, to present such people to the living as are suitable and possess the appropriate qualities, replacing their predecessor's position and with the same stipend. In presenting the candidate, the rules of Patronage must be maintained.

Source: (a) *Monumenta Henricina.* Vol. 12 (1454-1456) (Coimbra, 1971), pp. 286-288; (b) *Recopilación de Leyes de los Reynos de las Indias.* Vol. I (Madrid, 1791) (^{R}1973), pp. 40-41 (Book I, Title VI, Law 16). — *Further Reading:* Sunquist, *Dictionary,* pp. 623-627 (Art. Padroado); A. da Silva Rego, *Le Patronage Portugais de l'Orient* (Lissabon, 1957); C. R. Boxer, *The Church Militant and Iberian Expansion, 1440-1770* (1978); T. R. de Souza, "The Portuguese in Asia and Their Church Patronage," in: M. D. David (ed.), *Western Colonialism in Asia and Christianity* (Bombay, 1988), pp. 11-29.

9. Goa as a Political and Ecclesiastical Center

Seized in 1510, the Indian city of Goa became the headquarters of the political administration of the Portuguese "Estado da Índia" in 1530. In 1534 it also became the seat of the bishopric, and in 1558 was raised to the rank of a metropolitan church, to which by the end of the century ten suffragan dioceses in India, Malaya, China and Japan were subordinated. The boundaries of the bishopric of Goa, as claimed by the church authorities, lay both within and outside of the Portuguese-controlled areas of Asia, and extended from the Cape of Good Hope in Africa all the way to China. Even after the demise of the Portuguese colonial kingdom in the seventeenth century, Goa remained in Portuguese possession until reclaimed by India in 1961.

a. The Raising of Goa to the Seat of the Bishopric (1534)

In 1534, Goa became the seat of the bishopric. The Papal Bull *Romanus pontifex* from Pope Paul III, 8 July 1539, defined the borders of the newly created diocese:

By the power of our apostolic authority, we ordain and order permanently that the boundaries of the Diocese of Goa shall extend from the Cape of Good Hope until and including India and from India to China, including all localities both on solid land and on islands, in all discovered and yet undiscovered areas, in which the aforementioned King John [of Portugal], we have heard, maintains fortresses and several cities, camps and sites in which a great number of those [Indian] Christians converted to the true faith as well as many Portuguese live. This is on the condition that the abovementioned King John readily agrees.

b. Complaints about the Immorality of Settlers and Clergy

The Dominican Friar Duarte Nunes, Apostolic Commissioner, in a letter to the Portuguese King on 12 January 1522:

As regards the life of the clergy and friars who are outside the monasteries, for the most part they are very corrupt, and through their bad example the piety of the Christians of the country is gravely destroyed. So let your highness send some person of upright life and well instructed, to bring them to a better state. For if this is not done, they will be of very little service to God or to your highness.

The Jesuit Friar Lancilotto around 1555:

There are innumerable Portuguese who buy droves of girls and sleep with all of them and this is known publicly. This is carried to such excess that there was one man in Malacca who had twenty-four women of various races, all his slaves and all of whom he enjoyed. . . . But other men, as soon as they can afford to buy a female slave, almost always use her as a girl friend *(amiga)*, beside many other dishonourable proceedings in my poor understanding.

c. Position of the Non-Christians (1522)

The Dominican Friar Duarte Nunes on 12 January 1522:

It would be a service to God to destroy these [Hindu] temples, just in this island of Goa, and to replace them by churches with saints. Anyone who wishes to live in this island should become a Christian, and in that case may retain his lands and houses just as he has them at present; but, if he is unwilling, let him leave the islands. . . . It may be that these people will not become good Christians, but their children will be . . . and so God will be served, and also your highness, by becoming the cause of salvation to so many lost Souls.

d. The Introduction of the Inquisition in Goa (1543)

In this very year [1543] it came to pass that a bachelor of medicine residing in Goa, named Jeronimo Dias, of the caste of New Christians, in the course of familiar discourses with his friends, spoke of certain things which were against our holy faith. The bishop, on being informed of this, ordered that he should be arrested and tried and that witnesses should be examined. When arrested, together with certain other persons who had discoursed with him, he continue to uphold certain things of the old law against our holy faith, all of which showed clearly that he was a Jew, and the proceedings were concluded. The bishop thereupon went to the residence of the Governor where a council was held, at which were also present the teacher Diogo [Borba], Friar Antonio, commissary of St. Francis and preacher, another Dominican preacher and the Vicar General [Miguel Vaz]. Having seen the papers of the case, they pronounced sentence, which was signed by the Bishop and ran as follows: "Having seen the sentence of the Holy Church, in which bachelor Jeronimo Dias, stands condemned in a case of heresy, the justice of our sire the King, pronounces sentence to the effect that in respect of the said case, by public proclamation your body be burnt alive and reduced to ashes, for heresy against our holy Catholic faith. In case you seek pardon and repent and confess your error and desire to die as a Christian, you shall be first strangled to death so that you may not feel the torments of fire." While the case was thus being dealt with by the Governor's council, teacher Diogo spoke to the bachelor and sternly rebuked him. As a result, the latter was made to repent and realize his error, so that when the secular sentence was pronounced as stated above, he heard it patiently, thus accusing himself of his sin in public. Soon he was sent to the prison, where he asked for confession and was confessed by teacher Diogo. He was taken to the pillory, accompanied as an act of mercy by teacher Diogo who accompanied him until he was strangled, and was burnt and was reduced to ashes.

Source: (a) Bullarium collectio, quibus . . . ius Patronatus . . . conceditur I (Olisipone, 1707), p. 173; quoted in: P. A. Jann, *Die katholischen Missionen* . . . (Paderborn, 1915), p. 90; (b) Neill, *History I*, pp. 115, 97; (c) Neill, *History I*, pp. 115; (d) A. K. Priolkar, *The Goa Inquisition* (Bombay, 1961), 22f. — *Further Reading:* Neill, *History* I, pp. 220, 235ff; A. M. Mundadan, *History of Christianity in India I* (Bangalore, 1984), pp. 437-459; RGG[4] 3, 1069f: Art. Goa.

D. Francis Xavier in Asia (1542-1552)

Like no other, the Basque Francis Xavier (Don Francisco de Jassu y Xaver) (1506-1552) epitomized the wide horizons of the Jesuit mission movement of the sixteenth century. Arriving in the city of Goa on 15 May 1543 from Lisbon (document 10a) he left the Portuguese enclave almost immediately and set out to work in the southern part of the Indian subcontinent, outside the Portuguese territory, among the already-christianized Paravas (document 10b and document 16). In 1545-1547 he worked in Melaka and in the Molucca Islands (document 11), from which (after a temporary return to India) he set off for Japan, arriving on 15 August 1549 (document 12a/b). From Japan, he set his gaze upon China (document 13). However his dream was not realized and he died, 3 December 1552, on the island of Sanzian near Canton.

10. India

a. Goa (1452)

Letter to the Fathers of the Society in Rome: Goa, 18 September, 1542:

[. . .] We are now in the fifth month since we arrived at Goa, the capital of India. It is a fine-looking city, entirely in the hands of Christians. It has a convent of Franciscans, really very numerous, a magnificent cathedral with a large number of canons, and several other churches. There is good reason for thanking God that the Christian religion flourishes so much in this distant land in the midst of heathen. [. . .]

b. South India: The Paravas (1542-1544)

Letter to Ignatius of Loyola in Rome: Tutikorin, 28 October 1542:

[. . .] We went through all the villages of the converts who were made Christians a few years ago. This country is too barren and poor for the Portuguese to live in, and the Christian inhabitants here have had no priests; they just know that they are Christians and nothing more. There is no one to say mass for them; no one to teach them the Creed, the Pater, the Ave Maria, and the Ten Commandments of God. [. . .] I went diligently through the villages one after another, and baptized all the children who had not yet been baptized. In this way I have christened a multitude of children who, as the saying is, did not know their right hand from their left. Then the young boys would never let me say office, or eat, or sleep, till I had taught them some prayer. It made me understand for the first time that 'of such is the Kingdom of Heaven.' Their petition was too pious for me to refuse it without impiety, so I began with the profession of belief in the Father, Son, and Holy Ghost, and then taught them the Apostles' Creed, the Pater Noster, and the Ave Maria. I have found very great intelligence among them: and if they had any one to instruct them in religion, I doubt not they would turn out excellent Christians.

Source: (a) H. J. Coleridge S.J. (ed.), *The Life and Letters of St. Francis Xavier.* Vol. I (London, ²1886), pp. 114-122, here 115; (b) ibid., I, p. 146. — *Further Reading, general:* G. Schurhammer, *Francis Xavier: His Life, His Times.* 4 Vols. (Rome, 1973-1982); L. M. Bermejo, *Unto the Indies: Life of St. Francis Xavier* (Anand, 2000); Sunquist, *Dictionary,* pp. 909f (Art. Xavier, F.); J. Meier (ed.), *Sendung — Eroberung — Begegnung* (Wiesbaden, 2005); Moffett, *Asia,* II, pp. 9ff, 62ff, 68ff; A. C. Ross, *A Vision Betrayed: The Jesuits in Japan and China* (Edinburgh, 1994).

11. Southeast Asia: The Sultanate of Ternate

Letter to the Fathers of the Society in Europe: Cochin, 20 January 1548:

After having visited all the Christian villages, I returned to Molucco [the Moluccas], where I again spent three months more in preaching twice on feast days, in the morning to the Portuguese, and in the afternoon to the converts. . . . I instructed the native wives of the Portuguese by themselves in the articles of the faith, the ten commandments, and the sacraments of confession and communion. . . . During the six months I stayed at Molucco, both the Portuguese, their wives and children, and also the native Christians, made great progress in piety. After Lent I quitted Molucco and sailed towards Malacca, having received very great proofs of affection, not only from the Christians, but also from the heathen. [. . .]

The Mussulman [Muslim] king of Molucco is under the sovereignty of the King of Portugal, and thinks it an honour to be so. Whenever he names him, he calls him his Lord. He speaks Portuguese well. . . . The king himself is prevented from becoming Christian less by his Mahometan [Muslim] religion than by his passions and the habits of a licentious life. Indeed, he has . . . been married a hundred times, and besides his hundred wives he has innumerable concubines.

The Mahometans in the Moluccas are very ignorant of the law of Mohammed. They have hardly any cacizes, and the few they have are very uninstructed and come from other countries. The king received me in the most friendly manner; so much so that the lords of his court did not like it at all. He sought my friendship, holding out hopes that he might one day embrace the Christian religion; he begged me not to keep at a distance from him because he professed Mahometanism [Islam] for he said Mahometans and Christians worshipped the same God, and a day would come when both would adopt one and the same religion. Every time I went to see him, he seemed highly delighted with my company; but I could never prevail upon him to become a Christian.

Source: H. J. Coleridge S.J. (ed.), *The Life and Letters of St. Francis Xavier.* Vol. I (London, [2]1886), pp. 385-391, here 388-390.

12. Japan

a. First Plans

Letter to the Fathers of the Society in Europe: Cochin, 20 January 1548:

[. . .] At Malacca, a Portuguese merchant, a man of great devotion and faith, told me a great many things about some very large islands which have lately been discovered. The country is called Japan. He told me that much more progress may be made there than in India in the propagation of the religion of Jesus Christ, because the whole nation in Japan surpasses others in its desire for knowledge. A certain Japanese came to me with this merchant. His name is Hanshiro, and he had made up his mind to come and talk to me

b. Experiences in Japan

Letter to the Jesuits at Goa: Kagoshima, 5 November 1549:

[. . .] On the very day of the Feast of our Blessed Lady's Assumption 1549. We could not make another port, and so we put into Cagoxima [Kagoshima], which is the native place of [our Japanese companion] Paul of the holy Faith [Hanshiro]. We were most kindly received there both by Paul's relations and connections and also by the rest of the people of the place. [. . .]

By the experience which we have of this land of Japan, I can inform you thereof as follows. Firstly, the people whom we have met so far are the best who have yet been discovered, and it seem to me that we shall never find among heathens another race to equal the Japanese. It is a people of very good manners, good in general, and not malicious; they are men of honour to marvel, and prize honour above all else in the world. [. . .] Of all the lands which I have seen in my life, whether those of Christians or of heathens, never yet did I see a people so honest in not thieving [. . .]. Here they are not surprised at people becoming Christians, and as a great part of them can read and write, they very soon learn the prayers [. . .]. They listen with great avidity to discourse about God and Divine things, especially when they can well understand what you say.

[. . .] They do not worship any gods under the form of beasts. Most of them venerate certain ancient men, who, as far as I have been able to ascertain, used to live after the fashion of the old philosophers; most of them worship the sun, some the moon. They listen willingly to things consonant to nature and reason; and although they are not them-selves free from crimes and wicked practices, yet, if you show them that their sin is contrary to reason, they readily acknowledge their guilt and obey the law of reason.

Source: (a) H. J. Coleridge S.J. (ed.), *The Life and Letters of St. Francis Xavier.* Vol. I (London, [2]1886), pp. 417-421, here 417 (slightly altered); (b) ibid., II, pp. 232, 237f. (slightly altered); cf. C. R. Boxer, *The Christian Century in Japan 1549-1650* (Berkeley, etc., 1967), pp. 401-405.

13. Plans for China

Letter to Ignatius in Rome: Cochin, 29 January 1552:

China, an immense empire, enjoying profound peace, regulated by a number of very wise laws, is governed by a single sovereign whose will is absolute. It is a most opulent empire, abounding in everything necessary for human life. A narrow strip of sea separates it from Japan. Its people are remarkable for intelligence, and employ themselves in study, chiefly of laws and human jurisprudence, and also of political science. The ambition of the greater part of the people is to gain a deep knowledge on this subject. The faces of the natives are pale and beardless, and their eyes are small. They have generally kind open dispositions, and are lovers of peace, which flourishes and is firmly established among them, without any fear of wars. Unless some new obstacles should arise and alter my plans, I hope to sail for China in this year 1552, whither I am attracted by the hope of being able to do good work in furthering greatly the service of God to the benefit of both the Chinese and Japanese nations. As soon as the Japanese learn that the Chinese have embraced the faith of Jesus Christ, there is reason to hope that the obstinacy with which they are attached to their own false sects will be lessened. So I am full of confidence that by the labours of our Society, the Chinese and Japanese will abandon their idolatrous superstitions and adore Jesus Christ, the Saviour of all nations.

Source: H. J. Coleridge S.J. (ed.), *The Life and Letters of St. Francis Xavier.* Vol. II (London, [2]1886), pp. 365-375, here 373.

E. INTERCULTURAL CONTACTS

14. The Philippines: Christian Conversion and the Demonization of Local Religion

In the course of the search for a westward passage to the Moluccas that became the first voyage around the world from 1519 to 1521, the Spanish expedition under the leadership of Ferdinand Magellan reached the islands that were later named the Philippines. On Cebu, Magellan won some local rulers to Christianity. It was symbolic of the connection between mission and colonization that it was Magellan, and not the priest who accompanied the expedition, who preached. The account of Magellan as missionary (a) preserved by the chronicler Pigafetta, gives insight into the ardent religious spirit of the Spanish conquistador and the Cebuanos' early perception of the meaning of baptism.

a. Magellan as Preacher (1521)

The captain [Magellan] said many things concerning peace, and that he prayed God confirm it in heaven. They [the Cebuanos] said that they never heard anyone speak such words, but that they took great pleasure in hearing them. The captain, seeing that they listened and answered willingly, began to advance arguments to induce them to accept the faith. Asking them who would succeed to the seigniory after the death of the king, he was answered that the king had no sons but only daughters, the eldest of whom was the wife of that nephew of his, who therefore was the prince. [They said that] when the fathers and mothers grew old, they received no further honor, but their children commanded them. The captain told them that God made the sky, the earth, the sea, and everything else, and that he had commanded us to honor our fathers and mothers, and that whoever did otherwise was condemned to eternal fire; that we are all descended from Adam and Eve, our first parents; that we have an immortal spirit; and many other things pertaining to the faith. All joyfully entreated the captain to leave them two men, or at least one, to instruct them in the faith, and [said] that they would show them great honor. The captain replied to them that he could not leave them any men then, but that if they wished to become Christians, our priest would baptize them, and that he would next time bring priests and friars who would instruct them in our faith. They answered that they would first speak to their king, and that they would become Christians, [whereat] we all wept with great joy. The captain-general told them that they should not become Christians for fear or to please us, but of their own free wills; and that he would not cause any displeasure to those who wished to live according to their own law, but that the Christians would be better regarded and treated than the others.

All cried out with one voice that they were not becoming Christians through fear or to please us, but of their own free will.

b. Filipino Religion as "The Work of the Devil"

Although Spanish accounts of pre-Hispanic Filipino religion differ in details, the general lines seem clear, at least for the major lowland peoples of Luzon and the Visayas. Typically these early missionaries interpreted the religion of the people as all the work of the devil, whose influence and presence they felt tangibly.

All their method of government and their religion is based on tradition and custom introduced by the devil himself, who used to speak to them in their idols and their ministers. They preserved these traditions in songs which they know by memory, having learned them as children by hearing them sung when rowing, when working, when rejoicing and celebrating, and much more when weeping in mourning for the dead. In these barbaric songs they tell of the fabled genealogies and vain deeds of their gods. Among them they make one a principal one and superior to all. This one the Tagalogs call *Bathala Mei-capal* that is to say, the god who is Maker or Creator, and the Visayans, *Laon*, which means Antiquity. They speak of the creation of the world, the beginning of the human race, the flood, the reward of glory, punishment, and other invisible things. Doing this they tell innumerable falsehoods and even vary a great deal in telling them, some doing it in one fashion, others in another. Thus it can best be seen that they are lies and fables [. . .]. To sum it up, their idolatry, like that of many other nations, consists in adoring and considering as gods their ancestors, particularly men who were outstanding for their deeds of valor or cruelty. In memory of their ancestors they have little idols, some of stone, others of straw, others of bone or of ivory or of a crocodile's tooth, others of gold, which they call *Iarawan*, which means idol, image, or statue. To these they had recourse in their necessities and offered to them their barbaric sacrifices. [. . .]

Although they did not have any temples, they had priests, men and women, whom the Tagalogs call *Catalonan* and the Visayas *Babailan*. This office was held by the one who had the best ability to deal with the devil, who deceived him, or with the blind people, to deceive them with a thousand tricks and deceptions [. . .].

Source (a) A. Pigafetta, "Primo viaggio intorno al mondo," in: E. H. Blair/J. A. Robertson (eds.), *The Philippine Islands* (Cleveland, 1903/09), pp. 33, 142-145; (b) P. Chirino S.J., *Relación de las Islas Filipinas i de lo que en ellas an trabaiado Los Padres dae la Compañia de Iesus,* Rom 1604 (= Manila, 1890), pp. 52-55; English text from J. N. Schumacher, *Readings in Philippine Church History* (Quezon City, 1979), pp. 13f. — *Further Reading:* Moffett, *Asia II,* 150ff; Sunquist, *Dictionary,* p. 509 (Art. Magellan, F.); pp. 654-657 (Art. Philippines).

15. Japan: Religious Debates between Jesuits and Buddhists (1551)

Just a few years after the Portuguese had reached Japan, Francis Xavier and two companions (Father Cosme de Torres and Friar Juan Fernandez) landed on the southern island of Kyushu in 1549. With the help of translators, they began their work. After an unsuccessful attempt to base themselves in the capital city of Miyako [Kyoto], they established themselves in the culturally and religiously significant city of Yamaguchi. There ensued a debate with representatives of Zen Buddhism, in which the Jesuits attempted to clarify the special position in the cosmos of human beings gifted with self-awareness. This conversation between Cosme de Torres and the Zen Buddhists on 20 October 1551 is preserved in the minutes by Juan Fernández, who knew the local language. It has been recognized as the "first documentation of the clash between Asian and European ways of thinking" (W. Reinhard).

After You, Reverend Father [Francis Xavier], had left, many questions were posed by the Japanese. They were quite taken aback when they saw that you, Reverend Father, had already left. Indeed, the house was full from morning till night, for they felt there was no one left who could overwhelm them with the grace and help of the Holy Spirit. Fr. Cosmos de Torres handled the questions, and I [J. Fernández] served as translator.

And since the Father had instructed me to write down the proceedings in Japanese always, what they asked and how he answered them, so I will here give Your Lordship the information that I have written down.

First many *Zen-shu*, priests and laypeople, came. We asked them what they were doing in order to become saints. They laughed and answered that there were no saints and therefore it was not necessary to seek out that path. For after the great Nothing had come into existence, it could do nothing but transform itself once again into Nothing.

We asked them many things in order to make it clear to them that there is a principle *(principio)* that gives all other things their beginning. They admitted that it was true by saying, "This is the principle out of which all other things emerge: humans, animals, plants. Every created thing has this principle inside it, and when a human or an animal dies, then they transform themselves into the four elements, back into what they have been before, and this principle returns to that which it is." This principle, they say, is neither good nor evil, knows neither pain nor bliss, neither lives nor dies: it is Nothingness.

We asked whether there is a difference between humans and animals. They answered that the two are alike in birth and death. But in one respect the animals are better; for they live their lives without worry, pangs of conscience or sadness; humans are different.

We asked what it is exactly that differentiates a human from the animals; that causes the human to feel sadness, worry and pangs of conscience.

They answered that, just as there are many kinds of animals who each live in a different manner, so too do men differ among themselves.

We said to them that even if there are many kinds of insects and other animals, each with a particular body form, they all, whether large or small, share the one characteristic of knowing neither good nor evil. The human, however, differs from them all in this respect, and is therefore unique.

They answered, "That may well be, but in that all are born, and die, and have a soul, humans and animals are one."

We told them that this was not the case. Even if one were to take a child soon after its birth and set it out among animals, so that it saw no humans, as soon as it had the bodily strength it would speak and know the difference between good and evil, and if it did something against reason, it would have pangs of conscience. And then we asked them to tell us the source for such pangs of conscience. [. . .]

They said that they knew well that the body was made up of four elements, but asked us from which substance had God made the soul?

We answered them: "When God created the world, he did not have to look out for the matter in order to make the sun and the moon, etc. Rather he created new things only through his word and his will. In the same way he also creates the soul without any matter, alone through his word and his will." [. . .]

Source: G. Schurhammer, *Die Disputation des P. Cosme de Torres S.J. mit den Buddhisten in Yamaguchi im Jahr 1551* (Tokyo, 1929), pp. 66-68.

F. Forms of Local Christianity

16. Southern India: The Mass Conversion of the Paravas (1535-1538)

Although initial motives for conversion to Christianity may have been mixed, the process often led to the formation of a committed new religious identity. The years 1535-1538 saw the mass conversion of the Paravas on the south Indian Fishery Coast. Formerly a privileged caste, the Paravas, who cultivated pearls, had become dependent on Arab-Indian merchants and were exposed to oppression from local Hindu rulers. In this situation they put themselves under the protection of the Portuguese, and this led to their acceptance of Christianity. A local Christian named João da Cruz played a significant role in these events. At the age of fifteen, he had been sent by the prince of Calicut to the court of King Manuel I in Lisbon, and had there converted. Returning to India, he set about the task of propagating his newfound faith with zeal mixing economic, political and religious interests in a peculiar way. The acceptance of the Catholic faith by the Paravas, at first superficial, proved permanent, and survived the transitions of rule from Catholic Portugal to the Calvinist Netherlands in the seventeenth century, to Britain in the nineteenth century and more recently to Indian independence. The Paravas thus established themselves as a Christian caste in South India. The following account was drawn up in 1580 by P. Manuel Texeira S.J., who was an acquaintance of eyewitnesses of these events. See also document 10b.

Since the Paravas were facing such trouble and persecution [from the local Muslims] and knew no other remedy, they sought advice from a Christian Malabari [i.e., South Indian], a distinguished man who had been in Portugal. . . . His name was João da Cruz and he had brought some horses as a gift for the kings of that land. They inquired of him what they should do in the midst of such hardship and distress. Since João da Cruz was a good Christian, he told them that the Mohammedans were exploiting the favor of the [Hindu] kings of the land, and consequently he knew of no other remedy for them than to turn to the almighty King of heaven and to the Portuguese for help. Since they were themselves Christians, the Portuguese would afford them naval support at sea, if they accepted our holy faith. And, he went on, the Portuguese would not only help them out of their current turmoil, but the Paravas, with their help, might obtain the pearl fisheries that the Mohammedans now had, fisheries which would then belong to the Paravas, who had worked until now as day laborers in the Muslims' fisheries. [. . .]

And it pleased our Lord that it should happen as João da Cruz had said to them. For the Paravas found his advice good and they all decided to become Christians; and they sent their *Patangatins,* that is, their leaders, with money to the city of Cochin, in order that they might become Christians and the Portuguese fleet might be brought to their aid and might bring with it also priests to baptize them. [. . .] The *Patangatins* and the rest who came with them were baptized in Cochin and took on the family name Da Cruz because of João da Cruz, who had given them such good advice. Since then has been a custom for the leaders and nobles to be called da Cruz.

After their baptism the fleet sailed to help them, and with it the Vicar of Cochin and some priests. And so the Paravas received help and their whole nation was baptized, an area 20-30 miles long; about 20,000 people were baptized, as some of them and some of the priests who were there still remember today [around 1580]. The pearl fisheries were given to them, and although the Muslims still fish a bit, they are now dependent on the Paravas, as João da Cruz had told them.

Source: G. Schurhammer, Die Bekehrung der Paraver (1535-1537), in: idem, *Gesammelte Studien.* Vol. 2: Orientalia (Rome, 1963), pp. 215-254, here: 222-226. — *Further Reading:* Schurhammer, ibid.; S. B. Kaufmann, "A Christian Caste in Hindu Society," in: *Modern Asian Studies* 15 (1981), pp. 203-234; A. M. Mundadan, *History of Christianity in India* (Bangalore 1, 1984), pp. 391-401; Neill, *History 1*, pp. 140ff; Gründer, *Welteroberung*, pp. 279ff.

17. Ceylon (Sri Lanka): The Martyrs of Mannar (1544)

The self-Christianization of the Paravas, who changed their residence with the seasons, led quickly to a Catholic presence on the Northwest coast of Ceylon as well, long before the Portuguese appeared there. Despite persecution by the Hindu rulers of Jaffna in 1544, the new converts in the region of Mannar, still today a stronghold of Sri Lankan Catholicism, held fast to their new faith.

It pleased God to bless the efforts of the priest [who was sent to Ceylon] so abundantly that in a short time he instructed and baptized a large number of the inhabitants of this Island. In those days, Mannar was a dependency of the Kingdom of *Giafanapatan* (such is the name of that part of Ceylon which is to the North); this king was a man doubly barbarous, by nature and by vices; rather a tyrant than king, since he had by force of arms imprisoned and deprived his elder brother, of the throne which was due to him by right of birth. Moreover he held his subjects in servitude, despoiling and causing the murder of such chiefs as might create an insurrection among the people. But above all, he was an implacable enemy of the law of Christ. . . . Now, this king, when he had intelligence of the conversion of the Mannarites, was so incensed that he would not leave one of them alive. He ordered that an army, sufficiently strong, should be at once got ready, which was despatched to Mannar in secret, to massacre those innocent people, so as to chastise them and terrify the others. The execution was by no means less cruel than the order. As many baptized persons as could be found, without any distinction of age or condition — women and men, children and babes — till alike were put to the edge of the sword. And such was the admirable effect of the grace of baptism in them, that when every one in turn was asked if he was a Christian, they, instead of denying it and thus saving their lives, avowed themselves to be Christian, and the fathers and mothers spoke for their babes who had not yet received the power of speech to speak for themselves, and courageously offered these along with themselves to death. Thus, in a short time, from, six to seven hundred were killed: and the chief spot . . . was afterwards called the Land of Martyrs in honour of these martyrs.

Source: S. G. Prakasar, *A History of the Catholic Church in Ceylon* (Colombo, 1924), pp. 42f.

G. St. Thomas Christians and the Portuguese
before 1599

The relationship between the Indian St. Thomas Christians and the Catholic Portuguese soon proved ambivalent. At first both sides were dependent on each other, but increasingly they became conscious of their religious differences. The St. Thomas Christians did not acknowledge the papacy, recognize seven sacraments, or require celibacy. Their ecclesiastical language was Syrian and they were under the Nestorian patriarch in Mesopotamia ("Babylon"), from whom they received their bishops. Portuguese attempts to latinize the St. Thomas Christians began early and intensified noticeably in the middle of the sixteenth century, due in part to the reception of the Council of Trent. These attempts came to a tragic climax at the Synod of Diamper in 1599, when the St. Thomas Christians were forced to join the Portuguese colonial church and their records were destroyed. This remains a traumatic memory for large sections of Indian Christianity of all denominations.

18. Growing Alienation (1516/18)

From a letter of the Portuguese priest Penteado to the King of Portugal 1516/18:

The Christians of St. Thomas do not care for communication with the Portuguese, not because they are not happy that they are Christians as we are, but because we are among them as the English and the Germans are among us. As regards their natural customs, their will is corrupted by their priests who say that just as there are twelve Apostles, even so, they founded twelve [different forms of ecclesiastical] customs, each different from the others.

Source: A. M. Mundadan, *The Arrival of the Portuguese in India and the Thomas Christians under Mar Jacob 1498-1552* (Bangalore, 1967), p. 83. — *Further Reading:* G. Schurhammer, *The Malabar Church and Rome* (Trichinopoly, 1934); P. A. M. Mundadan, *History of Christianity in India.* Vol. I (Bangalore, 1984), pp. 283-347; Moffett, *Asia II*, pp. 12ff.

19. Campaigns for the Latinization
of the St. Thomas Christians (1550)

Mateo Dias, a St. Thomas Christian priest serving the Portuguese, in a letter to the King of Portugal in the year 1550, on the current situation:

On this coast there are many St. Thomas Christians, over forty thousand souls, who formerly had the [Nestorian] Patriarchs of Babylon [i.e., Mesopotamia] as their prelates. In their name there came men from Babylon as bishops, to instruct them in the Catholic faith, which they did, not without some errors. Among other things they ordained the natives, but without the permission to say mass. And now there are here two from the said Babylon, who first did everything after the manner of Babylon, until Your Highness sent Fr. Alv[arez] Penteado, who with much diligence and zeal brought the said two Babylonians to the obedience of the Holy Mother Church and obtained for them a salary from Your Highness, and now they no longer do anything after the Babylonian custom and they are very honest and obedient towards the [Roman Catholic] Holy Mother Church. One, however, of those [Indian priests] ordained by one of the Babylonians above mentioned, is going about teaching St. Thomas Christians the Babylonian custom without fear of God or of the Holy Mother Church, . . . and he has already created much confusion amongst them.

Source: A. M. Mundadan, *History of Christianity in India.* Vol. I (Bangalore, 1984), pp. 319-320.

20. Forced Integration at the Synod of Diamper (1599)

The Synod of Diamper (Udayamperur) was convened by the Archbishop of Goa, Aleixo de Menezes S.J., who compelled the St. Thomas Christians of Kerala to repudiate their traditions and place themselves under Roman jurisdiction. It signified the temporary end of the independence of St. Thomas Christianity in India. Not until 1653 did at least a fraction of the St. Thomas Christians manage to free themselves from this forced union.

Session III. Decree VIII [Ending the connection to the Nestorian Patriarch of Babylon/Mesopotamia]. Till the very time of the most illustrious Metropolitan [the Archibishop of Goa Aleixo de Menezes S.J.] entering into his diocese, there was [among the St. Thomas Christians] a certain heresy twice repeated in the holy sacrifice of the mass, and twice more in the divine office, in calling the Patriarch of Babylon, the universal pastor, and head of the catholic church, in all places, and as often as they happen to name him; a title that is due only to the most holy father, the Bishop of Rome, successor of the prince of the Apostles, St. Peter, and vicar of Christ on earth: the Synod therefore command in virtue of obedience, and upon pain of excommunication to be ipso facto incurred, that no person of this bishopric, secular or ecclesiastical, shall from henceforward presume, . . . to bestow that title on the said Patriarch of Babylon, or on any other prelate, besides our lord, the Bishop of Rome [. . .].

Session III. Decree XX [Condemning Nestorianism]. This present Synod, together with all the priests and faithful people of this diocese, doth embrace all the holy general councils received by holy mother church, believing and confessing all that was determined in them, . . . condemning all that they have rejected and condemned; but especially it doth with great veneration receive and embrace the first holy council of Ephesus [in 431], consisting of 200 fathers, firmly believing all that was therein determined, and rejecting and condemning whatsoever it condemned; but above all, the diabolical heresy of the Nestorians, which has been for many years preached and believed in this diocese; which together with its author Nestorius and all his followers, the said council [of Ephesus in 431] did reject and anathematize [. . .].

Session III. Decree XXI [Submission to Council of Trent]. Furthermore, this present Synod, with all the priests and faithful people of this diocese, embraces the last holy and sacred council of Trent [1545-1563], and does not only believe and confess all that was determined and approved of therein, and reject and anathematize all that the council rejected and condemned [. . .] by which only it is resolved to govern itself as to all matters relating to the government of the church, and the reformation of the manners of this faithful and catholic people, any customs, though immemorial, in this bishopric, to the contrary notwithstanding.

Session III. Decree XXII. [Submits the St. Thomas Christians to the Inquisition in Goa]. This present Synod, together with all the priests and faithful people of this diocese, doth with great submission and reverence, submit itself to the holy, upright, just, and necessary court of the holy office of the inquisition, in these parts established; and being sensible how much the integrity of the faith depends upon that tribunal, . . . being, after the example of all other bishoprics in the province, willing that all matters of faith should be judged of by the same court, . . . and notwithstanding the said holy office has not hitherto, by reason of this church's having been separated, and had little or no correspondence with the apostolical see, or with any of the churches that are subject to it [. . .].

Source: M. K. Kuriakose, *History of Christianity in India* (Madras, 1982), pp. 39-43. — *Further Reading:* Neill, *History 1*, pp. 191-219; RGG[4] 2, 825f: Art. Diamper, Synode von; J. Thaliat, *The Synod of Diamper* (Rome, 1958); J. Tekkedath, *History of Christianity in India* (Bangalore, 1982), pp. 2, 64ff; T. de Souza, "The Indian Christians of St. Thomas and the Portuguese Padroado," in: K. Koschorke (ed.), *Christen und Gewürze* (Göttingen, 1998), pp. 31-42; Moffett, *Asia II*, 13ff; G. Nedungatt (ed.), *The Synod of Diamper Revisited* (Rome, 2001); B. Puthur (ed.), *The Life and Nature of the St. Thomas Christian Church in the Prediamper Period* (Kochi, 2000); S. Zacharia (ed.), *The Acts and Decrees of the Synod of Diamper 1599* (Edamattam, 1994).

II. ASIA 1600-1800

A. Forms of Catholic Presence

21. Religious Orders in the Philippines

The Spanish-ruled Philippines was the only country in Asia to see the development of a comprehensive Catholic presence. The evangelization — and also to a great extent the "pacification" — of the islands lay in the hands of the religious orders, among whom the country was divided in 1594. This form of organization remained decisive for the history of Filipino Catholicism.

Report of Governor Francisco Tello (July 9, 1598)

The Order of St. Augustine, the first order to be founded in these islands [in 1565], has occupied the Tagalog provinces, Pampanga, Ylocos, and Pintados. It has in them 60 houses with 108 priests and preachers, and 53 lay brothers. They must establish more houses, both for the entries into new regions and the new discoveries which are to be made; and in order to provide sufficient instruction. For all this, it will be necessary to send annually 20 religious. If these should come from Nueva España [Mexico], . . . it would be much less expensive to the royal treasury to do this, and they will be more suited for this country, because they have already begun to have experience of Indians.

The Order of St. Francis has occupied the province of Camarines, where it has 40 houses, with 120 religious, 23 of whom are lay brothers, and the rest priests, preachers, and confessors. They need 50 religious, both that they may provide sufficient instruction, and for the houses that they are to establish.

The Order of St. Dominic occupies the province of Cagayan, where it has 12 houses, with 71 religious. For the houses which they are to establish in that province, and that the province may have sufficient instruction, they must have 20 priests sent to them every year. For they receive as many lay brothers in the islands as they need.

The Society of Jesus, which is the most recently established, has 12 houses, which lie in the province of Pintados, the islands of Camar [Samar], Leite, and Babao [Eastern Samar]. They have in them 43 religious, of whom 23 are priests, preachers, and confessors, and the rest lay brothers. For the houses that they are still to establish, and in Mindanao, where these religious will have charge of the work of pacification, they will need 50 priests at one time. . . . For they are reaping a great harvest in this country. They have two colleges here, one in Manila, and the other in the city of Santissimo Nombre de Jesús, where Latin is taught to the Spaniards and the Christian faith to the natives, with much care.

The superiors of these orders are religious of good ability, and among the other members of the orders are many good linguists, who are accomplishing much for the conversion of the natives. As a result, this continues to increase daily.

Source: J. N. Schumacher, *Readings in Philippine Church History* (Quezon City, 1979), pp. 17f. — *Further Reading:* P. Fernandez, *History of the Church in the Philippines (1521-1898)* (Manila, 1970), pp. 19ff; *TRE* 16, 1996, pp. 514ff (Art. Philippinen); Sunquist, *Dictionary* (Art. Philippines); Moffett, *Asia II*, pp. 153ff.

22. Jesuits at the Court of Mogul Emperor Akbar I

In accordance with a concept of mission to the elites, Jesuits in Asia were frequently active at the courts of non-Christian rulers. The third ruler of the Turkish-Persian Mogul Dynasty of Northern India, Akbar I (1556-1605), presented an extraordinary opportunity by inviting them to his court, first in Fatehpur Sikri and then in Lahore. The hope that Akbar, who was given to organizing religious debates among Hindus, Muslims, Parsi, Jesuits and others, would convert proved illusory. However a Jesuit presence at the Emperor's court continued for almost two hundred years. Antonio Monserrate S.J. on Akbar I, who died on 26 October 1605:

He was a prince beloved of all, firm with the great, kind to those of low estate, and just to all men, high or low, neighbour or stranger, Christian, Muslim or Hindu. . . . He lived in the fear of God, to whom he never failed to pray four times daily, at sunrise, at sunset, at midday and at midnight, and, despite his many duties, his prayers on these four occasions . . . were never curtailed. . . . Akbar was one of the most fortunate monarchs of his time. . . . Scarcely ever did he engage in any enterprise which he did not bring to a successful conclusion . . . but he missed the greatest thing of all: the knowledge of the true God and his only Son Jesus Christ who came to save mankind.

Source: Neill, *History I*, p. 90. — *Further Reading:* ibid., I, pp. 166-190; C. H. Payne, *Akbar and the Jesuits* (London, 1926); A. Camps, *Jerome avier S.J. and the Muslims of the Mogul Empire* (Schönech, 1957).

23. The Persecution of Christians in Japan

With the unification of Japan under Toyotomi Hideyoshi (1582-1598), a half-century of unprecedented church growth came to an end. Persecution of Christians began in 1597 and became increasingly violent in the ensuing years. Under the Shogun Iemitsu Tokugawa (1623-1651), the country sealed itself off from the outside world (a). For more than 200 years Japanese were forbidden to leave their country and Europeans were not permitted to enter. In the period 1614-1636, the church in Japan was almost completely extinguished. The few believers remaining were forced to publicly recant their faith by a formal oath and by stamping on holy images (b). Despite cruel persecution, a minority survived underground into the nineteenth century (see document 59).

a. Edict on the Closure of the Land (June 1636)

1. No Japanese ships may leave for foreign countries.
2. No Japanese may go abroad secretly. If anybody tries to do this, he will be killed, and the ship and owner(s) will be placed under arrest whilst higher authority is informed.
3. Any Japanese now living abroad who tries to return to Japan will be put to death.
4. If any *Kirishitan* [Christian] believer is discovered, you two *Nagasaki bugyo* [officials] will make a full investigation.
5. Any informer(s) revealing the whereabouts of a *bateren* [priest] will be paid 200 or 300 pieces of silver. If any other categories of *Kirishitans* are discovered, the informer(s) will be paid at your [officers] discretion as hitherto. [. . .]
7. Any foreigners who help the *bateren* or other criminal foreigners will be imprisoned at Omura as hitherto.
8. Strict search will be made for *bateren* on all incoming ships. [. . .]
11. If any deportees should try to return or to communicate with Japan by letter or otherwise, they will of course be killed if they are caught. . . .
12. *Samurai* [members of the knights' estate] are not allowed to have direct commercial dealings with either foreign or Chinese shipping at Nagasaki.

b. "Oath of Apostasy" (1645)

We have been Christian believers for many years. Yet we have found out that the Christian religion is an evil religion. It regards the next life as the most important. The threat of excommunication is held over those who disobey the *padres'* orders, whilst they are likewise kept from associating with the rest of humanity in the present world and doomed to be cast into Hell in the next. It further teaches that there is no salvation in the next life unless sinners confess their faults to the *padres* and receive their absolution. In this way, the people were led to place their trust in the *padres*. Yet all this was done with the design of taking the lands of others. When we learned this, I became an adherent of the Hokke sect and my wife of the Ikko sect.

We hereby witness this statement in writing before you, worshipful magistrate. Hereafter we shall never revoke our apostasy, not even in the secret places of the heart. Should we even entertain the slightest thought thereof, then let us be punished by God the Father, God the Son, and God the Holy Ghost, St. Mary, and all Angels and Saints. Let us forfeit all God's mercy, and all hope like Judas Iscariot, becoming a laughing-stock to all men, without thereby arousing the slightest pity, and finally die a violent death and suffer the torments of Hell without hope of salvation. This is our Christian Oath [were we to have remained Christians].

We tell you frankly that we have no belief whatsoever in Christianity in our hearts. Should we be guilty of any falsehood in this respect, now or in the future, then let each and both of us be divinely punished by *Bonten, Taishaku, Shiten-daijo,* the great and small deities of the sixty and more provinces of Japan, particularly *Gongen* and *Mishima-daimyojin* of the two regions of *Idzu* and *Hakone, Hachiman-daibosatsu, Tenman-daijizai-Tenjin,* especially our own tutelary deity *Suwa-daimyojin,* and all the minor deities. This is our formal oath.

> Second year of Shoho [1645]
> Kuyusuke, his wife

[. . .] The apostate foreign padre-Chuan [Christovão Ferreira], the apostate Japanese padres-Ryojun [= Thomas Araki?], Ryohaku [uncertain].

(Countersigned:) We hereby certify that the above-mentioned Kyusuke and his wife have become members of the Ikko sect. Saishoji Temple Head Priest, Shusan.

Source: (a) C. R. Boxer, *The Christian Century in Japan 1549-1650* (Berkeley, 1967), pp. 439f. (b) Ibid., pp. 441f. — *Further Reading:* Boxer, ibid., pp. 363-400; A. C. Ross, *A Vision Betrayed* (Edinburgh, 1994), pp. 93-117; Neil S. Fujita, *Japan's Encounter with Christianity* (New York, 1991), pp. 108ff, 147ff; Moffett, *Asia II,* 79ff; England, *ACT I,* pp. 53ff.

B. ACCOMMODATION STRATEGIES AND THE RITES CONTROVERSY

24. Matteo Ricci in China (1583-1610)

The work of Matteo Ricci (1552-1610) marked the beginning of a significant Jesuit presence in the Middle Kingdom which was sustained in the face of imperial hostility in the eighteenth century until the dissolution of the order in 1773. In 1583 Ricci and his Italian compatriot Michele Ruggieri received permission to reside in the coastal region of southern China. By 1601 he had established himself in Beijing and there gained access to the emperor's court. Ricci is probably the most important representative of the approach of "accommodation" to Asia's advanced civilizations. The strategy was shaped by the objective to win over the educated classes and emphasized scholarly disputation rather than public preaching. Unlike the Jesuits in Japan, Ricci took Confucian tradition as his system of reference rather than Taoism or Buddhism which he regarded as idol worship. He engaged positively with the classical Confucian documents, where he discovered what he considered to be a monotheistic faith. Ricci believed that his translation of these writings into Latin was as significant a part of his work as his production of theological writing in Chinese. His writings, especially his tract *On Friendship* and his dialogical catechism from 1603-1604 *The True Meaning of the Lord of Heaven* (T'ien-chu shih-i [Tian-zhu shi-yi]), were widely circulated.

a. Letter from November 13, 1584

The *Catechism* that we have made and printed in the Chinese language, by the grace of the Lord, has been very well received. In it, by means of a dialogue between a Gentile and a Father from Europe, there are presented all the things necessary to be a Christian in good order, good letters, and good language. In it the principal sects of China are refuted, and there are the *Ten Commandments*, the *Pater Noster*, and the *Ave Maria* [in Chinese translation] [. . .].

The prefect [of our city Zhaoqing] had me make a map in the manner of ours of Europe, but with the distances and names of countries in the Chinese language. And he immediately printed it without my reviewing. . . . He esteems it so much that he keeps the print with him, not wanting anyone to learn about it except those to whom he slowly presents it, the more important persons of China. The building of our little house in Chao ch'ing is almost finished, and although it is small, all the nobility come to see it — so much so that we have no rest. This year the prefect that has been so favorable to us has been made *limsitao*, that is, governor of many cities. . . . This should be no little help at the proper time for the propagation of the Gospel.

We have experienced many tribulations, even to the point of being accused falsely of very serious things at the suggestion of the ancient adversary. But from all this God has freed us. . . .

b. Theory and Practice of Accommodation

Letter from 12 October 1596:

Since the scholars and the most important people here do not hold the local bigwigs in high esteem, I've taken on the general appearance of one their scholarly preachers, so that I don't make the mistake of looking like a bigwig myself [. . .] I think we will not open a church at the present time, but rather a house of preaching, . . . although I preach more effectively through conversations than through formal sermons.

From his tract: "On the Various Sects in China that Contradict Religion"

In no other heathen people that we Europeans know of have there existed so few misconceptions about the true nature of religion than in ancient China. Indeed I find in their books [the Confucian classic writings] that they have always revered the highest deity, which they call King of Heaven or Heaven and Earth (heaven and earth seem perhaps to be considered like a living being, like a live body with the highest deity as its soul). . . . They never accepted such improper teachings about the King of Heaven and his servants, the other spirits, as our Romans, the Greeks, the Egyptians and other foreign peoples did. We may therefore have hope that many of their ancestors were saved through the natural law — that special help which God customarily grants to those who strive for it to the best of their abilities.

Letter from 15 February 1609:

In olden times they [the Chinese] followed the natural law precisely as well as we do in our homelands. For 1500 years this people has hardly worshipped any idols, or only those idols which are not as reprehensible as those in ancient Egypt, Greece and Rome. Certain deities were even quite virtuous and well-known for their good deeds. Indeed, in the oldest and most influential scholarly books, they venerate only Heaven, Earth, and the Lord of both. On closer analysis, I find very little in their books which contradicts the light of natural reason and much that is in accordance with it. Their natural philosophers are also no worse than others.

c. "The True Meaning [of the Doctrine] of the Lord of Heaven" (1603)

Ricci on this text:

This book does not deal with all the mysteries of our holy faith — these should only be explained to catechumens and [baptized] Christians — but only with some fundamental concepts that can be proven naturally and be understood through the natural light of reason. . . . Such as; there is in the universe one Lord and creator of all things, who preserves everything; the soul is immortal and God will repay good and bad deeds in the hereafter; it is false to believe in the transmigration of the soul into the body of another person or into animals, which many people here do — and other things of that sort.

d. A Chinese Voice on Ricci

The philosopher Li Zhi (1527-1610), who had met Ricci several times in Nanjing, to a friend:

I have safely received your questions on the subject of Li Xitai [Ricci]. Xitai is a man from the regions of the great West who has traveled over 100,000 *li* to reach China. [. . .] He then stayed for about twenty years in Zhaoqing, and there is not a single one of our books that he has not read. [. . .] He asked someone who was learned in the commentaries of the Six [Confucian] Classics to give him all the necessary explanations. Now he is perfectly capable of speaking our language, writing our characters and conforming to our conventions of good behaviour. He is an altogether remarkable man. Although personally he is extremely refined, his manner is as simple as can be. [. . .] Among all the people I have ever seen, there is not his equal. [The fact is that] people err through an excess of either inflexibility or compliancy — either they make a show of their intelligence or their minds are limited. They are all inferior to him. But I do not really know what he has come to do here. I have now met him three times and I still do not know what he is here for. I think it would be much too stupid for him to want to substitute his own teaching for that of the Duke of Zhou and Confucius. So that is surely not the reason.

Source: (a) M. H. Reinstra, *Jesuit Letters from China 1583-1584* (Minneapolis, 1986), pp. 24f. (b) Tacchi Venturi, *Opere storiche del P. Matteo Ricci S.J.* Vol. II (Macerata, 1913), pp. 50f; Fonti Ricciani I (Rome, 1942), pp. 108f; Tacchi Venturi, Opere storiche 2, p. 385; (c) Fonti Ricciani 2, 291; Chinese-English Edition in: D. Lancashire/P. Hu Kuo-Chen (eds.), *Matteo Ricci: The True Meaning of the Lord of Heaven* (St. Louis/Taipei, 1985); (d) J. Gernet, *China and the Christian Impact* (Cambridge, 1985), pp. 18f. — *Further Reading:* J. Gernet, *China and the Christian Impact* (Cambridge, etc., 1987); A. C. Ross, *A Vision Betrayed: The Jesuits in Japan and China 1542-1742* (Edinburgh, 1994); G. Minamiki, *The Chinese Rites Controversy from Its Beginnings to Modern Times* (Chicago, 1985); D. E. Mungello, *The Chinese Rites Controversy: Its History and Meaning* (Nettetal, 1994); Reinhard, *Expansion 1*, pp. 184-195; R. Malek (ed.), *"Western Learning" and Christianity in China.* 2 Vols. (Nettetal, 1998); D. E. Mungello, *The Great Encounter of China and the West, 1500-1899* (New York, etc., 1999); G. Criveller (ed.), *Preaching Christ in Late Ming China* (Taipei, 1997); Moffett, *Asia II*, pp. 108ff; England, *ACT I*, pp. 29ff.

25. Roberto de Nobili in South India (1606-1656)

In an apologetic document to Pope Paul V from 1619, Roberto de Nobili S.J. (1577-1656) gives an account of the beginnings of the Jesuit mission in the independent South Indian principality of Madurai. In order to win the favor of the leading Brahmin elite, de Nobili made a great effort not only to study the classical Indian languages and philosophy, but also to conform outwardly in issues of clothing, eating habits and customs. He interpreted the caste system not as a religious but as a socio-cultural phenomenon and accepted it within the church.

With the permission of Father General [of the Jesuit Order] I left Rome in 1603 and after two years spent in travelling I arrived at Goa. Soon after I came to Cochin, and thence to Madura. There I remarked that all the efforts made to bring the heathens to Christ had all been in vain. I left no stone unturned to find a way to bring them from their superstition and the worship of idols to the faith of Christ. But my efforts were fruitless, because with a sort of barbarous stolidity they turned away from the manners and customs of the Portuguese and refused to put aside the badges of their ancient nobility.

When I noticed that certain Brahmins were highly praised because they led lives of great hardship and austerity . . . they contrived to keep perpetual chastity and weaken their bodies by watching, fasting and meditation, I could, to win them to Christ, conform myself to their mode of life in all such things which were not repugnant to the holiness of Christian doctrine. . . . Therefore I professed to be an Italian Brahmin who had renounced the world, had studied wisdom at Rome (for a Brahmin means a wise man) and rejected all the pleasures and comforts of the world.

I had already learned Tamil and Sanskrit, which among them holds the same place as the Latin among us, and was pretty well acquainted with their books which, although it is contrary to their customs, they had allowed me to read. In a short time I went through them and found it clearly stated in them that [wearing] the thread [as a distinguishing mark of caste] and the long tuft [of the Brahmans], which are the object of the present controversy, indicated the nobility of their family and not their worship or religion, and that the nobles, specially the Brahmins, the Rajahs and the merchants were thus specially distinguished from the rabble and lower classes. For as they apply their laws whether secular or religious to all social actions without any expectation, the way they speak of their thread show that it is a badge of their rank or family but not of their religion [. . .].

My efforts were not in vain. By God's grace in two years nearly two hundred persons embraced the faith of Christ. At the sight of the present and the prospect of the future harvest our joy was very great, but it was soon damped by unexpected rumours. Among our Fathers there was no agreement regarding this new method; some did not approve this mode of life, nor the wearing of the thread [by converts]. Shortly after a superior, . . . forbade me to carry on with my work and baptize neophytes, until that question of the thread was more closely examined. Not only this order affected all the neophytes, but many others who desired to embrace the Christian religion. That is why the Archbishop of Cranganore [in South India] thought he must consult Your Holiness by letters. [. . .]

Source: M. K. Kuriakose, *History of Christianity in India* (Madras, 1982), pp. 50-52. — *Further Reading:* P. R. Bachmann, *Roberto de Nobili 1577-1656* (Rome, 1972); Sunquist, *Dictionary,* pp. 233f (Art. De Nobili, R.); England, *ACT I,* pp. 41ff, 206ff.

26. Indochina: Instruction of the "Propaganda" of 1659

Among Rome's many statements on the issue of inculturation is the Instruction of 1659 of the Propaganda Congregation, founded in 1622 as Rome's mission center to counter the Iberian monopoly of missionary patronage. The Instruction contained guidelines for the "Vicars apostolic" who were sent to China and Indochina. The outstanding feature of the Instruction is its differentiation between the gospel that should be preached and the European manifestation of that gospel. It also attempts to sever the connection between ecclesial and political claim to power, which characterized patronage mission. The document produced little response in the seventeenth century, but has been rediscovered in modern discussions, especially within Catholic missiology.

The most important reason that causes this Holy Congregation to send you as Bishops into these areas is that you have made the effort in every way to form the youth [of these lands] in such a way so as to produce suitable priests, ordained by you and put in place to serve the Christian cause under your leadership with the utmost zeal. You should always hold this goal before your eyes: to encourage as many and good [candidates] as possible to become ordained, to educate them properly and to promote them at the right time.

Should any of them prove themselves worthy of the office of bishop, [however,] you are most strongly forbidden from bestowing this honor upon them. Instead, you should first inform the Holy Congregation of their names, gifts, age, and further significant aspects: how and where they could be consecrated, which dioceses might be transferred to them, and countless other factors, of which you will soon be informed. [. . .]

Do not waste an effort upon this, and by no means should you advise these people to alter their customary rites and customs unless they obviously contradict religion and common decency. What could be more absurd than to import France, Spain, Italy, or another part of Europe into China? You should import not these, but faith, which does not reject or injure the rites and customs of any people — so long as they are not wrong — but on the contrary, wishes to preserve and protect them. And since nearly all humans by nature appreciate and love what is theirs, and especially their own nation above all others, there is no stronger ground for hate and estrangement as the alteration of native customs, above all those which the people since time immemorial have practiced and to which they have become accustomed. Such hatred occurs particularly when you wish to introduce customs of your own land to replace those which have been abolished. For this reason, never substitute customs of those people with European ones, but rather come to love them. Admire and praise that which deserves praise. When that is not quite appropriate, never give false praise and flattery. [In such situations], rely on your own cleverness: [preferably] make no judgment at all but at least do not casually and freely dismiss it. However, the false things that do exist should be condemned through hints and through silence rather than through words, all the while nevertheless realizing [each] opportunity to eliminate it gradually and unnoticeably, by encouraging their spirits to favor the acceptance of the truth. [. . .]

Source: Instructio Vicariorum ad Regna Sinarum, Tochini et Cocinae profiscentium, printed in: H. Chappoulie, *Rome et les missions d'Indochine au XVIIe siècle.* Vol. I (Paris, 1943), pp. 396-400.
— *Further Reading:* Sunquist, *Dictionary,* pp. 384f (Art. Instruction of 1659).

27. China: Emperor K'ang Hsi's Edict of Tolerance (1692)

The Europeans are very quiet; they do not excite any disturbances in the provinces, they do not harm to anyone, they commit no crimes, and their doctrine has nothing in common with that of the false sects in the empire, nor has it any tendency to excite sedition. . . . We decide therefore that all temples dedicated to the Lord of Heaven, in whatever place they may be found, ought to be preserved, and that it may be permitted to all who wish to worship this God to enter these temples, offer him incense, and perform the ceremonies practised according to ancient custom by the Christians. Therefore let no one henceforth offer them any opposition.

Source: S. Neill, *A History of Christian Missions* (Harmondsworth, 1971), pp. 189f. — *Further Reading:* C. von Collani, "A Note on the 300th Anniversary of the Kangxi Emperor's Edict of Toleration" in: *Sino-Western Cultural Relations Journal* 14 (1992), pp. 62-63.

28. Prohibition of Chinese Rites by Clement XI (1704)

Ricci's policy of accommodation was not undisputed in his own ranks. However, the biggest controversy ensued after his death. This centered around two main points: his evaluation of ceremonies honoring Confucius (and the ancestors), and the issue of a suitable translation of the concept of God in Chinese. There was strident opposition to Ricci's "civil" understanding of the rites performed in honor of Confucius, as well as his theistic interpretation of the "King of Heaven" in the Confucian documents. The "Rites Contro-versy" lasted more than 100 years, and remains noteworthy as a local argument that be-came significant for the global church. It was not only rival religious orders in Asia who spoke up on the matter. From at least 1645, Rome was also involved, publishing a series of partially contradictory statements which concluded with an unambiguous prohibi-tion of the Chinese rites (and thereby of a church model based on the cultural traditions of China) by Pope Benedict XIV in the 1742 papal bull *Ex quo singulari*. This signaled the end of the Jesuit mission in China and to a large extent also of the Jesuit efforts in India, against which an analogous papal bull, *Omnium Sollicitudinem* from 1744, is directed. The official dissolution of the Jesuit order in 1773 just dealt their work a final blow. The follow-ing is an earlier statement by Pope Clement XI from the year 1704 inserted in the bull *Ex quo singulari* of Pope Benedict XIV from 1742.

Because one cannot appropriately give expression to the highest God *(Deus optimus maximus)* with European vocabulary among the Chinese, the phrase *Tien Chu* should be allowed as description of this true God, that is, Lord of Heaven: a word which, as it is well known, is accorded respect through long use among the Chinese missionaries and believers. The terms *Tien* (heaven) and *Xang Xu* (highest emperor), however, should be fully rejected.

For this reason the hanging of plaques with the Chinese inscription *King Tien* ("dedicated to the veneration of heaven") cannot be allowed in Christian churches nor may those already hung be allowed to remain.

Moreover, believers in Christ cannot under any circumstances whatsoever be permitted to preside over, assist or participate in the celebrations of the of-ferings that are brought by the Chinese to Confucius and to the ancestors in the yearly ceremonies of the equinox, because these celebrations are tainted with superstition. Likewise it is forbidden for these same believers in Christ to carry out ceremonies, rites and offerings in the Confucian temples that are called in Chinese *Miao,* to honor Confucius each month at new moon and full moon. These ceremonies are normally held by the Mandarins or the highest officials, other officers and writers. Sometimes [they involve] Mandarins, governors or judges before they take office or least after their appropriation while at other times writers who, after obtaining their degrees, immediately proceed to the temple of Confucius. [. . .]

And furthermore it shall not be tolerated that the above mentioned Chris-tians help or take part in any sort of offering, rite or ceremony, together with pa-gans or separately, at ancestor shrines in private houses, at the graves of the an-cestors, or at the graveside before the burial of the deceased, as would usually be done to honor them. No, on the contrary: since it has been proven, according to all that that was said here, and after our meticulous and mature discussions, that the above mentioned cannot be completely separated from superstition, it fol-lows that the adherents to the Christian law should not even be permitted to submit public or secret *protestatio* (protest) in advance, for they would be carrying this out not as a religious, but a civil act and even a political cult of the dead to whom they offer nothing and from whom they expect nothing.

Source: E. Schmitt (ed.), *Dokumente zur Geschichte der europäischen Expansion III* (München, 1987), pp. 484-487. — *Further Reading:* see above under document 24; Moffett, *Asia II*, pp. 120-142.

C. COLONIAL FORMS OF PROTESTANTISM

29. Trading Companies as Colonial Rulers

Portugal and Spain's colonial monopoly (see documents 8; 223a) did not last long. From the end of the sixteenth century, other European — mainly Protestant — powers were increasingly attracted to the lucrative Asian market. Playing a leading role were the British, the French, the Danes and the Swedes, but above all the Dutch, who ousted the Portuguese from large parts of South and Southeast Asia by the middle of the seventeenth century. These European newcomers were generally organized into privileged, partially state-supported, trading companies. The Dutch East India Company (*Vereenigde Oost-Indien Compagnie,* V.O.C.), founded in 1602, and the British East India Company, which originated in 1600, achieved special significance. Primarily economically oriented and showing very little interest in missionary activity, the new Protestant rulers maintained a generally modest colonial church structure, which focused almost exclusively on ministry to the Europeans living in their territories.

a. The Charter of the Dutch East India Company (V.O.C.), 1642

1. Within the territories of the Dutch East India Company no other religion will be exercised, much less taught or propagated, either secretly or publicly, than the Reformed Christian Religion as it is taught in the public churches of the United Provinces. Whoever will be found holding any other religious services, whether Christian or heathen, will have his possessions confiscated and will be put in chains and expelled from the country; or he will, according to the circumstances, receive a punishment involving limb of life. [. . .]

b. The Charter of the English East India Company (1698)

And we do hereby further will and appoint, that the said Company, hereby established, and their successors, shall constantly maintain a Minister and Schoolmaster in the Island of St. Helena, when the said Island shall come into the hands or possession of the same Company; and also one Minister in every

Garrison and superior Factory, which the same Company, or their successors, shall have in the said East Indies, or other the parts within the limits aforesaid; and shall also, in such Garrison and Factories respectively, provide, or set apart, a decent and convenient place for Divine Service only; and shall also take a Chaplain on board every ship which shall be sent by the same Company to the said East Indies, or other the parts within the limits aforesaid, which shall be of the burthen of 500 tons, or upwards, for such voyage [. . .]. And we do further will . . . , that all such Ministers as shall be sent to reside in India, as aforesaid, shall be obliged to learn, within one year of their arrival, the Portuguese language, and shall apply themselves to learn the native language of the country where they shall reside, the better to enable them to instruct the Gentoos, that shall be the servants or slaves of the same Company, or of their agents, in the Protestant Religion.

Source: (a) V. Perniola (ed.), *The Catholic Church in Sri Lanka.* Vol. I: The Dutch Period (Colombo-Dehiwala, 1983), p. 17 (= SLNA 1/2387, 4f); (b) C. J. Grimes, *Towards an Indian Church: The Growth of the Church of India in Constitution and Life* (London, 1946), pp. 223f.

30. The English in Bombay (1698)

The Government here now is English. The soldiers are under Martial Law, the commoners under Common Law. The President is the Chief Judge with his Council at Surat; under him is a Justiciary, a Court of Pleas, and a Court for Arbitration and the presenting of all complaints.

The President has unlimited control and is the Vice Regis, he also has an advisory Council here, and when he walks or rides abroad either for pleasure or on duty, he is accompanied by a guard and a cavalry unit which are constantly kept at the ready in the stables. He has his chaplains, physician, surgeons, and household; his linguist, and his Mint-Master: At meals he has his trumpets usher in his courses, and soft music at the table: If he moves out of the Chamber, the silver staves wait on him; if downstairs, the guard receives him [. . .]. He always has a parasol of state carried over him: And those of the English inferior to him, have a train suitable for their station. [. . .]

To avoid the presence of unchaste women and to propagate their colony, the Company have sent out English women; but they beget a sickly generation; and as the Dutch will observe, those thrive better that come of an European father and Indian mother: Which . . . may be attributed to their living at large, not debarring themselves wine and strong drink, which immoderately used, inflames the blood, and spoils the milk in these hot countries. . . . The Natives abhor all heady liquors [. . .].

Source: J. Fryer, *A New Account of East-India and Persia in Eight Letters* (London, 1698), pp. 68-70 (modernized version). — *Further Reading:* Moffett, *Asia II*, p. 236.

31. Life in Dutch V.O.C. Churches

The Asian colonial empire of the Dutch East India Company (V.O.C.) existed from the middle of the seventeenth to the end of the eighteenth century, in Ceylon, South India, the Moluccas, and parts of what would later become Indonesia and Formosa (Taiwan). Their limited attempts to propagate the Reformed faith met with at best only moderate success. In this period the V.O.C. sent a total of 254 preachers and about 800 lower-ranked church employees into its Asian territories. There were some isolated but note-worthy experiments, such as the construction of seminaries for the training of native church leaders in Ceylon (1692 in Jaffna, 1696 in Colombo). However, the colonial church straitjacket and a lack of cultural adaptation in Dutch Calvinism strangled local initia-tives. Endeavors to build native congregations in colonial Ceylon failed due to the lack of language skills of the Dutch pastors (a) who were frequently moved from one post to an-other. Attempts at an independent stance on colonial ethics in Dutch Indonesia fell vic-tim to disciplinary measures by the colonial authorities (c).

a. Language Problems of the Preachers in Ceylon (1750)

The Political *Commissaris* [in the meeting of the Church Consistory of Co-lombo, on 16.12.1750] also tabled an extract of a letter received from Batavia [Ja-karta, the Asian VOC base], in which that [V.O.C.] Government strongly urges the *Predikants* [preachers] to devote more time and attention to acquiring a good knowledge of the native languages so that they could preach in them. While expressing their satisfaction at the progress already made in this connec-tion by the Revs. Messrs. Bronsvelt, Scults and Fybrands they are pleased to note that the Rev. Mr. Silvius, who has recently come over [from the Nether-lands to Ceylon], will also devote himself to such studies. They consider that a period of one and a half years should be sufficient to enable one to acquire a sufficient knowledge of a language to be able to preach in it, and they hope that they will not delay so long as the Rev. Mr. Wermelskircher, who in spite of so many years' work and experience here [after nine years' sojourn in Ceylon], ac-cording to reports, has not yet been able to make but a fair degree, of progress in these studies [of the Singhalese language].

b. Cultural Pressure to Conform (1643)

From a Church order of Batavia/Jakarta from 1643:

It will also be necessary to impress upon the native Christians that they must also align their outward behavior with that of the Dutch.

c. Indonesia: Conflicts with Colonial Authorities (1655)

In 1655 pastors of the Church of Batavia (Jakarta) refused to hold a government-ordered intercessory service for a fight against rebels on the island of Ambon, on the grounds that the war was "unjust." The highest-ranking council of the V.O.C. in Amsterdam, the Council of the "Heren XVII," issued an order to the governor of Batavia to take drastic measures in the case of a repeat offense.

The Church Consistory of Batavia [Jakarta] has testified to the General Governor [of Batavia] that some of its members were having scruples about the intercessory service and the blessing of our weapons ordered by the government for the war in Ambon, and were therefore causing a nuisance. They claimed that our war was unjust and that we had in fact ourselves instigated it through noncompliance with the treaties we had made. They claimed we therefore had no right to praise the Lord God for his benevolent blessing upon our weapons and to thank him. Since we [the highest-ranking council of the V.O.C. in Amsterdam] find this [behavior] to be quite an unsightly development with dangerous consequences, we were compelled to make mention to Your Excellency [the General Governor of Batavia] of these circumstances and to seek assurance that Your Excellency — in the event that this case should repeat itself or a similar one materialize — release such preachers who refuse to celebrate these intercessory services as You have ordered . . . from their service to the Compagnie and the church, and send them on the first available ship homewards. For such matters and decisions can most assuredly not be left to the discretion of the preachers . . . much less may they dispute or contest the commands of Your Excellency, since it is Yours to command and to direct . . . and theirs to obey and to fulfill Your commands.

Source: (a) Sri Lanka National Archives, Minutes of the Dutch Reformed Church Consistory 16.12.1750. vol. IV4A/2, 6; (b) C. W. van Boetzelaer, De Protestantse Kerk in Nederlands-Indie ('s-Graavenhage, 1947), p. 47; (c) ibid., pp. 61f. — Further Reading: J. van Goor, Jan Kompenie as Schoolmaster: Dutch Education in Ceylon 1690-1795 (Groningen, 1978); Th. Müller-Krüger, Der Protestantismus in Indonesien (Stuttgart, 1968), pp. 39-59; C. R. Boxer, The Dutch Seaborne Empire 1600-1800 (London, 1977), pp. 113-154; Reinhard, Expansion 1, pp. 108-129; Moffett, Asia II, pp. 213ff, 222ff; Sunquist, Dictionary, pp. 253f (Art. Dutch United East-India Company).

D. INDIGENOUS FORMS OF CHRISTIANITY

32. Catholic Underground Church in Ceylon

With the end of Portuguese rule in Ceylon in 1658, Catholicism also seemed to have disappeared from the island. The practice of "Popery" was severely punished by the new Dutch rulers, and Catholic believers either fell back *en masse* into their old "heathen" ways — whether Buddhism or Hinduism — or attended the churches which had been turned into Reformed ones. Others went underground. Around the end of the seventeenth century, however, a revival of Ceylonese Catholicism became noticeable. It became so dynamic that it soon outstripped the membership of the colonial Calvinist churches, still under Dutch rule (1658-1796). By the middle of the eighteenth century Catholics were the strongest Christian group on the island. This is a notable example of the independent development of a model of Christianity first founded in the colonial context. — From the minutes of the emergency session of the Dutch Church Consistory of Colombo from December 2, 1751:

The President said that the time was now due for the despatch of the annual reports to the Superiors and the *Classes* [Church Councils] in Holland. . . . On deliberating over the matters to be mentioned in this report, it was resolved, . . . to send a detailed report on the daily increasing pernicious creeping influence of Popery in these Ceylon quarters, which in spite of all the wholesome orders and *plakkaats* [public displays] issued by the authorities, has nevertheless, as was apparent in the recent school visits, again raised its head so much and so vigorously that the so called [Catholic] priests and vagabonds . . . have no longer any respect or regard [for the Dutch religious or political authorities in Ceylon], and openly by day practice their seductive religious exercises with the pealing of bells and the exposition of their idolatrous images; yes, and they even baptise and marry the people in the land in their own sheds at their meeting-places, and incite them to openly blaspheme the doctrines and the teachers of the Reformed religion; and in places where they have a strong influence, especially like in the district of Negombo [close to Colombo], act with oppression and scorn of the members of the Reformed Church. It was also resolved to represent to the *Classes* and Synods [in the Dutch motherland] our embarrassment regarding Roman Catholic baptisms solemnised by the so-called priests in these parts where they have no legitimate authority, and as we therefore have no confirmation of their authenticity we are faced with great reasons for doubt as to whether they are duly ordained priests or base vagabonds. . . .

Source: Sri Lanka National Archives, Minutes of the Dutch Reformed Church Consistory 2.12.1751, vol. IVA/2 p. 51. — *Further Reading:* R. Boudens, *The Catholic Church in Ceylon under Dutch Rule* (Rome, 1957); K. Koschorke, "Dutch Colonial Church and Catholic Underground

Church in Ceylon in the 17th and 18th C.," in: K. Koschorke (ed.), *Christen und Gewürze* (Göttingen, 1998), pp. 95-105; Sunquist, *Dictionary*, pp. 871f (Art. Vaz, Joseph).

33. Autonomously Founded Communities in Korea (since 1784)

The beginnings of the Catholic Church in Korea are unique. They reach back to an initiative by Confucianist scholars at the end of the eighteenth century who in hermetically sealed Korea came into contact with Christian doctrine, or "Western knowledge," through Jesuit tracts written in Chinese. They wished to learn more, and sent Seung-Hoon Lee to Beijing in 1783 as a delegate with the annual tribute commission, where he was baptized in the North Church with the baptismal name "Peter." After his return to Korea in 1784, he in turn won over and baptized his colleagues, who then propagated the new teachings and began to produce theological literature first in Chinese and then in Korean, in the midst of rapidly intensifying, bloody persecutions. By 1794 the Catholics numbered 4,000. The growth continued for fifty years before the first European missionary, Frenchman Pierre Maubant, arrived in the country in 1836. The following document, an excerpt from a letter from "Peter" Seung-Hoon Lee from 1789, provides a fascinating insight into the self-organization of the nascent church as well as the accompanying doubt about the legitimacy of the path they had forged.

a. "Peter" Seung Hoon Lee on the Situation in the Year 1789

From a letter to the French missionaries of Pei-t'ang (North Church) at Peking in 1789:

Immediately upon my arrival [in February 1784 from Peking] in my country [Korea] I felt it my most pressing duty to study my [Christian] religion as set forth in the books which I had brought with me and to preach it to my relatives and friends. In the course of this work I became acquainted with a scholar who had come into possession of a book of our [Christian] religion, to the study of which he had devoted himself for several years. His efforts had not been unavailing, for he had gained some knowledge of the less easily comprehended points of our religion, but his faith and his fervor far surpassed his knowledge. It was he who taught and encouraged me; we helped each other to serve God and to lead others to serve Him, to the number of a thousand who embraced the faith and earnestly pleaded to be baptized; at the unanimous desire of all, I baptized several of them according to the rite observed at my own Baptism in Peking. In the meantime the persecution broke out; my family was the worst to suffer, and I was obliged to withdraw from the companionship of my Brothers in Christ. In order not to bring about a discontinuance of Baptism, I delegated two other persons to take my place. One of them was the above-mentioned scholar, and the other was the one who suffered greatly in the persecution, and who died in the autumn of 1785, a year after his arrest.

During the spring of 1786, the Christians held an assembly to discuss how to confess and hear confessions [. . .]. Toward autumn of that year a second assembly was held, at which it was decided that I should celebrate Holy Mass and that I should confer the Sacrament of Confirmation: not only did I yield to their request, but I conferred the same power to celebrate Holy Mass on ten other persons. For these ceremonies I followed the procedure laid down in various books [which I had brought with me from Peking], both prayer books and books of hours (primers) adding certain parts and omitting others. For the prayers I made selections from our prayer books. [. . .]

Since 1784 the number of those who listen to our preaching has gone on increasing: those who worship God within a thousand *li* [about 250 miles] amount to a thousand persons; the persecution goes on in five or six districts, many Christians have been arrested, thrown into jail, beaten, threatened, won over by promises; in short no means has been spared to make them renounce their religion. The number of outstanding cases of constancy, resolution and courage is also very great, more than ten [Christians] among them having sealed their faith with their blood.

b. Korean Underground Theology: Extracts from the "Essentials of the Lord's Teaching" by Chong Yak-jong Augustine (ca. 1796)

"The Essentials of the Lord's Teaching" (Chu-Gyo Yo-Ji), by Chong Yak-jong Augustine, who was martyred in 1801, is the first Christian theological work written in Korean. Clearly inspired by Matteo Ricci's "True Meaning" (see document 24c), the articles deal with Confucian, Buddhist, Taoist and Shamanist worldviews.

I. Man's mind by itself knows the existence of the Lord

As a general rule, when man looks up to heaven, he knows that the Master is above there. If he undergoes illness, pains and distress, he looks up to heaven, implores the Lord to heal him and wishes to he delivered. When he faces the thunder and lightening, he remembers his bad sins, and his soul is alarmed and afraid. If there is no Master in heaven, why should each man's soul react like this? [. . .]

II. All creation cannot come into existence by itself.

In all creation there is not a single thing which brought into existence its own body. Plants bear fruit and propagate seeds. Animals have a mother and father and are conceived and born, men are also born from their parents. Those parents were born from their grand-parents. If we got back gradually, obviously there will be a first-born man. Who gave birth to this man? If we say that he was born because he had parents, then who gave birth to those parents? Necessarily the first existent man was brought into existence without parents. And we have to say that this man by himself brought forth his body. This man by himself came into the world, but the next man cannot come into the world by himself. By this fact we deduce that necessarily there must be a person who brought into existence the first man. [. . .]

XVIII. Buddha and the Bodhisattva are men brought into existence by the Lord. There is only one person who has no beginning and originally exists. All creation was brought into existence and started by Him. All kinds of things cannot come into being by themselves, because they cannot spontaneously exist. In the world's room, the countless things, and the ghosts and man, all were created and came into being by the Lord's infinite ability. Not a single thing came spontaneously into being. Buddha and the Bodhisattva are also men who were brought out by the Lord. They were born from their parents' inner parts. They have a soul. They have flesh. They are as we are. Even if by agreement among men, someone is considered to be a little more able, a little more good [than others], it is not more than man's ability and man's goodness. Why does a man rise higher above other men? Compared with the Lord's infinite ability and infinite goodness, it is as one ten-thousandth. When Buddha and the Bodhisattva were in this world they did not get the Lord's help, then what goodness did they have?

c. The First Martyrs (1791)

In 1791, the first martyrs of the Korean Church, "Paul" Yun Chi-Ch'ung and "John" Kwon Sang-yon were executed. The proceedings were based on the charge that they had violated religious duties by disregarding the Confucian rites at the funeral of their mother.

From the minutes of the trial before the Chinsan Magistrate:

The governor then turned to James Kwon.
"And you," he asked, "what books have you studied?"
"I have studied the book of the True Doctrine of God [by Matteo Ricci], and that of The Seven Mortification."
"Where did you get them?"
"I read them with my cousin Yun Chi-ch'ung, who lent them to me."
"Did you also make copies of them?"
"I did not."
"Have you omitted the sacrifices [in honour of the ancestors]?"
"I have."
"And burnt the tablets [in honour of the ancestors]?"

"I have the boxes at home still, which the magistrate noted on his visit."

The governor then asked his relationship with various other persons, and continued, "One of our relatives has spread the rumor, at the capital, that you have burnt the tablets [in honour of the ancestors] — what is one to believe?"

"Since I gave up sacrificing, my relatives regard me as an enemy, and reprimand me, saying 'This fellow will surely go so far as to burn his tablets.' Their words of blame, in spreading, become news, and that is the way they conclude that I must undoubtedly have burnt my tablets."

Source: (a) J. Chang-mun Kim, J. Jae-sun Chung (eds.), *Catholic Korea, Yesterday and Today* (Seoul, 1964), pp. 28-30; (b) H. Diaz, *A Korean Theology. Chu-Gyo Yo-Ji: Essentials of the Lord's Teaching by Chóng Yak-Jong Augustine (1760-1801)* (Immensee, 1986), pp. 281-283, 307-309; (c) J. Chang-mun Kim, J. Jae-sun Chung (eds.), *Catholic Korea, Yesterday and Today* (Seoul, 1964), p. 35. — *Further Reading:* Diaz, *A Korean Theology;* Moffett, *Asia II,* pp. 311ff; Sunquist, *Dictionary,* pp. 446-449 (Art. Korea); England, *ACT I,* pp. 59ff; England, *ACT III,* pp. 474ff.

E. Tranquebar 1706 and Its Consequences

Protestant missionary activity in Asia can only properly be spoken of from 1706 when two German missionaries, Bartholomäus Ziegenbalg (1682-1719) and Heinrich Plütschau (1677-1746), began their work in the Danish settlement of Tranquebar on the southern coast of India, thus inaugurating the era of the Danish-Halle Mission. The mission was characterized by the coincidence of many different factors unique in Protestantism up to that point, including the initiative of the Danish King Frederik IV (1671-1730), the availability of motivated personnel through the Halle Pietism movement, a theology of missions that was focused on the salvation of the individual soul, and, as a direct consequence, a sensibility to the regional culture. Their goal was the founding of an indigenous church. Intensive study of the language (document 34 from a writing by Ziegenbalg), religious dialogues (document 35), publication of books — though hampered by censorship by the Halle headquarters — (document 37), and conflicts with local colonial authorities on issues such as the treatment of baptized slaves (document 36) are characteristic of this program. It reached a watershed with the ordination of the first Indian Protestant pastor in 1733 (document 38) and received attention not only in Europe but also in the emerging overseas churches of Africa (see document 141).

34. First Lutheran Communities and Church Buildings

The quick learning of the [Tamil] language is a clear witness that God has been with us. This language is indeed very difficult to learn, and in the beginning we did not have any opportunity to learn it well. Further we could not get books about this language and its [grammar] rules. Yet by God's help we could advance within a year so far that we could catechize and preach in this language. We have learned the basics [of this language] just as it is written in the Tamil books and spoken by the Tamil people. For this purpose we have acquired several books. [. . .] The blessed learning [i.e., mastery] of the language has actually motivated us, to more cheerfully begin and extend this [mission] work. Hence, within a year of our arrival we started to form a Tamil congregation and a Portuguese congregation. We needed a separate place to preach the divine Word and administer the holy Sacraments. With God's blessing and support, and despite our poverty, we could erect a small church building [in 1707] and name it the *New Jerusalem*. For six years we have been abundantly, yet plainly preaching to our congregations the Word of God both in Tamil and Portuguese.

Source: Unprinted manuscript, in: Mission Archives of the Francke Foundations II C 5: Apologia (from 8 September 1713), pp. 54-55, dated September 8, 1713; translated by D. Jeyaraj. — *Further Reading:* D. Jeyaraj, *Inkulturation in Tranquebar* (Erlangen, 1996); Neill, *History 2*, pp. 28-48; Moffett, *Asia II*, pp. 237ff; Sunquist, *Dictionary*, pp. 662f (Art. Plütschau, H.); pp. 852f (Art. Tranquebar); pp. 935f (Art. Ziegenbalg, B.); D. Jeyaraj, *Bartholomäus Ziegenbalg: The Father of Modern Protestant Mission — An Indian Assessment* (New Delhi, 2006).

35. Religious Dialogue with Hindu Brahmans

The priest said [to Ziegenbalg]: "There are many religions and sects in this world. Among us Tamil people alone there are 360 sects. We also see that many such sects are found among you Christians. . . . As only one God rules this world we can say nothing but the fact that all these different religions have actually come from God. Correspondingly all religions point to salvation. . . . If any person has firmly decided to attain salvation, that person could attain it — no matter which religion this person belongs to. Salvation might be easier to attain in one religion than in another. . . ." The following reply was given to him: "The fact that many kinds of religions and sects are found among the people on this world does not originate with God, as you understand it, rather they came about through the delusion of Satan. Moreover they originated and developed after the Fall through the confusion of human mind and will. As a result, of the two religions [i.e., Christianity and other non-Christian faiths and sects] one must be true and the other false. While one religion alone can come from God, the other religions must have been introduced either [directly] by the devil or [indirectly] by the enticements of the devil or by the foolish mind of the [spiritually] blind people. These religions are contrary to one another. Hence, one religion leads the people to salvation and the other to hell. . . ." They [i.e., Ziegenbalg's dialogue partners] asked us, whether we consider the entirety of their religion or only some aspects of their religion to be false and erroneous. The following response was given to them: "Due to the light of nature some general truths are indeed found among you. You have written about them in your books. You also mention them in your discussions. For example, you say that there is only one God, who should be known, loved and feared. [Further you say that] the soul is undying. [You also believe that] after this present time [here on earth] there will be another life, in which people receive either a reward or a punishment. This judgment will depend on how they lived their life here on earth, whether they have avoided all kinds of sins and done all kinds of good things . . . etc. You understand that these and other kinds of teachings agree with the [teachings] of the Word of God and the divine truths that are written in our conscience. [. . .] But when you teach that this one divine Being has been manifested in different gods, who have sinful qualities . . . , you differ in these things widely from the truth of the divine Word, and also generally from the light of nature. You have chosen weary . . . paths for your own peril."

Source: Dialogue with a Brahmin Priest dated January 23, 1714, printed in the *Halle Reports*. Vol. I (Halle 1716), Continuation 9, pp. 694-695; translated by D. Jeyaraj.

36. Conflicts with the Colonial Authorities

a. The Imprisonment of Ziegenbalg (November 1708–March 1709)

We [B. Ziegenbalg and H. Plütschau, the missionaries in Tranquebar] wish to illustrate the evil consequences [of the conflicts between us and the Danish colonial authorities in Tranquebar]. Their hearts are hardened in such a way that they neither think of God nor of our most gracious King [Friedrich IV]. Further they do not reflect on [the teachings of] the Lutheran religion. But under their [power and] authority they make everything happen. They especially wanted to pacify their anger towards me. Finally they came with [drawn] swords and loaded guns, seized me violently while I was praying at home and brought me to Fort [Dansborg]. They made me stand in front of them and asked several questions. In reply I did not speak a word, but called on my most gracious King. I told them that they should accuse me of anything they had against me in his presence. Then they put me in a prison and told the soldiers to strictly guard me every day. They sent a decree to my colleague [Plütschau] and ordered him, on pain of extreme punishment, neither to preach any weekly sermon in the [Danish] Zion Church [built in 1701] nor to hold any Bible study at home. All Europeans [in Tranquebar] were asked to take a fresh oath obliging themselves not to have any contact with us. Our congregation was completely scattered. Our interpreter [i.e., the Tamil mother tongue speaker, Alagappan, who was also fluent in German, Danish, Dutch, and Portuguese], who helped us greatly in the Tamil language, was also arrested and banished from the city [of Tranquebar]. All my things, including the books that I have translated into Tamil, were sealed and daily guarded. [. . .] In this manner the name of God was blasphemed; the work of our most gracious King was reproached; the Lutheran religion was criticized among the non-Christians [literally: heathens] and the Roman Catholics. All our European neighbors [i.e., the Dutch and English East India Company settlements on the Coromandel Coast] were grieved. The holy name of Christ was dishonored among the non-Christians [literally: heathens] and the Muslims. After the enemies had fiercely ravaged for two months, and were about to receive God's punishment, they sought for all kinds of opportunities to free me from prison.

b. Slave Trade as One of the Controversial Issues

[On 14 September 1708, Commanding Officer of Tranquebar A. Hassius penned a long letter to Ziegenbalg and Plütschau, in which he defended the slave trade:] You [Ziegenbalg and Plütschau] think that someone has sold the slaves in an unchristian manner. It is not certain whom you mean. You admonish me that this [sale of the slave] was done without your knowledge, and you wish that such a merciless act should never take place. I understand that you extend your presumptuousness and suppose that if a master has permitted his slave to accept the Lutheran religion and get baptized, you immediately wish to assume jurisdiction not only over the slave but also over his master. If this assessment is correct, we wish to know the Lutheran Pope, who has entrusted you with such authority.

Source: (a) Mission Archives of the Francke Foundations: I C 2:9, Ziegenbalg's letter dated August 15, 1709, and printed in: A. Lehmann (ed.), Alte Briefe aus Indien (Berlin, 1957), pp. 93-97, translated by D. Jeyaraj; (b) Mission Archives of the Francke Foundations: II C 14:1, p. 35, translated by D. Jeyaraj.

37. Ziegenbalg's Unpublished Work: "Malabarian Heathenism" (1711)

From Ziegenbalg's Preface, dated May 28, 1711:

11. [The books of the Tamil people] show the great deception of the devil and the appalling [spiritual] errors, which the South Indians have become subjected to. However, these books help us understand, how far the Tamils, on account of the light of their reason, have advanced in the knowledge of God and in natural

things. These books also reveal how, the Tamils, within their natural powers often lead such a virtuous life that would shame many [European] Christians. It is evident that the South Indians are far more greatly concerned about the life [after death] than the Christians are. [. . .] 13. [. . .] I have written this book for the following reasons: Firstly, my [missionary] successors should have some reliable source of information, which will prevent them from going through a great deal of difficulty that I had to go through and yet help them understand the [religious] principles of the South Indians. [. . .] If the Tamil people] know that the missionary knows at least something about their religions, they will listen to the Word [of God], and they will also highly esteem the missionary. If a person can explain Christian teachings to them in their own language and show them the paradoxes of their inaccurate [religious] beliefs, then they will be convinced of the truth of our Christian teaching and the falsehood of their image worship. [. . .] 14. The second reason for writing this book is as follows: Currently, the Christians in contemporary Europe have an opportunity to receive more detailed information about the situation of the South Indians than they received in former times. On the one hand, they will have sympathy towards the South Indians [. . .]. On the other hand, they will be challenged to take the practice of their Christianity seriously because they will know [literally: hear] how [sincerely] the South Indians perform severe austerities and fasts, how they observe several wearisome ceremonies and many other tedious things so that they can attain salvation. Thus, the Christians in Europe will . . . earnestly pray for their conversion and take every opportunity to support this [missionary] work.

15. The third reason addresses the Lutheran theologians in Europe, who will learn . . . from this book the [religious] teachings [of the Tamil people], and will be able to advise us how appropriately we should do the things here and what we as teachers of the Tamil people [literally: heathen] should especially be mindful of. Now the Lutheran theologians in Europe have an opportunity to discuss the situation of the Tamil people [literally: heathen] among themselves. Then they can communicate their opinions through letters. The fourth reason is to help Christian teachers and preachers to efficiently use the teachings of the Tamil people [literally: heathen] to refute atheism that is now flourishing in Europe. Despite the fact that the Tamil people [literally: heathen] are not Christians, their books state that they believe in a divine being that has created everything, rules over everything, and will one day reward the good and punish the evil. [. . .] As the Christians [in Europe] deny both [aspects of eschatology] and think that things happen by chance. As a result, they lead a more wicked life than the Tamil people [literally: heathen] do.

Source: W. Caland (ed.), *Ziegenbalgs Malabarisches Heidenthum* (Amsterdam, 1926), pp. 11-13, translated by Daniel Jeyaraj.

38. Ordination of the First Indian Pastor, Aaron (1733)

When Ziegenbalg talked about Tamil Christians in 1709, he also thought of Tamil pastors. However, concrete steps for ordaining a Tamil Lutheran Christian were only taken in 1729. At that time the central office in Halle authorized the missionaries in Tranquebar "to ordain an able person of Indian nation for the office of a pastor." On December 28, 1733, the Tamil Catechist Aaron was ordained and installed as the first Indian Protestant pastor. The inspiration for this action came, among other things, from the reports on the Native American clergy in New England. The congregations in Tranquebar were also actively involved in choosing their pastor from three proposed candidates. The following text is taken from the announcement in Tamil.

Beloved in the Lord!

After we have considered this matter for long time and requested our authorities in Europe for advice, we have decided to ordain a man, who belongs to you and to your nation. We want to give him the care of the churches in the country side. We ourselves cannot do this job. Hence, a faithful shepherd is needed. He will be able to deal with the people in the country side more efficiently than we could ever do; he will also preach them the Word of God and administer the sacrament. Until now God has been sending you servants from Europe. Therefore you should not think that a shepherd of your own nation will be incompetent. If a person is called and equipped by the Holy Spirit to undertake this work, no other special qualification is necessary. God is not partial. He loves all people who obey Him (Acts 10:34-35).

Among Christians every people group has its own shepherd. Hence, without any hesitation you can request God for your own shepherd. Through this ordination we can together work against the 'heathenism.' Therefore pray for this matter in your church, homes and assemblies that God might choose a shepherd who will please Him.

Source: Tranquebar Archives in the Tamil Library of the Leipzig Evangelical Lutheran Mission in Leipzig/Germany, Box 23: *Tamulische Schriftstücke von der Ordination Aarons.* Translation: D. Jeyaraj. — *Further Reading:* D. Jeyaraj (ed.), *Ordination of the First Protestant Indian Pastor Aaron* (Madras/Chennai, 1998).

III. ASIA 1800-1890

A. THE GENERAL SITUATION IN THE EARLY 19TH CENTURY

The end of the first Colonial Era brought with it the disintegration of its ecclesiastical structures. In India, the French clergyman Abbé J. A. Dubois (1779-1848) lamented the almost complete decline of Catholicism on the subcontinent (document 39). In neighboring Ceylon the British traveler and East India Company chaplain Claudius Buchanan (1766-1815) described the collapse of the Reformed Church on the island after the end of the Dutch rule in 1796 (document 40). At the same time he attempted to awaken interest in his native England for new forms of Protestant missionary activities in British India.

39. India: Decline of Catholicism (1815)

The Christian religion of the catholic persuasion was introduced into India a little more than three hundred years ago, at the epoch of the Portuguese invasions [in the sixteenth century.] [...] The low state to which it is now reduced, and the contempt in which it is held, cannot be surpassed. There is not at present in the country (as mentioned before) more than a third of the Christians who were to be found in it eighty years ago, and this number diminishes every day by frequent apostasy. It will dwindle to nothing in a short period; and if things continue as they are now going on, within less than fifty years there will, I fear, remain no vestige of Christianity among the natives. The Christian religion, which was formerly an object of indifference, or at most contempt, is at present become, I will venture to say, almost an object of horror. It is certain that during the last sixty years no proselytes or but a very few have been made. [...] In fact, how can our holy religion prosper amidst so many insurmountable obstacles? A person who embraces it becomes a proscribed and outlawed man; he loses at once all that can attach him to life. A husband, a father is forthwith forsaken and deserted by his own wife and children, who obstinately refuse to have any further intercourse with their degraded relative. A son is unmercifully driven out of his paternal mansion, and entirely deserted by those who gave him birth.

Source: J. A. Dubois, *Letters on the State of Christianity in India* (London, 1823), pp. 1-14. — *Further Reading:* Moffett, *Asia II*, pp. 176ff.

40. Ceylon: Collapse of the Reformed V.O.C. Church (ca. 1796)

In the time of Baldaeus, the Dutch preacher and historian, there were thirty-two Christian Churches in the [Northern] province of Jaffna alone. At this time there is not one Protestant European Minister in the whole province. I ought to except Mr. Palm, a solitary Missionary, who has been sent out by the London [Mission] Society. [. . .] Most of those handsome Churches, of which views are given in the plates of Baldaeus's history, are now in ruins. Even in the town and fort of Jaffna, where there is a spacious edifice for Divine Worship, and a respectable society of English and Dutch inhabitants, no Clergyman has been yet appointed. The only Protestant preacher in the town of Jaffna is *Christian David,* a Hindoo Catechist sent over by the [Danish-Halle] Mission of Tranquebar. [. . .] The Dutch ministers who formerly officiated here have gone to Batavia [Jakarta, Indonesia] or to Europe. The whole district is now in the hands of the Romish priests from the College of [Indian] Goa; who perceiving the indifference of the English nation to their own religion, have assumed quiet and undisturbed possession of the land. [. . .]

I find that the south part of the island is in much the same state as the north, in regard to Christian instruction: There are but two English Clergymen in the whole island. [. . .] I was not surprised to hear that great numbers of the [Singhalese] Protestants every year go back to [Buddhist] idolatry. Being destitute of a Head to take cognizance of their state, they apostatize to Boodha, as the Israelites turned to *Baal* and *Ashteroth.* It is perhaps true that the religion of Christ has never been so disgraced in any age of the Church, as it has been lately, by our official neglect of the Protestant Church in Ceylon.

Source: *The Works of the Rev. Claudius Buchanan. Comprising His 'Christian Researches in Asia'* (Albany, 1812), pp. 53-61.

41. Debates about the Admission of Missionaries to British India (1813)

Through the expansion of its influence and the elimination of rivals, the British East India Company managed to bring the Indian subcontinent as far as the Indus River under its direct or indirect control by 1818. Primarily interested in commerce, the Company refused to allow missionary activity in its territories. Protestant pioneers such as the English Baptist William Carey in Danish Serampore (see document 43) and the American Baptist Adoniram Judson in Burma had initially to restrict their activities to areas outside British control. The British East India Company's charter had to be renewed by the British Parliament every 20 years and Evangelicals campaigned for the acceptance of clauses that would permit mission. In 1792 they failed. Despite the resistance of the Company (a), the Evangelicals were successful in lobbying parliament and in 1813 the Charter opened India for British missionaries (b). In the 1833 Charter missionaries also of other nationalities were also allowed.

a. Protests against the So-called "Missions Clauses"

From the judgment from P. Bensley, one of the directors of the British East India Company, in the parliamentary hearing of 23 May 1813:

So far from approving the proposed clause or listening to it with patience, from the first moment I heard of it I considered it the most wild, extravagant, expensive, and unjustifiable project that ever was suggested by the most visionary speculator.

b. The Charter of 1813

It is the opinion of this [Parliamentary] committee that it is the duty of this country to promote the interests and happiness of the native inhabitants of the British dominions in India, and that such measures ought to be adopted as may lead to the introduction among them of useful knowledge, and of religious and moral improvement. That, in the furtherance of the above objects, sufficient facilities shall be afforded by law to persons desirous of going to and remaining in India for the purpose of accomplishing these benevolent designs: Provided always, that the authority of the local governments respecting the intercourse of Europeans with the interior of the country be preserved, and that the principles of the British Government, on which the natives of India have hitherto relied for the free exercise of their religion, be inviolably maintained.

Source: (a) J. Richter, *A History of Missions in India* (Edinburgh/London, 1908), p. 151; (b) Neill, *History II*, p. 153. — *Further Reading:* Richter, *History of Missions in India*, pp. 1501ff; Neill, *History II*, pp. 146ff, 151ff.

42. The Reorganization of Protestantism in Indonesia (1817)

In South Africa, Ceylon and the Moluccas the British took advantage of Napoleon's occupation of Holland to acquire the Netherlands' colonial territories. Indonesia however, after having temporarily become a British territory, came back under Dutch rule in 1815 and remained a Dutch colony until 1942. Under the British some missionary activity had been permitted, but with the return of the Dutch the former V.O.C. Church was reorganized into the Protestant Church in the Dutch Indies. It was effectively a state church, and some areas were sealed off against Christian missionary activity. The Royal Resolution Text 5 from 4 September 1817 announced the plans of the Dutch crown for the Church in what is now Indonesia.

We have taken into consideration the necessity of laying down some regulations with regard to both the general ecclesiastical matters of all colonies of this State and in particular with regard to the relationship between the Reformed Church of the Netherlands and the Reformed Church in the East Indies, in anticipation of those which will then be affected by this arrangement of the leadership of the Reformed Church, and of those arising in the context of the religious affairs of the Church in the East and West Indies etc.

Source: C. W. Th. van Boetzelaer, *De Protestantsche Kerk in Nederlandsch-Indië. Haar ontwikkeling van 1620-1939* ('s-Gravenhage, 1947), pp. 285f. — *Further Reading:* Th. Müller-Krüger, *Der Protestantismus in Indonesien* (Stuttgart, 1968), pp. 86ff; Moffett, *Asia II*, pp. 367ff; *WCE I*, pp. 374ff; Sunquist, *Dictionary*, pp. 374ff (Art. Indonesia).

B. Southern Asia: A New Beginning in Serampore (1800)

The new upsurge of the Christian mission at the beginning of the nineteenth century was shaped primarily by the Protestant missionary movement, which was then entering its "great century" (K. S. Latourette). At first the movement was supported not so much by the established churches but rather by dissenting groups and Christians affected by the evangelical revival in Great Britain, continental Europe and the United States. In India, the activities of English Baptist William Carey (1761-1834) and his friends became significant. By 1800 they established themselves in Bengal in the small Danish colony of Serampore outside of British-ruled Calcutta. Through a variety of activities — including preaching on the streets, the study of local languages, the translation of the Bible into many Indian and Asian languages, the production of evangelical tracts and the establishment of a Protestant school system — they introduced a new era of Christian presence on the Indian subcontinent and beyond.

43. William Carey on Methods of Evangelization (1796)

From W. Carey's Journal, 11 January 1796:

I wish to say something about the manner of my preaching but scarcely know how. As a specimen, however, I will just describe the season at a large village, about four miles from Mudnabatty [in Bengal], called Chinsurah. I went one Lord's Day afternoon to this place, attended by a few persons from Mudnabatty. When I got into the town, I saw an idolatrous temple, built very finely with bricks. [. . .] I however mounted the steps, and began to talk about the folly and wickedness of idolatry. [. . .] we began by singing the hymn 'O who besides can deliver.' By this time a pretty large concourse of people was assembled, and I began to discourse with them upon the things of God. It is obvious that giving out a text and regularly dividing it could not be of any use to those who never heard a word of the bible in their lives; I therefore dwelt upon the worth of the soul and its fallen state . . . and the impossibility of obtaining pardon without a full satisfaction to divine justice. I then inquired what way of life consistant with the justice of God was proposed in any of their shastras. They, said I, speak of nine incarnations of Vishnu past, and one to come, yet not one of them for the salvation of a sinner. There were only to preserve a family, kill a giant, make war against tyrants, &c.; all which God could have accomplished as well without these incarnations. An incarnation of the Deity, said I, is matter of too great importance to take place in so ludicrous a manner and for such mean end purposes. [. . .] I then observed how miserable they were, whose religion only respected the body, and whose shastras could point out no salvation for the sinner. [. . .] This is the method of preaching I use among them; nothing of this kind affronts them; many wish to hear; many, however, abhor the thoughts of the gospel. The Brahmins fear to lose their gain; the higher castes, their honour. . . . Thus we have been successful.

Source: E. Carey, *Memoir of William Carey* (London, 1836), pp. 255-258. — *Further Reading:* Neill, *History II*, pp. 186-211; Moffett, *Asia II*, 253ff; Sunquist, *Dictionary*, pp. 119-121 (Art. Carey, W.); K. S. Latourette, *The Great Century: North Africa and Asia* (Grand Rapids, [7]1980), pp. 65ff; RGG[4] 4, 96f: Art. Indien IV (K. Koschorke); E. D. Potts, *British Baptist Missionaries in India 1793-1837* (Cambridge, 1967); S. K. Chatterjee, *William Carey: The Father of Modern Missions in the East* (Serampore, 2004); G. Bond, *William Carey and the Dawn of Modern Mission* (London, 1992); M. Dewanji, *W. Carey and the Indian Renaissance* (Delhi, 1996).

44. Bible Translations and Book Printing (1811)

Serampore quickly developed as a center of translation and printing for the region. By 1820, the New Testament had been translated into Bengali, Sanskrit, Oriya, Hindi, Marathi, Punjabi, Assamese and Gujarati. Although some work was hasty and revision was soon needed, parts of the Bible were translated into a total of forty of the languages of India and other Asian countries such as the Maldives, Burma, Java and China. For many Indian and East Asian languages, printed characters were produced here for the first time. From an 1811 letter from William Ward, a close co-worker of Carey:

As you enter, you see your cousin, in a small room, dressed in a white jacket, reading or writing, and looking over the office, which is more than 170 feet long. There you find Indians translating the Scriptures into the different tongues, or correcting proof-sheets. You observe, laid out in cases, types in Arabic, Persian, Nagari, Telugu, Panjabi, Bengali, Marathi, Chinese, Oriya, Burmese, Kanarese, Greek, Hebrew and English. Hindus, Mussulmans and Christian Indians are busy, — composing, correcting, distributing. Next are four men throwing off the Scripture sheets in the different languages; others folding the sheets and delivering them to the large store room; and six Mussulmans do the binding. Beyond the office are the varied type-castors, besides a group of men making ink; and in a spacious open-walled-round place, our paper-mill, for we manufacture our own paper.

Source: P. Carey, *William Carey* (London, 1925), p. 283. — *Further Reading:* Sunquist, *Dictionary,* pp. 79-88 (Art. Bible Translation).

45. The Founding of Serampore College (1818)

Serampore College was established in 1818 "for the instruction of Asiatic and other youth in Eastern literature and European science," and is still an important institution today. Excerpts from the first prospectus of 1818:

1. The College shall secure the instruction in the Sungskritu [Sanscrit] language of all the native Christian youth admitted, and of a certain number in Arabic and Persian, for which purpose, the ablest native teachers shall be retained in these languages, at adequate salaries.
2. It shall secure their being further instructed in the various shastrus of the Hindoos; and in the doctrines which form the basis of the Pouranic and Buddhist systems. They shall also be instructed in those which relate to Hindoo Law.
3. They shall also be instructed in the sacred scriptures, which they shall regularly study and in lucidation of which lectures shall be constantly delivered. [. . .]
4. They shall be further instructed in general history, chronology, geography, astronomy and the various branches of natural science [. . .].
6. It shall further secure instruction of a certain number in the English language; and a number selected for that purpose in Latin and Greek.
8. The College shall admit such Hindoo and Muslim Youth as wish to enlarge their minds, to its various lectures without any restriction; and at the direction of the committee, admit as many parts from all parts of India as may support themselves or be supported by some friend to study under the various teachers in the College. [. . .]

Source: M. K. Kuriakose, *History of Christianity in India* (Madras, 1982), pp. 94f.

46. Ecumenical Visions

Due to practical necessity and the network of relationships among those involved in evangelical revivals, the early Protestant missionary movement fostered cooperation across denominational borders. Already in 1806, William Carey had envisioned a world missionary conference (b) — a plan that would only come to fruition one hundred years later with the Edinburgh Conference 1910 (see documents 70ff). In South India, Protestant contact was made with St. Thomas Christians. Anglican missionaries recognized many common features and sought to support them without taking control, as they accused the Catholics of doing (a).

a. Relations with the St. Thomas Christians (1806)

In the creeds and doctrines of the Christians of Malabar, internal evidence exists of their being a primitive church; for the supremacy of the Pope is denied, and the doctrine of transubstantiation never has been held by them. They also regarded, and still regard, the worship of images as idolatrous, and the doctrine of purgatory to be fabulous. Moreover they never admitted as sacraments, extreme unction, marriage, or confirmation. All which facts may be substantiated on reference to the Acts of the Synod assembled by Don Alexis de Menezes, Archbishop of Goa at Diyamper, in the year 1599.

The Christians on the Malabar Coast are divided into three sects. 1. The St. Thomas or Jacobite Christians. 2. The Syrian Roman-Catholics. 3. The Latin Church.

b. William Carey's Proposal for a World Missionary Conference (1806)

The Cape of Good Hope is now in the hands of the English; should it continue so, would it not be possible to have a general association of all denominations of Christians, from the four quarters of the world, held there once in about ten years. I earnestly recommend this plan, let the first meeting be in the Year 1810, or 1812 at furthest. I have no doubt but it would be attended with very important effects; we could understand one another better, and more entirely enter into one another's views by two hours conversation than by two or three years epistolary correspondence.

Source: (a) C. Buchanan, *Christian Researches in Asia* (London, 1812), p. 148; (b) M. K. Kuriakose, *History of Christianity in India* (Madras, 1982), p. 82. — *Further Reading:* Neill, *History II*, pp. 237ff.

C. Mission as a Means of Modernization

The effects of the Protestant missionary movement were felt far beyond the circle of baptized members. Mission became a means of modernization — through the construction of schools, hospitals and printeries that preceded or accompanied evangelistic efforts, the introduction of technical inovations and various social activities. These actions triggered effects in the traditional Asian societies that went far beyond the limited sphere of the mission churches.

47. The Education System

The British colonial chaplain Munro in 1816, on the introduction of Protestant Christianity in South India:

An efficient and extended system of education, particularly in English language, will attribute more effectively than any other plan to the early and substantial advancement of the Protestant religion in India. The prevalence of the Portuguese language has substantially promoted the propagation of the Roman Catholic religion. Indeed from the situation of the Portuguese in India, strong arguments may be adduced for the diffusion of the English language, as a means of supporting the British Power, as well as of extending the Protestant religion; for the name and influence of the Portuguese nation have been preserved by the prevalence of their language, long after the subversion of their power by the Dutch; and if the Portuguese were in a state to undertake conquests in India, their design would be greatly facilitated by the extension which their language and customs have obtained. [. . .]

Source: M. K. Kuriakose, *History of Christianity in India* (Madras, 1982), p. 92. — *Further Reading:* Neill, *History II*, pp. 307ff; M. A. Laird, *Missionaries and Education in Bengal 1793-1837* (Oxford, 1972); Moffett, *Asia II*, pp. 260ff; Sunquist, *Dictionary,* pp. 97f (Art. Buchanan, C.).

48. Medical Missions in China

The English Physician G. Tradescant Lay at the first annual assembly of the Medical Missionary Society in China on 27 September 1839 in Canton:

I am so impressed [by the medical missionary work hitherto achieved in Canton] that I have determined to make the system of gratuitous relief for the sick in some sort universal. I may not succeed in my first attempts, but I will continue, while life and health last, to pursue my object till I have attained it. We have societies for giving the bible, the gospel, useful knowledge, and so on, to the world — we will have also a Society for giving the benefits of rational medicine to the world. . . . Physicians must throw their skill in the healing art at the feet of the Savior, and be ready to use it when and where he shall direct. The number who should go to heathen lands [as missionary physicians] cannot well be named. It is sufficient to say that one pious physician at least could be advantageously useful; and fully employed in every congregation of heathen.

Source: Chinese Repository 7 (1838/39) 460f, partly quoted in: Chr. H. Grundmann, *Gesandt zu heilen! Aufkommen und Entwicklung der ärztlichen Mission im 19. Jahrhundert* (Gütersloh, 1992), pp. 173f. — *Further Reading:* C. Grundmann, *Sent to Heal! The Emergence and Development of Medical Missions in the 19th C.* (1999); H. Balme, *China and Modern Medicine* (1921); Sunquist, *Dictionary,* pp. 529-533 (Art. Medical Work).

49. Struggle Against the "Social Evils" of Hinduism

The Anglican Bishop of Calcutta, Henry Wilson, in a briefing from 5 July 1833 on the elimination of the caste system within the church:

The distinction of castes then must be abandoned, decidedly, immediately, finally; and those who profess to belong to Christ, must give this proof of their having really put off concerning the former conversation the old, and having put on the new man in Christ Jesus [cf. 2 Cor 5:17]. The Gospel recognises no distinctions, such as those of caste, imposed by a heathen usage, bearing in some respects a supposed religious obligation, condemning those in the lower ranks to perpetual abasement, placing an immoveable barrier against all general advance and improvement in society, cutting asunder the bonds of humane fellowship on the one hand, and preventing those of Christian on the othersuch distinctions, I say, the Gospel does not recognise; on the contrary, it teaches us that God 'hath made of one blood all the nations' of men; it teaches us that 'whilst the princes of the gentiles exercise authority upon them, and they that are great, exercise authority upon them, it must not be so amongst the followers of Christ, but that whosoever will be great amongst them, is to be their servant, even as the Son of Man came not to be ministered unto, but to minister and to give his life a ransom for man' [cf. Lk 22:25]. [. . .]

In the practical execution, however, of the present award, dear Brethren, much wisdom and charity, united with firmness, will be requisite.

1. The catechumens preparing for baptism must be informed . . . of the Bishop's decision, and must be gently and tenderly advised to submit to it. [. . .]

2. The children of native Christians will, in the next place, not be admitted to the holy communion without this renunciation of caste. [. . .]

3. With respect to the adult Christian already admitted to the holy communion, I should recommend that their prejudices and habits be so far consulted as not to insist on an open direct renunciation of caste. [. . .]

4. In the mean time it may suffice that overt acts, which spring from the distinction of castes, be at once and finally discontinued in the church. Whether places in the church be concerned, or the manner of approach to the Lord's table, or procession in marriages . . . or differences of food or dress — whatever be the overt acts, they must, in the church and so far as the influence of ministers goes, be at once abandoned. [. . .]

Source: H. Bower, *An Essay on Hindu Caste* (Calcutta, 1851), pp. 110-115. — *Further Reading:* Neill, *History II*, pp. 403ff; G. A. Oddie, *Social Protest in India: British Protestant Missionaries and Social Reform 1850-1900* (Delhi, 1978); D. Forrester, *Caste and Christianity* (London/Dublin, 1980).

50. Burma: A Missionary at the Royal Court in Mandalay (1868)

From a report of the Anglican missionary J. E. Marks on 20 October 1868:

In 1863 I met, in Rangoon, the Thonzay Mintha (prince), one of the sons of the King, who had fled from the capital [Mandalay, of Upper Burma still independent of Britain]. I gave him several Christian books in Burmese, and spoke to him about their contents. He became reconciled to the King, and, on his return to Mandalay, asked me to come and see him at the capital. [. . .]

We passed Ava and Amerapoora, and reached the capital city of Mandalay on the 8th October [1868], where we were most hospitably received by Captain Sladen, who had but recently returned from his expedition. On the following day the *Kulla Woon* came to tell me that the King had been very impatient about my coming . . . and would appoint an early day for an audience. On Saturday I went out to see the city. It is large and well laid out, the streets wide and at right angles, but the houses mean and irregular. The city is enclosed by an embattled high brick wall, with several imposing gateways. [. . .] A hill on the N. E. is completely covered with Buddhist buildings and emblems. There are in Mandalay more than 20,000 yellow-robed Buddhist priests, &c. On Sunday we had English service at the Residency, but very few people attended, the notice having been imperfectly circulated. [. . .]

On Monday, October 11, we had our first interview with the King of Burmah. [. . .] As the King entered every Burman bowed his head to the ground and kept it there. [. . .]

He then asked me what requests I had to make to him, assuring me that all were granted before I spoke. I said that I had four requests to make: — 1. Permission to labour as a Missionary in Mandalay. 2. To build a church for Christian worship according to the use of the Church of England. 3. To get a piece of land for a cemetery. 4. To build, with his Majesty's help, a Christian school for Burmese boys. With regard to the first, the King said very courteously that he welcomed me to the royal city: that he had impatiently awaited my arrival. . . . I was to choose . . . a piece of land for a cemetery. That with regard to the church and school his Majesty would build them entirely at his own cost. I told him that the Bishop of Calcutta had most liberally offered 100 £, towards the church. The King replied, 'It is unnecessary, I will do all myself.' He directed me to prepare the plans, adding that the school was to be built for 1,000 boys. The King said that it was his wish to place some of his own sons under our care, and he sent for nine of the young princes, fine intelligent-looking lads of about ten years of age, and formally handed them over to me. He handed me a hundred gold pieces (worth 50 £.) to buy books, &c. for the school. The King talked about . . . his desire to do all the good in his power, and especially to be friendly with the English. He asked me whether I would procure machinery for him from Europe. I said that, with every desire to oblige his Majesty, I must decline all commercial or political business; that my province was simply that of a religious teacher. The King was evidently pleased with my answer. [. . .]

Source: J. E. Marks, *A Visit to the King of Burmah at Mandalay, in Oct. 1868* (London, n.d.) (= 1869?), pp. 3-12. — *Further Reading:* Moffett, *Asia II*, pp. 322ff; *WCE* I, pp. 519ff; *RGG*[4] 5, 837f: Marks, John Ebenezer (D. O'Connor); Sunquist, *Dictionary,* pp. 574 (Art. Myanmar).

D. Public Response, Non-Christian Voices

51. The Hindu Reformer Rammohun Roy (1772-1833)

Raja Rammohun Roy (1772-1833) was one of the leading representatives of the cultural life in Bengal. A lifelong Hindu, he called Jesus the "perfect teacher" and attempted to reform popular Hinduism in the light of the ethical teaching of Jesus and specifically of the Sermon on the Mount. He declined the offer of the Serampore missionaries to become a Christian and instead founded the *Brahmo Samaj*. This played an important role in the Hindu Revival of the nineteenth century (cf. documents 62ff), and yet through it many individuals also found their way to the Bible and to the Christian church.

a. "The Commandments of Jesus the Leader for Peace and Happiness" (1820)

I . . . confine my attention at present to the task of laying before my fellow creatures the words of Christ, with a translation from the English into Sungskrit, and the language of Bengal. I feel persuaded that by separating from the other [doctrinal] matters contained in the New Testament, the moral precepts found in that book, these will be more likely to produce the desirable effect of improving the hearts and minds of men of different persuasions and degree of understanding. For historical and some other passages [in the New Testament] are liable to the doubts and disputes of free-thinkers and anti-Christians, especially miraculous relations, which are much less wonderful than the fabricated tales handed down to the natives of Asia, and consequently would be apt at best to carry little weight with them. On the contrary, moral doctrines [in the New Testament], tending evidently to the maintenance of the peace and harmony of mankind at large, are beyond the reach of metaphysical perversion, and intelligible alike to the learned and unlearned. This simple code of religion and morality is so admirably calculated to elevate men's ideas to high . . . notions of one God, who has equally subjected all living creatures, without distinction of caste, rank, or wealth, to change, disappointment, pain, and death, and has equally admitted all to be partakers of the bountiful mercies which he has lavished over nature, and is also well fitted to regulate the conduct of the human race in the discharge of their various duties to God, to themselves, and to society, that I cannot but hope the best effects from its promulgation in the present form.

b. "An Appeal to the Christian Public" (1823)

In perusing the twentieth number of [the journal of the Serampore missionaries] "The Friend of India," I felt as much surprised as disappointed at some remarks made in that magazine by a gentleman under the signature of "A Christian Missionary," on a late publication intitled, "The Precepts of Jesus" [. . .] [The critic] is correct . . . in ascribing the collection of these Precepts to Rammohun Roy; who, although he was born a Brahmun, not only renounced idolatry at a very early period of his life, but published at that time a treatise in Arabic and Persian against that system; and no sooner acquired a tolerable knowledge of English, than he made his desertion of idol worship known to the Christian world by his English publication — a renunciation that, I am sorry to say, brought severe difficulties upon him, by exciting the displeasure of his parents, and subjecting him to the dislike of his near, as well as distant relations, and to the hatred of nearly all his countrymen for several years. [. . .] It is, however, too true to be denied, that the Compiler of those moral precepts separated them from some of the dogmas and other matters, chiefly under the supposition, that they alone were a sufficient guide to secure peace and happiness to mankind at large — a position that is entirely founded on and supported by the express authorities of Jesus of Nazareth — a denial of which would imply a total disavowal of Christianity. [. . .]

Source: (a) R. Roy, *The Precepts of Jesus and Guide to Peace and Happiness: Extracted from the Books of the New Testament* (Calcutta, 1824), pp. XXVIIf. (b) Ibid., pp. 101-110. — *Further Reading:* S. Ahluwalia, *Raja Rammuhun Roy and the Indian Renaissance* (New Delhi, 1991); M. M. Thomas, *The Acknowledged Christ of the Indian Renaissance* (Madras, 1970), pp. 13-20; R. B. Baird (ed.), *Religion in Modern India* (New Dehli, 1991), pp. 1-16; Sajal Basu (ed.), *Rammohun Roy — Prophet of Modern India* (Calcutta, 2003); Sunquist, *Dictionary,* pp. 93f (Art. Brahmo Samaj).

52. Religious Debates in Colonial Ceylon (1873)

Between 1865 and 1899 major debates between Christians and Buddhists took place in Ceylon (Sri Lanka), and the 1873 debate at Panadura became the most significant. This involved the Sinhalese Methodist preacher David de Silva and the Buddhist monk Mohottivatte Gunanda Thera. It received attention not only in Ceylon but also in published form brought Buddhism to the attention of the co-founder of Theosophism, H. S. Olcott in the United States (see document 64).

Precisely as the clock struck eight, the Rev. David de Silva rose to address the crowd. He stated that before engaging in the controversy it was necessary to explain the reasons for holding it. On the 12th of June [1873] last he delivered a lecture in the [Methodist] Wesleyan Chapel, Pantura, on the teachings Buddha with reference to the human soul on the 19th of the same month it was taken exception to by the Buddhist party, and denounced as untrue. The present occasion was, therefore, appointed to shew what the doctrine of Buddhism was with reference to the soul, and he hoped that the Buddhist party would, if possible, meet his arguments properly; and that the assembly would judge for themselves what statements were to be received as sound. He stated that Buddhism taught that man had no soul and that the identical man received not the reward of his good or bad actions. According to Buddhism, the *sattâ*, sentient beings, are constituted in the five *khand-hâs* [factors of existence], namely the organised body, *wedanák-khandha,* the sensations, *sannak-khandha,* the perceptions, *sankharak-khandha,* the reasoning powers, and *winnanak-khandha,* consciousness. In proof of this, he quoted the following from *Sanyouttanikaya,* an extract from Buddha's sermons, and from the *Sutrapitaka* [collection of his sermons]. [. . .] From these authorities it is clear that Buddhism teaches that everything which constitutes man will cease to be at death, and that no immortal soul existed therein, and if then man was only a brute what need had he of a religion? Can he possess any moral principle? [. . .]

The [Buddhist] Priest Migettuwatte [Mohattiwatte Gunanda] then commenced his reply. He said that much penetration was not needed to form a correct opinion of the Rev. Mr. Silva's lecture to which they had all listened. It was a very desultory and rambling speech. . . . In his exposition of the Pali extracts, made from Buddha's discourses, he was not more successful, because he completely failed to convey to those present the correct meaning in intelligible language. [. . .] And with reference to Christianity, the Priest went on to say that the Christian was not a true religion, and by embracing it no being can thereby hope to enjoy bliss in a future life. [. . .] Christians, wherever they went, commenced propagating their religion by giving the object of their worship the name of a being already held in veneration by the nations [. . .]. It would thus be seen that the Christians adapted themselves to different nations with the intention of deceiving them.

Source: J. M. Peebles (ed.), *Buddhism and Christianity Face to Face, or an Oral Discussion Between the Rev. Migettuwatte, A Buddhist Priest, and Rev. D. Silva, A Wesleyan Clergyman, held at Pantura, Ceylon* (London, n.d. [= 1878]), pp. 22f, 27f, 31, 35f. — *Further Reading:* H. Bechert, *Buddhismus, Staat und Gesellschaft. I.* (Frankfurt, 1966), pp. 43ff; R. F. Young, G. P. V. Somaratna, *Vain Debates* (Wien, 1996); Moffett, *Asia II*, pp. 341ff.

53. Japan: Buddhist Voices on Christianity

J. D. Davies, an American missionary in the mid 1870s, reporting on Buddhist activities in Kyoto:

The priests have recently bought one hundred and twenty copies of the New Testament and some commentaries, and have put the school at work studying the Bible every day. What will come of it I do not know, but the priest who bought the books told the bookseller that they were bound to see what Christianity was. [. . .]

A Buddhist anti-Christian tract published in 1881 opens with the statement that:

Christianity is spreading like fire on a grassy plain, so that in capital and country there is no place where it is not preached.

The Buddhist journal *Meikyo shinsi* laments the fact that Buddhism is losing ground daily:

Buddhism besieged: *Ten-dai shiu,* without a scholar; *Shin-gon shiu,* neither men nor money; *Zen shiu,* its time is past — it hangs like a forgotten fruit; *Jodo shiu,* no sect is to be seen.

Source: N. R. Thelle, *Buddhism and Christianity in Japan: From Conflict to Dialogue 1854-1899* (Honolulu, 1987), pp. 78, 57, 57.

E. Northeast Asia: A Forced Opening

Christian missions in Northeast Asia were for a long time officially prevented. Only in 1853-54 under American pressure did Japan begin to open itself to the outside world, and the Japanese ban on Christianity was not lifted until 1878 (document 56). Similarly in China, a gradual opening to Western missions began following the first Opium War in 1840-1842. However the "protection" of Christianity by the European powers left an unfortunate legacy. In the French version of the Peking Convention of 1860, France unilaterally extended the rights of the Catholic missions beyond what was stated in the original Chinese version (document 55). On the other hand, Protestant missionaries such as the German Karl Gützlaff firmly believed in the principle of an autonomous propagation of Christianity through Chinese evangelists, and tried to operate independently in the so-called treaty ports and other areas. In Vietnam, persecutions of Catholics, a minority which had been in existence since the seventeenth century, began in 1832 (document 57). In Korea, a few American Protestants started missionary activity in 1884-1885. Cooperating with Korean Christians living in the diaspora, their efforts led to the founding of fast-growing Protestant congregations (document 58).

54. Karl Gützlaff's "Chinese Accounts"

Karl Gützlaff (1803-1851), deeply influenced by the German pietist movement, generated a great enthusiasm in Europe for overseas missions through his passionate "Chinese Accounts" from 1841 to 1846. He was convinced that Chinese could only be successfully evangelized through "native evangelists." Naïve as well as adventurous, Gützlaff, through his education of Chinese preachers, indirectly also contributed to the Taiping Rebellion (see document 61).

Journal from 17 May 1831:

My work in Siam [Thailand] is now completed. . . . My eye is directed now entirely on China, not of my own choice but out of conviction that the Lord is sending me along this path and that my commitment belongs there. I want to lay the 100 million [Chinese people] on the heart of the High Priest, the Lord Jesus. He must pave the way and make his glorious gospel victorious. Not that I am capable of anything on my own; rather, the almighty Jesus is the rock of my trust. I must fight insurmountable obstacles. . . . The whole guidance of the Lord is wonderful. [. . .]

Account from 6 June 1841:

After I had made a stopover here [in Macao] for a few days, I received another command to ship myself off to Schusan [Zhoushan] and Ningpo [Ningbo], where we arrived at the end of April. The warlike preparations and the repeated attempts to shoot us dead notwithstanding, I found the opportunity to spread the Word of God. . . . Since all efforts to compel the Emperor toward peaceful convictions were futile, the fight [the British-Chinese Opium War, 1840-42, in which Gützlaff served the British as translator and negotiator] will probably end only in Peking. The consequences will be tremendous. As Christians, we have nothing to do with war, our duty is to hasten to the throne of grace and there to beseech our savior to open wide the door of his gospel. . . . The present struggle will be epoch-making in the world's history; here is nothing less at stake than whether China shall be able to close its doors to every stranger forever. The Emperor believes that all power is exclusively his . . . and anticipates the help of the idols in this fight. Our Lord Christ lives, the myriads of this land are his, and he shall bring about the day of affliction with unending love.

Account from 27 June 1846:

Journeying. This shall always remain our chief labor because it was in just this way that the gospel was spread by his apostles. Not to mention the less important areas, we have undertaken quite long expeditions to Lantao, Taipan, . . . to Haihong, now a permanent station, to Kweitschen [Guilin], Tamtsui [Guishan], to Taichu (messengers who had been sent there just came . . . to tell us of how they were robbed by thieves) . . . to Formosa and the south-west area of Fokien [Fujian], to Kweilin [Guilin]in Kwangsi Guangxi]. There a Christian association has sprung up, even without our help, and we wish, should it please the Lord, to donate a little chapel in this faraway city. [. . .]

Source: Gaihans (Karl Gützlaffs) Chinesische Berichte 1841-1846, ed. by the Chairmen of the Chinese Foundation (Vorstand der Chinesischen Stiftung) (Kassel, 1850), pp. 1-6, 274 — Further Reading: Moffett, Asia II, pp. 295ff; Sunquist, Dictionary, pp. 318f; J. G. Lutz, "The Legacy of K. F. A. Guetzlaff," IBMR 24 (2000), pp. 123-128; H. Schlyter, Karl Gützlaff als Missionar in China (Lund, 1976); B. E. K. Sng, Liang Afa: China's First Preacher (Singapore, 1998); Th. Klein/ R. Zöllner (eds.), Karl Gützlaff (1803-1851) und das Christentum in Ostasien (St. Augustin, 2005).

55. China: Forced Missionary Protectorate (from 1842)

a. The Nanjing Convention (August 29, 1842)

Article II. His Majesty the Emperor of China agrees that British Subjects, with their families and establishments, shall be allowed to reside, for the purpose of carrying on their Mercantile pursuits, without molestation or restraint at the Cities and Towns of Canton, Amoy, Foochow-fu, Ningpo, and Shanghai, and

Her Majesty the Queen of Great-Britain, etc., will appoint Superintendents or Consular Officers, to reside at each of the above-named Cities or Towns, to be the medium of communication between the Chinese Authorities and the said Merchants, and to see that the just Duties and other Dues of the Chinese Government as hereafter provided for, are duly discharged by Her Britannic Majesty's Subjects.

b. The Bejing Convention of 1860

Chinese version:

In agreement with the imperial edict which was issued by the distinguished Emperor Tao-kuang on 20 March 1846, the religious and charitable institutions that were confiscated during the persecutions targeting Christians shall be restored to their proprietors through the mediation of the French Legate in China, to whom the imperial government [of China] will surrender them, with the churchyards and other building that belong to them.

French version:

It shall be proclaimed as soon as possible in the whole land, according to the conditions of the imperial edict of 20 March 1846, that it is allowed for each and every person in every part of China to propagate and practice Catholicism, to gather for the preaching of doctrine, to construct churches and hold worship services, and furthermore shall each man who imprisons Christians without thought of their confessional differences be appropriately punished; and such churches, schools, cemeteries, parcels of land and edifices as formerly belonged to persecuted Christians shall be paid for and the money shall be transferred to the French representative in Peking to be given out to the Christians in the affected places. The French missionaries will furthermore be allowed to rent or purchase property in all provinces and erect there as many buildings as they please.

Source: (a) H. F. MacNair, *Modern Chinese History: Selected Readings* (Shanghai, 1923), pp. 175f. (b) J. Richter, *Das Werden der christlichen Kirche in China* (Gütersloh, 1928), p. 109. — *Further Reading:* Moffett, *Asia II,* pp. 297ff; England, *ACT III,* pp. 92ff.

56. Japan: Gradual Steps towards Legality

After more than two hundred years of self-imposed isolation, Japanese ports were forcefully opened in 1854 by an American fleet under Commodore M. C. Perry. Before that, foreigners were not allowed to set foot in the country without proving that they did not adhere to the Catholic religion (a). The American actions hurled the country into crisis (b), followed in the 1870's by an imitation of Western models. The Protestant missions benefitted in only a limited way at first. Initially, missionaries were only allowed to work as teachers or physicians in the foreign quarters of the port cities. The first Protestant congregation in Japan was founded in 1872 by eleven secretly baptized Christians. The proscription of Christianity was only officially lifted in 1878 (d), and religious freedom laid down in the first constitution of Japan, the "Meiji constitution" of 1889 (e).

a. The Trial of a Foreigner

In 1848 the American businessman Ranald MacDonald, administrator of the Hudson Bay Company in Oregon, landed in Japan. He was put on trial by the governor of Nagasaki and sent back on the next ship. From his account:

In entering [the governor's reception hall] . . . I saw a bronze plate, round, about six inches in diameter [5 by 15 centimeters], flat on the ground, with something delineated on it which — stooping to examine — I took to be the virgin and child. Told to put my foot on it, being a Protestant, I unhesitatingly did do. [. . .] [The Governor's ceremonial grand entrance was quite impressive. The Japanese translator] Murayama repeated his injunction to bow low. Still angry, I didn't. I *"Kitu"* (or *"Kotow"*) to no man! [. . .] Curious to read my fate at the hands of His Excellency, I looked him fearlessly but respectfully, full in the face. So did he me. I had just quickly, before that, looked around, and saw every one, even the soldiers, flat on their faces, the hands being placed on the ground, and the forehead resting on them. They all remained in this position for quite a time, say ten or fifteen seconds during which, in dead silence, the Governor and I stared at each other. At length, rising from his sitting position, . . . leaning towards me, the Governor addressed me a few words, deep toned and low [. . .]. Afterwards — for I could not at the time — I asked Murayama what he said. He answered: "He said you must have a big heart." [. . .]

MacDonald is asked about his origins, circumstances and religion:

One of the questions — as on a former occasion — was whether I believed in a God in Heaven. I said Yes! — Then I was asked what was my belief as to a God in Heaven. I answered, first, that I believed in One God, and that He was constantly and everywhere present. Then Murayama — as if not satisfied with the answer — asked what I believed in respect to God in Heaven. I answered by beginning to recite the "Apostles' Creed," in my English prayer book, having been brought up an Episcopalian — my father's creed and my own; but when I had said "And in Jesus Christ, his only Son," born of the virgin Mary"; Murayama suddenly stopped me, saying, quickly, in a whisper "that will do ! what will do!" He then proceeded to translate my answer, to the Governor [. . .]. [The Japanese report records Moriyama's translation of MacDonald's confession of faith; it reads:] There is no God, no Buddha. I strive only to develop my spirit and my will and to worship heaven, in order to attain clear understanding and happiness. [Moriyama's false translation saves MacDonald's life. He is told that he, like every Western 'barbarian', would be expelled to Batavia/Jakarta as soon as possible, but that it would take a year, because the yearly Dutch ship had only recently sailed.]

b. Forced Opening (1853ff)

Following the appearance of American gunboats in 1853 Japan's political council, the *Bakufu*, witnessed violent debates in one of which the Prince of Mito, Tokugawa Nariaki, made this statement:

It is my conviction that the first and most essential task of the *Bafuku* is to choose between war and peace, and to follow this chosen policy without swaying. [. . .] I will offer ten reasons why we may never choose a policy of peace.

1. Even though our country is not so large, the barbarians have still feared and respected us till now. [. . .] However, although the Americans know very well that it is forbidden, they sailed into the Bay of Uraga and they insist upon trading here. [. . .] If the *Bafuku* does not chase them away, or tries to negotiate with them, then it will be impossible to maintain our national pride. This is the first reason.

2. The prohibition of Christianity is the highest law of the *Tokugawa* [dynasty, ruling since 1615]. To this very day, public prohibitions have been posted in every single location, even in the most remote parts of the country. If the Americans were allowed to return, then this religion would again rear its head, no matter how strict the prohibitions are, and we would never be able to justify that to the spirit of our forefathers. That is the second reason.

3. To trade our gold, silver, copper and iron for worthless foreign goods would mean a huge loss for us and would be of no benefit. [. . .]

c. First Conversions (1865)

From the account of one of the first American Presbyterian missionaries:

Yano, Ritizan, a shaven-headed Buddhist, . . . who held an inferior position, was selected by the Shogun's Council of State as a language teacher for Dr. S. R. Brown. On my arrival, November 11th, 1861, he became my teacher. With him I undertook the translation of St. John, more to translate the Gospel for him than for the use of others. In the summer of 1864 he became quite weak. I was disturbed by his inability to keep to the schedule, and asked him if he would be willing for me to seek a blessing for our translation work. On his consenting, I made my first impromptu Japanese prayer, which seemed to impress him much. One day, while explaining a picture of the baptism of the Ethiopian eunuch [cf. Acts 8,26-39], he suddenly said to me: "I want to be baptised; I want to be baptised because Christ commanded it." I warned him of the law against Christianity and the possibility that, even if he escaped the penalty, his son might not. The son, being consulted, said that whatever would please his father should be done. On the first Sabbath in November his baptism took place in the presence of his wife, son, and daughter.

d. Repeal of the Anti-Christian Edict (1878)

From the annual report of the Protestant Missionary Conference of Japan in Osaka, April 1883:

The next event to be recorded is the removal of the edict against Christianity [cf. document 24] from the public notice-boards throughout the Empire. This took place in virtue of a decree of February 24th, 1878. It was an event of the weightiest consequence to the work of the missions; for, although the removal of the obnoxious edict was finally decreed, because the authorities might presume that its subject matter, having been before the eyes of the nation for more than two centuries, "was sufficiently imprinted on the people's minds," and although the Government by no means intended publicly to declare by its action that the prohibition of Christianity had now been abrogated and religious toleration granted, yet the event itself conveyed, in the general estimation of the people, the idea that liberty of conscience was henceforth to be allowed, and it virtually amounted to as much. It was especially calculated to do so, when taken in connection with the almost entire disestablishment of the various Buddhist sects (by decree of February 23rd, 1871), the release of many hundreds of Roman Catholic Christians (in March and April, 1873), and the perfect immunity practically accorded to the Protestant church recently organized at Yokohama without the slightest attempt at secrecy and under the very eyes of the authorities. There is no doubt that the people generally regarded the removal of the edict in question as being equivalent to a repeal of the laws which had for generations prohibited Christianity under the most severe penalties, and there can be as little doubt that the Government was not at all disinclined to see so favorable a construction put upon its action, especially in foreign parts. [. . .] The year 1878, finally, is remarkable for having witnessed the arrival of by far the largest number of missionaries that ever came to Japan in any one year, either before or after. [. . .] During these fourteen years there arrived 20 married missionaries, 6 single female, and 5 single male missionaries, making a total of 31; while in the year 1878 there arrived 16 married missionaries, 7 single female, and 6 single male missionaries, making a total of 29.

Source: (a) R. MacDonald, *The Narrative of His Early Life on the Columbia under the Hudson's Bay Company's Regime . . . 1824-1894* (ed. and annot. from the original ms. by W. S. Lewis) (Portland, Ore., 1890), pp. 216-220; (b) G. C. Schwebell, *Die Geburt des modernen Japan in Augenzeugenberichten* (Düsseldorf, 1970), pp. 119-121; (c) O. Cary, *A History of Christianity in Japan: Roman Catholic, Greek Orthodox, and Protestant Missions.* Vol. II (Tokyo, 1976) (= New York, 1909), p. 56 (slightly altered); (d) Proceedings of the General Conference of the Protestant Missionaries of Japan, held at Osake, Japan, April 1883, ed. by the Publishing Committee (Yokohama, 1883), pp. 54-57. — *Further Reading:* TRE 16, 1987, pp. 527ff: Art. Japan II (K. Ogawa); Moffett, *Asia II,* pp. 504ff; England, *ACT III,* pp. 22ff, 300ff.

57. Vietnam: Edict against the Christians (1851)

Indochina had been a favorite field of activity for French Catholic missionaries from the middle of the seventeenth century. By the beginning of the nineteenth century Christianity had become established. It proved impossible to drive it out even though the religious politics of the Vietnamese rulers — who had freed themselves from Chinese rule with the help of the French — changed and Christians were persecuted with increasing brutality. While Christian teaching spread quickly in the lower classes, where economic and social hopes were pinned on this new doctrine of salvation, the alliance between mission and European trade and political interests was judged increasingly critically by the Confucianist-educated higher class. In the years 1882-1884, Vietnam became a French protectorate. The anti-Christianity edict printed below, from the Vietnamese Emperor Tú Dúc, dates from 30 March 1851. The violent persecution of Christians in the years following has been judged in different ways: on the one hand as an act of national self-assertion (in the historiography of communist Vietnam), on the other hand as an example in a long series of anti-Christian persecution measures (the official Roman-Catholic position).

The doctrine of Jesus comes from the Europeans: it forbids ancestor and spirit worship. To mislead men and bemuse its adepts it talks of Heaven and holy water. Its propagators, well knowing that the law of the kingdom cannot tolerate such an evil doctrine, present to the people an image of a tortured Jesus, their master, to seduce the ignorant and make them confront death without repentance. What a deplorable illusion! What a strange obsession!

In the reign of King Minh Mang this senseless cult was severely prohibited by several decrees: every time a Christian refused to abandon it he was very rigorously, promptly and remorselessly punished. From the time of Thieu Tri many orders were given to renew prohibition of this perverse doctrine. Except for the aged and infirm, no refractory Christian was ever granted exception.

That is why our venerable predecessors have always acted with consumate care, rigour and prudence to eliminate its inherently evil principles. By the faithful observance of ritual and by the study of music and a respectable style of clothing they have attained a high level of culture. The basis of our own civilisation is proper behaviour; but it would soon be degraded if the doctrine of these men with hearts of savages and the habits of animals were to be put into practice. [. . .]

Here is the advice which our officials give: That the priests from Europe should be thrown into our rivers or into the depths of the sea for the glory of the True Religion. Annamese [Vietnamese] priests, whether they agree to trample on the cross or not, shall be cut in half so that all may know the severity of the Law. We have examined these proposals and find them in conformity with true reason. [. . .]

Source: P. J. N. Tuck, *French Catholic Missionaries and the Politics of Imperialism in Vietnam: A Documentary Survey* (Liverpool, 1987), pp. 34f. — *Further Reading:* Moffett, *Asia II*, pp. 360ff; Sunquist, *Dictionary*, pp. 876-880 (Art. Vietnam).

58. Korea: Protestant Beginnings (since 1884)

The beginnings of Korean Protestantism are usually connected with the arrival of the first American missionaries in the country in 1884-1885, which until then had been sealed off from the outside world. However, as already noted, well before that date, Koreans living in Japan, China and Manchuria had accepted the new faith. Through their work as Bible translators and their propaganda among their countrymen they set the stage for the sudden sweep of Christianity in Korea.

a. Korean Christians in the Diaspora

Yi, Su-jong, or Japanese: Rijutei, was an extra member of the Special Envoy of the Korean government to Japan . . . following the military riot of 1882. . . . He was a court annalist and held the title of a general, Sun-Yak-Chang-Koon . . . , a fourth degree military title of the rear rank. [. . .] As soon as he reached Japan, he came into contact with the Japanese agriculturist, Tsuda Sen, who was a Christian. Yi was touched by a scroll [with the text] of the Sermon on the Mount in Chinese, which was hung up on the wall of Tsuda's guest room, and took interest in the [Christian] faith. . . . He was soon converted and baptized by a Japanese pastor. American Missionaries in Tokyo seized the opportunity of his presence and engaged him for the translation of the Bible into Korean. [. . .] He . . . taught the Korean language in the Tokyo University and wrote a book and articles on the Korean language. In the home politics [in Korea], he was a protege of the reactionary Min faction, but in Japan he caught a glimpse of modernism and embraced the new faith. [. . .] He had returned home [to Korea] in May, 1886, and . . . he was . . . put to death . . . by the reactionary government.

b. The First American Missionaries

From a 1902 visitation report on the beginnings and the current state of the Presbyterian mission in Korea:

It was not till September 20, 1884, that the first Protestant missionary, Dr. H. N. Allen . . . arrived in Korea, and not till July, 1886, that Dr. Underwood baptized the first 17,935 catechumens, exclusive of adherents and children. Our own mission easily leads all the others, with over 4,000 baptized adults, about 15,000 adherents and 251 organized "groups" or congregations. And the growth continues at the rate of over 1,000 accessions on examination [prior to baptism] yearly. Hundreds more only want the visit of a missionary to be received. Ninety-two were baptized at a single service in Pyeng Yang, just before my arrival. Wherever I went, I found not only full but crowded churches. I looked with mingled awe and gladness on a congregation of 1,000 worshippers in Seoul, and of 1,800 in Pyeng Yang, and when in the latter city, which was not opened as a station until 1894, I found the whole congregation in four sections studying the Bible in the Sunday-school, and packing the great church for the Wednesday evening prayer meeting, the wonder increased. In 1898, the Pyeng Yang Station reported that its field contains 4,000,000 of people, living in forty-four counties of North and South Pyeng An Provinces, and ten counties of Whang Hai Province. In all but one of these counties the Gospel has been preached with the result that the whole region is in a ferment, and groups of inquirers are springing up in every direction.

[. . .] From the beginning, Korean Christians have not been allowed to expect paid employment from the missionaries, nor have they received it, except in comparatively few and clearly exceptional cases. They have been taught to live the Gospel, and to spread it without pay among their countrymen. We are now seeing the fulfillment of the prophecy made in the Mission Report of 1896, in which it was said that "the native Christians have by word of mouth, and by printed page, and by the testimony of reformed lives, carried the Gospel into hundred of town and villages. . . ." The believers meet in one another's houses until they are strong enough to build, unaided, a church. The edifice is usually a very humble one, but it is as good as the houses in which the members live, and sometimes, as in Sorai and Pyeng Yang, it is the most notable building in the community. The people prize it because it costs them something, and because it is their own.

Source: (a) Lak-Geoon G. Paik, *The History of Protestant Missions in Korea, 1832-1910* (Pyeng Yang, 1929), p. 78; (b) Report of a Visitation of the Korea Mission of the Presbyterian Board of Foreign Missions, by Rev. Arthur J. Brown, D.D., Secretary (New York, 1902), pp. 8f. — *Further Reading:* Moffett, *Asia II*, pp. 528ff; Sunquist, *Dictionary,* pp. 446-449 (Art. Korea); 451f (Art. Korean Christian Church in Japan); England, *ACT III*, pp. 491ff; E. N. Hunt, *Protestant Pioneers in Korea* (Maryknoll, 1980); Wi Jo Kang, *Christ and Caesar in Modern Korea* (New York, 1990), pp. 9ff; T. K. Thomas (ed.), *Christianity in Asia* (Singapore, 1979), pp. 67ff (Kyoung Bae Min); Sook Jong Lee, "The Beginnings of the Early Korean Protestant Church . . . ," in: K. Koschorke (ed.), *Transcontinental Links . . .* (Wiesbaden, 2002), pp. 87-105.

F. Indigenous Versions of Christianity

59. Japan: The "Hidden Christians" of Nagasaki (1865)

In 1865, members of the *Kakure Kirishitan,* the "hidden" Christians of Japan, who had survived 200 years of persecution underground, came into contact with a European visitor to the country, the French priest Bernard Petitjean (1829-1884). In other parts of Japan, the *Kakure Kirishitan* kept themselves hidden until the beginning of the twentieth century (a). Petitjean later received a copy of their holy book, the *Tenchi Haaijmari no Koto* ("The Beginning of Heaven and Earth"), in which the creation story and other biblical stories merge with Buddhist mythology and other syncretic elements (b).

a. First Contacts with Western Visitors (1865)

From a report of the French priest B. Petitjean:

On March 17, 1865, about half past twelve, some fifteen persons were standing at the church door. Urged no doubt by my guardian angel, I went up and opened the door. I had scarce time to say a Pater when three women between fifty and sixty years of age knelt down beside me and said in a low voice, placing their hands upon their hearts: 'The hearts of all of us here do not differ from yours.' 'Indeed!' I exclaimed, 'Whence do you come?' They named the village, adding: 'All there have the same heart as we.'

Blessed be Thou, O my God, for all the happiness which filled my soul! What a compensation for five years of barren ministry! Scarcely had our dear Japanese opened their hearts to us than they displayed an amount of trustfulness which contrasts strangely with the behaviour of their pagan brethren. I was obliged to answer all their questions and to talk to them of *O Deusu Sama, O Yasu Sama,* and *Santa Maria Sama,* by which names they designated God, Jesus Christ, and the Blessed Virgin. The view of the statue of the Madonna and Child recalled Christmas to them, which they said they had celebrated in the eleventh month. They asked me if we were not in the seventeenth day of the Time of Sadness (Lent); nor was Saint Joseph unknown to them; they call him *O Yasu Sama no Yofu,* 'the adoptive father of our Lord.' In the midst of this volley of questions, footsteps were heard. Immediately all dispersed; but as soon as the newcomers were recognised, all returned laughing at their fright. 'They are people of our village,' they said, 'They have the same hearts as we have.' However, we had to separate for fear of awakening the suspicions of the officials, whose visit I feared.

b. From Their Scripture "The Beginning of Heaven and Earth"

In the beginning *Deusu* [God, deus] was worshiped as Lord of Heaven and Earth, and Parent of humankind and all creation. *Deusu* has two hundred ranks and forty-two forms, and divided the light that was originally one, and made the Sun Heaven, and twelve other heavens. The names of these heavens are Benbo or Hell, Manbo, Oribeten, Shidai, Godai, Pappa, Oroha, Konsutanchi, Hora, Koroteru, and a hundred thousand Paraiso and Gokuraku.

Deusu then created the sun, the moon, and the stars, and called into being tens of thousands of *anjo* just by thinking of them. One of them, *Jusuheru,* the head of seven *anjo,* has a hundred ranks and thirty-two forms. *Deusu* is the one who made all things: earth, water, fire, wind, salt, oil, and put in his own flesh and bones. Without pause *Deusu* worked on the *Shikuda* [Monday, port. Segunda], *Terusha, Kuwaruta, Kinta, Sesuta,* and *Sabata.* Then on the seventh day *Deusu* blew breath into this being and named him *Domeigosu-no-Adan* [Sunday-Adam], who possessed thirty-three forms. So this is the usual number of forms for a human being. For this reason the seventh day of one cycle is observed as a feast day. *Deusu* then made a woman and called her *Domeigosu-no-Ewa* [Sunday-Eve], had the man and woman marry, and gave them the realm called *Koroteru.* There they bore a son and daughter, *Chikoro* and *Tanho,* and went every day to *Paraiso* to worship *Deusu.*

One day while *Deusu* was away, *Jusuheru* seized the opportunity to deceive the anjo and said, "As I'm also like Deusu, worship me from now on." Hearing this, the *anjo* worshiped him saying, "Ah, behold, behold!" [. . .] [Here follows the story of the fall of mankind]

What a pitiful sight it was, for *Ewa* and *Adan* too lost the glory of heaven and were transformed on the spot. They offered the *Salve Regina,* cried out to heaven, and bowed to the ground. Tears of blood flowed from their eyes, and although they had a thousand regrets it was no use. This incident is the origin of the Contrition *orassho* [repentance].

After some time had passed, *Ewa* and *Adan* turned to *Deusu* and implored, "Please let us taste again the glory of heaven." *Deusu* listened and answered them, "If that is your wish, you must repent for more than four hundred years. Then I will invite you to *Paraiso*. But you, *Ewa*, will become a dog in Middle Heaven." Ewa was then kicked and disappeared to who knows where. "As for you, children of *Ewa*, you must live on the earth, eat beasts, and worship the moon and the stars, and repent. At some later time I will show you the way to heaven."

Source: (a) O. Cary, *A History of Christianity in Japan.* Vol. I (Tokyo, 1976) (= New York 1909), pp. 1, 282f; (b) C. Whelan, *The Beginnings of Heaven and Earth: The Sacred Book of Japan's Hidden Christians* (Honolulu, 1996), pp. 39-41. — *Further Reading:* A. M. Harrington, *Japan's Hidden Christians* (Chicago, 1992); S. R. Turnbull, *The Kakure Kirishitan of Japan* (Richmond, 1999); Ikuo Higashibaba, *Christianity in Early Modern Japan: Kirishitan Belief and Practice* (Leiden, etc., 2001); Moffett, *Asia II,* pp. 502ff.

60. South Asia: Migrants as Multipliers (1854)

Often Christianity spread without any missionary influence, especially through Christian migration from other areas of Asia. This happened, for example, on the tea plantations in Ceylon's highlands:

As [the Anglican missionary] Mordoch rode about among the estates, he discovered little groups of Christian *coolies* from [South Indian] Tinnevelly. An English planter, not long out from a Christian home in his native land, was astonished one Sunday morning to hear hymn-singing in the coffee-store, not far from the bungalow. Going down to ascertain from whence it proceeded, he found a hundred of his *coolies* gathered together, under the leadership of one of themselves, for a service. Such gatherings were found on more than one estate where Christian *coolies* were engaged in holding services regularly without minister or sacrament.

Source: R. Potter Butterfield, *Padre Rowlands of Ceylon* (London, [1928]), pp. 43f. — *Further Reading:* N. C. Sargant, *The Dispersion of the Tamil Church* (Madras, 1962), pp. 64f.

61. China: The Taiping Rebellion (1850-1864)

The Taiping Rebellion was one of the most important and tragic rebellions in Chinese history and brought the ruling Manchu Dynasty to the brink of destruction in the middle of the nineteenth century. It has been called the Chinese "version of Old Testament Protestant Christianity" by authorities such as John K. Fairbank. Its leaders regarded themselves as Christians, preached the biblical message to the exclusion of all other doctrines (despite various syncretic elements), championed a puritan ethic and aimed at friendly contact with missionaries and other representatives of the West. Yet they remained independent in their actions and theology. The military suppression of the group in 1864 (supported in the end by the Western powers) claimed millions of victims. The movement began in 1837 with a vision experienced by the movement's founder and later "King," Hong Xiuquan (1814-1864), which he later interpreted, in light of the biblical promises, as a commission to bring about the fall of the Manchu Dynasty and to drive out from China Confucius and other "demons" (a). Among his followers, the precise knowledge of this vision was regarded as indispensable, together with a catechism which consisted of the Ten Commandments and Christian prayers (b). The Taiping presented themselves as true Christians (c) and regarded Taiping China as an equal member in the family of "Christian" — that is, Western — "nations" (d).

a. The Vision of Hong Xiuquan

Afterwards they entered another large hall, the beauty and splendour of which were beyond description. A man, venerable from his years, with golden bears, and dressed in a black robe was sitting in an imposing attitude in the highest place. As soon as he observed Hong Xiuquan, he began to shed tears, and said — 'All human beings in the world are produced and sustained by me; they eat my food and wear my clothing, but not a single one among them has a heart to remember and venerate me; what is however still worse, they take my gifts, they take my gifts, and therewith worship demons; they rebel against me, and arouse my anger. Do thou not imitate them.' Thereupon he gave Hong Xiuquan a sword, commanding him to exterminate the demons, but to spare his brothers and sisters; a seal by which he would overcome the evil spirits and a yellow fruit, which Hong Xiuquan found sweet to the taste. [. . .]

In another version of the vision one of the demons is identified as Confucius:

Our Heavenly Father, Supreme Lord and August God thus reproached Confucius: 'Why do you teach people in such a muddle-headed way that they do not know Me on earth? Is your name, on the other hand, greater than Mine?' At first Confucius tried to argue, but then became tongue-tied and speechless. [. . .] All the angels also blamed him. Hence he secretly fell down from Heaven, intending to join the devils. Our Heavenly Father, Supreme Lord and August God immediately dispatched the Lord [Hong Xiuquan] and an angel to pursue Confucius, [and] tie him up [. . .].

b. The Ten Commandments and the Lord's Prayer among the Taiping

The little journal that every rebel in the year 1854 possessed and which is today still in countless hands, has the following content.

It begins with the Ten Commandments: "1. Honor God and worship him. (Explanation: Whoever does not worship God is breaking this commandment.) 2. You shall not worship evil spirits. 3. You shall not take the name of the Lord your God in vain. (Note: The original name of God is Jehovah. All who abuse the name of God are breaking this law.) 4. Every seventh day you shall praise God and extol his virtues. 5. Honor your father and your mother. (Note: Whoever rebels against his parents or is disobedient to them is breaking this commandment.) 6. You shall not commit murder or hurt anyone. (Note: Whoever murders, kills himself; whoever hurts others, hurts himself. Whoever kills or hurts others is breaking this commandment.) 7. You shall not commit adultery or act badly in any other way. [. . .] 8. You shall not steal, rob or plunder. (Note: Heaven has regulated wealth and poverty, therefore each one should help the other. Whoever steals or plunders is breaking this law and will go to hell). 9. You shall not speak any untruth. [. . .] 10. You shall not covet. (Interpretation: Whoever desires to satisfy evil passions or craves for riches or loves the hunt, gluttony, opium or gambling is breaking this commandment).

Whoever holds these aforementioned ten commandments of heaven and does not besmirch his soul will certainly go to heaven and enjoy eternal bliss; whoever does not keep them and besmirches his soul will go to ruin and suffer eternal misery. We shall therefore make every effort to keep these ten commandments!"

Then comes the *praise section,* which corresponds with the Sabbath and is the praise of the Holy Trinity. [. . .]

Another *prayer* laid down in this little booklet is the following:

"Highest Lord and God, Heavenly Father, we your unworthy children who kneel here remember that you, our heavenly Father, created heaven and earth, mountains and seas, sun and moon, humans and all things in six days. We ask you, that you may bless the brothers and sisters of all nations. [. . .] Bless us brothers and sisters; give us our daily bread and garments, turn away accident and disadvantage from us, so that we have peace in this world."

c. Taiping as a Popular Movement

From the account of American missionary Rev. Dr. Walter H. Medhurst (1796-1857) on a mission gathering in Shanghai enthusiastically taken over by Taiping supporters:

Having obtained admission into the city of Shanghae this afternoon, I proceeded to one of the chapels belonging to the London Missionary Society, where I commenced preaching to a large congregation, which had almost immediately gathered within the walls. I was decanting on the folly of idolatry, and the necessity of worshipping the one true God, on the ground that he alone could protect his servants . . . when, suddenly a man stood up in the midst of the congregation, and exclaimed: "That is true, that is true! The idol must perish and shall perish. I am a *Kwang-se*-man, a follower of *Thai-ping-wang;* we all of us worship one God *(Shang-te),* and believe in Jesus, while we do our utmost to put down idolatry; everywhere demolishing the temples and destroying the idols, and exhorting the people to forsake their superstitions. When we commenced two years ago, we were only 3,000 in number, and we have marched from one end of the empire to another, putting to flight whole armies of the Mandarins' troops; that were sent against us. If it had not been that God was on our side, we could not have thus prevailed against such overwhelming numbers; but now our troops have arrived at Tien-tsin, and we expect soon to be victorious over the whole empire." He then proceeded to exhort the people in a most lively and earnest strain to abandon idolatry, which was only the worship of devils, and the perseverance in which would involve them in the miseries of hell; while by giving it up, and believing in Jesus, they would obtain the salvation of their souls [. . .]. "While continuing here, we make it our business to keep the commandments, to worship God, and to exhort each other to do good, for which end we have frequent meetings for preaching and prayer. What is the use, then," he asked, "of you Chinese going on to burn incense, and candles, and gilt paper [. . .]." He went on to inveigh against the prevailing vices of his countrymen, particularly opium-smoking. "That filthy drug," he exclaimed, "which only defiles those who use it, making their houses stink, and their clothes stink, aud their bodies stink, and their souls stink, and will make them stink for ever in hell, unless they abandon it."

"But you must be quick," he adds; "for *Thai-ping-wang* is coming, and he will not allow the least infringement of his rules, no opium, no tobacco, no snuff, no wine, no vicious indulgences of any kind; all offences against the commandments of God are punished by him with the severest rigour, while the incorrigible are beheaded. Therefore repent in time."

d. Taiping China and the "Christian Nations"

From an account of the British representative Thomas T. Meadows on his visit to the court of the Prince of Taiping in Nanjing in the year 1853, in which he communicated the desire of the British government to remain neutral in the conflict between the ruling Manchu Dynasty and the Taipings:

To all this the Northern Prince listened, but made little or no rejoinder; the conversation, in so far as directed by him, consisting mainly of inquiries as to our religious belief, and expositions of their own. He stated that, as children and worshippers of one God, we were all brethren; and after receiving my assurance that such had long been our view also, inquired if I knew the heavenly rules *(Tien-teaou)*. I replied that I was most likely acquainted with them, though unable to recognize them under that name; and, after a moment's thought, asked if they were ten in number. He answered eagerly in the affirmative. I then began repeating the substance of the first of the Ten Commandments, but had not proceeded far before he laid his hand on my shoulder in a friendly way, and exclaimed, 'The same as ourselves! the same as ourselves!' while the simply observant expression on the face of his companion disappeared before one of satisfaction, as the two exchanged glances.

He then stated, with reference to my previous inquiry as to their feelings and intentions towards the British, that not merely might peace exist between us, but that we might be intimate friends. He added, we [the Britons] might now, at Nanjing, land and walk about where we pleased. He reverted again and again, with an appearance of much gratitude, to the circumstance that he and his companions in arms had enjoyed the special protection and aid of God, without which they would never have been able to do what they had done against superior numbers and resources [of the Manchu government].

Source: (a) H. F. MacNair, *Modern Chinese History: Selected Readings* (Shanghai, 1923), pp. 337f (slightly altered); (b) *Evangelisches Missionsmagazin* 7, 1863, pp. 164-179 ("Die Lage der Taiping in China"), pp. 175-177; Chinese text in: P.-K. Cheng, M. Lestz (eds.), *The Search for Modern China* (New York, 1999), pp. 140-143; (c) A. F. Lindley, Ti-Ping Tien-Kwoh, *The History of the Ti-Ping Revolution.* Vol. I (London, 1866), pp. 164f. (d) Ibid., I, 140f. — *Further Reading:* R. G. Wagner, *Reenacting the Heavenly Vision: The Role of Religion in the Taiping Rebellion* (Berkeley, 1982); idem, "Understanding Taiping Christian China," in: K. Koschorke (ed.), *Christen und Gewürze* (Göttingen, 1998), pp. 132-157; J. Spence, *God's Chinese Son* (London, 1996); Moffett, *Asia II,* pp. 298ff; Sunquist, *Dictionary,* pp. 814f (Art. Taiping Rebellion).

IV. ASIA 1890-1945

A. RELIGIOUS REVIVAL AND POLITICAL NATIONALISM

European observers, and even quite a number of Asians, may have considered traditional Asian religions antiquated and destined to gradual extinction. Nevertheless around the end of the nineteenth century in various regions they experienced a noticeable upsurge. This religious-cultural revival was in many ways connected with the beginnings of political nationalism and presented the mission churches with a new challenge. At the same time, these movements were often influenced by Christian ideas and the organizational forms of missionary Protestantism.

62. Religious Revival as a Pan-Asian Phenomenon

The Ceylonese journal *The Hindu Organ*, 18 January 1899, on "Present-day Hinduism":

Everywhere throughout the East there is a revival of [Asian] learning and literature, and the work of rescuing the glory of the Oriental religions from the forgotten past is going on apace. In India, Burmah, Siam, Annam [Vietnam], Japan and even in China, which . . . sent a representative to the Parliaments, the need for religious and moral education is largely felt. Not that our ancestors did not pay to the subject as much attention as is now attempted to be paid to it, they went further in that respect than we who live amidst the materialistic tendencies of the present age can conceive of. In fact, our ancestors lived, moved, and had their being in religion.

Source: The Hindu Organ (Jaffna), 18.1.1899, p. 41.

63. Hindu Renaissance in India

a. Change of Public Opinion in India

From a letter of the colonial official Valentine Chirol, 23 May 1910, to the Viceroy Lord Minto:

. . . When I first came to India — say 30 years ago — the ambition of young India was to be, intellectually at least, more English than the English. The superiority of Western literature and Western ethics was as generally recognized as that of Western science and Western methods of government. Somewhere in the 80's the pendulum began to swing back coincident with the slackening of our interest in, and control over, native education — and already in the 90's the movement had set in which has developed into the extraordinary Hindu revival in the last few years — back to the Vedas [Hindu scriptures, back to Kali-worship . . . back to the golden age when, before the advent of the wicked Eng-lishman, prosperity reigned and all the virtues flourished! In the three potential storm centres, Bengal, Deccan and Punjub, we are, I am convinced, face to face with the same phenomenon. . . .

b. The Goals of the Indian National Congress (1885)

The Indian National Congress was founded in 1885, at first as a government-supported association of elites, both English and Indian, rather than the nationalistic revolutionary movement it developed into by 1905. Englishman A. O. Hume, one of the founding members of the Congress and its honorary president, delivered a speech about its goals on 30 April 1888:

It is desirable at the outset to explain that the Congress movement is only one outcome, though at the moment the most prominent and tangible, of the la-bours of a body of cultured men, mostly born natives of India, who some years ago banded themselves together to labour silently for the good of India. To un-derstand the Congress thoroughly it is necessary to understand . . . the basic principles . . . :

First: The fusion into one national whole of all the different and, till re-cently discordant, elements that constitute the population of India.

Second: The gradual regeneration along all lines, mental, moral, social and political, of the nation thus evolved. . . .

Third: The consolidation of the union between England and India, by se-curing the modifications of such of its conditions as may be unjust or injurious to the latter country.

c. Revival as an Inter-Religious Phenomenon

The British missionary and scholar of religion J. N. Fahrquar in 1915 on religious move-ments in contemporary India:

. . . The most prominent characteristic of the long series of religious move-ments [in contemporary India] we have dealt with is the *steady advance of the ancient faiths.* The earlier [religious] organisations were very radical indeed in the treatment they proposed for the troubles of the time, and adopted great masses of Christian thought and practice. But as the years passed, men found courage to defend an ever larger amount of the old theology, until a number undertook to prove every scrap of the ancient structure good. *Hinduism, Islam, Buddhism, Jainism and Zoroastrianism* each leaped up into new vigorous activity, every prominent sect experiencing a mysterious *awakening*. Finally, under the impulse of national feeling, the tables were completely turned: not only the religions but everything Oriental was glorified as spiritual and ennobling, while everything Western received condemnation as hideously materialistic and degrading. [. . .]

The dominance of Christianity in the religious development of the last 100 years may be clearly seen in this that, almost without exception, the methods of work in use in the [non-Christian] movements have been borrowed *from [Christian] missions*. This is the more noticeable since India, in the past, had the genius to produce a series of methods of religious propagation unmatched in the history of the world.

Source: (a) M. Nath Das, *India under Morley and Minto* (London, 1964), p. 20; (b) B. N. Pandey (ed.), *The Indian Nationalist Movement, 1885-1947: Selected Documents* (London, 1979), pp. 5f; (c) J. N. Farquhar, *Modern Religious Movements in India* (New York, 1915), pp. 430, 442.

64. The Rise of Buddhism in Ceylon (Sri Lanka)

An upswing of Buddhism began to emerge in Sri Lanka in the 1870s and in 1880 the conversion of the American theosophist H. S. Olcott (1832-1907) brought Buddhism to the attention of a wider public. The opening of Buddhist schools broke the monopoly of Christian missions in education. Olcott's oft-reprinted "Buddhist Catechism" emphasized the rational character of Buddhist teachings and their compatibility with modern science (a). A missionary observer described the changed situation around 1900 (b).

a. The "Buddhist Catechism" from H. S. Olcott (1881)

Part V: Buddhism and Science

325. *Question:* Has Buddhism any right to be considered a scientific religion, or may it be classified its a "revealed" one?

Answer: Most emphatically it is not a revealed religion. The Buddha did not so preach, nor is he to be so understood. On the contrary, he gave it out as the statement of eternal truths, which his predecessors had taught like himself. [. . .]

327. *Question:* Do Buddhists accept the theory that everything has been formed out of nothing by a Creator?

Answer: The Buddha taught that two things are causeless, viz., *Akasha* [ether] and *Nirvana* [extinction]. Everything has come out of *akasha*, in obedience to a law of motion inherent in it, and, after a certain existence, passes away.

Nothing ever came out of nothing. We do not believe in miracles; hence we deny creation, and cannot conceive of a creation of something out of nothing. Nothing organic is eternal. Everything is in a state of constant flux, and undergoing change and reformation, keeping up the continuity according to the law of evolution.

328. *Question:* Is Buddhism opposed to education, and to the study of science?

Answer: Quite the contrary: in the *Sigalowada Sutta* in a discourse preached by the Buddha, He specified as one of the duties of a teacher that he should give his pupils "instruction in science and lore." The Buddha's higher teachings are for the enlightened, the wise, and the thoughtful. [. . .]

b. The Situation around 1900

The whole character of Buddhism has changed during the last few years. Whereas some time ago the mass of the people knew nothing of Buddhism, and had for their religion little more than devil-worship, Buddhism is now a popular force opposed to Christianity. It is taught in schools which vie with our own, and are like them supported by Government grants. . . . By its institution of *pan-sil* it continually presents to its disciples an elevated morality, requiring them to observe these five precepts: not to kill, not to steal, not to lie, not to be impure, not to drink strong drinks. . . . And finally it is supported by the traditions of the past and the strong feeling of conservatism and attachment to ancient customs by which the Singhalese are peculiarly animated: they are now from a kind of patriotism setting themselves in many ways against Western fashions, and reverting in dress and manners to ancient usage.

Source: (a) H. Steel Olcott, *The Buddhist Catechism* (Colombo, n.d.) (ca. 1897, reprint 1985), p. 76; (b) Report for the year 1900 of the Society for the Propagation of the Gospel (London, 1900), p. 78. — *Further Reading:* H. Bechert, *Buddhismus, Staat und Gesellschaft* . . . (Frankfurt, etc. 1966), pp. 1, 43ff; G. D. Bond, *The Buddhist Revival in Sri Lanka* (Columbia, 1988); S. R. Prothero, *H. S. Olcott (1832-1907) and the Construction of "Protestant Buddhism"* (Ann Arbor, 1990); Moffett, *Asia II*, p. 580.

65. Japan's Victory over Russia 1904-1905 and the Asian Elites

No other event near the turn of the twentieth century contributed as much to the formation of a pan-Asian identity among the Western educated elites of the continent as the victory of "Asian" Japan over "Western and Christian" Russia in the war of 1904-1905. C. F. Andrews, a British missionary and later a friend and co-worker of Gandhi, reported on reactions in India:

The effect of the Japanese successes upon the educated people of North India has been startling and immediate. A wave of enthusiasm has passed through all our cities which has given rise to new hopes and new ideals. . . . It is . . . the awakening of a new national spirit and the turning of all eyes in India to Japan as the true model for the East. After a passive, fatalistic acquiescence in the advance of the West as inevitable, there has now arisen an active hope that the East may work out her own salvation in her own Eastern way, and that India may one day take her place side by side with Japan as an independent nation. . . . Students who before were anxious to go to Oxford or Cambridge are now eager to go to Tokyo, and some have already started. [. . .]

The air was full of electricity. The war between Russia and Japan had kept the surrounding peoples on the tip-toe of expectation. A stir of excitement passed over the North of India. Even the remote villagers talked over the victories of Japan as they sat in their circles and passed round the *huqqa* (pipe) at night. One of the older men said to me, 'There has been nothing like it since the mutiny' [in 1856/57, which briefly threatened British rule in India].

Source: C. F. Andrews, "The Effect of the Japanese Victories upon India," in: *The East and West* (October 1905), 361-372, 362; idem, *The Renaissance in India: Its Missionary Aspect* (London, 1912), p. 4.

B. Attempts at Indigenization in the Protestant Churches

66. Programmatic Statements

Reacting to the growing nationalism in Asia at the turn of the nineteenth century, some Protestant missionary churches increased their efforts to create a "native," non-Western, "national" form of Christianity. Such endeavors at indigenization addressed many aspects of ecclesiastical life and were found simultaneously in very different and geographically remote Asian churches. They were often connected with a "fulfilment theology," which understood Christianity as the fulfilment (Matt. 5:17) — and not the denial — of Asia's religious aspirations which were seen as parallel to those of the Hebrews before Christ. This movement was supported both by anonymous Christian laypeople and by prominent indigenous church leaders, such as the Indian Surendra K. Datta (1878-1942) (a) and the Chinese theologian T. C. Chao (1888-1979) (c). Missionaries who encouraged this movement included the British teacher A. G. Fraser (1863-1962) who worked in Ceylon from 1904-1924 and was also connected with the international network of the Protestant Missionary Movement (b).

a. Indian Christians and the Vision of an Indian Church (1908)

There are many indications which point to Christianity becoming the standard round which [in India] all the moral forces of the country tend to rally. [. . .]

Indian theology:

The Indian Church has failed on the whole to produce a distinctive theology capable of reaching the minds and hearts of the people. The religious history of India would lead us to look for something of this kind. Yet the nearest approach to a distinctively Indian interpretation of Christ has come from a non-Christian sect, the Brahmo Samaj. [. . .]

Native church/hymnology:

[. . .] There are signs of an indigenous hymnology in southern India . . . and to a lesser degree in the north. [. . .] We can see how the growing hymnology of the southern Indian Church, if fired by God's Spirit, may give utterance to divine truth in a language that will be understood by the people. [. . .] [*Self-government:*] The Indian Church is not self-governing. Western sectarianism has been perpetuated to the detriment of Indian Christianity. Yet there are movements towards union. [. . .] [*Self-propagation:*] [. . .] [The Indian Church] alone has the capacity of overcoming the inaccessibility, both physical and mental, of the millions in whose hearts the light of truth has not yet dawned.

b. A Missionary's Voice from Ceylon (1908)

To-day the National Movement is anti-Christian. I have met men profoundly convinced of the truth of Christ, wistfully desirous of accepting Him, yet turning away because to accept Him seemed treachery to their people and nation. On the other hand, where it was made clear that Christ was no foreign Lord but the one who alone could solve their National and Social problems, I have seen a leader of high rank accept Him. National feeling is against our Lord to-day, not because He is holy, not because He is the Saviour, but because He is Western, and not seen to be . . . the Saviour of India. [. . .] Now to win the national feeling for Christ, it is first necessary to show that we preach no English Christ but Him who was and is the Son of Man. [. . .] We must in our educational missions learn to preach the Christ of India and Ceylon. [. . .] we must set aside picked men, giving them ample leisure. Then we shall be able to teach our native clergy a theology conditioned by the East. [. . .] Those going to work amongst Buddhists will be care-fully and sympathetically trained in the Buddhist Scriptures and lore, and taught to relate the revelation of our Lord to the lesser truth that was given by Buddha, and so in regard to the other faiths. Christ came not to destroy but to complete all [Mt 5:17] that is best and truest in their ancient learning and faith [. . .]. Only in the power of the risen Lord and Christ can a disciple fulfill the ethic of Buddha. Secondly, in our secular curriculum we must aim at making good Indian citizens. [. . .]

c. Characteristics of a Native Church in China (1924)

A native church [in China] is one that preserves and reconciles all truths contained in the Christian religion and in the ancient civilization of China, and that expresses the religious life and the experiences of Chinese Christians in a way that is appropriate and natural for them.

Source: (a) S. Kumar Datta, *The Desire of India* (London, 1908, ⁴1911) (230ff: Chapter VII: The Indian Church), pp. 234, 255f, 257, 259f. (b) A. G. Fraser, "The Problem before Educational Missions in Ceylon," in: *Pan-Anglican* (1979), p. 62. — *Further Reading:* England, *ACT I*, pp. 208ff, 464ff.; Sunquist, *Dictionary,* p. 301 (Art. Fraser, A. G.).

67. Demands for a "Native Bishop" (1899)

In addition to the call for cultural authenticity, the demand for ecclesiastical self-governance was a central component of the indigenization program. Indian Christians repeatedly voiced a demand to have their own Indian bishops, noting the example of Bishop Crowther in Nigeria as a precedent (see documents 150, 165a). In 1912 V. S. Azariah was consecrated as the first Asian Anglican bishop. In a report about the conference of the Church Missionary Society in Allahabad, India in 1899, the *Indian Christian Guardian,* mouthpiece of the Christian intelligentsia of the country, criticized the cautious stance of the Anglican church leaders:

It was acknowledged by all that India is sadly behind-hand as regards the Episcopate. No Native of the soil, in connexion with our [Anglican] Church, has yet been consecrated bishop. Beyond doubt, the Conference took a step forward in declaring that the time has come for a little "holy boldness," and in advocating, and that with perfect unanimity (there was not a single dissentient voice) the appointment of Indian Suffragan Bishops. If care is exercised, and the type of Episcopacy adopted for our native brethren be the simple and more primitive one of North Africa, rather than the pretentious one which prevailed in the Roman Empire when the Church began to adopt the grandeur of the State, we see no reason why an Indian Episcopate should not prove a great success. Anyhow, it cannot be right always to hold a large and growing Native Church [like the Indian Church] in leading-strings, nor can it be fair to govern it for ever by a foreign episcopate. At least let a beginning be made by the appointment of Native Suffragan Bishops where the right [Indian] men are forthcoming. . . .

Source: Indian Christian Guardian, Vol. 3 (1899).

68. Christian Ashrams (1921)

The indigenization movement was interested in the manifold cultural forms and expressions of the Christian faith. Local traditions played an increasingly important role in church architecture and the shaping of worship services and liturgy. Christian Ashrams also have to be seen in this light. This idea of a Christian community based on indigenous models had been discussed in India since the beginning of the twentieth century in the National Missionary Society, an assembly of Indian Christians, and was realized first in 1921 with the founding of the Christukula Ashram in North Arcot. Savarirayan Jesudason, one of the two founders of this Ashram, relates the principles and forms of this undertaking:

To some rare few of these [members of the ashram who look at it as a new form of Christian Community overcoming the barriers of race, class, caste and sex] the presence of God is so real that without depending on any human companionship they go everywhere as wandering prophets or *Sadhus* [saints] of the Kingdom; for others their fullest life purpose can only be fulfilled in loving comradeship in a group of those likeminded with themselves, devoting their whole life and energies for the fulfillment of a God-given vision. . . . For some of these who seek to fulfill their mission in life in such an intimate comradeship, the permanent membership of the ashram family is intended. We fully realized that permanent membership under these conditions could not be lightly undertaken. . . . So we also welcome those who desire to come for shorter periods for one or two years, whether they come with the purpose of later permanently joining the ashram family, or whether because of their other circumstances or obligations they can only be with us temporarily. These of course are not expected to make any decision as regards property or marriage, but share for the time being in the common life of the family.

Source: Savarirayan Jesudason, Ashrams Ancient and Modern: Their Aims and Ideals (Vellore, 1937), pp. 36ff. — Further Reading: England, ACT I, pp. 372ff; Sunquist, Dictionary, pp. 43f (Art. Ashram Movement); P. Pattathu, Ashram Spirituality: A Search into the Christian Ashram Movement against Its Hindu Background (Satpaakashan, 1997).

C. Local Ecumenical Initiatives and Edinburgh 1910

69. Protests against Western Denominationalism

a. Voices of Indian Christians (1897/98)

The search for a "native" form of Asian Christianity was strongly associated with the protest against the confessional splintering of missionary Protestantism. In an article from the year 1898 the *Christian Patriot,* a voice of educated Indian Christians, described the obstacles in the way of an independent Indian church.

There are, however, other respects in which the tendency to Anglicization has hampered the growth of an indigenous church. For example the way in which the various missions have tried to perpetuate on oriental soil the peculiar distinctions of the West, which are the outcome of social and political circumstances peculiar to the countries in the West. It is this kind of Anglicization that has wrought real mischief. Not long ago we had a series of articles in our columns in which we discussed the adaptability of the *Book of Common Prayer* of the Church of England to the Indian Church. We discussed the question calmly and moderately, and yet it raised quite a storm of indignant protest from church dignitaries. . . .

The *Indian Christian Guardian* takes a similar position:

Yet even in this event, the eye of hope . . . would fain discern the time when the deplorable sectarian differences which characterize our Western Christianity, and which have acquired a foothold to no small extent in India, shall be superseded by a freer and fuller growth growth of Christian doctrine and spiritual life [in India]. . . . We warn . . . not only against the English [Anglican] and Roman [Catholic] missions, but also against the Scotch, German and American missions.

b. The Mood around 1910

The Anglican Bishop of Bombay, James Edwin Palmer, comments on the situation in India:

I have heard it said often, that if we, foreign missionaries, left India in a body today, all Indian Christians would very quickly unite and form one Indian Church. I have heard said it again and again that it is only we foreign missionaries who keep the Indian Christians from unity.

Source: (a) *Christian Patriot* 18.6.1898; *Indian Christian Guardian* 1 (1897), p. 67; (b) Bp. E. J. Palmer, *Reunion in Western India: Papers and Articles by the Bp. of Bombay* (Bombay, 1910), pp. 3ff; "The Hope of the Reunion of Christendom."

70. The World Missionary Conference in Edinburgh 1910 as a Catalyst

In an unprecedented way, the World Missionary Conference in Edinburgh 1910 reacted to impulses and developments in the "mission fields" of Asia and Africa, which it passed on to missionary headquarters and churches in the West, and then subsequently returned to their origins. The emergence of national movements in Asia and a growing interest in modernity was understood as a unique chance to christianize the continent. This would, however, demand a higher degree of cooperation among the missions and churches. On the eve of WWI, Edinburgh provided impulses not only for the whole modern ecumenical movement. It inspired debates especially in Asia, where they led to concrete results in Asia more quickly than in the churches of the West. See also document 287.

a. An Analysis of the Situation in Asia

Throughout the non-Christian world [in Asia and Africa] world there are unmistakable signs of the awakening of great peoples from their long sleep. Through the whole of Asia a ferment is in process, which has spread from the intellectual leaders, and is fast taking possession of the masses. It affects over three-fourths of the human race, including peoples of high intelligence and ancient civilisation. [. . .] It is difficult to believe that two generations ago *Japan* was even more completely closed to Western influence than was China. Since then she has, however, proved herself in some respects the most brilliant nation in the world. She has achieved greater progress in one generation than any other country has achieved in two, if not in three generations. [. . .] *Korea* was known yesterday as "The Land of the Morning Calm." To-day it is vibrating with the spirit of the modern world, and the age-long isolation of the hermit nation has ceased. [. . .] The educational system has been reformed along modern lines [. . .]. A new literature is being evolved under the influence of the Christian Church. [. . .] *China* has a longer unbroken history than any other people in the world. For four thousand years she has been the same changeless and unchanging empire, entirely self-centred and self-satisfied, with a profound contempt for everything foreign. Yet to-day she too has turned her face from the past and has begun to learn from other nations. [. . .] *India,* in common with all other lands in the East, is in a state of change and unrest. Great and surprising transformations have taken place in the past few years [. . .]. One notes the growing sense of concern on the part of many outside the missionary and Christian community over the ills which afflict the great masses of the people of this land — ills intellectual, social, and religious. [. . .]

b. Message from the Conference on World Christianity

To the members of the Church in Christian lands.

. . . We members of the World Missionary Conference assembled in Edinburgh desire to send you a message which lies very near to our hearts. During the past ten days we have been engaged in a close and continuous study of the position of Christianity in non-Christian lands. [. . .] Our survey has impressed upon us the momentous character of the present hour. We have heard from many quarters [in Asia and Africa] of the awakening of great nations, of the opening of long-closed doors, and of movements which are placing all at once before the Church a new world to be won for Christ. The next ten years will in all probability constitute a turning-point in human history, and may be of more critical importance in determining the spiritual evolution of mankind than many centuries of ordinary experience. If those years are wasted, havoc may be wrought that centuries are not able to repair. On the other hand, if they are rightly used, they may be among the most glorious in Christian history.

Source: (a) J. R. Mott, *The Decisive Hour of Christian Missions* (London, [2]1911), pp. 2-20; (b) World Missionary Conference, 1910. Vol. IX (Edinburgh, etc. [1911]), p. 108. — *Further Reading:* H.-R. Weber, *Asia and the Ecumenical Movement 1895-1961* (London, 1966), pp. 56ff, 130ff, 143ff; K. Baago, *A History of the National Council of Churches* (1965); Sunquist, *Dictionary,* pp. 258-265 (Art. Ecumenical Movement).

71. Edinburgh in Asia: The China Conference of 1913

In 1912-1913 a series of continuation conferences of the Edinburgh World Missionary Conference took place in a number of Asian countries. They first led to the founding of national missionary councils, and then, beginning in 1922, to national Christian councils, with which the foundations of future ecumenical cooperation in Asia were established. In China the national conference (Shanghai, 11-14 March 1913) took place during the revolutionary upheaval following the fall of the Manchu Dynasty in 1911 and with a Methodist Christian (Sun Yat-Sen) as the first president of the People's Republic of China.

1. China as a Republic. Thus far the most striking event of the twentieth century is unquestionably the swift change by which the most ancient of empires [1911] has adopted a republican form of government. Whatever may be our forecast of the future of China, it is evident that, as related to the work of the evangelization of this land, the step which has been taken is one of transcendent importance. [. . .]

III. The Chinese Church. — 1. The Unity of the Church of Christ in China.
This Conference prays with one accord for that unity of all Christians for which
our Lord Himself prayed, that the world may know and receive Him as God the
Son, the Saviour of all mankind, and . . . earnestly desires the unity of the whole
Church of Christ in China.

2. Freedom of Development in Form and Organization. This Conference re-
joices that the Churches in China, for the most part, have been organized as
self-governing bodies, and believes that in respect of form and organization,
they should have freedom to develop in accord with the most natural expression of the spiritual instincts of Chinese Christians. At the same time it is essential for these Churches to maintain cordial relations with the Churches of the
West, that they may receive and absorb every good influence which those
Churches can impart.

3. Chinese Recognition of the Churches as Truly Indigenous. In order that
Christianity may appeal with force to the minds and hearts of the Chinese people and win their growing national consciousness for the service of Christ, it is
of the utmost importance for the Churches to be so developed that the Chinese
them-selves may recognize them as having become truly native. [. . .]

8. Developing the Indigenous Character of the Churches. As methods by
which to develop the indigenous character of the Churches, the Conference
makes the following recommendations:

(1) The Chinese Churches should be organized with local and district representative councils, wherever these do not already exist.

(2) Representative Chinese should have a share in the administration of
foreign funds used for the work of the Chinese Church.

(3) Church buildings should, wherever possible, be erected on grounds
separate from the foreign missionary residences.

(4) In the management of the evangelistic, educational and other work of
the Church, there should, to the fullest possible extent, be joint control by, Chinese and foreign workers. All positions of responsibility open to Chinese Christians should, as far as is practicable, be related to Chinese organizations rather
than to foreign Missionary Societies. [. . .]

*IV. Chinese Christian Leadership — 1.Imperative Need for Able Chinese
Christian Leadership.* In view of the great awakening in China, and the present
unprecedented opportunity owing to the friendly attitude of the people, especially the student class, towards the influence and teachings of our Lord, it is the
united opinion of the Conference that there is an imperative need for able Chinese Christian leadership. [. . .]

Source: *The Continuation Committee Conference in Asia 1912-1913* (New York, 1913), pp. 319-367.
— Further Reading: H.-R. Weber, *Asia and the Ecumenical Movement* (London, 1961), pp. 130ff;

C. H. Hopkins, *John R. Mott 1865-1955* (Grand Rapids, 1979), pp. 386ff; N. Koshy, *A History of the Ecumenical Movement in Asia.* Vol. I (Hong Kong, 2004); Sunquist, *Dictionary,* pp. 258-265 (Art. Ecumenical Movement); p. 583 (Art. National Christian Conference China, 1913).

72. Local Forms of Cooperation

At the local level, ecumenical initiatives of indigenous Christians began early. At the invitation of the Madras "Native Christian Association" a first meeting of all churches, including the Catholics, took place at the end of April 1899 to protest against the new inheritance tax laws that put Christians at a particular disadvantage. Similar interdenominational ventures were planned for the future.

On Saturday evening, [April] the 29th instant, the Indian Christians of the Madras Presidency held a very successful meeting at the Victoria Public Hall to consider the question of succession duties. . . . The meeting was in one respect unique as it was the first occasion on which Roman Catholics, Anglicans and Protestants belonging to the Indian races met together in a common cause. The meeting was also happy in its choice of the President, the Right Reverend Bishop Theophilus Mayer, who was proposed to the fauteuil [chair] by Dr. S. Pulney Andy, and was accepted by all present with acclamation. The legal, historical and practical sides of the question were respectively dwelt on by Mr. Satya Joseph, Mr. Pragasa Mudaliar and Mr. Devadoss Pillai. . . . It was unanimously resolved that the meeting should place on record its sense of the grievance to which the [Christian] community is subjected by the compulsory levy of succession duties . . . , whereas other Indian communities are exempt from such compulsion and such interference [by the Government]. A committee was also appointed for the purpose of drawing up a memorial on the subject to the local Government as well as the Government of India.

Source: Christian Patriot, May 6th 1899: "Native Christians and Succession Duties."

D. Developments in Catholic Asia

73. Foundation of an Indian Hierarchy

The Catholic Church of India only gradually recovered from its nadir at the beginning of the nineteenth century (see document 39). For a long time it was overshadowed by Protestant missions, whose numbers were low in comparison but whose influence in Asian societies was strongly felt. The church was paralyzed by ongoing struggle over jurisdiction between Portugal — which insisted on its traditional patronage rights

("Padroado," see documents 8, 228f) in the filling of ecclesiastical posts, even though it no longer controlled any territory in Southeast Asia apart from the enclave in Goa — and the pontifical mission headquarters *(Propoganda fide)*, which attempted to take into account the changed political realities and to erect independent church structures. The Concordate of 1886 put a temporary end to the bitter feuds and enabled the creation of a unified hierarchy for all of India. Seven church provinces were established, of which, Goa, was put under the control of the *Padroado* and the rest (Agra, Bombay, Verapoly, Calcutta, Madras, Pondicherry) under the *Propaganda*. At the same time, changes were carried out in the Catholic school system and other areas of ecclesiastical life.

Concordate of 1886:

Art. I. In virtue of former Pontifical concessions, the exercise of the Patronage of the Crown of Portugal shall continue, conformably to the rules of Canon Law, in the Cathedral Churches of the East Indies subject to the modifications expressed in the present Concordat. [. . .]

Art. VI. The Portuguese Government undertakes to provide for the suitable endowment of the above-mentioned dioceses [the Archdiocese of Goa with the Dioceses of Cochin, Mylapore and Damaun], with Chapters, clergy and seminaries, and effectively to co-operate in seconding the action of the bishops for the foundation of schools, orphanages and other charitable institutions necessary for the good of the faithful and for the evangelization of the pagans.

Art. VII. As to the four dioceses of Bombay, Mangalore, Quilon and Madura [being subject to the Propaganda], which are to be established by the institution of the hierarchy in the Indies [South Asia], the Metropolitans with their suffragan bishops shall, on the occasion of the vacancy of an episcopal See . . . form of their free choice a *terna* or list of three, which they shall communicate to the Archbishop of Goa, who shall forward it to the [Portugese] Crown. Within a period of six months the latter must present to the Holy See one candidate out of the three comprised in the list. . . .

Art. VIII. The Sovereign Pontiff shall have the nomination of the first Archbishops and bishops of the four dioceses mentioned in the preceding article, which shall be founded as soon as the ecclesiastical hierarchy has been constituted.

Art. IX. The Christian communities of Malacca and Singapore, at present under the extraordinary jurisdiction of the Archbishop of Goa, shall be subject to the jurisdiction of the bishop of Macao.

Art. X. The patronage of the [Portugese] Crown being thus regulated, the Holy See shall enjoy throughout the rest of the Indies full power to nominate the bishops, and to adopt such measures as it deems expedient for the good of the faithful. [. . .]

Source: M. K. Kuriakose, *History of Christianity in India* (Madras, 1982), pp. 239-246, here: pp. 239-241. — *Further Reading:* C. B. Firth, *An Introduction to Indian Church History* (Madras, 1983), pp. 215-232; A. Meersman, "The Catholic Church in India since the Mid-19th Century," in: H. C. Perumali u.a. (eds.), *Christianity in India* (Alleppey, 1973), pp. 248-266.

74. Indigenous Bishops in China

Following Pope Benedict XV's (1914-1922) declaration *Maximum illud* of 30 November 1919, the formation of an indigenous clergy became a central agenda item for pontifical missions policy. His successor Pius XI (1922-1939) consecrated six Chinese bishops in 1926 and the first Japanese bishop in 1927.

In order to make the work of propagating the faith in this enormous land more efficacious, the Holy Father [Pius XI] first concerned himself with the unification of the work of the entire missionary forces. This happened on two fronts. First, on 15 August 1922, the Apostolic Mission was established in China and Msgr. Celso Constantini was named the first Apostolic Delegate to China. [. . .] From then on the unification was promoted by the *first Chinese Plenary Council.* In a text from 20 January 1924, in which he set forth both the meaning and the tasks of this meeting, Pius XI had given his delegate instructions to convene this council. The council had been prepared earlier, but its launch was prevented by the outbreak of the war. . . . At the council in Shanghai from 15 May to 12 June 1924, all Chinese missions officials, including the two indigenous leaders who had been named Apostolic Prefects in that year, met together for the first time to advise one another on the ways and means of propagating the faith, to set guidelines to avoid fragmentation and to provide the unity necessary for their work. [. . .] [In his letter to the participants of the council,] the Pope indicates which paths should be taken to adapt to the Chinese mentality, and he expresses his joy that he be granted the opportunity to pursue and develop an effort in China that would display in remarkable measure the generosity of the Catholic Church and would be accommodating towards the justified nationalism of the Chinese, the *native clergy and episcopate.* In 1924, two native priests had already been promoted to Apostolic Prefects, Cheng He-de Odoric, O.F.M. (d. 1928) for Pu-qi and Sun De-zhen Melchior, C.M. for Li-sien. To crown the whole achievement, the Holy Father personally consecrated six Chinese priests as bishops in St. Peter's Basilica in Rome on 28 October 1926. On this day he demonstrated to the whole world that the Catholic Church still today is truly "catholic" (that is, universal) and recognizes no difference between races and nations. This consecration signified the first major step on the path to a new missions policy in China.

Source: J. Beckmann, "Pius XI. und die Mission in China" (in: *Kath. Missionsjahrbuch der Schweiz*), 1928, pp. 10-13. — *Further Reading:* J. Metzler, *Die Synoden in China, Japan und Korea 1570-1931* (Paderborn, etc. 1980), pp. 181ff; J.-P. Wiest, *Maryknoll in China 1918-1955* (New York, 1988), pp. 252ff.

75. The Abolition of the Anti-Rites Oath (1939)

Also during the pontificate of Pope Pius XI, the oath against Chinese rites was abolished. This oath had been demanded of all priests and missionaries working in China or among the Chinese since Pope Benedict XIV's 1742 ban on Chinese rites (see document 28). A 300-year series of church declarations on the question of Chinese rites thus came to an end amid the confusion of the undeclared Japanese-Chinese war and the difficulties faced by Christians in Japanese-ruled Korea who were required to follow Shinto forms of worship. In 1935 and 1936 declarations related to Japan and Manchuria emphasized the civil character of the rites in honor of Confucius and of ancestor worship. The instruction *Plane compertum est* of the Propaganda Fide (from 8 December 1939), addressed to the Chinese churches, begins with these words:

It is abundantly clear that in the regions of the Orient some ceremonies, although they may have been involved with pagan rites in ancient times [*cum ethnicis ritibus connexae*], have — with the changes in customs and thinking over the course of centuries — retained merely the civil significance [*civilem tantum servare significationem*] of piety towards the ancestors or of love of the fatherland or of courtesy towards one's neighbors.

Source: G. Minamiki, *The Chinese Rites Controversy* (Chicago, 1985), p. 197. — *Further Reading:* ibid., pp. 197-203; D. E. Mungello, *The Chinese Rites Controversy* (Nettetal, 1994), pp. 83-108.

E. Independent Church Movements

As in Africa (see documents 170ff), there were also in Asia various attempts in many regions to establish independent churches around the end of the nineteenth century. The supporters were mainly members of the emerging class of Western-educated indigenous Christians. They strove much more quickly than the Western missionaries toward the goal — *theoretically* supported by the Westerners as well — of realizing the establishment of a self-governing native church. Analogous movements could be found at that time in Catholic Asia as well, although under different conditions.

76. Ceylon: Petition for an "Independent Native Church" (1878)

The authoritarian policies of the Anglican Bishop of Columbo, R. S. Copleston, were the catalyst for many protests and petitions by indigenous Christians in the years 1876-1879. The petitions, some of them with hundreds of signatures and marks, demanded not only an end to many specific grievances, but also the establishing of an Independent Native Church in colonial Ceylon, today Sri Lanka.

To the Committee of the Church Missionary Society, London

Most respected and honorable Gentlemen,

The humble petition of the Christians connected with the Tamil Cooly Mission of Ceylon regarding the formation of an *Independent Native Church* — humbly scheweth [shows]:

I. That we do not find in the New Testament that it was the practice of the Apostles when new Churches were founded to subjugate them to foreign control. They were left to grow up and become established as an independent body, assisted by the Apostles who had first preached the Gospel to them, but not controlled by any foreign authority. [. . .]

III. The oriental manners and customs of the Native Christians make it extremely desirable that they should have liberty to frame a constitution and rules of Church Government suited to their needs. In many respects the laws of the English [Anglican] Church are unsuited to adopt them to our circumstances. . . . We are also unable to add prayers to local blessings, or the spread of the gospel in our country, or to remove difficulties in the liturgy and simplify them so that uneducated people may more easily understand the services.

IV. The Ecclesiastical laws of England are so uncertain, and their administration in Ceylon especially has been so arbitrary and uncontrolable, that we are not able to obtain justice in the English Church. [. . .]

V. In the appointment of Bishops of the English Church the interests and requirements of the Natives are not considered. [. . .] We wish to have a voice in the election of our own Bishops, and to appoint men who are qualified by knowledge, experience and sympathy, to watch over our interests. [. . .]

VII. [. . .] We have no desire to create a schism. We ask for the liberty which was claimed by the Church of England 300 years ago when it threw off the authority of the Pope of Rome. We trust still to continue in fellowship with the Church of England, which we shall always regard with affection as our mother Church. But we ask for freedom, and the right of independent existence.

Source: K. Koschorke, "Kirchliche Unabhängigkeitsbestrebungen im kolonialen Ceylon. Eine Denkschrift einheimischer Christen aus dem Jahr 1878" (in: *NZM* 54, 1994, pp. 131-136), pp. 132f.
— *Further Reading:* ibid.; C. P. Williams, *The Ideal of the Self-Governing Church* (Leiden, 1990).

77. India: The "National Church of India" (Madras 1886)

In Protestant India, repeated demands had been made since the 1860s for the establishment of an Indian national church to which all Indian Christians, irrespective of their denominational affiliation, would belong. The most important example was the National Church of India, established in 1886 in Madras. It remained in existence only until 1930, but nevertheless played an important role as a point of crystallization for the Protestant intelligentsia of South India. It also influenced debates in the mission churches about closer cooperation.

a. Setting Goals

The main object with which this Church was started was clearly enunciated at the very outset [of the founding assembly on 12 September 1886 in Madras]. It is neither more or less than to bring together, into closer sympathy than exists at present, the Indian Christians of several denominations, and thus let non-Christian brethren see that though [the Indian] Christians agree to differ in certain points [of Church organization], these differences are yet neither so great nor so essential but that they may unite together for worship in spite of them. That this object is beginning to be appreciated by the most intelligent portion of the Native Christian Community is no doubt apparent from the fact of so many brethren of different denominations coming forward to help us in this movement.

b. Account of an Assembly

On the evening of Tuesday, the 13th instant [September 1887], was celebrated, in the Evangelistic Hall, Esplanade [in Madras], the first Anniversary of the national Church of India, Dr. S. Pulney Andy was in the chair, and about three hundred native Christian ladies and gentlemen were present. A few non-Christian friends and sympathizers also graced the occasion with their presence. The proceedings commenced at half past six [p.m.] with the singing of the hymn 'Stand up! Stand up for Jesus.' Then Mr. P. B. Ragaviah, B.A., offered a short prayer invoking God's blessing. Next Mr. C. Appasawmy Pillai read the first twenty four verses of the 4th Chapter of St. Paul's Epistle to the Ephesians. Then was read by Mr. J. P. Cotelingum, M.A., the first Report of the National Church of India, printed copies of which had been previously distributed among the audience. . . . The expenses of the Church which amounted Rs. 318 have been fully met by voluntary contributions. After the Report had been read, a Tamil lyric was given out by Mr. Kathirvela Mudaliar, and was to the accompaniment of native music.

Then Mr. W. L. Venkatara . . . was called upon by the Chairman to address the meeting in English. [From his speech:] The National Church is now an accomplished fact, whatever folks may say to the contrary. . . . Now I think I can mention three very good reasons which ought to enlist our heartiest sympathies on behalf of the National Church. 1. The good old missionary pioneers — most of them, at least — forgot that the doctrines and ritual that separate one sect of Christians from another in Europe are . . . the resultant of various forces at work in the civil and religious history of Europe; and that to bequeath to us the legacy of tradition . . . was neither necessary nor advisable. . . . The [Indian] National Church is an attempt to give tangible form to the impatience which with all thoughtful Indian Christians regard needless division and difference in the Church. [. . .]

2. [The native Christians are still trapped in their dependence on the mission churches.]

3. [For this reason, it is of utmost importance that Indians administer Church's finances.]

c. National Church and Mission Churches

The need for a United Church in India [is] very great. [. . .] [There is need for a] church that will not reflect Scotch Presbyterianism, nor English Anglicanism, nor German Lutheranism; but which will combine into a harmonious whole the best features of all denominations, and be suited to the social instincts and national characteristics of the native converts. Christianity has in India been molded too much after European pattern, and Missionaries have been a little over-anxious to perpetuate their own Church peculiarities.

d. Indian National Church and Indian National Movement

The object and aim of the National Church movement is to establish in India a Church which shall . . . be characterized by its sympathy with the National sentiments and aspirations of Indians, and profit by oriental modes of thought and religious peculiarities in the local development of spiritual truths [. . .].

There appears to be all the material for the development of the National Church movement in existing. Christian churches of almost every denomination, with a strong tendency to emphasize the conservatism of the national character and thought, exist everywhere. The movement is not very widespread at present, but it probably will set in like a flood, as soon as denominational Christian societies withdraw from supporting Christian churches, in order to direct attention more exclusively to purely Evangelistic operations in India and other localities.

Source: (a) National Church of India. First Annual Report 1886-87, in: Collection of papers collected with the movement of the National Church of India (Madras, n.d.), pp. 31-78, here: p. 34;

(b) ibid., pp. 37-41; (c) National Church of India. Proceedings at the first anniversary (Madras, n.d.), p. 49; (d) National Church of India. Third Annual Report 1888-89. Proceedings at the third anniversary (Madras, n.d.), p. 107. — *Further Reading:* K. Baago, *Pioneers of Indigenous Christianity* (Madras, 1969); G. Thomas, *Christian Indians and Indian Nationalism 1885-1950* (Frankfurt, 1979), pp. 78ff; Sunquist, *Dictionary,* pp. 368f (Art. Indian Independent Church Movements); R. Hedlund, "Emerging Indigenous Christianity in India and Asia" (19th and 20th c.), in: K. Koschorke (ed.), *Transcontinental Links . . .* (Wiesbaden, 2002), pp. 273-292.

78. Japan: Kanzo Uchimura's "Non-Church" (1901)

One of the most prominent early representatives of Protestant Japan was Kanzo Uchimura (1861-1930). He emphasized the importance of being both Japanese and Christian, and derived from that declaration the necessity of *not* belonging to a mission-led ecclesiastical organization of a particular denomination. His "Non-Church Movement" (Mukyôkai) still exists today.

On relating to the Roman Catholic Church and to the Protestant mission churches in Japan:

The gospel that I believe in is Jesus Christ, the crucified. I protest against every teaching and every edifice of doctrine that goes beyond or fails to arrive at this simplest of all teachings. Protestantism as I understand it, means Christ *against* human inventiveness, faith *against* the church. It means simplicity that is exerted against complications, a living organism against dead organizations.

On the principles of the "Non-Church" Movement:

My "Non-Church" is not an "ism" for the sake of an "ism." It was an "ism" for faith. It was a consequence of the conviction that one is saved not by works, but by faith. . . . It was not an "ism" for the purpose of attacking the church. It was an "ism" for the purpose of defending the faith. Belief in the cross stands at the forefront, and as a result of that comes the "Non-Church." The cross forms the primary 'ism', the "Non-Church," on the other hand, forming only a secondary 'ism.' For this reason, I have sometimes attacked the church fiercely, because there were some people whose faith did not reflect the truth of the gospel. I say this to make my position clear. I don't belong to the "Non-Church" that has become the fashion today. I don't have the courage to attack the current weak church. I want to represent the gospel of the cross honorably for the rest of my life. This gospel will, when necessary, destroy and rebuild the church. I am a representative of the "Non-Church" in the sense that I am indifferent to church problems as such. I want to be a "Non-Church" representative who rejects all churches described as "churches" and all isms described as "isms."

Source: A. Dohi u.a., *Theologiegeschichte der Dritten Welt: Japan* (München, 1991), pp. 70f (translated from: K. Uchimura, *Collected Writings* [Japan: Zenshû], Vol. 32, 1983, pp. 347f). — *Further Reading:* Hiroshi Miura, *The Life and Thought of Kanzo Uchimura* (Grand Rapids, 1996); S. Kaplan, *Indigenous Response to Western Christianity* (New York, 1995), pp. 75-94; Sunquist, *Dictionary,* p. 609 (Art. Non-Church Principle); pp. 858f (Art. Uchimura Kanzo).

79. Philippines: Aglipay's "Iglesia Filipina Independiente" (1898-1902)

In the nineteenth century, indigenous secular priests were often the moving force of the anti-colonial movement in the Catholic Philippine Islands. With the collapse of Spanish rule in 1898, their hopes for a Filipino national church were bound up with the idea of a Filipino hierarchy (a). When Rome refused to name a Filipino bishop, the nationalist priest Gregorio Aglipay (1860-1940) founded the "Iglesia Filipina Independiente." This attracted a sizeable constituency and is still today the strongest non-Roman Catholic Church in the country. Their initial attempts to make contact with North American Protestant missionaries, active in the country since 1898, were unsuccessful (b).

a. Aglipay's Manifesto of October 21, 1898

My beloved brethren: Inasmuch as the Revolution tends to liberate the Filipino people from Spain, it is also necessary that we also work to throw off the yoke with which the Spanish clergy pretends to subjugate us so that we may be worthy successors of the Filipino priests who sacrificed themselves in defense of our unquestionable rights which were usurped with the greatest arrogance by the [Spanish] friars who made themselves Lords of our beloved country. The Revolutionary Government of the Philippines is supporting us in our aims because it cannot recognize as head of the Filipino clergy any Spanish bishop, for the powerful political influence of the [Spanish] clergy in the Spanish government is proverbial.

b. Unsuccessful Contact with Protestants

In August of 1901 he [Gregorio Aglipay] sought a private conference with several Protestant ministers to discuss the religious situation in the Philippines, outline his own plans and seek some kind of cooperation if union of effort proved impracticable. He took the initiative. It was his first contact with the Protestants whom he had always denounced as the offscourings of the earth. Senor Aglipay, with great cleverness, set forth the situation as he saw it. He pictured the [Filipino] popular hatred of the [Spanish] friars as we had seen it. He pointed out the systematic ill-treatment of the native clergy by the foreign friar and the unrest which this caused in the entire native community. He showed us proofs of the passionate fervor of all Filipinos for their own islands. He then told us that he proposed to lead in the establishment of an Independent Catholic Church in the Philippines and that he wished us to make common cause with him. The first item on the program was separation from the Papacy and complete autonomy in the Philippines. His next step was to stand for the "Catholic doctrine in its purity." Other details were of less importance. We [Protestant missionaries from the U.S.A] pointed out to him the impossibility of any attempt to unite with a movement which did not make the Scriptures the rule and guide in doctrine and life, and urged him to study the situation more carefully and throw his strength into the Protestant movement.

Source: (a) L. B. Whitemore, *Struggle for Freedom. History from the Philippine Independent Church* (Greenwich, 1961), p. 73; (b) Ibid., p. 98. — *Further Reading:* P. S. Acutegui/M. A. Bernad, *Religious Revolution in the Philippines.* Vol. 1 (Manila, 1960/1966); J. N. Schumacher, *The Revolutionary Clergy . . . 1850-1903* (Manila, 1981); G. H. Anderson (ed.), *Studies in Philippine Church History* (New York, 1969), pp. 223-255; *RGG*[4] 1, pp. 184f: Art. Aglipay, Gregorio; *TRE* 26, 1996, pp. 514ff: Art. Philippinen; Moffett, *Asia* II, pp. 563ff; Sunquist, *Dictionary*, pp. 10f (Art. Aglipay, Gregorio); pp. 359f (Art. Iglesia Filipina Independiente).

F. DEVELOPMENTS IN THE 1920S AND 1930S

80. Korea: Christians and the Independence Movement (1919)

In contrast to other Asian countries, Korea was not the victim of Western colonialism, but — following its annexation by Japan in 1910 — of foreign rule by an Asian nation. From the beginning Christian groups played a significant role in Korean resistance to Japanese rule. On 1 March 1919, a Declaration of Independence of the Korean People was delivered in Seoul, accompanied by nationwide demonstrations. Sixteen of the 33 signatories were Korean church leaders. Document a is an eyewitness account of a Korean Presbyterian pastor on the simultaneous events in Pyongyang, and document b is from the account of a British merchant on the subsequent Japanese oppression.

a. The Independence Movement of March 1, 1919

Pyongyang Chosen, March 1st, 1919

This has been a memorable day in the history of this country. Yi Tai Wang, former Emperor of Korea, passed away recently and day after tomorrow has been set as the day for the funeral. He is to be buried at state expense and as a prince of the Japanese Empire. The ceremonies are to be according to the Shinto rites and it is reported that the Koreans are very much offended at this as they want the funeral to be conducted according to their own national ceremonies. [. . .]

A few days ago it was announced that Memorial Services would be held in this city [Pyongyang] in memory of the late emperor. One meeting was to be held in the compound of the Seungduk (Christian Boys' School), another meeting at the compound of the Methodist Church and a third one at the headquarters of the Chondo Kyo. The latter is a half religious, half political organization which is widely spread throughout the country.

There has been considerable suppressed excitement for some days among the Koreans and we have had various rumors that something important was going to take place at that time. [We] decided to attend the meeting. We found the courtyard full of people, we estimated the crowd at about three thousand. We were shown seats well forward. . . . The pupils from all our church schools were there and also many from the government schools.

In front of the entrance was erected a speaker's stand and around and back of this were seated several of the pastors and officers of the Presbyterian churches of the city. Rev. Kim Sondu, pastor of the Fifth Church and moderator of the General Assembly, was speaking when I entered. Pastor Kang Kyuchan of the Fourth Church had already spoken reviewing the life history of the late emperor. [. . .] After the benediction had been pronounced Kim Sondu read two passages of Scripture as follows: 1 Pet. 3:13-17 and Rom. 9:3. It was evident from his intonation as he read these words that something serious was on the docket.

Then, Chung Ilsun, a graduate of the college and now helper in the Fourth Church, took the platform and said he had an important communication to read. He said it was the happiest and proudest day of his life. . . . There was a great cheer went up from the audience. He then proceeded to read what was virtually a declaration of independence of the Korean people. After he had finished another man took the floor and explained just what the people were expected to do, saying that nothing of an unlawful nature was to be permitted in the least but that the people were to follow the instructions given and make no resistance to the [colonial] authorities nor attack the Japanese people or officials. Kang Ryuchan then addressed the people relative to the subject of national Independence. . . . A large Korean flag was then fastened to the wall back of the speakers' stand and then the crowd went wild shouting, "Mansei!," the Korean for Hurrah, and waving the flags. It was then explained to them that they were all to form in procession and parade the streets waving flags and saying nothing but "Mansei, Mansei!"

b. Massacre in a Village Church

On Tuesday, April 15th [1919], early in the afternoon some [Japanese] soldiers had entered the village [Cheamri, close to Suwon] and given orders that all the adult male Christians and members of the Chundo-Kyo were to assemble in the church, as a lecture was to be given to them. In all some twenty-three men went to the church as ordered. . . . They soon found out the nature of the plot, as the soldiers immediately surrounded the church and fired into it through the paper windows. When most of them had thus been either killed or injured the devilish soldiers set fire to the thatch and wooden building that readily blazed.

Source: (a) Kim Yong-Bock, *Historical Transformation, People's Movement, Messianic Koinonia,* Diss. theol. (Princeton, 1976), pp. 427f. (b) H. Heung-Wo Cynn, *The Rebirth of Korea: The Reawakening of the People, Its Causes, and the Outlook* (New York/Cincinnati, 1920), pp. 68f. — *Further Reading:* Kim Yong-Bock, *Historical Transformation* (see above), pp. 403-476; Wi Jo Kang, *Christ and Cesar in Modern Korea* (New York, 1997), pp. 27ff, 51ff; Sunquist, *Dictionary,* pp. 450f (Art. Korea Independence Movement 1919); England, *ACT III,* pp. 505ff.

81. China: The Anti-Christian Movement (1922-1925)

The 1922 conference of the World's Student Federation in Shanghai, unfortunatly titled "The Christian conquest of China," sparked a fresh outbreak of xenophobic and anti-Christian agitation. This differed from the Boxer Rebellion of 1900 in that it spread quickly through the major cities, supported particularly by students and intellectuals. From a Chinese Christian:

On March 10th, 1922 a telegram was sent out from Shanghai as a manifesto against the World's Student Christian Federation. The telegram was signed by the Anti-Christian Federation. Five days later a fortnightly magazine called "The Vanguard" came out with a special number on the Anti-Christian Student Federation, publishing the manifesto and the names of the constituent organizations as well as three articles on the Anti-Christian movement and a reprint of three others which had appeared elsewhere. The main line of argument was (1) that science and religion are incompatible; (2) that Christianity is the tool of imperialism and capitalism and is a means of oppressing the weaker nations.

On March 21st [1922] a telegram was sent out from Peking to all parts of the country signed by seventy-seven persons connected with various educational institutions in Peking. This announced the organization of the Anti-Religious Federation, its object being as therein expressed to further the truth of science and to do away with the moral restraints of religion. [. . .]

Following this outbreak of activity very little was done in an open way until the summer of 1924. In a number of places mission schools suffered from strikes and there was a tendency towards concentration upon Christian education as a point of attack. [. . .] During the summer and autumn of 1924, four important educational conferences took a distinctly anti-Christian line. The fifth annual conference of the Young China Association held at Nanking in July 1924 passed the following resolution: "That we strongly oppose Christian education which destroys the national spirit of our people and carries on a cultural program in order to undermine Chinese civilization." [. . .]

The sixth national conference of the Student's Union held in August 1924 in Shanghai decided to start a movement for the restoration of educational rights and for the denunciation of educational enterprises started by foreigners in order to spread religion.

Source: N. Z. Zia, "The Anti-Christian Movement in China," in: *The China Mission Year Book 1925*, pp. 51-55. — *Further Reading:* J. T. Chao, *The Chinese Indigenous Church Movement 1919-1927* (Ph.D. diss., Univ. of Pennsylvania, 1986), pp. 135-168; J. G. Lutz, *The Anti-Christian Movements of 1920-1928* (Notre Dame, Ind., 1988); England, *ACT III*, pp. 130ff, 135ff, 153ff.

82. India: Gandhi on Christianity

a. On Conversions (1920)

In an interview with British journalist Millie Polak in the year 1920, Mahatma Gandhi explained why he did not convert to Christianity:

Gandhi: I did once seriously think of embracing the Christian faith. The gentle figure of Christ, so patient, so kind, so loving, so full of forgiveness that he taught his followers not to retaliate when abused or struck, but to turn the other cheek. I thought it was a beautiful example of the perfect man.

Mrs. Polak: But you did not embrace Christianity, did you?

Gandhi: No. I studied your Scriptures for some time and thought earnestly about them. I was tremendously attracted to Christianity, but, eventually I came to the conclusion that there was nothing really in your Scriptures that we had not got in ours, and that to be a good Hindu also meant that I would be a good Christian. There was no need for me to join your creed to be a believer in the beauty of the teachings of Jesus or to try to follow his example.

Mrs. Polak: Of course, it is what a man is that counts, not what he calls himself. But, tell me, do you believe in conversion, in changing from one form of faith to another?

Gandhi: What do you feel yourself?

Mrs. Polak: It does not please me, some how. I could not do it.

Gandhi: I think that is right. If a man reaches the heart of his own religion, he has reached the heart of the others, too. There is only one God, but there are many paths to Him.

b. Western Christianity and the Sermon on the Mount (1921)

I consider Western Christianity in its practical working a negation of Christ's Christianity. I cannot conceive Jesus, if he was living in the flesh in our midst, approving of modern Christian organizations, public worship or modern ministry. If Indian Christians will simply cling to the Sermon on the Mount, which was delivered not merely to the peaceful disciples but a groaning world, they would not go wrong, and they would find that no religion is false; and that if all live according to their lights and in the fear of God, they would not need to worry about organizations, forms of worship and ministry. The Pharisees had all that, but Jesus would have none of it, for they were using their office as a cloak for hypocrisy and worse. Co-operation with forces of Good and non-cooperation with forces of Evil are the two things we need for a good and pure life, whether it is called Hindu, Muslim or Christian.

Source: (a) *M. K. Gandhi, The Message of Jesus Christ,* ed. by A. T. Hingorani (Bombay, 1986), pp. 23-25; (b) ibid., pp. 33ff. — *Further Reading:* M. M. Thomas, *The Acknowledged Christ of the Indian Renaissance* (Madras, 1970), pp. 135-165; R. Ellsberg (ed.), *Gandhi on Christianity* (New York, 1991); G. Pattery (ed.), *Gandhi — The Believer* (New Dehli, 1996).

83. Tambaram (1938) as an Ecumenical Event

Asia's growing significance in international ecumenism was demonstrated in many ways by the World Missionary Conference of 1938. The choice of venue was Tambaram, South India, near Madras. For the first time just over half of the delegates came from the so-called "young churches" of the non-European world, bringing their own topics and perspectives to the debate. During the preparation for the conference, a group of critical Indian Christians issued a significant contribution to the topic of the conference, the relationship between Christianity and culture. (a) Asian delegates such as Indian bishop V. S. Azariah were impressed by the ecumenical character of this assembly meeting as the clouds of world war again gathered. (b) African participants utilized the conference to make contact with Asian church leaders (see document 185) and also, like South African pastor S. S. Tema, to speak with Gandhi.

a. The "Rethinking Christianity in India" Group

In Europe and other Christian countries, Christians see Jesus only. In the unique situation in India . . . we see Jesus in the company of other founders of religion or saviours of men — Buddha, Rama, Krishna. Christianity moves and has its being in the midst of live, active religions commanding the homage of millions. . . . In India, these religions are in numbers and influence such as to compel mutual attention and respect. The life and destiny of [Indian] Christians has to be studied in this vital context. [. . .]

The missionary, forced by the logic of the situation, undertakes a comparative study of religions [from a certain perspective] in his field. His conviction that Christianity alone can be the true religion predetermines and conditions his enquiry. [. . .] [Indian Christians see things in a different way. They are] dissatisfied with what the Church offers . . . as Christianity [and have] been led to seek for help in rediscovering the message of Christianity from a study of the life and experience of earnest seekers after salvation in other religions. . . . The convert of today regards Hinduism as his <u>spiritual mother</u> who has nurtured him in a sense of spiritual values in the past. He discovers the supreme value of Christ, not in spite of Hinduism but because Hinduism has taught him to discern spiritual greatness. [. . .]

The signal contribution of Karl Barth to the theological thinking of the day is the merciless cutting of the globe of religion into the original core and the accumulated tradition called by him religion. The religion of Christ is not the same as Christ. To belong to the religion of Christ is not necessarily to come into contact with Jesus and to be dominated by Him. As a religion, Christianity is no better or worse than other religions. The supremacy we claim or we should claim is not for Christianity, but for Christ. [. . .]

b. Tambaram and the "Young Churches"

The outstanding impression left on my [V. S. Azariah's] mind by the Tambaram gathering is the Ecumenical character of the Assembly, which brought home to me, more vividly than anything else, the strength of the Churches in the Mission Field. Not merely their number, but the contribution their representatives made to the life, the devotions and the counsels of the Conference are memories not to be easily forgotten. The strength of our fellow Christians in China, in South Africa, in Java, in the Philippines and South America was a revelation to me. [. . .] The fellowship in Christ which leapt over barriers of race, language and denomination was most inspiring. At the Christmas celebration, I noticed the South African White and the South African Bantu and Negro, the Chinese and the Japanese, the Burmese and the Indian, the French and the German delegates kneeling side by side before the symbols of our redemption. Where would such a thing be possible except at the foot of the Cross?

Source: (a) P. Chenchiah, "Jesus and Non-Christian Faiths," in: D. M. Devasahayam/A. N. Sudarisanam (eds.), *Rethinking Christianity in India* (Madras, 1938), pp. 49-64, here: pp. 49-54; (b) Yale Dale Library, Mott Papers 4/61: Letter of Bishop V. S. Azariah to J. R. Mott from 12.1.1939. — *Further Reading:* F. Ludwig, *Zwischen Kolonialismuskritik und Kirchenkampf*

(Göttingen, 2000), pp. 137-174; S. B. Harper, *In the Shadow of the Mahatma: Bishop V. S. Azariah* ... (Grand Rapids, etc., 2000); England, *ACT I*, pp. 375ff.

G. The Asian Churches during World War II

84. Japan: Forced Unification (1941)

At the beginning of World War II pressure on Japanese Christians to take part in the national Shinto cult was growing. Critics of the official militarism were dismissed from their jobs or, like prominent Christian Toyohiko Kagawa in 1940, arrested for distributing pacifistic propaganda. Under massive pressure from the government, the *Nippon Kirisuto Kyodan* (United Church of Christ in Japan) was founded in 1941, a merger of 34 Protestant denominations. As the war progressed, the *Kyodan* supported various religious and intellectual actions of the totalitarian regime. Already in 1940 the "National Christian Assembly" had expressed itself in this way:

We Japanese are proud to acknowledge the glorious history of the Tenno which has continued for 2600 years without interruption since the rule of the first Tenno Jinmu. Today we the Christians in Japan gather together and humbly offer our homage to the Tenno. The contemporary world situation is very disturbed and we must not loose sight of that fact. In the West we see war damage and in the East we have the China Incident [Japan's undeclared long-running war against China]. . . . In such a world, however, the destiny and power of our nation moves ever on, without any mistakes. We have no doubt that these developments are due to the providence of heaven and the practices of the Emperor and his subjects, incomparable throughout the world.

Facing the changing situation of the world, the state renews its policy and struggles for the establishment of the New Order of Greater Asia. We Christians will respond positively to this national policy. We are resolved to participate in this great work of inspiring the national spirit by abolishing denominational differences and uniting together in an ecclesiastical merger, and rendering devoted loyalty to the Empire.

On this memorial day, accordingly, we declare the following:

1. We will propagate the Gospel of Christ and save the soul of the nation.
2. We will accomplish the union of all Christian churches in this nation.
3. We will inspire the national spirit, and uplift the national morality, and renew the national life.

October 17, Shouwa 15 (1940)
National Christian Meeting for the Celebration of Tenno Era 2600

Source: Proceedings of the 18th General Assembly of the National Christian Council in Japan (26.-27.11.1940) (Tokyo, 1940), pp. 46f, translated by A. Dohi (slightly altered). — *Further Reading:* A. Dohi, "Christianity in Japan," in: T. K. Thomas (ed.), *Christianity in Asia* (Singapore, 1979), pp. 35ff; H. Drummond, *A History of Christianity in Japan* (Grand Rapids, 1971), pp. 250ff; *TRE* 16, 1987, pp. 525ff: Art. Japan II; K. Ishihara, "The United Church of Christ in Japan," in: N. Ehrenstrom/W. G. Muelder (eds.), *Institutionalism and Church Unity* (New York, 1963).

85. Persecution of Christians in Territories Occupied by Japan

The Japanese expansion into Indochina, South Asia and the Pacific had immediate consequences for Christian communities in these regions. Suspected by the new rulers of being covert supporters of the West, they were often subject to persecution in the newly conquered areas. This was also true for the island of Formosa (Taiwan), which had been annexed by Japan in 1895.

At first they [the Japanese] acted by prohibiting assemblies for worship, the circulation of the Bible, and the passing on of the Gospel from individual to individual. Then, as the people continued to meet in secret, and more and more villages came to be gripped by the message, they moved on to sterner measures. The leaders of the various groups were condemned to forced labour, thrown into prison or beaten. As Japan in its conflict with China and America, was driven to struggle ever more urgently for its own existence, the [Taiwanese] believers were treated as enemies of Japan. Now they were subjected to strict interrogation, often accompanied by torture. In some cases sentences of death were pronounced. The police attempted to collect the Bibles and to destroy them. In most cases, however, the Christians managed to conceal them. The [Taiwanese] Church was driven to maintaining an underground existence.

Source: S. Neill, *Colonialism and Christian Missions* (London, 1966), pp. 212f.

86. India: Fear of Marginalization (1944)

The entry of British India into the Second World War and the prospect of post-war independence confronted Indian Christians with a dilemma. On the one hand, they supported demands for national sovereignty. On the other hand, Christian communities, and especially Protestants who had given up claims for communal representation in the debates about the future political order, saw themselves threatened with marginalization. In a March 1944 statement the Anglican Bishop V. S. Azariah of Dornakal, a respected leader of Indian Christians, expressed the ambivalence of their position.

The Congress Party of India demands that Britain immediately surrender the entire government into the hands of the peoples of India, and if that is not done it cannot cooperate with Britain in the war against Axis aggressors [Germany and Italy]. The Muslim League [in India] also demands self-government, but stipulates that those provinces where Muslims are in a vast majority should be constituted after the war into a Muslim Dominion. In the interests of the sixty million of the depressed classes, Dr. Ambedkar violently objects to the Congress demands. [. . .] In this conflicting situation the Indian Christian hardly knows what his attitude ought to be. Certain considerations emerge from the fact that he is both a follower of Christ and a citizen of India.

With trembling conviction Indian Christians see that they must be on the side of India's freedom. If China, Japan, Persia, and Turkey can hold their heads up as independent nations, their motherland should have the same status. The Indian Christian has vague fears that the freedom he desires for his country may spell deprivation of his own liberty and his fundamental religious rights. Would India's freedom mean a return to the old caste tyranny? Congress leaders have never given the slightest consideration to clearing these doubts. [. . .]

Source: Yale Dale Library, Mott Papers: V. S. Azariah, "The Indian Christian's Dilemma Today, 1944." — *Further Reading:* S. B. Harper, *In the Shadow of the Mahatma: Bishop V. S. Azariah and the Travails of Christianity in British India* (Grand Rapids, etc., 2000); Sunquist, *Dictionary,* p. 49 (Art. Azariah, V. S.)

V. ASIA 1945-1990

A. THE CHURCHES AND NATION BUILDING IN THE 1950S

87. India: Church Union and Hindu Nationalism

The year 1947 brought political independence to India and also saw the formation of the Church of South India (a). This was the first merger of Episcopal and non-Episcopal churches worldwide and as an act of ecclesiastical independence by Indian Christians attracted wide attention in the international ecumenical community. In the Constitution of 1950, India defined itself as a secular state, and established the principle of religious freedom (b). Nevertheless as a result of growing Hindu nationalism the Christian minority found itself exposed to repressive measures and the restriction of their missionary activities and ecumenical contacts (c).

a. The South India Church Merger in 1947

From the Constitution of the Church of South India in 1947:

2. *The Purpose and Nature of the Union.* — The Church of South India affirms that the purpose of the union by which it has been formed is the carrying out of God's will, as this is expressed in our Lord's prayer — 'That they may all be one . . . that the world may believe that Thou didst send me'. It believes that by union the Church of South India will become a more effective instrument for God's work, and that there will become a more effective instrument for God's work, and that there will be greater peace, closer fellowship and fuller life within the Church, and also renewed eagerness and power for the proclamation of the Gospel of Christ. It hopes that it may be a greater release of divine power for the fulfilment of God's purpose for His world. [. . .]

8. *Necessary Elements in the Life of the Church of South India.* — The Church of South India recognizes that episcopal, presbyteral, and congregational elements must all have their place in its order of life, and that the episcopate, the presbyterate, and the congregation of the faithful should all in their several spheres have responsibility and exercise authority in the life and work of the Church, in its governance and administration, in its evangelistic and pastoral work, in its discipline, and in its worship.

b. Articles on Religion in the Indian Constitution of 1950

25. (1) Subject to public order, morality and health and to the other provisions of this Part [of the constitution], all persons are equally entitled to freedom of conscience and the right freely to profess, practise and propagate religion.

(2) Nothing in this article shall affect the operation of any existing law or prevent the State from making any law — (a) regulating or restricting any economic, financial, political or other secular activity which may associated with religious institutions of a public character to all classes and sections of Hindus. [. . .]

26. Subject to public order, morality and health, every religious denomination or any section thereof shall have the right (a) to establish and maintain institutions for religious and charitable purposes; (b) to manage its own affairs in matters religious; (c) to own and acquire movable and immovable property; and (d) to administer such property in accordance with law.

27. No person shall be compelled to pay any taxes, the proceeds of which are specifically appropriated in payment of expenses for the promotion or maintenance of any particular religion or religious denomination.

28. (1) No religious instruction shall be provided in any educational institutions wholly maintained out of State funds. [. . .]

(3) No person attending any educational institution recognized by the State or receiving aid out of State funds shall be required to take part in any religious instruction that may be imparted in such institution or to attend any religious worship that may be conducted in such institution on or in any premises attached thereto unless such person . . . has given his consent thereto.

c. Restriction of Missionary Activities

From the recommendations of the official government Niyogi Committee in 1956:

1. Those Missionaries whose primary object is proselytization should be asked to withdraw. The large influx of foreign Missionaries is undesirable and should be checked.

2. The best course for the Indian Churches to follow is to establish a United Independent Christian Church in India without being dependent on foreign support.

3. The use of medical or other professional services as a direct means of making conversions should be prohibited by law. [. . .]

9. An amendment of the Constitution of India may be sought, firstly to clarify that the right of propagation has been given only to the citizens of India and secondly that it does not include conversion by force, fraud or illicit means.

10. Suitable control on conversions brought about through illegal means should be imposed. If necessary legislative measures should be enacted. [. . .]

13. Circulation of literature meant for religious propaganda without the approval of the State Government should be prohibited. [. . .]

Source: (a) M. K. Kuriakose, *History of Christianity in India* (Madras, 1982), pp. 378-381; (b) ibid., pp. 388f; (c) Report of the Christian Missionary Activities Enquiry Committee. Vol. I (Madhya Pradesh, 1956), pp. 131f, 163-165. — *Further Reading:* B. Sundkler, *Church of South India 1900-1947* (London, 1954); K. M. George, *Church of South India (1947-1999)* (Delhi, 1999); Sunquist, *Dictionary,* pp. 175f (Art. Church of South India); D. E. Smith, *India as a Secular State* (Princeton, 1963), pp. 207ff (re: Niyogi Committee).

88. Indonesia: Monotheism as State Doctrine (Pancasila)

On 17 August 1945, Indonesia declared its independence, although this was not recognized by the Netherlands until 1950. In view of the religious and cultural diversity of the 11,000-island country the national leaders proposed neither a secular constitution nor the Islamic state desired by the Muslim religious majority. Instead they proclaimed a policy of "five pillars" or principles *(pancasila)* to provide a binding element between the five recognized religions of Islam, Protestantism, Catholicism, Hinduism and Buddhism. This secured a legal basis for the continuing existence of Christian churches.

a. From the Declaration of Independence (1945)

By the grace of God Almighty and moved by the high ideal for a free national life, the People of Indonesia declare themselves independent. In order to establish a form of government in the Indonesian nation which protects the whole population and its territory, and to promote public welfare, to raise the standard of living and to help achieve a world order based on independence, eternal peace and social justice, the national independence is embodied in the Constitution of the Indonesian State, set up as a republic with sovereignty vested in the people and based on:

- Belief in One God,
- Just and Civilized humanity
- The Unity of Indonesia, and
- Democracy wisely guided and led by representation, creating
- Social justice for the whole Indonesian people.

b. President Sukarno on the Five Basic Principles (Pancasila)

I have put forward four principles:

1. Indonesian Nationalism
2. Internationalism or Humanitarianism
3. Consensus or Democracy
4. Social Welfare

We hope that the fifth principle will create a Free Indonesia with the devotion to one God . . . the principle of belief in God, but every Indonesian should believe in his own God. Christians should worship God according to the teachings of Jesus Christ. Moslems according to the teachings of the Prophet Mohammad. Buddhists should carry out their religious duties according to their own scriptures.

But let us all have belief in God. The Indonesian state shall be a state in which every person can freely worship God namely without "religious egoism." And Indonesia should be a state which has a Belief in God! [. . .]

Source: (a) M. P. M. Muskens, *Partner in Nation Building* (Aachen, 1979), pp. 180f (slightly altered); (b) ibid., pp. 173f. — *Further Reading:* F. Cooley, *The Growing Seed: The Christian Church in Indonesia* (Jakarta, 1981), pp. 30ff; D. Becker, *Die Kirchen und der Pancasila-Staat* (Erlangen,

1996); E. Darmaputera, *Pancasila and the Search for Identity . . . in Indonesian Society* (1988); Sunquist, *Dictionary*, pp. 374-380 (Art. Indonesia); pp. 634f (Art. Pancasila); England, *ACT II*, pp. 159ff.

89. Japan: Japanese Christians' Confession of Responsibility (1946)

The defeat of Japan in 1945 resulted in a collapse of traditional values and an ideological vacuum in which Christianity temporarily experienced an enormous upswing. Japanese Christians even dreamt of the Christianization of the entire land. In contrast to other segments of Japanese society, they also admitted Japan's "responsibility" for the events of World War II. The following text is taken from the 9 June 1946 "Statement of the National Christian Council for a Christian Movement for the Founding of a New Japan."

We Japanese painfully recognize our responsibility for World War II. Given that Christians believe in the gospel of peace, we are especially moved, after deep reflection, to acknowledge our sin and express our repentance. We are persuaded that the heavenly Father, favoring infinite forgiveness, will open the way of regeneration from death with abundant grace. Facing war damages beyond description and the painful sufferings of our people, we are resolved anew to bear our cross.

We are determined that we will build a new Japan on the basis of Christ's Cross and will aim to establish a moral order of the world. At this regular gathering on the day of Pentecost in 1946, we pray for the Christianizing of all Japan, for the renewal of our faith through Christ, and for the expansion and strengthening of the Church of Christ. By means of Christian solidarity throughout Japan, we will take the agonies of the nation upon ourselves, tirelessly playing our part by serving this nation amid famine, perplexity, destitution, and suffering. We will promote, therefore, the three-years project of the Christian Movement to establish a new Japan.

We resolve that:

1. We will christianize Japan through the Gospel of Christ.
2. We will make every endeavor to relieve eighty millions people from near famine.
3. We will preserve the purity of men and women in the midst of suffering and uplift the morality of the people.

June 9, Shouwa 21 (1946)   National Christian Meeting

Source: Nihon Kirisuto Kyodan (ed.), *Collection of Sources on the History of the Nihon Kirisuto Kyodan* (Jap.). Vol. III (Tokyo, 1998), p. 194. Translation: A. Dohi. — *Further Reading:* J. M. Philips, *From the Rising of the Sun: Christians and Society in Contemporary Japan* (Maryknoll, 1981), pp. 1-16; Sunquist, *Dictionary*, pp. 411f (Art. Japan); England, *ACT III*, pp. 363ff.

B. UNDER COMMUNIST RULE

90. China: Christians in the People's Republic

The Communist takeover of 1949 under the leadership of Mao Zedong represented a profound turning point for the churches of China. The religious policies of the communists were controlled exclusively by the Party, according to the principle of the dictatorship of the proletariat. This at best provided for some isolated alliances with religious groups (a). Traditional Chinese religions were expected to rid themselves of their "feudalistic" ties, and Christian churches were attacked for their alleged ties to Western "imperialism." With the escalation of the Korean War in 1951, American missionaries were expelled from the country and all foreign financial support was cut off (c). In 1949, Chinese church leaders revised their relationships with overseas missions (b), and in 1950, left-wing Protestant Christians took steps toward the formation of the "Three-Self Movement." This adopted a version of the late nineteenth-century missionary vision of the establishment of indigenous churches based on the principle of self-propagating, self-financing and self-governing churches, and coupled it with a demand of strict loyalty to the new regime (d). The majority of Protestant congregations joined this movement, with significant groups going underground, but initial attempts to form a similar patriotic organization among Catholics failed and it was not until 1958 that some priests were consecrated bishops without Rome's consent (e). The Chinese Catholic church split into a "patriotic" official wing and an underground church that remained faithful to Rome.

a. Mao Zedong (1893-1976) on Religion

From Mao's text: "The Chinese Revolution and the Chinese Communist Party" (1939):

The imperialist powers have never slackened their efforts to poison the minds of the Chinese people. This is their policy of cultural aggression. And it is carried out through missionary work, through establishing hospitals and schools, publishing newspapers and inducing Chinese students to study abroad. Their aim is to train intellectuals who will serve their interests and to dupe the people.

From "On Religion and the United Front (1940)":

Communists may form an anti-imperialist and anti-feudal united front for political action with certain idealists and even with religious followers, but we can never approve of their idealism or religious doctrines.

b. Chinese Christians Writing to the Overseas Missions (1949)

We Christians in China feel the urgency to undertake an examination of our work and of our relationship to the "old" churches in the face of historical changes in China. We don't have to question our faith, because our fundamental belief in Christ cannot be shaken. . . . The challenge for us consists of finding new paths. When that means that we should love our neighbor, in the fullest sense — in our daily lives and in our society — then we should accept this challenge. . . . It has never been easy to carry the cross and it will be no easy task in the New China either. More than ever, a true Christian spirit must manifest itself in whichever form it might appear.

c. Expulsion of Foreign Missionaries

From the Regulations of the administrative affairs for the control of Christian organizations, issued by Chou En-lai to a conference of 151 Protestant leaders in Peking (April 16-21, 1951):

1. Chinese Christian churches and other organizations should immediately sever all relations with American Mission Boards, and with Mission Boards [in China] which receive a major part of their funds from America. Such Mission Boards shall immediately cease all activities in China.

2. Americans who are now working in Chinese Christian churches and other organizations shall be treated according to the following rules:

(1) Those who by word or deed work against the People's Government shall be dismissed from their work, and given appropriate punishment by the Government.

(2) Those desiring to leave the country may do so.

(3) Those who are not reactionary and whom the church or other organizations wish to employ and support may continue their work, but may not hold any administrative position.

3. Self-supporting churches and organizations which have been carrying on service projects, such as medical and benevolent organizations, may, if their finances are sufficient, continue these activities. But a Board of Managers must be organized, which will be responsible for ensuring that government regulations are obeyed.

d. The Protestant "Three Self Movement"

Minutes from a conference of Protestant church leaders in 1954:

The churches of New China on the basis of "Love-country Love-church" are showing a new spirit. [. . .] We thank the Lord that during the past four years, by the grace of the Lord and the determination of both laymen and pastors, the

Chinese Church has not only made progress in its spiritual work, but has attained a sense of solidarity which it never had before.

Today believers love their church more than ever and are willing to take responsibility for it, giving generously of both money and time. Many pastors have a firmer faith, seeing more clearly God's upholding providence, and are more zealous in caring for their flocks, rightly divining the word of truth, and training Christians in the spirit of Love-country Love-church. Accordingly the sense of fellowship between pastors and laymen is constantly growing.

The partitions which [Western] imperialism had raised between the [various denominational] churches are gradually being destroyed, and members and workers of different churches who formerly had little or nothing to do with each other are now increasing in fellowship. [. . .] The Christian young people of Shanghai, Peking, Wuhan, Canton, Amoy and Nanjing have had interdenominational summer and winter conferences and Christmas and Easter programs. We have truly come to realize what a pleasant thing it is for brethren to dwell together in unity.

e. Consecration of Bishops without Rome's Consent

Controversies arose about the validity of the consecration of bishops performed without the consent of Rome. The issue was debated in 1959 in Hong Kong at an assembly under the chairmanship of the Prefect of the Congregation of Faith, where Cardinal Liénart of Lille explained:

The [Catholic] Christians in China number several million, and they can only continue to exist if they behave loyally to the government of their country. Can we rebuke them for that? Can we hold it against them for consecrating Chinese bishops themselves to replace the missionary bishops that were driven out, without first receiving the proper authorization of the Pope as they should have? In the complete absence of relationship between the Holy See and the current government in China, this was unfortunately impossible for them.

Source: (a) D. MacInnis, *Religious Policy and Practice in Communist China* (New York/London, 1972), p. 12; (b) Evangelisches Missionswerk (ed.), *China und seine Christen — ein eigener Weg* (Hamburg, etc., 1982), p. 20; (c) D. MacInnis, *Religious Policy . . .*, pp. 27f; (d) ibid., pp. 101-104; (e) R. Malek/M. Plate (eds.), *Chinas Katholiken suchen neue Wege* (Freiburg, etc. 1987), pp. 40f. — *Further Reading:* MacInnis, *Religious Policy* (see above); P. L. Wickeri, *Seeking the Common Ground* (1988); Sunquist, *Dictionary,* pp. 143ff (Art. China); p. 846 (Art. Three-Self Patriotic Movement); England, *ACT III,* pp. 59ff, 64ff.

91. North Korea: Kim Il Sung on the Sermon on the Mount

For Korea, the end of World War II brought not only liberation from Japanese occupation but also the onset of national division. On 9 September 1948, the People's Republic of Korea was declared in the Soviet-controlled North, with Kim Il Sung (1912-1994) as its Prime Minister and dictatorial leader. Christianity was regarded as an instrument of the Americans controlling the South, and as far as possible eliminated. Still today, remnants of Christian churches in North Korea remain severely restricted. The Korean War (1950-1953) brought unending suffering to the divided land, and led to the flight of numerous Christians from North Korea into South Korea. Kim Il Sung on the relationship between Christianity and American imperialism:

The United States had sent to our country missionaries under the mantle of relation long ago to build churches in many places and disseminate Christianity and ideas of U.S. worship, and made preparations over tens of years to dominate Korea some day. This was an insidious trick of the United States to [establish] . . . its influence in Korea under the cloak of religion.

The U.S. missionaries preached to the Koreans, "Whosoever shall smite thee on thy right cheek, turn to him the other also." This implies that the Korean people must not resist but remain submissive even if the United States encroaches upon their freedom. The Korean patriots and people, however, were not fooled by this deceptive preaching of the United States. Our people answered to the U.S. rascals, "If you slap us once, we will return two slaps" and did so indeed. Yet, some of the [Korean] pastors and church elders, taken in by such a religious propaganda, are trying to sell our country for dollars. . . . There is a tendency among the Christians towards unconditional worship of America, and the reactionary pastors dislike our Party which enlightens and politically awakens the people, and come out against its policies because it becomes more difficult to attain their ends if our people get awakened.

Source: M. Sawa, "Human Rights of Christian Minority in North Korea," in: *The Northeast Asia Journal of Theology* 28/29 (1982), pp. 49-78, 60f. — *Further Reading:* Sawa, ibid.; Wi Jo Kang, *Christ and Cesar in Modern Korea* (New York, 1997), pp. 71-80; Sunquist, *Dictionary,* pp. 453f (Art. Korean War).

92. North Vietnam: Massive Flight of Catholic Christians (1954)

Comparable developments took place in Vietnam, which was divided in 1954. The first Indo-China war in 1954 led to around one million believers leaving Communist North Vietnam for the South. A majority of the priests (618) also migrated south, only 375 remaining in the North. Official church instructions, such as the letter from Archbishop Dooley to Bishop Kue (Hanoi) of 28 July 1954, could not prevent this flight:

All those [Catholic priests] who have the chance to guide souls — after the example of the perfect Priest [Christ] who did not abandon his flock — should stay with their faithful, excepting certain cases where, for special reason, written authorization to leave is received, delivered by the competent superiors.

Source: C. Lange, "The Catholic Church in Vietnam" in: *Teaching All Nations* 14 (1977), pp. 17f. — *Further Reading:* Sunquist, *Dictionary,* pp. 876-880 (Art. Vietnam); England, *ACT,* pp. 583ff; *WCE* I, pp. 802ff.

C. DEVELOPMENTS IN THE 1960S

93. Sri Lanka: Nationalization of Church Schools

The 1960s in Sri Lanka were characterized by a new wave of Sinhalese nationalism. After political independence in 1948, Sri Lankans aspired to overcome the cultural legacy left by the former colonial power. In 1961 Sinhala replaced English as the administrative language. Although it was the language of the majority of the Sri Lankan people, it brought discrimination against the Tamil minority. Ceylon was renamed Sri Lanka, the Western calendar was abolished in favor of the traditional lunar one, and the official status of Buddhism was strengthened. Along with these changes came a *kulturkampf* mentality, which led to the national takeover (without compensation) of the mostly Catholic private schools, which until then had been supported by the state. From the parliamentary debate of 2 January 1961:

The Government regrets to announce that its generosity and patience [in regard to the Schools issue] has been thoroughly abused by certain proprietors [i.e., the church schools]. The only option now open to the Government, forced on it by the [church] schools, is the introduction of an appropriate Bill in Parliament. The Government proposes to recall Parliament in order to introduce the necessary legal steps to take over and place under government ownership all schools, together with buildings and lands. There will be no compensation.

Proclaimed by Mr C. P. de Silva, Leader of the House, sitting on 2nd January, 1961.

Source: Ceylon Daily News, January 3, 1961. — *Further Reading:* K. M. de Silva, *A History of Sri Lanka* (Oxford/Kalkutta, 1981), pp. 527f; H. Bechert, *Buddhismus, Staat und Gesellschaft . . .* (Frankfurt, 1966), pp. 1, 348ff; K. M. de Silva, *A History of Sri Lanka* (Dehli, etc., 1990), pp. 525ff, 528ff; G. P. V. Somaratna, *The Events of Christian History in Sri Lanka* (Colombo, 1997).

94. Burma: Buddhist Nationalism and the Churches

In 1962, the new government under General Ne Win announced a "Burmese path to socialism," associated with a policy of self-imposed isolation. For Christian churches, the majority of which were Baptist, this meant completely breaking off all foreign missionary and ecumenical contacts. This was also seen as an opportunity for reorientation and openness towards Burmese society. Isolation also led to intensified cooperation within the church, dialogue with Buddhists, and social engagement. From a 1977 Burmese voice in this debate:

In this present time the role of the Church in Burma is to move out into the world. It also has the serious task to penetrate the country's struggle with Christ's purpose. There is the common ground where we can work hand in hand with people of different faiths using common words such as "justice" "freedom" "peace" because the common structures of human existence confront us with common human questions. . . . It is vital that as Christians we meet our fellow human beings on that ground.

The situation of social change in Burma is inevitably a situation of tension and potential strife. If the church is to respond to this situation with the message of reconciliation, it must show in its own life the marks of reconciliation. The Churches in Burma cannot effectively proclaim the Gospel of love and reconciliation while they are divided confessionally, racially, and socially. We have learnt bitter lessons of the past divided Church with Communalism and barriers of denominations lacking in co-ordination and strategy. They have been competitive more than co-operative. The task of the Church in Burma is to repentance and renewal. [. . .]

Times have changed. Christians cannot and must not be confined in their own Ghettos. The Church's responsibility is now derived from a deeper insight on the moving god working in history and among men. The mission of God can be seen at work beyond the Churches. Christian presence and participation is the order of the day. Churches should explore means to co-ordinate their programmes with secular organizations and the Government.

Source: U Pe Thwin, Summary of the thesis submitted to the Faculty of the South East Asia Graduate School of Theology (Rangoon, 1975), pp. 16-17 (typed ms.). — *Further Reading:* England, *ACT II,* pp. 55ff, 93ff.

95. China: Christians during the Cultural Revolution

The "proletarian cultural revolution" of the years 1966-1976 was accompanied by an excessive Mao cult and aimed to eliminate all "remains of the bourgeoisie and of feudalism" in the party, the government, the army, and society. It resulted in intensified perse-cution of religious communities and the destruction of the remaining church structures. Nevertheless Christian communities survived underground, and some experienced a major upswing after the end of the Mao era.

a. Cultural Revolution as a Permanent Process

From an article of the *Bejing Review* from 25 May 1976 on the 10th anniversary of the Cul-tural Revolution:

The present major Cultural Revolution is only the first; in the future there will inevitably be more. In the defensive struggle against the right-wing wind, Chairman Mao has ascertained: "After the democratic revolution, the workers, poor farmers and peasants did not stand still — they want the revolution. But some of the party members don't want to move forward. Many have drawn back and have taken action against the revolution. Why? Because they have be-come high officials and want to protect the interests of the high officials. . . . Will a revolution be needed in 100 years? Will a revolution be needed in 1000 years? Revolution is always necessary. One part of the people will always feel oppressed; lower officials, students, workers, farmers and soldiers don't want to be oppressed by the big shots. That's why they want revolution."

b. "Reject Revisionist Religious Superstition"

From a Red Guard paper, *Hung Wei Pao*, 9 March 1967:

We must destroy whatever is unprofitable to the people; whatever benefits the people must be established. Without this, how can we carry forward our cul-ture? Can it be that the proletarian revolutionary faction can both criticize and perpetuate the religious superstitions of the exploiting class? [The answer is:] No!

c. Closures of Churches and Religious Buildings

The following poster was hung on the former YMCA building in Bejing on 22 August 1966:

There is no God; there is no Spirit; there is no Jesus; there is no Mary; there is no Joseph. How can adults believe in these things? . . . Priests live in luxury and suck the blood of the workers. . . . Like Islam and Catholicism, Protestantism is a reactionary feudal ideology, the opium of the people, with foreign origins and contacts. . . . We are atheists; we believe only in Mao Tse-tung. We call on all people to burn Bibles, destroy images, and disperse religious associations.

Source: (a) Evang. Missionswerk (ed.), *China und seine Christen* (Hamburg, etc., 1982), p. 27; (b) D. MacInnis, *Religious Policy and Practice in Communist China* (New York/London, 1972), p. 288; (c) R. A. Bush, *Religion in Communist China* (Nashville, 1970), p. 257. — *Further Reading:* England, *ACT I*, pp. 468ff, 490ff; *ACT III*, pp. 188f.

96. South Korea: Explosive Church Growth

The South Korea of the 1960s and 1970s saw extraordinary growth in the Christian churches. The number of Christians rose from 600,000 in 1950 to 1,140,000 in 1960, 2.2 million in 1970 (according to an official church estimate). In 1980, the year official government religious statistics were first generated, the number of Christians was recorded as 7,280,627. By 1983 Christians represented the largest religious community of the country, with 23% of the population. Various historical, theological and sociological factors have been identified as factors in this growth: the congregational principle and a tradition of self-government in Korean Protestantism, the identification of Christianity with the nationalistic movement during the time of the Japanese occupation, the role of the churches in the post-war processes of modernization and urbanization, and the sensitivity towards social and human rights issues encouraged by Minjung theology and other influences (see document 101). Korean Christians increasingly saw themselves as "missionary churches" sending people to places such as Guam, the Philippines, Singapore, India, and further afield, and a Korean Foreign Mission Association was founded in 1972. Due to the conviction that Korean churches were a better model for Asian Christianity than the churches of the West, Koreans also began to see themselves as a "chosen land." From Harold Hong, former President of the Methodist Theological Seminary in Seoul:

It would be unfair . . . to say that the Korean people were more receptive and responsive to the Christian gospel than any other nation in Asia. But we strongly believe that we are now the chosen people of God and that we are under the special providence of God. This strong faith has actually made the Korean church the most rapidly growing.

Source: D. N. Clark, *Christianity in Modern Korea* (Lanham/New York, 1986), p. 37. — *Further Reading:* Ro Bong-Rin/M. L. Nelson (eds.), *Korean Church Growth Explosion* (Seoul, 1983); W. Blair, *The Korean Pentecost* (Edinburgh, 1977); M. R. Mullins, R. F. Young (eds.), *Perspective on Christianity and Culture in East Asia* (New York, etc., 1995); Kim Byong-Suh, "The Explosive Growth . . . A Sociological Analysis," in: *International Review of Mission* 74 (1985), pp. 59ff; Sunquist, *Dictionary,* pp. 446-449 (Art. Korea).

97. Indonesia: The Coup of 1965 and Its Consequences

A coup attempted on 30 September 1965 by a left-wing military group was suppressed within a few days by General Suharto, who later came to power. The Communist party was disbanded and thousands of its members and other suspects incarcerated: many more (ca. 300,000) were killed. Before the coup d'etat, Christian churches had stressed their loyalty to Sukarno as the nation's founding father. At the same time, they had warned of the growing Communist influence and called for the observance of the principles of *Pancasila* (see document 88). In the ideological vacuum and fear resulting from the coup, people flocked to join the Christian churches.

In the area of proclamation of the gospel to the individuals, accounts have been coming in that reveal an almost unprecedented situation. Thousands of people in various regions are presenting themselves for instruction in the faith and baptism into the Christian community. Some come out of disillusionment with their traditional faiths (animism, Hinduism or Islam); some out of fear of being branded atheist (Communist); some out of awareness that in a time of revolutionary change some firm direction and lasting values are essential: some out of recognition that for a man on his own (secularist or Communist) there is no salvation, no hope, no joy, no strength to go on in suffering and frustration. . . .

From the village of Tiglingga in North Sumatra, for example, reports say that 15 ministers from six different communions joined in baptizing more than 2,000 people into one church on a Sunday in June, 1966. Several local congregations in Central Java have doubled their membership during 1966. The General Secretary of the Council of Churches, the Rev. S. Marantika, after giving instruction to a group of former Communist leaders in a Djakarta prison, baptized more than 20 in October, 1966. In some areas the number of people registering for instruction and baptism is so large that local congregations have been mobilized to the limit to provide the needed ministry.

Source: F. L. Cooley, *Indonesia: Church and Society* (New York, 1968), p. 113. — *Further Reading:* England, *ACT II*, pp. 159ff.

98. The Second Vatican Council (1962-65) and Its Reception in Asia

Just as in Latin America (see documents 301ff), the Second Vatican Council triggered an awakening in Catholic Asia in many areas of ecclesiastical life. Its impact was comparable to that of the 1910 Edinburgh World Mission Conference among Asian Protestant churches fifty years earlier. Remarkable experiments were carried out in ecumenical cooperation, interreligious dialogue, inculturation of worship and social action. In a personal statement, Filipino bishop Julio X. Labayen expressed his views on the significance of the Vatican Council for the Asian churches.

I am most enthusiastic about the recent growth of the basic Christian communities [in the Philippines]. . . . I think they will prove to be the major influence in the church of the future. [. . .] I am also enthusiastic about the growth of all ecumenical activities in Asia and the Philippines — those between the Christian churches, those with the traditional religions of Asia, and those also with dedicated secularists, including Marxists, of good will. Vatican II, I believe, has helped us to see that our small Asian church is relative in the building up of God's kingdom, and this has turned us to closer cooperation with all others who dream and work for the kingdom or for the true liberation of the people. [. . .] I am, thirdly, very enthusiastic about the understanding we have reached on the relationship between the Basic Christian Communities (the Church) and the peoples organizations (the secular world). I think this understanding would have been impossible without Vatican II. [. . .] The Church and the secular world cooperate but they clearly follow their own dynamisms. This is a precious inheritance of Vatican II. It allows us full freedom to work with people of all faiths and all persons dedicated to bettering the life of the poor.

Source: J. X. Labayen, "Vatican II in Asia and the Philippines," in: *Ecumenical Review* 37 (1983), pp. 275-282, 276f. — *Further Reading:* P. Phan, "Reception of Vatican II in Asia," in: K. Koschorke (ed.), *Transcontinental Links . . .* (Wiesbaden, 2002), pp. 243-258.

99. The "Christian Conference of Asia" (1973)

In 1973 numerous Protestant churches in Asia came together to form the Christian Conference of Asia (CCA). Prior to this date ecumenical cooperation had been organized mainly on a national or regional level. The goal of the coalition was the cooperative witness of the Asian churches in the revolutionary upheaval of the time and an independent ecumenical voice for Asia that was not just part of the World Council of Churches. At the 1977 CCA Assembly in Penang, Malaysia, the Group for Mission and Evangelism delivered a statement on the situation in Asia which was widely quoted:

The dominant reality of Asian suffering is that people are wasted: Wasted by hunger, torture, deprivation of rights. Wasted by economic exploitation, racial and ethnic discrimination, sexual suppression. Wasted by loneliness, non-relation, non-community. The base and sinful instincts of people are exploited and their noble instincts are suppressed and ridiculed. Our Task: in this situation we begin by stating that people are not to be wasted, people are valuable. Made in God's image, redeemed by the Christ who died for them, people have his promise of abundant life, not wasted life. Therefore, we affirm that God is a living God, the God of love and that the Spirit of God works with his people in freeing and uniting them. This is our message: to share his life-style through our style; to offer his hope by offering ourselves in proclaiming the Gospel; to share Christ thus is our mission.

Source: Yap Kim Hao, *From Prapat to Colombo: History of the Christian Conference of Asia (1957-1995)* (Hong Kong, 1995), pp. 82f. — *Further Reading:* ibid.; Sunquist, *Dictionary,* pp. 162f (Art. Christian Conference of Asia).

100. The Concept of Contextualization (1972)

Ever since the term was coined in 1972, the concept of contextualization has played a significant role in the debates of Asian theologians. It soon displaced the traditional model of indigenization — that is, the attempt to make missionary Christianity "native" in cultural terms — which was felt to be too static and to have very little relation to the modern developments in Asia. The concept of contextualization was first formulated in the discussions of the Presbyterian Church of Taiwan (above all by Shoki Coe). The Theological Education Fund (TEF) of the Ecumenical Council of Churches made contextualization the central concept of its Third Mandate in 1972 — excerpted below — and it rapidly gained acceptance in ecumenical debates.

Contextualization means all that is implied in the familiar term 'indigenization' and yet seeks to press beyond. Contextualization has to do with how we assess the peculiarity of Third World contexts. Indigenization tends to be used in the sense of responding to the Gospel in terms of a traditional culture. Contextualization, while not ignoring this, takes into account the process of secularity, technology, and the struggle for human justice, which characterize the historical moment of nations in the Third World.

Source: C. Lienemann-Perrin, *Training for a Relevant Ministry: A Study of the Contribution of the Theological Education Fund* (Madras, 1981), pp. 174f. — *Further Reading:* ibid., 62ff, 173ff; England, *ACT III,* pp. 673ff.

101. Minjung Theology in Korea

Minjung theology is a specific Korean form of liberation theology which developed in Korea in the 1970s. It developed out of the struggle of church-related and other groups fighting for human rights under an authoritarian regime. In this situation, the *minjung,* the suffering, alienated and exploited people were understood as the subjects of their own history, not the objects of somebody else's, in both the Biblical texts and in the Korean historical experience.

The most prominent reality of the recent democratic struggle in S. Korea has been the realization that the people *(minjung)* are the central actors, or subjects of history. There has been an increase of concern on the theme of minjung among students, writers and socially conscious Christian groups such as Korean Student Christian Federation, Urban Industrial Mission movement, Catholic Young Workers movement and Christian intellectuals.

This broad concern on the theme of the *minjung* as central historical subject represents a newly emerging historical consciousness in Korea, both in the society at large and in the church. Growing awareness of the reality of the people — a process of historical conscientization — has been brought about through various processes: (1) transformation of social perception through physical exposure and involvement in the suffering, struggle and aspirations of the people; (2) critical reflection on social reality; and (3) actions and movements for social justice and grassroots democracy (in factories, slums, and rural villages) where the people live.

In a recent Christian Youth gathering held in a provincial city of Korea in September 1976, *minjung* became the central theme of the entire conference. Some of the themes that emerged in this meeting should be introduced here.

"Who are the *minjung* and where are they?

In a word, they are the have-nots. They are farmers, fishermen, laborers, unemployed, soldiers, policemen, salarymen, small shopkeepers, small producers. They suffer political suppression, economic exploitation, social humiliation, and cultural alienation."

The *minjung*'s condition of life is described as oppression, exploitation, 'nobodyness', silence, and loss of subjectivity *(chuch'e song)*.

The *minjung* have been robbed of their subjectivity not only in their expressions and actions, but also in their feelings and thoughts. The consciousness of *minjung* is determined by the ruling echelon of that particular society at a given time. Thus, they cannot handle their own destiny and they become unable to discern even their own will and interests; and finally, they are consumed by the sense of habitual frustration.

These conditions of the people rise basically due to the unjust power structures — the structural evil. Thus, the people's life is understood in terms of power relations or power contradictions. [. . .]

It is clear that the historical motive power of the national independence struggle in Korea [during the Japanese occupation 1910-1945] is the *minjung*. Often, when nationalism is referred to, the national bourgeoisie is regarded as the central force of the nationalist movement. However, in the Korean situation there was no rise of a national bourgeois class during the time of nationalist struggle; the nationalist movements such as March First Movement [in 1919, see document 80] were sponsored and carried out in the main by the grassroots structures of the Korean people, including Tonghak Religion and Christianity (Protestantism), which may be regarded as religions of the oppressed masses.

Source: Kim Yong-Bock, "The Minjung (People) as the Subject of History," World Student Christian Federation Dossier Nr. 13, 1977, quoted in: J. England, *Living Theology in Asia* (London, 1981), pp. 25-27. — *Further Reading:* Sunquist, *Dictionary,* pp. 552-555 (Art. Minjung Theology); England, *ACT III,* pp. 556ff; Kim Yong-Bock, *Messiah and Minjung,* 1992; David Kwang-Sun Suh, *The Korean Minjung in Christ,* 1991.

102. Theology of Liberation and Asian Religiosity

In the multi-religious context of South Asia, Sri Lankan Catholic theologian Aloysius Pieris discusses reasons for Christianity's lack of success in Asia:

Any christological inquiry into Asian cultures will stumble against the fact that neither Jesus nor the religion he founded has won large-scale acceptance in Asia. Gautama the Buddha and Muhammad the Prophet are household names in the East, but Jesus the Christ is hardly invoked by the vast majority (over 97 percent) of Asians. Yet Jesus was no less an Asian than were the founders of Buddhism and Islam. Even of the few who believe in him, how many recall that God's Word had chosen to become Asian in wanting to be human? And how is it that the first Asians who heard him on our behalf and gave us the normative interpretations of his divine sonship made a significant breakthrough in the West but failed to penetrate the complex cultural ethos of Asia?

Asia's later disillusion with the "colonial Christ" no doubt added to this estrangement. But it also revealed that Christ could make sense in our cultures only to the extent that we use the soteriological idiom of "non-Christian" religions. I infer this from the fact that, when Jesus reentered the continent of his birth as the white colonizers' tribal god seeking ascendancy in the Asian pantheon, it was often the non-Christian religions that awakened the cultural ego of subdued nations in their collision with Christian powers, so that after four centuries of colonialism, Asia has surrendered only about two percent of its population to Christianity! If the Philippines went over to Christendom, it was because no other major Asian religion had struck institutional roots there earlier. The rapid rate of Christianization in South America, contemporary Africa, and Oceania, in contrast to Asia's persistent defiance of the Christian kerygma, confirms my thesis: the door once closed to Jesus in Asia is the only door that can take him in today — namely, the soteriological nucleus or the liberative core of various religions that have given shape and stability to our cultures.

I stress *soteriological* and *liberative,* for there is also a *sinful* and *enslaving* dimension to Asian religion. In a theological discourse such as this, therefore one must discern the authentic core of an Asian religion from its perverted forms. [. . .]

Source: A. Pieris, *An Asian Theology of Liberation* (Faith Meets Faith series) (Maryknoll, 1988), pp. 206-211.

D. Trends at the End of the 1980s

103. Political Liberalization: Christians in China

With the end of the Cultural Revolution in 1977 (see document 95), the situation of Christians and other religious communities in China began to improve, even though the Communist Party — despite its partial liberalization in the economic sector — held firmly to its ideological monopoly and repeatedly sanctioned persecution against Christian groups such as the Catholics who had remained loyal to Rome. Churches were re-opened in 1979, centers of theological education were reactivated and attendance at worship services skyrocketed. In autumn 1982, in a presentation on "The Church in China," Bishop Ding Guangxun, president of the (post-confessional) Chinese Council of Churches, advocated an independent path for the Chinese churches. He urged them to allow neither the former Western mission churches nor the current model of Latin American liberation theology (see document 340ff) to control or influence them in ecumenical affairs.

Since the end of the Cultural Revolution the policy of religious freedom has returned. Of course there are difficulties here and there. But thanks to the policy of religious freedom that is included in the National Constitution [from 1982], these can always be publicly discussed and settled.

Clearly a policy of religious freedom on the part of the state cannot of itself bring the church very far in its life and witness. We must develop a theological self-identity that will lead us in all of our decisions, so that we can realize more and more our existence as the church of Jesus Christ in the midst of the Chinese people.

The church's first priority must be to concentrate on its message. It can both humble and inspire us to see how Christians in other countries [such as Latin America] are laboring for the cause of the societal and political liberation of the people. . . . In their reference to the [biblical] motif of the exodus from Egypt and in their commitment to a fundamental change in the society, we find clues there, with thankfulness and repentance, for how we Christians in China in the time before our liberation [through the founding of the People's Republic of China in 1949] should have behaved. It would be . . . a gross simplification to say that Christians in China take a negative view of the theology of liberation of our Latin American brothers and sisters. But coming from our situation we cannot help but confirm that the reconciliation between God and humans in Jesus Christ stands in the middle of the message that God gave us. [. . .]

In order to secure the development and blossoming of a church in China which is just as Chinese as the English church is English, we must build a protective wall against [false forms of] "internationalism," which lack respect for legitimate national efforts. Christians want to express their support and love of their nation. This is not some narrow-minded nationalism of people who defend their country, right or wrong. [. . .]

Source: China heute [St. Augustin] Nr. 3/1983, pp. 2-5; Nr 4/1983, pp. 3-6. — *Further Reading:* D. E. MacInnis, *Religion in China Today: Policy and Practise* (1989); G. Th. Brown, *Christianity in the People's Republic of China* (Atlanta, 1983); T. Lambet, *The Resurrection of the Chinese Church* (Wheaton, Ill., 1994); D. Aikman, *Jesus in Beijing* (Lanham, Md., 2003); Sunquist, *Dictionary,* pp. 139-146 (Art. China); 146 (Art. China Christian Council); England, *ACT III,* pp. 189ff.

104. The "Rosary Revolution" in the Philippines

A wave of political liberalization seized some non-socialist countries of Asia as well. In the Philippines (1986) and in South Korea (1987), Christian groups played decisive roles in the overthrow of authoritarian regimes. In the Philippines, the 21 August 1983 assassination of the opposition leader Ninoy Aquino, on his return from exile in the United States, led the Catholic hierarchy to break openly with the Marcos regime which had been ruling the Philippines under martial law since 1972 (document a, an excerpt from a July 1984 statement of the Conference of Bishops). Peaceful demonstrations in Manila in February 1986 (c), coordinated by the ecclesiastical broadcasting station *Veritas* (b), accelerated the end of the regime.

a. Rebellion against the Marcos Regime (July 1984)

The murder [of Ninoy Aquino by the military on 21 August 1983] shocked us [the members of the Catholic conference of Bishops] all as no other killing has in recent history, and for many of us it was the one, single event that shook us out of our lethargy and forced us to face squarely the violence that has through the years been building up and becoming practically an ordinary facet of our life as a nation. . . . For years now we have been, for all intents and purposes, in a state of war. . . . This is the hard reality we are faced with now.

b. The Ecclesiastical Broadcasting Station "Veritas" (February 1986)

The tone set by the station, and also by the Cardinal [Sin] and other leading churchmen, constituted a moderating influence. It was responsible, serious, sorrowful, but neither inflammatory nor provocative. The nation was kept informed at a time when other media tended only to disinform; and this probably contributed immeasurably to the rapid erosion of the credibility of both the government and the controlled media.

c. Massive Demonstrations (February 1986)

Most important of all: they [the 1-2 million demonstrators in Manila] came with rosaries in their hands and prayers on their lips. Most of them were scared to death. In the back of their mind they knew that the full force of Marcos' legions — numbering some 250,000 fully armed troops — could be let loose on them. But they came anyway. Their spiritual leader [Cardinal Sin] had told them to go.

Source: H. Wooster, "Faith at the Ramparts: The Philippine Catholic Church and the 1986 Revolution," in: D. Johnston/C. Sampson (eds.), *Religion, the Missing Dimension of Statecraft* (New York, 1994), pp. 153-176, here: pp. 160, 163. — *Further Reading:* C. N. Tate, "The Revival of Church and State in the Philippines," in: E. Sahliyeh (ed.), *Religious Resurgence in the Contemporary World* (Albany, 1990), pp. 142-159; Sunquist, *Dictionary,* pp. 654-657 (Art. Philippines); pp. 657f (Art. Philippines, Martial Law); England, *ACT II,* pp. 375ff.

105. Islamic Fundamentalism: Christians in Pakistan

In a gathering of the Diocesan Council of the Church of Pakistan on 24 October 1991, the Anglican Bishop of Lahore, Alexander J. Malik, described the difficulties of the Christian minority in Pakistan in the midst of an Islamic environment increasingly influenced by fundamentalist tendencies:

(1) Christian children face many difficulties in obtaining places for higher level study. College places are not awarded on merit, but are generally obtained by cheating in exams and bribing the examiners. Christians, who are mostly very poor, do not stand a chance.

(2) Christians have an identity crisis. This is because the Pakistani press tends to present an image of Pakistan as a completely Islamic nation, belonging only to Muslims. [. . .]

(4) Christian women are being converted to Islam by force. This used to happen only in small Christian villages, but now it is occurring in the cities as

well. The women are kidnapped by Muslim young men and forced to convert to Islam. The police do nothing to help the Christians, as they prefer to help rich rather than poor people.

(5) There is no provision for Christian religious education in government schools whereas Islam is a compulsory subject. At one point the government formed a committee to discuss this issue, but after meeting twice the committee was dissolved. [. . .]

Source: International Institute for the Study of Islam and Christianity (ed.), *The Status of the Church in the Muslim World* (London, 1992), p. 37 — *Further Reading:* Sunquist, *Dictionary,* pp. 628-631 (Art. Pakistan); England, *ACT I,* pp. 414ff, 447ff; *WCE I,* pp. 570ff; P. Sookhdeo, *A People Betrayed — The Impact of Islamisation on the Christian Community in Pakistan* (Fearn, 2002).

106. Warning of Exaggerated Contextualization (1982)

In Seoul in August 1982, a meeting was organized by the Asia Theological Association for the purpose of discussing perspectives for an "evangelical theology for the third world." The Asian participants cautioned against the uncritical acceptance of Western models, but also against the "syncretistic" tendencies of certain Asian theological concepts. Instead they advocated the model of "evangelical contextualization."

Those of us in Asia will have to grapple with such questions as the resurgence of indigenous religions, the struggle for justice in the face of oppression, totalitarian ideologies and regimes, the tensions between traditional values, corruption, and modern consumerism. To this end we need to develop our [own] hermeneutical tools. We must proclaim the finality of Jesus Christ in the context of universalistic and syncretistic tendencies expressed in some Asian theologies. The distinctive Asian qualities of spirituality, meditation and devotion, self-sacrifice and servanthood are to be tested and utilized in developing our theology. We identify with suffering people in Asia and will seek to develop guidelines for our churches' life and witness in oppressive societies. [. . .]

Biblically oriented Asian theology must set up certain propositions and circumscribed limits in order to avoid theological confusion and thus promote evangelical harmony and cooperation. We need to pay attention to three areas in our attempt to contextualize theology. First, the essential biblical doctrines such as the uniqueness and finality of Jesus Christ and the unique revelation in the Bible cannot be compromised. Second, the priority of biblical exegesis must be emphasized to make adequate application to different contexts. Third, we must pay careful attention to the historic creeds to find out how God worked in the lives of Christians in centuries past.

Source: Bong Rin Ro/R. Eshenaur (eds.), *The Bible and Theology in Asian Contexts: An Evangeli-cal Perspective on Asian Theology* (Taichung/Taiwan, 1984), pp. 25, 74f.

107. A New Urgency for Interreligious Dialogue (1986)

Interreligious dialogue has always been a constitutive part of the Asian experience, as emphasized by Wesley Ariarajah, a Methodist theologian from Sri Lanka and from 1981-1992 chair of the Dialogue Program of the World Council of Churches in Geneva. He also emphasizes the relevance of Asia's experience of the Asian churches in dealing with multi-religious contexts for world Christianity.

We live together with people of other faiths. In Asia, we are surrounded by them; they are our neighbours and colleagues; our life story, in many ways, is wound up with theirs. When a person in Asia accepts Christ, in the majority of cases, his or her immediate relatives — parents, brothers and sisters — remain true to the faith they had belonged to. We, therefore, share our racial, national and linguistic identities with people of other faiths; we struggle hand in hand with them to shape our lives in more humane ways; we work together with them in seeking peace and in our common duty to build up our nation.

We do all of this as Christians; our faith penetrates our whole lives; all of our decisions are shaped by it, whether they have to do with the so-called "secu-lar" areas of our lives or the religious ones. We also believe, as a Christian com-munity, that we have overcome the barriers of race, class and other divisions that separates us into 'us' and 'them'; we cannot exist as an isolated community.

The God whom we confess in Christ is God of all peoples; at least, that is what we believe in. Thus, we see the urgency of interreligious dialogue as flow-ing out of our beliefs, and the demand of our faith.

Source: W. Ariarajah, "Dialog" in: *Zeitschrift für Mission* 12, 1986, pp. 137-151, 144f (English ver-sion authorized by the author). — *Further Reading:* England, *ACT I*, pp. 514ff.

AFRICA

I. AFRICA 1450-1600

A. Ancient African Christianity

108. Leo Africanus on Africa and Ethiopia

The early church counted northern Africa as one of the centers of the Christian world. Christianity expanded south of Egypt into Nubian land (Sudan), as well into Aksum (which was to become Ethiopia) during the fourth and fifth centuries. The church's influence remained steady, even after the Muslim expansion during the seventh century. In Europe, the Ethiopian ruler was identified with the legendary "Prester John." This is evident in the report of Leo Africanus (1494?-1552), who was born in Granada as Al-Hassan Ibn-Muhammad al Wezzani, and who was active as a jurist in Moroccan Fez. During one of his many trips he was captured by Christian pirates and, on account of his erudition, was not sold into slavery, but presented to Pope Leo X (1513-1521), who enabled his release. After his conversion and baptism he composed in 1526 an account of both of his trips to Africa in 1509 and 1516.

This land of Negroes had a mighty ruler, which taking his name of the region, is called Niger [. . .] Our Cosmographers affirm that the said river of Niger is derived out of Nilus, which they imagine for some certain space to be swallowed up by the earth [. . .] And here is to be noted, that . . . that land of Negroes by which Nilus is said to run . . . is not to be called any member of portion of Africa [. . .]: The said country is called by the Latines Aethiopia. From thence come certain religious friars seared or branded on the face with an hot iron, who are to be seen almost ouer Europe, and especially at Rome. These people have an Emperor, which they call Prete Gianni, the greater part of that land being inhabited by Christians. However, there is also a certain Mohamedan among them, which is said to possess a great dominion.

Source: Leo Africanus, *The History and Description of Africa* (translated into English by John Pory, edited by Robert Brown (London, 1896), pp. 124, 125, slightly modernized. — *Further Reading:* Pekka Masonen, *Leo Africanus: The Man with Many Names* (in Al-Andalus-Magreb. Revista de estudios árabes e islámicos, vol. VII-IX, fasc. 1, 2002, 115-143; http://www.uta.fi/~hipema/leo.htm); D. Rauchenberger, *Johannes Leo der Afrikaner. Seine Beschreibung des Raumes zwischen Nil und Niger nach dem Urtext* (Wiesbaden, 1999).

109. Ethiopia according to the Kebra Nagast

Christianity in Ethiopia can be traced back to the early fourth century with the missionary activities of Frumentius. Most Ethiopians, however, refer to Biblical texts such as Acts 8 (Philip and the Eunuch) or 1 Kings 10:1-13 or 2 Chronicles 9:1-11 upon which the *Kebra*

Nagast ("Glory of Kings") is based. The Kebra Nagast originated in the ninth or tenth century and was used as a mythical justification for the Salomonic dynasty which came to power in 1270.

a. The Conversion of the Queen of Sheba

And the Queen . . . said: "[. . .] We worship the sun according to what our fathers have taught us to do. [. . .] We call him 'Our King' and we call him 'Our Creator' and we worship him as our god, for no man hath told us that besides him there is another god. But we have heard that there is with you, Israel, another God whom we do not know, and men have told us that He hath sent down to you from heaven a Tabernacle and have given unto you a Tablet of the ordering of the angels, by the hand of Moses the Prophet. This also we have heard — that He Himself cometh down to you and talketh to you, and informeth you concerning his ordinances and commandments."

And the King [King Solomon] answered and said unto Her: "Verily, it is right that they (i.e., men) should worship God, Who created the universe, the heavens and the earth, the sea and the dry land, the sun and the moon . . . , the trees and the stones . . . , the wild beasts and the crocodiles . . . , the fish and the whales. . . , the clouds and the thunders, and the good and the evil [. . .] For He is the Lord of the Universe, the Creator of angels and men. And it is he Who killeth and maketh to live, it is He Who inflicteth punishment and showeth compassion, Who raiseth up from the ground him that is in misery, Who exalteth the poor from the dust, Who makes to be sorrowful and Who maketh to rejoice, Who raiseth up and who bringeth down. [. . .]. And as concerning what thou sayest, that 'He hath given unto you the Tabernacle of the Law', verily there hath been given unto us the Tabernacle of the God of Israel, which was created before all creation by his glorious counsel. [. . .]"

And the Queen said: "From this moment I will not worship the sun, but will worship the Creator of the sun, the God of Israel. And that Tabernacle of the God of Israel shall be unto me my Lady, and unto my seed after me, and unto all my kingdoms that are under my dominion. [. . .]" Then she returned to [her] house. And the Queen used to go [to Solomon] and return continually, and hearken unto his wisdom, and keep it in her heart.

b. Menyelek, the Son of Solomon and the Queen of Sheba

And he (King Solomon) worked his will and they slept together. And after he slept there appeared unto King Solomon (in a dream) a brilliant sun, and it came down from heaven and shed exceedingly great splendour over Israel. And when it had tarried there for a time it suddenly withdrew itself, and it flew away to the country of Ethiopia, and it shone there with exceedingly great brightness for ever, for it willed to dwell there. [. . .]

And the Queen departed and came into the country of Bala Zadisareya nine months and five days after she had separated from King Solomon. And the pains of childbirth laid hold upon her, and she brought forth a man child, and she gave it to the nurse with great pride and delight. And she tarried until the days of purification were ended, and then she came to her own country with great pomp and ceremony. [. . .] And the child grew and she called his name Bayna-Lehkem.

Source: E. W. Budge, *The Queen Sheba and Her Only Son Menyelek* (London, etc., 1922), pp. 27-38. — *Further Reading:* M. F. Brooks, *A Modern Translation of the Kebra Nagast: The Glory of Kings* (Lawrenceville, 1996); G. Colin (ed.), *La Gloire des Rois* (Kebra Nagast) (Geneva, 2002); T. Tamrat, *Church and State in Ethiopia 1270-1527* (Oxford, 1972); E. Ullendorff, *Ethiopia and the Bible* (London, 1968); E. Ullendorff, "The Queen of Sheba in Ethiopian Tradition," in: J. B. Pritchard/Gus W. Van Beek (eds.), *Solomon & Sheba* (London, 1974), pp. 104-114; E. Ullendorff, *The Ethiopians* (Wiesbaden, [2]1990).

110. Saga Za-àb: Ethiopian-Egyptian Contacts (1540)

From the beginning the congregations in Ethiopia were on good terms with Alexandria, and until the attainment of the autocephalous (independent) church in 1959 the Ethiopian Church recognized the Egyptian Coptic Metropolitan as its head. These relations are described by the Ethiopian Saga Za-àb who was sent to Portugal by the Ethiopian King Lebna Dengel in 1527. His descriptions were published in the work of the Portuguese humanist Damian/Damiao de Góis, "Fides, Religio Moresque Aethiopium" of 1540:

First, one must know that our Patriarch [Metropolitan] is chosen in a solemn rite by the vote of our monks in Jerusalem, who live there near the Holy Sepulcher of the Lord — that is in the following way: After the Patriarch [Metropolitan] has died, our king, the Beloved John, immediately sends someone unburdened with baggage to Jerusalem to those aforementioned monks living there, who, after receipt of the message and the alms which the king, our Lord, sends to the Holy Sepulcher as a gift, immediately choose by majority vote another Patriarch [Metropolitan]. It is also traditionally proper to elect only someone who is an Alexandrian and whose character is irreproachable. After he has been elected, they seal their votes and give them over by hand to the envoy that was sent for that purpose. He hurries quickly to Cairo. As soon as he has arrived, he hands over for reading the outcome of the election to the Alexandrian Patriarch, who has his permanent seat there. After it has become known, whom of the Alexandrians they have chosen, he sends back with the envoy to Ethiopia the so greatly honored chosen man, who must be, according to ancient order, a monk of the Order of Holy Anthony the Eremite, with whom a courier promptly departs for Ethiopia, where he will be received by all with great joy and honor. At least one year and occasionally one more year elapses in this undertaking, and in the mean time the Beloved John, at the will of the order, meets according to the will of the orders regarding the income of the Patriarch [Metropolitan]. The most important task of the Patriarch [Metropolitan] is to consecrate [candidates] into the holy orders, which no one, excepting himself, can confer or deny. In other respects, he transfers to no one an office of bishop or a churchly benefice. That is the concern only of the Beloved John, who distributes all at his discretion.

Source: S. Uhlig/G. Bühring, *Damian de Góis' Schrift über Glaube und Sitten der Äthiopier* (Wiesbaden, 1994), pp. 88f, 269ff.

111. Francisco Alvarez: Traces of Nubian Christianity

The Portuguese traveler Francisco Alvarez visited Ethiopia between 1520 and 1540. In his account, first published in 1540, he also gives some information about Nubia. In this territory in today's Northern Sudan, various Christian empires had been founded since the sixth century. From the fifteenth century onward, they were conquered by Muslims.

When we were in the country of Prester Johannes (i.e., Ethiopia) six men from that country (Nubia) came as messengers to the Prester. They asked him to send them priests and monks in order to teach them. He decided not to send them to them. They said that these people had received everything from Rome (maybe meaning Constantinople which was the "Rome of the East"), and that it is a very long time since a Bishop dies whom they had received from Rome. And because of the wars of the Moors (Muslims), they could not get another one, and so they lost all their clergy and their Christianity and thus the Christian faith was forgotten.

Source: F. Alvares, *Ho Pereste Joam das indias. Verdadera informacam das terras do Preste Joam* (Lisbon, 1540); quoted in: R. Werner/W. Anderson/A. Wheeler, *The History of the Sudanese Church Across 2000 Years* (Nairobi, 2000), p. 109. — *Further Reading:* G. Vantini, *Christianity in the Sudan* (Bologna, 1981), T. Hägg, *Nubian Culture Past and Present* (Stockholm, 1986); Sundkler/Steed, *History,* pp. 30-34; W. B. Anderson & O. U. Kalu, *Christianity in Sudan and Ethiopia,* in: *Kalu, African Christianity,* pp. 75-116.

B. European Expansion and New Discoveries

112. The Rise of Portugal: Schedels World Chronicle (1493)

The World Chronicle of the Nuremberg humanist Hartmann Schedel (1440-1514) was published in 1493. It documented not only the rise of Portugal under Prince Henry the Navigator (1394-1460), but also the relationships of the then largest German imperial city to the first European overseas expeditions. The text mentions Martin Behaim, who made the first globe in 1493 (still omitting the Americas).

In the following years Henry noticed that the territory of the kingdom of Portugal was too small. Thus a burning desire arose in him to expand the kingdom. Accordingly he traveled the Spanish sea with a great force and discovered there — advised and instructed by the same ones who themselves knew their way in the world and on the sea — countless uninhabited islands. Among other things, via ship he reached an uninhabited inland which nonetheless was rich with water and was fertile and wooded, so that it was suitable for colonization and human habitation. So he sent countless families there for settlement. Besides other fruits so much sugar was found there that all of Europe could be supplied thereby. This island is called Madeira, and the sugar from there is called Madeira-sugar. Thereafter, Henry discovered many other islands. . . . Then in 1483 AD, King John of Portugal — a lord with far-reaching plans — supplied more galleons with all the necessities of life and sent them out to travel to the south behind the Columns of Hercules[1] and to explore Ethiopia. And for these galleons he appointed two commanders, namely Jacob Canus, a Portuguese, and Martin Behaim, a German from Nuremberg [. . .].

Source: H. Schedel, *Liber chronicarum* (Nuremberg, 1493), p. CCLXXXV; translated and published into German by W. Spiewok, "Der Beitrag der deutschen Humanisten für die Entdeckungsfahrten portugiesische Seefahrer im späten Mittelalter," in D. Buschiner/W. Spiewok (eds.), *Das große Abenteuer der Entdeckung der Welt im Mittelalter* (Greifswald, 1995), pp. 95-104. — *Further Reading:* The German National Museum (ed.), *Focus Behaim Globus* (Nuremberg, 1992); C. R. Boxer, *Four Centuries of Portuguese Expansion* (Berkeley, 1961); C. R. Boxer, *The Portuguese Seaborne Empire, 1415-1825* (London, 1969); P. E. Russell, *Prince Henry "the Navigator": A Life* (New Haven, 2000).

1. The Columns of Hercules: classical term for different points on the edge of the world, especially for the rocks on either side of the Strait of Gibraltar.

113. The Papal Privileges of Portugal

After Portugal had launched its European expansion overseas, it acquired papal rights for colonial territories. Of decisive significance was the bull of January 8, 1455, *Romanus Pontifex*, with which Pope Nicholas V (1447-1455) sanctioned the earlier advances of the Portuguese on the African coast. He transferred to the Portuguese King Afonso V and Prince Henry the lands, harbors, islands and seas of Africa, together with patronage over the churches, a trade monopoly and the right to sell "infidels" into slavery. But even his predecessors, Martin V (1417-1431) and Eugene IV (1431-1447) had supported the undertaking of the colonial expansion: Sixtus IV (1471-1484) had discharged a corresponding papal bull (cf. document 8a). The Portuguese traveler and historian Joao de Barros (1496-1579) summarized this development.

With the discovery of these lands, the prince's main objective was to bend the barbarian nations under the yoke of Christ, as well as to advance the honor and glory of these kingdoms along with enriching the imperial inheritance. And when he learned of the inhabitants of those lands from the prisoners which Antao Concalves and Nuno Tristao had taken, he wanted Pope Martin V, who then presided over the Church, to announce this news as though they were first fruits due him, because this work had been completed to the honor of God and for the furthering of Christian belief. And he also wanted to ask the Pope that since he had pursued this enterprise for so many years and thereby . . . had expended a great part of his wealth, that it might please him [the Pope] to make a perpetual gift to the crown of all the lands that would be discovered on this ocean beyond Cape Bojador up to and including India. And that for those who in the course of these conquests had found death, he should grant a plenary indulgence in perpetuity for their souls, since God had set him on the seat of St. Peter. [. . .] He entrusted this business that was of such great importance to a knight of the Order of Christ, named Fernao de Lopez do Azevedo who belonged to the council of the king. [. . .] And as a result of this mission which he carried out, the prince was granted not only his request, but also many other blessings and privileges, which are the property of the Order. [. . .] Later, at the requests of King Dom Alfonso and his son King Dom Joao, Pope Eugene IV and Pope Nicholas V as well as Pope Sixtus granted to them and their heirs through bulls the perpetual gift of all they discovered on the ocean from Cape Bojador (in present-day Mauritania) up to and including the east coast of India, together with all kingdoms, dominions, lands, conquests, harbors, islands, trading companies, exchanges and fisheries, amid countless harsh excommunications, prohibitions and interdicts should other kings, princes, rulers or communities penetrate or be able to penetrate these lands and neighboring seas, as contained in detail in their bulls.

Sources: João de Barras, *Die Fahrten entlang der Westküste Afrikas und die Entdeckung der Inseln Porto Santo und Madeira und des Cabo Verde,* in G. Pögl/R. Kroboth (eds.), *Heinrich der Seefahrer oder die Suche nach Indien* (Wien, 1989), pp. 282ff. *Further Reading:* V. Y. Mudimbe, "Romanus Pontifex and the Expansion of Europe," in: V. L. Hyatt/R. M. Nettleford (eds.), *Race, Discourse and the Origin of the Americas: A New World View* (Washington, 1995).

114. Mission and Violence

The majority of the capital necessary to push into West Africa came out of the treasury of the Order of the Knights of Christ. Henry the Navigator was the grandmaster of this order. At least indirectly, the idea to missionize was thus present during the ensuing expansion. A report by the court chronicler Gomes Eana de Zurana (ca. 1420-1472) published in 1481 shows that this religious and idealistic objective could go hand-in-hand with the enslavement of Africans. At this time it was taken for granted that Senegal was an outflow of the Nile River.

Having passed beyond the land of Sahara, as we have said, the Portuguese saw the two palms which Dini Dias had already reported, and they understood that here began the Land of the Negroes which filled them with great joy. [. . .] When the men in the caravels saw the first palms . . . they knew they were near the River Nile, where it casts itself into the sea of the Ponent, and which is called the River of Canaga. [. . .] They cast anchor, and sent a boat ashore with Estavam Affonso, a squire of the Infante's, and seven men. They found a hut, in which they captured a young man who was wholly naked, and who carried a short lance. [. . .] This young negro was afterwards educated according to the orders of the Infante, and he was taught all such things as a Christian should know — and many a Christian does not know them as well as this young Negro knew them. He was taught the Pater Noster and the Ave Maria, and the articles of the faith and the precepts of the law and the works of mercy, and many other things beside, for the purpose of the Infante was to give him such instruction as would enable him to become a priest, so that he might preach the faith of Jesus Christ in his own country.

Source: G. E. de Zurara, *Crónica dos Feitos da Guiné* (Lisbon, 1481) (= Lisbon 1949), English translation in "Chronicles of Azurara," in: Virginia de Castro e Almeida, *Conquests and Discoveries of Henry the Navigator* (London, 1936), pp. 195-197.

115. Explorations: Vasco da Gama in Mozambique

In 1487 the Portuguese rounded the Cape of Good Hope for the first time. On his way to India, Vasco da Gama also passed Mozambique. The account of an anonymous author not only indicates the European interest in Prester John, but also informs us about the trade and contact network along the East African coast.

The people of this country are of a ruddy complexion and well made. They are Mohammedans, and their language is the same as that of the Moors. Their dresses are of fine linen or cotton stuffs, with variously coloured stripes, and of rich and elaborate workmanship. They all wear toucas with borders of silk embroidered in gold. They are merchants, and have transactions with white Moors [i.e., Indians], four of whose vessels were at the time in port, laden with gold, silver, gloves, pepper, ginger and silver rings, as also with quantities of pearls, jewels and rubies, all of which articles are used by the people of this country. [. . .] These Moors, moreover, told us that along the route which we were about to follow we should meet with numerous shoals; that there were many cities along the coast, and also an island one half the population which consisted of Moors and the other half of Christians who were at war with each other. The island was said to be very wealthy.

We were told, moreover, that Prester John resided not far from the place, that he held many cities along the coast, and that the inhabitants of those cities were great merchants and owned big ships. The residence of Prester John was said to be far in the interior, and could be reached only on the back of camels. These Moors had also brought hither two Christian captives from India. This information, and many other things which we heard, rendered us so happy that we cried with joy, and prayed God to grant us health, so that we might behold what we so much desired.

Source: Vasco da Gama's Logbook, from the translation in: E. G. Ravenstein (ed.), *A Journal of the First Voyage of Vasco da Gama* (London, 1898); extracts in: B. Davidson, *The African Past* (Boston, 1964), pp. 122-128, here: 124, 125. *Further Reading:* G. Bouchon, *Vasco Da Gama* (Lille, 1997).

116. Destruction of Eastern African City States (1505)

Da Gama also made an intermediate stop at Mombasa and Malindi. Both were independent city states. Malindi seems to have been the main rival of Mombasa at this time and took the side of the Portuguese invaders. Mombasa and Kilwa, however, resisted the invasion. These cities were attacked, plundered and burnt down by the Portuguese in 1505. The report of Francisco d'Aleida is probably based on an account of the German Hans Mayr, who was on board the *San Rafael* commanded by Captain Fernan Suarez.

On Tuesday, 22 July, they entered the harbour of Kilwa at noon, with a total of eight ships. [. . .]At dawn on Thursday, 24 July, the vigil of the feast of St. James the Apostle, all went in their boats to the shore. The first to land was the Grand-Captain [Vasco da Gama], and he was followed by the others. They went straight to the royal palace, and on the way only those Moors who did not fight were granted their lives. At the palace there was a Moor leaning out of the window with a Portuguese flag in his hand, shouting: 'Portugal! Portugal!' This flag had been left behind by the admiral [Vasco da Gama] when he had arranged for Kilwa to pay a tribute of 1,500 ounces of gold a year. The Moor was asked to open the door, and, when he did not do so, the door was broken down with axes. They found neither the Moor nor anyone else in the Palace, which was deserted. [. . .] As soon as the town had been taken without opposition, the Vicar-General and some of the Franciscan fathers came ashore carrying two crosses in procession and singing the Te Deum. They went to the palace, and there the cross was put down and the Grand-Captain prayed. Then everyone started to plunder the town of all its merchandise and provisions. [. . .] On 9 August the ships left Kilwa for Mombasa, sixty leagues up the coast. The ship Sam Rafael reached there on 14 August, but the Grand-Captain arrived with the other ten ships a day earlier. [. . .] The Grand-Captain met with the other captains and decided to burn the town that evening and to enter it the following morning. [. . .]

Source: Portuguese text in: E. Axelson, *South-East Africa, 1488-1530* (London, 1940), pp. 231-239; English translation in S. P. Freeman-Grenville, *The East African Coast* (Oxford, 1962), pp. 105-111. — *Further Reading:* M. N. Pearson, *Port Cities and Intruders: The Swahili Coast, India, and Portugal in the Early Modern Era* (Baltimore, 1998).

C. Encounters

117. A Portuguese Ambassador in Benin (1516)

The Kingdom of Benin was one of the largest non-Muslim empires in black Africa. At its maximum it extended from Onitsha in the east into the present-day nation of Benin. Its capital was located at Benin City, in what is now southwestern Nigeria. In 1514, Oba (chief) Ozolua sent a mission to Lisbon to announce his interest in Christian instruction and to request weapons. Since the Portuguese had as little interest in this as the court of Benin had in Portugal's wish for the sale of slaves, there was no real basis for a trade agreement. The missionaries who arrived in 1515 were unsuccessful in the long run. However, the report of the Portuguese ambassador in Benin, Duarte Pires, to King Manuel of Portugal on December 20, 1516 shows that the prospects looked more positive under Ozolua's son, Esigie (who probably ruled from 1516-1547).

Most high and mighty king and prince, our lord. [. . .] Sir, . . . the king of Benjm [Benin] is pleased with what I said in favour of your highness, and he desires to be your very good friend and speaks nothing save what concerns Our Lord and your interest; [. . .] The favour which the king of Benjm accords us is due to his love of your highness; and thus he pays us high honour and sets us at table to dine with his son, and no part of his court is hidden from us but all the doors are open. Sir, when these priests arrived in Benjm, the delight of the king of Benjm was so great that I do not know how to describe it, and likewise that of all his people; and he sent for them at once; and they remained with him for one whole year in war. The priests and we reminded him of the embassy of your highness, and he replied to us that he was very satisfied with it; but since he was at war, that he could do nothing until he returned to Benjm, because he needed leisure for such a deep mystery as this; as soon as he was in Benjm, he would fulfil his promise to your highness, and he would so behave as to give great pleasure to your highness and to all your kingdom. So it was that, at the end of one year, in the month of August, the king gave his son and some of his noblemen — the greatest in his kingdom — so that they might become Christians; and also he ordered a church to be built in Benjm; and they made them Christians straightway; and also they are teaching them to read, and your highness will be pleased to know that they are very good learners. Moreover, sir, the king of Benjm hopes to finish his war this summer, and we shall return to Benjm; and I shall give your highness an account of everything that happens.

Source: Portugese text in: Torre de Tombo, Corpo chronolico, pt. I, maso 20, no. 18; English translation in: T. Hodgkin, *Nigerian Perspectives* (London, ²1975), pp. 127f. — *Further Reading:* A. F. C. Ryder, *Benin and the Europeans* (London. 1960), pp. 49-52; Art. Benin (A. Adogame) in RPP I.

118. An African Ambassador from Benin in Portugal

King Esigie of Benin actually sent an ambassador to Portugal, about whom both the court chronicler Ruy De Pina (1440-1523) (a) and African sources (b) report.

a. Ruy de Pina's Account

The king of Beny [= Benin] sent as ambassador to the [Portuguese] king a Negro, one of his captains, from a harbouring place by the sea, which is called Ugato [Ughoton], because he desired to learn more about these lands, the arrival of people from them in his country being regarded as an unusual novelty. This ambassador was a man of good speech and natural wisdom. Great feasts were held in his honour, and he was shown many of the good things of these kingdoms. He returned to his land in a ship of the king's, who at his departure made him a gift of rich clothes for himself and his wife: and through him he also sent a rich present to the king of such things as he understood he would greatly prize. Moreover, he sent holy and most catholic advisers with praise-worthy admonitions for the faith to administer a stern rebuke about the here-sies and great idolatries and fetishes, which the Negroes practise in that land.

b. Local African Recollections

It is said that John Affonso d'Aveiro came to Benin City for the second time during this [Esigie's] reign. He advised the Oba to become a Christian, and said that Christianity would make his country better. Esigie therefore sent Ohen-okun of Gwatto with him as an Ambassador to the King of Portugal, asking him to send priests who would teach him and his people the faith. In reply the King of Portugal sent Roman Catholic missionaries and many rich presents, such as a copper stool (Erhe), coral beads and a big umbrella, with an entreaty that Esigie should embrace the faith. [. . .] John Affonso d'Aveiro with the other missionaries remained in Benin to carry on the mission work, and churches were built at Ogbelaka, Idunmerie and Akpakpava (Ikpoba Road), the last named being the 'Holy Cross Cathedral'. [. . .] The work of the Mission made progress and thousands of people were baptized before the death of the great missionary John Affonso d'Aveiro, who was buried with great lamentations by the Oba and the Christians at Benin City.

Source: (a) Ruy de Pina, Chronica del Rey Dom João II, Kap. 24 Atlantida 1950, English transla-tion in: T. Hodgkin, *Nigerian Perspectives* (London, [2]1975), p. 125; (b) This compilation of vari-ous oral traditions is published in J. Egharevba, *A Short History of Benin* (Ibadan, 1953, [4]1968) p. 27; T. Hodgkin, *Nigerian Perspectives*, pp. 125f.

119. South Africa: Between Aggression and Martyrdom

Since India could be reached only by sailing around Africa, all those traveling to India came into contact with the "Black Continent" during stays at Portuguese posts. At times missionaries could be pulled into military campaigns. The Dominican, Nicolas de Rosario, had begun a return trip from India to Portugal in 1588 when his ship, *S. Thomé,* capsized at the Cape of Good Hope. Nicolas was rescued and made a trip to the fort in So-fala. There he came upon a Dominican House with monks. However, the Portuguese em-broiled him in a conflict with the people of Zimba.

Andre de Santiago, moved by the harm the Zimbas were doing in the vicinity, determined to go in search of them and fight them, and try to defeat them be-fore their power and reputation increased. [. . .] But on arriving, the enterprise was found to be more difficult than was supposed on first setting out, for the enemy's town was surrounded with a strong palisade [. . .] He immediately requested the Captain at Tete to come to his assistance with as large a force as possible. Pero Fernandes de Chaves made no delay, it being a common cause, and thinking it was likely to be a long siege, asked Friar Nicolas . . . to accompany the expedition for the administration of the sacraments and the consolation of all. He could refuse nothing which was for the service of God and the good of souls, and set out with them. The barbarians . . . lay in ambush in a dark and thickly wooded pass [. . .]. Our people came on their way with no attempt at military order . . . devoid of precautions . . . in short as men who neither feared nor considered the enemy. The latter, as soon as they were well into the thicket, raised a thundering cry which rent the clouds, and fell upon them with such fury that before they could draw their swords all the Portuguese and half-breeds were slain to a man. [. . .] Friar Nicolas, who was found to be still alive and was recognised as a religious, they carried to their town, covered as he was with mortal wounds; there they bound him hand and foot to a high tree-trunk and finished killing him with arrows, in hatred of our holy religion, saying that the Portuguese only made this war upon them by the advice of their cacizes (for thus the Kaffirs[1] call our priests in the language of the Moors of the coast, their ancient neighbours). He is said to have suffered death not only with patience but with joy, his eyes upraised to heaven. . . .

Source: G. M. Theal, *Records of South-Eastern Africa* (Cape Town, 1964), pp. 1, 358-361 refers to L. Caregas, *History of the Order of Saint Dominic in the Kingdom and Conquests of Portugal* (Lissabon, 1767), Book III/Chapter XXXIV.

D. African Catholicism in the Congo

120. Lopez: The Beginnings of the Church in Congo (1491)

The king of the Congo empire, which had been founded in the twelfth century, ruled an area that stretched from the south of the lower Congo to the Atlantic coast of what is to-day Angola, as well as to the western regions of the present Democratic Republic of Congo. A Portuguese expedition landed near the capital in 1482. The report by O. Lopez describes the friendly relations which were established.

These Portingalles conversing familiarly with the Lorde of Sogno, who was uncle to the King, and a man well stroken in yeares, dwelling at that time in the

---

1. Kaffirs (arab. Kafir = Unbelievers), derogatory name in early European accounts for the Xhosa, a Bantu group in Mozambique and South Africa.

Port of Praza (which is the mouth of Zaire) were well entertained and esteemed by the Prince, and reverenced as though they had been earthly Gods, and descended down from heaven into those countries. But the Portingalles told them that they were men as themselves were, and professors of Christianitie. And when they perceyued in how great estimation the people held them, the foresaide Priest and others beganne to reason with the Prince touching the Christian religion, and to shew unto them the errors of the Pagan superstition, an by little and little to teach them the faith which wee profess, insomauch as that which the Portingalles spake unto them, greatly pleased the Prince, and so became converted.

With this confidence and good spirit, the Prince of Sogno went to the Court, to enforme the King of the true doctrine of the Christian Portingalles, and to encourage him that he would embrace the Christian religion which was so manifest, and also so holesome for his soules health. Hereupon the king commanded to call the Priest to Court, to the end he might himself treat with him personally, and understand the truth or that which the Lord of Sogno had declared unto him. Whereof when he was fully enformed, he converted and promised that he would become a Christian. [. . .]

Source: O. Lopez, *Relazione del Reame di Congo* (Rome, 1591); Duarte Lopez, *A Report of the Kingdom of Congo* (London, 1597, Amsterdam, 1970) pp. 119, 120. *Further Reading:* John Thornton, "Early Kongo-Portuguese Relations: A New Interpretation," *History in Africa* 8 (1981), pp. 183-204.

121. The Manikongo Complains about Unfit Priests (1514)

The king of the Congo (Manikongo) Nzinga Memba/Dom Afonso I (1465[?]-1543) was already Christian when he became king in 1506. During his long reign, he established the distinctive Catholic character of his kingdom. He supported close connections to the Portuguese crown and to the Curia in Rome. His letter to King Manuel of Portugal, dated November 5, 1514, shows that in this early period, criticism in either direction was possible.

Very esteemed and great Prince and Lord: We, King Afonso, through the grace of God, King of the Congo, Lord of the Ambundus, etc., commend ourselves to Your Highness as the King and Lord whom we love dearly. [. . .] We reported [in a letter that was sent earlier] that our kingdom had already become Christian and requested Your Highness to send some priests or brothers to us to instruct and to help us to grow in faith. Likewise we have sent our son King Henry and our nephew Rodrigo de Santa Maria so that Your Highness could instruct them. [. . .] Countless men and women converted and became Christians.

Thereafter we called together all our brothers, sons, and nephews as well as the sons of our servants. There were at least four hundred men and young people. We raised high a stockade with many thorns so that they could not swing themselves over and flee. Then we entrusted these young people to the holy orders for instruction. At the same time we raised more stockades next to the first one. In this enclosure there were four cells in which the priests could live together as prescribed in the rules for their order. But these priests remained there only three or four days; then Jovo de Santa Maria [an abbot of the Canons Regular who had been active in the Congo since 1508] promptly released those who had been gathered together. Two priests begged us to allow them to return to Portugal as Your Highness had sent them here to serve God and to set a good example, and now others had destroyed this good arrangement. They wanted to go so that they would not have to witness so great an injustice. The two priests in question were Antonio de Santa Cruz and Diogo de Santa Maria. Father Aleixo died from grief. At the same time other priests begged us to appoint Pedro Fernandez as abbot, but under no circumstances to live under him in the monastery; rather the opposite: to exempt them from this union and let everyone live by themselves. We answered them that it was not in our power to make a secular priest into a priest of the order. Then they all went their separate ways. They moved into separate huts and there welcomed the young people for instruction. They came daily and begged us for money. As we gave them some, they all began to trade — to buy and to sell. In view of this disorder we asked them, for the sake of the love of our Lord's will, [at least] to buy only true slaves and above all to buy no women, in order not to set a bad example and not to represent us as liars in the eyes of the people to whom we had preached. Without bothering themselves about that, they began to fill their houses with women of ill repute. Father Pedro Fernandez took a woman into his house who bore him a mixed-race child. For this reason, the young people who he taught and sheltered in his house fled and told their parents and relatives of the situation. All began then to mock and to laugh at us. They said that all things were probably lies, and that we had deceived them for our own reasons and for white objectives. We were very saddened and did not know how we should respond. [. . .]

Source: A. Brásio (ed.), *Monumenta Missionaria Africana* (Lisbon, 1952), 1/1, pp. 294-323, German translation in: Schmitt, *Dokumente 3*, pp. 453ff. — *Further Reading:* L. Jadin/M. Dicorato (eds.), *Correspondance de Dom Afonso, Roi du Congo 1505-1543* (Bruxelles, 1974), pp. 77-101; Art. Afonso I (A. Hastings) in *RPP 1*. John Thornton, "Perspectives on African Christianity," in: Vera Lawrence Hyatt & Rex Nettleford (ed.), *Race, Discourse and the Origin of the Americas* (1995), pp. 169-198.

122. Complaints about the Slave Trade (1526)

Sir, Your Highness [of Portugal] should know how our kingdom is being lost in so many ways that it is convenient to provide for the necessary remedy, since this is caused by the excessive freedom given by your factors and officials to the men and merchants who are allowed to come to this Kingdom to set up shops with goods and many things which have been prohibited by us, and which they spread throughout our Kingdoms and Domains in such an abundance that many of our vassals, whom we had in obedience, do not comply because they have the things in greater abundance than we ourselves; and it was with these things that we had them content and subjected under our vassalage and jurisdiction, so it is doing a great harm not only to the service of God, but to the security and peace of our Kingdoms and State as well.

And we cannot reckon how great the damage is, since the mentioned merchants are taking every day our natives, sons of the land and the sons of our noblemen and vassals and our relatives, because the thieves and men of bad conscience grab them wishing to have the things and wares of this Kingdom which they are ambitious of; they grab them and get them to be sold; and so great, Sir, is the corruption and licentiousness that our country is being completely depopulated, and Your Highness should not agree with this nor accept it as in your service. And to avoid it we need from those [your] Kingdoms no more than some priests and a few people to teach in schools, and no other goods except wine and flour for the holy sacrament. That is why we beg of Your Highness to help and assist us in this matter, commanding your factors that they should not send here either merchants or wares, because it is our will that in these Kingdoms there should not be any trade of slaves or outlet for them. Concerning what is referred above, again we beg of Your Highness to agree with it, since other wise we cannot remedy such an obvious damage. Pray Our Lord in His mercy to have Your Highness under His guard and let you do for ever the things of His service. I kiss your hands many times.

At our town of Congo, written on the sixth day of July./Joao Teixeira did it in 1526./

The King, Dom Affonso.

Source: Visconde Paiva-Manso, *Historia do Congo* (Lissabon, 1877); English translation in: B. Davidson, *The African Past* (London, 1967), pp. 191ff.

E. Ethiopia and Portugal

123. The Ethiopian King to the Pope (1524)

Ethiopian Christianity had survived the expansion of Islam primarily because it was farther from the center of Islamic power than for instance Egypt or Nubia. Under Amda Siyon (1314-1344) the kingdom had clearly been expanded. He had conquered Ifat and had compelled the Muslim rulers to establish a new kingdom farther to the east in Harara. At the same time he expanded his borders to the south and west. These conquests also opened a wide mission field to the Ethiopian Church; in particular, Christianity was extended through the establishment of monasteries of holy men. Under Zara Yaqob (1434-1468) the nation was centralized and stabilized. Nevertheless after his death there were separatist movements everywhere. One who profited from this development was the Sultan of Harare, with whom the Muslims had found refuge. Against this background can be seen the efforts of King Lebna Dengal (Dawid II, 1508-1540) to intensify the contacts with Rome that had been in place already since the 1200s.

In the name of God, the Father, the Almighty, the Creator of heaven and earth, of that is visible and invisible. [. . .] Oh blessed Holy Father, I submit to you reverently, that, in you, there is all peace, and you well deserve all that is good, and so it is just that all submit to your obedience, as the holy apostle has written down, by God. [. . .] Oh Holy Father, so mighty: Why have you not sent anyone to us, whereby you might bring security to my land and be my salvation in temptation, as you are the shepherd and I am your sheep? [. . .] Persistently I beg you, Your Holiness, that they may wish to send to me some holy images, and especially images of the Holy Virgin Mary, whereby the name of Your Holiness may often be in my mouth and in my thoughts, and I may draw constant joy from your gifts. For this reason, I also fervently request that you send me learned theologians and scholars who can make images and also swords and weapons of war of all sorts as well as gold and silver smiths and wood workers, in particular builders (architects) who can build houses of stone. [. . .] Now we must turn to other matters, and even as I ask you, Holy Father, give an answer to my question: Why do you not urge the Christian kings, your sons, to lay down their weapons and, as is fitting for brothers, to desire agreement of one with another, as they are your own sheep and you are their shepherd? Your Holiness knows best what was written in the Gospel which says, "Any kingdom that is divided against itself will be destroyed." If the kings are in agreement in their convictions and are in a secure alliance, then they will easily annihilate all Muslims and destroy and tear down the grave of the pseudo-prophet with a favorably fortuned surprise raid. Therefore take pains, Holy Father, that between them true peace will come and a secure bond of friendship will be forged; exhort them to help me and to desire assistance, since I, in the region neighboring my kingdom, am surrounded on all sides by Muslim Moors who are most evil.

Source: The letter of Paulus Jovius is translated into German and published in S. Uhlig/ G. Bühring, *Damian de Góis' Schrift über Glaube und Sitten der Äthiopier* (Wiesbaden, 1994), pp. 37-41, 195-201. — *Further Reading:* Hastings, *Africa*, pp. 130-147; W. B. Anderson & O. U. Kalu, "Christianity in Sudan and Ethiopia," in: Kalu, *African Christianity*, pp. 75-116.

124. The War against the Muslims in the King's Chronicle

In the year 1529 Ahmed Gran of the Islamic state Adel began a *jihad* against Ethiopia. In less than ten years the Christian kingdom was almost completely overcome. Gran was recognized as King, the churches and monasteries were plundered and a great number of Christians were forcibly compelled to convert. However, with the help of a Portuguese expedition in 1541, there was a turn of events. The following selections from the Ethiopian king's chronicle describe this period.

In the name of the Father, of the Son and of the Holy Ghost — of the three in one God! [. . .] At no other time had our land been so divided, and never had an enemy penetrated so far as to take control. Rather, our kings had defeated many [enemy] kings, as for example Anda-Seyon had defeated ten Islamic kings although they had unexpectedly attacked him before he could gather together his army. However, the invasion of the enemy into our land began at the time of King Lebna-Dengel, the son of her majesty Na'od; his reign was named Wanag-Sagad; Wanag means "lion." You see, with the help of our Lord Jesus Christ, we have written down here for you the report concerning the persecution and a description of the agony of the deaths of the Ethiopian people and the destruction of all churches ordered at the time of this event. [. . .] One year later Gran returned. On the 17th of Ter[1] he set out from the land of Adal and came to Dawaro on the 2nd of Yakkatit[2] according to the information of the inhabitants of this land. He delivered a tremendous blow at Ayfars on the 5th of Miyazia.[3] Then fell Eslam-Sagad, Takla-Jyasus and many princes. He (Gran) now ruled Sawa. That was in the Year of Grace 183. On the 24th of the month of Hamle[4] he burned (the monastery) Dabra-Libanos. On the 5th of Nahase the *Ras* Wasan-Sagad died. [. . .] After that his son,

---

1. The Ethiopian year consists of twelve months, each with thirty days, and one month with five days, except in leap year when there are six days. *Ter* overlaps with our January and February.

2. *Yakkatit* overlaps with February and March.

3. *Miyazia* overlaps with April and May.

4. *Hamle* overlaps with July and August.

Galawdewos (Claudius),[5] came into power at a young age. His reign was named Asnaf-Sagad. He came [to Bur through the middle of G(we)lo-Mahwada] and met there unexpectedly on the *Wazir* Asa (Arab.: 'Isa), *Garad* Esman (Arab.: 'Utman), Del-Ba-Iyasus, Iyoram and many other Malasay. He defeated them on the 11th of Tahsas[6] and killed many of them. He appeared dreadful to them, as a terrible lion or a bear with a newborn cub. He left there unharmed, and they could not stand against him. They said, "Who can fight against someone who has the Lord with him?" He was able to do this through the power of the Holy Ghost who was over him — he who had not yet learned the art of war and he stood in battle on this day as one who was eternal. He set out from there and moved into the land called Semen. He left from there, cutting through the Takkaze, and came to the land of Sard, where he celebrated Easter, the memorial celebration of the resurrection of our Lord Jesus Christ. As he stayed there, *Garad* 'Emar moved in close to him. He approached him in battle order and on the 29th of Miyazya they entered into battle. It was said [later], "We have never before seen such a brave hero who is so young, and still more, who fears death no more in the middle of a great army than in a small (troop)." Thereafter he moved away from there and came into the land of Sema. [. . .] In this year the Franks (Europeans) of da Gama from Portugal came under their captain King Cristovam (Dongestobu). They killed Abu 'Esman Nur and set up their quarters for the rainy season in Dabarwa. Gran, however, spent the rainy season in Darasga.

Then, in the Year of Grace 194, the young Prince Minas (in prison) was deported to the Ottoman Empire [literally: Rome = Byzantium or its successor; here: to Yemen]; he had left Dambeya in the month Maskaram.[7] Gran broke camp in the month of Tahsas and marched into the land of Tegra. The Franks also broke camp in Dabarwa, and Sabla-Wangel, the mother of the king, moved with them; she supported them with sound advice and supplied them with food and equipment. They met up with Gran in the land Aynaba and entered into battle on the 29th of Maggabit.[8] He was attacked with musket shot, and still he was not killed. Gran spent the rainy season in Zobel. Queen Sabla-Wangel spent the rainy season with the Franks in Ofla.

In the Year of Grace 195, battle broke out on the 2nd of Maskaram. The captain fell. In the month of Teqemt[9] King Asnaf Sagad came to the region and met with his mother and surviving Franks in the land of Semem. After they

5. Galawdewos/Claudius was one of the most important Ethiopian rulers who reigned from 1540-1559.

6. *Tahsas* also overlaps with the months January and February.

7. The Ethiopian year begins with *Maskaram* (September/October).

8. *Maggabit* cuts across the months of March and April.

9. *Teqemt* overlaps the months of October and November.

had conferred, they established a field camp in Sewada. On the 17th of the month of Hedar[10] he (King Asnaf Sagad) entered into battle at Waggara. He killed Sid Mahammad [Muhammad], 'Esman ['Utman] and Talila. Those that remained scattered themselves like smoke. Many surrendered and because of that they carried a heavy burden. On the 19th he proceeded to Darasge. He burned the houses (of the unbelievers) and captured their equipment and possessions. He returned to Sewada and remained there two months. But Gran marched from Darasga over to Dambeys. [The king] broke camp from Sewada and came to Wayna-Daga on the 5th of Yakkatit where he halted. Gran left Darasga and camped in the vicinity of the kings. The army of Gran and the army of the kings stayed in one and the same place! Do you realize the grace of the Lord who strengthened the enslaved *(agertaaweyan)* and their young king and put them in position to halt in the vicinity [of the enemy] and see him face to face [stand up to them]! Not as before, when they feared and trembled if they heard his name, as he stayed in Sawa and the Christians [as far away as] in Tegre trembled as though he had already come upon them! Even though the grace of the Lord remained with him through his travels, they laughed at him and mocked him. On [the 27th of] Yakkatit Gran set out arrogantly, trusting in his canon and in the Turkish (troops); and he said, "Tell me, how many years have I chased after you? Will you face me today?" But the king, trusting in the Lord and the prayers of our beloved Virgin Mary, engaged him. The soldiers of the king, who competed with each other to be the first, killed him [Gran] before the king arrived. He fell in the Pass of Zantara. He died at the command of the Lord on Wednesday at the third hour. His army dispersed as oven ashes that are scattered. [. . .]

Source: M. Kropp (ed.), *Die Geschichte Lebna-Dengel,* Claudius and Minas (Louvain, 1988) pp. 3-26. — *Further Reading:* J. Cuoq, *L'Islam en Éthiopie des origines au XVIe siècle* (Paris, 1981).

125. The "Confessio Fidei" of Emperor Galawdewos (1555)

The Roman Catholic Church had become interested in subjugating the Ethiopian Church to the Pope in Rome as early as the thirteenth century. After the war with Gran the Portuguese intensified their pressure on the young King Galawdewos (Claudius, 1540-1559). As a response, Galawdewos wrote a treatise which became known as his confession and which emphasized the traditions of his country. Church and monastic life had become indigenous; circumcision and the celebration of Sabbat as well as of Sunday were important features of the Ethiopian Church.

10. The month of *Hedar* overlaps the months of November and December.

And we go along the path of the king [= Christus], plain, true, and we do not deviate, neither right nor left, from the doctrine of our fathers, the Twelve Apostles, and of Paul, the fount of wisdom, and of the 72 disciples, and of the 318 Orthodox [men] who assembled [in the year 325] at Nicaea, and of the 150 [in the year 381] at Constantinople, and of the 200 [in the year 431] at Ephesus. Thus I preach and thus I teach, I Claudius, King of Ethiopia; and my regal name is 'Asnaf Saegaed, son of Waenag Saegaed, son of Na'od.

And as to the pretext of our observing (alternative readings: honouring) the day of the earlier sabbath, it is not that we observe it like the Jews who crucified Christ saying: his blood is upon us and upon our children (Mt 27:25). For those Jews do not draw water and do not light fire and do not cook meals and do not prepare bread and do not move from house to house. We, however, honour it by offering up on it the sacrifice (eucharist) and perform on it the supper (agape) as our fathers, the Apostles, have commanded us in the Didascalia.[1] It is not that we observe it like Sunday which is the new day of which David said: This is the day which God has made for us to rejoice and be glad on (Ps. 118:24). For on it our Lord Jesus Christ was resurrected, and on it the Holy Spirit descended upon the Apostles in the upper chamber of Zion. And on it he became man in the womb of Saint Mary, virgin at all time. And on it he will come again for the reward of the righteous and the requital of the sinners.

And as to the institution of circumcision, it is not that we are circumcised like the Jews, for we know the word of the teaching of Paul, fount of wisdom, which says (Gal. 5:6): circumcision is of no avail, and lack of circumcision does not empower either — but rather the new creation which is faith in our Lord Jesus Christ.

And furthermore he says to the Corinthians: he who has taken circumcision let him not take (off) the foreskin [1 Cor 7:18]. We possess all the books of Paul's teaching and they instruct us as regards circumcision and as regards the prepuce. But the circumcision which we have is according to the custom of the country — like the scarification of the face (practiced) in Ethiopia and Nubia; and like the perforation of the ears among Indians. What we do is not for the observance of the laws of the Pentateuch but rather in accord with the custom of the people. And concerning the eating of pork, it is not that it is forbidden to us by virtue of observing the laws of the Pentateuch like the Jews. Whoever eats of it, we do not detest him nor do we consider him unclean; and whoever does not eat of it, we do not compel him to eat of it. As our father Paul wrote to the

---

1. Didaskalia (Greek: Teaching): Ancient Christian Church order written by an anonymous author from Syria. The text emerged during the third century, but mentions the Council of Apostles as its origin.

Romans, saying: Let not him who eats (of it) reject him who does not eat (of it); God accepts all of them (Romans 14:39). [. . .]

Source: Hiob Ludolf, *Commentarius ad suam Historiam Aethiopicam* (Frankfurt, 1691), pp. 237-241, translated by E. Ullendorff, "The Confessio Fidei of King Claudius of Ethiopia," in: *Journal of Semitic Studies* 32/1 (1987), pp. 159-176.

126. Lent and Easter in the Ethiopian Church

The Portuguese Miguel de Castanhoso (died ca. 1565) arrived in Massawa in 1541. He gave an account of the war but also described the rites and ceremonies of the Ethiopian Church.

Their fast is very strict, for they eat nothing that has suffered death, nor milk, nor cheese, nor eggs, nor butter, nor honey, nor drink wine. Thus during the fast days they only eat bread of millet, wheat, and pulse, all mixed together, spinach, and herbs cooked with oil [. . .] This fast follows the old law, for they do not eat at midday, and when the sun is setting they go to church and hear Mass, and confess, and communicate, and then go to supper; and they say their Mass so late on fast days, because they say they can only receive the Holy Sacrament because of the fast. On saints' days and on Sundays, they say Mass at midday, as in the Church of Rome, and the Mass is always chanted, with deacon and sub-deacon, and a veil before the altar. The host is of very choice wheat unmixed, and they make a cake as large as a large host *(como huma hostia grande),* which is cooked in an earthen mould and has a cross in the centre, and around it some Chaldee letters, which are those of the consecration. With this cake or host, all the friars and those who have confessed for this purpose, communicate. Every Sunday the King, the Queen, the nobles, all of noble birth, and all the people confess and communicate. They enter the Church barefooted, without any kind of slipper; they do not spit in the church, and if they want to do so, they have a cloth into which they spit, as they consider it a dirty habit.[1] [. . .] They always pray standing; they bow frequently, and kiss the earth, and then stand again, and thus they take the body of the Lord. In the holy week the sacred offices are performed with great decency, beginning on the eve of Palm Sunday with gathering them (palms) and on Sunday they are consecrated with full ceremony as in Portugal, for all the women place crosses of wild olive leaves on their heads, in their head dresses, and the men carry away palm branches in their hands, which they take into their houses. On the day of the resurrection there was a very solemn procession, with many wax candles, and very large

1. The Portuguese did spit in the church, and this custom surprised the Abyssinans.

ones, so many, that truly I say there are more wax candles collected there than there should be in Portugal. [. . .]

Source: Miguel de Castanhoso, "História das cousas que o mui esforcado capitao Dom Cristóvao da Gama fez nos reinos do Preste Joao com quatrocentos portugueses que consigo levou, 1563," English translation in: R. S. Whiteway, *The Portuguese Expedition to Abyssinia in 1541-1543, as Narrated by Castanhoso* (London: Hakluyt, 1902), pp. 89, 90.

II. AFRICA 1600-1800

A. SLAVE TRADE

127. Early Accounts of Africans Captured by Europeans

The first African slaves appeared in Portuguese market places in the middle of the fifteenth century. Despite the fact that the slavery which had already existed in many African lands served as a foundation and essential element of the new trade relations, the "trans-Atlantic trade triangle" (i.e., weapons and jewelry from Europe to Africa, slaves from Africa to Latin America, sugar and agricultural products from Latin America to Europe) that grew out of this marked an entirely new stage. The African slaves were ripped from their homeland and thrown into a system in which not only they but also their children had little chance of advancement and hope for freedom. According to some estimates, by the end of the nineteenth century around 10 million Africans had been taken and sold in the New World. Gomes Eana de Zurana (ca. 1420-1472), the Portuguese court chronicler, reports the beginnings.

But when he had accomplished his voyage, . . . Antam Goncalvez, . . . spoke to them in this wise: "Friends and brethren! We have already got our cargo, as you perceive, by which the chief part of our ordinance is accomplished . . . but I would know from all whether it seemeth to you well that we should attempt something further, that he who sent us here may have some example of our good wills; for I think it would be shameful if we went back into his presence just as we are, having done such small service. [. . .] O how fair a thing it would be if we, who have come to this land for the cargo of such petty merchandise, were to meet with the good luck to bring the first captives before the face of our Prince. [. . .] "See what you do," replied the others, "for since you are our captain we must obey your orders . . . even to the laying down of our lives in the event of the last danger. But we think your purpose to be good. . . ."

. . . they saw a naked man following a camel . . . and as our men pursued him there was not one who felt aught of his great fatigue. But though he was only one, and saw the others that were many, yet he had a mind to prove that those arms of his right worthily and began to defend himself as best as he could, shewing a bolder front than his strength warranted. But Affonso Goterres wounded him with a javelin, and this put the Moor in such fear that he threw down his arms like a beaten thing. [. . .] And, as they were going on their way, they saw a black Mooress come along [. . .] and though some of our men were in favour of letting her pass to avoid a fresh skirmish. . . . Antam Goncalvez bade them go at her, for if (he said) they scourned that encounter, it might make their foes pluck up courage against them. And now you see how the word of a captain prevaileth among men used to obey; for, following his will, they seized the Mooress. [. . .] I cannot behold the arrival of these ships, with the novelty of the gain of these slaves before the face of our Prince, without finding some delight in the same. [. . .] But thy joy was solely from that one holy purpose of thine to seek salvation for the lost souls of the heathen. [. . .] And in the light of this it seemed to thee, when thou sawest those captives brought into thy presence, that the expense and trouble thou hadst undergone was nothing: such was thy pleasure in beholding them. And yet the greater benefit was theirs, for though their bodies were no brought into some subjection, that was a small matter in comparison of their souls, which would now possess true freedom for evermore.

Source: G. Eanes de Zurara, *Crónica dos Feitos da Guiné* (Lisbon, 1481) (= Lisbon 1949), English translation in: *Goes Eanes de Zurara, the Chronicle of the Discovery and the Conquest of Guinea* (translated by C. R. Beazley), Vol. 1 (New York, 1896) pp. 40-51, 98-100.

128. Joachim Nettelbeck: Trade in Africa

Joachim Nettelbeck (1738-1824) was initially captain of a slave ship, but decided against trading in slaves and became a distiller of liquor. His account below shows the interdependence of trade.

Here at one time human beings were seen as goods to be exchanged for the products of the European skilled industry, and so such articles would be chosen depending mainly on which need or luxury had become indispensable to the black Africans. Guns of all kinds and gunpowder in small barrels of thirty-two, sixteen or eight pounds were of prime importance. Almost as desirable was tobacco, either cut or in leaf form, together with tobacco pipes and liquor, either in half anchors or in cellar bottles of twelve, eight or six sized accordingly. Calico fabrics of all sorts and colors lay in bolts of twenty-one to twenty-four cubits, as was also the case with linen and silk cloths, which were worked in weavings of from six to twelve (cubits). Only a few might go without a good supply of linen cloth, three cubits long and half so wide, which there were worn as body-wrap clothing. The rest of the cargo was filled with all kinds of small wares such as small mirrors, knives of all kinds, colored coral, sewing needles and thread, *fayence,* flints, fishing hooks and the like.

Once accustomed to having these different articles from Europe, the Africans on the coast as well as those farther inland could not and would not do without them and thought incessantly about how to obtain the things which could be exchanged for the desired goods. Therefore the entire land was from then on divided into small regions which were hostile to one another, and all prisoners which they took were sold either to the black slave traders or were immediately taken away to the European slave ships. Sometimes, if such spoils of war were lacking, and they needed new supplies of goods, their chiefs, who exercised despotic power over their subjects, would seize which of them was the most dispensable. But it often happened that a father was dragged away from his son, a man from his wife and a brother from his brother to be sold at the slave market. One can easily understand that all these lands found themselves in a most miserable state; but just as little could it also be denied that the original reason for all this misery stemmed from the Europeans, who up until then through their eager insistence had encouraged and undertaken kidnapping.

Source: *Lebensbeschreibung des Seefahrers, Patrioten and Sklavenhändlers Joachim Nettelbeck. Von ihm selbst aufgezeichnet* (Leipzig, 1821/1823), new ed. by J. C. L. Haken (Nördlingen, 1987), p. 185; reprinted also in H. Pleticha (ed.), *Afrika aus erster Hand* (Würzburg, 1972), p. 139.

129. A Protestant on the Portuguese Slave Trade

Since the Portuguese and Spaniards controlled the seas, some time elapsed until Protestant empires engaged in overseas expeditions. However, in the seventeenth century the Dutch and the English played a prominent part in the slave trade, although at first their attitude had been quite ambivalent. In 1631, the Dutch West India Company started trading in human commodity. In the same year the second edition of Hugo Grotius' work, *De Iure Belli et Pacis,* was published which legitimized slave trade. The question of whether slaves should be converted to Christianity remained controversial. In this context the Protestant Kaplan H. C. Monrad, who stayed in Guinea from 1805-1809, gives the following account of the Portuguese ships:

So far as my experience goes, they (the slaves) are treated the most humanely by the Portuguese who come from Brazil. On their ships only a few slaves under cover are chained. Most of them are on deck and are partly mingled with the crew. In spite of this, I do not know of a single case of a Portuguese ship being overrun, as it is called, i.e., the crew being attacked and killed by the slaves. In nearly every such Portuguese ship a priest is to be found, and as soon as the slaves come on board they are baptised and have a crucifix hung round their necks. Then they are good Christians who must be treated humanely. The Portuguese captains are often dissatisfied with their Padres (sometimes there may be good reasons for this, for I have found extremely ignorant and empty heads among them) and accuse them of creating intrigue and causing trouble among the crew instead of teaching slaves. But usually the real reason is undoubtedly that these Padres keep a strict eye on the captains and inform against them and bring them to book on their return if they have treated the slaves cruelly.

Source: H. C. Monrad, *Gemälde der Küste von Guinea* (Weinmar, 1824), pp. 307, 105f. Translated in: H. W. Debrunner, *A Church between Colonial Powers: A Study of the Church in Togo* (London, 1965).

130. Account of the Slave Trade by an African Priest

Philip Quaque (1741-1816) grew up in Cape Coast, the town outside the walls of Cape Coast Castle, the principal British trading port on the West African coast. In 1754 he was sent to England for education, sponsored by the Society for the Propagation of the Gospel in Foreign Parts (S.P.G.), and he was ordained as a priest of the Church of England, the first African to attain this distinction. In 1766, the Reverend Philip Quaque returned to the Gold Coast as a missionary to his own people. Over the next half-century, he wrote a series of letters to S.P.G. headquarters in London. The text that follows is an extract of a letter dated February 8, 1786:

On Tuesday the 18th of last October, happened a most . . . unhappy circumstance in the Road of Mouri belonging to the Dutch settlement, where was riding at anchor a Dutch ship full of slaves almost ready to take her departure from the coast. But the ill treatment of the unfeeling Captain incensed the poor captives so highly that they rose upon the ship's crew in his absence and took possession of the vessel. They consisted in number about 150. But the most dreadful circumstance of all is that after having laid their scheme with subtlety and art, and decoying as many of their countrymen who came far and near to plunder on board and near the ship, and also some white sailors from an English ship in hopes of relieving them, were all indiscriminately blown up to upwards of three or four hundred souls. This revengeful but very rash proceeding we are here made to understand to be entirely owing to the Captain's brutish behaviour, who did not allow even his own sailors, much more the slaves, a sufficient maintenance to support nature. If this is really the case, can we but help figuring to ourselves the true picture of inhumanity those unhappy creatures suffer in their miserable state of bondage, under the different degrees of austere masters they unfortunately fall in with, in the West Indies. [. . .] it is easy to conceive that the evils which they seem to complain of, to bear an affinity to the excess of burden the Children of Israel suffered in the reign of Pharaoh, King of Egypt, under their task masters.

Source: M. Priestley, "P. Quaque of Cape Coast," in: P. Curtin (ed.), *Africa Remembered: Narratives by West Africans from the Era of the Slave Trade* (Madison, 1967), pp. 99-139, here: 132. — *Further Reading:* F. L. Bartels, "Philip Quaque, 1741-1816," in: *Transactions of the Gold Coast and Togoland Historical Society* (Achimota, 1955), 1, part V, pp. 135-177; H. Debrunner, "Sieckentroosters, Predikants and Chaplains: A Documentation of the History of Dutch and English Chaplains to Guinea before 1750," in: *Bulletin of the Society of African Church History* 1 (1965), pp. 73-89.

131. Mission to Slaves in South Africa (1658)

In 1652, a chartered trading corporation, the Dutch East India Company (VOC), set up a half-way station at the Cape. The first commander, Jan van Riebeek (1619-1677), was influenced by Reformed piety. He felt that something must be done for the intellectual and moral welfare of the 227 slaves who had arrived from Angola and from West Africa in 1658. A school was opened, of which the nurse Pieter van der Stael was appointed teacher. We have the following entry of the establishment of this school in Van Riebeek's "Journal":

1658. April 17. Began holding school for the young slaves, the chaplain being charged with the duty. To stimulate the slaves to attention while at school, and to induce them to learn the Christian prayers, they were promised a glass of brandy and two inches of tobacco, when they finished their task. All their names were taken down, and those who had no names (presumably Christian names) had names given them. [. . .] All this was done in the presence of the Commander, who will attend for some days to bring everything into order, and to bring these people into proper discipline, in which at present they appear to promise well.

Source: D. Moodie (ed.), *The Record; or, A Series of Official Papers Relative to the Condition and Treatment of the Native Tribes of South Africa* (Cape Town, 1838-1842) p. 124, quoted in: J. Du Plessis, *A History of Christian Missions in South Africa* (Cape Town, 1911, [N]1965), p. 30. *Further Reading:* J. N. Gerstner, "A Christian Monopoly: The Reformed Church and Colonial Society under Dutch Rule," in: R. Elphick/R. Davenport (eds.), *Christianity in South Africa* (Berkeley 1997), pp. 16-30.

B. Catholic Rulers

132. The King of Warri (West Africa) to the Pope (1652)

Christian missions were not much more than an appendix to the colonial enterprise during this period in West Africa. An exception was the small kingdom of Warri near Benin in what is today Nigeria. During the late sixteenth century a son of the king was baptized by Augustinian monks from Sao Tome. He became the first of a series of Christian rulers. When the first mission which the Sacred Congregation of the Propaganda Fide dispatched had gone to Benin, one of his successors, probably Dom Antonio, recommended to the pope that it would be more successful to send Capuchins to Warri. The following is an extract from the letter, written originally in Portuguese, dated November 20, 1652. A Capuchin mission, composed of Italians, eventually succeeded in reaching Warri in ca. 1656 and spent about four years travelling in the kingdom.

I have been informed of the fervent zeal that burns in the breast of Your Holiness to spread the Holy Faith in these parts, which, because they have not been watered by the blood of Jesus Christ or any apostle or saint, are deprived of the light of the faith. Also I have heard that to remedy this Your Holiness dispatched a mission of fathers called Capuchins to the Kingdom of Benin, a people neighbouring mine, who rejected the favour offered them and expelled the fathers from their Kingdom; nor did they tell the fathers anything about me and my Kingdom. I truly believe, Holy Father, that Your Holiness intended these priests to come to me, judging by their information that the King of Benin was a Christian who desired ministers of the Gospel. I am that king, and my kingdom is on the same coast adjoining Benin and distinguished from it only by the fact that mine is called Oery [Warri]. Such is my need of disinterested ministers to spread the faith in my kingdom that it has almost gone to perdition, for it is more than seven years since a priest has been here, and those who used to visit came only once a year [. . .] I wondered that none came for so long: they tell me that they have no bishop in Sao Tome and so few priests that they are in almost the same straits as myself. I leave it to Your Holiness to imagine how many are falling away from the Faith. I am acting as preacher myself, as far as I am able, urging my subjects to trust in the mercy of God that all will soon be set in order. This can only be done, I believe, by Your Holiness. I beg you therefore by the blood of Our Lord Jesus Christ to come to my aid and send me a mission of Capuchin fathers who because they are disinterested (as I am informed) will do great good to me and my kingdom. As a faithful Christian I kneel and kiss the feet of Your Holiness, and, like other Christian kings, I offer to Your Holiness the obedience of myself and my kingdom, not to Your Holiness alone, but to all who shall afterwards be elected canonically to that dignity. Again I beg Your Holiness to send me the fathers as soon as possible, and, if possible, to instruct the Prefect of the fathers in Portugal to see that every year some priests are sent with the ships that come from Lisbon to Sao Tome, and from there to my kingdom to trade. I will give them all the help in my power and reliable interpreters so that they may bring my neighbour, the King of Benin, and others to the faith. I beseech Your Holiness to send me some relics for myself and my kingdom.

I am writing to my cousin King John of Portugal asking him to help me by assisting the fathers with their passage and the necessary provisions. I believe he will do this for the Portuguese have often done me favours; also, because they introduced the faith into my kingdom and my forebear King Dom Domingos married a Portuguese lady, I hold them in great brotherly affection. [. . .]

Source: Archivio della Sacra Congregazione di Propaganda Fide: Scritture Riferite nei Congressi. Africa, Angola, Congo, Senegal. Vol. III.a fol. 249, quoted and translated in: T. Hodgkin, *Nigerian Perspectives* (London, ²1975) pp. 176-178.

133. Warri: Complaints about Shortage of Priests (1692)

The kings of Warri remained interested in attracting Christian missionaries to their country. This extract is from a letter, written in Portuguese, from the Olu of Warri, who signs himself Dom Domingos II, to Father Francesco da Monteleone, the Italian Prefect of the Capuchin Mission in Sao Tome. It would seem to have been written late in 1692.

I received a letter from Your Excellency written on 15th August last year, and with it came the Reverend Fathers to the very great joy of myself and my chiefs. We gave thanks to God for them. But . . . it was the misfortune of myself and my subjects that we were not able to do so much as we would have wished for these Reverend Fathers, although we have always shown them every due regard and assisted them as far as our resources allow, as Your Excellency knows. I realize that it could not meet with their entire satisfaction, nor be according to their desires. At any rate Your Excellency must know that matters here are in such a state that everyone is suffering in some degree because the Ijaw [a neighbouring ethnic group] are stopping me from going to Benin, and my subjects are unable to cultivate their farms, which is a great hardship. As . . . there is no perfect happiness in this life, and my misfortune has given me further proof of this in the loss of those two servants of God, Father Gioseppe Maria and Father Bernardino. I have felt their loss deeply, and now I have to lament the departure of Father Protasio because he finds himself without a companion. Neither my persuasions and prayers nor those of my chiefs have been able to dissuade him from his determination to leave. [. . .] I well know that the Reverend Fathers will make many accusations against us, but everyone, including Your Excellency, knows full well how little help we have received from the Fathers for many years past, and how few labourers there have been in this vineyard, so it is naturally full of blemishes. But if the work goes forward without interruption, it will undoubtedly bear fruit. The Reverend Father has promised me that he will come back, if God so wills and Your Excellency approves. His companion or companions should be of his age and disposition so that they may bear the fatigue and labour of the service of God and the conditions of life in this land. As Your Excellency will learn, the hospice is almost complete after our manner of building, and I shall begin the construction of a church on the plan that the Reverend Father has left me. May God be pleased to bring him back so that he may see it finished and praise the Lord therein.

Source: T. Hodgkin, *Nigerian Perspectives* (London, [2]1975), pp. 188f. (from: Archivio della Sacra Congregazione di Propaganda Fide: Scritture Riferite nei Congressi. Africa, Angola, Congo, Senegal. Vol. III.a, 37-39). — *Further Reading:* A. Ryder, *Benin and the Europeans* (London, 1960), pp. 11-16.

134. Zimbabwe: Baptism of King Manamotapa (1652)

Catholic missionaries (in this case Dominicans) were also successful in Zimbabwe in converting the king to the Catholic faith. But unlike in the Congo or in Warri, Christianity scarcely took root among the African people. The church remained an element within the colonial structures and isolated. The testimony of the baptism of the emperor and king Manamotapa was signed by the said emperor, as well as by the secretary, and sealed with the royal seal.

Dom Dominic Manamotapa, by the grace of God king and lord of Mocharanga, Boessa, Borongha, Quiteve, Monghos, Inhaxamo, &c., make known to all to whom these presents shall come, that during the life of our father and lord the king Philip, we, being prince of these kingdoms, were brought up by the Religious of St. Dominic, to whose care the said king, our father, consigned us in the days of our early youth, and by them we were instructed and catechised and many times persuaded, until we desired to embrace the holy faith of Jesus Christ, and to receive the waters of holy baptism, and though we fervently desired the fulfillment of this our longing, being firmly convinced that this was the true path, in which the fathers walked; nevertheless we deferred the effect of our desire until such time and season as God our Lord should have done us the grace of bringing us to the actual possession of this our kingdom, wishing to imitate in this particular all that was done by the king our father, who being instructed and cathechised in the doctrines of the holy faith, by Friar Emanuel Sardigna, of the said order of St. Dominic, would not receive holy baptism until he was in possession of his kingdoms. [. . .] We omitted no occasion of encouraging the holy work of the said fathers [of St. Dominic], and hearing that some of our nobles showed some reluctance to receive the waters of holy baptism, we ordered them to be summoned to our presence, and making use of the doctrine learned from the said fathers, we made them an exhortation by means of which they were fully convinced and resolved to become Christians. The fathers did not fail, for many days following, in catechising the said nobles, and their instructions came to an end on the feast of St. Dominic. On this day we issued from our palace with great pomp, accompanied by all the nobles, the soldiers of the garrison, and by the aforesaid, religious who walked on each side of our person. On arriving at their church, richly decorated and prepared with great magnificence, we prescribed the order in which the waters of baptism were to be administered, which was in this manner following: we caused Friar Giovanni de Melo to baptize us and the queen our consort, Friar Salvador of the Rosary being godfather and bestowing upon us the name of Dom Dominic, the day being consecrated to that saint, and upon the queen the name of Dona Louisa. Then we ordered the two chief nobles of our kingdom to be baptized, Inigomaxa receiving the name of Dom John, and Inevinga that of Dom Sebastian, and after these two Inhamafunhe our friend by the name of Dom Peter —

Manamotapa, The King
Antonio Suarez, Secretary and interpreter

Source: G. M. Theal, *Records of South-Eastern Africa* (Cape Town, 1964), pp. 2, 445-448. — *Further Reading*: P. Schebesta, *Portugals Konquistamission in Südostafrika. Missionsgeschichte Sambesiens und des Manamotaporeiches* (Steyl, 1966).

C. Catholic Experiments and Failures

135. Sierra Leone as Base

Sierra Leone was used as a base by the Portuguese colonial mission. The account of Francisco de Lemos Coelho indicates that there was also some disappointment about missed opportunities.

After this coast of Guinea was discovered and during this period it began to be settled by the Portuguese, there is no record of any priest being sent expressly for the conversion of the pagan people, the Lord Bishop of this island — to which all this coast is suffragan — being content to send a vicar to the town of Cacheu . . . to administer the sacraments to the inhabitants there . . . and when this benefit was extended further, it was only to send a cleric to administer the sacraments to the inhabitants of a specific settlement, such as, in the past, Geba, and today, Farim. At the same time, they also sent a Visitor, who made his way along all these rivers administering the sacraments to those he found there, while also making inquiries about points relevant to an ecclesiastical visitation [. . .]

Source: Francisco de Lemos Coelho, *Description of the Coast of Guinea, 1684* (Liverpool, 1985); translated and edited by P. E. H. Hair from D. Peres, *Duas decricoes seiscentistas da Guiné de Francisco de Lemos Coelho* (Lissabon, 1953); cf. P. E. H. Hair, "Christian Influences in Sierra Leone before 1787," *Journal of Religion in Africa* 27 (1997), pp. 3-13, 11.

136. Egypt: Report of a Jesuit (1723)

The first Catholic German mission newspaper, *Neuer Welt-Bott*, was published by Joseph Stöcklein (1676-1733) in Augsburg from 1725. It contains letters from Jesuit missionaries, in particular original letters from German Jesuit missionaries. This report from Cairo came from the French Jesuit Sicard. Rather than proving the ignorance of the Copts it indicates the ignorance of the author about the Copts.

I have written Your Reverence quite often, that the Copts in Egypt are a strange people far removed from the kingdom of God; they can only be understood by those who remain in heresy; then, although they say they are Christians, they are such only in name and appearance. Indeed many of them are so odd that outside of their physical form scarcely anything human can be detected in them. Likewise the Son of God excludes no single family of the world from his kingdom, no matter how miserable it may be . . . and so in any event we should not omit to teach the ignorant Copts in the faith as incapable as they always are of learning its mysteries without incontestable effort. We throw the good seed onto this unthankful ground, which certainly is thickly covered with weeds, but is not so unfruitful that we would not have the comfort of a small step each year. Certainly our last harvest in the past year was nothing to despise, then the single conversion of one Coptic priest, who God has converted through our efforts into the true church, will undoubtedly draw a number of similar Copts to him, whose ignorance is so great, that they blindly believe everything that the priest of the land tell them. [. . .]

Source: A third, still shorter letter from Fr. Claudii Sicard to Fr. Carolum Fleuriau, written from greater Cairo on July 2, 1723, in *Neuer Welt-Bott*, or *Allerhand So Lehr- als Geistreiche Briefe, Schriften und Reis-Beschreibungen, Welche von denen Missionariis der gesellschaft Jesu/aus Indien und andern über Meer gelegenen Ländern biß Anno 1731 in Europa angelangt seynd, 19. Teil* (Augsburg, 1732), 42/120.

137. Gold Coast: Traditions Difficult to Overcome

The Dutch had removed the Portuguese from Fort Elmina (Gold Coast/Ghana) in 1637. Michael Hemmersam, a goldsmith from Nuremberg, paid a visit to Sao Jorge da Mina on behalf of the Dutch West Indies Company toward the end of 1639. During his five years' stay, the Portuguese were driven from the entire Gold Coast, enabling the Dutch to rule over almost the entire trade for a short time. Hemmersam's book was published in 1663 and reprinted in 1669.

They confess and believe that there is a God who is good and does them no evil. But they must keep their *fetisso* (fetish) as their friend by sacrificing to him, so that he will not let anything bad happen to them for (they say) he is easily angered. Such fetisso among them vary. One person believes in a tree, another in a stretch of water, some in stone(s) or pieces of wood. When they eat or drink, they lay or pour a little (food or drink) on their fetissum, so that he may be willing to protect them and keep them in good health.

Some also believe in fishes and regard them as sea-gods. Some believe in crocodiles, and faithfully advised us to do them no harm. Whenever we heard about their superstition, we contradicted it, telling them that they believed in the Devil. We spoke to them about God from Holy Scripture and had the impression that we had converted them. But they still stuck to their opinion. Although some liked what we told them, they were nevertheless afraid of the other Moors and said their fetissos might punish them if they believed not in him but in us Christians.

The French, English, Portuguese and Spaniards have in the past sent many priests to convert them. When they attended mass, they took the paternoster in their hands, but afterwards they lived in as heathen a manner as before, for there is no foundation laid in them. My general at that time had a school set up, intended to have the children instructed in reading, prayer and godly living, but because their language was peculiar and German was too hard for them to imitate, the school made no progress.

Source: M. Hemmersam, *Guineische und West-Indianische Reißbeschreibung de An. 1639 biß 1645 von Amsterdam nach St. Joris de Mina, Nürnberg,* ed. by S. P. l'Honoré Naber (The Hague, ᴿ1930), translated in: A. Jones, *German Sources for West African History 1599-1669* (Wiesbaden, 1983) pp. 118f.

138. "We are no better than our forefathers" (1704)

One of the best known and most reliable descriptions of West Africa of the late seventeenth and early eighteenth centuries is that of the Dutchman Willem Bosman (1672-?), who emigrated as a 16-year-old and became a high-ranking Dutch official in Elmina (modern-day Ghana). In his report of 1704 (first published in Utrecht), he was concerned with the Catholic mission and the indigenous people's resistance to it. His description of the coast of Guinea was very popular, being republished in 1709, 1719 and 1737, and translated into English, French, and German.

Slave-Coast: . . . Whilst I was there, there was also an Augustine monk which came from St. Thomè, in order, if possible, to convert the Blacks to Christianity, but in vain. Polygamy is an obstacle which they cannot get over. As for all other Points they might have got Footing here, but the Confinement to one Wife is an insuperable Difficulty. This Priest invited the King to be present at Mass, which he also did. And when I saw him next, asking him how he lik'd it, he said very well, and that it was very fine: but that he chose rather to keep to his Fetiche.

This Priest in my Company being once in Discourse with one of the King's Grandees, who was a witty Man, said in a menacing Manner, that if the Finasians continu'd their old Course of Life, without Repentance, they would unavoidably go to Hell, in order to burn with the Devil; To which the sharp Fidasian reply'd Our Fathers, Grandfathers, to an endless Number, Liv'd as we do, and Worship'd the same Gods as we do, and if they must burn therefore, Patience, we are not better than our Ancestors, and shall comfort ourselves with them. After this the Priest left off, and Perceiving that all his Pains at Fida were likely to be fruitless, he desir'd me to introduce him to the King to take his Leave of him, which I did shortly after.

Source: William Bosman, *Description of Guinea Coast* (first published in Dutch 1704, first English edition 1705; New Edition with an Introduction by John Ralph Willis and Notes by J. D. Fage and R. E. Bradbury, New York, 1967). *Further Reading:* J. G. Platvoet, "Dutch Merchants, Missionaries and Academics on African Religions, 1594-2000," in: Ludwig/Adogame, *European Traditions*, pp. 75-96.

139. Execution of Three Capuchins in Ethiopia (1684)

In the seventeenth century the Portuguese, Rome and the Jesuits continued their efforts to convert Ethiopia to Catholicism. When King Susenyos himself converted to the Catholic faith in 1622, the realization of this goal appeared to be within reach. However when the "Patriarch" Alphonsus Mendes, who had been sent to Ethiopia by the pope in 1625, insisted that many Ethiopian customs, including circumcision, be abolished, a wide-ranging resistance arose, which in the end led to the abdication of Susenyos and to the expulsion of the Jesuits. Furthermore, other Roman Catholic missionaries were no longer allowed into the country. The failure of a Capuchin mission is reported in the life story of Peter Heylings (1607-1662), who had traveled to Ethiopia in 1632. The biography was published by the orientalist Johann Heinrich Michaelis:

Now it happened that the Abyssinian Abba Gregorius, who was made known in Germany through Herr Ludolf,[1] wanted to leave India to return to his homeland, and in 1647 he arrived in Suaquen. [. . .] There three Capuchins thought that in him they had gotten a good scholar, or even that he might deliver a letter to the great Negus. They drafted a letter in a thoroughly thoughtless manner, which roughly contained the following: How they, as clergy, had been sent from Italy by the Pope, as the high priest of all Christians, to the King of Kings of the Ethiopians and his subjects to make known the truth of the Roman Catholic faith. They thus requested permission to come into his kingdom, not doubting that His Majesty would grant them permission to enter. Gregorius, who traveled alone ahead, was to bring this letter along, which he — not without reason — refused to do. Therefore, the letter was sent with some Arabs and delivered early in 1684, but the king took it without grace. He became angry and said: There was reason to complain that he was not only plagued by the Portuguese from the Orient or India, but also by the Italians from the Occident, that he and his people could have no peace in his land. For this reason, he wrote a letter to Suaquen, that the three clerics should be executed, which the *bascha* also did without much hesitation, in hope of some good gain. In order to insure that he would receive a reward from the Negus, he took the scalps of the beheaded monks, stuffed them with straw and sent them to the Negus so that he could see from the hair that they were Europeans, and from the shaved crown, that they had been priests. . . .

Source: H. Michaelis, *Sonderbarer Lebens-Lauff Herrn Peter Heylings aus Lübec und dessen Reise nach Ethiopien* . . . (Halle, 1724), Kap. LXXX: 88ff. (Text has been slightly modernized.)

140. Gold Coast: Lutheran Mission Initiatives (1673)

The way to Africa was cleared for Protestant powers in Europe with the destruction of the Spanish Armada in 1588. England, the Netherlands, Denmark, Sweden, Brandenburg, and Kurland made use of this opportunity during the seventeenth century. At first they built trading posts chiefly in West Africa, and with this came sporadic efforts at mission work. As such, Wilhelm Johann Müller (1633-?) worked as a Danish Lutheran chaplain in the Gold Coast (today Ghana) at the behest of the Danish trading company from 1622-1670. His writing also manifests serious attempts at mission:

Most, especially those who come into contact with the Christians living there, are able to say that there must be an almighty Creator of Heaven and Earth,

1. Hiob Ludolf (1624-1704), Founder of the Ethiopian Studies in Germany, published a dictionary, a grammar, and a cultural guide of Ethiopia.

whom they call Jan Commè or Jan Compo, he being a distinguished man who enables us Whites, called by them in Portuguese filhos de Deos (children of God), to buy all good things, particularly nice food and drink, good clothes and shoes and expensive goods; yet they still lack the ability to recognize the true living God. They do not desire to believe in the almighty Creator of Heaven and Earth, let alone fear, love and have faith in Him. From such blindness of the heart comes all evil. [. . .] If one speaks to them of God, of the Godhead, in particular of Christ . . . then one hears the blind people say all kinds of insulting and mocking things.

Sometimes it is asked: as Jan Commè or Jan Compo is such a great Lord and so without doubt has a large number of wives, did he not have more than just one son? This impertinent question arises from the fact that these blind people seek their grandeur and high status in polygamy and that they do not understand what it means to be God's son from everlasting to everlasting.

Concerning the conception and birth of our Saviour, Jesus Christ, they have their carnal ideas in the same way as the Turks, since they consider it impossible that a woman can become pregnant without the action of a man and give birth without losing her virginity. According to the Annunciation of the Angel Gabriel, with God nothing is impossible; yet these blinded people are not prepared to understand or learn this. If one tells them of Christ's suffering and death, they ask: "What evil had he done? He must have sinned, or else his father, Jan Comme, would not have let people deal so cruelly with his son."

Source: W. J. Müller, *Die Africanische auf der Guineischen Gold-Cust gelegene Landschafft Fetu* (Hamburg, 1763), 1676 (Nachdruck: Graz, 1968), pp. 87-98, translated in A. Jones, *German Sources for West African History 1599-1669* (Wiesbaden, 1983), pp. 176, 177. *Further Reading:* R. Debusmann/F. Ludwig, "From Distance to Difference," in: Ludwig/Adogame, *European Traditions*, pp. 65-74.

141. An African Pastor Concerning India as Model

J. E. J. Capitein (1717-1747), a former slave, completed his Ph.D. at the University of Leiden and was ordained as the first black African pastor. In a letter to the Board of Directors in Amsterdam he complained about the state of things in the Dutch colony Elmina in today's Ghana and about the colonial authorities' lack of interest in spreading the gospel among the indigenous population. He referred to the better working conditions of his colleagues in the Danish colony of Tranquebar in Southern India (about the work of the Danish-Halle mission in Tranquebar cf. documents 34ff). The letter demonstrates that there was an awareness among the emerging African Christian elite of conditions in other continents across confessional and colonial networks.

Most Noble and Honourable Gentlemen! Your Excellencies! [. . .] Not only legitimate but also illegitimate children have been baptised here from the earliest times. Moreover, . . . I have discovered that there are still baptised illegitimate children of Europeans in our dependent Crom and possibly elsewhere. These have not received any instruction from their parents since their baptism, and have not been committed to teachers for that purpose, but have been raised in heathendom, and there remain. For this reason, I could use the freedom which Your Excellencies have granted me to baptise some of the school-going children of the heathen as they make progress and (show themselves) fit for it. However, I fear that, as long as we have no suitable seminary, . . . in which these children may be shut off (from heathen influences) and cared for, they may fall back into heathen ways. Accordingly, I shall defer administration of the holy sacrament until such times as Your Excellencies have lent a favourable ear to the Historical Foreword of the late Rt Revd Mr H. Velse, now a blessed inhabitant of heaven. In his *Accurate reports concerning the establishment of Christendom among the heathens on the coast of Coromandel and Malabar by the Danish missionaries at Tranquebar,* paragraphs 46-53, the reasonable and sensible means are gathered, whereby a minister in these parts may contribute both to the spreading of the Gospel of the glory of the blessed God and to the advancement of the interests of your Excellencies company. Neither of these purposes can truly be achieved unless the servants of God here are given more freedom in their ministry and are provided with the appropriate means to carry out their work, so should these things appear quite out of the question, Your Excellencies will allow me hereby to request in the most humble and respectful manner that I be relieved of my duties.

Source: D. N. A. Kpobi, *Mission in Chains: The Life, Theology and Ministry of the Ex-slave Jacobus E. J. Capitein (1717-1747) with a Translation of His Major Publications,* 1993, pp. 246-249; translation from A. Eekhof, *De Negerpredikant-Jakobus Elisa Johannes Capitein* (1917). *Further Reading:* David Nii Anum Kpobi, *Saga of a Slave: Jacobus Capitein of Holland and Elmina* (Legon, 2001); D. N. A. Kpobi, "African Chaplains in Seventeenth Century West Africa," in: Kalu, *African Christianity,* pp. 140-171.

142. The Moravians in South and West Africa

a. Georg Schmidt on the Cape (1744)

In South Africa in 1652, the settlement of Cape Town was established by the Dutch as an intermediate station on the sea-route to India; the two Danish-Halle missionaries, Ziegenbalg and Plütschau, had also stopped here enroute to India. After they had reported concerning the situation in South Africa, the board of directors of the Dutch East India Company turned to the Herrnhuter Brotherhood to take on the second great Pietist mission endeavor. These are the first two German missionaries sent to South Africa: Georg Schmidt and Carl Christian Reindorf. Georg Schmidt (1709-1785) came to Herrnhut in 1725 from the Catholic Kunewalde in Moravia, where he, with the followers of Zinzendorf, experienced a spiritual awakening on August 13, 1727. In 1737 he began his trip to South Africa. After a stop in Cape Town, he settled in Zoetelmelks-vlei, where he took up missionary work among the Hottentots (known today as the Khoikhoi). Below, Schmidt describes an evening gathering that took place in the house of the Khoikhoi African who came with him from Cape Town.

They were lovers of tobacco. So I gave them some and smoked with them. In that way I was able to talk a bit with the Africans, as though I had come to them out of free love, wanting nothing more from them than to acquaint them with the Savior and to help them to work so that they might be able to live. The African said, "This is good, Baas (sir). The others cannot speak Dutch." Then I asked him, if they knew that there was an even greater Baas, who had given them their cattle and everything that they had. He said, "Yes." What did he call that one? He said, "Tui'qua." I said, "Dear people, this Tui'qua, is the Savior, the Redeemer. He became human, and was crucified on a cross for us, and he will make you all to be holy people. Upon hearing this, they said nothing. [...] With time, many more of them from the "corral"[1] came to hear me. Even though they could not understand me, I taught them to read Dutch, and through that I told one or the other of them — as much as they could understand — a bit about the Savior. But they had all kinds of superstitions. When I told them, that they were being swindled (by superstitions), the African said, "I can understand that this is true," and he no longer believed in it (the superstitions).

Nine months later I asked Fate (through casting lots)[2] if I should look for another place, since I was so near the company post, so that more Hottentots would come to me. Fate decided: Yes. I considered two places. Fate dictated: Go to Sergeantsrevier. So I moved on the 23rd of April 1738 with 18 Hottentots, small and large, to Sergeantsrevier and began again to build a house and to cultivate a garden and as soon as I could, to hold fellowship meetings with them. Then an "awakening" began among them, so that in a short time, large and small began to pray together, and in particular Wilhelm was one of the best. So I said to them, "Dear people, it is good, that we should have a bit of order," and I divided them into fellowship groups. They observed all days, and I took care of as many of them as I could, and in the mornings I let them gather in their fellowship groups to pray and in evenings I gathered them all together. [...] But as the earliest con-

1. Here the European was referring to the settlement of the Khoikhoi as a "corral" or kraal.

2. The custom of asking "Fate through casting lots" and accepting the result as God's decision comes from the founder, Nikolas von Zinzendorf (1700-1766), who himself turned to casting lots and found application in many areas in the early history of the Moravians.

verts began to look after their cattle, so that no harm would come to them, they then had to continue alone in daily prayer. Then some became annoyed with others who had their cattle nearby, and they disagreed with each other . . . and first one then another began to leave their fellowship groups. [. . .] A farm laborer also said to them, "If your people become learned, then the Company will turn them into slaves." As they mulled that over, I said nothing to them about it, until I heard it (myself). [. . .] In March of 1742, I obtained ordination for the congregation. On the 29th while underway from the Cape, I baptized Wilhelm by a body of water and gave him the name Joshua. On the 2nd of April I baptized the African at my residence and gave him the name Christian. [. . .] On the 4th of September I had to return to the Cape for a council meeting concerning the baptisms. The governor asked me, in the presence of the council, who had given me permission to baptize. I said, "The superintendents of our church." He said, "The superintendents of your church have no say here; they cannot ordain you in this district." I said, "I was not ordained by this district, but by the Hottentots." He said, "The Hottentots are also under (the jurisdiction of) the preachers." [. . .] Shortly thereafter, a speech was made to the people, that I would not be allowed to baptize, and I could do nothing more among the Hottentots. This went so far, that my Hottentots also heard it. They became confused by it, even the ones who had been baptized, and they no longer came to me for fellowship.

b. Moravian Baptisms Rejected (1743)

Resistance of the Reformed Pastors in the Cape to Georg Schmidt became stronger. In December 1743 the Amsterdam Classis decided to nullify Schmidt's baptisms. In 1744 the Moravians had to leave the Cape Colony.

We desire (and will also endeavor to secure) that certain suitable persons holding the Reformed faith shall be appointed to instruct the unfortunate Hottentots and others beyond the mountain in the Christian religion. The baptism of the Herrnhutters has been declared illegal by the Synods of South- and North-Holland. On this ground our Classis disapproves of the baptisms of Schmidt, the Herrnhutter, and approves of the action of the governors and yourselves. The Classis, however, is also of opinion that you should not insist upon Schmidt's recall by the seventeen [the chief governing body of the Dutch East India Company]. On the contrary the Classis requests you to do all in your power to assist the simple Europeans also, of whom you made mention, to obtain good instruction. [. . .]

Source: (a) "Kaapsche Cyclopaedia," No. 48; (b) Spoelstra I, p. 195; (c) Spoelstra II, p. 76, quoted in: J. Du Plessis, *A History of Christian Missions in South Africa* (Reprint, 1965), pp. 56-59.

c. Carl Christian Reindorf: The Beginnings in West Africa (1737)

The Moravians were also active in West Africa. In the eighteenth century they tried three times (1737, 1768, 1770) to start missionary work in the Gold Coast (Ghana), but the work was interrupted by the frequent deaths of their agents (often caused by yellow fever). It is significant that the first missionary was an African, Christian Jacob Protten Africanus (1715-1769). The mission's beginnings were reported by the African pastor and historian Carl Christian Reindorf (1834-1917), who wrote a history of the Gold Coast and Asante in 1895:

By the suggestion of Governor Hendrik von Suhm, then in command of the Danish settlements on the Gold Coast, Pastor Schwane, who acted in the capacity of a Chaplain on the Coast during a period of six years, was instructed to bring two Mulatto youths of the Government school to Copenhagen to be educated at the expense of the Government. Two youths were selected, but one of them being prevented by illness, Protten took his place. So he and the other youth were brought to Denmark in the year 1727. The mother of Protten appears to have been a daughter of king Ashongmo, who emigrated to Popo [in present day Benin/Dahomey] in 1680; and his father a soldier in the castle of Christiansborg. On the 17th of November 1727, Protten was baptized in Copenhagen and got the name "Christian Jakob." He began to study in 1728-1732. In 1735 he was asked to return to his native country, but found no confidence to do so, when fortunately he met Count Zinzendorf in Copenhagen, and after eight days of intercourse with him, he expressed a desire to become a missionary. In July 1735 he accompanied Zinzendorf to Herrnhut, where the case was laid before the Society. Henry Huckoff was appointed by the Conference to accompany Protten to Africa as the first Moravian missionaries. Zinzendorf proceeded with Protten to Holland and got passage for them. In March 1737 they set sail for Africa, and arrived at Elmina on the 11th of May. It was the intention of the Society first to establish their mission at Elmina under the Patronage of the Dutch Government. But on their arrival at Elmina, Protten proposed coming to Akra, and his brother missionary was obliged to accompany him down. But 35 days after their arrival in the country, poor Huckuff found his grave at Akra the 15th June 1737.

In September Protten went to see his relations in Popo. There he was kept against his will and did not return before October 1739. From this time up to 1762, he never was permanently employed in direct missionary work, nor settled in one place. In 1741 he returned to Germany. In 1743 he made a trip to St. Thomas, returned to Germany in 1745 and married there a pious Mulatto-lady, the widow of a Moravian missionary, on the 6th June 1746.

d. C. J. Protten Africanus: Letter of Application (1735)

In 1735, C. J. Protten Africanus applied for admittance into the Moravian Brotherhood:

On the 14th of August, 1727, after enduring all kinds of danger we finally arrived at the Copenhagen Rhede, which means the Lord rules and uses the strength of his arm. On the 17th of November in that same year I was baptized along with one other man from Africa (Frederik Pedersen Svane), after which we both were examined. Thereafter we were assigned to do blacksmith work because that was supposed to be very profitable in Africa. But we did not care for this kind of work, and we did not let the minister rest until he had gotten permission for us to be allowed to study, which was granted, and we were allowed to study for 4 years. [. . .]

(1735) The director Pastor Pleß called on me and my fellow countryman and asked us if we would like to return to Africa, and when we answered yes, he promised to provide for our trip, taking care of our expenses himself, and we were to travel on a ship that was ready to sail (on which our fellow countryman was also leaving). [. . .] I felt very uneasy that I had made this promise to Pleß; I was proud, and so that I would not arrive in Africa under an obligation, I wanted to make a scene. I sought the counsel of Prof. Reus(s), who I was with. His advice was: I should go to Pleß and say straight out, that I refused to be under obligation to go to the pagans; I did (speak to Pleß) and that relieved my uneasiness. Graf von Zinzendorff came to Copenhagen. Reus(s) asked if I wanted to go to Herrnhut. I answered that I wanted to go to Holland. Now I became very uneasy that I had no (skilled) work, and I really wanted to learn to work with my hands. But I could not imagine a more comfortable place to do that than at Herrnhut. I returned on that account to Reuß, asking that if the Herrnhuter was still there — I did not know that the Graf himself was still there — whether I could talk to him regarding my trip, which I did. And on the third day thereafter, I went with them to Herrnhut. Since I have come here, I have often been uneasy and have been irritated with myself. But the Lord uses the strength of His arm. I am a witness that He is an almighty majesty with whom all is possible that is desired; He is holy, He is holy, who is His friend.

Source: (a) Georg Schmidt's Account, September 8, 1744, in: B. Krüger/H. Plüddemann/J. du P. Boeke/H. C. Bredekamp/J. L. Hattingh, *Das Tagebuch und die Briefe von Georg Schmidt, dem ersten Missionar in Südafrika (1737-1744)* (Bellville, 1981) pp. 478-487; (b) C. Spoelstra, *Bouwstoffen voor de geschiedenis der Nederduitsch-Gereformeerde Kerken in Zuid-Afrika* (Amsterdam, 1906-1936), pp. 2, 76, quoted in: J. Du Plessis, *A History of Christian Missions in South Africa* (Cape Town, 1911) ([N]1965), pp. 56-59; (c) C. C. Reindorf, *History of the Gold Coast and Asante* (Basel, 1895), pp. 221-222; (d) Moravian Archives in Herrnhut, quoted in: P. Sebald,

"Christian Jacob Protten Africanus (1715-1769) — erster Missionar einer deutschen Missions-gesellschaft in Schwarzafrika," in: W. Wagner (ed.), *Kolonien und Missionen* (Münster/Ham-burg, 1994), pp. 109-121. — *Further Reading:* (a) K. Müller, *Georg Schmidt. Die Geschichte der ersten Hottentottenmission 1737-1744* (Herrnhut, 1923); J. Du Plessis, *A History of Christian Missions in South Africa* (Cape Town, 1911) ([N]1965); H. Beck, *Brüder in vielen Völkern* (Erlangen, 1981), pp. 98-106; D. Chidester, *Savage Systems* (Charlottesville, 1996), pp. 31-34; (c) P. Jenkins (ed.), *The Recovery of the West African Past: African Pastors and African History in the Nineteenth Century. C. C. Reindorf & Samuel Johnson* (Basel, 1998), p. 13; (d) J. F. Sensbach, *Rebecca's Revival: Creating Black Christianity in the Atlantic World* (Cambridge, Mass., 2005), pp. 162-230.

D. Protests against the Slave Trade

143. The "Encyclopédie" on the Slave Trade (1765)

The slave trade was attacked from various quarters during the second half of the eighteenth century. Leading protagonists of the enlightenment spoke out against this obvious limitation of freedom. Important in this regard was the "Encyclopädie" which was published between 1751 and 1772 by Denis Diderot (1713-1784) and Jean Le Rond D'Alembert (1717-1783). The "Encyclopädie" covered many topics and became a crucial tool for spreading rational views. The article about "Negroes" by Le Romain appeared in the 11th volume in 1765.

To justify this loathsome commerce, which is contrary to natural law, it is argued that ordinarily these slaves find the salvation of their souls in the loss of their liberty, and that the Christian teaching they receive, together with their indispensable role in the cultivation of sugar cane, tobacco, indigo, etc., softens the apparent inhumanity of a commerce where men buy and sell their fellow men as they would animals used in the cultivation of the land.

Source: Le Romain, 'Commerce', in: *L'Encyclopédie,* 1765, cf. M. Craton, *Slavery, Abolition and Emancipation* (London, 1976) pp. 207f. — *Further Reading:* F. Ludwig/A. Adogame, "Introduction," in: Ludwig/Adogame, *European Traditions,* pp. 1-22; J.-G. Bidima, "The Dialectic of the French Enlightenment for Africans," in: Ludwig/Adogame, *European Traditions,* pp. 97-108.

144. The *Zong* Insurance Case (1783)

Nothing so stung the public into awareness of the evils of the slave trade as the publicity given to the case of the *Zong.* The crime committed on March 19, 1783, mobilized the resistance against slavery in Great Britain. The *Zong* insurance case was made known by Granville Sharp (1735-1813) who had been engaged in the anti-slavery struggle since 1769.

The ship Zong, or Zung . . . sailed from the island of St. Thomas, on the coast of Africa, the 6th September, 1781, with four hundred and forty slaves (or four hundred and forty-two) and seventeen Whites on board, for Jamaica . . . between the time of her leaving the coast of Africa and the 29th of November 1781, sixty slaves and upwards, and seven White people, died; and a great number of the remaining slaves, on the day last mentioned, were sick [. . .] it was proved that they did not discover till that very day, the 29th November (or the preceding day) that the stock of fresh water was reduced to two hundred gallons: yet the same day, or in the evening of it, . . . before there was any present or real want of water, "the master of the ship called together a few of the officers, and told them to the following effect: — that, if the slaves died a natural death, it would be the loss of the owners of the ship; but if they were thrown alive into the sea, it would be the loss of the underwriters (i.e., the insurance company)": . . . [T]wo or three or some few following days, the said Luke Collingwood picked, or caused to be picked out, from the cargo of the same ship, one hundred and thirty-three slaves, all or most of whom were sick or weak, and not likely to live; and ordered the crew by turns to throw them into the sea; which most inhuman order was cruelly complied with.

Source: Prince Hoare, *Memoirs of Granville Sharp* (London, 1820) in: C. M. Craton, *Slavery, Abolition and Emancipation* (London, 1976), pp. 47ff.

145. William Wilberforce: Speech at the Parliament (1789)

The Quakers were prominent among the first Christian pressure groups to abolish slavery. Nine of the twelve members of the Society of the Abolition of the Slave Trade, founded in 1787, belonged to this denomination. Then also representatives of other denominations, as for instance John Wesley *(Thoughts upon Slavery)* spoke out against the trade in human merchandise. On the side of the Anglicans, the "Clapham sect," a revivalist group which met in the London suburb of Clapham, was important. The political spokesman of this group was William Wilberforce (1759-1813). The influence of Wilberforce and the Clapham sect on the British decision to abolish the slave trade has been emphasized by some authors (Coupland, Sternberger), while others (E. Williams) point to the changing economic conditions as determining factor. The following are extracts from a speech Wilberforce gave at the British parliament in May 1789.

What a striking view . . . of the wretched state of Africa is furnished by the tragedy of Calabar! Two towns, formerly hostile, had settled their differences and by an intermarriage among their chiefs had pledged themselves to peace. But the trade in slaves was prejudiced by such pacifications, and it became, therefore, the policy of our traders to renew the hostilities. This policy was soon put into practice and the scene of carnage was such that it is better perhaps to refer Gentleman to the Privy Council's report than to agitate their minds by dwelling on it.

The Slave Trade, in its very nature, is the source of such kind of tragedies. It is a trade in its principle inevitably calculated to spread disunion among the African princes, to sow the seeds of every mischief, to inspire enmity, to destroy humanity, and it is found in practice, by the most abundant testimony, to have had the effect in Africa of carrying misery, devastation and ruin wherever its baneful influence has extended.

Source: W. Wilberforce, Speech in the House of Commons, 12.5.1789, Parliamentary History, XXVII, pp. 41-55, 62f; quoted in: R. Coupland, *Wilberforce* (Oxford: Clarendon Press, 1923), pp. 120, 121. — *Further Reading:* B. Stanley, Christian missions, antislavery and the claims of humanity, c. 1813-1873, in: Gilley/Stanley, *World Christianities*, pp. 443-457; S. Jacobson, *Am I Not a Man and Brother?* (Uppsala, 1972); D. E. Williams, *Capitalism and Slavery* (Chapel Hill, 1944).

146. Olaudah Equiano on His Enslavement (1789)

Olaudah Equiano (1745-1797) from South Eastern Nigeria was seized by slave-hunters at the age of ten and was shipped successively to Barbados, Virginia and England. Baptized and renamed Gustavus Vassa, he was for many years a mariner, fighting in the Seven Year's War and sailing frequently to the Mediterranean, Caribbean and North America. Purchasing his freedom in 1766, he took part in Lord Mulgrave's Arctic expedition of 1773. Converted to Calvinism, Equiano became one of the most prominent opponents of the slave trade. His autobiography is one of the most influential works in antislavery literature.

One day, when all our people were gone out to their works as usual and only I and my dear sister were left to mind the house, two men and a woman got over our walls, and in a moment seized us both, and without giving us time to cry out or make resistance they stopped our mouths and ran off with us into the nearest wood. Here they tied our hands and continued to carry us as far as they could. [. . .]

The first object which saluted my eyes when I arrived on the coast was the sea, and a slave ship which was then riding at anchor and waiting for its cargo. These filled me with astonishment, which was soon converted into terror when I was carried on board. [. . .] When I looked round the ship too and saw a large furnace or copper boiling and a multitude of black people of every description chained together, every one of their countenances expressing dejection and sorrow, I no longer doubted of my fate; and quite overpowered with horror and anguish, I fell motionless on the deck and fainted. [. . .] I now saw myself deprived of all chance of returning to my native country or even the least glimpse of hope of gaining the shore, which I now considered as friendly; and I even wished for my former slavery in preference to my present situation, which was filled with horrors of every kind, still heightened by my ignorance of what I was to undergo. [. . .] In a little time after, amongst the poor chained men I found some of my own nation, which in a small degree gave ease to my mind. I inquired of these what was to be done with us; they gave me to understand we were to be carried to these white people's country to work for them. I then was a little revived, and thought if it were no worse than working, my situation was not so desperate: but still I feared I should be put to death. [. . .] At last, when the ship we were in had got in all her cargo, they made ready with many fearful noises, and we were all put under deck so that we could not see how they managed the vessel. [. . .]

The closeness of the place and the heat of the climate, added to the number in the ship, which was so crowded that each had scarcely room to turn himself, almost suffocated us. This produced copious perspirations, so that the air soon became unfit for respiration from a variety of loathsome smells. [. . .] The shrieks of the women and the groans of the dying rendered the whole a scene of horror almost inconceivable. [. . .] One day, when we had a smooth sea and moderate wind, two of my wearied countrymen who were chained together (I was near them at the time), preferring death to such a life of misery, somehow made through the nettings and jumped into the sea: immediately another quite dejected fellow, who on account of his illness was suffered to be out of irons, also followed their example, and I believe many more would very soon have done the same if they had not been prevented by the ship's crew, who were instantly alarmed.

Source: O. Equiano, *The Interesting Narrative of the Life of Olaudah Equiano, or Gustavus Vassa, The African: An Authoritative Text* (edited by W. Sollors) (New York, 2001), pp. 32, 38-41. — *Further Reading*: V. Carretta, *Equiano, the African: Biography of a Self-made Man* (Athens, 2005); M. Diedrich/H. L. Gates/C. Pedersen, *Black Imagination and the Middle Passage* (New York, 1999); G. I. Jones, "Olaudah Equiano of the Niger Ibo," in: P. D. Curtin (ed.), *Africa Remembered: Narratives by West Africans from the Era of the Slave Trade* (Madison, 1967), pp. 60-98; P. D. Morgan/Sean Hawkins, *Black Experience and the Empire* (Oxford/New York, 2004).

147. Opposition to the Anti Slavery Movement

The slave trade existed in Africa even before the arrival of Europeans there. If this had not been the case, then the rapid growth of transatlantic trade of slaves would not have been possible. Nevertheless, the export of imprisoned Africans to America marked a complete change, as this text of H. C. Monrad makes clear. Monrad pointed out that the economic structure of West Africa had become dependent on the slave trade, and, therefore, it was difficult to suddenly abolish it.

The slave trade had existed throughout the history of Africa; however, the (situation in) the most ancient times, when nations of that part of the world carried on the slave trade amongst themselves, can probably not be compared to the gruesome practices which the Europeans introduced later. Although the negroes have no scruples to rob the life of their slaves, I have not had the opportunity to experience that they torture them or overtax their strength. The negroe does not view being a slave in his own land as a great calamity; but being taken from his land is the same for him to being killed. If one considers the fate of the slaves on their trip to the West Indies and their treatment without bias, it also has to be admitted that it would be more humane, at least in most places, to chop them down, than to carry them away from their homelands. [. . .]

It is sure that the negroe princes as well as the Europeans who do business in Africa regard the abolition of the slave trade with displeasure. When the Danish government ordered that after a certain number of years the slave trade should cease, our governor in Guinea — I don't know why — informed the King of *Ashantee* through a delegation of Black Africans from Accra while at the same time delivering some presents to him, which was always done at such noteworthy occasions. The king responded: "The king of Denmark is free to do as he pleases in his country; but in my country I will do as I please." This answer was greatly admired there. I do not believe, though, that the delegation had intended [. . .] to encourage the king to send slaves; although the number of slaves sent to the coast after this time does not speak against this. For a long time those who were not friends of the slave trade were pounced on in Guinea, especially Wilberforce (philanthropist and Member of the English Parliament who strongly urged the abolition of slavery). Some took him to be a poor cleric who, in order to earn money, had taken up the plight of Black Africans in Parliament. I noticed that he was not only a talented and noble statesman, but also a wealthy man. That a wealthy man could be so mistaken and could seek to shine in such a way, seemed unbelievable. [. . .]

Source: H. C. Monrad, *Gemälde der Küste von Guinea und der Einwohner derselben* (Weimar, 1824), pp. 297-301.

III. AFRICA 1800-1890

A. ABOLITION OF THE SLAVE TRADE AND MISSION

148. Liberated Slaves and Sierra Leone

From the late 1780s Protestant Christianity impinged upon Africa in a new and dynamic way. As a "Province of Freedom" for liberated slaves, Sierra Leone played a crucial role. After a first unsuccessful attempt of colonization in 1787, there was a new initiative by Africans who had been British servicemen and slaves and then had settled in Nova Scotia in Canada. Their spokesman was Thomas Peters. Peters organized a petition of blacks from Nova Scotia and carried it personally to London. The directors of the newly formed Sierra Leone Company accepted Peter's petition and in March 1792 the Armada of sixteen ships with a party of altogether 1190 men and women landed in Freetown. The description of the landing scenes (a) compares the arrival to the return of the Israelites from captivity.

The settlers faced many difficulties and their community dwindled. However, in 1808 the British declared Freetown, the peninsula and its environs a Crown Colony. They established a naval base at Freetown, from which they policed the African coast in an effort to enforce the 1807 act of the British Parliament banning the slave trade. An article from the magazine of the *Basler Mission* describes events that followed.

a. Arrival of Afro-Americans from Nova Scotia (1792)

Their pastors led them ashore, singing a hymn of praise. . . . Like the Children of Israel which were come out again of the captivity they rejoiced before the Lord, who brought them from bondage to the land of their forefathers. When all had arrived, the whole colony assembled in worship, to proclaim to the . . . continent whence they or their forbears had been carried in chains — "The day of Jubilee is come, Return ye ransom sinners home."

b. A "Flourishing Christian Black African Nation"

We all know that the English government has worked with much energy and has done extraordinary work these past many years to suppress the slave trade everywhere. To that end they stationed a number of war ships or "preventive squadrons" as they were called, on the coast of West Africa, which had the task of laying in wait for slave ships. When they met a slave ship, the English would capture the ship, sentence the owners and burn or sell the ship, giving freedom to any black Africans they found. The freed black Africans were usually brought to the English colony of Sierra Leone, which consists entirely of such freed slaves and, under English protection, is a flourishing Christian black African nation. But even though Sierra Leone is a very beautiful country and the situation there is advantageous and desirable for the black Africans who have been relocated there, nevertheless the Africans still cannot forget their homeland. Homesickness is a yearning that is as characteristic for them as it is for the Swiss. And because of this many of these colonists — often after ten or twenty years in the colony — were moved by the sweet yearning for home and set out to search for the land of their birth and youth, even though they were in danger there of being captured and sold again as slaves. In the years from 1839 to 1842 more than 500 such colonists left Freetown in Sierra Leone in order to return aboard a coastal ship which they had purchased to Abbeokuta [in modern-day Nigeria], the place from which they had once been dragged off as slaves. Among them were many who had found in Sierra Leone not only bodily freedom and timely well-being but also that true freedom which is given by God's Son. Many who longed to see their fathers, mothers and brothers again also carried inside the stronger desire to bring to their relatives the sweet name of Jesus in which they themselves had found peace, salvation and blessedness.

Source: (a) Lamin Sanneh, *Abolitionists Abroad: American Blacks and the Making of Modern West Africa* (Cambridge, Mass./London, 1999), p. 52; cf. C. Fyfe, *A History of Sierra Leone* (London, 1962), pp. 36-37; (b) A. Ostertag, "Der Weg der Trübsal" (in *Evangelisches Missions-Magazin* 1, 1857, p. 50). — *Further Reading:* C. Fyfe, *A History of Sierra Leone* (London, 1962); A. F. Walls, "A Christian Experiment: The Early Sierra Leone Colony," in: G. J. Cuming (ed.), *The Mission of the Church and the Propagation of the Faith* (Cambridge, 1970), pp. 107-129; Jehu Hanciles, *Euthaniasia of a Mission: African Church Autonomy in a Colonial Context* (London, 2002).

149. The Tasks of the Church Missionary Society

Founded in 1799, the Church Missionary Society had its first field of activity in Sierra Leone where it started to provide a Christian education for the liberated slaves. As the letter indicates the tasks were far-reaching. It was difficult for the CMS to carry them out, since many missionaries died and Sierra Leone soon acquired a reputation for being the "white man's grave." The former slaves who had become Christians took over a leading role.

In a Minute laid before His Majesty's Government in the year 1817, it was proposed by the Committee of the Church Missionary Society, that the Society should take on itself, in addition to its expenditure for the benefit of Sierra Leone, the whole charge of paying the Schoolmasters and Schoolmistresses of the Colony; Government undertaking the support of a Second Chaplain, and appointing the Salary annually voted in the Estimates to the Superintendents of the Seven Country Parishes of Sierra Leone to the same number of clergymen with the assignment of Glebe and the erection of Parsonage Houses.

This arrangement was adopted; and has, in substance and so far as circumstances would allow, been acted upon. It has, however, been found impracticable to supply the number of Teachers adequate to the increasing demands of the Colony; and some new position has in consequence become necessary. The Society has endeavoured to supply, from year to year, the requisite number of Teachers; but the climate has been so fatal to the health and lives of those who have been sent, as greatly to counteract its exertions. The Society has indeed from the beginning encountered some losses in its attempts to benefit the population of the Colony: from the commencement of its efforts in that quarter in the year 1804 to the present time it has sent out Seventy Adult Europeans: of these only Twenty-five are now living in Africa, Seven having returned, and Thirty-eight having fallen victims in this difficult and hazardous service. [. . .] The difficulty of supplying a Colony with an adequate number of Instructors has been much augmented since the period of the arrangement before mentioned, by the increase of the Liberated Africans. [. . .]

The Committee beg to remark, in reference to this branch of the subject, that, as they have every prospect of being able to bring forward, in due time, the Liberated Africans themselves to take charge, under the respective Clergymen of the Country Parishes, of the education and civil superintendence of their Towns, the expense incurred by Government for such Towns will be likely gradually to decrease, as Natives shall be substituted for Europeans. [. . .]

Source: Public Record Office, London: Colonial Office 267/43: Letter to the Secretary of State from the Church Missionary Society, dated 12 April 1824, quoted in: C. Fyfe, *Sierra Leone Inheritance* (London, 1964), pp. 137f.

150. A Freed Slave: Samuel Ajayi Crowther (1837)

Without a doubt the most prominent among the freed slaves was Samuel Ajayi Crowther (ca. 1806-1891). He was ordained in 1843, and was consecrated as the first black African Anglican Bishop in 1864. He describes his path from slavery to baptism in a report to the leadership of the Church Mission Society (cf. document 165).

I suppose some time about the commencement of the year 1821, I was in my native country, enjoying the comforts of father and mother, and the affectionate love of brothers and sisters. From this period I must date the unhappy, but which I am now taught, in other respects, to be called blessed day, which I shall never forget in my life. I call it unhappy day, because it was the day in which I was violently turned out of my father's house, and separated from relations; and in which I was made to experience what is called to be in slavery — with regard to its being called blessed, it being the day which Providence had marked out for me to set out on my journey from the land of heathenism, superstition, and vice, to a place where His Gospel is preached. [. . .] Our conquerors were Oyo Mahomedans, who led us away through the town. [. . .] The town on fire — the houses being built with mud. [. . .] The flame was very high. We were led by my grandfather's house, already desolate; and in a few minutes after, we left the town to the mercy of the flame, never to enter or to see it any more. Farewell, place of my birth, the play-ground of my childhood, and the place which I thaught would be the repository of my mortal body in its old age! [. . .] On the next morning, our cords being taken off our necks, we were brought to the Chief of our captors — for there were many other Chiefs — as trophies at his feet. In a little while, a separation took place, when my sister and I fell to the share of the Chief, and my mother and the infant to the victors. [. . .] Now and then my mistress would speak with me and her son, that we should by and bye go to the Popo country, where we should buy tobacco, and other fine things, to sell at our return. Now, thought I, this was the signal of my being sold to the Portuguese who, they often told me during our journey, were to be seen in that country. Being very thoughtful of this, my appetite forsook me, and in a few weeks I got the dysentry, which greatly preyed on me. I determined with myself that I would not go to the Popo country; but would make an end of myself, one way or another. In several nights I attempted strangling myself with my band, but had not courage enough to close the noose tight, so as to effect my purpose. [. . .]

About this time, intelligence was given that the English were cruising the coast. This was another subject of sorrow with us — that there must be war also on sea as well as on land — a thing never heard of before, or imagined practicable. This delayed our embarkation. [. . .] After a few weeks delay, we were embarked, at night in canoes, from Lagos to the beach, and on the following morning were put on board the vessel, which immediately sailed away. [. . .] On the very same evening, we were surprised by two English men-of-war, and on the next morning found ourselves in the hands of new conquerors, whom we at first very much dreaded, they being armed with long swords [. . .] After nearly two months and a half cruising on the coast, we were landed at Sierra Leone, on the 17th of June 1822. The same day we were sent to Bathurst, formerly Leopold, under the care of Mr. Davey. Here we had the pleasure of meeting many of our country people, but none were known before. They assured us of or liberty and freedom, and we very soon believed them. [. . .] From this period I have been under the care of the Church Missionary Society, and in about six months after my arrival at Sierra Leone, I was able to read the New Testament with some degree of freedom, and was made a Monitor, for which I was rewarded with sevenpence-halfpenny per month. The Lord was pleased to open my heart to these things which were spoken by His servants; and being convinced that I was a sinner, and desired to obtain pardon through Jesus Christ, I was baptized on the 11th of December, 1825, by the Rev. J. Raban.

Source: Letter of S. A. Crowther, Feb. 22, 1837, published in: Church Missionary Record 8/1837, 217-223, cf. Curtin, *Africa Remembered,* pp. 299-315. — *Further Reading:* J. F. A. Ajayi, *A Patriot to the Core: Samuel Ajayi Crowther* (Ibadan, 1992); A. F. Walls, "Samuel Ajayi Crowther," in: G. Anderson et al. (eds.), *Mission Legacies* (Maryknoll, 1994), pp. 132-139.

151. Afro-American Missionaries for Liberia (1833)

There were also initiatives in the USA to resettle former slaves in Africa. Supported by the state, colonization societies started around 1820 to establish settlements along the coast of today's Liberia. In 1839 most of these settler colonies united in the Commonwealth of Liberia declared their independence on July 16, 1847. The resettlement program was accompanied by missionary endeavours:

Could we find men suitable, it would probably be for the interest of the mission, as well as the colony, and the interest of our Colored friends in general, to call as many of them into the field, as auxiliaries, as could conveniently be supported. Their constitutions, it is thought by some, are better suited to the climate than that of the white man's, and it would have a tendency to allay the many petty and fearful jealousies that exist here against white influence. The whole colony, with a few exceptions, seems strangely fearful of the authority of white men in any form. Time and patience, and love, however, I doubt not, will soon correct the evil.

Source: Melville B. Cox, Monrovia to the American Colonization Society, May 4, 1833, quoted in: T. W. Shick, "Rhetoric and Reality: Colonization and Afro-American Missionaries in Early Nineteenth Century Liberia," in: S. M. Jacobs (ed.), *Black Americans and the Missionary Movement in Africa* (Westport/London, 1982), pp. 45-62, 53. *Further Reading:* Jehu Hanciles, "Back to Africa: White Abolitionists and Black Missionaries," in: Kalu, *African Christianity,* pp. 191-217.

152. Reform Program to Abolish the Slave Trade

Since neither the blockade by the British preventive squadron nor the anti-slavery treaties with other European powers were sufficient to effectively undermine the slave trade, the anti-slavery movement became more and more concerned with reforming the social and economic structures of West Africa and with liberating the African people from their dependence on the slave trade. Thomas Fowell Buxton (1786-1845) outlined a basic reform program in his book *The African Slave Trade and Its Remedy* (1840). The aim was to establish an African middle class which could take over leading positions in all areas of social life (a). A summary of the proposed step is given in the Program of the Society for the Extinction of the Slave Trade (b).

a. Commerce, Civilization, Christianity

We must elevate the minds of her (Africa's) people and call forth the resources of her soil. [. . .] Let missionaries and schoolmasters, the plough and the spade, go together and agriculture will flourish; the avenues to legitimate commerce will be opened; confidence between man and man will be inspired, whilst civilization will advance as the natural effect, and Christianity operate as the proximate cause, of this happy change.

b. Program of the Society for the Extinction of the Slave Trade and for the Civilization of Africa, June 1839

Adopt effectual measures for reducing the principal languages of Western and Central Africa into writing; prevent or mitigate the prevalence of disease and suffering among the people of Africa; encourage practical science in all its various branches; investigate the system of drainage best calculated to succeed in a climate so humid and so hot, assist in promoting the formation of roads and canals, the manufacture of paper and the use of the printing press; afford essential assistance to the natives by furnishing them with useful information as to the best mode of cultivation, as to the productions which command a steady market and by introducing the most approved agricultural implements and seeds. The time might come when the knowledge of the mighty powers of steam might contribute rapidly to promote the improvement and prosperity of that country.

Source: (a) T. F. Buxton, *The African Slave Trade and Its Remedy* (London, 1840), pp. 282, 511, quoted in: J. F. A. Ajayi, *Christian Missions in Nigeria 1840-1891* (London, 1965), pp. 10, 11. (b) Prospectus of the Society for the Extinction of the Slave Trade and for the Civilization of Africa, instituted June, 1839, published in: *The African Slave Trade and Its Remedy*, pp. 8-16, cf. Ajayi, pp. 16, 17. *Further Reading:* M. A. B. Gaiya, "Thomas Fowell Buxton (1786-1844): His Impact on Christian Mission in Africa," in: Ludwig/Adogame, *European Traditions*, pp. 129-141.

B. New Missionary Societies

153. Samuel Johnson: The Anglican Yoruba Mission

The outset of the nineteenth century marked a new epoch for Christian missions. The Protestant missionary movement started in England. In 1795 the interdenominational

London Missionary Society was founded, followed in 1799 by the Anglican Church Missionary Society (C.M.S.), which worked from 1808 onwards in Sierra Leone. C.M.S. was financially better off than the continental missionary societies which were established soon afterwards and was therefore in a good position to open up new fields such as the Yoruba region in Western-Nigeria. The following account was written by the African pastor and historian Samuel Johnson (1846-1901).

Christianity was introduced by the Church Missionary Society in 1843, first into Abeokuta via Badagry, and then from thence to Ibadan in May 1851, and also to Ijaye. On January 10, 1852, the C.M.S. removed their base from Badagry to Lagos. From Abeokuta, mission stations were planted at the Oke Ogun and Egbado districts, from Ibadan missions were planted at Iwo, Modakeke, Ife, Osogbo and Ilesa. Missions were established also at Oyo and Ogbomoso before the Iyae war broke out in 1860, which put a stop to the progress of missions all over the country. The intertribal wars which followed and which convulsed the greater part of the country, and devastated vast areas, prevented its growth northwards, but at Abeokuta where it was first planted, it grew so rapidly that at the time of the British occupation, Christian adherents could be numbered by thousands; schools had been established, and evangelistic work among the surrounding kindred tribes systematically undertaken and was being vigorously carried on. The Bible in the vernacular was the most potent factor in the spread of the religion.

Source: S. Johnson, *The History of the Yorubas: From the Earliest Times to the Beginning of the British Protectorate* (Lagos, 1921), p. 39. — *Further Reading:* P. Jenkins (ed.), *The Recovery of the West African Past: African Pastors and African History in the Nineteenth Century* (Basel, 1998).

154. Negotiations of the Basel Mission in Ghana (1835)

The first mission society of the nineteenth century in German-speaking lands was the "Basler Mission" which was established in 1815 to enable an interdenominational and ecumenical effort and to work in close cooperation with British missions. In the early years, more than at any other time, countless missionaries who had been trained in Basel worked for the British Church Missionary Society. Naturally they also developed their own mission fields. In 1836 the missionary A. Niis reports about the negotiations to establish a mission station in Akropong in Ghana (then the Gold Coast).

At the beginning of the mutual discussions, the three delegates from Christiansburg, Usue and Labode had to step forward and publicly announced in front of the gathering that the three towns approve a settlement [of the white man] in Akropong. The soldier, who had been sent by his Danish governor to accompany me and who followed me everywhere on foot, asked the noble, on behalf of the governor, to kindly accept me and to offer me assistance, as I had need, and to allow me his protection everywhere, and the other two by him agreed as well. The noble answered this with a loud and friendly "Yes," and also with many solemn and shining promises. He testified loudly to his joy that he had lived to see the day that a white man might be accepted into his village, who might decide to stay by him and to teach his people and children about the "good." The noble continued that he [the white man] should always be loved, honored and highly esteemed among his people. He should count on the fact that we would always give him help in need. [He said,] We only asked these things of the white man: (1) that he does not bring any dogs here; (2) that on Monday and Friday he does not do any field work; (3) that he does not kill the giant snake; and (4) that he does not shoot any of the black apes. These things were forbidden by the fetish. I said that my presence here had a much different goal than to seek sensual pleasure and wealth; I made this known to them and the gathering dispersed.

Source: Various portions taken from the diary of the missionary Andreas Niis during his stay among the Aschanti people on the West Coast from the 19th of March until the 7th of October in 1835, in: *MNGPM* 1836, pp. 510-564, specifically pp. 513ff. — *Further Reading:* W. Schlatter, *Geschichte der Basler Mission 1891-1915.* 3 Vols. (Basel, 1916).

155. Alexander Merensky: "Openings" in Swaziland (1860)

Between 1855 and 1858 Alexander Merensky (1837-1918) received training at the Berlin Mission which had been established in 1824, after which he was sent to South Africa. Upon his arrival, he and his companions traveled about 1400 km by foot and ox cart to the Emmaus Mission-station in Zululand. From there, he began his work in a new mission field to the Swazi people who lived farther to the north. His report demonstrates how difficult communication was.

Since then no group had attempted to secure a new foothold for the Gospel into Swasiland until in April of 1860 we finally were able with difficulty to clear a way into that forgotten region. [. . .] The king greeted us with the Dutch-South African [Afrikans] word "Morro Baas," but he looked upon us with considerable disdain, and it certainly happened by intent, that just then servants brought large bowls full of meat for his dogs to fall on greedily. [. . .] The king gave more attention to our rifles than to our words. Our statement that we had been sent to bring the living word of God to him moved him to ask whether a king had sent us, but soon he cut short all discussion by explaining that Missionary Allison had talked in a similar manner, and that through him, he had lost many people. We did not handle this very wisely as we should have let the matter drop when we noticed that his *Induna* (councilors) grumbled when we asked what had happened, but the king explained the matter in his way: "Allison preached," so he told us, "that it is a sin to kill a man; thereupon the *abataki* (witch-doctor) sought refuge with him; all the deadbeats ran there, because they believed they would be safe there; finally my own brother fled to him and I was forced to kill the entire bunch." In further discussion about the commandments of God he called out: "The commandment 'You shall not kill' is of no use to me and my people! I must be able to kill whoever I want to kill, what should I use for punishment when a messenger does not deliver his message quickly; what should my soldiers eat if they don't carry out war campaigns?" He cut short our discussion that man must obey God's commandments and that Christian people have become great and powerful because they have followed God's commands with these words: "We Swazi have always done it this way." Finally he ruled, that we should teach the youngsters to read and write and other people should be taught other skills, but the older people should be left as they were.

Source: A. Merensky, *Mein Missionsleben in Transvaal,* Ed. von U. van der Heyden (Berlin, 1996), pp. 35, 40. — *Further Reading:* J. Richter, *Geschichte der Berliner Missionsgesellschaft 1824-1924* (Berlin, 1924).

156. Casalis and Chief Moshesh in Lesotho (1833)

Eugène Casalis (1812-1891) was sent to South Africa in the fall of 1832 by the Paris Mission (Société des Missions évangeliques de Paris) which had been established in 1822. He was commissioned to start missionary work among the Basutos. Together with other missionaries he established the stations Morija in 1833 and Thaba Bossiou in 1838. In his biography Casalis, who was director of the Paris Mission between 1855 and 1882, reports about his talks with chief Moshesh.

At night Moshesh made us seat ourselves by his hearth, in the house of his chief wife. [. . .] The repast finished, he took great pleasure in repeating what we had said in public, and in taking explanations. It was thus that he discovered, to his great surprise, that our teaching was based on facts, or real history, and was not, as he had thought at first, composed of myths and allegories. 'You believe, then', said he to me one evening, pointing me to the stars, 'that in the midst of and beyond all these, there is an all-powerful Master, who has created it all, and who is our Father? Our ancestors used, in fact, to speak of a Lord of heaven, and we still call these great shining spots (the Milky Way) you see up above, "the way of gods," but it seemed to us that the world must have existed for ever, except, however, men and animals, who, according to us, have had a beginning, — animals having come first, and men afterwards. But we did not know who gave them existence. We adored the spirits of our ancestors, and we asked of them rain, abundant harvests, good health, and a good reception amongst them after death.' 'You were in darkness, and we have brought you the light. All these visible things, and a multitude of others which we cannot see, have been created and are preserved by a Being all wise and all good, who is the God of us all, and who has made us to be born of one blood.' This last assertion appeared incredible to the chief's advisers. 'What!' said the boldest, 'that can never be! You are white; we are black: how could we come from the same father?' To which the chief replied without hesitation: 'Stupids! In my cattle are white, red, and spotted cattle; are they not all cattle? Do not they come from the same stock, and belong to the same master?' This argument produced more impression among them than it would have done amongst us.

Source: E. Casalis, *My Life in Basutoland* (Cape Town, 1889, 1971), pp. 219-27.

157. A Catholic Voice: Cardinal Lavigerie (ca. 1877)

Not only Protestant but also Catholic missions experienced a new impetus in the nineteenth century. Charles Lavigerie (1825-1892), Archbishop of Algiers (from 1867) and Carthage (from 1884), developed missionary activities which aimed at the indigenization of Christianity. He established the missionary organization of the White Fathers in 1868. He became Apostolic delegate for North Africa in the same year and in 1878 for the interior of Africa. An important aim was to recruit sufficient workers.

The education we provide for selected Africans should leave them truly African, as far as material life is concerned. [. . .] We should aim at giving selected Africans an education which will give them the greatest possible influence over the members of their own communities, while at the same time not putting too great a burden on the resources of the mission.

It is a piece of good fortune that the Holy See, under attack from all sides, has now a great opportunity. We can see Pius IX. crowning his Immortal Pontificate by such an act, or his successor similarly inaugurating this. What profound emotion would grip the world when it witnessed such a sign of power and moral grandeur.

A Pontifical Bull addressed to the leaders of Missions in Equatorial Africa, announcing this great crusade of humanity and faith, calling for the creation of an army of apostles ready to march to death to save life and to restore liberty to the poor children of Cham: such an act would be one of the greatest events of the century and indeed of the whole history of the church. We would not then need to worry too much about the projects of the Brussels Conference.[1] Let the Conference march with the explorers; we march with God and humanity.

Source: F. Renault, *Cardinal Lavigerie: Churchman, Prophet and Missionary* (London, 1994), pp. 224ff. — *Further Reading:* H. Gründer, "'Gott will es' — Eine Kreuzzugsbewegung am Ende des 19. Jahrhunderts" (in: *Geschichte in Wissenschaft und Unterricht* 28, 1977, pp. 210-224); F. Renault, *Lavigerie, l'esclavage africaine et l'Europe 1868-1899.* 2 Bde. Paris 1971. "Zu Lavigerie vgl. X. de Montclos, Charles Lavigerie," in: M. Greschat (ed.), *Gestalten der Kirchengeschichte* (Stuttgart, 1985), pp. 9, 196-207.

C. Livingstone and Other "Explorers"

158. Egypt: Napoleon and Coptic Christians

Napoleon's (1769-1821) Egypt campaign of 1798 initiated a new epoch in the relationship between Europe and Africa. This was the time when systematically organized journeys to explore the interior of Africa began. The Ottoman Empire's loss of power also led to the question of the new political order in Egypt and the position of the Coptic Christians. However, there was a big difference between intentions (a) and "Realpolitik" (b).

a. Intentions (1798)

I have received the message sent to me by the Coptic nation. It is my pleasure to protect this nation which from now on will never be subjected to disrespect. When time permits, as will soon be the case, I will allow this nation to practise its religion in public, as is the case in Europe, where everyone practises his own religion.

b. Orders (1800)

The Copts are nothing but a minority hated by the Muslims and they have brought this hatred upon themselves. We should ensure justice and freedom for them, but it is not wise — and even dangerous — to be allied with them and to grant them privileges. Therefore their leaders and those of the Greek and Syrian communities will attend the meetings of the diwan (only) on a consultative basis.

Source: (a) Letter of Bonaparte to Mu'alim al Jawarhi, December 7th, 1798, quoted in: A. C. Thibaudeau, *Histoire de la Campagne d'Egypte sous le Règne de Napoleon le Grand* (Paris, 1839),

1. Brussels Conference: King Leopold II invited Africa 'experts' to Brussels in 1876 to discuss the 'opening of Africa to civilization.'

pp. 2, 71; cf. also J. Tagher, *Christians in Muslim Egypt: An Historical Study of the Relations be-tween Copts and Muslims from 640 to 1922* (Altenberge, 1998), p. 180. (b) Paragraph 4 of the order of 10 vendémiaire of the 10th year of the French Revolution (October 1800) quoted in Tagher, ibid., p. 188.

159. Explorations in Africa: An "Open Door for Missions"

Political stability in the post-Napoleonic era was a precondition for the intensified explo-ration of Africa by Europeans. The Africa Company (London), founded in 1788, played an important role in this enterprise. The upper Nile, the coastal region, the Congo, the Zam-bezi and the Niger were explored by the Englishmen M. Park, H. Clapperton, D. Living-stone, R. F. Burton, J. H. Speke, V. L. Cameron, the American H. M. Stanley and others. The discoveries by Livingstone and Stanley aroused particular enthusiasm in mission circles.

If a "new Columbus" had discovered an unknown part of the world, we could attach to his discovery no greater significance than to the famous deed of the American Henry M. Stanley. [. . .] Towards the end of 1874 he reentered the "Dark Continent" from the east, embarking on a path never taken by a Euro-pean to *Ukerewe-Lake* (Lake Victoria-Nyanza) before, whose banks he explored along its entire length, staying for a time with King Mtesa of Uganda and ar-ranging for the establishment of an evangelical mission (Church M.S.) there. He also discovered the region between the *Ukrewe* and the *Mwutan* (Albert Nyanza), as well as the most important discharge of the first-named lake in the west, and he found a couple of smaller lakes, which he named Alexandrian-Nyanza, after the Alexandrian-Nile, which he regarded as the source of the River Nile. Later we find him active in Tanganyika.

Here was an open door for missions, the likes of which had not been found since the beginning of their work: a wide and, in parts, heavily populated re-gion that had not previously been influenced directly by European forces had been opened up to them. Such virgin ground they had never before experi-enced for their work, or such was the case in only a few exceptional circum-stances. The mission societies should not allow these opportunities to escape. As soon as the first trade steamer goes up the Livingstone (river), a mission steamer should accompany it.

Source: "Die Erschließung Innerafrikas durch Stanleys Entdeckung des Livingstone" (in: *Allgemeine Missions-Zeitschrift*, 1878, pp. 1-11). — *Further Reading:* J. E. Flint (ed.), *The Cam-bridge History of Africa*, vol. 5, ca. 1790–ca. 1870 (Cambridge, 1976); R. I. Rotberg, *Africa and Its Explorers* (Cambridge, Mass., 1970).

160. Heinrich Barth: A German in Muslim West Africa

German travelers, such as Eduard Vogel, Gustav Nachtigal, Gerhard Rohlfs, Eduard Flegel and Heinrich Barth, contributed to European knowledge about Africa. Heinrich Barth (1821-1865) was commissioned by the British government to explore the continent and published his experiences in five volumes. In the account of his visit to Yola he reported his reflections on praying together with Muslims:

I had a visit from two very handsome and amiable young Fulbe, and, in my rather morose mood [Barth was very ill at the time] refused their urgent request, made in the most simple and confidential way, to say the fatha [fatiha], or the opening prayer of the Koran, with them. I have always regretted my refusal, as it estranged from me many people, and, although many Christians will object to repeat the prayer of another creed, yet the use of a prayer of so general import as the introductory chapter of the Koran ought to be permitted every solitary traveller in these regions, in order to form a sort of conciliatory link.

Source: Barth's entry 24 June 1851, quoted in A. H. M. Kirk-Greene (ed.), *Barth's Travels in Nigeria: Extracts from the Journal of Heinrich Barth's Travels in Nigeria 1850-1855* (London, 1962), p. 15.

161. Johann Rebmann: On Mount Kilimanjaro (1848)

Johannes Rebmann (1820-1876), a Swabian missionary in the services of the Anglican Church Missionary Society, was the first European to penetrate Africa from its Indian Ocean coast and to discover Mount Kilimanjaro. He submitted his findings to the Royal Geographical Society, but his description of a snowcapped mountain in eastern equatorial Africa was doubted by these "experts." The account of his ascent is included in the travelogue of his associate, Johann Ludwig Krapf, another German who worked for the CMS.

May 25 (1848). I ascended today a mountain about two thousand feet high [. . .] Kilimanjaro was veiled in clouds, other wise I might have seen it invested with the silver crown, by which it seems to claim the title of king of the mountains of Eastern Africa. Before I descended from the noble mountain on which I had enjoyed so grand a view, I prayed from the depths of my heart, as regards all the populations around, — 'Thy kingdom come.' On the way back to my gloomy hut we visited several of the King's residences, which were, however, nothing more than the usual African huts covered with withered grass and impenetrable to light and air. This evening I heard the people of Jagga, too, pray to the souls of the dead, which they call Warumu; but instead of rice and palm-wine, like the Wanika, they place milk on the graves. This custom, diffused wide and far in Eastern Africa, proves a strong yearning after life in a future state. On the 26th of May Rehani, the king's vizier, came to me early, and asked me all sorts of questions respecting my supposed supernatural gifts; and as the rain kept him with me, I had time to lay before him the chief articles of our faith, so that the name of Christ has at least been named in this country, and the people know that I am His servant, and not a trafficker or dealer in magic and lies.

Source: J. L. Krapf, *Travels, Researches, and Missionary Labours during an Eighteen Years' Residence in Eastern Africa* (London, 1860), pp. 240, 241. *Further Reading:* Sundkler/Steed, *History,* pp. 510-519.

162. David Livingstone: Conversion of Sechele

The Scottish explorer and missionary David Livingstone (1813-1873) set out for Southern Africa in 1840. He reached the Zambezi in 1851. His missionary endeavors often failed. He was also not very successful among the Bakuena (in today's Botswana). However, the king of this ethnic group, Sechele, converted to Christianity. Livingstone gives the following account:

On the first occasion in which I ever attempted to hold a public religious service, he (Sechele, chief of the Bakuena) remarked that it was the custom of his nation, when any new subject was brought before them, to put questions on it; and he begged me to allow him to do the same in this case. On expressing my entire willingness to answer his questions, he inquired if my forefathers knew of a future judgment. I replied in the affirmative, and began to describe the scene of the "great white throne, and Him who shall sit on it, from whose face the Heaven and earth shall flee away," etc. He said "You startle me — these words make all my bones to shake — I have no more strength in me: but my forefathers were living at the same time yours were, and how is it that they did not send them word about these terrible things sooner? They all passed away into darkness without knowing whither they were going." I got out of the difficulty by explaining the geographical barriers in the North, and the gradual spread of knowledge from the South, to which we first had access by means of ships, and I expressed my belief that, as Christ had said, the whole world would yet be enlightened by the Gospel. Pointing to the great Kalahari desert, he said: "You never can cross that country to the tribes beyond; it is utterly impossible even for us black men, except in certain seasons, when more than the usual supply of rain falls, and an extraordinary growth of water-melons follows. Even we who know the country would certainly perish without them." Re-asserting my belief in the words of Christ, we parted; and it will be seen further on that

Sechele himself assisted me in crossing that desert which had previously proved an insurmountable barrier to so many adventures.

As soon as he had an opportunity of learning, he set himself to read with such close application that, from being comparatively thin, the effect of having been fond of the chase, he became quite corpulent from want of exercise.[. . .]

Sechele continued to make a consistent profession for about three years; and perceiving at last some of the difficulties of his case, and also feeling compassion for the poor women, who were by far the best of our scholars, I had no desire that he should be in any hurry to make a full profession by baptism, and putting away all his wives but one. [. . .]

When he at last applied for baptism, I simply asked him how he, having the Bible in his hand, and able to read it, thought he ought to act. He went home, gave each of his superfluous wives new clothing, and all his own goods, which they had been accustomed to keep in their huts for him, and sent them to their parents with an intimation that he had no fault to find with them, but that in parting with them he wished to follow the will of God. On the day on which he and his children were baptized, great numbers came to see the ceremony. Some thought, from a stupid calumny circulated by enemies to Christianity in the south, that the converts would be made to drink an infusion of "dead men's brains" and were astonished to find that water only was used at baptism.

Source: David Livingstone, *Missionary Travels and Researches in South Africa* (London: John Murray, 1857), pp. 15-18a. *Further Reading:* T. Jeal, *Livingstone* (London, 1973); A. Ross, *David Livingstone* (London/New York, 2002); Sundkler/Steed, *History,* pp. 427-438; A. F. Walls, "David Livingstone," in: G. Anderson et al., *Mission Legacies* (Maryknoll, 1994), pp. 140-147.

D. Mission Initiatives and African Rulers

163. Madagascar

a. Delegation of the King Radama I to England (1820)

The establishment of Christianity in Madagascar is bound together with the history of the kingdom of Merina, which remained independent until 1895. The London Missionary Society, founded in 1795, had made first contact there in 1820. The society postponed its 1821 annual meeting in London until May, because the Madagascar envoys had arrived and the messenger Ratefinahary had a letter from Radama I, written in Tananarivo on October 29, 1820, to deliver to the Director of the London Missionary Society.

At the time that Sir Farquhar, Governor, and I (Radama I) ratified a treaty that meant the end of the slave trade in Madagascar, a missionary, M. David Jones, accompanied by ambassadors of Great Britain, arrived in Antananarivo, the capital of my kingdom, to visit me and to ask where he could settle in my kingdom.

After careful examination of the plan for his mission, I happily agreed. [. . .] I was satisfied with the explanation from M. Jones, your missionary, who confirmed that the ambassadors of your society sought nothing other than to enlighten the spirit through conviction, to bring understanding of truth through explanation and through the search for happiness. Therefore I request from you gentlemen that you send to us as many missionaries as you are able to; they may be accompanied by their wives and children if they wish. Until then, while you are making this possible, you must send workmen with craft skills. [. . .]

I promise you that your missionaries will enjoy protection, respect and peace from my people. . . . The missionaries, who we urgently and quickly desire, are those who teach the Christian religion, but also any of a variety of workmen who are skilled in weaving, carpentry and joining, and spinning. . . . I hope, gentlemen, to receive a prompt and satisfactory answer from you. — Yours most faithfully — Radama Mpanjaka

b. Missions Prohibited by Queen Ranavalona I (1835)

In Madagascar the Bible was more and more understood as a book that held the traditions of the strangers' ancestors. Therefore missions were regarded as threatening loyalty toward the Malagasy royalty. In 1835 the widow of Radamas, Queen Ranavalona I (Ranavalomanjaka, ca. 1788-1861), sent out the following edict:

Antananarivo, February 26, 1835. To the English or French strangers: I thank you for the good that you have done in my land and my kingdom, where you have made known European wisdom and knowledge. Do not worry yourselves — I will not change the customs and rites of our ancestors. Nevertheless, whoever breaks the laws of my kingdom will be put to death — whoever he may be. I welcome all wisdom and all knowledge which are good for this country. It would be a waste time and effort to grab the customs and rites of my ancestors. Concerning religious practice — baptism or assemblies — it is forbidden for my people who inhabit this land to take part whether on Sunday or during the week. Concerning you, strangers, you can practice according to your own manners and customs. Nevertheless, if skilled handwork and other practical skills exist, which can profit our people, exercise these skills that good will come. These are my instructions which I make known to you. Ranavalomanjaka.

Prohibition for the inhabitants, not to celebrate a cult of ancestors for the forefathers of the strangers: [. . .] I do not forbid you to pray, but your customs are not those of our forefathers; you change our customs. [. . .] I will not allow this to happen in my lands and in my kingdom. So says Ranavalomanjaka.

Concerning baptism, assemblies, prayers outside of school . . . how many lords rule in this land? [. . .]

c. Resolution on Missionary Supervision

When the missionaries of the London Missionary Society returned in 1870, they wrote the following resolution:

That whilst fully and heartily embracing the principle that the church in Madagascar should be ultimately independent; whilst always acting with this principle before them; and whilst doing their utmost to raise and educate a native agency for securing this desirable end; yet the missionaries would wish to impress upon the Directors the undeniable facts, that, for some time to come, the natives must be incompetent for their duties (many of the preachers being but poor readers and worse writers), and that the number of European missionaries, including the expected additions, will be altogether inadequate to meet the present crisis and marvelous revolution in the religion of the island.

d. The Missionaries' Criticism of College Students

[. . .] They think they are equal to anything, and hence we have them swelling about and preaching with white neck ties, black gloves, gold chains, and rings etc. etc., in fact getting fairly spoiled through the grand idea of a college, whereas they could get all they get now, and a great deal more in a far more humble and satisfactory way.

Sources: (a) D. Ralibera (ed.), *Madagascar et le Christianisme* (Paris/Antananarivo, 1993), p. 202; (b) ibid., p. 226. (c) Fiangona Jesosy Kristy Madagaskara (Church of Jesus Christ in Madagaskar), Madagascar District Committee Minute Book, 21.1.1870, quoted in: B. A. Gow, *Madagascar and the Protestant Impact* (London, 1979), p. 160; (d) L. M. S. M B13/F/2: Matthews to Mullens, 25 July 1876, quoted in: Gow, p. 162. — *Further Reading:* F. Raison-Jourde, "The Madagascan Churches in the Political Arena and Their Contribution to the Change of the Regime," in: P. Gifford (ed.), *The Christian Churches and the Democratisation of Africa* (Leiden, 1995), pp. 292-301; Sundkler/Steed, *History,* pp. 487-499.

164. Buganda (Uganda)

a. Religious Debate at the Court of Uganda's King

The growth of the church in Buganda, a central part of the later Uganda, is one of the most significant chapters of African church history. The king played an important part in it right from the beginning. In 1879 Kabaka Mutesa (who ruled between 1856 and 1884) organized a debate between the Anglican missionary Alexander Mackay and the Catholic Simeon F. Lourdel. The Church Missionary Society had started work in Uganda in 1877; the White Fathers came to the East African country in 1879.

The king wanted to know more about the differences between Protestant and Catholic. Addressing himself to Father Lourdel, he said "Read me something and give me your prayer." Lourdel then took the Swahili catechism of the Holy Ghost Fathers and read the first chapters, with Mutesa listening attentively. In effect, he knew that language perfectly. When the Father finished, he slyly asked Mr. Mackay what he thought of the reading. Mackay replied: "Very good. I did notice, however, that he called the Holy Virgin the Mother of God, which is false: God, having no beginning, can not have a mother." "Excuse me," interjected Lourdel, "he did not begin as God, that's true, but he began as a man; and, when he became a man, he wished to be born of a mother." The king indicated that he understood the distinction; Mackay did not persist on that question, but shifted to another point. "The Catholics say that their leader is impeccable and thus put him in the place of God. That is impossible." Lourdel responded "Distinguish please, between impeccability and infallibility. We affirm the latter but not the former." Mackay did not persist.

b. Uganda's Martyrs: The Report of Denis Kanyukas

A third group at court were Muslim Arabs who had been there for 50 years. Although Kabaka Mutesa had twice declared Buganda an Islamic state, he mistrusted their increasing influence. This was one reason why he had decided to admit Christian missionaries into the country; his aim was to play off the three groups against each other. Under his successor Mwanga (who ruled between 1884-1897) Catholic and Anglican missionaries lost their privileged position. One reason lay in the fact that the Arabs whose trade monopoly was threatened by the European powers applied increasingly aggressive methods. In October 1885 James Hannington, the first Anglican Bishop of Eastern Equatorial Africa, was murdered by a follower of Mwanga. This was followed by persecutions of Christians of both denominations.

We set out with unconcealed joy, walking in single file; Gyavira, Mugaga, Kizito and myself, each of us with a silent prayer on his lips. After ten minutes march, we encountered Senkole and his following, their faces streaked with soot. He held in his hand the Sacred Fuse with which, as we filed past him, he tapped on the head each of those singled out for death. Me, he allowed to pass untouched, as if to say "Not fit for martyrdom! Too small, my boy." "My poor Kamyuka," whispered Mugaga to me, "you are going to miss the rendezvous in Heaven." Already, Senkole had singled out Charles Lwanga, our gallant leader, declaring, "You, I am keeping for myself, to sacrifice to Kibuka, Mukasa and Nnende. You will make a prime offering."

In taking leave of the rest of us, Charles said, "My friends, we shall before long meet again in Heaven. I stay here and go on ahead of you. Keep up your courage and persevere to the end." [. . .] When all the victims had been laid on the pyre, the executioners brought more wood, which they piled on top of them. While this was being done, I heard the Christians, each reciting the prayers which came to his mind at that supreme moment. When Mukajanga saw that all was ready, he signaled to his men to station themselves all round the pyre, and then gave the order "Light it at every point." The flames blazed up like a burning house and, as they rose, I heard coming from the pyre the murmur of the Christian's? voices as they died invoking God. From the moment of our arrest, I never saw one of them show any lack of courage. The pyre was lit towards noon.

c. Invitation to All European Nations (1890)

After unsuccessful attempts to liberate himself from the Arabs, Mwanga had to escape in 1888. He prepared his return with the help of the "Catholic party." The plan could be realized after Catholics joined forces with the Protestants who supplied arms. In the treaty of October 1889 the ministries were equally divided between Catholics and Protestants. Since Kabaka Mwanga was now interested in not becoming too dependent on one European power alone, he signed a treaty with the German Carl Peters in February 1890. When shortly afterwards an agent of the Imperial British East African Company, P. F. Jackson, arrived, Mwanga explained his standpoint to the British Consul Evans-Smith.

I inform you of the news of Uganda. How that when the Mahommedans had driven me out I dwelt on an island. I sent to Mr. Jackson to help me, and he refused, and said "I cannot help you now."

So we fought ourselves and drove them out. When I returned to Mengo Mr. Peters, the German, came and asked me for a Treaty of Commerce, and I gave it to him. Then Mr. Jackson came and wanted a Treaty to farm the Customs of the land and to put his flag up, and that I should enter into his hands, and I refused, and my people refused.

Now, I am sending two of my people to the English Consul, and the French

Consul, and the German Consul, named Samuel Mwemba and Victor Senkezi, great people at my Court, that they may know your counsel. If they want to help us, what repayment should we make to them? Because I do not want to give them (or you) my land. I want all Europeans of all nations to come to Uganda, to build and to trade as they like.

So I beg you to allow guns and powder to reach Uganda, that we may thoroughly drive out the Mahommedans. — I am, etc., Mwanga, King of Uganda

d. Further Developments: British and Protestant

In Buganda, assigned to the British sphere of influence through the Helgoland-Zanzibar treaty struck between Germany and England in 1890, civil war broke out in 1892 between Protestants and Catholics. As a result the Catholics withdrew to the southern province of Buddu; Mwanga found protection with the Germans. Since, however, the agent of the East Africa Company, Captain D. F. Lugard, wished to give greater political and economic accessibility to the area, he offered Mwanga a treaty. The Anglican pastor H. W. Kitakule reports:

I am writing to you a second time to tell you about Uganda. In my first letter I told you how we fought with the Catholics and drove out King Mwanga.

Well, when we had driven out the Catholics King Mwanga ran away and reached Kiziba, which is German territory, and remained there. We sent him many written requests that he would return to his throne, but he refused, and applied to the Germans to come and help him. They refused. So then Mwanga sent us a written proposal, saying "I wish to return to my throne," we invited him and he run away from the Catholics and returned to us and we restored him to his throne. Further we assigned to all the Catholics a district of Uganda, viz. Budu, and there they lived apart. We told them "we do not wish to mix with the Catholics again."

At the present time we Protestants have possessed ourselves of a very large district, and all the islands; and now the Mohammedans are applying to us to assign them a district, where they may settle and cease fighting with us: but the terms are not yet fully agreed upon. We hope that the Protestants will now have chief power in Uganda, and I think the land will perhaps be at peace. King Mwanga proposed to make a formal statement to us of his wish to be a Protestant, but we told him "Remain for a time in the Catholic Religion," as he was, because he was not yet a true or sincere believer. King Mwanga had hoisted the English flag and it is now flying before his house.

e. Triumph Song of the Ugandan Protestants

I don't want to sit where a papist sits
I don't want to eat where a papist eats
I don't want to dip my fingers in the same plate with a papist
For we the English defeated the papists.

Sources: (a) J. Mercui, L'Ouganda, la Mission Catholique et les Agents de la Compagnie Anglaise, 1893, 10-11 quoted in: D. Robinson/D. Smith, *Sources of the African Past* (New York, 1979), pp. 92-93. (b) D. A. Low (ed.), *The Mind of Buganda: Documents of the Modern History of an African Kingdom* (Berkeley/Los Angeles, 1971), pp. 11-12. (c) Public Record Office, London, F. O. 84/2064, quoted in Low, ibid., p. 26; (d) Zanzibar Secretariat Archives E. 143, quoted in Low, ibid., p. 27; (e) Q. J. Waliggo, "The Catholic Church in the Buddu Province of Buganda 1879-1925," Ph.D. thesis, Cambridge, 1976, D. 85-85, quoted in Hastings, *Africa*, p. 465. *Further Reading:* Hastings, *Africa*, pp. 371-385; Isichei, pp. 145-150.

E. African Christian Elite

165. West Africa

a. Samuel Ajayi Crowther: Concerns (1860)

Former slaves played an important role in the formation of the West African Christian elite. Samuel Ayaji Crowther, who was ordained as the first black African Anglican bishop (see document 150), became a symbolic figure. In 1860 he expressed concerns about taking over this position:

1. I am totally unfit. 2. The European missionaries have a greater claim to this right than any native has. 3. As man I know something of the feeling of man. . . . The plan of placing a native in a higher position where Europeans have to take a part . . . is very premature. 4. The use that has been made of my name in the English News Papers when the Bishopric of S. Leone was vacant has not done me good in this mission. 5. I myself never for a moment felt that I was called. . . . 6. My own young family claims my attention in their settlement of life.

b. O. Payne: The Significance of Bishop Crowther (1892)

During the 1880s, Bishop Crowther was deprived of power by young English missionaries who tried to legitimate their actions by pointing to problems in the Niger Mission. When Crowther died on December 31st, 1891, it took a long time (60 years!) until the next African Anglican bishop was ordained. Representatives of the African Christian elite were vehemently opposed to the evaluation of Crowther's episcopate as unsuccessful. The clergy and representative laymen of the Lagos native church expressed their protest in a Memorial of December 7, 1892, addressed to the Archbishop of Canterbury and the proper authorities of the Church of England.

The Episcopate of the late Bishop Crowther was in our humble opinion a successful one. It covered the space of 27 years, whilst before it was constituted, the Bishop, who was an ordinary clergyman had founded the Niger Mission in 1857, had always been its leader. The facts of his Mission — e.g., thousands of converts won from the most debasing kind of heathenism and idolatry, and many of them from cannibalism, infanticide and other cruel practices, also; Christian congregations, Churches and Schools here and there in what was before a moral and spiritual wilderness; Niger-born Native agents among those serving the Mission and Church, and the aggressive character of the profession of Christianity by those converts especially in the Delta, and all this within the last 32 years-facts testified by all who know the Niger. [. . .] This success, we respectfully submit, supplies a warrant for the continuation of the Native Episcopate.

The elevation of the late Bishop Crowther to the Episcopate in 1864, was declared by the C.M.S. which, under God, was mainly instrumental in bringing it about, . . . to be an experiment to prove the capacity of negroes for evangelizing important sections of the African Continent by themselves, and without the stimulus of the presence and supervision of Europeans, and for exercising the higher offices in the Church — an experiment whose success was very generally desired in England, especially on account of the very heavy mortality which had always prevailed among European missionaries in the African mission all through its long course. The clergy and lay agents that worked under this Episcopate, which was often exercised amidst circumstances of peculiar difficulty and trial, were almost always natives.

But attempts have been made the last few years on account of moral weakness discovered in some of the infant Churches that have been gathered in, and serious faults in some of the agents and the like, to pronounce the experiment a failure, and the negro incapable of a responsible trust and for an independent life; and, in spite of the century of training and teaching he has had, unfit still to be set free from his pupilage and the leading strings of European superintendence.

We on our part do not find ourselves able to subscribe to this pronouncement with the facts of the mission to which we have already referred before us, and also the fact that some of the Apostolic Churches of which we read in Scripture were not exempt from serious faults. [. . .]Christianity has seen about a century in West Africa generally, and yet it to this day wears the character of an exotic. [. . .] It is our conviction that one of the reasons for the character which Christianity now manifests in Africa is the fact that it has been held too long in a state of dependence; and that it has been too long in the habit of look-ing to its foreign parent for immediate guidance and direction in almost every-thing, and this, you will admit, does not make much for the development of that manly independence and self-reliance which are so essential for the devel-opment of a strong people and a vigorous institution.

c. James Africanus Horton: Africa's Potential (1868)

Dr. James Africanus Horton (1835-1883) also came from a family of liberated slaves and grew up in Freetown (Sierra Leone). After the completion of his studies in medicine in London and Edinburgh he worked for the British army in Ghana. From 1865 onwards he wrote about political themes. Although he regarded British rule and Christian mission as useful for Africa, he emphasized the abilities of the Africans for self-government

Rome was not built in a day, the proudest kingdom in Europe was once in a state of barbarism worse than now exists amongst the tribes chiefly inhabiting the West Coast of Africa, and it is an inconvertible axiom that what has been done can again been done. If Europe, therefore, has been raised to her present pitch of civilization by progressive advancement, Africa too, with a guarantee of the civilization of the North, will rise into equal importance. The nucleus has been planted, it is just beginning to show signs of life and future vigour; it shouts out legitimate as well as extraneous buds. Political capital is made of the latter by narrow-minded persons; whilst the liberal-minded, with more philos-ophy and generosity, make ample allowances for these defects, and encourage the legitimate growth. We may well say that the present state of Western Africa is, in fact, the history of the world repeating itself.

Source: (a) Archive of the Church Missionary Society, Birmingham: Crowther to Venn April 4, 1860, quoted in: P. Beyerhaus, *Die Selbständigkeit der jungen Kirchen als missionarisches Problem* (Wuppertal-Barmen, 1956), p. 133; (b) Memorial, dated Dec. 7, 1892, addressed to the Arch-bishop of Canterbury and the proper authorities of the Church of England, from the clergy and representative laymen of the Lagos native church, published in: T. Hodgkin, *Nigerian Perspec-tives* (London, [2]1975) pp. 309ff; (c) J. A. Horton, Letters on the Political Condition of the Gold Coast since the Exchange of Territory between the English and Dutch Governments, on January 1, 1868, in: Africanus Horton, *The Dawn of Nationalism in Modern Africa* (chosen and intro-duced by Davidson Nicol) (London: Longman, 1969), p. 177. — *Further Reading:* F. Ludwig, *Kirche im kolonialen Kontext. Anglikanische Missionare und afrikanische Propheten im südöstlichen Nigeria, 1879-1918* (Frankfurt/Bern, 1992).

166. South African Voices

a. Tiyo Soga: Race Discrimination in South Africa (1857)

After completing his studies at Lovedale (South Africa), Glasgow and Edinburgh, Tiyo Soga (1829-1871) was ordained as the first African Presbyterian minister in 1856. After his return to South Africa in 1857, he wrote about race discrimination.

The prejudices here against colour, which I anticipated, gave way on my arrival in a most remarkable manner, so far as I am personally concerned. [. . .] I have found that only in Britain the Black man is admitted to be quite as capable of mental and moral improvement as the white man. In this colony, as in America, by a strange perversion of logic, some men seem to argue in relation to the black man: "Dark in face, therefore dark in mind."

b. John Tengo Jabavu: New Forms of Slavery (1889)

John Tengo Jabavu (1859-1921) was born at Healdtown and later attended the famous Wesleyan School there. In 1883, he passed the high school examinations conducted by the University of the Cape. According to Jabavu, *Imvo*, published in Xhosa and English, was read throughout southern Africa.

When a Native young man begins to read English literature, he should take to easy and entertaining books such as Voyages and Travels, especially those written by persons who visited unknown lands for the first time. The Discovery of the New World by Columbus, Lord Ansons's Voyage Round the World, Captain Cook's Voyages and John William's Missionary Enterprise, are books of this class. The trash of so-called adventures, written by litterateurs like Ballantine and Kingston should be shunned. They are mere dreams written by persons who never saw one of the countries they pretend to describe. [. . .]

There are . . . reasons of a special kind why Kafir young men should learn from books the social problems of the Native races in other parts of the world. Here (South Africa) there is a hostile (Afrikaner) bond who seek to deprive the Natives of education and to cut them out of all hold on the soil. Experience elsewhere shows, that this means perpetual slavery not of the bondsman, now abolished, but slavery of the nominal freeman, who as he cannot own a foot of ground must yield up to the landlord all the fruits of his labour in return for the merest pittance on which a human being can live.

Source: (a) A. Chalmers, *Tiyo Soga: The Model Kaffir Missionary* (London, 1897) p. 147, quoted in: J. M. Chirenje, *Ethiopianism and Afro-Americans in Southern Africa, 1883-1916* (Baton Rouge/ London, 1987), p. 16; (b) J. T. Jabavu, "Education through Books," Editorial, *Imvo Zabatsundu*,

Aug. 29, Sept. 5, 1889, quoted in: J. M. Chirenje, ibid., pp. 33f. — For more important source material see J. W. Hofmeyr/J. A. Millard/J. J. Froneman (eds.), *History of the Church in South Africa: A Document and Source Book* (Pretoria, 1991) — *Further Reading:* D. Williams, *Umfundisi: A Biography of Tiyo Soga 1829-1871* (Lovedale, 1978); D. Williams (ed.), *The Journal and Selected Writings of the Reverend Tiyo Soga* (Cape Town, 1983); C. Saunders (ed.), *Black Leaders in Southern Africa* (London, 1979), pp. 127-156; D. D. T. Jabavu, *The Life of John Tengo Jabavu* (Lovedale, 1922).

IV. AFRICA 1890-1945

A. "Scramble for Africa"

The "Scramble for Africa" characterizes the period of intensified European rivalry which led to the partition of Africa among European colonial powers. The opening of this phase is usually linked to the Berlin "Congo" Conference (1884/85), called at the invitation of Germany and France, at which were discussed the conditions of trade in West Africa and traffic regulations on the Congo and the Niger rivers. Even before 1885, however, an increase in political interventions due to worsened economic conditions can be observed. At the end of the scramble, there were only two independent states in Africa: Ethiopia and Liberia.

167. Declarations of Intentions and Objectives

a. Cecil Rhodes: The Englishmen as Tools of God

Cecil Rhodes (1863-1902) was one of the main protagonists of British imperialism. It was mainly due to his initiative that Bechuanaland (Botswana) became a British colony. When he was prime minister of the Cape colony (1890-1896) the British South Africa Company which he had founded acquired Rhodesia (Zimbabwe and Zambia).

I contend that we are the first race in the world, and that the more of the world we inhabit the better it is for the human race. I contend that every acre added to our territory means the birth of more of the English race who otherwise would not have been brought into existence. Added to this, the absorption of the greater portion of the world, under our rule, simply means the end of all wars. [. . .]

Therefore, if there be a God, and He cares anything about what I do, I think it is clear that he would like me to do what He is doing Himself. And as He is manifestly fashioning the English speaking race as the chosen instrument by which He will bring in a state of society based upon Justice, Liberty and Peace, He must obviously wish me to do what I can to give as much scope and power to that race as possible. Hence, if there be a God, I think what he would like me to do is to paint as much of the map of Africa British red as possible, and to do what I can elsewhere to promote the unity and extend the influence of the English-speaking race.

b. A. Mackay: England's Destiny as a "Christian Nation" (1886)

Many missionaries supported the imperialist claims of their homelands. Alexander Mackay (1849-1890), leader of the Church Missionary Society in Uganda, not only forcibly advocated Buganda's incorporation into the British East India Company's sphere of influence, but also engaged in general reflections on the task of Europeans in Africa.

Can nothing be done to waken our Christian land from its lethargy regarding the sufferings and dreadful wrongs endured by our helpless fellow-Christians in Africa? Will you all allow them to continue to be murdered, and tortured, and hunted for their lives for decades of years, merely because they are far away, and it will cost a little diplomacy, and a little effort, and perhaps a little expense, to secure them the bare rights due to humanity? I can scarcely believe it. [. . .] We cannot fail to see that England can only fulfill her destiny as a Christian nation by occupying herself continually, at home and abroad, in furthering the cause of Christ. As private individuals, we are to spread the truth and relieve the distressed, and by our lives adorn the doctrine of holiness. As a nation, we are to bring the weight of our influence and power to bear, on a larger scale, on the evils existing among our masses at home and the dark places of the earth abroad. These are beyond the power of private effort.

c. Friedrich Fabri: "A New India" (1879)

In Germany the call for colonies — a "place in the sun" — was expressed by missionaries and in mission strategies. Colonial politics, economic and missionary interests were intermingled to some extent for Friedrich Fabri (1824-1891), inspector of the Rhenish mission from 1857 to 1884, a distinguished publicist on expansion and a colonial politician.

Now should Germany, being in need of colonial possessions, not participate mightily in the competition that has arisen especially in these extensive lands [in central Africa]? . . . Central Africa can indeed become a new India. . . . But first, a very important piece is missing: the mass cultivation of valuable products. Her population must be stimulated, if not educated, to their cultivation by increased demands. . . . Above all, mission endeavors of a practical pedagogical character, such as educating to work, would be valuable here; next and with that [would be] capital and people for plantations and large trade undertakings. [. . .] If our German trade estate wants to take part in the development and exploitation of Central Africa, then the significance of establishing German mission settlements at suitable locations on the west and east coasts cannot be underestimated.

d. Colonization and Mission in German East Africa (1886)

The most important mission society to be established from colonial political motives was the "Evangelical Mission Society for German-East Africa." The African traveler and colonial propagandist Carl Peters (1856-1918) played a role in its 1886 founding.

A short while ago, the German-East Africa Evangelical Mission Society was called into existence in Berlin, a new [mission] field was opened to the German mission efforts. . . . From now on an opportunity will be given to to him [i.e., the German missionary] to work where the fatherland was beginning to lay down new roots. No longer will a foreign country, hostile to all German efforts, reap what German industry and German work has sewn.

e. Warning against a Nationalist Understanding of Missions (1885)

Within the German mission, there were other voices than those of Fabri and Peters. The conference of the German mission society welcomed colonial occupation, but at the same time they warned against a nationalistic understanding of the tasks of evangelization.

1. The representatives of the boards of the German mission societies who gathered in Bremen felt themselves compelled to publicly proclaim their thankful appreciation that their missionaries who had worked in English, Dutch and Danish colonies had always received the same protection from the respective colonial governments and the same benevolent welcome as had been extended to the missionaries from their own nations. 2. They [the supervisors] at the same time speak of the hope that the German colonial governments in the newly acquired regions will protect and support not only the German mission ventures, but also, in recognition of the international character of missions, that they extend the same benevolent treatment to the missions of other nationalities as the German missionaries had received earlier from foreign colonial governments.

f. Bruno Gutmann on the Lutheran Mission (1909)

For some time in German Lutheran mission circles the idea of the "order of creation" was stressed. Bruno Gutmann (1876-1966), who was a representative of those associated with this mission concept, was active from 1903 to 1920 and again from 1925 to 1939 in the central region of Kilimanjaro (Tanzania) for the Leipzig mission. Gutmann regarded the life-styles and traditions of the Africans as God-given and benevolent. In his view, the assignment of the mission was to spread faith and at the same time to preserve the traditional social order and the traditional culture. While on the one hand this concept contributed to an appreciation of the African culture, on the other hand it left little room for development and could also be interpreted as racist.

The wide breach created by a new culture, often only technically superimposed, significantly endangers the independent development of these native peoples, and with an external assimilation rashly achieved causes even greater internal devastation. Because of this, forces in themselves harmful within these cultural stream find little hindrance and resistance in the spirit of the people. These forces get at the people's life-nerve before impulses for renewal have found time to unite with a people still healthy and open to development, or to fertilize and nurture it toward further, indigenous development. [. . .] And the Lutheran mission which in itself embodies the growth impulses of Lutheran Christianity, may maintain as its essential characteristic that it seeks to preserve understanding for everything vital that belongs to a people and would like to see the spiritual powers of that people involved in constructing a new moral and religious world view in custom and use.

g. Portuguese Colonial Mission in Mozambique (1896)

The Portuguese Mission of the Catholic Church was without any doubt on the side of the colonial power. This becomes evident in the instructions of the Marine and Overseas Ministry to Bishop Barros in 1896:

The Missions shall assume the character of national institutions, thus always being obligatory in: 1. their subordination to the Bishop of Mozambique; 2. the use and teaching of the Portuguese language; 3. always having the Portuguese flag hoisted at the Centre of the Mission; 4. the defence of the rights of Portuguese sovereignty, in their propaganda and exercising their missionary functions 5. rendering all their assistance to Portuguese authorities, to which is due their subordination in general terms.

Source: (a) W. T. Stead (ed.), *The Last Will and Testament of C. J. Rhodes* (London, 1902), pp. 57f, 97f. (b) A. MacKay to his father, Uganda, July 11, 1886, in A. M. Harrison/A. MacKay, *Pioneer*

Missionary of the Church Missionary Society in Uganda (London, 1970), pp. 280-283; (c) F. Fabri, *Bedarf Deutschland der Colonien? Eine politisch-okonomische Betrachtung* (Gotha, 1879), quoted in: Raupp, *Mission*, pp. 412ff; (d) "Mission in Ostafrika," in: *Kolonial-politische Correspondenz 1886*, quoted in: Raupp, *Mission*, pp. 414-417; (e) Resolution of the Conference for German Missions on Nov. 29, 1885, cp. Raupp, *Mission*, pp. 418f; (f) B. Gutmann, *Dichten und Denken der Dschagga-Neger*, 1909; Foreword, quoted in: Ernst Jäschke, *Gemeindeaufbau in Afrika. Die Bedeutung Bruno Gutmanns für das afrikanische Christentum* (Stuttgart, 1981), pp. 35f; (g) Minister of Marine and Overseas Affaires an Bischof D. Antonio Barroso, 23.6.1896, quoted in: A. Brásio, D. Antonio Barroso, *Missionário, Cientista, Missiólogo* (Lissabon, 1961), pp. 595f; English translation in: A. Helgesson, *Church, State and People in Mozambique* (Uppsala, 1994), p. 101. — Further Reading: K. J. Bade, *Imperialismus und Kolonialmission* (1982); A. Porter, "Missions and Empire," in: Gilley/Stanley, *World Christianities*, pp. 560-575; A. Porter (ed.), *The Imperial Horizons of British Protestant Missions 1880-1914* (2003); B. Stanley, *The Bible and the Flag* (1990); J. C. Winter, *Bruno Gutmann 1876-1966* (1979).

168. Rebellion and "Pacification Efforts"

a. Namibia: Herero-Nama Rebellion (1904)

As the structure of the colonial system penetrated more and more into African life, there was increasing primary resistance. The colonial powers reacted to this with "pacification" efforts. The 1904 Hereo-Nama rebellion in German Southwest Africa (Namibia) was especially brutally put down. The Rhenish Mission (Rheinische Mission) had contributed to compel chiefs such as the Nama captain, Hendrik Witbooi, to acknowledge German rule. (1) On November 14, 1904, Witbooi, after appealing to God, withdrew the protectorate treaty agreement. (2) While remaining loyal to the colonial power, the missionaries drew attention to the social causes of the rebellion of Hereros. (3) Therefore, the Rhenish mission was considered as hostile in colonial chauvinistic circles. This is indicated in the article in the *Koloniale Zeitschrift*.

(1) [H. Witbooi: "God has heard our weeping"] "As you point out, I have for ten years stood in your law, under your law, and behind your law — and not I alone but all the chiefs of Africa. For this reason I fear God the Father. All the souls which have for the last ten years perished from all the nations of Africa and from among all the chiefs, without guilt or cause, and under treaties of peace, accuse me, I will have to answer a great reckoning to God Our Father in Heaven. He has heard our weeping and the prayers and sighs, and he has redeemed us, for I stood in front of him and asked him to wipe our tears away in his own time. God in Heaven has now broken the contract."

(2) [The missionaries of the Rhenish Mission concerning the matter of the rebellion:] The system used by many white traders of excessive credit and its consequences — the continued cattle and land foreclosures, [is] a system that

... of necessity must bring about the economic decline of the black African people [. . .]. For many years we have already seen in these notoriously well-known evils the source of growing bitterness toward the indigenous people, and we see in them now at least one of the main causes of the horrible rebellion. [. . .] The Hereros grasped onto this last desperate means, because their existence was simply being undercut.

(3) [*Koloniale Zeitschrift:* "The mission has become black"] The mission [possesses] . . . the impertinence to advocate for the colored rabble, that not even the tiniest hair of their head might be crumpled. . . , whereas a holy wrath should wreak havoc [among the vermin], so their lust to burn, murder and rob will be driven out for all times. [. . .] the Mission has become black and stands against the whites in the protectorate. [. . .] The German mission has damaged our colonial efforts in the extreme.

b. Ghana: The "Christian Companies" of the Basel Mission

In other places the mission societies supported battle efforts directly. In 1874, and again in 1896 and 1900, so-called "Christian companies" of the Basel mission congregations participated in the English campaigns against the Asante. In the 1900 campaign the Englishman, Captain Benson, asked the missionaries of the mission station in Begoro for advice and help. Otto Lädrach reported about the consultation as follows:

The result of our consultation . . . with Captain Benson was the decision of the station's conference to place me with the indigenous Christians under his command and to prove to the English government that, as before, the Basel mission was also ready in this time to serve and to help as needed with the best possible forces to secure peace in the land and to promote the well-being of the negor people. The captain fully agreed with our proposal to unite the negroe Christians of all Akem villages into a "Christian company" so that they might better stick together, and might be less exposed to pagan temptations. The experiences made before with such "Christian companies" on the Gold Coast had not been bad, otherwise the English government would not have instructed the legislative body in Bern to warmly thank the mission committee in Basel for the energetic achievements of the Christian negroes, who had provided good and worthwhile service.

Source: (a1) Hendrik Witbooi Papers 1989, 159, quoted in F. Ansprenger, *Politische Geschichte Afrikas im 20. Jahrhundert* (München, 1997), p. 14; (a2) G. Haußleiter, "Der Sturm im Hereroland" in: *Berichte der Rheinischen Missionsgesellschaft* (Barmen, 1904), pp. 105-110, quoted in: Raupp, *Mission,* pp. 429f; (a3) "Unsere Gouverneure" (in: *Koloniale Zeitschrift* 1904, 78f), quoted in: Raupp, *Mission,* p. 430; (b) O. Lattrach, *Im Lande des Goldenen Stuhls: Erinnerungen aus Afrika* (Basel, 1920), quoted in: H. W. Debrunner, *Schweizer im kolonialen Afrika* (Basel, 1991), p. 70. — *Further Reading:* H. Drechsler, *Let Us Die Fighting: The Struggle of* the *Herero and Nama against German Imperialism, 1884-1915* (London, 1980); R. I. Rotberg/A. A. Mazrui (eds.), *Protest and Power in Black Africa* (New York, 1970); M. Crowder, *West African Resistance* (London, 1971); also the case study of Hargreaves and Ranger in: H. L. Gann/P. Duignan (eds.), *Colonialism in Africa*, vol. 1 (Cambridge, 1969), pp. 199-219, 293-324.

169. African Christians and Adaptation of European Ideas

a. Carl Christian Reindorf: "Rule, Britannia," 1895

The opposite pole to resistance was collaboration and assimilation to European ways of life. Especially the emerging Christian elites, who often owed their status to the missions were oriented to European values. In doing this, they were selective. In West Africa, for instance, many African Christians supported the idea of British imperialism. Appeals to the ideal of freedom could offer some protection against colonial encroachments and support their own emancipation efforts. An example is the poem of the African pastor C. C. Reindorf who worked for the Basel Mission in the Gold Coast:

Rule, supremely rule, Britannia, rule
Thy acquired colony on the Gold Coast!
Protected from the tyrant and the slaver
By blood of the noble sons shed on fields,
Besides thousands and thousands of pounds.
Destined by Heaven to have the rule,
Godly, justly, fatherly, therefore rule.
For years and years ago hadst thou to spend
And nothing, or at least not much to gain
Because the Danes and the Dutch
Had each their government on the Gold Coast.
The foes by land and sea hast thou vanquished;
Two inner and dangerous foes exist:
Ignorance and funeral custom.
The policy to allow ignorance
To exist and then to rule, rule at ease,
Is never the spirit of Britannia.
By thee no nation e'er was paralysed.
Its mission's duty the gospel to preach,
The government's classical education.
One word, and the funeral custom will die,
And all will sing "Rule, Britannia, rule!"
Superstition will then flee far away,
And Christianity will rule supremely.

b. Togo: Pastor Robert Kwamis' Luther Play (1900)

There were also Africans who were regarded as being especially "German friendly." Included in this group were colleagues of the Northern German Mission such as Pastor Robert Kwami (1879-?), who had been educated from 1894-1897 at Westheim in Württemberg. He presented a key episode in German church history in his homeland Togo, albeit in an Africanized form. In 1900 Superintendent D. A. Schreiber reported as follows:

Four groups of actors entered the broad square of the station at the same time. Depicted on a banner off to one side was the stronghold of Freiberg where a knight lay with his soldiers. At the announcement that Tetzel would be coming to sell indulgences, the soldiers hurried to Tetzel to confess their sins and receive indulgences. Last of all, the knight himself went there to receive an indulgence for a sin which he wanted to commit. Thereupon Tetzel withdrew from his followers, and the knight together with his soldiers also withdrew to a place in the shadows, and Tetzel took his money box. In the meantime, Luther, who had seen and heard all of this, had nailed his 95 Theses to the church. A young student carried a sign with the inscription: Wittenberg. Thereupon the knight turned around, read the theses, and became more than a little excited. A soldier brought Luther the message: "You must leave for Worms immediately!" His students wanted to hold him back, but he went to the Diet at Worms, whose proceedings were exactly like an African 'palaver,' that is, when a case is tried. Luther gave his defense and was mercifully dismissed by the emperor. At the end, all of the participants in the play sang, "A Mighty Fortress is our God." The actors were very proud and the audience was very pleased; the entire event under the palms was an extremely and splendidly colorful picture in the light of the setting sun.

Source: (a) C. C. Reindorf, *History of the Gold Coast and Asante* (Basel, 1895), p. 341; (b) E. Reinke, *Ein afrikanischer Zeuge Jesus Christi: aus dem Leben und Wirken von Robert S. Kwami, Pastor und Präses der Ewekirche in Togo, Westafrika* (Bremen, 1932), pp. 5f. — *Further Reading:* W. Ustorf, *Die Missionsmethode Franz Michael Zahns und der Aufbau kirchlicher Strukturen in Westafrika (1862-1900): eine missionsgeschichtliche Untersuchung* (Erlangen, 1989), pp. 266-270; F. Ludwig, "Zwischen Vereinnahmung und Selbstbehauptung," in: *Zeitschrift für Missions- und Religionswissenschaft* 2 (2002), pp. 98-114.

B. Concepts of Ecclesiastical Independence

170. Ethiopianism in West Africa

The concept "Ethiopianism" denotes African Christian communities which at the end of the nineteenth century in South and West Africa broke from the European mission churches primarily because of racial discrimination but which remained similar to them in organization, dogmatic position and liturgical forms. A key text for the Ethiopian movement was Acts 8, which was interpreted by Edward Wilmot Blyden (1832-1912) in 1882. Blyden, who was born in the West Indies, became an outstanding scholar, Pan-Africanist and politician in West Africa. After Bishop Crowther had been deprived of power, Blyden also became one of the leading advocates of African Independent Churches (cf. document 165b).

a. E. W. Blyden, "Philip and the Eunuch" (1882)

It is evident that the Gospel of Jesus Christ is designed for all countries and all climes — for all nations and races; but it is also evident that we have this treasure in earthen vessels, which subjects it to human conditions and limitations. The constitutions of mortal men, who are to be instruments of proclaiming the glad tidings, are now adapted to all countries and climates; yet the command is "Go ye into all the world and preach the gospel to every creature (Mk 16:15)." This was the parting injunction of the Saviour to His disciples. But he had told them before, that the Spirit of Truth, whom He would send to them after his departure, would explain what he had said unto them, and guide them unto all truth. Now, after the Spirit had come, and had filled the disciples with power for their mission, and they began to organise for aggressive work, it was found necessary to add to the number of evangelistic agents. Accordingly, under the direct inspiration of the Holy Spirit, seven men were chosen as evangelists, among whom was Philip. This man, after the murder of Stephen, went away from Jerusalem, and preached with great success in the city of Samaria. The injunction not to enter into any city of the Samarians had been withdrawn, and the whole world was now opened to the preachers of the gospel. They went over into Europe, penetrated farther eastward into Asia, went south to Arabia. But there lay Ethiopia, with its inhospitable climate and difficulty of access. What was to be done? The Spirit which was to guide them into all truth met the emergency. An African had come up in search of truth to Jerusalem, and, having completed his mission, was returning to his home, and was so far on his journey as to have reached the southern confines of the Holy Land, when Philip the Evangelist received a message concerning him: "The angel of the Lord spake unto Philip, saying, Arise and go toward the south, unto the way that goeth down from Jerusalem unto Gaza, which is desert. And he arose and went, and behold a man of Ethiopia, an eunuch of great authority under Candace, queen of the Ethiopians, who had the charge of all her treasure, and had come to Jerusalem for to worship, was returning; and, sitting in his chariot, red Esaias the prophet. Then the Spirit said unto Philip, Go near und join thyself to this chariot."

Now, this incident I take to be a symbolic one, indicating the instruments and the methods of Africa's evangelization. The method, the simple holding up of Jesus Christ; the instrument, the African himself. This was the Spirit's application and explication of the command. "Go ye into all the world" etc. — giving the gospel to a man of Ethiopia to take back to the people of Ethiopia.

We are told that after the singular and interesting ceremony, "The Spirit of the Lord caught away Philip, that the eunuch saw him no more; and he went on his way rejoicing." Philip was not to accompany the eunuch, to water the seed he had planted, to cherish and supervise the incipient work. If he desired to do so — and perhaps he did — the Spirit suffered him not, for he caught him away.

b. James Johnson: Christian Revival in Africa

Even if he never belonged to an African Independent Church, the Anglican James Johnson (1835-1917) can be counted among the leading representatives of Ethiopianism. In his writings he demanded the emancipation of African congregations from European control. In 1892 he established the Anglican Niger Delta Native Pastorate Church which was outside of missionary control. In 1900 he became assistant bishop. He advocated a stronger integration of Christianity into African culture, such as retention of African names after baptism, moderate stance toward polygamy.

Africa is to rise once more; Ethiopia is to stretch out her hands unto God, her tears are to be wiped off her eyes; her candlestick is to be replaced; her scores of Cathedrals and Bishops are to be restored, her Christian colleges are to be re-established, her native literature is to revive, and science again is to dwell in her, the word of the Lord above all is to cover her as the waters do the mighty deep: where this shall be the case then she will take her place with the most Christian, civilized and intelligent nations of the Earth.

c. James Johnson: Church Union Perspectives in Nigeria

At the fifth Lambeth Conference, the central assembly of Anglican bishops in London in 1908, Johnson urged union of the Nigerian churches.

You have created institutions in the country in connection with our different churches, but there is this before us. We are a poor people, we are not rich. Here the Church of England has its own institutions, and other churches have their own institutions in the same country, in the same district, it may be in the same town. The number of our Christians is small. We cannot keep up these institutions ourselves when you withdraw, and you cannot always be supporting us. We want to be independent, and not only independent, but self-governed. But how can we do this when we are divided in the way we are divided? I am most anxious to see the time when we shall be united, and I cannot express my joy at the discussion of this subject of the reunion of divided Christians in Europe here, because it will have a great effect upon us in the mission field, where I think every day we need to become united and become a strong Church.

d. Mojola Agbebi: Inaugural Sermon in the "African Church" (1902)

The background of Mojola Agbebi's (1860-1917) family also lay in Sierra Leone. He had an interesting ecclesiastical career — from 1868 to 1877 he was first a student and then a teacher in schools of the Church Missionary Society in Lagos, before he was employed by the Catholic Mission in Porto Novo. Afterwards, he worked for the Methodists and then for the Baptists. From 1888 onwards he began establishing his own independent churches. Agbebi is one of the pioneers of African nationalism, which he expressed in his personal life by taking on an African name (originally he was David Brown Vincent) and by wearing African clothes.

[. . .] Tastes differ. English tunes and metres, English songs and hymns, some of them most unsuited to African aspiration and intelligence, have proved effective in weakening the talent for hymnology among African Christians. In one of the churches planted up-country, I have found necessary to advise that for seven years, at least, no hymn books but original hymns should be used at worship. African Christians dance to foreign music in their social festivities, they sing to foreign music in their churches, they march to foreign music in their funerals, and use foreign instruments to cultivate their musical aspirations. [. . .] We are come to the times when religious developments demand original songs and original tunes from the African Christian.

[. . .] The African Moslem, our co-religionist, though he reads the Koran in Arabic and counts his beads as our Christian brother the Roman Catholic does, and though he repeats the same formula of prayer in an unknown tongue from mosques and minarets five times a day throughout Africa, yet he spreads no common prayer before him in his devotions and carries no hymn book in his worship of the Almighty. His dress is after the manner of the Apostles and Prophets, and his name, though indicating his faith, was never put on in a way to denationalize or degrade him. Islam is the religion of Africa. Christianity lives here by sufferance. [. . .] European Christianity is a dangerous thing. What do you think of a religion which holds a bottle of gin in one hand and a Common Prayer in another? Which carries a glass of rum as a vade-mecum to a 'Holy' book? A religion which points with one hand to the skies, bidding you 'lay up for yourselves treasures in heaven,' and while you are looking up grasps all your worldly goods with the other hand, seizes your ancestral lands, labels your forests, and places your patrimony under inexplicable legislations? A religion which indulges in swine's flesh and yet cries 'Be ye holy, for I am holy.' A religion which prays against 'those evils which the craft and subtlety of the devil or man worketh against us,' and yet effects to deny incantation, charms or spells and satanism — a religion which arrogates to itself censorial functions on sexual morality, and yet promotes a dance, in which one man's wife dances in close contact, questionable proximity and improper attitude with another women's husband. O! Christianity, what enormities are committed in thy name.

Source: (a) E. W. Blyden, "Philip and the Eunuch: Discourse Delivered in the United States in 1882," in: E. W. Blyden, *Christianity, Islam and the Negro Race* (Edinburgh, 1887, 1967), pp. 160f; (b) C. M. S. CA1/09(a), "Text of Sermon Preached by the Rev. James Johnson at Trinity Church, Kissy Road on 13 May 1867 on Behalf of the Native Pastorate Auxiliary," quoted in: E. A. Ayandele, *Holy Johnson: Pioneer of African Nationalism 1836-1917* (New York, 1970), p. 45. (c) Lambeth Palace Library, LC 66, Proceedings of the Fifth Lambeth Conference, 9th July 1908; (d) M. Agbebi, Inaugural Sermon (New York, 1903). Delivered at the celebration of the anniversary of the 'African Church', Lagos, 21 December 1902, in: A. Langley, pp. 72-77. — *Further Reading:* (a) H. R. Lynch, *Edward Wilmot Blyden* (London, 1970); (b) E. A. Ayandele, *Holy Johnson: Pioneer of African Nationalism 1836-1917* (London, 1970); (e) A. Akiwowo, "The Place of Mojola Agbebi in the African Nationalist Movements 1890-1917," *Phylon* (Atlanta, 1965), pp. 122-139. *General:* O. U. Kalu, "Ethiopianism and the Roots of Modern African Christianity," in: Gilley/Stanley, *World Christianities*, pp. 576-592.

171. Ethiopianism in South Africa

a. Nehemia Tile's Thembu Church

One of the first Ethiopianist Churches in South Africa was founded by Nehemia Tile, who broke away in 1882 from the Wesleyan Methodist Church to form the Thembu National Church with the chief, Ngangelizwe, as the head of the church. Tile died in 1891 and on his tombstone he is called the "Founder of the Ethiopian Church of Africa in 1884." A description of his church is given by another early independent leader, the Rev. L. N. Mzimba, in 1926:

The first definite movement of the independent spirit started forty-two years ago. Rev. Nehemia Tile separated himself from the Wesleyan Church, and

founded a Church of his own organization. We are told that his movement began with Native assistants. Their position was a trying one. In many stations
they did most of the work, but as they were not ordained, they could not celebrate marriages, baptize, or dispense the Lord's Supper. They had also a lower
salary and status than the White missionary. They felt much more isolated both
from the blacks and whites. Being somewhat educated they wished to better
their position, and the more ambitious wished to make a rapid ascent of the social ladder. They also had an awakening sense of power and racial responsibility.
Social and political avenues were closed against them, but the Church seemed
to offer a highway to increased influence. They were no doubt also moved by
the bearing of the white man, many of whom would not worship in the same
building as them.

b. "Ethiopia shall soon stretch out her hands unto God"

The most often quoted Bible passage in regard to the Ethiopian Movement is the promise in Psalm 68:31 "Princes shall come out of Egypt; Ethiopia shall soon stretch out her
hands unto God," to which the "Petition to God" of the New Kleinfontein and Boksburg
Native Vigilance Association of 1908 refers:

We feel that our sympathies should be broad enough to include the whole of
the African races when we approach our Maker. For instance, the atrocities
which our brethren are suffering under the administration of the Congo Free
State should appeal to us with a loud voice for our sympathy and prayers. Undoubtedly the time has come for the sons of Africa to stretch forth their hands
unitedly, as was prophesised to us in Psalm 68 verse 31. . . . [God] will bless us
and send a wave of his spirit, which will pass through the whole of Africa from
the Cape to Egypt, the effects of which will be felt even by our brethren in
America, who come from the same original stock as ourselves.

Source: (a) Rev. L. N. Mzimba's account is quoted in: L. Kretzschmar (ed.), *Christian Faith and
African Culture* (Umtata: University of Transkei, 1988), p. 34, and also published in J. W.
Hofmeyr/J. A. Millard/C. J. J. Froneman, *History of the Church in South Africa: A Document and
Source Book* (Pretoria: University of South Africa, 1991), p. 139. (b) Andre Odendaal, "Vukani
Bantu! The Beginnings of Black Protest Politics in South Africa to 1912," pp. 110-111, quoted in:
G. M. Fredrickson, *Black Liberation: A Comparative History of Black Ideologies in the United
States and South Africa* (New York/Oxford, 1995), p. 89.

172. Prophetic Movements in Southern Africa

a. Isaiah Shembe: Emphasis on African Identity

A second wave of African Independent Churches emerged out of a charismatic renewal. They were established by charismatic leading personalities acknowledged as prophets by their followers. Since these churches spread more dynamically than Western imported denominations, their significance in the ecumenical movement is increasing. There are probably more than 400 such churches in Congo (the former Zaire) and the largest of them, the Kimbanguist (cf. document 206), claims a membership today of several million adherents. In South Africa, Isaiah Shembe (1870-1935) played a leading role. He was baptized in 1906 by the African National Baptist Church. In 1911 he established his own Nazareth Baptist Church (ibandla lamaNazaretha). Five years later he started to proclaim visions and revelations. Today the Nazareth Baptist Church is by far the largest African Independent Church among the Zulu speaking people of Southern Africa. Its congregations can now be found in all the provinces of the Republic of South Africa, and its missions have spread the message to Swaziland and Mozambique. Isaiah Shembe's son and successor in the leadership of the movement, Johannes Galilee Shembe, appointed an archivist, Petros Musawenkosi Dhlomo, who started to collect stories. They were later published by H. J. Becken, G. Oosthuizen and I. Hexham.

Every nation shall believe in God according to the way in which he has created them. Your reward will be perfect, when you will not desire anything else, and when you will be content with what God has given to you. There is nothing wrong in having shrinked hair, God created them in this way, and you ought not to be ashamed of them.

Shembe had been sent to bring the Brown people back to God, so that they may serve God as they are. When you want to understand this in the right way, read Daniel 7:9 "Thrones were placed, and one who was ancient of days took his seat, his raiment was white as snow, and the hair of his head like pure wool of sheep."

Do you see what nation has this hair like wool of sheep? Are these not our shrinked hair? Why then do we not understand that this gift of God, which we had received from our creator, is good? We ought to be proud of it and rejoice, because God has given us this majesty. The one of whom was said that he was the ancient of days, whose throne was fire flames, and who was clad in white: this was Mvelinqangi. [. . .] We Brown people knew Mvelinqangi. [. . .] You see the statue of the great Shembe, he stands on one leg, while the other leg rests on a chair. What does this mean? One foot stands in heaven, the other one on earth, because he was sent by Mvelinqangi to us here. This statue is a document with an important message, it says: The foot which stand on the chair is the foot in heaven, and the other foot stand on the earth, where he has been sent.

Shembe said: "Jesus has said: The one who will come in my name will do the works, which I have done, and he will do greater works than these, because I am going to our Father." Also the great Shembe was sent, and after him others would be sent to continue his work and do even greater things than he has done.

b. Early Accounts of Visions and Miracles

[. . .] When we were in the homestead of Dludlana at Amanzimtoti, a thunderstorm came up at sunset time. The man of God stood on the veranda and looked at the West. Then he said with a loud voice: "Hau!" I asked him: "What has happened, our father?" He said: "My child, it looks as if today a lightning will slip out of the hand of the angel. Indeed, it slipped out and killed a boy at KwaMashu."

At another time, a girl by the name of Bella Ngcobo was very sick here in the village of Ekuphakameni; she peeled off like a snake and had been sick for a long time. When their native doctors were unable to help her, she was brought here to the village of Ekuphakameni. The man of God asked Jehova: "From what disease does this girl suffer?" He was praying in another house and told the girl to stay outside [. . .]. When he prayed for her, the demon went out, and the girl was healed by the God of Ekuphakameni.

c. John Chilembwe (Malawi) on the First World War

In Nyasaland (Malawi) John Chilembwe (1870-1915) played a central role. He had studied in institutions of the Church of Scotland, but then he had turned to the Baptists and stayed in the USA, where he came to know Afro-American ideas. After his return, and assisted by Afro-American Baptists, he founded the Ajana Providence Industrial Mission near Blantyre. During the First World War he became a leading charismatic figure who sharply attacked the Europeans.

Will there be any good prospects for the natives after the end of the war? Shall we be recognised as anybody in the best interests of civilisation and Christianity after the great struggle is ended? . . . In time of peace the Government failed to help the underdog. In time of peace, everything for the European only. [. . .] But in time of war it has been found that we are needed to share hardships and shed our blood in equality.

Source: (a) Joseph Mthethwa, "Epuphakameni," quoted in: Irving Hexham/S. G. Oosthuizen, *The Story of Isaiah Shembe*, Volume 3 (New York: Edwin Mellen Press, 2001), pp. 70, 71. (b) Esther Zungu remembers early experiences with Shembe, in: Irving Hexham/S. G. Oosthuizen, *The Story of Isaiah Shembe*, Vol. 1 (New York: Edwin Mellen Press, 1996), pp. 66, 67.

(c) *Nyasaland Times* Nr. 48, 26.11.1914, quoted in: G. Shepperson/T. Price, *Independent African: John Chilembwe and the Origins, Settings and Significance of the Nyasaland Native Rising of 1915* (Edinburgh, 1958), pp. 234f. — *Further Reading (General):* T. O. Ranger, "Religious Movements and Politics in Subsaharan Africa," in: *African Studies Review* 29 (1986), pp. 1-69; W. Ustorf, "Das Heilen in den unabhängigen Kirchen Schwarzafrikas," in: *Zeitschrift für Mission* 13 (1987), pp. 198-210; F. Ludwig, "Afrikanische prophetische Bewegungen," in: W. Wagner (ed.), *Kolonien und Missionen* (Münster, 1993), pp. 294-308.

173. Prophetism in West Africa: Garrick Braide in Nigeria

Prophetic movements spread rapidly in West Africa also. Today the Celestial Church of Christ, the Cherubim and Seraphim Church and the Christ Apostolic Church count among the largest of these churches, with several million members. There are congregations in many U.S. and European cities. The first prophetic-healing movements were established by William Wadde Harris (ca. 1860-1929), who found many adherents in the Ivory Coast and in the Gold Coast from 1913 onwards, and by Garrick Sokari Braide. In the following, the mass movement founded by Braide in the Niger Delta in 1915 is given as an example. Among the reasons for Brade's success was his sharp attack on African Traditional Religions which allowed for the burning of cultural objects and direct competition with the old powers. He was compared to Elijah by his followers (a). In this context, the exorcism of evil spirits was important, too (b). However, the movement was not without opposition in the African population. Some members of the Anglican Niger Delta Native Pastorate Church strongly condemned the movement (c). Church leaders such as James Johnson were concerned about the extent of the belief in Braide's healing miracles. (d) Nevertheless the movement was defended in the West African press against the attacks by the ecclesiastical and colonial authorities (e).

a. Competition with "Rain Doctors"

At another occasion certain club people of the town were having a big dance, that would last for several days, but fearing that the rain would disturb them they went and hired some Ibo Dibias or fetish doctors from the interior who dealt in charms and who were supposed to have some certain power over the clouds by being able to draw down the rain with charms and to stop it from raining at any time of the season. These Ibo-dibias receiving money from the club people started practising their charms until one day Garrick came across two of them and the following short dialogue ensued: [. . .] "Do you think that you and your colleagues possess any real power over the clouds?" "Yes, we have the power." [. . .] "You are only deceiving the people." [. . .]

He was walking away quickly when the head dibia who was almost mad with rage called him back and challenged him that as the club people were preparing for the big dance that evening, he should call upon his God to send down the rain if he was able and see whether he (the dibia) on his own part will not be able to stop it from raining and give the club people a fine evening to dance. On receiving this challenge he was going away when all of a sudden something unnatural came upon him; he immediately turned round and called upon them to stand and see the great power of God.

Having said this he lifted up his hands towards heaven and kneeling down in the public street prayed like Elijah of old, and no sooner he arose from his knees than the clouds began to gather and within five minutes there was a heavy torrent of rain . . . which filled all who were present with great wonder.

b. Liberation from Evil Spirits

In the Niger Delta there is a little juju town [. . .] containing few houses. A large lake is situated in one side, one palm tree is in the midst of this lake. Women are forbidden to approach this lake, the chief juju is residing in this lake mentioned above. The inhabitants of this little village have a firm belief that the moment a woman got near this juju lake she will die instantaneously or be barren for ever.

[. . .] On one occasion Garrick Braide arrived at this little village with his wife Jene Bene Marion and asked her to walk round where women are forbidden to go. When she walked round, he went near this well, with her together with these people that went with him. He offered a short and audible prayer for the deterioration of that juju causing women to be childless. Shortly after he had left there, after some months, the lake dried up. His wife has had three children after she has been there.

c. Rejection of the Movement as "Blasphemical"

In short, this infamous movement has taught the [Anglican] Delta Church a very big lesson. [. . .] I have carefully watched and examined the proceedings of the 'New Prophet Movement', and found nothing true, honest, just, pure, lovely of good report, virtuous or praiseworthy in it at all. [. . .] The Movement has done and is still doing much havoc among the Ogonis and Andonis, much blasphemy and profanation. The following are some conspicuous features of vice in the 'New Movement' here and elsewhere: (a) People are induced to throw away all European medicines, and told that the 'Prophet Movement' would strike a blow at the Government by depriving it of revenues derived from litigations, hospitals and spirits. (b) Illiterate young men are sent to the bushmen as teachers, just to get the money from them. (c) Any heathen polygamist is baptized without a word of instruction in the rudiments of Christianity, if only he believes in their doctrine; and (d) After such sudden and hasty baptism for which certain sums of money have been paid or gifts made, anyone is eligible either on the same or following day to partake of what they call the Lord's Supper, using tombo for wine. . . .

d. James Johnson, Elijah II

Garrick's person is considered as so sacred and so filled with power that even the water he bathes in is regarded as charged with healing and other virtues and is readily drunk or washed with. It is eagerly sought after or scrambled for by chiefs and people, rich and poor, sick and whole alike; and it has even been drunk by church agents. The vegetable matters with which many, especially women, used often to rub their bodies for adornment are now being commonly dispensed with in favour of the clay which earth makes when mixed with this water, either on account of the healing and other virtues believed to have entered into it, or as a charm to bring good luck or to secure protection against evil. . . .

e. Defense of the Movement in the West African Press

Nothing in the religious world of West Africa has happened since the beginning of missionary efforts that can be regarded as being equal to events that have been happening in Church matters recently in the Niger Delta Regions. [. . .] Many gross and in some cases malicious misrepresentations have appeared in English and American papers. The movement [which] is the outcome of the way God has been pleased to use Mr. Garrick Braide. To say that the Movement has 'undermined Government authority and Christian influence and that only the great loyalty — shown by the more important chief has held in check its most dangerous aspects' is incorrect, unfair and unjustifiable. [. . .] On the contrary it has been of the greatest help possible to the Administration in having so quietly and with proper Christian influence moved thousands of natives to voluntarily and gladly renounce gin and other vile drinks, it has been the means of rendering the inhabitants of some districts formerly troublesome to be peaceful and more industrious. Hundreds of Christ Army Church members in the Ogoni district — fresh converts to Christianity through this movement — have told me over and over that before their conversion they were very wicked to strangers including Europeans. . . .

To say that he made money through his faith healing power is misrepresentation. Garrick always instructed his patients after recovery when they offered him money to go and give it to the Church . . . as the cure was effected through the power and will of the Christian God and not by his own. If the patients were pagan he urged them to accept Christ who is the saviour of mankind. Through this many converts were made into the Delta Pastorate Church. . . .

Source: (a) A. C. Braide, *The Life of Prophet Garrick Sokari Braide alias Elijah II,* undated (unpublished source material, collected by H. W. Turner and E. M. T. Epelle in the 1960's and archived in the Selly Oak Colleges, Birmingham). (b) M. A. Kemmer, *Short Report on the Work of Garrick Braide of Bakana alias Elijah II,* in: ibid. (c) A. O. J. Pepple, "Report of Ogoni Mission, 1918," *Western Equatorial Africa Diocesan Magazine,* 24 July, 1919, pp. 171-173. (d) J. Johnson, "Elijah II," *Church Missionary Review* 67 (1916), pp. 455-462. (e) S. A. Coker, "The Truth About Garrick Braide Lately Designated Elijah II," *Lagos Weekly Record* (10.2.1917). — *Further Reading:* A. Adogame/L. Jafta, "Zionists, Aladura and Roho: African Instituted Churches," in Kalu, *African Christianity,* pp. 309-332; A. Anderson/E. Tang, "Independency in Africa and Asia," in: McLeod, *World Christianities,* pp. 107-127; D. Shank/J. Murray, *Prophet Harris, The Black Elijah* (Leiden, 1995); G. M. Haliburton, *The Prophet Harris* (London, 1971); A. Adogame, *Celestial Church of Christ* (Frankfurt/Bern, 1999); J. D. Y. Peel, *Aladura* (London, 1968); H. W. Turner, *History of an African Independent Church* (Oxford, 1967).

174. Uganda: Orthodox and Independent

The African Orthodox Church has its background in the Pan-African Movement in the USA. A member of the Universal Negro Improvement Association, the Anglican Priest George Macguire strived to establish a united black church which should be affiliated with the Orthodox Church. Macguire was ordained as a bishop by the Jacobite episcopus vagans Rene Joseph Vilatte. The ordination was declared null and void by the Syrian-Jacobite patriarch of Antioch, but at that time the African Orthodox Church had already established herself in Africa. The South African Daniel William Alexander, who up to this time had served the Ethiopian Church, was consecrated second bishop during the 1920s. In Uganda, too, there was an interest in becoming affiliated with the Orthodox Church; here the Anglican Reuben Sseseya Mukasa was the driving force. On his invitation, Bishop Alexander visited Uganda from October 1931 until July 1932. Mukasa was baptized and ordained, later taking on the name Reuben Spartas. He established the African Greek Orthodox Church which was not only independent from missionary churches but could also claim a more ancient tradition than those.

a. Constitution of the African Greek Orthodox Church (Extract)

The African Greek Orthodox Church shall be controlled by the Africans under the supervision and guidance of the Holy Ghost through the spiritual, physical and fraternal help and protection of the Holy Patriarchal Sea [*sic*] of Alexandria, Egypt. It shall be an absolutely independent church in all her administration.

b. Reuben Spartas: The Orthodox Faith as the "Indisputable Faith"

My breaking with the Anglican Church was not inconsistent with my desire for the reunion of the Christian Church. Far from it. As a layman within the Anglican fold my chances of being heard about the need for reform were very few indeed. In the end I might have found myself expelled as an heretic. In addition I had discovered that the Orthodox faith was the indisputable faith and far more true and original than the Anglican. I could not move the whole of Anglicanism into the Orthodox faith, but I could myself leave Anglicanism and join Orthodoxy. Once inside Orthodoxy, and a leader of an Orthodox Church, I could with propriety draw the attention of the whole of Anglicanism to the need for reunion. Inside Anglicanism I was speaking with the voice of an insolent child who presumes to teach his grandmother to suck eggs. As one of the leaders of an older and truer church, I would, and do, speak with better authority on the question of reunion.

c. Spartas in Greece: An Article in Pantainos (1947)

You will remember that during the summer we had among us an African clergyman, named Spartas. He is the religious head of the natives, who hitherto belonged to an eastern heresy and expressed years ago, in the time of Patriarch Meletios, their desire to return to the Orthodox Church. Our Patriarch, although accepting them, has postponed this matter first because of many difficulties and secondly due to the difficulties arising from the recent war. . . . It will be necessary to build in these countries Orthodox Churches and Orthodox Schools, which the Greeks will also attend. It will be also necessary to give the more keen of the Africans higher education, either here (in Egypt) or in Greece. Hospitals with doctors and nurses will have to be founded, dependent on the Church alone; and a cathedral with all necessary accessories will have to be built. All this will incur heavy expenditure, but we trust that the Greeks there will contribute, as so generously as present; and we hope that the Governments will not be indifferent.

Source: (a) Constitution of the Orthodox Uganda and Kenya Churches, Kampala, 1943, quoted in: F. B. Welbourn, *East African Rebels: A Study of Some Independent Churches* (London, 1961), p. 83. (b) Welbourn, p. 84, refers to H. R. T. Brandreth, *Episcopi Vagantes and the Anglican Church* (London, 1961). (c) Pantainos 11th January 1947 (original in Greek), quoted in Welbourn, p. 92. *Further Reading:* Horst Buerkle, "Reuben Spartas und die Anfänge der griechisch-orthodoxen, Kirche in Uganda," in: K. Nikolakopulos, *Orthodoxe Theologie zwischen Ost und West* (Festschrift Nikolau) (Frankfurt, 2002), pp. 495-508; Francis Kimani Githieya, *The Freedom of the Spirit: African Indigenous Churches in Kenya* (Atlanta, 1997); Stephen Hayes, "Orthodox Mission in Tropical Africa," *Missionalia* 24 (1996), pp. 383-398.

C. Developments within the Roman Catholic Church

175. White Fathers: "Folk Mission" at Lake Victoria

The concept of "folk mission," the Christianization of a ethnic group through the conversion of the chief and the adaptation of elements of the traditional social order to ecclesiastical structures, had been developed among Lutherans such as especially the Leipzig missionary Bruno Gutmann (cf. documents 167f). There were some similar attempts in other Protestant missions to indigenize Christianity. This concept was also used in the Catholic Church, as for instance in the Ungoni-region in the South, where the Benedictines made language spoken by the upper class the language of mission, or on the Ukerewe island in Lake Victoria, where the White Fathers supported a successful contender to the throne and thereby gained influence in the new Christian kingdom.

Before he began to rule, this king asked the fathers of the Catholic mission if he could receive the blessing of the Catholic Church for his work in the sight of all the people. [. . .] When he reached the church door the Father Superior asperged the king and together they went to the altar. [. . .] The Father Superior asked the king: "From whom have you received the dignity of kingship?" The king replied before all the people: "I have received the dignity of kingship from God." "Why have you received this dignity?" "That I may rule my people with justice and so care for them that they may gain heaven." [. . .] Then the Father Superior blessed the king.

Source: *Rafiki yangu,* Jan. 1910, quoted in: J. Iliffe, *A Modern History of Tanganyika* (Cambridge, 1979), pp. 218f.

176. The White Fathers and Rwanda's Ethnicities (1913)

During the civil war in Rwanda in 1994, one of the most Christianized African countries of Africa with 50% Catholics and 12% Protestants, at least 800,000 human beings were killed. The clashes between Hutus and Tutsis had a background in the colonial period in which the idea of ethnic identities was fostered. During German colonial rule (1897-1916) the Tutsis were systematically favored as the ruling elite. Since 1913 only Tutsis were trained in the government school in Kigali. Although this view of the Tutsis as the apex of the societal pyramid was shared by the Catholic missionaries (a), the White Fathers also worked among the Hutus which brought them into conflicts with the German colonial administration (b). Since the 1950s, many Catholic missionaries saw it as their aim to protect the rights of the Hutus. The concept of ethnic identity therefore also had a denominational component.

a. A Missionary Chronicle about Hutus and Tutsis (1905)

The greatest obstacle to evangelisation is the way the country is administered. The king has all the important chiefs as his clients; they in their turn have all the minor Tutsi, and these, the influential Hutu; it all forms a compact mass which is difficult to attack. They all agree that to frequent the whites is to become their clients and to set up as a rebel against the king; you cannot serve two masters, they think, God and the king.

b. Catholic Mission and German Colonial Rule

[. . .] The government turns to the Protestants, who set themselves up as German masters and wish above all else, as they never cease writing, to reach the Tutsi. [. . .] The government therefore reproaches us with, at least, working to form an anti-government party; if it were true we would be working against ourselves, against God by whom we have been sent, and so forming an anti-Catholic party; . . . it is our duty to convert the chiefs.

Source: (a) Chroniques Trimestrielles, No 114, March 1905, 143, quoted in: I. Linden, *Church and Revolution in Rwanda* (Manchester, 1977), p. 61; (b) Archives of the White Fathers, Rome: Classe to confrères, 17.4.1913, in: ibid., p. 111. — *Further Reading:* T. P. Longman, "Christianity and Democratisation in Rwanda: Assessing Church Responses to Political Crisis in the 1990s," in: P. Gifford (ed.), *The Christian Churches and the Democratisation of Africa* (Leiden, 1995), pp. 188-204.

177. Jesuits and "Paganism" in Madagascar (1924)

After Madagascar had been incorporated into the French colonial empire in 1896, the Catholic mission won countless followers. Catholicism was not only successful because it was the religion of the French conquerors (while Protestantism had been associated with the national resistance), but also on account of certain affinities to traditional religion. The Jesuit Pierre-Zavier Morel reports on some difficulties:

How many, more or less superstitious customs still accompany circumcision, which our *Betsiléos* take on! Certain days of the week are unlucky. In isolated villages one should be on one's guard against a burial undertaken on a Thursday. In others no one would dare set out on a journey on a Monday. Also, the *vaki-ra* is still practiced by our Christians. It consists in men taking each other's blood, drinking it and swearing themselves to friendship. Two blood brothers or blood sisters are friends for life and to death. All is held in common with them, all is allowed between them. Should I also broach the topic of the amulet?

Only rarely does one meet Christians who wear an amulet which adorns the throat, the arm or the head of the pagans. But how many with hardly any reservation wear the medallion or perhaps voluntarily the scapular, as if it were somehow also an amulet only of a different kind. The blessing of the palms, the blessing of the candles, but above all the Ash Wednesday ceremony always attracts a huge crowd. There are Christians who neglect the Easter communion, but for nothing in the world would they neglect to receive the cross of ashes. [. . .] And one of the most frequent attacks of the Protestants consists in that their saying: "The Catholics practice different superstitious customs than the pagans, and although it is a question of different customs, nevertheless they are superstitions." The answer is simple, but their attack is nevertheless an argument for the fact that this is a weak point among our Malagasy.

Source: P.-X. Morel S.J., *Madagassische abergläubische Bräuche,* Ambalavao, January 1924, in: D. Vacchi/A. Vuylsteke, *Die Jesuiten und die Welt* (Paris/München, 1991), pp. 150-155.

178. Basutoland: The First Ordination of an African (1931)

In the Catholic Church the transfer of responsibility to the Africans also had decisive significance. In the first ordination of a Black African, Raphael Mohasi was ordained on December 12, 1931. in Basutoland; Emmanuel Mabathoana followed on June 28, 1934. In the official celebratory inauguration of the seminar for Apostolic delegates held on December 14, 1930, the representative of the superintendents explained the historic importance of this event:

For us this day will truly be significant as an important date in our history. Seventy years have passed since our Chief Moshesh transferred to Father Gérard the place where we are now gathered. The Lord God has blessed the work of our missionaries so that many Basutos have since become Catholics. But today the Lord has visited us in a particular way because He has chosen among our sons those who will become His servants and priests. Fortunate are the parents who have given their children to the Lord God, because they will receive a rich crown in heaven. Happy are the young men who were chosen by Jesus to be his representatives on earth. There is no more beautiful calling than to the priesthood, which opens the portal of heaven to humankind. [. . .]

Source: M. Bierbaum, "Die Entwicklung der katholischen Mission im Basutoland," *Missionswissenschaft und Religionswissenschaft* 1 (1938), pp. 133-149, here: p. 141.

179. South Africa: New Orientation in Education (1928)

Of further importance was the recognition of the necessity for a program of comprehensive training. This new orientation toward education was made clear in the 1928 statement of the bishop's conference in Kimberley (South Africa).

Today, as the development of the land strides forward with giant steps, it is no longer sufficient to support a large number of small poor mission schools, which are directed from afar by one missionary and can only be visited from time to time. Such schools cannot impart the needed knowledge and the robust faith which the black and colored brothers need. It is essential that our priests, brothers and sisters receive a well-rounded basic education to enable them to teach according to stable, modern methods; they must be equipped to teach and defend the true and enduring principles of religion and morality which are the sole basis of their education of the youth.

Source: Bishop's Archives, Kimberley, cited in: J. J. Hagel, "Schulsturm in Südafrika," *ZMR* 39 (1955), pp. 283-296, here: p. 291.

180. Aims in Zimbabwe: An "African Lourdes" (1943)

As in many other African regions Christianity spread rapidly in Manicaland in Eastern Rhodesia (Zimbabwe) after 1910. Indigenous missionaries played an important role in the "spiritual revolution." Patrick Kwesha (ca. 1900-1963) who had emigrated to Johannesburg in 1922, worked among the migrant workers from Manicaland. His model was Francis of Assisi. In 1943 he described his vision for Manicaland as follows:

My only wish which led my whole life was that of going back to Rhodesia and start(ing) an out-school of Our Lady of Lourdes in the valley of Samanga, which also would mean the opening of the world's second Lourdes, or Lourdes of Africa. I wanted that school to be a mission and a training centre for boys and girls and a centre of religious civilisation, but all to be conducted by African priests, brothers and sisters, as the valley is very hot for Europeans. And the order of the religious group was to be the Fransiscans of the family of St. Joseph. I wanted Our Lady to be served fully in this valley like she is served at Lourdes of France, or more than that. I wanted God to be fulfilled with His covenant by these children of Mary of this her valley, and His grateful servants to rise up among them, and that some of them, as apostles, may swarm over the whole of Manyikaland, as the bees, and banish all heathenism, Protestantism and superstition, and establish a pure and holy Kingdom of God and glory of Mary, so that from that God may be called God of Manyikaland as He was called God of Israel, and Our Lady to be called Queen of Manyikaland as she is called Queen of Angels and Saints.

Source: Red Notebook, Written by Patrich Kwesha. 1943 Johannesburg, in possession of Augustine Kwesha, quoted in: T. Ranger, "Taking on the Missionary's Task: African Spirituality and the Mission Churches of Manicaland in the 1930s," in: *Journal of Religion in Africa* 29, no. 2 (1999), pp. 175-205, here: pp. 185f.

D. THEMES OF THE 1920S AND 1930S

181. New Interest in Africa

a. Joseph H. Oldham, International Missionary Council

While the World Missionary Conference in Edinburgh 1910 had focussed on Asia, during the 1920s the International Missionary Council became more and more interested in Africa. Its General Secretary, Joseph Oldham (1874-1969), played a leading role in this development. He also took a stance in political questions and was especially critical of the colonial politics in Kenya which favored the interests of white settlers. He made strong statements against forced labor, but despite his many initiatives concerning Africa he wrote in 1928:

In Africa we are at the first beginning of things. It is within our own lifetime that tropical Africa (in fact nineteenth twentieths of the continent) has been brought . . . into the main stream of world history.

b. The African Ecumenist J. E. K. Aggrey, 1919

At the beginning of the 1920s the question of educational possibilities for Africans took on central significance. Decisive impulses came from Afro-American experiences in the USA, especially from the Tuskegee Institute founded by Booker T. Washington in 1881. At Tuskegee, Afro-American students were trained under Afro-American leadership. Toward the end of the First World War the view prevailed in a few American mission societies that change in thinking was also required in the African mission schools. In 1919 and 1920 a commission of the Phelps Stoke Institute which was founded in 1909 visited various regions of the continent. A member of the commission, the African ecumenist James Emman Kwegyir Aggrey (1875-1927), gave the following report of the situation:

It seems to me that this is the psychological moment for Africa, and I believe you are destined metaphorically to stoop down and kiss the Sleeping Beauty Africa back into life from her centuries of sleep.

c. J. E. K. Aggrey Called to Achimota (Ghana)

There were also initiatives from some progressive colonial administrators. In the Gold Coast, general governor G. Guggisberg developed an interest in questions of education. A committee which had been commissioned by Guggisberg recommended establishing a new institution close to the village Achimota (near Accra) which would serve as a secondary school and as a training institution for teachers. Principal of the School was Oldham's brother-in-law, A. G. Frazer, the assistant principal the African J. Aggrey. After receiving the call in 1924, Aggrey wrote:

I return at the urgent call of my native country to give her my very best. [. . .] The Principal is a godsend to Africa. He wants the very best for Africa, and he can insist on the best if we unite to back him. He and I are working hand in hand. We consult each other in all important matters. Both of us desire and ask the wholehearted advice, counsel, constructive criticism and cooperation of all loyal Africans, because Achimota is destined to be *the* University for Africa.

d. The Nigerian Bishop Oluwole on the London Africa Institute

In 1926 the International Institute for African Languages and Cultures (Africa Institute) was founded. Missionary Societies had played an important role in its establishment. It aimed at studying African languages and cultures, producing literature in the "vernaculars" for education and in intensifying international cooperation. The London based Institute also edited its own journal *Africa*. In this academic journal articles were also published which were critical of missionaries. The Nigerian Bishop Oluwole learned of the new publication by reading a review in which an article of the colonial officer Rattray was summarized. Rattray had stated that the Christian Africans were "denationalised" and asked whether it would not be better to keep Christianity away from Africa. Oluwole reacted vehemently:

Just fancy! "The alternative of withholding Christianity" from the African. Captain Rattray or his Reviewer might not know, but Lord Lugard, whatever may be his opinion of the African Christian, knows, from his experience in Uganda and Nigeria, that it is too late for the day to speak of withholding Christianity from Africa. The International Institute of African languages and Cultures is said to be intended for the good of the African race. I have read somewhere that it is the outcome of missionary initiative, and it is highly spoken of by men whom we trust and respect. One is therefore anxious that its good object is strictly kept in view by the learned members, and that they pursue their researches in a way that will futher the interests of the peoples whose progress is at stake. Those who intend the good of the African should be very careful not to irritate him by writing or speaking contemptuously of him.

Source: (a) Yale Dale Library, Mott Papers 66/1195: *Oldham to John Mott,* September 1928; (b) E. Smith, *Aggrey of Africa* (London, 1929), p. 116; (c) Aggrey and Chief Coker, Accra, 18.10.1924, quoted in: ibid., 233f; (d) Bishop I. Oluwole, Address to the Synod by the President. The First Session of the Fourth Synod of the Diocese of Lagos (in: *Western Equatorial Africa Diocesan Magazine,* 34-297, September 1929, 202-215, here: 209). — *Further Reading:* K. Clements, "Friend of Africa": J. H. Oldham (1874-1969), "Missions and British Colonial Policy in the 1920s," in: F. Ludwig/A. Adogame, *European Traditions,* pp. 175-186; K. Clements, *Faith on the Frontier: A Life of J. H. Oldham* (Edinburgh, 1999); J. W. Cell, *By Kenya Possessed: The Correspondence of Norman Leys and J. H. Oldham* (Chicago, 1976).

182. South Africa: "United we stand, divided we fall" (1920)

During the 1920s there was a strong endeavour toward church union. In addition to official negotiations, as for instance in South India (cf. document 87), there were also numerous local initiatives, such as a conference organized by a Mr. Mkize in South Africa. In an article published in *Church Chronicle* his introductory speech was summarized as follows:

[When] he had called the conference together he stated: 1. That he might put before it the desirability of the union of all native Churches. The present Churches must be broken up and a new one built on love must be built up. He considered that the time had come for native Christians of all denominations to unite and form one native national Church. The Church was brought to the natives by white people in a divided state and naturally we are following their divisions. [. . .] 2. If on the other hand it was said, as some white people did, that the time had not yet come for Christians to have a native Church, that seemed to him a frank confession of failure on their part, and if after so many years of labour among natives they had failed to make a man of him, the sooner they left the native to go on by himself the better. 3. If natives are to maintain their nationality they are bound to unite as one man and learn a lesson from the negroes of America and do away with our racial difference. United we stand — divided we fall, and unity is strength. He thought that no good can come from mixing up as we are doing with white people — it is the source and the cause of our weakness. Besides white people have no true love for natives. [. . .] 4. He believed that there was a colour bar in the Church as well as in the State. He maintained that the Church showed its mind with regard to this colour bar in that she is careful never to promote any native minister or clergyman, however faithful or long his service in his Church might be. But on the contrary junior and inexperienced white men were often quickly promoted to positions and placed over black ministers and clergy who were old enough to be their fathers. Shame! Many white ministers had not come out here for the good of the native, but for their own good, to help their white brothers to take away our country and its wealth of which the owners of the country got nothing at all. Many of the native clergy ought to be Bishops, but they are treated as boys. All this must be put to a stop. 5. As to Education, the white man was so careful as to give the native so little of it, in order that he might always be able to keep him down under the white man. And to get better education, a few natives have had to go overseas or to America. [. . .]

Having finished his address, Mr. Mkize was inundated with a shower of questions, such as he was asked for instance to state what he proposed should be done with those native Churches which had already left the white man and were not under the control of white people — and also to state what he proposed should be done with those native Christians who still worshipped in white men's churches and were still under their control. Mr. Mkize's reply was that whilst he was there not to ask any one to give up or leave his Church, at the same time he did think that all natives should unite and form one national native Church.

Source: "Towards Reunion," *Church Chronicle* (April 1, 1920, and April 15, 1920), contributed by a native priest.

183. Italian Occupation of Ethiopia and Nigerian Critique

The resistance movement to the Italian occupation of Ethiopia in 1935 had far-reaching consequences for the history of emancipation. Its impact can be compared to the effects of Japan's victory against Russia in 1905 (cf. document 65). Pan-African consciousness took on new dimensions. The silence of the Vatican called forth a wave of criticism from African church leaders. Pope Pius XI had actually warned of an Italian invasion prior to the outbreak of war, but during the hostilities he avoided any moral judgment. This gave the impression that the pope not only tacitly accepted the Italian aggression, but even actively supported it. This becomes especially clear in a report of the *African Church Chronicle* which was published in Nigeria:

If there had been any doubt whatever on this question the recent action of the Pope, as reported in the Nigeria Daily Telegraph of September 2nd 1935, in blessing the chaplains going with the Italian forces being despatched by Mussolini to East Africa to invade Abyssinia, the only remaining independent sovereign state in Africa, in order to satisfy Italian greed for colonial expansion, has gone far to confirm this viewpoint that the church is national and embodied in each state.

Many Africans are naturally amazed at the action of the Pope, and although no two things can be contradictory to each other in their nature than that the acclaimed chief representative on Earth of the Prince of Peace should participate in any movement that might lead to War and an aggressive and un-provoked War at that, it should be remembered that the Pope is after all a hu-man being like the ordinary run of mankind and therefore heir to human weaknesses, in spite of the traditional claim for him by his adherents of infalli-bility. He is an Italian besides and it is natural that he should be interested and not be indifferent in matters affecting the destiny of his country. [. . .]

The African Church is the home church of the Africans, it is the first stan-dard in that struggle for Self-Determination which at present confronts the whole continent of Africa. It is a protest against foreign ecclesiacism, it is a bul-wark against the Spiritual Enslavement of Africa, it is the training ground for the Africans to demonstrate to the world that they are capable of Self-Government.

Source: "Back to the Land or Nationalism in Religion," *The African Church Chronicle* (Oct.-Dec. 1935), pp. 4f. — *Further Reading:* S. K. B. Asante, *Pan-African Protest: West Africa and the Italo-Ethiopian Crisis, 1934-1941* (London, 1977).

184. Max Yergan: Christianity and Social Renewal

Max Yergan, born in 1892 in North Carolina, came from a family which had committed it-self to the tradition of Ethiopianism — the Christianization of Africa by Africans. To Max Yergan this tendency became even stronger when he studied at St. Ambrose Episcopal Academy and the Baptist Shaw University. As a student, he became a member of the Black YMCA and after his graduation in 1914 he worked for a short while for the YMCA in Bangalore, later in East Africa and then in South Africa.

a. Christianity and Communism (1932)

I have no desire to contrast Christianity with communism, but I cannot refrain from observing that communism offers to Christianity its supreme opportu-nity as a force for social regeneration, and there is no place in the world where this is more true than here in Africa.

b. Support of the Freedom Struggle in Africa

Conditions in Africa must not be regarded as settled. They are not settled be-cause European nations will not permit them to be, and because Africans will never be content to live under the hardships imposed upon the light of our awakened concern for all human affairs and in the light of accurate knowledge of the facts. It is also urgently necessary that we do what we can to help improve this condition.

Source: (a) YMCA Archives, New York, South Africa Reports, 1906-1927, Box 67: Report of Max Yergan, South Africa, June 30, 1932, quoted in: D. H. Anthony III, "Max Yergan in South Africa: From Evangelical Pan-Africanist to Revolutionary Socialist" (*African Studies Review* 34/2, Sept. 1991), pp. 27-55, here: 42. (b) Schomberg Center for Research in Black Culture, New York: Schomberg R 6, Box 7.

185. Tambaram 1938: African Experiences in India

Tambaram 1938 (cf. document 83) was the first conference of the International Missionary Council in which a significant number of Africans took part. It therefore offered a unique opportunity for the 15 delegates from the continent. For the first time, West Africans exchanged views with South Africans about African Independent Churches. For the first time, they discussed questions like the tolerance of polygamy in an international setting. Prominent among the West African delegates was the Nigerian assistant bishop Alexander Babatunde Akinyele (1875-1968) (a). For South Africa, Albert John Luthuli (1898-1967) played a leading role. As president of the African National Congress (and one of the predecessors of Nelson Mandela), he was one of the most well known participants of the meeting: in 1960 he was the first black African to receive the Nobel Peace Prize. In his Memoirs he reported about the journey to India (b).

a. Report of Bishop Alexander B. Akinyele (Nigeria)

From the heat of political and economic turmoil, people gathered and forgot who they were and what their differences were. One night was spent in prayer for peace. Another session was devoted to music, and after the Africans sang, it was generally agreed that we were especially talented along that line. Let us consecrate that to God.

In the African group meetings, one of the first questions raised was that of monogamy and polygamy. I was surprised to find that polygamy as practised here is not practised in the East. And so we came to see that monogamy and polygamy are no matters of individual conscience, but that monogamy is the will of God for His people.

As compared with India, we are not nationalistic at all: We are half tribalistic and half nationalistic. In India the people have gone much further towards unity and self-determination. We need to be less tribalistic and more nationalistic. [. . .]

b. Reminiscences of Albert Luthuli (South Africa)

The leader of our delegation was a Dutch Reformed Minister. Even when South Africa had been left laying far behind in the wake of our ship, white South African attitudes clung to him. We, for some reason, were travelling second class, while the Europeans were travelling first. On the first Sunday out the delegation leader sought us to say: "Well, gentlemen, the other white passengers might object if you come to the first class to worship there. Would you make your own arrangements here?"

We accepted this. It was nothing new. It scarcely aroused comment until other white delegates came to inquire about our absence. We told them the reason and they were taken aback. On the following Sunday we were invited across to the first-class lounge for multi-racial worship. The boat did not sink. [. . .]

The Conference itself was a great privilege, bringing as it did contact with Christian leaders from all over the world, some of them giants. I think what made the deepest impression on me was not the high level of debate (it was high), but the thrill of seeing world-wide Christianity in miniature. For the first time I saw the result of the command: "Go ye into all the world and preach the Gospel." What had hitherto been vague became precise. Added to this was my delight in a sense of the vigour of Christianity. It was alive and active, grappling with its problems and facing its challenges. We do not see much of that in South Africa.

I was sad about South Africa. When I learned (for the first time) that there are African Anglican Bishops in West Africa, I thought it an adverse comment on South Africa, where so far there are none after this long time. Why? Has the Church been unable to train Africans, or has it tried only half-heartedly? Or has the rigour of the West African climate made Europeans feel more temporary there, readier to hand over and go? [. . .]

Source: (a) *The Nigerian Baptist,* 17-18, September 1939; (b) Albert Luthuli, *Let My People Go: An Autobiography* (London, 1962), pp. 78, 79. — *Further Reading:* F. Ludwig, *Zwischen Kolonialismuskritik und Kirchenkampf. Interaktionen afrikanischer, indischer und europäischer Christen während der Weltmissionskonferenz in Tambaram 1938* (Göttingen, 2000).

E. NATIONAL MOVEMENTS AND CHRISTIANITY

186. Kwame Nkrumah: The Significance of J. E. K. Aggrey

Many African nationalists had been educated in missionary schools. One significant example is Kwame Nkrumah (1909-1972), the first president of Ghana which became independent in 1957 as the first black African state. Before he studied in the U.S. he had attended Achimota College close to Accra. He was particularly impressed by the ecumenist and assistant principal J. E. K. Aggrey.

But the figure to whom all Africans looked that day was Dr Kwegyir Aggrey, assistant vice-principal and the first African member of the staff. To me he seemed the most remarkable man that I ever met and I had the deepest affection for him. It was through him that my nationalism was first aroused. He was extremely proud of his colour but was strongly opposed to racial segregation in any form and, although he could understand Marcus Garvey's principle of 'Africa for the Africans' he never hesitated to attack this principle. He believed that conditions should be such that the black and the white races should work together. Co-operation between the black and the white peoples was the key note of his message and the essence of this mission, and he used to expound this by saying: "You can play a tune of sorts on the white keys, and you can play a tune of sorts on the black keys, but for harmony you must use both the black and the white." I could not, even at that time, accept the idea of Aggrey's as being practicable, for I maintained that such harmony can only exist when the black race is treated as equal to the white race; that only a free and independent people — a people with a government of their own — can claim equality, racial or otherwise, with another people.

Source: The Autobiography of Kwame Nkrumah (Lagos/Nairobi, 1957), p. 14. — *Further Reading:* Sundkler/Steed, *History,* pp. 636-643.

187. Herbert Macaulay: Criticism of Missionary Work

Herbert Macaulay (1864-1946), who founded the Nigerian National Democratic Party (NNDP) in 1922, was a grandson of Bishop Crowther and had been a member of the Anglican Church. But as a nationalist he also assigned high value to African traditional religions:

It was said by a professor some time ago that the African should have been left with his ancestor-worship and that Christianity should not have been allowed to supplant it in certain parts of the continent. Ancestor-worship, it will be readily admitted is Aero-worship, nation-worship, in short it is patriotism. And it is the loss of this spirit and its displacement, by a cult which Africans have as yet not quite understood to the extent of being able to relate it to the practical problems of society, that is responsible for the deplorable absence of the meaning of patriotism.

Source: H. Macaulay, "Religion and Native Customs." Editorial *Lagos Daily News* (18.1.1932) (Mss in: Dike Library Ibadan, Macaulay Collection, Box 6).

188. Nnamdi Azikiwe: Religious Tolerance

With Nnamdi Azikiwe (1904-1996), son of a teacher who had been trained by the Church Missionary Society (C.M.S), and himself a student of several missionary schools, Nigerian nationalism reached a new stage. In the 1940s, Azikiwe founded the National Council of Nigeria and the Cameroons (NCNC), an efficient nationalist organization. When Nigeria attained her political independence in 1960, he became the first president. Regarding the relationship of religion and the state he experimented with various models. Since he was interested in realizing national unity in a religiously pluralistic country, the ideas of tolerance and national identity became central to him. These reflections were already given expression in his work *Renascent Africa,* submitted in 1937. They were clearly formulated in the leading article "Religious Toleration" published in the *West African Pilot* of January 1939:

[. . .] The Muslims must be ready to live in peace and harmony with Christians, and the Christians must be prepared to be citizens along with pagans and atheists and others. That is the crux of our ideal in a new Africa. [. . .] His Holiness the Pope and the Archbishop of Canterbury regard themselves as belonging to the same brotherhood of religion. And the Moderator of the Scottish General Assembly feels that he is discharging the same sacred duty as the head of the Greek Orthodox Church. Why then should the African Church, established in Nigeria, by those who feel the call to do so, not receive recognition at the hands of those who believe otherwise?

Source: "Religious Toleration," *West African Pilot* (25.1.1939), p. 4. — *Further Reading:* M. Crowder, *West Africa under Colonial Rule* (London, 1968), pp. 454-481; G. Grohs, *Stufen afrikanischer Emanzipation* (Stuttgart etc., 1967), pp. 163-167.

189. National Church of Nigeria (1948)

As the religious wing of the National Council for Nigeria and the Cameroons, the National Church of Nigeria was founded in 1948 with the aim of religiously supporting the national conscience. The foundation was partly conditioned by the experience that Africans were not allowed access to all meetings of the missionary churches. The program of the National Church was outlined in a pamphlet by K. O. K. Onylana. The title page shows an African woman holding a torch in front of a map of the African continent. The subtitle reads: "The torch of New Religious Civilization coming from Africa."

The name "church" is misleading in that the National Church of Nigeria discarded basic tenets of the Christian faith in favor of a program integrating different religions. Thus, for instance, the belief that Jesus Christ is the son of God was rejected for the reason that the African background does not permit worship of a man born of a woman as a God.

Sick and tired of an explosive world, and wishing to end religious quarrels that peace may return like doves among men, the Africans whose traditional attitude in all matters pertaining to worshipping of God is one of laissez faire, have formed the National Church of Nigeria to teach humanity "live and let live" even in religion. [. . .]

We the renascent youths of New Africa gather to form the National Church of Nigeria. It is to teach mankind tolerance and elevate the soul of man from the low level of intolerant jealousy to the glorious height of spiritual balance in all matters of religion in order that this world once more shall be a Garden of Eden in which the lion and the lamb shall lie together in happy companionship and enjoy the bounties of nature on the basis of equality — a veritable Kingdom of God on earth in which the universal brotherhood of man under the fatherhood of one God shall be a reality.

Source: National Archives Ibadan, RP 2/19: K. O. K. Onylona, *The National Church of Nigeria, Its Catechism and Credo* (Yaba, undated), pp. 1f.

190. Kaji Tovalou Houenou: Protest (1924)

There were also resistance movements in the French colonies. One of the leading nationalists was Kaji Tovalou Houenou from Dahomey who founded the "Ligue universelle de défense de la race noire" in Paris in 1924. He was connected to the Communist party and to the pan African ideas of Marcus Garvey. When he returned to West Africa, he was put under house arrest.

We, Negroes of Africa, we raise our indignant protestation against the fate of our brothers in America. Shame to those Americans who feign to be civilized, but who have not yet condemned, by law, the outrage of lynching, and who continue to torture 15 million of our brothers! [. . .] We demand respect for the territorial integrity and the national independence of the rare African states, or states of African origin, which still possess their autonomy. Abyssinia, Liberia, Haiti and St. Domingo are striking proofs of the organizing and political genius of Negroes, notwithstanding the persistent sabotage by nations eager for conquest.

We claim the right to judge and to be judged — a judicial court should be instituted, and above all, we claim the right to be educated. It is necessary to organize compulsory education in the colonies. The education of the native is the best means of assuring his evolution and his adaptation to European civilization. It is necessary to develop Africa for the benefit of the Africans and not exclusively for the profit of the white man, and to assure freedom of commerce and industry.

Source: M. K. T. Houenou, "Opportunity" (July 1924), pp. 203-207, quoted in: A. Langley, pp. 228-238. — *Further Reading:* M. Crowder, *West Africa under Colonial Rule* (London, 1968), pp. 433-453.

191. Jomo Kenyatta: Christianity and Individualism (1938)

In his work *Facing Mount Kenya*, which was published in 1938, the Kenyan nationalist Jomo Kenyatta (ca. 1891-1978) emphasized the values of traditional African culture and attacked Western individualism, which had also been represented by Christian mission. In 1947, Kenyatta became president of the Kenya African Union (later the Kenyan African National Union). From 1963 to 1964 he was prime minister of Kenya, from 1964 to 1978 its president.

We can see [. . .] that the early teachers of the Christian religion in Africa did not take into account the difference between the individualistic aspects embodied in Christian religion, and the communal life of the African regulated by customs and tradition handed down from generation to generation. They failed, too, to realize that the welfare of the tribes depended on the rigid observance of these tribal taboos and rights, through which all the members of a tribe, from kings and chiefs down to the lowest and most insignificant individual, were bound up as one organic whole and controlled by an iron-bound code of duties. The agencies of the Western religious bodies, when they arrived in Kenya, set about to tackle problems which they were not trained for. They condemned customs and beliefs which they could not understand. Among other things, the missionary insisted that the followers of the Christian faith must accept monogamy as the foundation of the true Christian religion, and give up the dances, ceremonies and feasts which are fundamental principles of the African social structure.

Source: J. Kenyatta, *Facing Mount Kenya* (London, 1938), in: R. Desai (ed.), *Christianity in Africa as Seen by Africans* (Denver, 1962), p. 100.

192. Waruhiu Itote: World War II as Turning Point

The two world wars marked turning points in the relationship between Africa and Europe, since on the one hand the idea of European superiority had been discredited and on the other hand Africans who had fought on the side of Europeans now demanded their own rights. This is illustrated by the autobiographical account of Waruhiu Itote (b. 1922), who later became one of the leading forest fighters in the Mau Mau war.

The following years (1944) I was at the Calcutta Rest Camp, where I met a tall and powerful Negro from the American South. An English-speaking Tanganyikan, Ali, was with me and the three of us started chatting. 'What's your real name?' I asked the Negro, when I read the name 'Stephenson' on his American Army bush jacket. 'What do you mean, 'real name'? That's my name right here, Stephenson' he replied. I explained that I meant his African name. [. . .]

'You guys', he said very clearly, 'are all looking at me as though I'm some freak, something strange, just because I don't have an African name. Well, I got this because somewhere, a long time ago, some Arabs shipped my people to America, and after that we all grew up in a Christian country. But the same thing can happen to people when the Christians come to them — you don't have to be taken to England to lose not only your names, but your whole way of life as well.' [. . .]

'All I can say' Stephenson went on, 'is that you shouldn't be misled by white Christians who tell you that they are superior with their holy names and their holy way of life. Jerusalem isn't in heaven, you know, it's just in Palestine and people are fighting there with bombs and shells, dying in so-called Holy Places.' This rather shocked me, for I had always believed Jerusalem to be in heaven. 'White Christians are fighting each other right now, so don't worry when they tell you not to fight for your own right', Stephenson told us, almost with a shout. 'But the whites who are fighting now will be heroes in their own countries forever and amen, while you Africans will be heroes for a day and then you'll be forgotten. If you want to be heroes, why don't you fight for your own countries?' [. . .] 'You should have demanded Independence as your minimum price for fighting,' he said.

Source: W. Itote, *Mau Mau General* (Nairobi, 1967), pp. 9-15, 23, 27-29, quoted in Langley, *Ideologies*, pp. 408-415.

193. Julius Nyerere and the Maryknoll Fathers

While in general the churches adopted either a "wait and see" or a negative attitude towards the national movements, there were also some instances in which certain missionary organizations supported some leaders. In Tanganyika (now Tanzania), Julius Nyerere (1922-1999), president of the Tanganyika African Association (since 1953) and of the Tanganyika African National Union (since 1954), had a reputation of being moderate. As a practicing Catholic he was supported by the Maryknoll Fathers.

The Maryknoll Fathers agreed to finance this trip from England and back to England because Julius Nyerere is a Catholic leader, a man from the Prefecture of Musoma, known and respected by our Fathers. Since it is the declared policy of the British authorities in Tanganyika to prepare leaders for eventual self-government, the Maryknoll Fathers felt that any help we could give Catholic leaders would be a help to the Church. He is a good Catholic, a man with moderate views in promoting the political ambitions of his people. He is not unaware that there are some hot-heads in his Union but he is trying to guide the union along a reasonable path. This union is registered with the government and is not a clandestine movement.

Source: Maryknoll Fathers Central Archives (New York: W. Collins), "Report on Julius Nyerere and His Relations with the Maryknoll Fathers in Tanganyika, British East Africa, Feb. 11, 1957"; cf. F. Ludwig, *Church and State in Tanzania* (Leiden, 1999).

V. AFRICA 1945-1990

A. "WIND OF CHANGE"

194. Harold Macmillan: Wind of Change (1960)

The wave of independence which had started in Asia after the Second World War reached Africa in the 1950s. Egypt became independent in 1952, Tunisia, Morocco and Sudan in 1956. Ghana followed in 1957, Guinea in 1958. The "Africa year" 1960 saw the independence of Cameroon, Congo-Brazzaville, Gabun, Chad, the Central African Republic, Togo, Ivory Coast, Dahomey, Upper Volta, Niger, Nigeria, Senegal, Mali, Madagascar, Somalia, Mauretania, and Congo-Leopoldville. It may therefore be justifiable to summarize these periods under the motto of a speech which the British Prime Minister Harold Macmillan delivered on a visit to Cape Town, South Africa, to the old Cape Colony Parliament on February 3, 1960.

Ever since the break-up of the Roman Empire one of the constant facts of political life in Europe has been the emergence of independent nations. They have come into existence over the centuries in different forms, with different kinds of Government, but all have been inspired by a deep, keen feeling of nationalism, which has grown as the nations have grown.

In the twentieth century, and especially since the end of the war, the processes which gave birth to the nation states of Europe have been repeated all over the world. We have seen the awakening of national consciousness in peoples who have for centuries lived in dependence upon some other power. Fifteen years ago this movement spread through Asia. Many countries there of different races and civilizations pressed their claim to be an independent national life. Today the same thing is happening in Africa, and the most striking of all the impressions I have formed is of the strength of this African national consciousness. In different places it takes different forms, but it is happening everywhere. The wind of change is blowing throughout this continent and, whether we like it or not, this growth of national consciousness is a political fact. We must all accept it as a fact, and our national policies must take account of it. [. . .]

Source: W. L. Arnstein, *The Past Speaks* (Heath, 1993), pp. 2, 386-389; H. Macmillan, *Pointing the Way, 1959-1961* (London, 1972). A taped reproduction is published in the British Library (ed.), *The Century in Sound* (London, 1999), p. 32. — *Further Reading:* R. Hyam/R. Louis (eds.), *The Conservative Government and the End of Empire 1957-1964.* 2 Vols. (London, 2000).

195. Pan-African Congress, Manchester (1945)

Pan-African congresses had been held from 1919 onwards (1919 and 1921 Paris, 1923 London, 1927 New York etc.). However, the congress in Manchester united many African leaders from British and French colonies for the first time. Regarding the political situation, the congress observed:

(a) That since the advent of British, French, Belgian and other Europeans in West Africa, there has been regression instead of progress as a result of systematic exploitation by these alien imperialist Powers. The claims of 'partnership,' 'trusteeship,' 'guardianship' and the 'mandate system' do not serve the political wishes of the people of West Africa. (b) That the democratic nature of the indigenous institutions of the peoples of West Africa has been crushed by obnoxious and oppressive laws and regulations, and replaced by autocratic systems of government which are inimical to the wishes of the people of West Africa. (c) That the introduction of pretentious constitutional reforms in West African territories are nothing but spurious attempts on the part of alien imperialist powers to continue the political enslavement of the peoples.

Source: A. Langley, pp. 758-760, 758.

196. First Conference of Independent African States (1958)

In May 1963 the Organisation for African Unity (OAU) was founded, after a first pan-African meeting had taken place in 1958 in Accra (Ghana).

We, the African States assembled here in Accra, in this our first conference, conscious of our responsibilities to humanity and especially to the peoples of Africa [. . .], and desiring to assert our African personality on the idea of peace, hereby proclaim and solemnly reaffirm our unswerving loyalty to the Charter of the United Nations, the Universal Declaration of Human Rights and the Declaration of the Asian-African Conference held at Bandung. We further assert and proclaim the unity among ourselves and our solidarity with the dependent peoples of Africa as well as our friendship with all nations. We resolve to preserve the unity of purpose and action in international affairs which we have forged among ourselves in this historic Conference, to safe-guard our hard-won independence, sovereignty and territorial integrity, and to preserve among ourselves the fundamental unity of outlook on foreign policy so that a distinctive African personality will play its part in cooperation with other peace-loving nations to further the cause of peace. [. . .] Recognising that the existence of colonialism in any shape or form is a threat to peace and security and independence of the African states and to world peace [. . .], [the Conference of Independent African States] [c]alls upon the Administering Powers to respect the Charter of the United Nations in this regard, and to take rapid steps to implement the provisions of the Charter and the political aspirations of the people namely self-determination and independence, according to the will of the people.[. . .]

Source: A. Langley, pp. 765-777. — *Further Reading:* F. Ansprenger, *Die Befreiungspolitik der Organisation für Afrikanische Einheit (OAU) 1963-1975* (München, 1975).

197. All Africa Conference of Churches (1963)

The Pan-African Movement also had an impact on the Church. The All Africa Conference of Churches was founded in Kampala in 1963 after a first preparatory meeting had taken place in Ibadan in 1958. The membership comprises Protestant, Anglican, Orthodox and Independent Churches. The main areas of work are theological education, youth and women ministries, work among refugees, literature and mass communication. The following is a message of the Inaugural Assembly.

We, three hundred and forty delegates and participants in the historic inaugural assembly of the All Africa Conference of Churches in Kampala (Uganda) [. . .] came here from one hundred churches in forty countries, and we found in the Cathedral on Namirembe Hill, that we, being many, are one body in Christ, and every one members of one another. On the Lord's day of April 21, 1963, most of us, the Lord's people, gathered at the Lord's table. We passed the Peace, we ate the bread, we drank the wine, and when we came out of the Lord's House, we said to ourselves: "Why did we have to come across Africa to discover this thing?" Now we ask you all the same question. Why, in Capetown and Dakar, in Douala and Nairobi, on the plains and by the rivers of this land, most we continue in those divisions which crucify the Lord until He comes?

Most of us here represented the Protestant Churches in Africa. One morning we shared in the ancient worship of the Orthodox Church of Ethiopia, led by our brother delegates from the Orthodox Christians in Africa, and we said: "This is the Lord's doing, and it is marvelous in our eyes. We were further blessed by having among us three official Roman Catholic observers."

We are deeply grateful to God that, at this assembly, the All Africa Conference of Churches has been duly constituted as a fellowship of consultation and co-operation within the wider fellowship of the universal Church. What was conceived at Ibadan in 1958 has become a reality at Kampala in 1963. We are confident that God will use the All Africa Conference of Churches as an instrument of his purpose to quicken the life of His church in Africa.

We have rejoiced that since Ibadan many new independent nations have been born in Africa. We identify ourselves with the aspirations of our people towards development of dignity and mature personality in Christ and we exhort the churches on this continent to participate wholeheartedly in the building of the African nation. We affirm that there is a larger freedom which God offers through His Son, so that men are liberated from the slavery of sin and fear, to live the rich, free, abundant life of the children of God. This is the Good News. [. . .]

Source: Drumbeats from Kampala. Report of the First Assembly of the All Africa Conference of Churches held at Kampala, April 20 to April 30, 1963 (London: United Society for Christian Literature, Lutterworth Press, 1963), pp. 15, 16.

198. "Unity and Freedom in the New Tanganyika"

In Tanganyika, the Catholic Bishops expressed their will to cooperate with the new government in the Pastoral Letter *Unity and Freedom in the New Tanganyika:* "All Catholics shall try to help build a soundly established Tanganyika, with ever growing dedication and enthusiasm." Social pluralism was given high priority:

[. . .] The Church, as ecclesiastical authority, has no jurisdiction over the State as a civil authority. As the civil authority has no direct competence in religious matters, so the ecclesiastical authority has no direct competence in civil matters. [. . .] but where the temporal and the supernatural join — in for instance in education, in legislation regarding marriage etc. — the Church has the right and the duty to give directions to the faithful in order to safeguard the religious aspect of these matters. Similarly whenever religious observances have also a civil aspect, the State has the right and the duty to exercise its function as guardian of the common good of all citizens [. . .] for the Church and for the individual Catholic collaborations with the State and loyal performance of our temporal duties do not mean the exclusion of religious influence in public life, much less a compromise as to religious beliefs and practises. It would therefore be an unrealistic stand for anyone who has the welfare of the community at heart. to consider religion and the State as two things which have nothing to do with each other. [. . .]

Source: Rhodes House Oxford 954.12r 42 (8) Unity and Freedom in the New Tanganyika, signed by Laurean Cardinal Rugambwa and 19 other bishops, Tabora 1960, p. 2; cf. Frieder Ludwig, *Church & State in Tanzania* (Leiden, 1999), p. 37.

199. Protestant Missions and Rebellion in Angola (1969)

Most of the African states attained political independence during the 1950s and early 1960s. There were however some exceptions. The Portuguese colonies Angola and Mozambique remained under Portuguese control until the mid-1970s. As the following document by the Information Service shows, Protestant missions here were seen as potentially subversive while the Catholic Church was still very much regarded as an ally of the colonial regime.

(1) Protestantism is widely disseminated throughout the Province. (a) There are technical indications that some Protestant missions assisted and certainly continue to favour subversion at least rendering a de-nationalizing function. [. . .] (c) At present, those Protestant missions which are potentially dangerous are the ones served by American and Canadian pastors. (d) The most important factor for the "adhesion" of the population to Protestantism is medical and scholarly assistance, which the Protestant missions provide in the areas of their influence. . . . (f) Such being the case, the best way of canceling, or attenuating the influence of Protestant missions among the African people appears to be the establishment of schools and sanitary posts where they are active. (2) Suggestion: We are here dealing with a delicate problem, which, however, appears necessary to tackle in a plan for counter-subversion. On one hand, open persecution of Protestant missions is not politically advisable. On the other hand their work in the medical and scholarly field has been of merit, and the Government is not in a position to dispense of their services, at least not presently. Such being the case [. . .] it is suggested that the orientation to follow should be this (a) Attempting to hinder the spreading of Protestant proselytizing, by intensification of sanitary and scholarly assistance of Catholic or official type, in zones where Protestant missions exercise a major influence over the African population. (b) Intensifying the relations between the official administration and the Protestant missions (1) to control the activities of the missions, observing and receiving, by discreet methods, information concerning their actions

(2) to obtain the cooperation of the missionaries, as it is known that some would be ready to cooperate with us.

Source: Direccao dos Servicos de Centralizacao e Coordenacao de Informacoes de Angola: Plano de Contra-Subversao, signed by Rairo Ladeiro Monteiro, O Chefe do Servico, Luanda, Jan. 6, 1969 (DMPL 1823 D), quoted in: Alf Helgesson, *Church, State and People in Mozambique* (Uppsala, 1994), pp. 333, 334.

B. African Churches and Nation Building

200. All Africa Conference of Churches: Africa in Transition

In the early 1960s, many African states had attained political independence. The Churches now faced new challenges such as identifying the role of Christianity in the independent nations, many of which were soon characterized by one-party systems. This is expressed in the AACC study "Africa in Transition" of 1962, which was based on various case-studies.

Gaining political independence . . . is not the end of the problem; yet no solution, however technically perfect, is acceptable to the African people, if it falls short of political independence, because without a national self-identity man cannot be fully man at this stage of human history. [. . .] As Christians throughout Africa studied the problem of nation-building, they began to sense the heavy burden they as citizens of newly independent countries must share. This is well illustrated in the Nigeria study on "Christian Responsibility in an Independent Nigeria," which contains a penetrating analysis of nationalism as socio-cultural, as well as politico-spiritual dynamic: "Since nationalism is subjective and largely based upon the feeling of unity and of common heritage or destiny, it is difficult to define objectively. In its original use it meant loyalty to an ethnic group as compared to patriotism which referred to loyalty to one's country, to the land in which one lived. In the modern nation-states the two have been combined and one usually thinks of nationalism developing among a group which shares such things in common as government, language, religion, race, a common heritage and common ideals. Divided as we are into tribal and linguistic groups and inhabiting a country which was created only sixty years ago, one would certainly question the extent to which Nigeria is a nation. [. . .] Here, however, as well as in much of Africa, the spirit of nationalism has developed more out of our hopes and aspirations than out of the common experience of past history. [. . .]

Freedom from colonialism . . . means the freedom and obligation of all nationals to participate in the nation's political life. Christians cannot evade it. In most African countries this is easier said than done for two reasons. In the first place, the Christian movement has of necessity for years been under the leadership of expatriate missionaries and rightly or wrongly as tradition has been established that "Christians are not to take part in politics." This tradition tends to condition the thinking of both the government and the church even after independence. [. . .] In the second place, the newly emergent nations lack the competent leadership to cope with the gigantic task of nation-building. The task is bound to be infinitely more complex for African than for Western nations . . . because in Africa . . . the present (what is) finds itself under the tension between the old (what used to be) and the new (what is to come). The old has not completely passed away and the new has not yet fully come, nor can the new be built on the foundation of the old. Neither the wisdom of the old tribal chief nor the technical competence of the Western-trained politician is sufficient. This problem, which is indeed at the heart of Africa today, can only be met through a corporate approach by responsible men and women of various professional skills and insights.

Source: All Africa Conference of Churches, *Africa in Transition: The Challenge and the Christian Response* (Geneva, 1962), pp. 18-21, 26-27. *Further Reading:* D. Maxwell, "Post-colonial Christianity in Africa," in: H. McLeod, *World Christianities,* pp. 401-421; M. A. Oduyoye, "Africa," in: J. Briggs/M. A. Oduyoye/G. Tsetis, *A History of the Ecumenical Movement,* Vol. 3, 1968-2000 (Geneva, 2004), pp. 469-493.

201. Kwame Nkrumah: Conciencism (1964)

With his concept of "Consciencism," the Ghanaian president Kwame Nkrumah (cf. document 186) developed a philosophy which could be used to justify his repressive system. During the freedom struggle of the 1950s, Nkrumah's support in the country had been overwhelming, and when, in February 1951, a general election was held to elect a legislature, he won it hands down. He was released from prison a few days later amidst wildly enthusiastic scenes, the singing of "Lead, Kindly Light" and the slaughter of a lamb at his feet. There were also articles which glorified Nkrumah in religious terms, such as the "Verandah Boys" Creed which was published in the *Accra Evening News* (document 202).

The philosophy that must stand behind this social revolution is that which I have once referred to as philosophical consciencism; consciencism is the map in intellectual terms of the disposition of forces which will enable African society to digest the Western and the Islamic and the Euro-Christian elements in Africa, and develop them in such a way that they fit into the African personality. The African personality is itself defined by the cluster of humanist principles which underlie the traditional African society. Philosophical conciencism is that philosophical standpoint which, taking its start from the present content of the African conscience indicates the way in which progress is forged out of the conflict in that conscience.

Source: Kwame Nkrumah, *Consciencism: Philosophy and Ideology for Decolonization* (New York: Monthly Review Press, 2nd edition, 1970), p. 79.

202. Ghana: "Verandah Boys" Creed

I believe in the Convention People's Party, the opportune Saviour of Ghana, and in Kwame Nkrumah its founder and leader, who is endowed with the Ghana Spirit, born a true Ghanaian for Ghana, suffering under victimizations: was vilified, threatened with deportation; he disentangled himself from the clutches of the U.G.C.C. (United Gold Coast Convention) and the same day he rose victorious with the "verandah boys," ascended the Political Heights, and sitteth at the Supreme head of the C.P.P. (Convention People's Party) from whence he shall demand Full Self-Government for Ghana. I believe in Freedom for all peoples, especially the new Ghana; the Abolition of Slavery, the liquidation of Imperialism, the Victorious end of our struggle, its glory and its pride, and the Flourish of Ghana, for ever and ever.

Source: Accra Evening News, quoted in: T. Bankole, *Kwame Nkrumah: His Rise to Power* (London, 1955), p. 81.

203. Léopold Senghor: Islam and Christianity (1964)

Léopold Sédar Senghor (1906-2001), who, although Catholic, served as the national president of predominantly Islamic Senegal from 1960 to 1980, was committed to a very different concept. Senghor formulated the principle of "Black pride" (the appreciation of African culture) and sought to create a bridge between Africa and Europe. He was as effective as a philosopher and poet, winning the 1968 German Publishers' Peace Prize. As a statesman, he was concerned with the question of peaceful coexistence among the different religious communities in the young African nations.

It is a sign of the times: In the past few years, since the acceleration of the "decolonizing" process, appeals have been drafted and efforts have been undertaken to organize cooperative efforts between the Muslims and Christians. Last year the rector of El Azhar-University invited Christians and Muslims to join in countering the onslaught of atheism. And in this same year, his Excellency Abdelkader Ei Fassi, ambassador from Morocco to Bonn, made a noteworthy speech entitled "A Muslim in the World of Christianity." From the Christian perspective, I could have termed the colloquies, which had been organized by the Jesuits in the heart of Morocco in the face of all the risks which countless priests had taken upon themselves, as an appeal from the Bishops of Maghreb to reach a peaceful solution to the Algerian conflict. Many of the priests had paid for remaining faithful to the ideal of Christendom by being imprisoned.

To this moral and religious foundation I add a political dimension. We cannot achieve true independence and build a modern African nation if we cannot overcome religious differences as well as race differences — if we are not diligent in fostering fruitful cooperation between Muslims and Christians.

Even if Muslims and Christians both worship the one uncreated God of Creation, as is testified to by the numerous named attributes of God, both here and there, they nevertheless do not conceive of God or worship God in the same ways. For Christians, God reveals himself to us in the mystery of the Trinity. Jesus is God and at the same time God's Son, who became man to save us from our sins. For Muslims, who reject the mystery of the Trinity, Jesus is only an extraordinary prophet of God. Even Mohammed, the last and greatest prophet, may not be confused with God. For Christians the Pope, who embodies the church, is the protector of God's Word. The Pope is unerring in his interpretation of Scripture. No such binding position has been imposed on the Muslims: They interpret the Koran freely. The priest is the important connecting link between God and the Christians. The Muslims have no clergy; they can turn directly to God by themselves.

Besides these differences in dogma and practice, Islam and Christianity preach the same virtues and strive for the same goal. The great commandment of Christianity is to love God above all else, and the second is to love all other humans as you would love yourself. And Mohammed said, "No one of you is faithful, if he does not love his brother as he loves himself." Jesus and Mohammed fought against both individualistic materialism and egoism, which have been characteristic of atheistic civilizations throughout time and have shaped the civilization of the twentieth century. In this battle, the will of God is evidenced as much in Islam as in Christianity.

Source: Léopold Senghor, *Negritude und Humanismus* (Düsseldorf/Köln: E. Diederich, 1967), pp. 234ff.

204. Julius Nyerere on the Church in Africa (1970)

In the Arusha Declaration of 1967, the ruling party in Tanzania TANU (Tanzania African National Union) under Julius Nyerere (cf. document 193) resolved to implement a new program which should lead Tanzania into economic independence. Central was the idea of "living together" (Ujamaa) and the development of rural communities ("villagisation"). The concept of African socialism marked a new period in Africa. The epoch of Nkrumah (who had lost power in 1966) was over, while Nyerere started to become influential. In his speeches and writings he also developed ideas on the role of the church. An example of this is a lecture which he gave to the Maryknoll Sisters in New York on October 16, 1970.

[. . .] in order to fulfill its own purpose of bringing men to God, the Church must seek to ensure that men can have dignity in their lives and in their work. It must itself become a force of social justice and it must work with other forces of social justice wherever they are, and whatever they are called. Further, the Church must recognize that men can only progress and can only grow in dignity by working for themselves, and working together for their common good. The Church cannot uplift a man; it can only help to provide the conditions and the opportunity for him to co-operate with his fellows to uplift himself.

What does this mean for those who give their lives to the church? First, it means that kindness is not enough; piety is not enough; and charity is not enough. The men who are now suffering from poverty, whether they are in the Third World or in the developed world, need to be helped to stretch themselves; they need to be given confidence in their own ability to take control of their own lives. And they need to be helped to take this control, and to use it themselves for their own purposes. They need their uhuru, and meaningful uhuru. This is important to the Church, as well as to mankind. For until men are in a position to make effective choices, few of them will become Christians in anything but name. Their membership of the Church will be simply another method by which they escape from a consciousness of their misery; if you like, religion becomes a kind of opium of the people. Everything which prevents a man from living in dignity and decency must therefore be under attack from the Church and its workers. For there is, in fact, nothing saintly in imposed poverty, and, although saints must be found in slums, we cannot preserve slums in order to make them breeding grounds for saints. A man who has been demoralized by the conditions under which he is forced to live is no use to himself, to his family, or to his nation. Whether he can be of much use to God is not for me to judge.

The Church has to help men to rebel against their slums; it has to help them do this in the most effective way it can be done. But most of all the Church must be obviously and openly fighting all those institutions, and power groups, which contribute to the existence and maintenance of the physical and spiritual slums — regardless of the consequences to itself or its members. And, wherever and however circumstances make it possible, the Church must work with the people in the positive tasks of building a future based on social justice. It must participate actively in initiating, securing, and creating the changes which are necessary and which will inevitably take place. Only by doing these things can the church hope to reduce hatred and promote its doctrine of love to all men.

Source: J. K. Nyerere, *Freedom and Development* (London, 1973), pp. 219, 220. — *Further Reading:* F. Ludwig, *Church & State in Tanzania* (Leiden, 1999).

205. Christian Council, Tanzania: Inevitable Change (1977)

Whereas in the 1960s the Tanzanian churches had been rather reserved towards the measures of the one-party system, in the 1970s critical voices grew more and more silent. In 1977 the Christian Council of Tanzania attempted to assume a principal role in the development of African socialism.

[. . .] Yet realising that such change cannot come overnight but eventually evolves only out of a long and bitter struggle with the external and internal forces of capitalism certain concrete steps have to be taken now in order to facilitate such change. Each of such steps, as it applies to changing the vocational educational system or to re-thinking the project and development strategies of the Churches, will have to be guided by a few essential conditions that are indispensable in Tanzania's struggle for building a socialist and self-reliant society:

  (i) It must clearly serve the objective interests of the direct producers, the workers and peasants, and help them concretely in their struggle for building a socialist and self-reliant society and for sufficing their basic needs.
 (ii) It must clearly attack the system of capitalism, the classes inside and outside our country that support it, from it and the exploitative and oppressive mechanism that reproduce this system.
(iii) It must clearly attack our economic dependency which is part of the international capitalist system, and contribute concretely towards disengagement from international capitalism by promoting the building of a nationally integrated and self-sustained socialist economy.

Source: Christian Council of Tanzania, Rural Vocational Education in Tanzania. Conclusions, Recommendations and Implementation, approved and passed by the Annual Conference of the CCT, Tabora, 8-9 Nov. 1977, quoted in: F. Ludwig, *Das Modell Tanzania* (Berlin, 1995), pp. 226-238.

C. African Theology

206. Lamin Sanneh: Translating the Message (1988)

Lamin Sanneh from Gambia taught at the Center for the Study of World Religions and at the University of Aberdeen in Scotland before becoming professor of missions and world Christianity at Yale Divinity School. His *Translating the Message: The Missionary Impact on Culture* (1988) became one of the influential books in Mission studies.

Christian missionaries assumed that since all cultures and languages are lawful in God's eyes, the rendering of God's word into those languages and cultures is valid and necessary. Even if in practice Christians wished to stop the translation process, claiming their own form of it as final and exclusive, they have not been able to suppress it. At any rate, Christian mission became the most explicit machinery for the cultivation of vernacular particularity as a condition of universal faithfulness to the gospel. In centering on the primacy of God's word, Christian translators invested the vernacular with consecrated power, lifting obscure tribes to the level of scriptural heritage and into the stream of universal world history. Almost everywhere vernacular participation in the Christian movement led to internal religious and cultural renewal, often with immediate consequences for political nationalism. The Christian view that culture may serve God's purpose stripped culture of idolatrous liability, emancipating it with the force of translation and usage.

Source: Excerpts from Lamin Sanneh, "Pluralism and Christian Commitment," *Theology Today,* 45:1 (April 1988), pp. 21, 27, 33; cf. Norman Thomas, *Classic Texts in Mission & World Christianity* (New York, 1995), pp. 279, 280

207. Kwesi Dickson: The Theology of the Cross (1984)

Kwesi Dickson is a Ghanaian Methodist who studied theology in Oxford. He has had a distinguished academic career and has taught mainly at the University of Ghana where he was Professor of Theology and Religion and Director of the Institute of African Studies.

No matter what the cultural perspective of the Christian might be, the matter of Christ's death and its significance cannot but be considered most central; Christians everywhere, from whatever cultural background, must react to this central belief. And yet it has been argued that the cross being such a central event, all talk of culture not only loses its significance, but also it amounts setting man's pride over and against the gospel; according to this argument, the gospel underlines the seriousness of sin which permeates human life and thought. This cannot be the last word, however, for as long as it is only flesh and blood which will stand beneath the Cross, the question of meaning and significance, in relation to human or cultural identities, arises. Indeed, the annals of the Church reveal that the Cross has been seen from different perspectives in accordance with prevailing cultural circumstances. [. . .]

African Thought. [. . .] 1. The African believes that death binds up relationships in society, revitalizing the living and underscoring their sense of community. Paul's language about the Cross clearly adumbrates this kind of understanding. He writes: 'The cup of blessing which we bless, is it not a participation in the blood of Christ? The bread which we break, is it not a participation in the body of Christ? Because there is one bread, we who are many are one body, for we all partake of the one bread. Consider the people of Israel, are not those who eat the sacrifices partakers in the altar?' (1 Cor 10:16-18). [. . .] It is evident that the kind of language Paul is using here relates his ideas very closely to the African experience and the goal of life. Not only is this kind of common meal as a sacred act widely known in African ritual, but also one of the life's goals, as already noted, is to maintain the social solidarity, and hence society's equilibrium. 2. It has been pointed out that one of the implications of the communal meal in Israelite sacrifice (as in sacrifice in African traditional religion) was that the worshipper and kinsmen had fellowship with God. Now the Cross is the supreme sacrifice in which Christ is both the initiator and the victim, so that in a singular sense by His death on the Cross Christ is linked to us. One very important piece of Old Testament legislation on sacrifice may be recalled: the victim for sacrifice was to be without blemish. Christ was the perfect victim; by his death he merits, to use an African image, to be looked upon as an Ancestor, the greatest of ancestors, who never ceases to be one of the 'living dead', because there always will be people alive who knew Him, whose lives were irreversibly affected by His life and work. He becomes the one with whom the African Christian lives intimately (as well as with other living dead) on whom he calls, and to whom he offers prayer. The physical Cross, like the staffs and stools looked upon as material representations symbolizing the presence of the ancestors, becomes the symbol of Christ's being the ever-living. 3. The Cross does not deny our human identities and the life-characteristics which go with them. Paul himself is an illustration of the truth of this assertion. He was a Jew who treasured the Jewish identity; the New Testament documents leave us in no doubt about this. Indeed, he found the Jewish national characteristics most helpful to him in his attempt to state Christian realities, hence the extent to which his language recalls institutions belonging to the 'Old Israel.' He describes the death of Christ using the language of the Passover, that great feast which his fathers had celebrated in Egypt and which was still celebrated in his time by Jews, and by Jewish Christians alike; it was indeed understood that every celebration was a participation in the first Passover. Paul needed the Jewish background in order to express most vitally the significance of the death of Christ, that was the only way in which he could speak meaningfully about something that meant so much to him.

Source: K. Dickson, *Theology in Africa* (New York, 1984), pp. 185-189; cf. J. Parratt, *A Reader in African Christian Theology* (London, 1987), pp. 82-94, 82, 89-92.

208. John Mbiti: The Biblical Basis for African Theology

John Mbiti was born in 1931 in Kitui in Kenya. After his studies in Uganda (Makerere), the USA and England (Cambridge) he taught at Birmingham, Makerere and Hamburg. He contributed to various commissions of the WCC. His books made an impact on the study of "African Traditional Religion" which in his opinion showed the same features every-where in sub-Saharan Africa, as for instance the belief in a creator God. When reflecting on the development of Christianity in Africa, he — like Sanneh — started with the transla-tion process:

The Bible has been translated in part or in full into nearly six hundred African languages and has become the basis of African Christianity, even though the lit-eracy rate ranges from about 7 percent to 85 percent of the population in Afri-can countries. It may seem to be a contradiction that while African Christianity is biblically grounded, many of the 185 million Christians on our continent to-day cannot read. The Bible is a closed book for those who cannot read it: they only hear it read or recited to them; nevertheless, through the translation and increasing use of the Scriptures the biblical world has been integrated with that of the traditional African world at all levels. The Bible is distributed extremely widely throughout what we may call 'Christian Africa', i.e., the Southern two-thirds of the continent and Madagascar. Its potential and actual influence in shaping African theology and Christianity is tremendous.

There are three main areas of African theology today: written theology, oral theology and symbolic theology. Written African theology is the privilege of a few Christians who have had considerable education and who generally ar-ticulate their theological reflections in articles and (so far only a few) books, mostly in English, French, German, or another European languages. Oral theol-ogy is produced in the fields, by the masses, through song, sermon, teaching, prayer, conversation etc. It is theology in the open air, often unrecorded, often heard only by small groups, and generally lost to libraries and seminaries. Sym-bolic theology is expressed through art, sculpture, drama, symbols, rituals, dance, colours, numbers etc. [. . .]

Theology is not produced by advice alone, and those who have enough advice to give about it should first use their advice for themselves; let them produce theological works and let these works speak for themselves. I say this to both African and overseas Christians. We are tired of being advised. Let the Bible be our human adviser and the Holy Spirit our Divine Adviser. [. . .] Like the African proverb that says that "the eyes of the frog do not stop the giraffe from drinking water in the pond," neither should the critical, sceptical, or advice-filled eyes of others prevent creative theologians from engaging in theological output.

I discern remarkable signs in the development of African theology. In this development the Bible is playing a crucial role, even if not in every case. African Christianity has the Bible at its forefront, and the Bible is shaping much of its development both explicitly and implicitly.

Source: J. Mbiti, "The Biblical Basis for Present Trends in African Theology," in: K. Appiah–Kubi/S. Torres (eds.), *African Theology en Route* (New York, 1979), pp. 83-94, here: pp. 83f, 90f.

209. Steve Biko: Black Consciousness (1973)

The South African politician and founder of the Black Conscious Movement Steve Biko (1946-1977) established the South African Students' Organisation. In 1973 he became honorary president of the Black People's Convention. In the same year he published the article "Black Consciousness and the Quest for a True Humanity." Between 1974 and 1977 he was arrested four times by the Apartheid Regime. During his last arrest, he was severely injured and died on September 12, 1977.

African religion in its essence was not radically different from Christianity. We also believed in one God, we had our own community of saints through whom we related to our God, and we did not find it compatible with our way of life to worship God in isolation from the various aspects of our lives. Hence worship was not a specialised function that found expression once a week in a secluded building, but rather it feathered in our wars, our beer-drinking, our dances and our customs in general. [. . .] There was no hell in our religion. We believed in the inherent goodness of man — hence we took it for granted that all people at death joined the community of saints and therefore merited our respect.

It was the missionaries who confused the people with their new religion. They scared our people with stories of hell. They painted their God as a demanding God who wanted worship 'or else'. People had to discard their clothes and their customs in order to be accepted in this new religion. [. . .] More than anyone else, the missionaries knew that not all they did was essential to the spread of the message. But the basic intention went much further than merely spreading the word. Their arrogance and their monopoly on truth, beauty and moral judgment taught them to despise native customs and traditions and to seek to infuse their own new values into these societies.

Here then we have the case for Black Theology. While not wishing to discuss Black Theology at length, let it suffice to say that it seeks to relate God and Christ once more to the black man and his daily problems. It wants to describe Christ as a fighting God, not as a passive god who allows to lie to rest unchallenged. It grapples with existential problems and does not claim to be a theology of the absolutes. It seeks to bring God back to the black man and to the truth and reality of his situation.

Source: Steve Biko, "Black Consciousness and the Quest for a True Humanity," in: Basil Moore (ed.), *The Challenge of Black Theology in South Africa* (Atlanta, 1973), pp. 36-47, here: pp. 42, 43.

210. Manas Buthelezi: Black Theology (1973)

Manas Buthelezi was bishop of the Central Diocese of the United Evangelical Lutheran Church of South Africa. In his writings he reflects critically on the role of Western Africa experts:

I am suspicious of 'African experts' who, without being invited, come from outside our black experience and propose theological as well as sociological programmes showing how the past cultural patterns can shape and condition our lives today. It must be a black man who best knows how to live as a black man today. [. . .]

If the Gospel means anything, it must save the black man from his own blackness. It must answer his basic existential question 'Why did God create me black?' This problem has partly been accentuated by linguistic usage. In many languages blackness is a symbol of evil, sin and ugliness; it is also a symbol of death and mourning. If St. John the Divine in the Book of Revelation describes the risen saints as dressed in white, he was merely following a certain language pattern and not some divinely inspired spiritual categories.

The Black Man must be enabled through the interpretation and application of the Gospel to realise that blackness, like whiteness, is a good natural face cream from God and not some cosmological curse. Here lies the contribution of Black Theology's methodological technique. Black Theology challenges established Christianity to engage in a dialogue with the black people who feel that somehow theology has not taken them into consideration. It cautions the preacher and minister to stop preaching a 'pie in the sky' religion, but instead to come down and toil with the black man spiritually and existentially in the sweat and dust of daily life. As soon as this objective has been realized, the whole world will know us as human beings and not merely study-curiosities to adorn the pages of doctoral dissertations.

Source: Manas Buthelezi, "An African Theology or a Black Theology," in: Basil Moore (ed.), *The Challenge of Black Theology in South Africa* (Atlanta, 1973), pp. 29-35, here: pp. 34, 35.

211. Kimbangu's New Jerusalem (1951)

The Kimbanguist Church (Église sur la Terre par le Prophète Simon Kimbangu/EJCSK) was established by followers of Simon Kimbangu from Nkamba in Congo who had initiated a great messianic movement in 1921. Charged with disturbing the public peace, he was arrested and imprisoned for thirty years. He died in 1951, and shortly after his death the EJCSK was founded by Diangienda, the third son of the prophet. Although there are many other organizations in western Congo which claim spiritual descent from Kimbangu, the EJCSK claimed Kimbangu's heritage exclusively for itself. In 1969 it was accepted into the World Council of Churches. The following is an extract of one of the few early theological texts which have been published:

Simon Kimbangu . . . raised the dead, caused the paralyzed to stand upright, gave sight to the blind, cleansed lepers, and healed all the sick in the name of the Lord Jesus. But he chased away those who practised witchcraft. [. . .] But in everything, whether raising the dead, healing the sick, or giving a blessing in the name of Jesus, first there must be prayer, then hymns, and then a teacher must read the Bible and teach the doctrines that change hearts, in order that all men shall leave their wickedness; for if that does not happen, then these blessings you have come to get become as fire to you. Believe in the Lord Jesus, he who saves you from your sins. For I am in obedience to Him. Now God our Father and his Son Jesus Christ are returned to us, so cease your wickedness. Every day the doctrine of repentance must be taught, and when it is finished the sick will be healed and the dead raised.

Now see how all the villages hasten to abandon their fetishes, see all the roads littered with fetishes of all kinds. People confessed their sins. Drums were broken, dancing forsaken. People struggled to seek out teachers. Churches were built overnight in all the villages. Those who had not cared to pray to God fought for places in church, and those who had no use for schools fought to enter the classroom.

Thus the words of Jesus were fulfilled, when he promised: "And I will pray the Father, and he shall give you another Comforter, that he may abide with you forever; Even the Spirit of truth, whom the world cannot receive, because it seeth him not, neither knoweth him: but ye know him; for he dwelleth with you, and shall be in you." (John 14:16-17) [. . .] With the work of the Lord God revealed by the hand of the Prophet, and the Heavenly Father made known to his people through his Prophet Simon Kimbangu, the hills of Satan also were revealed, their eyes fired with jealousy and envy. What kind of hills were these? The prophets of Satan, missionaries, the Belgian government. These hills stood up strongly to fight against the Church of Our Lord Jesus Christ on earth by his prophet Simon Kimbangu. Why were these hills so jealous? They knew that Jesus had given his power to the people of Africa, and that the city the Lord God had hidden, Jerusalem had descended here in Africa. But they should also know three reasons which surely show that God and Jesus surely cared for us: 1. When Jesus was born, and Herod wanted to kill him, he went to hide in Egypt (Matthew 2:13-15) 2. When Jesus was taken to be executed, Simon the African carried his cross (Mark 15:21) 3. God loves all peoples, because he made them (Acts 10:35).

Source: W. MacGaffey, "The Beloved City: Commentary on a Kimbanguist Text," *Journal of Religion in Africa* 2 (1969), pp. 129-147, here: pp. 138, 139. — *Further Reading:* A. M. Gampiot, *Kimbanguisme et identité noire* (Paris, 2004); M. L. Martin, *Kimbangu: An African Prophet and His Church* (Grand Rapids, 1971); W. Ustorf, *Afrikanische Initiative. Das aktive Leiden des Propheten Simon Kimbangu* (Frankfurt/Bern, 1975).

D. Church and Apartheid in South Africa

212. Ideology of Apartheid

Apartheid, an Afrikaans word meaning "separateness," denoted the South African policy applied by the Boer minority rule between 1948 and 1993. This policy of segregation rested on the assumption that races are the fundamental divisions of humanity. According to a law of 1983, South African society was divided in the four races of 22.7 million black Africans, 4.7 million whites, 2.8 million coloreds and 900,000 Asians. The main protagonists of Apartheid were the Boers, mainly Dutch immigrants. Their self-understanding of being a chosen race is illustrated by the poem of J. D. du Toits (1877-1953) (a). The politics of Apartheid were theologically supported by the Dutch Reformed Church (in the Republic of South Africa) and the Nederduitsch Hervormde Kerk van Afrika (b).

a. J. D. du Toits: The Boer Trekkers — A New Israel

But see! The world becomes wilder;
the fierce vermin worsen,
stark naked hordes,
following tyrants,

How the trekkers suffer,
just like another Israel,
lost in the veld — by enemies surrounded,
but for another Canaan elected,
led forward by God's plan.

b. Die Nederduitse Gereformeerde Kerk of Transvaal (1951): Internationalism Is Not Christian

The human attempt to restore unity, the internationalism and cosmopolitanism which emphasizes . . . the absolute fraternity of all people, is not derived from the Christian teachings . . . but is produced by pure humanist tendencies which decree that the human being should be the centre and measurement of all things. [. . .] From the French Revolution the principle of binding of international solidarity is the slogan of freedom, equality and fraternity. Communism on the other hand emphasises class division. [. . .] It is evident that God had ordained national governments in order to maintain law, order and justice but never did he institute any international government. [. . .] Thus the division of nations is to be directly derived from the authority of God and represents the social embodiment of the divine structure of authority. But this structure of authority extends further: The humanistic claim to equality is unscriptural because it does not take into account the fact that God has decreed structures of authority within every society. As the child cannot be equated with the parent, the labourer cannot be equated with the employer nor the subject with the authorities, so there are also differences in status within the nation. According to the Word of God the idea that Christianity ought to diminish differences in race, nation and status is most certainly wrong. [. . .]

Source: (a) V. E. d'Assonville (ed.), *Totius: Versamelde Werk* (Cape Town, 1977), vol. 10, 48, quoted in: I. Hexham, *The Irony of Apartheid: The Struggle for National Independence of Afrikaner Calvinism Against British Imperialism* (New York, 1981), p. 37; (b) Agenda van die 22ste Sinode van die Ne. Geref. Kerk van Suid-Afrika (1951), pp. 184, 187, quoted and translated in: J. Kinghorn, *Modernization and Apartheid: The Afrikaner Churches*, in: R. Elphick/T. R. H. Davenport, *Christianity in South Africa: A Political, Social and Cultural History* (Oxford, 1997), pp. 135-154, 144. — *Further Reading:* J. F. Noller, *Theorie und Praxis der Apartheid* (Frankfurt am Main/Bern/Las Vegas, 1977); RPP 1: Art. Apartheid (D. J. Smit).

213. Attitudes of the Churches

As a violation of human rights and democratic principles, the politics of Apartheid were faced by constantly growing national and international criticism. The resistance move-

ment included not only "black" African political organizations, but also some white opposition groups. The member churches in South Africa of the World Council of Churches
first made efforts towards a diplomatic solution and distanced themselves cautiously.
(a) Since these attempts were not fruitful and since it was more and more recognized
that rejection of Apartheid was not only a question of ethics but also a question of faith,
the two churches which supported this racist ideology — the Nederduitse Gereformeerde Kerk (in the Republic of South Africa) and the Nederduitsch Hervormde Kerk van
Africa were excluded from the World Alliance of Reformed Churches in 1982 (b). This led
to embittered reactions (c). Since 1968, when all political opposition was suppressed,
the South African Council of Churches (SACC) became more and more the 'voice of the
voiceless' within South Africa and was therefore itself persecuted by the state authorities. The prophetic calling of the church was central for the public witness of the SACC, as
is expressed in the Kairos document of 1985 (d). In the process of transition and overcoming of the Apartheid regime, the most representative gathering of South African
churches assembled in Rustenburg in November 1990 (e). Members of the Dutch Reformed churches publicly confessed their fault, formally declaring it was acknowledged
that support for Apartheid was a guilt, its theological legitimation a heresy and a sin, and
that concrete forms of compensation were demanded.

a. Cautious Distance: Cottesloe Consultation Statement (1961)

We have met as delegates from the member churches in South Africa of the
World Council of Churches, together with representatives of the World Council
itself, to seek under the guidance of the Holy Spirit to understand the complex
problems of human relationship in this country, and to consult with one another on our common task and responsibility in the light of the Word of God.
[. . .]

1. We recognize that all racial groups who permanently inhabit our country
are a part of our total population, and we regard them as indigenous. Members
of all these groups have an equal right to make their contribution towards the
enrichment of the life of their country and to share in the ensuing responsibilities, rewards and privileges. 2. The present tension in South Africa is the result
of a long historical development and all groups bear responsibility for it. This
must also be seen in relation to other parts of the world. The South African
scene is radically affected by the decline of the power of the West and by the desire for self-determination among the peoples of the South African continent.
3. The Church has a duty to bear witness to the hope which is in Christianity
both to white South Africans in their uncertainty and to non-white South Africans in their frustration. 4. In a period of rapid social change the Church has a
special responsibility for fearless witness within society. 5. The Church as a
body of Christ is a unity and within this unity the natural diversity among men
is not annulled but sanctified. 6. No one who believes in Jesus Christ may be ex-

cluded from any Church on the grounds of his colour and race. The spiritual unity among all men who are in Christ must find visible expression in acts of common worship and witness, and in fellowship and consultation on matters of common concern. 7. We regard with deep concern the revival in many areas of African society of heathen tribal customs incompatible with Christian belief and practice. We believe this reaction is partly the result of a deep sense of frustration and a loss of faith in Western civilization. (The whole Church must participate in the tremendous missionary task which has to be done in South Africa, and which demands a common strategy.) 9. Our discussions have revealed that there is not sufficient consultation and communication between the various racial groups which make up our population. There is a special need that a more effective consultation between the Government and leaders accepted by the non-White people of South Africa should be devised. The segregation of racial groups carried through without effective consultation and involving discrimination leads to hardship for members of the groups affected. [. . .]

b. Exclusion of the World Alliance of Reformed Churches (1982)

[. . .] 1. The General Council of the WARC affirms earlier statements on the issue of racism and apartheid ('separate development') made in 1964 and 1970, and reiterates its firm conviction that apartheid ('separate development') is sinful and incompatible with the Gospel on the grounds that: (a) it is based on a fundamental irreconcilability of human beings, thus rendering ineffective the reconciling and uniting power of our Lord Jesus Christ (b) in its application through racist structures it has led to exclusive privileges for the white section of the population at the expense of the blacks; (c) it has created a situation of injustice and oppression, large-scale deportation causing havoc to family life, and suffering to millions. 2. The General Council expresses its profound disappointment that, despite earlier appeals by the WARC General Councils, and despite continued dialogue between several Reformed Churches and the White Dutch Reformed Churches over twenty years, the Nederduitse Gereformeerde Kerk (in the Republic of South Africa) and the Nederduitsch Hervormde Kerk van Afrika have still not found the courage to realise that apartheid ('separate development') contradicts the very nature of the Church and obscures the Gospel from the world; the Council therefore pleads afresh with these Churches to respond to the promises and demands of the Gospel. 3. The General Council has a special responsibility to continue to denounce the sin of racism in South Africa as expressed in apartheid ('separate development'). It is institutionalised in the laws, policies and structures of the nation; it has resulted in horrendous injustice, in the suffering, exploitation and degradation of millions of black Africans for whom Christ died; and it has been given moral and theological justification by the white Dutch Reformed Churches in South Africa who are members of the WARC and with whom we share a common theological heritage in the Reformed tradition. 4. Therefore, the General Council, reluctantly and painfully, is compelled to suspend the Nederduitse Gereformeerde Kerk (in the Republic of South Africa) and the Nederduitsch Hervormde Kerk van Afrika from the privileges of membership in the WARC (i.e., sending delegates to General Councils and holding membership in departmental committees and commissions), until such time as the WARC Executive Committee has determined that these two churches in their utterances and practise have given evidence of a change of heart. [. . .]

c. Response of the Dutch Reformed Church

[. . .] By this decision the World Alliance of Reformed Churches wants to prescribe to us how to arrange the life and practice of our Church and what our attitude ought to be towards socio-political problems in our land while, at the same time, it holds before us by implication a political policy which is said to be good and right. We reject this claim by the Alliance: 1. To deprive us of our obligation and privilege to organize our Church life in a manner which is constantly tested against the demands of Holy Scripture, and to strive for the best practical way in which to fulfil our apostolic calling to be the Church of Jesus Christ giving due consideration to our experience within the unique South African ethnic situation (volkere-situasie). 2. To prescribe for us a political choice whereby we become a partner of those forces which, with disregard to the truth, with misuse of theology, and with reckless promotion of revolution, proclaim the objectives of godless communist imperialism. We claim the privilege as a Church of Jesus Christ to make our own choice what we regard to be responsible politics within our situation with full responsibility towards God and with a good conscience in relation to him. 3. To make a dogmatic pronouncement, with arrogant hypocrisy, concerning the political policy and circumstances in South Africa in response to misrepresentations, malicious exaggeration, and the calculated suppression of specific information. [. . .] The Nederduitsch Hervormde Kerk cannot comply with the requirements set by the World Alliance and it, therefore, has no choice but to withdraw.

d. The "Moment of Truth": The Kairos Document

In June 1985 as the crisis was intensifying in the country, as more and more people were killed, maimed and imprisoned, as one black township after another revolted against the apartheid regime, as the people refused to be oppressed or to co-operate with oppressors, facing death day by day, and as the apartheid army moved into the townships to rule by the barrel of the gun, a number of theologians who were concerned about the situation expressed the need to reflect on this situation to determine what response by the Church and by all Christians in South Africa would be most appropriate.

The time has come. The moment of truth has arrived. [. . .] It is the KAIROS or moment of truth not only for apartheid but also for the Church. [. . .] What the present crisis shows up, although many of us have known it all along, is that the Church is divided. [. . .] In the life and death conflict between different social forces that has come to a head in South Africa today, there are Christians (or at least people who profess to be Christians) on both sides of the conflict-and some who are trying to sit on the fence! [. . .] Our present KAIROS calls for a response from Christians that is biblical, spiritual, pastoral and, above all, prophetic. [. . .]

It would be quite wrong to see the present conflict as simply a racial war. [. . .] The situation we are dealing with here is one of oppression. [. . .]

This is our situation of civil war or revolution. [. . .] Throughout the Bible God appears as the liberator of the oppressed. He is not neutral. He does not attempt to reconcile Moses and Pharaoh, to reconcile the Hebrew slaves with their Egyptian oppressors or to reconcile the Jewish people with any of their late oppressors. Oppression is sin and it cannot be compromised with, it must be done away with. God takes sides with the oppressed. As we read in Psalm 103:6 (JB) "God who does what is right, is always on the side of the oppressed."

In other words a tyrannical regime has no moral legitimacy. [. . .]

A regime that is in principle the enemy of the people cannot suddenly begin to rule in the interests of all the people. [. . .] As Christians we are called upon to love our enemies (Mt 5:44). It is not said that we should not or will not have enemies or that we should not identify tyrannical regimes as indeed our enemies. But once we have identified our enemies, we must endeavor to love them. That is not always easy. But then we must also remember that the most loving thing we can do for both the oppressed and for our enemies who are oppressors is to eliminate the oppression, remove the tyrants from power and establish a just government for the common good of all the people.

e. Rustenburg Declaration

5.1. Confession and forgiveness necessarily require restitution. Without it, a confession of guilt is incomplete.

5.2. As a first step towards restitution, the Church must examine its land ownership and work for the return of all land expropriated from relocated communities to its original owners. 'White' schools must be opened to people of all races and programmes of affirmative action embarked upon at all levels of black education. [. . .] 5.6. Conference asks Churches to make available financial and human resources to enable the work of reconstruction and renewal of South African society. Conference asks Churches to cooperate in programmes for the welcoming back and rehabilitation of exiles.

Sources: (a) Charles Villa-Vicencio, *Between Christ and Caesar. Classic and Contemporary Texts on Church and State* (Cape Town, 1986), pp. 211-213, here: p. 212; (b) John W. de Gruchy and Charles Villa-Vicencio, *Apartheid Is a Heresy* (Cape Town: David Philip, 1983), pp. 168-173, here: pp. 171-172; (c) ibid., pp. 173-175; (d) http://www.bethel.edu/~letnie/AfricanChristianity/SAKairos.html; Charles Villa-Vicencio, *Between Christ and Caesar,* pp. 251-269; (e) C. Alberts/F. Chikane (eds.), *The Road to Rustenburg* (Cape Town, 1991). *Further Reading:* E. Lorenz (ed.), *Politik als Glaubenssache? Beiträge zur Klärung des Status Confessionis im südlichen Afrika und in anderen soziopolitischen Kontexten* (Erlangen, 1983); D. M. Balia, *Christian Resistance to Apartheid. Ecumenism in South Africa 1960-1987* (Ammersbek bei Hamburg, 1989); (b) J. W. De Gruchy, *The Church Struggle in South Africa* (London, ²1986, Minneapolis, 2005); J. W. De Gruchy, *Liberating Reformed Theology* (Grand Rapids, 1991); (e) L. Alberts/F. Chikane (eds.), *The Road to Rustenburg* (Cape Town, 1991).

E. Conflicts and New Beginnings

214. Tensions between Christians and Muslims

a. Sudan: "Here We Stand United in Action for Peace"

The political situation in Sudan, the largest territorial state in Africa, is characterized by regional conflicts between the Arab-Islamic North and the South whose Bantu population follows either African traditional religions or Christianity. In the Missionary Societies Act of 1962, missionary work, religious media and the activities of social organizations were forbidden. In 1964 all missionaries in southern Sudan were deported. The tensions escalated since 1983 when the military regime of Numeiri started to Islamize the South and to introduce Islamic Law (Sharia). After the fall of Numeiri it was not possible to resolve the conflict, since a strong party, the National Islamic Front, insisted on the upholding of sharia. The document "Here We Stand United in Action for Peace" (1996) was the first attempt of the Sudanese Churches to contribute directly to the search for peace in Sudan at the national level. The document mandated the international Christian community to speak about the suffering of the Sudanese people and the need for a sustained peace process, knowing they were speaking for the Sudanese Church. The document was backed both by the Sudan Council of Churches as well as by the New Sudan Council of Churches.

Whatever political solution is chosen by the people, we believe that peace and harmony will depend on the following principles being followed. (i) A recognition that all human beings are created by God and are precious and equal in his sight. (ii) Acceptance that cultural, linguistic and social diversity is a gift of God's creation, and not to be suppressed. It is rather to be celebrated and recognized as a national richness and resource. (iii) Freedom of religious expression, worship and witness. (iv) A recognition that a lasting and true peace must be based on justice and full and equal rights for all citizens. (v) Participation in political, social and economic life should be open to all irrespective racial, ethnic, social and religious background. (vi) A resolve to steadily widen the effective participation of all the people in political processes and decision making. (vii) Political and social conflicts should be solved peacefully. (viii) An openness to trusting dialogue between alienated political, social and religious groups within society. As leaders of the Sudanese Church we commit ourselves to defend and promote these principles and to work for reconciliation at all levels. We commit ourselves to pray for peace, for reconciliation, for those who suffer, for the oppressed and for the oppressor.

b. Nigeria: Demands to Restrict Sharia (1978)

In Nigeria, with 130 million inhabitants the most populous country of Africa, there were also tensions between Christians and Muslims. As a consequence of their politics of "Indirect Rule," a modified sharia legislation had continued to exist under British colonial rule in Muslim-dominated Northern Nigeria. The law system was reformed just before the coming of political independence; the sharia courts now only decided cases in civil law and no longer in criminal law. However, in the 1970s as well as in the 1990s and 2000s there were attempts by Muslims to strengthen sharia legislation. When in 1976 a new constitution was developed, the question of what role the Islamic law should play resurfaced. Spokesmen of Christian groups demanded a restriction of sharia law:

1. Restrict Sharia courts to where they already exist at the state level (1), provided they are not used as a means of victimization of non-Muslims in such states. (2) Restrict the jurisdiction on Sharia courts to persons or civil law, invalidating discriminating consequences on Christian parties (3) Whereas official representation is given to Islam the Federal level should be also granted to other religions. We recommend equal treatment with Government Fund, e.g., sponsoring religious projects and obligations like pilgrimages, Islamic Religious teachers in schools or colleges buildings and mosques etc. (4) We call for a separation between the state and religion in all its ramifications as stated in section 17 of the Draft Committee. We advise that Nigeria should have a uniform judicial system for all her citizens, irrespective of their religious and cultural backgrounds. Hence all the non-common laws should be put in a melting pot, or else preferential treatment for a particular religion will call for strong agitations by other religious groups.

Source: (a) "Here We Stand United in Action for Peace." The Position of the Sudanese Church on the Current Conflict in the Country. Our Vision for Sudan's Future (Morges, Switzerland, Sept. 25th, 1996) (Extracts), quoted in: R. Werner/W. Anderson/A. Wheeler, *The History of the Sudanese Church Across 2000 Years* (Nairobi, 2000), p. 658; (b) Quoted in L. Rassmussen, *Christian-Muslim Relations in Africa: The Cases of Northern Nigeria and Tanzania Compared* (London, 1993), p. 65. — *Further Reading:* J. O. Hunwick (ed.), *Religion and National Integration in Africa* (Evanston, 1992); H. B. Hansen/M. Twaddle, *Christian Missionaries & the State in the Third World* (Oxford, 2002).

215. Ghana: Dialogue Efforts since 1987

There were regional differences in Ghana between the more strongly Christianized South and the primarily Islamic North. For Christians living in the north, ecumenical dialog initiatives such as the "Islam in Africa Project" of 1959 (in 1987 renamed the "Project for Christian-Muslim Relations in Africa" [PROCMURA]) were important. The Reverend Dr. Johnson Mbillah describes the realization of the program this way:

In Ghana we have our own "North-South" conflict. [. . .] For many reasons, the North is poorer. The climate is much more arid. We can barely eke out a subsistence economy and in the greater region, it is impossible to cultivate vegetables and fruit for market. While still developing politically, the government in Ghana always gave preferential treatment to the South. Basically this neglect [of the North] had begun earlier under British colonial rule. While in the South, for decades prior to independence, a school and educational system had been built — in large part through mission efforts — the British forbad Christian missionaries admittance to the North and justified this prohibition by referring to the numerous Muslim believers there. Because of this, the school system began to catch on only after independence, but still it had not generally penetrated [into the North], especially not among girls and young women. [. . .] In the North, we especially value a program which had existed earlier, which had been vigorously reactivated in 1991: the "Project for Christian-Muslim Relations" (PROCMURA). We know how important it is for believers from different religions to learn to live together.

Since the 1970s, Islam has become a religious missionary community in Ghana. For years, there have been Koran schools in the North. The state worked towards making the old Koran schools into Islamic schools that would be similar to the Christian schools. In other words, that academic and cultural education would stand in the foreground rather than religious instruction. In Islamic schools, however, more value was placed on the religious devotion of the boy and girl students than in the Christian. Furthermore, since the 1970s, Islamic lands of the Middle East supported the Muslims of Ghana in their missionary zeal in ideas and financially with, for example, videos from Saudi Arabia or Iran. The Muslims also obtained funds for education and health programs, the development of agriculture, the building of mosques, and efforts to expand their [Islamic] beliefs. Accordingly, Christian communities were supported by their sisters and brothers overseas. Initially Christians in Ghana reacted with fear and missionary counter-activities. At PROCMURA we say, "Let us not react aggressively or fearfully. Let us recognize that Muslims are our neighbors and friends. We must engage [each other] in dialog." [. . .] We have begun a four-year course program especially for pastors and evangelists. The pastors should learn to understand the central thoughts of Islam, the meaning of the Koran for Muslims, their vision of God, their understanding of Jesus, and much more. We have established district committees, in which ordinary parish members participate on an honorary basis in order to learn to understand Islam and their Muslim neighbors and their beliefs. These parishioners then also pursue work intended to enlighten individual congregations and families. To know another faith means also to discover and grow stronger in your own faith. [. . .]

Source: Recommendations given at Ibadan in 1978 by the CSSN, the Ibadan Christian (inter-denominational) Islam in Africa project, the Protest Action Committee, cited in: L. Rassmussen, *Christian-Muslim Relations in Africa: The Cases of Northern Nigeria and Tanzania Compared* (London, 1993), p. 65. — *Further Reading:* Project for Christian-Muslim Relations in Africa — Ghana Area Committee Report. Revised: R. Freise, in EMS, *Länderheft Ghana* (Stuttgart, 1994), pp. 46-47. L. Sanneh, *Piety & Power: Muslims and Christians in West Africa* (New York, 1996).

216. Churches and Civil Society

In the early 1990s, the African churches were facing new challenges. After the end of the cold war, many countries in Africa went through a period of political transition and democratisation. Until 1990, only one ruling party failed to be re-elected (the conservative Labour Party of Mauritius in 1982). There were several democratic changes in 1991: on the Cape Verde Islands, in Benin and in Zambia, in many other countries, opposition against the ruling one-party and military regimes emerged. Recognizing the failures of the past (a), churches played an important role in such resistance. In Malawi, the silence of the churches was dramatically broken on March 8, 1992 when a Pastoral Letter signed by all the Catholic bishops (b) was read in every Catholic church. The Letter was sharply critical of President Dr. Kamuza Banda and the Malawi Congress Party. Although the bishops' lives were threatened, so much pressure was built up that the Government was forced to abandon the one-party system as well as the "Life Presidency" of Dr. Banda. In the elections of 1994, he was defeated. The struggle in Kenya which is described in Archbishop David Gitari's account (c), started earlier and lasted longer than in most other African countries — it was only in 2002 that Daniel arap Moi was deprived of power. A particular development took place in Zambia which was declared a "Christian nation" by President Chiluba in December 1991 (d).

a. All Africa Conference of Churches, Proceedings (1991)

We recognise that the sorry state of our continent is not only to be blamed on external factors but also on internal forces. In particular, we recognise that the absence of security for citizens, the pervasive lack of accountability, democracy and respect for human dignity whereby a majority of the African people are denied the freedom to apply their physical and mental capacities in efforts of their choice, to associate and express themselves freely, and to participate in developmental and other matters affecting them is responsible to a large extent for Africa's predicament that has ironically seen Africa's conditions crucially deteriorate since independence. Furthermore, it has hindered all popular mobilization efforts making them totally impossible in some places.

b. Malawi: Pastoral Letter "Living Our Faith" (1992)

[. . .] In our society we are aware of a growing gap between the rich and the poor with regard to expectations, living standards and development. Many people still live in circumstances which are hardly compatible with their dignity as sons and daughters of God. Their life is a struggle for survival. At the same time a minority enjoys the fruits of development and can afford a life in luxury and wealth. We appeal for a more just and equal distribution of wealth. [. . .]

[H]uman persons are honoured — and this honour is due to them — whenever they are allowed to search freely for the truth, to voice their opinions and to be heard, to engage in creative service of the community in all liberty within the associations of their own choice. Nobody should ever have to suffer reprisals for honestly expressing and living up to their convictions: intellectual, religious or political.

We can only regret that this is not always the case in our own country. We can be grateful that freedom of worship is respected; the same freedom does not exist when it comes to translating faith into daily life. Academic freedom is seriously restricted; exposing injustices can be considered a betrayal; revealing some evils of our society is seen as slandering the country; monopoly of mass media and censorship prevent the expression of dissenting views; some people have paid dearly for their political opinions; access to public places like markets, hospitals, bus depots etc. is frequently denied to those who cannot produce a party card; forced donations have become a way of life. This is most regrettable. It creates an atmosphere of resentment among the citizens. It breeds a climate of mistrust and fear. This fear of harassment and mutual suspicion gen-

erates a society in which the talents of many lie unused and in which there is little room for initiative. [. . .] We urgently call each one of you to respond to this
state of affairs and work towards a change of climate. [. . .]

c. Kenya: Anglican Archbishop Gitari's Account (1987-1997)

[. . .] another interesting incident was in 1987 when I preached a series of sermons Sunday after Sunday during June. These were being reported by newspapers every Monday and I was attacked by politicians from the moment I
preached the first sermon. The third sermon I preached at a place called St. Peter's, Nyeri, from Daniel chapter 6 about Daniel who was a very able civil servant, transparent and accountable. The king could not find a better person than
him. Yet because he was a Jew, some started plotting against Daniel. The king
was quick to sign a decree that nobody should worship any other than the king
for thirty days, without having given the people enough time to debate the motion that they were bringing. So the king made a terrible mistake. When Daniel
was put in the lion's den, he was very sorry but he could do nothing, because
when the king had signed a law it could not be repealed. And the king was very
sorry. As I mentioned Daniel, someone telephoned Daniel arap Moi to say the
bishop had spent the whole day attacking you. He was of course very furious
with me and then the Vice-Chairman of KANU issued a statement that Kenya
does not want to hear irrelevant Old Testament Books expounded with this foreign culture.

So the following Sunday I preached on the Second letter of Paul to Timo-
thy, which reads "All Scripture is inspired by God." And I said that here we have
to choose between two authorities, the chairman of KANU who says Daniel
chapter 6 is irrelevant and Paul who says all Scripture is inspired by God. And I
asked the congregation which authority we should follow, with the press there
with fourteen pressmen with their cameras. The whole congregation said 'Paul'.
I think the president found his people were loosing the battle and in his next
speech he said, "Let the bishop speak." And I wrote a book with the title *Let the
Bishop Speak.*

My final example took place in 1997 when the church leaders were really
trying to fight so that the constitution would be changed before the elections,
which were going to come in December. We went and saw President Moi as
church leaders. We told him "Please let us change the constitution so that we
can be more democratic!" We gave him a memorandum and he told us of
members of the opposition who met at Ufungamano House, which is near my
cathedral in Nairobi, to protest. The police came and beat them up and the only
sanctuary they could find was in the All Saint's Cathedral, so they all poured
into the cathedral. The police followed them there with tear gas. They were

beaten, bleeding inside the cathedral. I was not there but the Provost told me all that had happened on that day which was shown on world television because the entire media fraternity was well represented.

I said I would cleanse the cathedral the following Sunday. So a week later about a thousand people were there, with the international press. I cleansed the cathedral by spraying holy water everywhere and then I preached from Daniel chapter five 'Mene mene, tekel, uparsin. . . .' As I was expounding those words I said "Mene means God has numbered the days of your reign and has brought it to an end, tekel, you have been weighed on the scales and found wanting, and parsin, your kingdom has been divided and given to the Medes and Persians." Then I said "The hand of God has not yet written at State House, Nairobi, but President Moi, if you don't do the following, the hand of God is going to write in State House, meme, mene, tekel and write the things which he must do." On Tuesday he invited me to State House and he told me: "I now agree you can change the constitution before the elections." [. . .]

d. President Chiluba Declares Zambia a Christian Nation (1991)

The Bible which is the word of God abounds with proof that a nation is blessed, whenever it enters into a covenant of God and obeys the word of God. 2 Chronicles 7:14 says 'If my people who are called by my name will humble themselves and pray and seek my face and turn from their wicked ways, then will I hear from heaven and forgive their sin and will heal their land.' On behalf of the people of Zambia, I repent of our wicked ways of idolatry, witchcraft, the occult, immorality, injustice and corruption. I pray for the healing, restoration, revival, blessing and prosperity for Zambia. On behalf of the nation, I have now entered into a covenant with the living God. [. . .] I submit the Government and the entire nation of Zambia to the Lordship of Jesus Christ. I further declare that Zambia is a Christian nation that will seek to be governed by the righteous principles of the Word of God. Righteousness and justice must prevail in all levels of authority, and then we shall see the righteousness of God exalting Zambia.

Source: (a) All African Council of Churches, Problems and Promises of Africa. Towards and Beyond the year 2000. A summary of the proceeding of the symposium convened by the AACC in Mombasa in November, 1991, S. 29; (b) "Living Our Faith: Pastoral Letter from Catholic Bishops 1992," in: Kenneth R. Ross (ed.), *Christianity in Malawi: A Source Book* (Bonn, 1996), pp. 203-215, here: pp. 205, 211-212; (c) David M. Gitari/Ben Knighton, "On Being a Christian Leader: Story Contesting Power in Kenya," *Transformation* 18/4 (October, 2001), pp. 247-262, here: pp. 254, 255; (d) *Times of Zambia*, Feb. 20, 1994, cf. P. Gifford, *African Christianity: Its Public Role* (London: Hurst, 1998), pp. 197-198; Isabel Phiri, "President Frederick J. T. Chiluba of Zambia: The Christian Nation and Democracy," *Journal of Religion in Africa* 33/4, pp. 401-426, here: 407. — *Further*

Reading: P. Gifford (ed.), *The Christian Churches and the Democratisation of Africa* (Leiden, 1995), pp. 261-275; H. B. Hansen/M. Twaddle (eds.), *Religion and Politics in East Africa: The Period since Independence* (London, 1995).

217. Independent Churches and Democratization

Africa is taking over a leading role in the spread of Christianity. The number of African Christians grew from less than 10 million in 1900 to ca. 360 million in 2002. The historian Philip Jenkins calculated that the number of African Christians will increase to 633 million in 2025, while Christianity in Europe will stagnate between 555 and 560 million. Independent African Churches as well as Pentecostal Churches played an important role in this process. They often did not express themselves explicitly politically; sometimes they are accused of cementing the status quo and the continuance of oppressive structures by their silence. Thus the South African President Pieter Willem Botha was invited in 1985 to the Easter Meeting of the Zion Christian Church. The three million members were the largest crowd to which a politician of the Apartheid regime ever spoke. Nevertheless the role of the independent African churches is much more complex, as the South African theologian Constance Baratang Thetele pointed out in 1978:

The independent churches in South Africa in many ways are both pre-revolutionary and actively revolutionary at the same time. They are pre-Revolutionary in the sense that they do not operate according to a set plan or strategy in trying to move society toward a definite goal. But they are revolutionary in their impact on the fabric of society, creating a change that provides the dispossessed people with a sense of hope and a vision for the future. They offer a place in society where people can begin to sense their role as creators of their own histories, rejecting a passive acceptance of the status quo and beginning to work out alternatives to dehumanisation.

Source: C. B. Thetele, "Women in South Africa: The WAICC," in: K. Appiah-Kubi/S. Torres (eds.), *African Theology en Route* (Maryknoll, 1979), pp. 150-154, 151. — *Further Reading:* J. Kwabena Asamoah-Gyadu, *African Charismatics* (Leiden, 2005); J. K. Asamoah-Gyadu, "Born of Water and the Spirit," in: Kalu, *African Christianity,* pp. 388-409; P. Njeri Mwaura, "Gender and Power in African Christianity," in: ibid., pp. 410-445; A. Cohen/R. Marshall-Fratani (eds.), *Between Babel and Pentecost: Transnational Pentecostalism in Africa and Latin America* (London, 2001); P. Gifford, *African Christianity: Its Public Role* (London, 1998); P. Jenkins, *The Next Christendom: The Coming of Global Christianity* (Oxford, 2002).

LATIN
AMERICA

I. LATIN AMERICA 1450-1600

A. The First Encounters and the
Perspectives of Victor and Victim

218. Columbus: First Contact with the "Indians" (1492)

Christopher Columbus (1436?-1506) undertook four expeditions (1492-1493, 1493-1496, 1498-1500, 1502-1504), landing on a Caribbean island for the first time on October 12, 1492. In this report on his first expedition he talks openly about the three elements which embody the mixture of mercantilism and apostolic spirit that one finds at the roots of European expansionism abroad: "God and profit," "faith and gold," or "God and gold." Columbus' report describes the newly discovered islands as a country in which "milk and honey" flow, inhabited by naïve, scarcely armed natives who, because they live without a discernible worship of idols, could easily be made into Christians. With this report the crafty Columbus wished to persuade the Crown to finance a second expedition, for the first expedition had effectively failed: he had "only" found natives, not, as expected, the flourishing commercial centers of Asia. Later Pero Vaz de Caminha's first report about the accidental discovery of the Brazilian coast in April 1500 reads much the same way. For centuries the discovery of the New World by Columbus has been celebrated as an epoch-making event, indeed as one belonging to salvation history. Since 1992 the point of view of the conquered has been more closely considered; according to this view, the Indian who had discovered Columbus had made an awful discover.

Since I know that you will be pleased at the great victory with which Our Lord has crowned my voyage, I write this to you, from which you will learn how in thirty-three days I passed from the Canary Islands to the Indies, with the fleet which the most illustrious King and Queen, our Sovereigns, gave to me. There I found very many islands, filled with innumerable people, and I have taken possession of them all for their Highnesses, done by proclamation and with the royal standard unfurled, and no opposition was offered to me. [. . .] The people of this island and of all the other islands which I have found and of which I have information, all go naked, men and women, as their mothers bore them, although some of the women cover a single place with the leaf of a plant or with a net of cotton which they make for the purpose. They have no iron or steel or weapons, nor are they fitted to use them. [. . .] But so they are, incurably timid. It is true that, after they have been reassured and have lost this fear, they are so guileless and so generous with all that they possess, that no one would believe it who has not seen it. [. . .] So it was found that for a thong a sailor received gold to the weight of two and an half castellanos, and others received much more for other things which were worth less. [. . .] They do not hold any creed nor are they idolaters; but they all believe that power and good are in the heavens and were very firmly convinced that I, with these ships and men, came from the heavens. [. . .] This belief is not the result of ignorance, for they are, on the contrary, of a very acute intelligence and they are men who navigate all those seas, so that it is amazing how good an account they give of everything. [. . .] In all these islands, I saw no great diversity in the appearance of the people or in their manners and language. On the contrary, they all understand one another, which is a very curious thing, on account of which I hope that their Highnesses will determine upon their conversion to our holy faith, towards which they are very inclined. [. . .] In conclusion, to speak only of what has been accomplished on this voyage, which was so hasty, their Highnesses can see that I will give them as much gold as they may need, if their Highnesses will render me very slight assistance; presently, I will give them spices and cotton, as much as their Highnesses shall command; and mastic, as much as they shall order to be shipped and which, up to now, has been found only in Greece, in the island of Chios, and the Seignory sells it for what it pleases. [. . .] So that, since Our Redeemer has given the victory to our most illustrious King and Queen, and to their renowned kingdoms, in so great a matter, for this all Christendom ought to feel delight and make great feasts and give solemn thanks to the Holy Trinity, with many solemn prayers for the great exaltation which they shall have in the turning of so many peoples to our holy faith, and afterwards for the temporal benefits, because not only Spain but all Christendom will have hence refreshment and gain.

Source: Letter of Columbus, describing the results of his first voyage, in: *The Journal of Christopher Columbus* (London, 1960), pp. 192, 194, 196-197, 200-201. — *Further Reading:* F. Fernández-Armesto, *Columbus* (London, 1996); R. Crosfield, *Columbus: A Discoverer and His Conscience* (Kirstead, 1998); M. B. Mignone (ed.), *Columbus: Meeting of Cultures* (Stony Brook, N.Y., 1993); K. Sale, *The Conquest of Paradise: Christopher Columbus and the Columbian Legacy* (London, 1992); U. Bitterli, *Die "Wilden" und die "Zivilisierten"* (München, [2]1991); J. Gil, *Mitos y utopías del descubrimiento*, vol. 1: *Colón y su tiempo* (Madrid, [2]1992); T. Heydenreich (ed.), *Columbus zwischen zwei Welten*, 2 vols. (Frankfurt, 1992); G. Wawor, T. Heydenreich (eds.), *Columbus 1892-1992* (Frankfurt, 1995).

219. Caribbean: On the Religion of the Tainos (1498)

In contrast to what Columbus stated in his first report, Ancient America was not a no-man's-land with respect to the history of religion. Rather, America took part in the general development of the history of religion, in which people had various systems of belief and practice. When Europeans encountered peoples like the Aztecs, Mayans, and Incas, whose religions had a certain analogy to Christianity on the surface since they had temples, priests, and public rites (processions, sacrifices, ritually elaborated worship services), the Indian "worship of idols" stood out vividly to the incomers. With respect to others who lived as hunters, fishers, and gatherers, or who were semi-nomadic and had retained more "shamanic religions," the Europeans often thought at first glance that they had met peoples without religion. The following report was written by Ramón Pané who studied the religion and culture of the Tainos, the inhabitants of Española (today Haiti and the Dominican Republic). The excerpt describes the typical ceremony of a shamanic religion, namely, the consultation with the "idol" in a drug-induced state.

And when they want to find out if they will achieve victory over their enemies, they enter into a house in which none but the leading men enter. And their lord is the first one who begins to prepare *cohoba* [sniffing a heady weed = tobacco], and he plays an instrument [before the idol]; and while he is makings the *cohoba*, none of those who are in his company speaks until the lord has finished. After he has finished his prayer, he stays awhile with his head lowered and his arms on his knees; then he lifts his head, looking toward the heavens, and he speaks. Then they all answer him aloud in unison; and after all have spoken, they give thanks, and he relates the vision he has had, inebriated from the cohoba he had inhaled through his nose and that has gone to his head. And he says he has spoken with the zemi and that they will achieve victory, or their enemies will flee, or there will be a great loss of life, or wars or hunger or another such thing, according to what he, who is drunk, may relate of what he remembers. You may judge in what state his brain may be, for they say they think they see the houses turn upside down, with their foundations in the air, and the men walk on foot toward the heavens. And they prepare this *cohoba* not only for the zemis of stone and of wood, but also for the bodies of the dead.

Source: Fray Ramón Pané, *An Account of the Antiquities of the Indians.* A new edition with an introductory study, notes, and appendixes by J. J. Arrom (Durham, 1999), p. 26. — *Further Reading:* E. G. Bourne, *Columbus, Ramon Pane and the Beginnings of American Anthropology* (Worcester, 1906); F. Bercht (ed.), *Taíno: Pre-Columbian Art and Culture from the Caribbean* (New York, 1997); G. Haslip-Viera (ed.), *Taíno Revival: Critical Perspectives on Puerto Rican Identity and Cultural Politics* (Princeton, 2001); W. Krickeberg (ed.), *Pre-Columbian American Religions* (New York, 1969); Dussel, *Church,* pp. 23-42.

220. Mexico: Moctezuma in Anticipation of Cortés (1519)

The report, recorded by the Franciscan missionary and ethnographer Bernardino de Sahagún (1500-1590) around 1570, describes the mood at the court of Moctezuma after the appearance of the Spanish; it follows a familiar pattern. The Spanish are viewed as messengers of the cultural hero or white God Quetzalcóatl, who had disappeared somewhere towards the west; they demand that rule be returned to them in his name, and they will open a new chapter in history. Similar sagas are also known, among others, from the Inca Empire. Here the cultural hero or white God is named Viracocha, which is why the Spaniards were generally given this name as well. The demise of the Indian cultures under the conquistadors and the process of evangelization was thus to be interpreted as a divinely-ordained *translatio imperii*. Mexico was conquered by Hernán Cortés in 1519-1521, Peru by Francisco Pizarro in 1533.

And then the year changed to the companion to follow, Thirteen Rabbit [1518]. But the year [Thirteen] Rabbit was about to come to an end, was at the time of closing, when [the Spaniards] came to land, when they were seen once again.

And then [the stewards] hastened to come to inform Moctezuma. When he heard of it, then he speedily sent messengers. Thus he thought — thus was it thought — that this was Topiltzin Quetzalcoatl who had come to land. For it was in their hearts that he would come, that he would come to land, just to find his mat, his seat. For he had traveled there [eastward] when he departed. [. . .]

And Moctezuma loudly expressed his distress. He felt distress, he was terrified, he was astounded; he expressed his distress because of the city.

And indeed everyone was greatly terrified. There were terror, astonishment, expressions of distress, feelings of distress. There were consultations. There were formations of groups; there were assemblies of people. There was weeping — there was much weeping, there was weeping for others. There was only the hanging of heads, there was dejection. There were tearful greetings, there were tearful greetings given others. There was the encouragement of others; there was mutual encouragement. There was the smoothing of the hair; the hair of small boys was smoothed. Their fathers said: "Alas, O my beloved sons! How can what is about to come to pass have befallen you" And their mothers said: "My beloved sons, how will you marvel at what is about to befall you?"

Source: Florentine Codex, *Fray Bernardino de Sahagún, General History of the Things of New Spain,* Book 12 — The Conquest of Mexico, Part XIII (Santa Fe, N.M., 1975), pp. 9, 25. — *Further Reading:* J. Lafaye, *Quetzalcóatl and Guadalupe: The Formation of Mexican National Consciousness, 1531-1813* (Chicago, 1976); P. Honoré, *In Quest of the White God: The Mysterious Heritage of South American Civilization* (London, 1975); T. Todorov, *The Conquest of America: The Question of the Other* (Norman, 1999); W. Krickeberg (ed.), *Pre-Columbian American Religions* (New York, 1969); Dussel, *Church,* pp. 218ff.

221. Mexico: Lament after the Conquest (about 1523)

This document was written by an anonymous author in Náhuatl, the Aztec *lingua franca,* during the first years following the conquest. It impressively describes the view of the conquered after the conquest, which was experienced as a catastrophe. It also gives an idea of the poetic and religious richness of Aztec culture.

Nothing but flowers and songs of sorrow
Are left in Mexico and Tlatelolco,
Where once we saw warriors and wise men.//
We know it is true
That we must perish,
For we are mortal men.
You, the Giver of Life,
You have ordained it.//
We wander here and there
In our desolate poverty.
We are mortal men.
We have seen bloodshed and pain
Where once we saw beauty and valor.//
We are crushed to the ground;
We lie in ruins.
There is nothing but grief and suffering
In Mexico and Tlatelolco,
Where once we saw beauty and valor.//
Have you grown weary of your servants?
Are you angry with your servants,
O Giver of Life?

Source: M. León-Portilla (ed.), *The Broken Spears: The Aztec Account of the Conquest of Mexico* (Boston, 1992), p. 149. *Further Reading:* M. León-Portilla, *Native Mesoamerican Spirituality: Ancient Myths, Discourses, Stories, Doctrines, Hymns, Poems from the Aztec, Yacatec, Quiche-Maya and Other Sacred Traditions* (London, 1980); idem (ed.), *El reverso de la conquista* (Mexico City, 1964); idem, *Aztec Thought and Culture: A Study of the Ancient Nahuatl Mind* (Norman, 1963); idem, *The Aztec Image of Self and Society: An Introduction to Nahua Culture* (Salt Lake City, 1992); N. Wachtel, *The Vision of the Vanquished: The Spanish Conquest of Peru through Indian Eyes, 1530-1570* (Hassocks, Eng.), 1977; Dussel, *Church*, pp. 218ff.

222. José de Acosta: Conquest and Evangelization (1590)

In the rapid conquest and evangelization of Latin America, Spanish authors saw a historical and theological analogy to events in European antiquity. At the end of the sixteenth century the Jesuit missionary to Peru, José de Acosta (1540-1600), interpreted the Aztec and Inca empires as well as the similarities to Christianity detected in the Indian religions as a providential *praeparatio evangelica*.

I will make an end of this historie of the Indies, showing the admirable meanes whereby God made a passage for the Gospel in those partes, the which we ought well to consider of, and acknowledge the providence and bountie of the Creator. Every one may vnderstand by the relation and discourse I have written in these bookes, as well at Peru as in New Spaine, whenas the Christians first set footing, that these Kingdomes and Monarchies were come to the height and period of their power. The Yncas of Peru, possessing from the Realme of Chile beyond Quito, which are a thousand leagues, being most aboundant in gold, siluer, and all kinds of riches: as also in Mexico, Monteçuma commaunded from the North Ocean sea vnto the South, being feared and worshipped, not as a man, but rather as a god. Then was it, that the most high Lord had determined that that stone of Daneil, which dissolved the Realmes and Kingdoms of the world, should also dissolve those of this new world. And as the lawe of Christ came whenas the Romane Monarchie was at her greatnes: so did it happen at the West Indies, wherein we see the iust providence of our Lord. [. . .] It was also a great providence of our Lord, that whenas the first Spaniardes arrived there, they founde ayde from the Indians themselves, by reason of their partialities and greate diuisions. [. . .] And therefore the law of Christ seemed vnto them, and doth at this day seeme iust, sweete, clean, good, and full of happinesse. And that which is difficult in our law, to beleeve so high and soveraigne Misteries, hath beene easy among them, for that the Divell had made them comprehend things of greater difficultie, and the self-same things which he had stolen from our Evangelicall law, as their maner of communion and confession, their adoration of three in one, and such other like, the which, against the will of the enemy, have holpen for the easie receiving of the truth by those who before had imbraced lies. God is wise and admirable in all his works, vanquishing the adversarie even with his owne weapon, hee takes him in his owne snare, and kills him with his owne sword.

Source: Joseph de Acosta, *The Natural & Moral History of the Indies* (New York, 1963), pp. 527, 529, 531. — *Further Reading:* S. G. McIntosh, *Acosta and the "De procuranda indorum salute": A Sixteenth Century Missionary Model with Twentieth Century Implications* (Mac Research, 1989); C. M. Burgaleta, *José de Acosta, S.J. (1540-1600): His Life and Thought* (Chicago, 1999); G. J. Shepherd, *An Exposition of José de Acosta's "Historia Natural y moral de las Indias," 1590: The Emergence of an Anthropological Vision of Colonial Latin America* (Lewiston, NY, 2002); M. Sievernich, "Vision und Mission der Neuen Welt Amerika bei José de Acosta," in: idem, G. Switek (eds.), *Ignatianisch* (Freiburg, 1990), pp. 293-313; Dussel, *Church*, pp. 43-52.

B. Legitimation and Criticism of the Conquest

223. Sources of Legitimation

The papal bull of concession *Inter Caetera* of Alexander VI (document a) is one of the most researched documents in church history. Still controversial is whether or not it truly concerns a "donation" under international law or a simple "investiture." Yet even the purely legalistic investiture interpretation does not change the facts: "that the Pope grants himself the *dominium* over, in this case the 'supreme ownership of', the discovered region or regions to be discovered" (Reibstein, *International Law*, 274). The papal bull belongs to the curial tradition which, since the middle of the fifteenth century, went hand in hand with the expeditions of the Portuguese. In marked contrast to the papal bull *Romanus Pontifex* of January 8, 1455, which Nicholas V had issued to the Portuguese royal house at the beginning of its expeditionary venture and which Callistus III had confirmed with his papal bull *Inter Caetera* of March 13, 1456 (cf. document 8), Alexander VI refuses to explicitly grant the Catholic Kings and their followers complete and free authority to wage wars of conquest against the Moors, pagans, and other enemies of Christ, wherever they might be. Nevertheless, he speaks first of submission *(subicere)* and then of conversion *(reducere)*. Moreover, he assigns to them, "together with all their dominions, cities, camps, places, and villages, and all rights, jurisdictions, and appurtenances, all islands and mainlands found and to be found, discovered and to be discovered." Since Portugal was not in agreement with the line of demarcation drawn by the Pope, the Spanish and Portuguese met in Tordesillas in order to fix, by way of a bilateral agreement (June 7, 1494), the line of demarcation from the North Pole to the South Pole and 370 leagues west of the Cape Verde Islands. The Portuguese could thus later claim rule over Brazil. The other European countries (France, England and the Netherlands), however, never recognized this line of demarcation and the Iberian monopoly.

Queen Isabella of Castile had forbidden the enslavement of the Indians in 1500. Yet in a decree from December 20, 1503, she ordered the implementation of the *encomienda* (document b), which was to have devastating consequences later and which the defender and "Father" of the Indians, Bartolomé de las Casas, called the "evil of evils" of the Spanish empire (concerning Las Casas cf. document commentary 227). The *encomienda* (from Lat. *commendare*, to entrust, to assign) or *repartimiento* (Lat. *repartire*, to allot) is an institution of the Spanish colonial system, not comparable to benefices in Europe. Introduced in Hispañola in 1504, under the charge of a Spaniard, in order to Christianize the natives better and make them more Hispanic, it degenerated into a slave-like serfdom. Although forbidden by the "New Laws" (1542), the Crown (for economic reasons and because the prohibition could not be implemented) had to tolerate the *encomienda*. As an institution, the *encomienda* continued to exist up to the end of colonial times, though with diminishing impact.

a. Alexander VI: Bull "Inter caetera" (May 4, 1493)

Alexander, bishop, servant of the servants of God, to the illustrious sovereigns, our very dear son in Christ, Ferdinand, king, and our very dear daughter in Christ, Isabella, queen of Castile, Leon, Aragon, Sicily, and Granada, health and apostolic benediction.

Among other works well pleasing to the Divine Majesty and cherished of our heart, this assuredly ranks highest, that in our times especially the Catholic faith and the Christian religion be exalted and be everywhere increased and spread, that the health of souls be cared for and that barbarous nations be overthrown and brought to the faith itself. [. . .]

In the islands and countries already discovered are found gold, spices, and very many other precious things of divers kinds and qualities. Wherefore, as becomes Catholic kings and princes, after earnest consideration of all matters, specially of the rise and spread of the Catholic faith, as was the fashion of your ancestors, king of renowned memory, you have purposed with the favor of divine clemency to bring under your sway the said mainlands and islands with their residents and inhabitants and to bring them to the Catholic faith.

Hence, heartily commending in the Lord this your holy and praiseworthy purpose, and desirous that it be duly acomplished, and that the name of our Savior be carried into these regions, we exhort you very earnestly in the Lord and by your reception of holy baptism, whereby you are bound to our apostolic commands, and by the bowels of the mercy of our Lord Jesus Christ, enjoin strictly, that inasmuch as with eager zeal for the true faith you design to equip and despatch this expedition, you purpose also, as is your duty, to lead the peoples dwelling in those islands and countries to deter you therefrom, with the stout hope and trust in your hearts that Almighty God will further your undertakings.

And, in order that you may enter upon so great an undertaking with greater readiness and heartiness endowed with the benefit of our apostolic favor, we, of our own accord, not at your instance nor at the request of anyone else in your regard, but of our own sole largess and certain knowledge and of the fullness of our apostolic power, by the authority of Almigthy God conferred upon us blessed Peter and of the vicarship of Jesus Christ, which we hold on earth, do by tenor of these presents, should any of said islands have been found by your envoys and captains, give, grant, and assign to you and your heirs and successors, kings of Castile and Leon, forever, together with all their dominions, cities, camps, places, and villages, and all rights, jurisdictions, and appurtenances, all islands and mainlands found and to be found, discovered and to be discovered towards the west and south, by drawing and establishing a line from the Arctic pole, namely the north, to the Antarctic pole, namely the south, no matter whether the said mainlands and islands are found and to be found in the direction of India or towards any other quarter, the said line to be distant commonly known as the Azores and Cape Verde. With this proviso however that none of the islands and mainlands, found and to be found, discovered and to be discovered, beyond that said line towards the west and south, be in the actual possession of any Christian king or prince up to the birthday of our Lord Jesus Christ just past from which the present year one thousand four hundred and ninety-three begins. And we make, appoint, and depute you and your said heirs and successors lords of them with full and free power, authority, and jurisdiction of every kind; with this proviso however, that by our gift, grant and assignment no right acquired by any Christian prince, who may be in actual possession of said islands and mainlands prior to the said birthday of our Lord Jesus Christ, is hereby to be undestood to be withdrawn or taken away.

Moreover we command you in virtue of holy obedience that, employing all due diligence in the premises, as you also promise — nor do we doubt your compliance therein in accordance with your loyalty and royal greatness of spirit — you should appoint to the aforesaid mainlands and islands worthy, God-fearing, learned, skilled, and experienced men, in order to instruct the aforesaid inhabitants and residents in the Catholic faith and train them in good morals.

b. Isabel of Castilla: The Encomienda (December 20, 1503)

Dona Isabel, by the grace of God etc. — Whereas my lord the king and I, by the instruction we sent to don Nicolás de Obando, chief commander of Alcántara . . . ordered that the Indians of the island Hispaniola should be freed and not subjected to servitude . . . and now I am informed that because of the great freedom these Indians have, they withdraw and turn away from conversation and communication with Christians, so that even when they are offered payment they do not want to work but go vagabonding about, and they cannot be catechized and attracted to convert to our holy Catholic faith, and that for this reason the Christians who live on that island have no one to work on their farms and upkeep and to help them collect the gold that is on that island, which is to the disadvantage of both sides, and that it is Our desire that these Indians be converted to our holy Catholic faith and be catechized in matters of faith, and because this can best be done through communication between the Indians and the Christians who are on that island and walking among them and dealing with them and both sides helping each other to work the island, populate it, make it fruitful, and gather the gold that is there so that these my kingdoms and their neighbors might benefit from it, I have sent this letter for that reason. Therefore I order you, our governor, as soon as you see this letter, to compel and force these Indians to deal and converse with the Christians on that island and work in its buildings and gather gold and other metals and do farm work and maintenance for the Christians who live on that island; and to arrange that each one be paid a daily wage and maintenance according to the quality of the land and the person and the work that you consider should be assigned them; and that every chief be responsible for a certain number of these Indians whom you will order to work where they are needed, and for bringing them together for festivals and other appropriate days to hear and receive doctrine in the things of faith at the designated places, and that each chief will come with the number of Indians that you designate to the person or persons whom you will name so that they will work at the tasks assigned by these persons and be paid a daily wage that you will determine. This they will do and fulfill as free persons, which they are, and not servants. And you shall order that these Indians be well treated; those who are Christians better than the others. And you shall not consent or allow that any person harm or wrong them. And neither group may do otherwise, or they will lose my favor, etc.

Source: (a) W. G. Grewe (ed.), *Fontes Historiae Iuris Gentium. Quellen zur Geschichte des Völkerrechts/Sources Relating to the History of the Law of Nations,* vol. 2, 1493-1815 (Berlin/New York, 1988), pp. 103-108; Lat.: *America pontificia primi saeculi evangelizationis 1493-1592,* ed. Josef Metzler (Vatican City, 1991), vol. 1, pp. 79-83; (b) B. de las Casas, *Historia de las Indias* vol. 2 (Obras completas vol. 4), ed. I. Pérez Fernández et al. (Madrid, 1994), p. 1341f (Book II, Chapter 12) — *Further Reading:* (a) H. Huiskamp, *A Genealogy of Ecclesiastical Jurisdictions: Schematic Outline, Illustrating the Development of the Catholic Church in Territories Assigned to Portugal by Treaty of Tordesillas in 1494* (Kampen, 1994); The earliest diplomatic documents on America. The papal bulls of 1493 and the treaty of Tordesillas, Berlin 1927; A. J. R. Brown, *The Treaty of Tordesillas and the Colonisation of the Wild Coast* (London, 2000); Dussel, *Church,* pp. 43ff., 53ff; A. García-Gallo, "Las bulas de Alejandro VI. y el ordenamiento jurídico de la expansión portuguesa y castellana en Africa e Indias" (in: *AHDE* 27/28, 1957-1958), pp. 461-829; P. de Leturia, "Der Heilige Stuhl und das spanische Patronat in Amerika" (in: *HJ* 46, 1926, pp. 1-71); idem, *Relaciones entre la Santa Sede e Hispanoamérica 1493-1835,* vol. 1 (Rome, 1959); (b) S. Zavala, *La Encomienda Indiana* (Mexico City, ³1992); idem, *Suplemento documental y bibliográfico a la Encomienda Indiana* (Mexico City, 1994); idem, *The Colonial Period in the History of the New World* (Mexico City, 1996); L. B. Simpson, *The Encomienda in New Spain* (Berkeley, 1982); Dussel, *Church,* pp. 53ff.

224. The Advent Sermon of Antonio Montesinos (1511)

The first community of Dominicans reached Española (the Dominican Republic/Haiti) in September of 1510. Since they had come in the spirit of strict observance and radical imitation of Christ, it did not take long for the undaunted Dominicans, in the best tradition of the Order, to make the connection between praxis and law, to detect the contradiction, and to decide to denounce the actions of their compatriots from the pulpit who "were excessively brutal and who knew no mercy or pity" (Las Casas). The prophetic sermon of Antonio Montesinos (d. 1540) on the fourth Sunday of Advent (December 21, 1511) represents a rebellion of conscience and belongs to those events that we should definitely call epochal in ecclesial and human history. Christianity had barely reached the New World in earthen vessels when the Dominicans, by means of this sermon, gave it back its own unique character as a "messianic" religion of the hungry and of those who thirst for justice.

Came the Sunday and the time to preach. Padre Fray Antón Montesino mounted the pulpit. He took as the basic document of his sermon, "I am the voice of one crying out in the desert" [Joh 1,23] [. . .]. "I have gotten up here to make you aware. I am the voice of Christ in the desert of this island. Therefore, it would be wise of you to pay attention, more than that, to listen with your whole heart, listen with every pore. That voice will be one you have never heard before, the harshest, hardest, most fearful, menacing you ever thought to hear. [. . .] You are all in mortal sin," he said, "you live in it, you die in it, because of the cruel tyranny you work on these innocent peoples. Tell me. By what right, with what justice, do you hold these Indians in such cruel and horrible servitude? By what authority have you made such hideous wars on these peoples? They were living on their own lands in peace and quiet. By what right have you wasted them, so many, many of them, with unspeakable death and destruction? By what right do you keep them so oppressed and exhausted? You give them no food, you give them no medicine for the illnesses they incur from the excessive work you put them to every day. And they die on you. Or, to put it better, you kill them. Just to get at gold, to acquire gold, day after day. And what steps do you take to have someone teach them? So they know their God and creator, so they are baptized, so they hear mass, so they keep fast-days feast days and Sundays? The Indians, are they not human beings? Do they not have rational souls? Are you not required to love them as you love yourselves? Do you not know this? Not understand this? How can you be so asleep, so deep in such a torpid dream? Take this for certain, in the state you are in, you can no more save your souls than Moors or Turks who neither have the Christian faith nor want it!"

Source: Indian Freedom: The Cause of Bartolomé de Las Casas 1484-1566, A Reader (Kansas City, 1995), pp. 141-142. — *Further Reading:* G. Gutiérrez, *Las Casas: In Search of the Poor of Jesus Christ* (Maryknoll, NY, 1993); B. Biermann, "Die ersten Dominikaner in Amerika," in: *ZMR* 5, 1947/1948, pp. 57-65, 107-121; B. de las Casas, *The Devastation of the Indies: A Brief Account* (Baltimore, 1992); M. A. Medina, *Una comunidad al servicio del indio* (Madrid, 1983); Dussel, *Church,* pp. 43ff, 201ff.; Delgado, *Gott,* pp. 143-176; Delgado, *Abschied,* pp. 29-78.

225. The "Requerimiento" and Criticism of It

After Montesinos' sermon the Crown convened a junta (commission) of theologians and jurists. On the one hand they developed the Laws of Burgos (1512) and Valladolid (1513) in order to limit the fierce exploitation of the Indians and of the *encomienda*. On the other hand they drafted the *requerimiento* (1513) in order to justify the crusades of conquest to the European public, with a subjugation demand or conquistador proclamation (cf. Deut. 20:10-12). The *requerimiento* (document a) is thus the first response to the colonial and ethical "discussion of ownership" which Montesinos had initiated with the question "with what right?" (cf. document 224). Later theologians like Francisco de Vitoria (1483-1546) harshly criticized the *requerimiento* and justified legal titles which were based, above all, on the *ius communicationis* and the *ius praedicandi*. The *requerimiento* was read out for the first time in 1514 by Pedrarias Dávila during the conquest of Darién (Panama). According to the *requerimiento*, which, among other things, refers to the papal bull of Alexander VI of 1493 (cf. document 223a), a war against the Indians is to be judged "just" after their refusal to submit to the sovereignty of the Pope and the Spanish King. Warfare according to the method of the *requerimiento* belonged to the accepted rules of the game in the confrontation between Muslims and Christians. On linguistic grounds alone, however, it must have appeared completely incomprehensible to the Native Americans. Las Casas' core criticism begins here (document b), but he also (cf. commentary to document 227) criticizes the appeal to the papal bull of concession and the absence of a voluntary treaty of submission.

a. The Requerimiento (1513)

On the part of the King, Don Fernando, and of Doña Juana, his daughter, Queen of Castille and Leon, subduers of the barbarous nations, we their servants notify and make known to you, as best we can [. . .] that the Lord our God, Living and Eternal, created the Heaven and the Earth, and one man and one woman, of whom you and we, and all the men of the world, were and are descendants, and all those who come afters us. [. . .] Of all these nations God our Lord gave charge to one man, called St. Peter, that he should be Lord and Superior of all the men in the world, that all should obey him, and that he should be the head of the whole human race, wherever men should live, and under whatever law, sect, or belief they should be; and he gave him the world for his kingdom and jurisdiction. [. . .] This man was called Pope, as if to say, Admirable Great Father and Governor of men. The men who lived in that time obeyed that St. Peter, and took him for Lord, King, and Superior of the universe so also they have regarded the others who after him have been elected to the pontificate, and so has it been continued even till now; and will continue till the end of the world. One of these Pontiffs, who succeeded that St. Peter as Lord of the world, in the dignity and seat which I have before mentioned, made donation of these isles and Tierra-firme to the aforesaid King and Queen and to their successors, our lords, with all that there are in these territories, as is contained in certain writings which passed upon the subject as aforesaid, which you can see if you wish. [. . .] Wherefore, as best we can, we ask and require you that you consider what we have said to you, and that you take the time that shall be necessary to understand and deliberate upon it, and that you acknowledge the Church as the Ruler and Superior of the whole world, and the high priest called Pope, and in his name the King and Queen Doña Juana our lords, in his place, as superiors and lords and kings of these islands and this Tierra-firme by virtue of the said donation, and that you consent and give place that these religious fathers should declare and preach to you the aforesaid. If you do so, you will do well, and that which you are obliged to do to their Highnesses, and we in their name shall receive you in all love and charity [. . .] and they shall not compel you to turn Christians, unless you yourselves, when informed of the truth, should wish to be converted to our Holy Catholic Faith, as almost all the inhabitants of the rest of the islands have done. [. . .] But, if you do not do this, and maliciously make delay in it, I certify to you that, with the help of God, we shall powerfully enter into your country, and shall make war against you in all ways and manners that we can, and shall subject you to the yoke and obedience of the Church and of their Highnesses; we shall take you and your wives and your children, and shall make slaves of them, and as such shall sell and dispose of them as their Highnesses may command; and we shall take away your goods, and shall do you all the mischief and damage that we can, as to vassals who do not obey, and refuse to receive their lord, and resist and contradict him; and we protest that the deaths and losses which shall accrue from this are your fault, and not that of their Highnesses, of course, nor of these cavaliers who come with us. And that we have said this to you and made this Requisition, we request the notary here present to give us his testimony in writing, and we ask the rest who are present that they should be witnesses of this Requisition.

b. Bartolomé de las Casas: Criticism of the Requerimiento (ca. 1526)

And first, let all prudent men consider — supposing that the Indians understood our language and its words, and the meaning of each: what news would it convey and what would they feel on hearing that there is a God in the world, creator of heaven and earth, who created mankind or men, when they believed in the sun as God or in other gods whom they believed to have made men and other things? With what reasons, testimonies, or miracles could we prove to them that the God of the Spaniards was more God than theirs, or that he more than the gods they believed in had created the world and men? If the Moors or Turks gave them the same order, affirming to them that Mohammed was the lord and creator of the world and of men, would they be obliged to believe it? . . .

And then, what feelings would they have — what love and reverence toward the God of the Spaniards would it inspire in their hearts, especially in the kings and lords — to hear that by God's order, St. Peter or his successor the pope had given their lands to the king of the Spaniards, while they believed themselves and their ancestors to be true kings and free and the ancient owners of the land from many years before; and that they and their slaves were being asked to accept as lord someone they had never seen or known or heard, not knowing whether he was evil or good, or whether he intended to rule them well or rob or destroy them, especially when his messengers were such fierce, barbarous men, so heavily armed? What could they, what should they in good reason assume or expect of such people?

Furthermore: Is it customary and right, in reason and natural law, to ask them to swear obedience to a foreign king without establishing a treaty or contract or covenant with them regarding the good and just way in which the king would rule them, and regarding the service that they are required to render, which treaty would establish from the beginning their choice and acceptance of the new king, or of a new successor if it is an ancient state?

Source: (a) W. G. Grewe (ed.), *Fontes Historiae Iuris Gentium. Quellen zur Geschichte des Völkerrechts/Sources Relating to the History of the Law of Nations,* vol. 2, 1493-1815 (Berlin/New York, 1988), pp. 68-70; (b) B. de las Casas, *Historia de las Indias,* vol. 3 (Obras completas vol. 5), ed. I. Pérez Fernández et al. (Madrid, 1994), pp. 1998f (Book III, Chapter 58). — *Further Reading:* B. Biermann, "Das Requerimiento in der spanischen Conquista" (in: *NZM* 6, 1950), pp. 94-114; Delgado, *Abschied,* pp. 29-78; J. A. Fernández-Santamaría, *The State, War and Peace* (Cambridge, 1977); L. Hanke, *The Spanish Struggle for Justice in the Conquest of America* (Dallas, 2002); G. Gutiérrez, *Las Casas: In Search of the Poor of Jesus Christ* (Maryknoll, 1993).

226. Pope Paul III on the Human Dignity of the Indians (1537)

During the first decades of conquest and evangelization a dispute arose over the human dignity of the Indians and their ability to believe. The missionaries were also divided into "indophobe" and "indophile" parties. In the mid-1530s, the latter addressed themselves to the Pope — thereby circumventing the patronage — with a request for a clarifying word. This led to the authoritative papal bull *Veritas Ipsa* (also called *Sublimis Deus*) of June 2, 1537, which maintained the human dignity of the Indians and their ability to believe. Las Casas and the "indophiles" always quoted and propagated this edict. The "intervention" of Pope Paul III resulted in a patronage conflict with Charles V which was not finally settled until the Treaty of Nice (1538).

Who is never deceived or deceiving, said, as we know, when He sent preachers out to preach the faith: "Go, and teach everyone" [Matt. 28:19]. All, He said, without exception, since all are capable or learning the faith. Satan saw and was jealous of humankind. He fights goodness always to destroy it. He concocted a novel way to prevent the world of God being preached to people for their salvation. He got certain of his lackeys, who wanted to satisfy their lust for riches, to affirm rashly that East and West Indians — and others like them who came into our ken recently, and therefore lacked a knowledge of our Catholic faith — were brute beasts, were to be subjected to our control wherever they were. These lackeys reduce them to slavery, they load them with afflictions they would never load on any beast of burden.

We are the unworthy Viceregent on earth of the Lord. We try with all our might to lead into the flock of Christ committed to our care, those who are outside the sheepfold. We are aware through what we have been told that those Indians, as true human beings, have not only the capacity for Christian faith, but the willingness to flock to it. We wish to provide apt solutions for the situation. The Indians we speak of, and all other peoples who later come to the knowledge of Christians, outside the faith though they be, are not to be deprived of their liberty or the right to their property. They are to have, to hold, to enjoy both liberty and dominion, freely, lawfully. They must not be enslaved. Should anything different be done, it is void, invalid, of no force, no worth. And those Indians and other peoples are to be invited into the faith of Christ by the preaching of God's word and the example of a good life.

Source: *Indian Freedom: The Cause of Bartolomé de Las Casas 1484-1566: A Reader* (Kansas City, 1995), pp. 214-215. (Lat.: *America pontificia primi saeculi evangelizationis 1493-1592*, ed. J. Metzler (Vatican City, 1991), vol. 1, pp. 364-366. — *Further Reading:* A. de la Hera, "El derecho de los indios a la libertad y a la fe" (in: *AHDE* 26, 1956), pp. 89-181; M. M. Martínez, "Las Casas-Vitoria y la Bula 'Sublimis Deus,'" in: A. Saint-Lu u.a. (eds.), *Estudios sobre Fray Bartolomé de Las Casas* (Sevilla, 1974), pp. 25-51; H. R. Parish, H. E. Weidmann, *Las Casas en México* (Mexico City, 1992); M. Delgado, "Der Konflikt zweier Universalismen," in: D. Büchel, V. Reinhardt (eds.), *Modell Rom?* (Köln, 2003), pp. 83-100; J. A. Fernández-Santamaría, *The State, War and Peace* (Cambridge, 1977); L. Hanke, *The Spanish Struggle for Justice in the Conquest of America* (Dallas, 2002); idem, *Pope Paul III and the American Indians* (Cambridge, Mass., 1937); G. Gutiérrez, *Las Casas: In Search of the Poor of Jesus Christ* (Maryknoll, 1993).

227. Two Controversial Interpretations of the "Compelle intrare"

Relying on the papal bull of concession *Inter Caetera* (cf. document 223a), the humanist and Aristotle expert Juan Ginés de Sepúlveda (d. 1573) advocated the political Augustinianism of the *ecclesia militans*, justifying military campaigns of conquest followed by forced conversion by the de facto dominating force. In contrast, Bartolomé de las Casas (1484-1566: defender of the rights of the Indians as well as of the values of their religions and cultures, denouncer of the conquest and the *encomienda*, defender of peaceful missionary work) insisted that the Gospel has nothing to do with violence and war and that the *compelle intrare* of Luke 14:23, the Bible passage with which Augustine justified the use of force against heretics and schismatics in the fifth century, is to be understood as persuasion of the intellect by rational means and by the gentle attraction and exhortation of the will. This view underlies all his work and his missiological treatise "De unico vocationis modo omnium gentium ad veram religionem," the first such treatise of the modern age. On the basis of Cajetan's commentary on Thomas Aquinas' *Summa Theologiae* II-II, q. 66, a. 8, it was crucial for him that the Indians represented a new type of pagans who had not been able to hear the Gospel until then and, therefore, against whom no coercion was permitted, unlike against the "heretics."

a. Juan Ginés de Sepúlveda (1544)

Leopoldo [one of the participants in the dialogue]: Nevertheless, we have not read that Christ or his Apostles obliged anyone to receive the faith or to hear the Gospel, but only invited them. . . . Truly I see no reason to think otherwise.

Demócrates [the other participant]: But St. Augustine does, for when a certain heretic raised a similar objection he replied: "Don't you understand that at that time the new seed of the Church was germinating, and the prophecy had not yet been fulfilled that says: 'May all kings fall down before him, all nations give him service'"? [Psalm 72:11] And in truth the more this is fulfilled, the more the power of the Church grows, not only to invite but also to oblige what is good, and this is what the Lord meant, for although he had great power he preferred to teach humility. And to confirm this opinion with evangelical doctrine St. Augustine added: "Christ gave ample evidence of this in the parable of the feast, when [the host] sent a slave to invite the guests, and when they would not come he told the slave: 'Go out at once into the streets and lanes of the town and bring in the poor, the crippled, the blind, and the lame.' And the slave said, 'Sir, what you ordered has been done, and there is still room.' Then the master said to the slave, 'Go out into the roads and lanes, and compel people to come in, so that my house may be filled.' [Luke 14:21-23] Notice that of the first group he said to invite them, and of the last he said to compel them. This represented the beginning of the still-growing Church, and the later stage when [the Gentiles] had to be compelled by force. . . ." In this way he affirmed that these barbarians should not only be invited but also compelled to the good, that is, to justice and religion, especially when the task can be carried out with so little effort and so few losses on both sides, and the barbarians can submit, and we can once and for all see salvation and great good for an almost infinite multitude of present and future human beings, which will last forever.

b. Bartolomé de las Casas (1551)

At this point I would like Sepúlveda and his associates to produce some passage from sacred literature where the gospel parable is explained as he explains it; that is, that the gospel (which is the good and joyful news) and the forgiveness of sins should be proclaimed with arms and bombardments, by subjecting a nation with armed militia and pursuing it with the force of war. What do joyful tidings have to do with wounds, captivities, massacres, conflagrations, the destruction of cities, and the common evils of war? They will go to hell rather than learn the advantages of the gospel. And what will be told by the fugitives who seek out the provinces of other peoples out of fear of the Spaniards, with their heads split, their hands amputated, their intestines torn open? What will they think about the God of the Christians? They will certainly think that [the Spaniards] are sons of the devil, not the children of God and the messengers of peace. [. . .]

From what has been deduced so extensively, it is evident what literal meaning was intended by Christ in the phrase from the parable cited above, "Force them to come in" [Luke 14,23]; that is, the compulsion signified here is that which concerns unbelievers who have never heard the truths of faith, and the compulsion is accomplished through the urgings of reason and human persuasion or through the spiritual and interior persuasion attained by the ministry of angels.

Source: (a) J. Ginés de Sepúlveda, *Demócrates Segundo o de las justas causas de la guerra contra los indios,* ed. Angel Losada (Madrid, 1984), pp. 69-71; (b) B. de las Casas, *In Defense of the Indians* (DeKalb, Ill., 1992), pp. 270, 303. — *Further Reading:* B. de las Casas, "Die Disputation von Valladolid (1550-1551)," in: *Las Casas* (WA) 1, pp. 337-436; J. A. Fernández-Santamaría, *The State, War and Peace* (Cambridge, 1977); L. Hanke, *The Spanish Struggle for Justice in the Conquest of America* (Dallas, 2002); G. Gutiérrez, *Las Casas: In Search of the Poor of Jesus Christ* (Maryknoll, 1993); L. Hanke, *All Mankind Is One: A Study of the Disputation between Bartolomé de Las Casas and Juan Ginés de Sepúlveda in 1550 on the Intellectual and Religious Capacity of the American Indians* (DeKalb, 1994); A. Losada, "The Controversy between Sepúlveda and Las Casas in the Junta of Valladolid," in: J. Friede, B. Keen (eds.), *Bartolomé de Las Casas in History* (DeKalb, 1971), pp. 127-234; B. de las Casas, *The Only Way* (New York, 1991); J. L. Phelan, *The Millennial Kingdom of the Franciscans in the New World* (Berkeley, [2]1970); Latourette, *Expansion III,* pp. 93ff.

C. Establishment of Colonial Church Structures

228. Pope Julius II: Kingly Patronage (1508)

The Catholic Kings of Spain, who had been named patrons of Granada because of their role in conquering that region, endeavored to gain that same patronage on discovering the New World. This patronage was shaped by the various bulls they had requested from the Pope. As was the custom, the kings drafted a document which they included with their request, and negotiated the final and definitive document with the Roman curia. Often the document had to be revised many times until the Kings were satisfied. The papal bull of concession *Inter Caetera* of Alexander VI issued on May 4, 1493 (cf. document 223a) already contained wording in the patronage tradition, even if it did not formally award the patronage. In this document a part of the New World was "given, granted and assigned" to the Catholic Kings and their successors for all times. At the same time they were solemnly admonished to appoint "worthy, God-fearing, learned, skilled, and experienced" men to evangelize the newly discovered peoples. This mandate to evangelize can be regarded as the birth of the Spanish patronage for the church overseas. A further step was the papal bull *Eximiae Devotionis* of November 16, 1501, with which Alexander VI conferred the tithes "of the islands and mainland of the West Indies" to the Catholic Kings "for all times." As this was still not enough for them, the kings exacted the bull *Universalis Ecclesiae* of July 28, 1508 from Julius II which was an explicit bull of patronage. The following excerpt is taken from this document. Even though there were to be further bulls to clarify other details (for example, Julius II's bull *Eximiae Devotionis* of August 8, 1510, concerning the tithe), the three named bulls had essentially established the patronage (mandate to evangelize, exclusive right to establish and endow parishes and cathedrals, and the tithe along with the right of presentation) for the church overseas.

Having in consideration the honor, the beauty and the security of the said island [Hispaniola] and of those kingdoms, whose kings have always been faithful to the Apostolic See, and considering the urgent petition presented to us some time ago and still presented to Us with due respect by the said king Fernando and the said queen Juana, and after long discussion with Our Brothers, the cardinals of the Holy Roman Church, in accordance with their advice we grant to king Fernando and queen Juana and to their successor kings of Castilla and León . . . the right of patronage and presentation of the appropriate persons for the above-mentioned churches of Yaguata, Magua and Baynua, as well as for the other metropolitan and cathedral churches and for the convents and monasteries; we also grant them the right to the place of honor after the high clergy in the metropolitan and cathedral churches, and in the churches of the convents and monasteries after the father superior; because of the great distance by sea we also grant them the right of presentation to Us and Our canonical successors, the Roman popes, for the other ecclesial benefits and holy positions in the islands and places named above, when these become vacant, naturally including those positions in the metropolitan and cathedral churches as well as in the churches of the convents and monasteries, when decisions must be made in consistory within a year after vacancies occur; for lesser benefits we grant them the said right of presentation before the local bishops; but we grant to the bishops the right to name the persons presented for lesser charges; and if the bishops do not name the persons presented within ten days, then any other bishop of that region, at the petition of king Fernando or queen Juana or the king who succeeds them, may freely and legitimately name the person presented.

Source: J. Metzler, ed., *America pontificia primi saeculi evangelizationis 1493-1592* (Vatican City, 1991), vol. 1, p. 106. — *Further Reading:* P. de Leturia, "Der Heilige Stuhl und das spanische Patronat in Amerika" in: *HJ* 46 (1926), pp. 1-71; idem, *Relaciones entre la Santa Sede e Hispanoamérica 1493-1835*, vol. 1 (Rome, 1959); J. Meier, "Die Anfänge der Kirche auf den Karibischen Inseln, Immensee 1991; M. Delgado, Der Konflikt zweier Universalismen," in: D. Büchel/V. Reinhardt (eds.), *Modell Rom?* (Köln, 2003), pp. 83-100; W. E. Schiels, "King and

Church: The Rise and Fall of the Patronato Real" in: *Jesuits Studies* (Chicago, 1961), pp. 105ff;
Dussel, *Church,* pp. 53-68.

229. Exercise of Patronage by Philip II (1574)

Attempts by the "indophile" party among the missionaries to move the Pope to interfere
directly in the Americas missions, in spite of patronage, led to "patronage conflicts."
These arose above all in the shadow of the bulls of Paul III in 1537 (cf. document 226) and
as a result of the failed attempt of Pius V during the "junta Magna" of 1568 to install a
nuncio in the American viceroyalties who was supposed to take care of direct contact
with Rome. As a result of these conflicts, Philip II provided for a stricter exercising of his
patronage rights through a law enacted June 1, 1574.

Whereas the right of Ecclesiastical Trust in all the Indies belongs to Us as a result
of having discovered and acquired that New World, built and endowed the
Churches and Monasteries therein at our expense and that of our ancestors the
Catholic Kings, and as willed to us by the Bull of the Sovereign Pontiffs for its
conservation and the justice we owe to it: We ordain and command that this
right of Patronage of the Indies be reserved exclusively and *in solidum* to Us and
to our Royal Crown, and may not be alienated from it in whole or in part; and
that any grace, mercy, privilege or other disposition made or granted by Us or
our royal descendants shall not be seen as granting a right of patronage to any
person, Church, or Monastery, nor shall it prejudice our said right of Patronage. . . . And our Viceroys, Audiences, and Royal Judiciaries shall proceed with
full rigor against anyone who fails to observe and uphold our right of patronage.

Source: Recopilación de Leyes de los Reynos de las Indias (Madrid, 1791) (^RMadrid 1973), pp. 1, 36
(book I, title 6, law 1). — *Further Reading:* P. de Leturia, *Relaciones entre la Santa Sede e
Hispanoamérica 1493-1835,* vol. 1 (Rome, 1959); A. Egaña, *La teoría del Regio Vicariato Español en
Indias* (Rome, 1958); M. Delgado, "Der Konflikt zweier Universalismen," in: D. Büchel,
V. Reinhardt (eds.), *Modell Rom?* (Köln, 2003), pp. 83-100; W. E. Schiels, "King and Church: The
Rise and Fall of the Patronato Real," in: *Jesuits Studies* (Chicago, 1961), pp. 105ff; Dussel, *Church,*
pp. 53-68.

D. MISSION AND MISSIONARIES

230. Mexico: The Missionary Method of the Franciscans (1596)

In their missionary work in Mexico the Franciscans made use of the children of the nobility whom they prepared in special schools for work in the missions. The children served
them as interpreters, but also as sources of information about "idol worship." The first

missionary methods were quite diverse and imaginative. In addition to translating the most important prayers and dogmas into the Indian languages, the Franciscans initially employed picture catechisms based on Aztec pictography. Many examples have been preserved and demonstrate the missionaries' ability to inculturate. Granted, at the end of the sixteenth century the author of this document, the Spanish Franciscan Jerónimo de Mendienta (1525-1604), sketches a rather romanticized picture of missionary work in Mexico. The Franciscans were accused of a *tabula rasa* assumption and of unnecessary rigor in the persecution of "idol worship."

[The children] had such good memory that they remembered a sermon or the story of a saint after hearing it once or twice, and repeated it later with good humor, boldly and correctly. . . . We have already said that the children taught by our religious brothers and sisters learned Christian doctrine easily; because of their intelligence they also learned in a few days from those who came from outside, using the common mode of instruction, that is: the teacher would say *"Pater noster,"* and the students would respond, *"Pater noster."* Then, *"qui es in coelis,"* and so on in the same manner. . . . Others tried a different method, more difficult in my opinion, but strange, which was to apply the words in their language which sounded similar to the Latin words, and to write them in order on a paper; not the words but the meaning of them, because they did not have other letters but painting, and they used symbolic characters to understand. Let us give examples: The word they have which most resembles *Pater* is *pantli,* which refers to a symbol that looks like a small flag, and stands for the number twenty. So to remember the word *Pater* they put the little flag that means *pantli,* and with it they say *Pater.* Their word closest to *noster* is *nochtli,* which refers to the plant the people here call Spanish tuna [cactus], which in Spain is called Indian fig, a fruit with a green shell covered with spines on the outside, very painful to anyone who grasps the fruit. Thus to remember the word *noster,* after the little flag they paint a tuna, which they call *nochtli,* and they continue in this way to the end of the prayer. . . . What I am describing was at the beginning of their conversion; later every Sunday and in religious observances, before the sermon and the mass the doctrine is always recited two or three times, when all the people are gathered in the church yard. . . . No other people in the world have had the care and curiosity that was shown in this New Spain for the christianizing doctrine and teaching of the Indian natives.

Source: G. de Mendieta, *Historia eclesiástica indiana,* vol. 1 (Madrid, 1973), pp. 137, 148f. — *Further Reading:* P. Borges, *Métodos misionales en la cristianización de América* (Madrid, 1960); Delgado, *Abschied,* pp. 191-234; J. G. Durán (ed.), *Monumenta catechetica hispanoamericana* (Siglos XVI-XVIII). 2 vols. (Buenos Aires, 1984-1990); J. L. Phelan, *The Millennial Kingdom of the Franciscans in the New World* (Berkeley, ²1970); W. Henkel, *Die Konzilien in Lateinamerika,* vol. 1: *Mexico, 1555-1897* (Paderborn, 1984); R. Ricard, *The Spiritual Conquest of Mexico: An Essay* on the Apostolate and the Evangelizing Methods of the Mendicant Orders in New Spain, 1523-1572 (Berkeley, 1974); J. Specker, *Die Missionsmethode in Spanisch-Amerika im 16. Jh.* (Schöneck-Beckenried, 1953); M. Cayota, *Siembra entre brumas* (Montevideo, 1990); Dussel, *Church*, pp. 46ff; Latourette, *Expansion III*, pp. 102ff, 113ff.

231. Peru: Evangelization of the Inca Empire (End of the Sixteenth Century)

The anonymous author of this document, probably the mestizo Blas Valera, analyzes the three ways of converting the Peruvian Indians during the sixteenth century. His — in part romanticizing — sympathy for the third way is quite noticeable. This third way was introduced after the Second Council of Lima (1567) and supported primarily by the Jesuits who arrived in Peru in 1569. It was based on the study of the Indian languages and cultures and allowed for an intensified missionization of the Inca Empire. The first period lasted until 1540, the second until 1567.

In Peru there have been three ways to christianize the natives. The first was by force and with violence, with no prior catechization or teaching, as was done in Puna, Tumbez, Cassamarca, Pachacama, Lima and other places, when the preachers were soldiers and the baptizers were laymen, and the people were brought for baptism in collars and chains, or bound together in a line or herd, realizing that if they didn't hold up their heads they would learn the taste of a sword or musket. . . . The second way to christianize the Indians was when they chose in free will to become Christians, moved by the saintly example of a good religious teacher or a devout Spanish layman (who were not lacking, but they were the least able teachers), but had no one to teach them the faith in their own language; it was enough for them to learn the Pater Noster, the Ave Maria and the Credo in Latin, to kneel before a cross raised in public in the mornings and evenings. . . . The third way that Peruvians could enter into Christendom was for Indians who not only wished to be baptized along with their children and wives, but had the good fortune to find people to teach them, whose good example inspired in them a strong faith and love of God. And if no one was available to teach them, they found ways to learn what they needed and teach it to their children. . . . And because they did what they should and could, God never failed them, he sent them some clear-minded ecclesiastics, clergy and regular, who with great and praiseworthy effort learned the language of that land; and these men dedicated themselves to preaching the gospel publicly, going from town to town, removing idolatry not only in external things, as the first and second group did who did not know the language, but also in hearts and wills; so that they did not need to find the idol and break it, or to tear out the old altars and oratories, but the Indians themselves shattered and burned all the idols and altars they found; those that were hidden they discovered and broke up.

Source: F. Esteve Barba, *Crónicas peruanas de interés indígena* (Madrid, 1968), pp. 181-187. — *Further Reading:* F. Armas Medina, *Cristianización del Perú* (1532-1600) (Sevilla, 1953); P. Borges, *Métodos misionales en la cristianización de América* (Madrid, 1960); J. Specker, *Die Missionsmethode in Spanisch-Amerika im 16. Jahrhundert* (Schöneck-Beckenried, 1953); G. Gutiérrez, *Las Casas: In Search of the Poor of Jesus Christ* (Maryknoll, 1993); K. Mills, *An Evil Lost to View? An Investigation of Post-Evangelisation Andean Religion in Mid-Colonial Peru* (Liverpool, 1994); P. J. de Arriaga, *The Extirpation of Idolatry in Peru* (Lexington, 1968); *Letter to a King: A Picture-History of the Inca Civilisation by Huamán Poma* (Don Felipe Huamán Poma de Ayala) (London, 1978); Dussel, *Church*, pp. 49ff, 286ff; Latourette, *Expansion III*, pp. 102ff, 145ff.

232. Guatemala: Agreement on Peaceful Missionization (1537)

Even if evangelization usually followed the conquest and was carried out under the protection of political coercion, the ideal of a peaceful, coercion-free evangelization promoted in Las Casas' "The Only Method of Attracting All People to the True Faith" never died. Las Casas himself practiced this method among the bellicose tribes in Guatemala. Successful at first, he had the Crown rename this region Verapaz ("Land of True Peace"). In his late work Las Casas (WA 3/1, 297) would write, full of wrath, that the Spanish rule was legitimate only in the province named Verapaz since it had been accepted by the Indians voluntarily, thanks to the missionaries. Before beginning his missionary work in Verapaz, Las Casas had had Alonso Maldonado, the governor of Guatemala, assure him in an agreement that the missionaries would work alone and that the *encomenderos* would not interfere. After a few years the experiment in Verapaz failed, largely due to the interference of Spanish colonists.

I, Lic. Alonso Maldonado, his majesty's Governor of this city and province of Guatemala, state that whereas you, Father Frey Bartolomé de las Casas, vicar of the house of Santo Domingo in this city, and the Religious who are here with you, have been moved to the service of our Lord God and to the salvation of souls and also to serve his majesty, to manage and work so that certain tribes of native Indians within the borders of this jurisdiction, who are not in obedience to our Lord King nor in conversation with the Spaniards, but rather are in rebellion and at war so that no Spaniard dares to go where they are, may come in peace, and you wish to secure and pacify them and bring them to royal subjection and dominion and that they may recognize his majesty as their lord so that they may be instructed in matters of the holy Catholic faith and that the Christian faith may be preached to them by you and the other Religious who hold that responsibility, and you have asked me to participate and give my approval; and whereas you fear that after you have brought the said Indians and tribes to peace and into the service of the King, if they are assigned to Spaniards they will be abused as has been customary and prevented from receiving the Christian faith and doctrine, and therefore you have demanded in the name of God and his majesty that if I promise and certify in the name of the crown that all the tribes and Indians which you bring in peace and subjection to his majesty, will be designated to the crown and will not be assigned or given to any Spaniard, then you would secure them and work with all your strength to bring them in that way, and that if I do not so promise you would not accept that responsibility, because you say that you cannot work fruitfully or bring them to become Christians or to receive instruction in good customs; and because this is a work of obvious service and glory to God for his majesty and the well-being and salvation of the native Indians of these tribes, and it is clear that his majesty desires nothing but that these infidels become Christians and be converted to God; therefore I state and promise you and give my word in the name and on behalf of his majesty . . . that I from here, with the powers given me by his majesty, will designate to the crown all that you secure and all their tribes, so that they may serve him as his vassals, and that I will not assign anyone to any Spaniard now or at any time, and I will order that no Spaniard molest them or approach them or their lands, on grave punishment of five years, in order that they shall not agitate, offend, or impede them from your preaching and their conversion.

Source: A. Saint-Lu, *La Vera Paz. Esprit évangélique et colonisation* (Paris, 1968), pp. 16-18. — *Further Reading:* M. Bataillon, "La Vera Paz," in: idem, *Études sur Bartolomé de Las Casas* (Paris, 1966), pp. 137-202; B. Biermann, "Missionsgeschichte der Verapaz in Guatemala" (in: *JGSLA* 1, 1964), pp. 117-156; A. Saint-Lu, *La Vera Paz* (Paris, 1968); G. Gutiérrez, *Las Casas: In Search of the Poor of Jesus Christ* (Maryknoll, 1993); K. Sapper, *The Verapaz in the Sixteenth and Seventeenth Centuries: A Contribution to the Historical Geography and Ethnography of Northeastern Guatemala* (Los Angeles, 1985); Bartolomé de las Casas (1474-1566) in the pages of Father Antonio de Remesal (Lewiston, N.Y., 2002); M. J. MacLeod, *Las Casas, Guatemala, and the Sad but Inevitable Case of Antonio de Remesal* (Pittsburgh, 1970); B. de las Casas, *The Only Way* (New York, 1991); Dussel, *Church,* pp. 46ff.

233. Brazil: Catholic and Calvinistic Activities

About the middle of the sixteenth century not only Spanish and Portuguese Jesuits came to Brazil, but also French Huguenots. The former evangelized in the region governed by the Portuguese, the latter in the shadow of the short-lived French attempts (1555-1558) to found the colony of France Antarctique in Brazil (in the Bay of Rio de Janeiro). Calvin sent fourteen fellow Christians to Brazil, among them Jean de Léry (1534-1613) who recorded the history of this early mission in the manner of a diary. Despite the denominational differences, the reports of the Jesuit Manoel da Nóbrega (1517-1570) and the Calvinist Léry exhibit structural similarities in terms of "civilized" Europeans towards foreign "savages." Just like Columbus in his first report (cf. document 218), they thought that the semi-nomadic Tupi Indians, who lived without permanent temples and places of worship, had no God. Both intuitively considered the shamans or sorcerers to be their main enemies, which is why they tried to unmask their "deceitful" practices. The theologically polemical point in Léry's report is also interesting where he compares the superstitious practices of the Tupis to Catholics' unquestioning faith in the Pope and their veneration of the saints.

a. Manuel da Nóbrega: On the Land and People of Brazil (1549)

These pagans do not worship anything, nor do they know God, only the thunder which they call Tupana, meaning something divine. So we have no better word to bring them the knowledge of God, than to call him Father Tupana. Among themselves they carry out a ceremony like this: Every few years some sorcerers come from distant lands, pretending to bring holiness; at the time of their coming the people clean the roads, and go out to receive them with dances and feasts according to their custom. . . . When the sorcerer arrives with great feasting, he enters a dark house and places a gourd in the shape of a human being in the most convenient place for his deception, and beside the gourd, assuming the voice of a child, he tells them not to be concerned with work, not to go out to work the fields, that the food grows by itself, and that they will never lack something to eat, and that the food will come to their houses by itself; and that their hoes will go out by themselves to dig, and the arrows will go hunting in the woods for their master, and that they must kill many of their enemies, and capture many for their banquets. And he promises them long life, and that the old women will become young girls, and that they should give their daughters to whomever they want, and he says and promises other such things to deceive them; thus they believe that something holy and divine is inside the gourd, saying these things, and they believe them. . . . And these sorcerers also use many tricks and charms on the pagans' illnesses. They are the greatest enemy we have here, and they sometimes make the sick people believe that we will stick knives, scissors, and other things in their bodies in order to kill them.

b. Jean de Léry: The Mission of the Hugenots in Brazil (1557)

In our conversation with them, when it seemed the right moment, we would say to them that we believed in a sole and sovereign God, Creator of the World, who, as He made heaven and earth with all the things contained therein, also now governs and disposes of the whole as it pleases Him to do. Hearing us hold froth on this subject, they would look at each other, saying "The!" — their customary interjection of astonishment — and be struck with amazement. As I will recount at more length, when they hear thunder, which they call Toupan, they are much afraid. Adapting ourselves to their crudeness, we would seize the occasion to say to them that this was the very God of whom we were speaking, who to show his grandeur and power made heavens and earth tremble; their resolution and response was that since he frightened in that way, he was good for nothing. And that, sad to say, is where these poor people are now. "What?" someone will now say, "can it be that, like brute beasts, these Americans live without any religion at all?" Indeed they do, or with almost none; I think that there is no nation on earth that is further from it. [. . .]

To proceed further into this matter, you must know that there are among them certain false prophets that they call caraïbes, who, going and coming from village to village like popish indulgence-bearers, would have it believed that by their communication with spirits they can give to anyone they please the strength to vanquish enemies in war, and, what is more, can make grow the big roots and the fruits [. . .] produced by this land of Brazil. [. . .]

If, when we seized the occasion to point out their errors, we told them that the caraïbes, who gave it out that the maracas ate and drank, were deceiving them; and also, that it was not the caraïbes (as they falsely boasted) who caused their fruits and their big roots to grow, but rather the God in whom we believe and whom we were making known to them — well, that had about as much effect as speaking against the Pope over here, or saying in Paris that the reliquary of St. Genevieve doesn't make it rain. Therefore these caraïbes charlatans hated us no less than the false prophets of Israel (fearing to lose their fat morsels) hated Elijah, the true servant of God, who similarly revealed their abuses; they began to hide from us, fearing even to approach or to sleep in the villages where they knew we were lodging.

Source: (a) S. Leite (ed.), *Monumenta Brasiliae*, vol. 1, 148-154; (b) Jean de Léry, *History of a Voyage to the Land of Brazil, otherwise called America* (Berkeley, 1990), pp. 135-136, 140, 145. — *Further Reading:* U. Bitterli, *Die "Wilden" und die "Zivilisierten"* (München, ²1991); A. Métraux, *La Religion des Tupinamba et ses rapports avec celle des autres tribus Tupi-Guarani* (Paris, 1928); M. Münzel, "Jupiters wilder Bruder," in: K.-H. Kohl (ed.), *Mythen der Neuen Welt* (Berlin, 1982), pp. 101-109; O. Reverdin, *Quatorze calvinistes chez les Topinambous* (Geneva, 1957); A. Züger, "Zur calvinistischen Mission in Brasilien im 16. Jahrhundert," in: *NZM* 14 (1958), pp. 218-219; Bastian, *Protestantismus*, pp. 50ff; T. L. Ferreira, *Padre Manoel da Nóbrega, fundador de São Paulo* (São Paulo, 1957); W. Krickeberg (ed.), *Pre-Columbian American Religions* (New York, 1969); Dussel, *Church*, pp. 51ff, 314ff; Latourette, *Expansion III*, pp. 160ff.

234. Language and Missionary Work

Two tendencies influenced the language policy of the church and of the Spanish Crown from the very beginning: on the one hand the gentle "Hispanicization" of the Indians which necessarily also involved their acquisition of the Spanish language; on the other hand the appropriate evangelization which made the acquisition of the Indian languages by the missionaries and the translation of the most important prayers and principles of belief appear expedient. Only after they had learned the Indian languages were the missionaries able to understand the world of Indian thought and feeling; after that, evangelization began with an irrepressible dynamism. The translation accomplishments such as, for example, the Our Father here (document a) in the Náhuatl translation of the Franciscan Alonso de Molina (d. 1579), were very bold. In December, 1578, Phillip II declared formal examination in Indian languages to be a formal condition for pastoral positions in Indian villages and parish communities. In the second half of the sixteenth century professorships for the main languages of the Inca and the Aztec Empires had been established at the universities of Lima and Mexico. The missionaries compiled grammars and dictionaries of the Indian languages as well as small and large catechisms and sermon manuals. Document b emphasizes, with conciliar authority, the principle of evangelization in the mother tongue. Practice, however, did not always correspond to theory. The repeated exhortations of Church and Crown on the importance of learning Indian languages thoroughly suggests many missionaries had failed in this regard. The process of translating Spanish into the Indian languages ran into difficulties when communicating abstract technical terms of Christian God-speak. The opinion prevailed — it was already crystallizing in the mid-sixteenth century — "that the mysteries of faith could not be described well and correctly even in the best and most complete Indian language without inconsistencies and deficiencies" (R. Konetzke). In the catechisms and sermon books we therefore always find words like God, Holy Trinity, person, faith, or Holy Spirit in Spanish. Nevertheless, the greatest and most admirable inculturation accomplishments of mission work in the Americas are to be found in the area of language.

a. Our Father in the Aztec Language Náhuatl (1546)

Totatzine in ilhuicac timoyetztica,	Our Father, Who art in heaven,
ma yecteneualo in motocatzin.	Hallowed be Thy Name.
Ma uallauh in motlatocayotzin.	
Ma chiaualo in tlalticpac in ticmonequiltia in iuh chiualo in ilhuicac.	Thy Kingdom come Thy Will be done, on earth as it is in Heaven.
Yn totlaxcal in momoztlae totechmonequi ma axcan xitechmomaquili.	Give us this day our daily bread.
Ma xitechmopopolhuili in tot-	And forgive us our trespasses,

latlacol in iuh tiquimpopolhuia in techtlatlacalhuia.	as we forgive those who trespass against us
Macamo xitechmotlalcauili inic amo ipan tiuetzizque in teneyeyecoltiliztli.	And lead us not into temptation.
Ma xitechmomaquixtitli in iuicpa in amoqualli.	But deliver us from evil.
Mayuh muchiua.	So be it!

b. Third Council of Lima: The Indians Should Be Taught in Their Own Language (1583)

The fundamental purpose of Christian instruction and catechesis is an understanding of the faith. . . . Therefore everybody should be taught in a way they can understand: the Spaniards in Spanish, Indians in their own language. Otherwise no amount of blessing will bring them benefit, as the apostle Paul affirms [1 Corinthians 14:6-19]. Thus no Indian should be obliged to learn the prayers or catechism in Latin, because it is sufficient and much better for them to say it in their language, and if some wish, they may also learn in Spanish which many of them have mastered. It is superfluous to require the Indians to learn any other language beside that.

Source: (a) J. Baumgartner, "Evangelisierung in indianischen Sprachen," in: Sievernich, *Conquista*, pp. 313-347, 326f; (b) F. L. Lisi, *El Tercer Concilio Limense y la aculturación de los indígenas sudamericanos* (Salamanca, 1990), pp. 128-129. — *Further Reading:* Lisi, ibid.; Borges, *Historia I*, pp. 509-520; R. Konetzke, "Die Bedeutung der Sprachenfrage in der spanischen Kolonisation Amerikas" in: *JGSLA* 1 (1964), pp. 72-116; Delgado, *Abschied*, pp. 78-112; *Doctrina cristiana y catecismo para la instrucción de los indios* (Madrid, 1985); R. Vargas, *Concilios Limenses*, 3 vols. (Lima, 1954); Dussel, *Church*, pp. 43-52, 60-80.

E. Religious Dialogue and Ethnographic Works

235. Mexico: Religious Dialogue between Aztecs and Franciscans (1524)

In 1564 the Spanish Franciscan Bernardino de Sahagún (1500-1590), who had come to Mexico in 1529, rewrote a religious dialogue (in Spanish and Mexican) from conversation notes recorded in Spanish and from Aztec sources. This dialogue had occurred in 1524 between the first twelve Franciscans of the Mexico mission and Aztec priests and noblemen. The Franciscans had made a great effort to implement the method of religious dialogue in Mexico as well. Yet the de facto existing conditions — this was also a dialogue between victorious Spaniards and conquered Aztecs — makes the dialogue appear as a kind of "spiritual *requerimiento*" in the name of the stronger Christian God. It is striking that in a section not documented here the Franciscans first emphasize that they are not gods, but humans, probably in an allusion to Acts 14:11-18. But they have no appreciation of the "unknown God" of the Aztecs, of the seeds of the Word among them, indeed the Franciscans insist that the Aztecs have lived in darkness and had no knowledge of the true God up to that time. Despite the best intentions of the Franciscans, this dialogue served rather to deepen the perplexity and despondency of the Aztecs who, after the defense of their gods and religious customs, respond with resignation: "Do with us as you like!" Even so, the Franciscans emphasize that the fault of the Aztecs is not very grievous because they belong to a new type of pagans who have not as yet been able to hear about the Gospel.

[*The Aztecs:*] You tell them, indeed, that we do not know Him, the Possessor of the Near, Possessor of the Surrounding, the Possessor of Heaven, Possessor of Earth. You tell them, indeed, that our gods are not real gods. It is a new word, this one you tell them, and because of it we are extremely frightened. Indeed, these our makers, these who came to be, these who came to live on the earth, did not speak in this way. Verily, they gave us their law. They followed them as true, they served them, they honored them, the gods. They taught us all their forms of serving, their modes of honoring. Thus, before them we eat earth, thus we bleed ourselves, thus we discharge the debt ourselves, thus we burn *copal*, and, thus, we cause something to be killed. They used to say that, verily, they, the gods, by whose grace one lives, they merited us. When? Where? While it was still night. And they used to say, indeed, they give us our supper, our breakfast, and all that is drinkable, edible, this our meat, the corn, the bean, the wild amaranth, the lime-leaved sage. They are those from whom we request the water, the rain, by which the things of the earth are made. Furthermore, they are rich themselves, they are happy themselves, they are possessors of gods, they are owners of gods, by which always, forever, it germinates there, it grows green there, in their house. Where? What kind of place is it, the place of Tlaloc? Hunger never occurs there, nothing is diseased, nothing is poor. And also, they give to the people prowess, courage, the chase, and the lip-grass, the instrument by which something is bound, the loincloth, the mantle, the flowers, the tobacco, the precious green stones, the fine plumes, the divine excrement. When, and where, were these thus summoned, when implored, when held as gods, when honored? It is already a very long time ago. When? At another time it was in Tula. When? At another time it was in Huapalcalco. When? At another time it was in Xucahtlapan. When? At another time it was in Tlamohuanchan. At another time it was in Yohualichan. When? At another time it was in Teotihuacan. Indeed, they, everywhere in the world, they caused the people to construct their mat, their seat, with stones. They gave to the people the lordship, the dominion, the fame, the glory.

And, perchance, now, are we those who will destroy it, the ancient law? The law of the Chichimecs? The law of the Toltecs? The law of the Colhuaque? The law of the Tepanecs? Already our heart is this way: through him one is made to live, through him one is given birth, on account of him one is made to grow, on account of him one is made to mature, by means of this one who is summoned, by means of this one who is implored. Hear, our lords, beware of doing something to them, this your precious tail, your precious wing, so much the more so that it will be abandoned, so much the more so that it will be destroyed. In this way also the old man, in this way also the old woman had her growth, had her increase in age. Oh, that the gods be not angry with us. Oh, that their anger, their wrath, not come. And let us beware that on account of that it not rise before us, on us, the tail, the wing. Let us beware that on account of that we not stir it up, let us beware that on account of that we not provoke it, by saying to it: no longer will it summon them, no longer will it implore them.

In the meantime, calmly, peacefully, consider it, our lords, whatever is necessary. Indeed, our heart is not able to be full. And, indeed, absolutely we do not yet agree to it ourselves, we do not yet make it true for ourselves. We ourselves will cause you injury to the heart. Indeed, here they lie, the possessors of water, the possesors of mountains, the lords, the speakers, these who carry it, these who bear it, the world. It is enough that we have already left it alone, we have lost it, we have had it taken away, we have had it prohibited, the mat, the seat. Indeed, [if] we will only remain there, we will only cause them to be restricted. Do it to us, whatever it is you will desire. Indeed, we return it all by this, by this we respond to it, your precious breath, your precious word, our lords.

[*The Franciscans:*] There it is told how they, the twelve Fathers, responded to them, those who offer incense. When it finished, their word having ended, the response of the ones who offer things, they, the twelve divine guardians, at once said it: If only you would not torment yourselves, our beloved, if only you would not understand it as an evil omen, our word, the one we told you: how, in what manner, no tone of the gods is real, all these whom you regard as gods, these whom you have continually implored.

Please hear it. If the gods were truly real gods, perchance, would we not also regard them as gods? Perchance, would we not also request from them our supper, our breakfast? And, likewise, would they not everywhere in the earth be summoned, be implored? Indeed, we are not merely inventing it, this which we now tell you. Indeed, we know it well, who they are, how they are, those whom you regard as gods, these whom you have continually implored; where, and in what manner they began, they commenced, who they were, beyond there, at first; and of what sort is their being, their heart, their function, their will, and from where they came. Indeed, we will tell you everything, we will cause you to hear it, if you desire it. And we will be able to cause you to have a full heart, because we guard it, the divine book, the divine word, there where it lies visible, it lies painted, it lies arranged all that which is His precious word, this one of the Possessor of the Near, Possessor of the Surrounding. This took place a very long time ago. And that divine word is very properly real, properly upright, properly that which is followed as true. And everywhere on the earth, in the world, it has been heard, it has been followed as true. There, from there we came, there they lie not a few possessors of water, possessors of mountains, and lords, speakers, the ones who are very old, the ones who are very strong, the ones who are very wealthy, the ones who are very much in possession of things.

And you, on this account, you do not regard them as God, you do not know to abandon them, these wicked ones, this one who is a deceiver of people. Because, indeed, you never heard it, the precious word of God. You did not guard it, the divine book, the divine word. It never came to reach you, His precious breath, His precious word, this one of the Possessor of Heaven, the Possessor of Earth. And, then, you are blind, you are deaf, as if in darkness, in gloom, you live. On account of this your faults are, furthermore, not very great. But now, if you do not desire to hear it, the precious breath, the precious word of God (this one He gives to you), you will be in much danger. And God, Who has commenced your destruction, will conclude it, you will be completely lost.

Source: Fray Bernardino de Sahagún, "The Aztec-Spanish-Dialogues of 1524," in: *Alcheringa*, vol. 4 (Boston, 1980), no. 2, pp. 52-193, here: 119-132. — *Further Reading:* W. Lehmann, *Sterbende Götter und christliche Heilsbotschaft* (Stuttgart, 1949); C. Duverger, *La conversion des indiens de Nouvelle Espagne, avec les "Colloques des Douze" de Bernardino de Sahagún (1564)* (Paris, 1987); M. Sievernich, "Inkulturation und Begegnung der Religionen im 16. Jahrhundert," in: Adveniat (ed.), *Entdeckung des Evangeliums in Lateinamerika* (Essen, 1990), pp. 28-47; H. Wißmann, *Sind doch die Götter auch gestorben* (Gütersloh, 1981); A. Zaballa, *Transculturación y misión en Nueva España* (Pamplona, 1990); M. León-Portilla, *Bernardino de Sahagun, First Anthropologist* (Norman, 2002); J. J. Klor de Alva (ed.), *The Work of Bernardino de Sahagun: Pioneer Ethnographer of Sixteenth-Century Aztec Mexico* (Albany, 1988); M. S. Edmonson, *Sixteenth-Century Mexico: The Work of Sahagún* (Alburquerque, 1974); L. Nicolau d'Olwer, *Fray Bernardino de Sahagún (1499-1590)* (Salt Lake City, 1987); R. Nebel, *Santa María Tonantzin Virgen de Guadalupe. Continuidad y transformación religiosa en México* (Mexico City, 1995).

236. Bernadino de Sahagún: Rehabilitation of the Aztec Culture (1577)

The Franciscan Bernadino de Sahagún (1500-1590) is considered to be the greatest ethnographer of the Aztec culture and the founder of modern ethnography. In the preface to his *magnum opus* he clearly expresses his intellectual interest: on the one hand the eradication of the "idol worship" that had remained after the first mission and on the other hand the rescue of the cultural memory and the honor of a conquered and humiliated people whose cultural achievements could certainly be compared to those of the "civilized" Europeans: all descended from Adam. The compensation theory, which appears at the end of the document and which played an important role in the theological disputations between Catholics and non-Catholics, is also interesting.

The sins of idolatry, idolatrous rituals, idolatrous superstitions, auguries, abuses, and idolatrous ceremonies are not yet completely lost. To preach against these matters, and even to know if they exist, it is needful to know how they practiced them in the times of their idolatry. [. . .]

All this work will be very useful to learn the degree of perfection of this Mexican people, which has not yet been known. [. . .] Thus they are considered as barbarians, as a people at the lowest level of perfection, when in reality (excluding some injustices their mode of governance contained) in matters of good conduct they surpass many other nations which have great confidence in their administrations. [. . .] As to the religion and the adoration of their gods, I do no believe there have been in the world idolaters to such a degree venerators of their gods, nor at such great cost to themselves as these of this New Spain. [. . .]

It is most certain all these people are our brothers, stemming from the stock of Adam, as do we. They are our neighbors whom we are obliged to love, even as we love ourselves. Whatever it may be that they were in times past, we now see through experience, that they are capable in all the crafts and they practice them. They are also capable in learning all the liberal arts and sacred theology, as has been seen through experience of those who have taught in these sciences. [. . .] They are no less capable of our Christianity; besides, they have been duly indoctrinated therein. It certainly seems, in our times, in these lands and with this people, that our Lord God has willed to restore to the Church that which the demon robbed her of in England, Germany, France, Asia and Palestine.

Source: Florentine Codex, *Fray Bernardino de Sahagún, General History of the Things of New Spain,* Part I (Santa Fe, N.M., 1982), pp. 45, 47, 49, 50. — *Further Reading:* G. Baudot, *Utopía e historia en México* (Madrid, 1983); M. Delgado, "Produktive Neugierde für das Fremde," in: P. Burschel e.a. (eds.), *Historische Anstöße* (Berlin, 1992), pp. 411-428; M. Erdheim, "Anthropologische Modelle des 16. Jahrhunderts," in: K.-H. Kohl (ed.), *Mythen der Neuen Welt* (Berlin, 1982), pp. 57-67; M. M. Marzal, *Historia de la antropología indigenista* (Lima, 1981); A. Pagden, *The Fall of Natural Man* (Cambridge, 1982); T. Todorov, *The Conquest of America: The Question of the Other* (Norman, 1999); M. León-Portilla, *Bernardino de Sahagun, First Anthropologist* (Norman, 2002); J. J. Klor de Alva (ed.), *The Work of Bernardino de Sahagun: Pioneer Ethnographer of Sixteenth-Century Aztec Mexico* (Albany, 1988); M. S. Edmonson (ed.), *Sixteenth-Century Mexico: The Work of Sahagún* (Alburquerque, 1974); L. Nicolau d'Olwer, *Fray Bernardino de Sahagún (1499-1590)* (Salt Lake City, 1987).

F. Failed Approaches to Indian Christianity

237. Inquisition Proceeding against an Indian Nobleman (1539)

The *Junta Magna* of 1568 decided to install the tribunal of the Holy Inquisition as an administrative body in Lima (1570) and in Mexico (1571) in order to monitor the early Christians and their offspring as well as the *conversos* from Judaism and Islam "in a most moderate and gentle way." It was explicitly stated in Philip II's directives that the Inquisition was not to take action against the Indians. Before the installation of the Inquisition Tribunal, the bishops of the West Indies had extensive inquisitional authority in their sees. The first bishop of Mexico, the humanist and Franciscan Juan de Zumárraga (d. 1548), organized a shameful legal proceeding against Don Carlos Ometochtzin, the Indian prince of Tezcoco, because he wanted to return to the religion of his ancestors and because he rejected the education of the youth practiced by the Franciscans in the colleges (among other things celibacy, cf. document 239). The legal proceeding and the burning of Don Carlos led to protests and to complaints to the Crown which censured Zumárraga's behavior and strictly forbade any repetition of the events. Upon closer examination one sees that Don Carlos aimed his criticism not only against the attempt of the Franciscans to introduce Christian ethics, but also against the disempowerment of the nobles and the promotion of the common Indians. The "Indian Christendom," which the Franciscans had dreamt of, suffered its first setback with the legal proceeding against Don Carlos. At first it was a mission project and essentially consisted in seeing the poor and virtuous Indians as "moldable wax" for the creation of a Christendom modeled on the Franciscan ideal. It was therefore initially a "Franciscanization of the Indians." A real Indian Christianity emerged only when the Indians themselves expressed their view of Christianity (cf. documents 242, 248f) — often against the resistance of the missionaries. The beginnings of an Indian Christianity can be characterized as a failure only insofar as one means by this the establishment of a native church with a native clergy.

The above-mentioned Don Carlos called this witness . . . and said to him: "Francisco, come, listen, brother . . . I'll tell you that in truth everything they teach at the School is a deception. . . . Look, the Franciscan monks have one kind of doctrine and one way of living and dressing and praying; and the Augustinian monks have another way; and the Dominican monks have another, as everybody can see. It was the same for those who kept our gods, that those in Mexico had one way of dressing and praying and offering and fasting, and those of other peoples, another. . . . Let us follow what our ancestors had and followed, and let us live in the way they lived. . . . It's not good for us to listen to the preaching of the religious fathers, it's their business, they make a point of not having women and not caring for the things of the world and women; let the fathers do what they say when they want to, it's their business, but it's not our business. . . . Brother, what harm do women or wine do to men? Do you think the religious fathers can stop Christians from having many women and getting drunk? So what can the fathers do to us? ... Let us get away from them and do what our ancestors did, with no one to stop us. There was a time when the common people did not sit on the mats and seats of the great. Now everyone does and says whatever they want. No one has the right to stop us or meddle in what we want to do. ... We are our own rulers."

Source: L. González Obregón (ed.), *Proceso criminal del Santo Oficio de la Inquisición, y del Fiscal en su nombre, contra Don Carlos, indio principal de Tezcuco* (Mexico City, 1910), pp. 40ff. — *Further Reading:* Delgado, *Abschied,* pp. 191-234; M. León-Portilla, "Los franciscanos vistos por el hombre náhuatl," in: *Estudios de cultura náhuatl 17* (Mexico City, 1984), pp. 261-339; Borges, *Historia I,* pp. 299-320; R. E. Greenleaf, *The Mexican Inquisition of the Sixteenth Century* (Albuquerque, 1969); idem, *Zumárraga and the Mexican Inquisition, 1536-1543* (Washington, 1961).

238. Pedro de Quiroga: Life Story of a New Convert (ca. 1563)

The Indian who narrates his life here, not without irony, is a literary figure. His account, however, is probably representative of many Indian biographies from the higher strata of society. Trained by three Spaniards — a conquistador, a merchant, and a hermit — he documents the ethical and religious diversity of the Europeans who had come to the Americas, including those Christians who appeared convincing because of the example of their lives. The Indians were thus able to criticize the colonial system while accepting Christianity as a liberating religion.

I am of the Ynca nation and a subject of the kings who conquered and occupied these kingdoms, people well esteemed and feared. ... You have spiritedly and forcibly attacked us and conquered us. ... I begged one of the captains, a well-mannered and valiant Spaniard, to protect me from your fury and from being killed, unlike the many thousands of Indians who lost their lives there that day. He used me for more than a few days. ... I had enough of this awful and wearying life ... and so I left the war and went to live with a merchant, whose life and condition seemed quieter and less harmful even to the Indians. ... He was the first to speak to me of your God, of becoming a Christian and accepting your religion. ... He taught me doctrine and instructed me in the things of the faith, although confusedly and briefly, without the preparation or means to do so, and thus I received without understanding the baptism and faith of Jesus Christ. ... Certainly I wanted to know, not more than I ought but enough to know how to be a man; and for this purpose God gave me a better master whom I had sought out and desired, a man you call a hermit, poorly dressed by his own choosing, who held in contempt all that you love and seek. He was a man of holy life and religious customs; he feared God and sought only heaven. I understood then that there were good and bad people among you, and that not everything was disorder as I thought. This good man abhorred your evil works, and with painful tears he wept for the harm you were doing us, comforting the people of my nation wherever he saw them suffering, proclaiming to us that God would have mercy on us and would stop punishing us if we called on him and sought to know and serve him. Because this man was good and just, I felt that you were persecuting him and that you hated him for what he said and did in favor of the natives of this miserable kingdom. Now because he saw my willingness and eagerness he began to teach me the true way and to instruct me in the holy faith of Christ. He fed me with doctrine, which I had not yet tasted, nor even knew that men were capable of such things. He gave me the doctrine as it was, and with such clarity and love of God and neighbor that whenever I remember this man my eyes cannot cease from weeping for his absence and death. God took him to himself because this earth was not worthy of such a man.

Source: P. Quiroga, *Coloquios de la verdad* (Sevilla, 1922), pp. 61-64. — *Further Reading:* M. M. Marzal, *Historia de la antropología indigenista: México y Perú* (Lima, 1981); F. Armas Medina, *Cristianización del Perú (1532-1600)* (Sevilla, 1953); Dussel, *Church,* pp. 286ff.

239. Mexico: Debates about a College for Indians (ca. 1570)

In 1536 the first Franciscans of the Mexico mission founded schools in order to instruct the children of Indian nobles in reading and writing, Latin, grammar and rhetoric, logic and philosophy, music and indigenous medicine. While their immediate goal was certainly to ascertain how well the Indians could learn, they also cherished the dream of being able to train a native clergy in the long term. Right from the beginning the project was controversial. But after the legal proceedings against Don Carlos (cf. document 237) it became clear to the Franciscans that the Indians most skilled in grammar had a greater propensity for marriage than celibacy, as Bishop Juan de Zumárraga recorded in a letter to Charles V in which he also reflected on the school at Santiago Tlatelolco (Mexico City) which was constantly being attacked in the 1540s and 50s by those opposing the indigenous people. From 1546 on the Franciscans entrusted Native Americans with the leadership of the school. Due to bad results, however, they found it necessary to take over the school again in 1570 or, rather, to found it anew. It existed until the seventeenth century, but was hardly able to provide the church in Mexico with any priests at all (there are some exceptions, but the research is not clear on this point). Sahagún, who from the beginning was an instructor at the above-mentioned college and held the Indians in high regard (cf. document 236), summarizes the arguments for and against the school.

The Spaniards and other religious who heard about this laughed and joked a lot, being very certain that no one would be able to teach Grammar to such backward people; but after working with them for two or three years, they came to understand every aspect of the art of Grammar, to speak and understand Latin, and to write in Latin, even to write epic poetry. . . . When [the Spaniards] saw their progress and that they were able to do even more, both the secular and ecclesiastical priests began to oppose this effort and raised many objections to prevent it. . . . They said that since these people were not going to become priests, it would do no good to teach them Grammar, that it would put them at risk of becoming heretics, and that they would know from Holy Scripture that the ancient Patriarchs had many wives at once, just as they did, and that they would no longer believe what we teach them, that no one may have more than one wife *in facie ecclesiae;* they raised other objections of this sort, and we told them that even if they could not become priests, we wanted to show how much ability they had. . . . To those who said we were giving them occasions for heresy, we answered that our intention was quite the opposite, that knowledge would help them better understand the things of faith; and that since they were also subject to the Most Christian Prince, if such things should happen it would be very easy to correct.

Source: R. Ricard, *La conquista espiritual de México* (Mexico City, 1986), pp. 344f. — *Further Reading:* R. Ricard, *The Spiritual Conquest of Mexico: An Essay on the Apostolate and the Evangelizing Methods of the Mendicant Orders in New Spain, 1523-1572* (Berkeley, 1974); Borges, *Historia I*, pp. 715-730; M. Cayota, *Siembra entre brumas* (Montevideo, 1990); Delgado, *Abschied*, pp. 191-234; L. Gómez Canedo, *La educación de los marginados durante la época colonial* (Mexico City, 1982); J. M. Kobayashi, *La educación como conquista* (Mexico City, 1985); F. Morales, *Franciscanos y mundo religioso en México* (Mexico City, 1993); E. C. Frost, *La historia de Dios en las indias. Visión franciscana del Nuevo Mundo* (Mexico City, 2002); Dussel, *Church*, pp. 375ff.

240. G. de Mendieta: No Indian Priests (1596)

In this document the Franciscan Mendieta (1525-1604) justifies denying ordination as well as membership in a religious order to the Indians. The statutes of the Franciscans were particularly strict in this regard. The early councils, such as the First Council of Mexico (1555) and the Second Council of Lima (1567), also forbade ordination and religious order status to the Indians as new Christians up to the fourth generation after conversion. The Third Council of Lima (1582) and the Third Council of Mexico (1585) were, however, less strict and, depending on the interpretation, even left the door open in well-founded cases to the ordination of Indians and mestizos. In the seventeenth century, interventions on behalf of the Indians increased. In his influential manual for Indian priests *(Itinerario para párrocos de Indios)*, the Dominican Bishop Alonso de la Peña Montenegro stated in 1668 that the ordination of Indians from a lawful marriage was not only not forbidden by the decrees of the Third Council of Lima and the laws of the Crown, but in fact considered to be expedient. In his opinion the Indians were capable of ordination and as natives who knew Indian languages and culture should even be preferred for the sinecure of the Indian parishes. This change of mindset resulted in the ordination of a considerable number of Indians and mestizos, above all in Mexico, even if the number given by the Jesuit Francisco Javier Clavijero, namely that thousands of Indians had been ordained priests since the end of the sixteenth century, is somewhat exaggerated.

"Why are such people not given the habit of religious orders, both lay and priestly, in the same way that the early Church chose Gentiles and Jews newly converted to the faith as priests and bishops? This would seem to be even more beneficial for the conversion and good Christendom of the whole country, since they know the languages and can preach and minister in them more appropriately and perfectly. And since the people will more willingly accept and receive doctrine from the lips of their fellow natives than from foreigners." This was answered in short order, by admitting that it was so in the early Church, and that it was right in that time, because God worked miracles in the newly converted and they became saints, and later offered themselves as martyrs by confessing the name of Jesus Christ. But in these times the Church, enlightened by the Holy Spirit and taught by the experience of the many lapses it has seen in new Christians, has ordered, as determined by the Holy Pontiffs Vicars of Christ, that descendants of the unfaithful to the fourth degree not be admitted to religious orders, and this prohibition in particular appears in the statutes of our order. . . . A great and learned foreigner from the Spanish kingdoms who came here [Jacobo Daciano], confident of his knowledge, presumed to affirm that this new Indian Church was wrong not to have native ministers from among the converted, as the early Church did; he was of the opinion that Indians should be given sacred orders and made ministers of the Church. And the most erudite and most religious father Fray Juan de Gaona convinced him of his error in public debate, and obliged him to do penance.

Source: G. de Mendieta, Historia eclesiástica indiana, vol. 2 (Madrid, 1973), pp. 60-61. — Further Reading: J. L. Phelan, The Millennial Kingdom of the Franciscans in the New World (Berkeley, ²1970); P. Nettel Díaz, La utopia franciscana en la Nueva Espana (1554-1604): el apostolado de Fray Gerónimo de Mendieta (Mexico City, 1989); L. González y González, Jerónimo de Mendieta. Vida, pasión y mensaje de un indigenista apocalíptico (Zamora, Mexico, 1996); Borges, Historia I, pp. 261-279; R. V. de la Rosa, "Reinheit des Blutes," in: Sievernich (Conquista), pp. 271-291; J. Specker, "Der einheimische Klerus in Spanisch-Amerika im 16. Jahrhundert," in: J. Beckmann (ed.), Der einheimische Klerus in Geschichte und Gegenwart (Schöneck-Beckenried, 1950), pp. 73-97; F. Zubillaga, "Intento de clero indígena en Nueva España en el siglo XVI y los jesuitas" in: Anuario de Estudios Americanos 26 (1969), pp. 426-469; Dussel, Church, pp. 375ff; Latourette, Expansion III, pp. 100ff.

II. LATIN AMERICA 1600-1800

A. Church and Mission in Colonial Society

241. Peru: Monasteries, Hospitals and the University in Baroque Lima (1629)

Between 1608 and 1622 the Spanish Carmelite and theology professor Antonio Vázquez Espinosa (d. 1630) traveled throughout Spanish America. In his work *Compendio y descripción de las Indias Occidentales* (1629) he left us a comprehensive description of the state of colonial society during the Baroque period. City centers blossomed. Male and female religious orders built their monasteries and convents there (document a). Hospitals were created for the care of the poor (document b) as well as schools and universities for training and education (document c). All in all, Lima and Mexico City had the same living standard as Spanish cities. Colonial society was a "mixed" society, in which each person had his or her place according to social rank: Spaniards, Creoles (descendants of Spaniards born in America), Mestizos (offspring of Indians and Spaniards), Indians, Blacks and Mulattos. Around 1600 a shared "American" identity budded among Creoles and Indians (cf. documents 259-262) which led to the battles for independence around 1800. In Baroque colonial society that form of Catholic Christianity took shape — in sacred art, in the feasts and processions, as well as in congregations, brotherhoods and on pilgrimages — which has been formative for Latin American popular piety up to the present.

a. Monasteries

This famous city has remarkable Dominican, Franciscan, Augustinian, Mercedarian, and Jesuit convents. [. . .]

[The Order of the Company of Jesus] it has a congregation of priests to which repair with exemplary confidence the Ecclesiastical Chapter, another congregation of students, and another of laymen, comprising 800 men of every station in the republic. [. . .] There is another congregation of boys in the decury. [. . .] There is another congregation, of Indians, and another, of Negroes; these all meet Sundays after noon in different chapels; there, after a few minutes' reading in public of spiritual lessons, they have their sermon; on some days the Father who has them in charge invites others to deliver the spiritual discourse. And since the slaves who hold the horses are many in number and stand out in the street in front of the gates of the College of San Pablo, one of the Fathers comes out and takes his position in a high spot and preaches to them, so that they may not be deprived of good doctrine and instruction. All these congregations, and particularly that of the laymen who are under the protection of Our Lady of Expectation, have their festival and communion every month; the Holy Sacrament is exposed with remarkable lavishness of elaborate decoration. [. . .]

This city has six nunneries, famous and remarkable both for their temples and for the large number of nuns, all of them subject to the monastic rule with clausure. The Convent of the Encarnación [. . .] the convent of La Concepción [. . .] They observe the Franciscan rule [. . .] the convent of the Santísima Trinidad, of the Order of St. Bernard. [. . .] The convent of Santa Clara is a later foundation; they were aided by the zeal of the sainted Archbishop Don Toribio Alfonso Mogrovejo. [. . .] Next in order comes the convent of the Barefoot Nuns of St. Joseph of La Concepción, under the same Franciscan rule. [. . .] The last in order of founding, but not in size, is that of Santa Catalina de Sena, of the Dominican Order and rule.

b. Hospitals

No less godly, and in fact unique in the world, is the Confraternity of La Caridad and its hospital [. . .] for poor sick women, and a refuge and seminary beyond compare for impecunious young ladies and girls. [. . .] Of no less importance for the education of girls is the retreat and convent of the Carmelite Order. [. . .] The daughters of leading persons are educated in this retreat [. . .] The Royal Hospital of San Andrés [. . .] can vie with the beast in the world, for it receives without limit or personal favor those ill with any disease, distributing them in different wards. [. . .] It has large number of men and women slaves for the service of the poor. [. . .] one Superintendent after another, in pious emulation, has tried to leave a memorial in improvements of wards, offices, infirmary, and wardrobe, which latter has to provide for over 500 beds. [. . .] The famous Hospital of Santa Ana was founded by that most devout churchman, Don Jerónimo de Loaysa, first Archbishop of Peru, for the care of the Indians [. . .] it can furnish what is needful for 1,000 beds; and as the Indians are used to their meals of Indian corn and herbs, seasoned with ají (chilli) or pepper, they prepare them for them after their fashion. [. . .] There is another hospital called the Espíritu Santo, in which they take care of sick sailors. [. . .] The hospital of San Diego belongs to the Brethren of San Juan de Diós; they take care of convalescents and the aged, providing them with the necessary sustenance.

c. University

The University and Royal Schools are so distinguished that they need envy no other in the world, since they were established by the Emperor Charles V, and later by Philipp II [. . .]; they enlarged, ennobled and enriched them, with the same privileges as the University of Salamanca; they endowed the professorial chairs of Prime with 1,000 assay pesos, and those of Vespers with 600, per annum. The Prime chairs are in Theology, Scholastics, Scripture, Law, and

Canons; the Vespers, in the Institutes, the Code, the Decretals, three in Philosophy, one in Indian language for the training of the priests who are to be parish
priests or dotrineros; before they are commissioned, they have to be examined
and certificated by the Professor of the language. The Professors are in major
part natives of the Indies and specially of this city. [. . .] This University's faculty
is important, for it comprises more than 80 Doctors and Masters; the members
of the Circuit Court join them, for at the end of the year the fees amount to
many ducats. The lecture halls in the schools are excellent, and the chapel very
fine, but the most remarkable feature is the amphitheatre, where they hold the
public functions and commencements; it is very large and imposing [. . .] and
the Chancellor gives him his degree, just as is done at Salamanca.

Source: A. Vázquez de Espinosa, *Compendium and Description of the West Indies* (City of Washington, 1942); (a) pp. 434, 437, 438, 439, 440, 441; (b) pp. 441, 442, 443, 444; (c) pp. 444, 445, 446.
— *Further Reading:* Borges, *Historia I*, pp. 699-714, 761-778; P. Morandé, *Cultura y
modernización en América Latina* (Madrid, 1987); L. Schell Hobermann, S. M. Socolow (eds.),
Cities & Society in Colonial Latin America (Albuquerque, 1986); Dussel, *Church*, pp. 287ff.

242. Mexico: The Cult of the Virgin of Guadalupe (1649)

"There are only flowers and songs of mourning here in Mexico, in Tlatelolco, yes it is
here, where sorrow is felt" — so laments an Aztec song immediately after the conquest
of Mexico by Hernán Cortés (cf. document 221). The religious dialogue of 1524 between
the first twelve Franciscans of the Mexico mission and Aztec priests and noblemen is
also marked by the bitter lament of the latter (cf. document 235). Toribio de Benavente
(Motolinía), one of these Franciscans, did not see a possibility to evangelize, as far as
one could tell, in the face of the dramatic confrontation between Spaniards and Aztecs
— unless God were to work a miracle. The longed-for miracle took place from December
9 to 12, 1531, on the hill Tepeyac, which was north of México-Tenochtitlán and where
there used to be a temple to the goddess Tonantzin Cihuacóatl ("our revered Mother
Snake Woman"): A dark-skinned virgin appeared four times to the baptized Indian Juan
Diego Cuauhtlatoatzin ("Talking Eagle") with the request that he should go to the
bishop (to the Franciscan Juan de Zumárraga) and tell him to erect a sacred shrine to
her, the perpetual Virgin Mary, on the hill Tepeyac. When Juan Diego called on the
bishop the third time, the miracle occurred — his cloak was imprinted with the miraculous image of Our Lady of Guadalupe: The Mexican "Guadalupe event" was born which
shares only its name with the Guadalupe tradition of the Spanish Extremadura (the
home of the Franciscans). Although the Franciscans were skeptical since they suspected
that the Indians only wanted to pray to their old goddess Tonantzin under the guise of
Our Lady of Guadalupe, the event nonetheless burrowed deeply into the collective
memory of the Mexicans as a constitutive element of their national and Catholic identities. A decisive factor here was the new perspective which the four "Guadalupe evange-

lists" (the Creoles Miguel Sánchez, d. 1674, Lasso de la Vega, d. 1660?, Luis Becerra Tanco, d. 1672, and Francisco de Florencia S.J., d. 1674) propagated during the "Marian" seventeenth century. They did not see syncretism in the Guadalupe event, but rather the expression of a very special divine preference for Mexico. The report of the appearance was not published until 1649. On July 31, 2002, the Indian Juan Diego was canonized in Mexico City.

It had been ten years since the *altepetl* of Mexico had been conquered and the weapons of war had been laid down, and peace reigned in the altepetls all around; likewise the faith, the recognition of the giver of life, the true deity, God, had begun to flower and bloom. Right in the year of 1531, just a few days into the month of Decembre, there was a humble commoner, a poor ordinary person, whose name was Juan Diego. They say his home was in Cuauhtitlan, but in spiritual matters everything still belonged to Tlatelolco. It was Saturday, still very early in the morning, and he was on his way to attend to divine things and to his errands. When he came close to the hill at the place called Tepeyacac, it was getting light. He heard singing on top of the hill, like the songs of various precious birds. [. . .] When the song had subsided and silence fell, he heard himself being called from the top of the hill. A woman said to him, "Dear Juan, dear Juan Diego." Thereupon he stepped forward to go where he was summoned. When he reached the top of the hill, he saw a lady standing there; she called to him to go over next to her. When he came before her, he greatly marvelled at how she completely surpassed everything in her total splendour. Her clothes were like the sun in the way they gleamed and shone. [. . .]

He prostrated himself before her and heard her very pleasing and courtly message, as if inviting and flattering him, saying to him, "Do listen, my youngest child, dear Juan, where is it that you are you going? [. . .] Know, rest assured, my youngest child, that I am the eternally consummate virgin Saint Mary, mother of the very true deity, God, the giver of life, the creator of people, the ever present, the lord of heaven and earth. I greatly wish and desire that they build my temple for me here, where I will manifest, make known, and give to people all my love, compassion, aid, and protection. For I am the compassionate mother of you and of all you people here in this land, and of the other various peoples who love me, who cry out to me, who seek me, who trust in me. There I will listen to their weeping and their sorrows in order to remedy and heal all their various afflictions, miseries, and torments. And in order that this my act of compassion which I am contemplating may come to pass, go to the bishop's palace in Mexico and tell him how I am sending you to put before him how I very much wish that he build me a house that he erect a temple for me on the level ground here. You are to relate every single thing that you have seen and beheld, and what you have heard."

Source: *The Story of Guadalupe: Luis Lasso de la Vega's Huei tlamahuiçoltica of 1649* (Stanford, 1998), pp. 61-67. — Further Reading: D. Brading, *Mexican Phoenix: Our Lady of Guadalupe* (Cambridge, 2001); S. Poole, *Our Lady of Guadalupe: The Origins and Sources of a Mexican National Symbol, 1531-1797* (Tuscon, 1995); V. Elizondo, *La Morenita: Evangelizer of the Americas* (San Antonio, Tex., 1980); J. Lafaye, *Quetzalcóatl and Guadalupe: The Formation of Mexican national Consciousness, 1531-1813* (Chicago, 1976); E. Chávez, *Our Lady of Guadalupe and Saint Juan Diego: The Historical Evidence* (Lanham, Md., 2006); R. Nebel, *Santa María Tonantzin Virgen de Guadalupe. Continuidad y transformación religiosa en México* (Mexico City, 1995).

243. Mexico: A Debate on the Erudition of Women (1690/91)

Sor ("Sister") Juanna Inés de la Cruz (1651-1695), called "the tenth muse of Mexico," was a woman with an astute mind and a brilliant, sharp pen. Indeed, she is one of the greatest poets in the Spanish-speaking world. She was admired in Baroque Mexico, but as a woman, she was also put in her place. In 1690 her polemical pamphlet *Carta Atenagórica* (Athenagorian Letter) was published. In it she criticized a sermon by the famous Portuguese Jesuit priest António Vieira (1608-1697), who, referring to Paul, had reprimanded women. This pamphlet was accompanied by a letter of the Bishop of Puebla, Manuel Fernández de Santa Cruz, dated November 25, 1690, which he had written under the pseudonym Sor Filotea de la Cruz (document a) and which contained both praise and reproach of Sor Juanna Inés de la Cruz. In response, she drafted her "Answer to Sister Philothea," from which document b was taken and in which the right of women to study and to take part in scholarly disputations is defended. The debate from Baroque Mexico seems quite modern today.

a. Filotea de la Cruz, The Letters (the Knowledge) That God Wants in Women (1690)

I do not subscribe to the commonplace view of those who condemn the practice of letters in women, since so many have applied themselves to literacy study, not failing to win praise from Saint Jerome. True, Saint Paul says women should not teach, but he does not order women not to study so as to grow wiser. He wished only to preclude any risk of presumptuousness in our sex, inclined as it is to vanity. Divine Wisdom took one letter away from Sarai and added one to the name of Abram, not because man is meant to be more lettered than woman, as many falsely claim, but because the *i* appended to the name of Sara connoted being swollen up and domineering (Gen. 17:5, 15). Sarai is interpreted as "My lady," and it was unfitting that one should be the lady of Abraham's house whose position was a subordinate one.

Letters that breed arrogance God does not want in women. But the apostle does not reject them, as long as they do not remove women from a position of obedience. [. . .] I do not mean you to modify your natural predisposition by giving up books, I do mean that you should improve it by sometimes reading the book of Jesus Christ. [. . .] You have spent much time studying philosophers and reading books. Surely it is only right for you now to better your occupation and to upgrade your books.

b. Sor Juana Inés de la Cruz: The Answer to Sor Filotea (1691)

There can be no doubt that in order to understand many passages, one must know a great deal of the history, customs, rituals, proverbs, and even the habits of speech of the times in which they were written, in order to know what is indicated and what alluded to by certain sayings in divine letters. [. . .]

All this requires more study than is supposed by certain men who, as mere grammarians or, at most, armed with four terms from the principles of logic, wish to interpret the Scriptures and cling to the *"Let women keep silence in the churches,"* [1 Cor 14:34] without knowing how to understand it rightly. So it is with another passage, *"Let the woman learn in silence"* [1 Tim 2:11]; for this passage is more in favour of than against women, as it says that they should learn, and while it is also written, *"Hear, O Israel, and be silent,"* [Deut 27:9] where the whole congregation of men and women are addressed, and all are told to be quiet, for whoever listens and learns has good reason to take heed and keep still. If this be not so, I would like these interpreters and expounders of St. Paul to explain to me how they understand the passage, *"Let women keep silence in the churches,"* [1 Cor 14:34] For they must understand it either materially, to mean the pulpit and the lecture hall, or formally, to mean the community of all believers, which is to say the Church. If they understand in the first sense [. . .], why then do they rebuke those women who study in private? And if they understand it in the second sense and wish to extend the Apostle's prohibition to all instances without exception, so that not even in private may women write or study, then how is it that we see the Church has allowed a Gertrude, a Teresa, a Brigid, the nun of Agreda, and many other women to write?

Source: (a) *A Sor Juana Anthology* (Cambridge, Mass., and London, 1988), pp. 200, 201; (b) Sor Juana Inés de la Cruz, *The Answer/La Respuesta, Including a Selection of Poems* (New York, 1994), pp. 87-91. — *Further Reading:* O. Paz, *Sor Juana, or, The Traps of Faith* (Cambridge, Mass., 1988); J. C. B. and E. L. Webster (eds.), *The Church and Women in the Third World* (Philadelphia, 1985); S. Merrim (ed.), *Feminist Perspectives on Sor Juana Inés de la Cruz* (Detroit, 1991); M. Knaster, *Woman in Spanish America: An Annotated Bibliography from Pre-Conquest to Contemporary Times* (Boston, 1977); H. Wustmans, "Und so lag die Welt erhellt in wahrerem Licht, und ich erwachte" (Frankfurt u.a., 2001).

244. Missionary Work in the Baroque Period

Missionary work during the Baroque period had two focal points: on the one hand, the eradication of the forms of Indian "idol worship" which had remained after the first period of evangelization and, on the other hand, the strengthening of Indian Christianity through catechesis and visitations. Visible elements of pagan religion (temples, idols, public rites) had been destroyed in the wake of the first evangelization. Now it was a matter of also ferreting out and destroying the covert "idol worship" of so-called syncretism or mixed religiosity. In the seventeenth century such campaigns took place above all in the Andes, whereas in Aztec Empire regions they were more prevalent in the late sixteenth century. The numerous directives for eradicating "idol worship," among which those of the Jesuit Pablo José de Arriaga (d. 1622) stand out, also contain exact descriptions of idol worship and are therefore a prime source for investigating Indian religions and syncretic forms of belief after the first evangelization. According to their "both/and logic" the Indians were in general willing to embrace Christianity but, understandably, they did not want to break with their former religious customs (document a). Document b, on the other hand, corresponds to the typical visitation report of a bishop during the Baroque period: The Christian piety of the common Indians is praised, even romanticized, and their oppression under the colonial system denounced. The author, Juan de Palafox y Mendoza (1600-1659), was Bishop of Puebla and, for a time, also the viceroy of Mexico; his report was addressed to the King.

a. Fr. José de Arriaga: The Indigenous Manner of "Doing Both Things at the Same Time" (1621)

An even more common error than the previous one [the Indians believed and said that their *Huacas* or "idols" were to them the same thing as the saints to Christians] is their tendency to carry water on both shoulders, to have recourse to both religions at once. I know a place where a cloak was made for the image of our Lady and a shirt for their huaca from the same cloth. They feel and even say that they can worship their huacas while believing in God the Father, Son, and Holy Ghost. Thus, for the worship of Jesus Christ they generally offer what they offer their huacas. They celebrate their festivals for Him and go to church, hear mass, and even take Communion.

b. J. de Palafox y Mendoza: On the Piety and the Life of the Indians (1640)

Every house, no matter how poor, has a prayer room they call the holy *cali*, which is the resting place of God and the saints, and there they display their images; whatever they can save from their labor and sweat is spent on these holy and useful ornaments, and that room is reserved for praying and making retreat with great reverence and silence before they take communion. On the day before communion, the women in particular begin a rigorous fast, and because they want their bodily purity to match the purity of their souls, they put on clean clothes and wash their feet, because they will enter the church with bare feet; and when they return from the church they perfume the saints in the house as a sign of reverence; and that day they either remain in prayer before their saints or spend the whole day in the church, or visit the churches in the city or place where they are, and all this with great humility and devotion, which we ministers of God can learn from. . . . They show a notable devotion and punctuality in praying and reciting doctrine aloud, and when they go to sing the mass; and their division in the churches, the men apart from the women, attending the churches with admirable reverence, their lowered eyes, the deepest silence, the humiliations and genuflections in unison, the uniform prostrations and great order, so that I doubt that any religious order possesses the perfection and observance practiced and offered with great humility by this external worship. . . .

And what I consider even more admirable, my Lord, is that with all their poverty of usage and feelings it is these native Indians, in their nakedness, who dress and enrich the world, and in the Indian women, everything ecclesiastical and secular. Because their nakedness, poverty and labor sustain and build the churches, increase the churches' income, aid and enrich the religious orders, and are largely responsible for maintaining the ecclesiastical life. In the secular realm, their labor supports and operates the mines, works the fields, practices the skills and arts of the republic, empowers the judges, pays the tributes, brings in the sales taxes, gives rest and relief to the public magistrates, serves their superiors, assists their inferiors, so that there is nothing high or low in which the Indians are not the hands and feet of these wide provinces; and if there were no more Indians there would be no more Indies, because it is they who protect the Indies and like solicitous bees they build the honeycomb for others to eat, and like gentle sheep they offer their wool to cover the needs of others, and like patient oxen they work the land to provide food for others.

Source: (a) *The Extirpation of Idolatry in Peru* by Father Pablo Joseph de Arriaga (Lexington, 1968), p. 72; (b) G. García (ed.), *Documentos muy raros para la historia de México* (Mexico City, 1982), pp. 635-636, 648. — Further Reading: (a) Delgado, *Gott*, pp. 193-224; idem, *Abschied*, pp. 113-190; P. Duviols, *La lutte contre les religions autochthones dans le Pérou colonial* (Lima, Paris, 1971); K. Mills, *Idolatry and Its Enemies: Colonial Andean Religion and Extirpation, 1640-1750* (Princeton, 1997); (b) R. Fernández Gracia (ed.), *Palafox* (Pamplona, 2001); Ch. E. Ph. Simmons, *Juan de Palafox y Mendoza: Reforming Bishop, 1640-1649* (Pullman, Wash., 1966); C. Alvarez de Toledo, *Politics and Reform in Spain and New Spain: The Life and Thought of Juan de Palafox, 1600-1659* (Oxford, 2000); BBKL 6, 1993, pp. 1443-1447: Art. Palafox y Mendoza (C. V. Collani).

B. Indian and Mestizo Voices

245. A Morning Prayer of the Evangelized Quechua (ca. 1600)

The missionaries translated central documents into various Indian languages, but they also preached in the languages of the natives and created new songs and prayers in which they adapted the mysticism of nature of the Indians in an attempt to channel it in a Christian way. At the same time they encouraged corresponding Indian initiatives. The present document is, for example, a hymn or psalm adaptation from the Quechuan area. One hundred five such hymns were collected from oral traditions at the onset of the twentieth century. They are of a simple and impressive lyricism, fitting perfectly with the poetic tradition of the Quechuan language.

The earth is awakening, letting its light shine
to honor its creator.
This earth is already sweeping the gray clouds away,
it has removed its black cloak
to honor its creator.
Inti, the lord of the stars, has already ascended aglow,
has spread his rays like golden hair
to honor his creator . . .
The fish are already splashing about in the lagoon of crystal-clear,
   rippling waters
to honor their creator . . .
Only humans who, after all, dwell in the house of God
have not dressed up
to honor their creator.
Only humans, who, after all, are God's children made in His image,
have not dressed up
to pay homage to God, their creator.
Only humans do not want to repent of their sins of the day and the night
and purify their lives
to pay homage to God, their creator.
Only humans do not want to hear
that they must renew themselves completely
to pay homage to God, their creator, everywhere in the world.
Our faith teaches us that we must live contritely,
otherwise God, our creator, will punish us.
Stones, trees, animals — everything that has been created
obeys God's commandment,
only humans always shun His voice . . .

You, my Father, who are the source of mercy,
make me believe and make me obey
your voice through your love, cleanse my impure words,
and loosen my stammering tongue
so that I may praise your immensity, you,
my most exalted creator, together with the angels for all eternity.

Source: Llaqtaq takiy. Lieder und Legenden der Ketschua, ed. W. Böhringer, A. Wagner, C. Muñoz (Frankfurt, 1988), pp. 30-32. — *Further Reading:* Delgado, *Abschied,* pp. 79-112; R. Konetzke, "Die Bedeutung der Sprachenfrage in der spanischen Kolonisation Amerikas" in: *JGSLA* 1 (1964), pp. 72-116; J. Lara, *La poesía quechua* (Mexico City, 1979); idem, *Quechua peoples poetry* (Willimantic, Conn., 1986); J. A. Lira, *Himnos quechuas católicos cuzqueños* (Lima, 1955); C. A. Sandoval, S. M. Boschetto-Sandoval (eds.), *J. M. Arguedas: Reconsiderations for Latin American Cultural Studies* (Athens, Ohio, 1998).

246. Garcilaso de la Vega: The Incas Looked for the True God (1609)

The common demonization of Indian religions by the missionaries, who even character-ized any analogies to Christianity found in them as a diabolical "mimicry" of the true reli-gion (as in the *opinio communis* advocated by the theologian and Peru missionary José de Acosta in 1590, cf. document 222), awakened the desire among educated Mestizos and Indians for an apologetic rehabilitation of the Indian cultures and religions. The author, the son of a Spanish captain and an Incan princess, attempts to present the Incans as worshipers of the unknown true God and advises the missionaries to call the Christian God by the Indian name, as one had done during the evangelization of ancient Europe.

Besides adoring the Sun as a visible god, to whom they offered sacrifices, and in whose honour they celebrated grand festival [. . .], the Kings Yncas and their *amautas,* who were philosophers, sought by the light of nature for the true su-preme God our Lord, who created heaven and earth, as we shall see further on by the arguments and phrases which some of them used touching the divine majesty. They called Him Pachacamac, a word composed of *pacha,* which means the universal world, and *camac,* the present participle of the verb *cama,* to animate, whence is derived the word *cama,* the soul. Pachacamac therefore means He who gives animation to the universe, and in its full signification it may be translated — "He who does to the universe what the soul does to the body." [. . .] It is true, what I am about say, that the Indians sought out the truth with this name and gave it to our true God, as the devil testifies, though, as the father of lies, he mixed up a lie with the truth. For when he saw our holy evangel preached, and that the Indians were baptised, he said to certain familiars of his, in the valley now called Pachacamac (from the great temple which was erected there to this unknown God), that the God whom the Spaniards were preaching about and Pachacamac were all one. [. . .] The word Pachacamac, which the Spanish historians so abominate, not understanding the meaning of the word, is really that of God; although their abhorrence of it is not wholly without reason, because the devil spoke in that gorgeous temple, making himself appear as God under that name, which he adopted for his own. But if any one should now ask me, who am a Catholic Christian Indian by the infinite mercy, what name was given to God in my language, I should say — *Pachacamac*. For in that general language of Peru there is no other word in which to name God save this; and all those that are given by historians are generally incorrect, for they are either corrupt or invented by the Spaniards.

Source: Ynca Garcilaso de la Vega, *First Part of the Royal Commentaries of the Yncas*, vol. I (New York, 1963), pp. 106-109. — *Further Reading:* Delgado, *Abschied*, pp. 113-190; M. M. Marzal, *Historia de la antropología indigenista* (Lima, 1981); F. G. Crowley, *Garcilaso de la Vega, el Inca and his sources in Comentarios reales de los Incas* (The Hague, 1971); L. A. Ratto, *Inca Garcilaso de la Vega* (Lima, 1964); Dussel, *Church*, pp. 287ff.

247. A Mayan Priest: Christianity as the Origin of All Evil (Seventeenth Century)

The Indian priests and magicians were naturally the most bitter enemies of the missionaries since they were specifically opposed and disempowered by them. The following document of a Mayan priest from the seventeenth century blames Christianity — with considerable rhetorical skill — for being the origin of all evil after the conquest and evangelization. Amid the reflections of the 1992 celebrations, this document was also cited approvingly by many theologians without any consideration of the literary uniqueness of the document or the intention of the author. In fact the document suggests various tracks for its interpretation — a reproach to their own Mayan priesthood because of its failure to read the signs at the time of the conquest, post-Christian syncretism, and nativistic chiliasm — and should also be read critically if one does not want to make an indiscriminate cult of victims *(victimismo)* from the perspective of those who suffered.

It was only because these priests of ours were to come to an end when misery was introduced, when Christianity was introduced by the real Christians. Then with the true God, the true *Dios*, came the beginning of our misery. It was the beginning of tribute, the beginning of church dues, the beginning of strife with purse snatching, the beginning of strife with blow-guns, the beginning of strife by trampling on people, the beginning of robbery with violence, the beginning of forced debts, the beginning of debts enforced by false testimony, the beginning of individual strife, a beginning of vexation, a beginning of robbery with violence. This was the origin of service to the spaniards and priests, of service to the local chiefs, of service to the teachers, of service to the public prosecutors by the boys, the youths of the town, while the poor people were harassed. These were the very poor people who did not depart when oppression was put upon them. It was by Antichrist on earth, the kinkajous of the towns, the foxes of the towns, the blood-sucking insects of the town, those who drained the poverty of the working people. But it shall still come to pass that tears shall come to the eyes of our Lord God. The justice of our Lord God shall descend upon every part of the world, straight from God upon Ah Kantenal, Ix Pucyola, the avaricious hagglers of the world.

Only by this was the divination,
And these were the diviners.
When misery came
From these many Christians
Who arrived
With the true divinity,
The True God.
For this indeed was the beginning of misery
For us,
The beginning of tribute,
The beginning of tithes,
The beginning of strife over purse snatching,
The beginning of strife with blowguns
The beginning of strife over promotions,
The beginning of the creation of many factions,
the beginning of forced seizure for debts,
The beginning of forced imprisonment for debts,
The beginning of village strife,
The beginning of misery and affliction,
The beginning of forcible separation,
The beginning of forced labor for the Spaniards
And the sun priests,
Forced labor for the town chiefs,
Forced labor for the teachers,
Forced labor for the public persecutors [. . .]
These were the very poor,
These were the very poor who did not rebel
At the oppression
That was inflicted on them.
This was the Antichrist

Here on earth,
The earth Lions of the towns,
The Foxes of the towns,
The Bedbugs of the towns
Are the bloodsuckers of the poor peasants here
For indeed the time is coming soon
Of the day of the coming
Of tears to the eyes
And the presence
Of our Lord
Who is God.
The justice of our Lord God will descend
Everywhere
In the world.

Source: Chilam Balam, "Eleven Ahau (Verses) 1645-1694," in: *Heaven Born Merida and Its Destiny: The Book of Chilam Balam of Chumayel* (Austin, 1986), pp. 109, 110. — *Further Reading: 1492-1992: The Voice of the Victims,* ed. L. Boff, V. Elizondo (London, Philadelphia, 1990); M. M. Marzal (ed.), *The Indian Face of God in Latin America* (Maryknoll, 1996); *The Maya: Diego de Landa's Account of the Affairs of Yucatán* (Chicago, 1975); Borges, *Historia II,* pp. 199-258; Dussel, *Church,* pp. 243ff.

248. Indian Brotherhood of the Virgin of Copacabana (1613)

In the shadow of evangelization, the Indian "idols" were frequently replaced by the Christian God, the Virgin, and pictures of the saints. The fact that sacred art was largely controlled by Indians and Mestizos around 1600 played an important role in the success of this substitution method. At first the Spanish Christians viewed the work of the Indians with mistrust because they feared that the new Indian Christians would not work according to the required standards and that their images might resemble their old gods. In the end, however, the Indian artists prevailed: The veneration of Our Lady of Copacabana on Lake Titicaca goes back to such a story from 1613 and ushered in a change in favor of the indigenization of sacred art in the Andes. The present document concerns the difficulties of an Indian artist to get the bishop to recognize a picture of the Virgin he had done because it did not quite correspond to the Iberian artistic canon. The last part of the document, which is not reproduced here, states that the Indian artist finally won recognition and that his Madonna was ceremoniously enthroned in the church in Copacabana. The Indians of Lake Titicaca now had their Brotherhood of Our Lady of Copacabana with an image created by one of their own.

Then I went to Choquisaca to ask the Lord bishop's permission to become a painter and create images for the fellowship of Our Lady; and I showed him an image of the Virgin painted on a board . . . with a petition saying that I want to be a painter and create images of the Virgin; and he replied that he did not want to give me permission to be a painter or to create images of the Virgin, and that if I wanted to be a painter I should paint a monkey with her young . . . and that if I painted and created images of the Virgin he would punish me severely. I left there saying Jesus, Holy Mary, may God and the Virgin his mother help me, because they said that her image was not good and that it looked like a man with whiskers, and they found many faults in it, saying that it was not the Virgin, and they told me angrily to stop doing it; after they saw the image of Our Lady they all laughed a lot, blaming the painter; all the Spaniards held it, looked at it and laughed; and they said that natives cannot make images or paintings of the Virgin; I was pretty discouraged and disheartened, because I had showed the image to the bishop and he had laughed at it. Then I went to the church to beg for Our Lord's mercy to be able to paint the image of Our Lady the right way, and so on. In my prayer I asked for permission to do this work and for a good hand to create images and to be a good painter.

Source: A. Ramos Gavilán, *Historia del santuario de Nuestra Señora de Copacabana* (Lima, 1988), pp. 234-237 — *Further Reading:* V. Salles-Reese, *From Viracocha to the Virgin of Copacabana: Representation of the Sacred at Lake Titicaca* (Austin, Tex., 1997); M. M. Marzal (ed.), *The Indian Face of God in Latin America* (Maryknoll, 1996); idem, *El sincretismo iberoamericano* (Lima, 1985); P. Morandé, *Synkretismus und offizielles Christentum in Lateinamerika* (Munich, 1992); Delgado, *Abschied*, pp. 113-190; Borges, *Historia I*, pp. 593-614, 835-854; Dussel, *Church*, pp. 73ff.

249. Chronicle of the Indian F. Guamán Poma de Ayala (ca. 1615)

The Indian Felipe Guamán Poma de Ayala (1532?-1615?) grew up in the care of Christian priests and was an assistant or interpreter for Cristóbal de Albornoz, the judicial visitor charged with the extermination of "idol worship" in the Andes in 1570. Later he spent 30 years traversing the Andes — as he said again and again — "in search of the poor of Jesus Christ." Along the way he led a campaign with pen and ink against corrupt *corregidores* (colonial provincial judges), *encomenderos* (quasi feudal lords of the colonial system), and *padres de doctrinas* (Indio-pastors) in order to denounce the deplorable state of affairs as well as to rehabilitate the suppressed and largely despised Indian culture. His work consists of around 1200 single sheets of paper of high quality with a format of 14.5 × 20.5 cm. They were sewn together into notebooks which were lost until 1908 and could only be printed for the first time in 1936. Around one-third of the pages have pen-and-ink drawings which provide valuable information about religious traditions, customs, societal structure, and agricultural techniques of the pre-Spanish past (vol. 1), but also critically present the conquest and early colonial society from an Indian perspective (vol. 2). The third section (vol. 3) consists of a fictional dialogue between the author and the Spanish king for the purpose of submitting good suggestions to the king for rectifying the deplorable state of affairs. Document a critically presents the turmoil of the time of conquest. Document b decries the exploitation of the Indians by their pastors who retained a great many house servants, treated them poorly, and — despite celibacy — harassed widows and virgins so much that a house for the children of these Indio-pastors had to be run in Lima. Document c describes the active participation of the Indians in the life of a parish community as they held various offices in the church and, in the absence of the pastor, led the parish independently.

a. The Conquest

They felt that they had this treasure in their power in the same way that a cat keeps a mouse within reach of its claws while it plays with it and, if the mouse escapes for a moment, lies in wait, pounces and gives all its attention to catching it again and always returns to the same place until the game is finished. The conquerors reached a point where they had lost the fear of death in their greed for riches. [. . .]

At first there was almost no mutual comprehension between the conquerors and the Indians. If a Spaniard asked for water he was likely to be brought wood. Then, as a new race of half-castes grew up, a mixture of the Quechua and Spanish languages became usual [but] was still not fully understood by either race. The conquerors were able to take over Indian land and property by learning only a few words in the native language. For instance they would call out in a loud voice. 'Don't be afraid: I am the Inca.' At this, the Indians would flee in terror without offering any resistance. [. . .]

Even under the reigns of the Incas there were highwaymen called pomaranra, who made their hiding-places in the deepest gorges and on the loneliest rocky hills. These ruffians, who had their own hierarchy of leaders, laid ambushes on the highways and lived by what they could steal and pillage. After the Conquest they became the willing tools of the Spaniards and were employed to rob their own Indian countrymen.

b. The Fathers and the Indians

These priests are irascible and arrogant. They wield considerable power and usually act with great severity towards their parishioners, as if they had forgotten that Our Lord was poor and humble and the friend of sinners. Their own intimate circle is restricted to their relations and dependants, who are either Spanish or half-caste.

They readily engage in business, either on their own or other people's account, and employ a great deal of labour without adequate payment. Often they say that the work is for ecclesiastical vestments, when really it is for the sale of ordinary clothing. Managers are taken on, but seldom get themselves properly rewarded. And the native chiefs are blamed if they do not arrange the immediate purchase of the goods.

The usual practice is for a priest to have a man and two girls in the kitchen, a groom, a gardener, a porter, and others to carry wood and look after the animals. Sometimes there are as many as the mules in the stables, not counting the beasts belonging to neighbours, and they all have to be sustained at the Indians' expense. Herds of 1,000 cattle, goats, pigs or sheep are a common-place and there are often hundreds of capons, chickens and rabbits, all requiring their own special arrangements, as well as market gardens. If a single animal is lost, the Indian held responsible has to pay for it in full. Since the servants are not even properly fed, it is no wonder that they avoid work. But there are always pretty girls attached to the household, who have been corrupted by the priests and bear them children. This kind of showy establishment is of course enormously costly.

A favourite source of income of the priesthood consists in organising the porterage of wine, chillies, coca and maize. These wares are carried on the backs of Indians and llamas and in some cases need to be brought down from high altitudes. The descent often results in death for the Indians, who catch a fever when they arrive in a warm climate. Any damage to their loads during the journey has to be made good at their own expense.

c. Ordinary Christian Indians

The Indians in our country are just as gifted as Castillians in their artistry and workmanship. Some of them are excellent singers and musicians. They make themselves masters of the organ, fiddle, flute, clarinet, trumpet and horn without any difficulty. They also become capable municipal clerks. [. . .] Some of them know Latin and study literature. If they were allowed to, they could perfectly well be ordained as priests. Above all they are loyal and admirable servants of the Crown, with no taste for rebellion.

Indians are skilful at all the decorative arts such as painting, engraving, carving, gilding, metalwork and embroidery. They make good tailors, cobblers, carpenters masons and potters. Also, by simply watching the Spaniards, the have learnt how to do well in trade.

In the same way the Indian girls learn reading, writing, music and needlework at the convents which they attend. They are just as clever and accomplished as Spanish girls at the domestic skills.

The clever ones among the Indians get themselves jobs with the Church, either as singers or clerks. Because of the incompetence or absence of the priests they soon find themselves burying the dead with all the proper prayers and responses. They take vespers and look after the music and singing, as well as intoning the prayers. On Sundays and holy days they conduct the ceremonies as well as any Spaniard. In default of a priest they baptize the babies with holy water, reciting the proper form of words, and this is allowed by the authorities in order to avoid any of the small creatures going to limbo for lack of baptism. On Wednesdays and Fridays Indians conduct the early morning service, these being the obligatory days, and they say the prayers for the dead. However, they get nothing but interference from the priests themselves, who usually refer to them dismissively as 'clever children'.

Source: Letter to a King: A Picture-History of the Inca Civilisation by Huamán Poma (Don Felipe Huamán Poma de Ayala) (London, 1978) (a) pp. 105, 113-114; (b) pp. 144-145; (c) pp. 186-197. — *Further Reading:* R. Adorno, *Guaman Poma and His Illustrated Chronicle from Colonial Peru: From a Century of Scholarship to a New Era of Reading* (Copenhagen, 2001); M. López-Baralt, R. Adorno, *Guaman Poma de Ayala: The Colonial Art of an Andean Author* (New York, 1992); R. Adorno, *The Nueva corónica y buen gobierno of don Felipe Guaman Poma de Ayala: A Lost Chapter in the History of Latin-American Letters* (Ann Arbor, Mich., 1983); G. Gutiérrez, *Las Casas: In Search of the Poor of Jesus Christ* (Maryknoll, 1993); Delgado, *Abschied*, pp. 113-190.

C. The Reductions (Settlements) of the Jesuits and Their Purpose

250. The Reductions of the Jesuits

The reductions (from Span. *reducciones,* Lat. *reducere*) were settlements of the indigenous peoples in colonial Latin America who had been semi-nomadic and widely dispersed before. There had already been reductions in the sixteenth century. For those in monastic orders, especially for the Franciscans of the Mexico mission, they were a form of *conquista espiritual* which included gentle subjugation and evangelization. Las Casas himself had practiced this method in the Verapaz region (Guatemala) in 1537 (cf. document 232). The Crown also thought that reductions were expedient, and enacted some laws to this effect, concerning, for example, the construction of a church in the middle of the settlement, the characteristics which a proposed location had to have (sufficient water, land, woods, fields, and grassland), or the prohibition of Spaniards (settlers and traders), Blacks, Mulattos, and Mestizos from settling in the reductions and Indian villages. The reductions in the settlement region of the Guaraní — on the border region between Spanish and Portuguese America — founded by the Jesuits in 1610 in order to practice the method of the *conquista espiritual* have an important place in cultural, political and church history (document a). The reductions could only really flourish after the defeat of the "Bandeirantes" or "Paulistines," who were Portuguese settlers from the region of São Paulo who fell upon the reductions to enslave the Indians. Document b is a report on such a raid of October 10, 1629, written by the Jesuit priests Justo Mansilla and Simón

Maceta. The priests accompanied the captured Indians to São Paulo and later traveled to Bahia to obtain the release of all the prisoners and compensation from the governor general. According to conservative estimates, there were around 100,000 people living in the reductions at the time the Jesuits were expelled in 1767-1768. Opinions are divided with respect to an appraisal of the Jesuit reductions. For some they were a "holy experiment" or a "realized utopia" which gently steered a cultural shift among the Guaraní under the conditions of colonialism; for others they were a clerical-paternalistic theocracy, even a kind of "spiritual concentration camp."

a. A. R. de Montoya: What Are the Reductions of the Jesuits? (1630)

Father Marciel de Lorenzana . . . founded the first reduction which the Society erected in that province [Paraguay]. "Reductions" are what we call towns of Indians who, formerly living in their old fashion in forests, hill country, and valleys, and along hidden streams in clumps of three, four, or six dwellings situated one to three or more leagues apart, have been through the Fathers' efforts assembled into large settlements, to a civilized, human way of life, and to the raising of cotton with which to clothe themselves — having previously been accustomed to live naked and leaving exposed even what nature has concealed. This reduction is called San Ignacio, located about twenty-five leagues from Asunción.

b. Paraguay: Atrocities of the "Bandeirantes" (1629)

For forty years the inhabitants of Sao Paulo have flaunted the laws of the King our Lord with no regard for them, nor for their great offense against God, nor for the punishment which they deserve. In their raids they continually capture and carry off by force of arms the free and emancipated Indians whom they keep for their own slaves or sell. [. . .] they have assaulted the reductions of the Fathers of the Company of Jesus of the Province of Paraguay and taken all the people whom we were instructing. [. . .] What is of gravest concern in this whole affair is that the Holy Gospel is now so disteemed and its Preachers so discredited that — with the door now completely closed to the preaching of the Gospel among all those heathen — the Indians imagine and repeat that we did not gather them to preach them the law of God, as we told them, but to deliver them by this subterfuge to the Portuguese. They also say that we tricked them by telling them so often that they were safe with us and that the Portuguese, being Christians and vassals of the same king, would not touch nor harm those who were with the Fathers, for they were then Christians and children of God. Therefore, since an action so atrocious goes unpunished and with no effective remedy, it seems to me that we shall be forced to abandon all these heathen, whom year after year we have been gathering together and instructing by order of His Holiness and Majesty with so much labor and hardship.

Source: (a) *The Spiritual Conquest: Accomplished by the Religious of the Society of Jesus in the Provinces of Paraguay, Paraná, Uruguay, and Tape Written by Father Antonio Ruiz de Montoya of the Same Society (1639)* (St. Louis, 1993), pp. 37-38; (b) "An account of the injuries perpetrated by certain citizens and inhabitants of the town of Sao Paulo de Piratininga of the captaincy of Sao Vicente of the state of Brazilk in plundering the settlements of the Fathers of the Company of Jesus in the mission of Guaira and Plains of the Iguacu in the jurisdiction of Paraguay with exceeding contempt for the Holy Gospel in the year 1629. Rendered by the Fathers Justo Mansilla and Simon Maceta of the Company of Jesus . . . ," in: R. M. Morse (ed.), *The Bandeirantes: The Historical Role of the Brazilian Pathfinders* (New York, 1965), pp. 82-86. — *Further Reading:* C. J. McNaspy, *Lost Cities of Paraguay: Art and Architecture of the Jesuit Reductions, 1607-1767* (Chicago, 1982); A. Armani, *Città di Dio e città del Sole* (Rome, 1977); F. J. Reiter, *They Built Utopia (The Jesuit missions in Paraguay), 1610-1768* (Potomac, Md., 1995); P. Caraman, *The Jesuit Republic of Paraguay* (London, 1986); G. V. O'Neill, *Golden Years on the Paraguay: A History of the Jesuit Missions from 1600 to 1767* (London, 1934); W. H. Koebel, *In Jesuit Land: The Jesuit Missions of Paraguay* (London, 1912); M. Haubert, *Des Indiens et des Jésuites du Paraguay au temps des missions* (Paris, 1967); B. Melià, *El Guaraní conquistado y reducido* (Asunción, 1988); idem, "Und die Utopie fand ihren Ort," in: *Sievernich* (Conquista), pp. 413-429; P. C. Hoffmann, *Der Jesuitenstaat in Südamerika 1609-1768* (Weißenhorn, 1994); K. Schatz, "Die Jesuitenreduktionen," in: B. Schlegelberger, M. Delgado (eds.), *Ihre Armut macht uns reich* (Berlin, 1992), pp. 74-89; M. M. Marzal, *La utopia posible* (Lima, 1992); W. Reinhard, "Gelenkter Kulturwandel im 17. Jahrhundert," in: *HZ* 223 (1976), pp. 529-590; H. Gründer, "Der 'Jesuitenstaat' in Paraguay. 'Kirchlicher Kolonialismus' oder 'Entwicklungshilfe' unter kolonialem Vorzeichen?" in: *Geschichte und Kulturen* 1 (1988), pp. 1-25; Borges, *Historia I*, pp. 535-548; Delgado, *Gott*, pp. 292-307; Dussel, *Church*, pp. 351-362; Latourette, *Expansion III*, pp. 153ff.

251. Paraguay: Everyday Life in the Reductions (1697)

Here the South Tyrolean Jesuit Anton T. Sepp (1655-1733) gives the reader a somewhat romanticized insight into the everyday life of the reductions. The modesty, simplicity and morality of the Indians warm the heart of the missionary whose report reminds one of the letters which many modern messengers of the faith send to friends and benefactors at home. Many reports by missionaries from the sixteenth and seventeenth centuries convey the impression that "the faith is alive" among the simple, unspoiled Indians.

As I said, almost all of these villages are high up on a hill on the Uruguay or Paraná rivers which are very rich in fish. According to the size of the tribe, families or dwellings they have seven hundred, eight hundred, nine hundred, and many even one thousand or more families. A family consists of: father and mother, daughter and son along with all the children. Thus there are seven, eight or more thousand souls to a village since the Indians are very prolific. The village has an extremely large, beautiful square at the church for promenading which is four hundred feet wide and just as long. The houses are placed on wide streets just like in the cities of Europe, but with this big difference: They are very low and the Indians live in them on the naked earth without any stone or wooden floors. The walls are not of stone, but of stamped earth. The roof is covered with straw except for a few which we have started to tile. The houses have neither windows nor a chimney or fireplace and are therefore pitch-black and filled with smoke all day. Thus when I visit the sick under my care, whom I usually call on every day, I almost suffocate because of the smoke; recently my eyes hurt, burnt and watered so much for fourteen days that I thought I was losing my sight. . . . The door of the house is three spans wide and six spans high. It is not made of wooden planks, but of ox hide. It is never locked because there is nothing in the house one could steal. As I said, this door leads into the living room, kitchen, bedroom, cellar and pantry since the living room, bedroom, cellar, kitchen and pantry are nothing other than one dark straw hut. In this hut there are father and mother, sister and brother, children and the children's children, four dogs and three cats, or even more, so many mice and rats that it is teeming with them, crickets, beetles, called cockroaches in Tyrol, and centipedes. And all of this in such a narrow, low, small hut. It is easy to imagine what kinds of unbearable odors this all produces. Nonetheless one still has to visit up to twenty or thirty bedridden people and old people in such a palace every day, administer the sacraments to them, support the dying, and console the housefather and housemother. This is how the visits are. Truly, truly, reverend fathers and beloved brothers, I really find my poor suffering Jesus in these poor, abandoned Indians. Here my heart is filled with inexpressible consolation whenever I enter such a stable of my Lord Jesus.

Source: Delgado, *Gott,* pp. 302-303. — *Further Reading:* J. Mayr, *Anton Sepp: Ein Südtiroler im Jesuitenstaat* (Bozen, 1988); M. M. Marzal, *La utopía posible* (Lima, 1992), pp. 1, 369-385; *BBKL* 9, 1995, 1390-1393: Art. Sepp v. Rainegg (N. M. Borengässer); K. Schatz, "Die südamerikanischen Jesuiten-Reduktionen im Spiegel der Berichte deutscher Missionare," in: J. Meier (ed.), *. . . usque ad ultimum terrae* (Göttingen, 2000), pp. 167-181; Dussel, *Church,* pp. 351-362; Delgado, *Gott,* pp. 292-295.

252. Paraguay: Sunday in the Reductions (1771)

The Jesuit José Cardiel (1704-1781), who was expelled from the reductions, describes the Sunday course of events there with understandable nostalgia. Here he not only gives us an insight into the catechetical methods in the autochthonous language, but also into the cloister-like aspects of life in the reductions: hour-long worship services, punishment of unexcused absentees by lashes. Until the end the reductions remained a guided experiment in cultural change in a zone protected from Spanish settlers and traders which, whatever their intention, brought considerable achievements in inculturation. First and foremost among them is the cultivation of the Guaraní language that blossomed thanks to the philological and catechetical work of the Jesuits: along with Spanish, it is Paraguay's official language today. The fine arts and music are also among these achievements, fields in which the talented Guaraní displayed all their skill.

Every Sunday at daybreak, while the Fathers are at prayer, they all [Indians] of all ages and both sexes gather in the plaza, the men and women, boys and girls divided and separated from each other as it is always done. When the fathers come out from their prayers, the doors are opened; the women enter the church through the three doors of the portico, and the men through the side doors. The boys remain in the patio of the Fathers; and the girls go to the cemetery. In the middle of the church, between the men and women, with their backs to the women, stand four Indians with the clearest voices, and everyone else is kneeling. The four begin the Lord's Prayer and other prayers, which everyone repeats. Then the others sit, while the four continue to stand. The four then begin the Catechism. Two of them say: Is there a God? The other two reply: Yes, there is. The first two continue: How many Gods are there? The other two reply: Only one. Everyone replies in the same way, and it continues in this order. . . . One supposes that it is all in their language; if it were in Latin or Spanish, which they don't understand, it would do them little good. . . . The boys and their leaders in the patio, and the girls in the cemetery, do everything that the men and women do in the church.

When this is done the Father whose turn it is to preach gives them a doctrinal homily, with the boys and girls coming in for this part. . . . At the end of the Mass, they all go to their places: the men and boys to the patio of the father, the women and girls to the cemetery; and later, in the patio, one of the most skilled leaders repeats the homily for everyone. . . . At the end of the homily, the Secretaries of each group take the roll of all ages and sexes, to see if anyone has missed the Mass: they report to the Priest, and he ascertains whether there was a reason. If the absence was not excused, the person is sought out and punished. The punishment is 25 lashes.

Source: J. Cardiel, *Las misiones del Paraguay* (Madrid, 1989), pp. 133-135. — *Further Reading:* J. Guillermo Durán (ed.), *Monumenta catechetica hispanoamericana (Siglos XVI-XVIII)*, 2 vols. (Buenos Aires, 1984-1990); B. Melià, *La création d'un langage chrétien dans les réductions des Guaraní au Paraguay*, 2 vols. (Strasbourg, 1969); idem, "Das Wort ist alles," in: B. Schlegelberger, M. Delgado (eds.), *Ihre Armut macht uns reich* (Berlin, 1992), pp. 110-124; F. J. Reiter, *They Built Utopia (The Jesuit Missions in Paraguay), 1610-1768* (Potomac, Md., 1995); Ph. Caraman, *The Jesuit Republic of Paraguay* (London, 1986); G. V. O'Neill, *Golden Years on the Paraguay: A History of the Jesuit Missions from 1600 to 1767* (London, 1934); M. Haubert, *Des Indiens et des Jésuites du*

Paraguay au temps des missions (Paris, 1967); B. Melià, *El Guaraní conquistado y reducido* (Asunción, 1988); idem, "Und die Utopie fand ihren Ort," in: *Sievernich* (Conquista), pp. 413-429; P. C. Hoffmann, *Der Jesuitenstaat in Südamerika 1609-1768* (Weißenhorn, 1994); K. Schatz, "Die Jesuitenreduktionen," in: B. Schlegelberger, M. Delgado (eds.), *Ihre Armut macht uns reich* (Berlin, 1992), pp. 74-89; M. M. Marzal, *La utopía posible* (Lima, 1992); M. Mörner (ed.), *The Expulsion of the Jesuits from Latin America* (New York, 1965); Borges, *Historia I*, pp. 535-548; Dussel, *Church*, pp. 351-362; Delgado, *Gott*, pp. 292-295; Latourette, *Expansion III*, pp. 153ff.

253. Franciscans in California (1787)

It was not the expulsion of the Jesuits (1767-1768), whose reductions were mostly taken over by the Franciscans, that brought the missionary expansion of the Catholic Church to a standstill, but rather the turmoil of the Enlightenment and the struggle for independence. At the end of the eighteenth century, however, such expansion was still unchecked when Franciscans, under the leadership of the Majorcan Junípero Serra (1713-1784), founded one mission after the other in the spirit of the reductions in today's state of California. Today only the melodic names of Californian cities between San Diego and San Francisco as well as the mission churches which have been lovingly restored here and there remind one of this. The Indians, whom the Franciscans had gathered together in settlements according to the *"conquista espiritual"* method and who had become acquainted with Christianity there as well as with the techniques of Western culture, have mostly perished — but not specifically during the Spanish colonial period.

We have not found any kind of "idol worship" in any of the numerous missions which have been established in the two hundred leagues between San Diego and here (San Francisco), but only a purely negative lack of faith. . . . We have found some forms of superstition and pointless rites among them, and some deceit among the old when they say that they are the ones who send the rain, cause the acorns to grow, have the whales come hither, make the fish, etc. But it is easy to persuade them and prove them guilty of deception. . . . Whenever they are sick they put it down to the fact that a hostile Indian has harmed them; and they cremate their dead which we have not been able to prevent up to now. . . . Thanks to the preaching of the faith they are gradually giving up polygamy and are gathered together in our holy Catholic faith; and all who have been gathered in the faith live in one place under the church bell and go to church twice a day to pray the Christian creed. The wheat, corn and beans they harvest are communal property. They are already harvesting fruit from Castile, like peaches and pomegranates, etc., which was planted from the very beginning.

Source: F. Palou, *Junípero Serra y las misiones de California* (Madrid, 1988), pp. 232-235; Francisco Palou, *Life of Fray Junípero Serra*. Transl. and annot. by Maynard J. Geiger (Washington, 1955). — *Further Reading:* M. J. Geiger, *The Life and Times of Fray Junípero Serra*, 2 vols. (Washington,

1959); M. F. Sullivan, *Westward the Bells* (New York, 1971); R. H. Jackson, E. Castillo, *Indians, Franciscans, and Spanish Colonization* (Albuquerque, 1995); J. A. Sandos, *Converting California: Indians and Franciscans in the Missions* (New Haven, London, 2004); M. J. Geiger, *Franciscan Missionaries in Hispanic California, 1769-1848: A Biographical Dictionary* (San Marino, Calif., 1969); P. H. Kocher, *California's Old Missions: The Story of the Founding of the 21 Franciscan Missions in Spanish Alta California 1769-1823* (New York, London, 1973); D. DeNevi, F. M. Noel, *Junípero Serra: The Illustrated Story of the Franciscan Founder of California Missions* (San Francisco, 1985).

D. Slavery

254. Alonso de Sandoval: Slavery and Mission (1627)

Up until the beginning of the seventeenth century newly arrived black slaves were rarely regarded as the targets of missionary efforts. The Jesuits were the first to introduce a change here. With his highly effective missionary manual *De instauranda Aethiopum salute* (1627), the Jesuit Alonso de Sandoval (1576-1652) sought to promote missionary work in his own order among the blacks. Slavery was an unfortunate reality for Sandoval, who did not concentrate on its abolition but instead tried to establish a pastoral approach to the blacks by means of a Jesuit Realpolitik. He and his student Pedro Claver (1580-1654), the "slave of slaves," did not just administer the sacraments but, within the existing framework among the blacks in the main Spanish American slave-trading center of Cartagena, practiced the most radical forms of love of neighbor which Jesus Christ admonishes his disciples to perform in the judgment passages of the Bible. Despite all their efforts, however, missionary work among the blacks in Latin America led a shadowy existence. In document a Sandoval describes the mistreatment of the slaves to arouse empathy among the Jesuits for the suffering of others; in document b he shows that the blacks are just as capable of belief as anyone else, for they, as human beings, are also endowed with both reason and a free will.

a. The Mistreatment of Black Slaves

And setting aside the whippings, which were endless, to refer to what happens in this regard; the mistreatment in the prisons, with running water and chains, shackles, handcuffs, pillories, leg irons, neck braces and other inventions with which they intimidate, imprison and punish them; who can describe it? One person said with astonishment (a person of such integrity that I am certain he would not exaggerate in seriously affirming his reaction to these things) that although he had been in prison for three years in Algiers, he had observed that the Christians punished their slaves more in one week than the Moors punished theirs in a year. . . . The inhumanity is so great that in this regard, in some houses it would be better to be an animal; as the emperor Octavian has said, in the house of Herod it is better to be a pig than a son.

b. On the Black Slaves' Capacity for Faith

Two things can be inferred from the above: first, that these Negroes are not animals as I have heard some around here say who consider them incapable of Christianity, nor should they be taken as childish or backward, because they are simply adult men and as such should be given baptism, if there is willingness and the other necessary acts on their part, and on our part, instruction in accordance with the ability we see in them, because in every nation there are differences in ability to understand. The second is that because these people do not have the same ability as Spaniards, the pastors and ministers of the Gospel have an obligation to teach them very slowly, taking more time to catechize them, because even we were not born educated, and in schools and doctrines we did not learn the things of faith as quickly as we want these poor people to learn whose ignorance is not from lack of understanding (which they have) but of our language; for they have free will and are able to use it in all the human activities we offer them; they dispute and make peace, marry, buy and sell, barter and exchange as we do. . . . Why should we, under the predocument of their ignorance, decline to work with people with so much need and so little opportunity?

Source: (a) Alonso de Sandoval, *De instauranda Aethiopum salute. El mundo de la esclavitud negra en América* (Bogotá, 1956), pp. 194-197; (b) ibid., pp. 341-346; (c) ibid., pp. 275-277. — *Further Reading:* Delgado, *Gott,* pp. 266-277; Margaret M. Olsen, *Slavery and Salvation in Colonial Cartagena de Indias* (Gainesville, 2004); R. Gray, *Black Christians and White Missionaries* (New Haven, 1990); M. Teipel, *Die Versklavung der Schwarzen* (Münster, 1999); CEHILA (ed.), *Escravidão negra e História da Igreja na américa Latina e no Caribe* (Petrópolis, 1987); H. Loth, *Sklaverei* (Wuppertal, 1981); Ch. Verlinden, "Die transatlantische Zwangsmigration afrikanischer Neger und ihre Folgen," in: G. Klingenstein et al. (eds.), *Europäisierung der Erde?* (Munich, 1980), pp. 73-94; Borges, *Historia I,* pp. 321-338; Dussel, *Church,* pp. 363-374; Latourette, *Expansion III,* pp. 98ff.

255. Afro-Brazilian Protests at the Curia (1684/86)

At the beginning of the 1680s we come across Lourenço da Silva de Mendouça as a recognized leader of the black community in Lisbon and Madrid. He was an Afro-Brazilian, probably of royal Congolese descent, who had been appointed procurator of the black "Brotherhood of Our Lady, Star of the Negroes" in Madrid in 1682. He traveled to Rome around 1684 to present Pope Innocent XI with a petition that opposed the bad treatment of Christian slaves by their Christian masters in America as well as the institution of "eternal slavery." The Congregation for the Propagation of the Faith, to which the petition was referred by the Pope, condemned the Atlantic slave trade and its organizational forms in two statements in 1684 and 1686.

From the petition of Lourenço da Silva (1684):

no one who has received the water of holy baptism should remain a slave, and all those who have been born or would be born to Christian parents should remain free, under pain of excommunication . . . remembering that God sent His own Son to redeem humanity and that He was crucified. [. . .]

From the declaration of the Congregation of Propaganda Fide: 6.3.1684:

New and urgent appeals on the part of the Negroes of the Indies to his holiness, and by him remitted to this holy Congregation, have caused no little bitterness to his holiness and their eminences on seeing that there still continues in those parts [Latin America] such a detestable abuse as to sell human blood, sometimes even with fraud and violence. This involves a disgraceful offence against Catholic liberty, by condemning to perpetual slavery not only those who are bought and sold, but also the sons and daughters who are born to them, although they have been made Christians.

To this is added an even greater grief on hearing how they are then so cruelly tormented that this results in the loss of innumerable souls, who are rendered desperate by such maltreatment perpetrated by those same Christians who should indeed protect and defend them; and, by the hatred which this conceives, the progress of missionaries in spreading the holy faith remains impeded.

Source: R. Gray, *Black Christians and White Missionaries* (New Haven, 1990), pp. 24, 19f (according to the Archives of the Propagation of Faith: Scritture originale riferite nelle Congregazioni generali, 490, fol 140). — *Further Reading:* Gray, ibid.; H. Fragoso, "Sklaverei in Brasilien," in: *Sievernich* (Conquista), pp. 167-200; J. T. López García, "Dos defensores de los esclavos negros," in: P. Richard (ed.), *Raíces de la teología latinoamericana* (San José, 1987), pp. 67-71; J. Meier, "Der Überlebenskampf der Negersklaven," in: W. Dreier (ed.), *Entdeckung, Eroberung, Befreiung* (Würzburg, 1993), pp. 66-81; V. Willeke, "Kirche und Negersklaven in Brasilien 1550-1888," in: *NZM* 32 (1976), pp. 15-26; Dussel, *Church*, pp. 363-374.

256. J. B. Labat: Negro Slaves in the French Antilles (ca. 1700)

During his stays on various islands of the Antilles (1694-1705), the Dominican priest Jean-Baptiste Labat (d. 1738) apparently kept a detailed diary which later formed the basis of the account of his journey that appeared in six volumes in 1722. The book soon went through a number of editions and was translated into several languages. In the following document Labat warns against black Islamic slaves and makes some suggestions concerning the better treatment of slaves. His work is full of often detailed recommendations to this effect, for Labat's goal was not the abolition of slavery, but the improvement of the living conditions of the slaves on the plantations.

Almost all the Negroes are idol worshipers; only a few who live in the area of Cape Verde are partial to the Moslem religion. If some of the latter are brought here to the islands, one must take care not to buy them since they never accept the Christian religion and are slaves to terrible vices as well. It is therefore extremely important that this religion does not slip in among the Negroes or steal its way into the country. . . . All the people who want to buy Negroes have them examined carefully to make sure they do not have any physical defects, a task which the house physician usually undertakes. Once they are purchased and taken to the plantations, one must above all try to moderate the insatiable avarice and the despicable cruelty of some of the plantation owners who send them to work immediately after their arrival and do not even allow them time to catch their breath. Whoever treats them in this way has neither pity nor powers of judgment for he does not even understand how to avail himself of his own advantage.

Source: Pater Labats Sklavenbericht: Abenteuerliche Jahre in der Karibik 1690-1705, ed. H. Pleticha (Stuttgart, 1984), pp. 190-191. — *Further Reading:* ibid.; R. Gray, *Black Christians and White Missionaries* (New Haven, 1990); G. Debien, *Les esclaves aux Antilles françaises XVII-XVIIIème siècles* (Basse terre, 1974); L. Peytraud, *L'esclavage aus Antilles françaises avant 1789* (Paris, 1879); Dussel, *Church,* pp. 363-374.

E. Colonial Protestantism

257. The Dutch in Brazil (ca. 1650)

During the seventeenth century, the Dutch inherited Portuguese colonial possessions not only in Africa and Asia (cf. documents 29ff, 142), but also in America. They established and briefly ran a colony in northeast Brazil (Pernambuco) from 1630-1654. The official religion there was Reformed Calvinism, with tolerance for Jews and Catholics. The following document from a Dutch Church source reports about the Tapúya Indian religion and the expansion of Reformed Christianity.

Their religious views form a peculiar mixture of idolatry, superstitions and that which the Catholic missionaries taught them. A few Indians know the articles of faith and the Lord's Prayer but only in their own language. [. . .]

Would not a mild, legally organized slavery be much better for this uncontrollable society than the unrestrained freedom for which it is not yet mature? The *Tapúya* must be under a civilized nation; otherwise, they will serve evil. On the request of the W.I.C. [Dutch West Indies Company], we sent missionaries to the savages. But where are the fruits of their efforts and labor? The Redskins still frolic in the hideous evils of prostitution and alcoholism, and do not think about curbing their passions. There is only one way to gradually tame them. One must take the children from them and educate the Indian boys and girls as Christians at the company's expense.

Source: H. Wätjen, *Das holländische Kolonialreich in Brasilien. Ein Kapitel aus der Kolonialgeschichte des 17. Jahrhunderts* (Gotha, 1921), pp. 259f. — *Further Reading:* F. L. Schalkwijk, *The Reformed Church in Dutch Brazil (1630-1654)* (Zoetermeer, 1998); C. R. Boxer, *The Dutch in Brazil 1624-1654* (Oxford, 1957); Bastian, *Protestantismus*, pp. 56ff; Latourette, *Expansion III*, pp. 166, 236; Dussel, *Church*, pp. 315f; Barrett, *WCE I*, pp. 130-138.

258. The Moravian Mission in the Caribbean (1739)

In 1732, the Bohemian Brethren sent missionaries to the Danish Virgin Islands for the first time. From 1736, Friedrich Martin worked in St. Thomas where, rather than work with expatriates, the Moravian missionaries turned to the black slave population. There were about 700 people, dispersed among 52 plantations, at St. Thomas when Nikolaus Ludwig Graf von Zinzendorf visited the mission area in 1739. The following is a report about the visit by the Moravian historiographer Christian Oldendoorp.

On the following day (it was Saturday, when the Negroes have the afternoon free), the Count [Zinzendorf] received a deeper impression of God's mercy prevailing among the Negroes. Two brothers, Friedrich Martin and Matthäus Freundlich, and two newly arrived couples went with him to the brother's plantation where hundreds of Negroes had gathered. Friedrich Martin fell to his knees under the open sky before the large gathering and with burning heart brought a thank offering before God in prayer for all the mercy and faith He had bestowed on the prisoners as well as on the large gathering of people. With joyful songs of praise, they went into the house, where there was room only for a small number of the gathered Negroes. After that, they took an hour to read the lesson, as was the usual custom, and then the church service began. After the singing, the Negro elder Abraham made a blessed and moving prayer to the Savior, which spiritually aroused the hearts of the entire gathering and filled them with divine comfort. Since Martin was still very weak, he requested the Count give a speech to the Negro community. He agreed and spoke of the faith of the apostle Thomas who recognized his Savior by his wounds and knew him as his Lord and God. How the certainly loud and tearful confession (that Jesus Christ was their Lord, who had redeemed them a lost and condemned people) of many hundred Negroes joyfully amazed him can be seen in his biography. [. . .]

On February 15th, he gave his parting speech to the Negroes, after which he read the following words in the Creole language: "My dear beloved friends, I have come a long way [from Europe] in order to see you, and it pleases me that I see among you the beginning of what I had hoped for more than six years ago when I sent my first brothers to teach you. . . . Fourthly I must earnestly say that your men and women are faithful, and your lead farmhands . . . are obedient, and that you do all your work with love and industriousness as if it was for yourself. You must know that Christ himself prepares each and every one of his children to work; for the Lord has created everything, kings, lords, farmhands and slaves; and for as long as we live in this world, each person must remain in the position that God has placed him and be content with God's will. [. . .] Fifthly, I hope that you would always think about the other Negroes or savages, who have been called to Jesus by the brothers everywhere. We also began this way with you, and so many brothers and sisters have died here while working for your souls and praying for you. I hope that you who have been the first will not be the last."

Source: C. G. A. Oldendoorp, *Geschichte der Mission der evangelischen Brüder auf den caraibischen Inseln St. Thomas, S. Croix und S. Jan,* Vol. 2 (Barby, 1777) (= Hildesheim etc. 1995), pp. 585f, 592-595. — *Further Reading:* H. Beck, *Brüder in vielen Völkern* (Erlangen, 1981), pp. 41-60; K. Hunte, "Protestantism and Slavery in the British Caribbean," in: A. Lampe (ed.), *Christianity in the Caribbean* (Kingston, 2001), pp. 86-125; Latourette, *Expansion III,* pp. 236-239; Dussel, *Church,* pp. 204f.

F. HERALDS OF INDEPENDENCE

259. Mexico: Against the Discrimination of the Creoles (1771)

During the eighteenth century the Creoles protested ever more frequently because of the discrimination they suffered vis-à-vis the "true" Spaniards born in the mother country. They were not allowed to become bishops or to hold the most important positions in the administration of justice and the military both because their loyalty was doubted and because it was assumed no one born in the Americas could be as competent and intelligent as Europeans. In the religious orders higher jobs were frequently rotated for the sake of peace, a Creole being elected superior after a Spaniard and vice versa. The structural discrimination against the Creoles is one of the main factors that led to the fight for independence. The following petition of May 2, 1771, from Mexico City to Charles III (Spanish King, 1759-1788) opposes such discrimination, making clear that the Europeans were the foreigners who should be discriminated against.

It is not the first time that ill disposure and prejudice damaged the estimation of the Americans and made them look as if they are unworthy of attaining any kind of honors. This war was led against us since the discovery of America. It was even questioned whether the native Indians are reasonable. There is not less injustice in the statement that we, who are born by European parents in this country, possess hardly enough brain to be humans. [. . .] The episcopal sees and other high ecclesiastical dignities were closed to us, as were in the worldly sphere the first-rate positions in the army, the administration and the judiciary. This means to overthrow international law. This is not only the way to loose America, but also to ruin the state. To allocate offices to natives and to exclude foreigners is a principle represented by the laws of all empires, adopted by all nations and given by natural reason and is engrained in the hearts and the wishes of the people. [. . .] But regarding the allocation of honorable offices, the European Spaniards here in America have to be regarded as foreigners, since the same reasons speak against them by which all people prohibited the employment of foreigners. The Europeans are foreigners in America by nature, though not by civil law.

Source: Archivo General de Indias (Sevilla) (Mexico City, 1684) (R. Konetzke, *Lateinamerika seit 1492* [Stuttgart, 1971], pp. 37-38). — *Further Reading:* D. A. Brading, *The First America: The Spanish Monarchy, Creole Patriots and the Liberal State, 1492-1867* (Cambridge, 1991); M. Delgado, *Die Metamorphosen des Messianismus in den iberischen Kulturen* (Immensee, 1994), pp. 65-88; A. Gerbi, *The Dispute of the New World: The History of a Polemic, 1750-1900* (Pittsburgh, London, 1973); J. Lafaye, *Quetzalcóatl and Guadalupe: The Formation of Mexican National Consciousness, 1531-1813* (Chicago, 1976); Borges, *Historia I*, pp. 281-298; Dussel, *Church*, pp. 220ff.

260. Peru: Uprising of Túpac Amaru II (1780-1781)

Túpac Amaru, who was beheaded by the Spanish in Cuzco in 1572, was the last legitimate ruler of the Incas. When the cacique José Gabriel Condorcanqui led his anti-colonial uprising in 1780-1781, he declared himself Túpac Amaru II. What did he want to achieve by this? Some researchers support the nativistic-messianic line of thought, seeing his uprising as the last step to an "Andean utopia." According to this theory, the Indian population had been waiting in hope since the deaths of Atahualpa and Túpac Amaru I for the mythical hero or Incan *redivivus* who would reestablish the old empire and gather the people together for the big battle against the foreign invaders. For Jürgen Golte, however, the uprising stemmed from the same dominant economic factors as the numerous peasant rebellions that shook the Andes during the 1760s and 70s. The uprising primarily targeted the trade monopoly of the *corregidores* or provincial judges under whom not only the common Indians suffered through arbitrary increases in the prices of products, but also those caciques who, like J. G. Condorcanqui, were landowners, haulage contractors, and mule traders. Document a shows that the leading caciques would have considered a broad alliance made up of the Creole middle class, the Mestizo lower middle class, and the Indian peasants against the *corregidores* and Europeans. However, the uncontrolled actions of the peasant armies developed their own dynamic and the conflict acquired a nativistic-messianic character. Out of fear of a siege, the Bishop of Cuzco even called the clergy to arms, a move which was criticized sharply by other bishops. Document b shows how skillfully Túpac Amaru used his "Exodus theology" to denounce the trade monopoly of the *corregidores* who carried on trade in front of church after Sunday Mass. After the uprising was quelled, Túpac Amaru was pulled apart by four horses in 1781 because he was judged to be a "rebel."

a. Indians, Mestizos and Creoles against the Europeans (1780)

Edict for the province of Chichas:

I, Don Jose Gabriel Túpac-Amaru, an Indian of the royal blood and principal lineage, inform the Creole residents of the province of Chichas and surrounding areas that, in view of the strong yoke that so cruelly oppresses us, and the tyranny of those who rule us with no consideration for our misfortunes, out of exasperation with them and their heartlessness, I have determined to shake off this unbearable yoke and contain the evil government that we suffer under the chiefs who comprise those bodies: for that reason the *corregidor* [magistrate] of this province of Tinta was publicly executed, a number of Spaniards having come from the city of Cuzco in his defense, followed by my beloved Creoles, who paid with their lives for their audacity and bravery. I only feel sorrow for the Creole compatriots, for it was not my intention that they come to any harm, but that we should live as brothers and come together in one body to destroy the Europeans. Viewing all this with mature accord, this aspiration is not at all opposed to our holy Catholic religion but seeks only to restore order, after having taken measures conducive to the support, protection and preservation of the Spanish Creoles, *mestizos,* Negroes and Indians, and the tranquility they deserve as compatriots, born in our lands, of the same origin as the natives, and having all equally suffered these oppressions and tyrannies at the hands of the Spaniards.

b. Criticism of Colonial Oppression under the Judges (1781)

A humble youth with a staff and sling and a rustic shepherd, with the help of divine providence, freed the unhappy people of Israel from the power of Goliath and Pharaoh: the reason was that the tears of those poor captives raised such voices of compassion, pleading for justice from heaven, that in a few years they left their martyrdom and torment for the promised land: but oh! in the end they attained their wish, with such sobbing and crying! But we, the unhappy Indians, though we sigh and weep more than they, in so many centuries have not been able to find relief; and although our monarch in his royal eminence and sovereignty has seen fit to free us with his royal *cédula* [proclamation], this relief and kindness has brought us greater anxiety, temporal and spiritual ruin: the reason is that the Pharaoh who pursues, mistreats and abuses us is not one but many, so iniquitous and depraved are the *corregidores,* their lieutenants, tax collectors, and other enforcers; diabolical and perverse men to be sure, who must have been born from the gloomy chaos of hell and sucked at the breast of the most disagreeable harpies, who are so ungodly, cruel and tyrannical that they make great saints of the Neros and Attilas whose iniquities are remembered in history, so that just to hear of them makes the body tremble and the heart cry out. Such evil is understandable in infidels; but the *corregidores,* who are baptized, malign Christianity with their works. . . . They scarcely hear the Sunday Mass with their ceremonious ostentation, and the neighbors learn from their bad example: they exile the faithful from the Churches with the help of their collectors and enforcers, so that the Indians and Spaniards are deprived of the spiritual benefit of the Mass: they stand guard at the doors of the Churches to take them to jail, and keep them there for two or three months until they pay their debts: they violate the Churches: they abuse priests to the point of bloodshed, and disrespect the sacred images: they prohibit the divine worship services, on the predocument of their cost; and mainly to advance their own interests: they strike fear in the cautious and timid parish priests in their homilies and sermons, who do not want the zeal of the faithful and obedience to God's precepts to be perturbed and chilled by such violence and extortions and insults; they chase out and wear down the love of God and the Saints; which leads to an even greater misfortune: that the parish priests and their assistants forget the duties of their ministry and aspire only to receive its benefits.

Source: (a) *Colección documental de la independencia del Perú,* vol. II, 2: *La rebelión de Túpac Amaru,* ed. C. D. Valcárcel (Lima, 1971), pp. 374f; (b) ibid., pp. 522-530. — *Further Reading:* L. E. Fisher, *The Last Inca Revolt, 1780-1783* (Norman, 1966); J. G. Condorcanqui (called Tupac Amaru), *The Last Inca, or the Story of Tupac Amaru,* 3 vols. (London, 1874); Delgado, *Gott,* pp. 308-316; I. Bouisson, H. Schottelius, *Die Unabhängigkeitsbewegungen in Lateinamerika 1788-1826* (Stuttgart, 1980); M. Burga, *Andean Millenarian Movements: Their Origins, Originality and Achievements, 16th-18th Centuries* (Washington, 1996); A. Flores Galindo, *Buscando un Inca* (Lima, 1987); L. L. Johnson, *Death, Dismemberment, and Memory: Body Politics in Latin America* (Albuquerque, 2004); J. Golte, "Determinanten der Entstehung und des Verlaufs bäuerlicher Rebellion in den Anden vom 18. zum 20. Jahrhundert," in: *JGSLA* 15 (1978), pp. 41-74; J. Klaiber, "Religión y justicia en Túpac Amaru," in: P. Richard (ed.), *Raíces de la teología latinoamericana* (San José, 1987), pp. 73-84; J. Pérez, *Los movimientos precursores de la emancipación en Hispanoamérica* (Madrid, 1977); J. Szeminski, *La utopía tupamarista* (Lima, 1983); Dussel, *Church,* pp. 287ff.

261. Juan Pablo Viscardo:
Letter to the Spaniards in America (1792)

The Jesuit Juan Pablo Viscardo (1748-1798) was a Peruvian Creole. After the expulsion of the Jesuits in 1767 he lived chiefly in London where, protected by the British government, he wrote a "Letter to the American Spaniards" in 1792. In this letter, which caused quite a sensation, he encouraged them to take the side of independence. The letter is filled with the optimism of the Enlightenment which Simón Bolívar and the other liberators of Latin America also shared: independence would turn Latin America into a new Promised Land of eternal peace for all the oppressed and peace-loving people of the world.

This time has arrived . . . and in spite of our poor efforts, freedom in its wisdom, the precious gift of heaven, surrounded by all virtue and followed by prosperity, will begin to reign in the New World and tyranny will be immediately exterminated. . . . The wise and virtuous Spaniard, who silently mourns the oppression of his fatherland, will applaud this undertaking in his heart. He will see the rebirth of the national glory of an enormous empire, transformed into a safe haven for all Spaniards, who in addition to the brotherly hospitality they have always found there will now be able to breathe freely under the rule of reason and justice. May it please God that this day, the happiest day that ever dawned, not only for America but for the whole world; may it please God that this day come soon. . . . How many people, fleeing from oppression or misery, will come to enrich us with their industriousness, with their knowledge, and to rebuild our exhausted population! In this way America will draw together the far corners of the earth, and its inhabitants will be bound together by the common interest of the one great family of brethren.

Source: J. L. Romero, L. A. Romero (eds.), *Pensamiento político de la emancipación* (Caracas, 1985), vol. 1, pp. 57f; J. P. Vizcardo y Guzmán, *Letter to the Spanish Americans.* A facsimile of the second English edition (London, 1810) (Providence, R.I., 2002). — *Further Reading:* D. A. Brading, *The First America: The Spanish Monarchy, Creole Patriots and the Liberal State, 1492-1867* (Cambridge, 1991); M. Batllori, *El abate Viscardo* (Madrid, 1995); D. A. Brading, G. Gutiérrez, M. M. Marzal, *Juan Pablo Viscardo y Guzmán (1748-1798),* 3 vols. (Lima, 1999); I. Bouisson, H. Schottelius, *Die Unabhängigkeitsbewegungen in Lateinamerika 1788-1826* (Stuttgart, 1980).

262. Mexico: Historical-Theological Emancipation
of the Creoles (1794)

About the middle of the sixteenth century, initially in the shadow of the first Jesuit mission in Brazil, we encounter the legend of Thomas according to which some of the rites and customs of the Indians are to be attributed to an original evangelization by the

Apostle Thomas. This legend served to legitimate the conquest and the forced conversion of the Indians since they had "reneged" on the received faith in favor of "idol worship." Around 1600, missionaries found traces of the Apostle in virtually all of America and identified him with the "white god" of the Indian traditions. Creole members of the religious orders, however, interpreted the Thomas tradition differently: The Indians were no longer to be blamed for the "idol worship," but the church which had apparently left them alone for so many centuries. The Creoles began to see themselves as Americans and considered the contempt and demonization of the Indian traditions to be an insult to their own slowly emerging cultural identity. The Creolization process of the Thomas tradition reached its climax at the end of the colonial period when the Dominican Servando Teresa de Mier (1763-1827) combined the Guadalupe tradition and the Thomas tradition in a sermon on the feast of Our Lady of Guadalupe in Mexico on December 12, 1794, in which he made clear that the Gospel and the Virgin of Guadalupe had not come to Mexico in the wake of the Spanish conquest and evangelization but rather during the apostolic period, during which the Virgin had appeared to the Apostle James in Spain. This view of history with its theological implications preceded political emancipation.

The image of Our Lady of Guadalupe is not painted on the cloak of Juan Diego but on the cape of St. Thomas, the apostle of this kingdom.
First proposition.

One thousand, seven hundred and fifty years ago the image of Our Lady of Guadalupe was already very famous, worshiped by the already Christian Indians at the summit of this Sierra of Tenanyuca, where St. Thomas built her a temple and placed her.
Second proposition.

Soon afterward apostate Indians of our religion vandalized the image, which they evidently could not erase, and St. Thomas hid it; then ten years after the conquest the queen of heaven appeared to Juan Diego asking for a temple, and the last time she gave him her ancient image to deliver to Senor Zumarraga.
Third proposition.

The image of Our Lady is a painting from the beginning of the first century of the Church; but its artistry and conservation are superior to all human industry, as the Virgin Mary herself was naturally imprinted on the living canvas in mortal flesh. Fourth proposition. . . .

Ah! If I had time to make you see that the Indians were Christians at the beginning of the Church, I could show you that they have knowledge not only of the one God with his sovereign attributes but also of the Trinity, the Incarnation, the Eucharist, and the other articles of our religion; communion, oral confession, the Lenten fasts practiced among them, along with other Church practices; the monastic institute conserved in Mexico until the conquest, all taught by St. Thomas and all distorted with the passage of time.

Source: Servando Teresa de Mier, *Obras completas*, vol. 1: *El heterodoxo guadalupano* (Mexico City, 1981), pp. 237-251. — *Further Reading:* M. Delgado, "Die Jungfrau von Guadalupe, der Apostel Thomas und die kreolischen Emanzipationsbestrebungen in Mexiko um 1800," in: K. Koschorke (ed.), *Transkontinentale Beziehungen in der Geschichte des Außereuropäischen Christentums* (Wiesbaden, 2002), pp. 315-327; J. V. Lombardi, *The Political Ideology of Fray Servando Teresa de Mier, Propagandist for Independence*, Cuernavaca 1968; *The Memoirs of Fray Servando Teresa de Mier* (New York, 1998); E. Marroquín, "Fray Servando Teresa de Mier," in: P. Richard (ed.), *Raíces de la teología latinoamericana* (San José, 1987), pp. 85-96; J. Lafaye, *Quetzalcóatl and Guadalupe: The Formation of Mexican National Consciousness, 1531-1813* (Chicago, 1976); D. A. Brading, *The Origins of Mexican Nationalism* (Cambridge, 1985); C. I. Archer (ed.), *The Birth of Modern Mexico, 1780-1824* (Wilmington, Del., 2003).

III. LATIN AMERICA 1800-1890

A. On the Path to Independence

263. The Bishop of Michoacán on the Situation around 1810

The French Revolution — more than the American Revolution — sparked Latin America's fight for independence. The "slave house," Haiti, already declared its independence in 1804. Spanish America was seething with unrest everywhere. But it was only after Spain's occupation by Napoleon in 1810 that the critical phase in the fight for independence began, which is apparent from this letter of May 20, 1810, from Bishop Manuel Abad y Queipo to the King. At that time almost every city voted for an autonomous government which then declared its independence from Spain or which resulted in formal independence later on. The invitation to representatives of Spanish America to the Cortes (the General Assembly of the Estates) of Cádiz in 1812 could no longer stop the independence process. Countries caught in the maelstrom of the "Bolivian" revolution strove to establish a republican government, whereas Mexico tended more towards a monarchy independent from Spain (1821). Brazil also opted for the monarchal solution (1822). Latin American independence was nourished by many intellectual roots, not least of all by the political theories of scholasticism (Francisco de Vitoria, Bartolomé de las Casas, Francisco Suárez), and it was in general a Creole phenomenon. The formal declaration of independence of the individual colonies normally occurred at a constituent assembly which had been convened and consisted of people of European descent with Spanish language and culture who viewed themselves as "Americans." The fight for independence in Spanish America ended with the Battle of Ayacucho (December 12, 1824).

Our possessions in America, and especially in this New Spain, are much inclined toward a general insurrection, unless your majesty's wisdom prevents it. The electric fire of the French Revolution, which is harming all the other nations at the same time, destroying some, causing agitation and commotion in others, has set in motion and gathered together in these countries the first elements of division and of a burning desire for Independence. . . . Our American people, viewing the character of the Spanish people as burnt out, thought the metropolis lost forever at the moment they saw it occupied; they also saw as impossible the reconquest and defense that those brothers had so heroically undertaken. From then on they naturally devoted themselves more intentionally to Independence and the means of achieving it, in the specific hypothetical case that the metropolis should not be recovered. . . .

That is the general inclination of our possessions in America, and particularly in this New Spain.

Source: Ernesto de la Torre Villar, *La Constitución de Apatzingán y los creadores del Estado Mexicano* (Mexico City, 1964), pp. 154-155. — *Further Reading:* D. A. Brading, *Church and State in Bourbon Mexico: The Diocese of Michoacán, 1749-1810* (Cambridge, 1994); idem, *The First America: The Spanish Monarchy, Creole Patriots and the Liberal State, 1492-1867* (Cambridge, 1991); idem, *The Origins of Mexican Nationalism* (Cambridge, 1985); J. Lafaye, *Quetzalcóatl and Guadalupe: The Formation of Mexican National Consciousness, 1531-1813* (Chicago, 1976); C. I. Archer (ed.), *The Birth of Modern Mexico, 1780-1824* (Wilmington, Del., 2003); I. Bouisson, H. Schottelius, *Die Unabhängig-keitsbewegungen in Lateinamerika 1788-1826* (Stuttgart, 1980); J. L. Romero, L. A. Romero (eds.), *Pensamiento político de la emancipación*, 2 vols. (Caracas, 1985); R. Vargas Ugarte, *El episcopado en los tiempos de la emancipación sudamericana* (Lima, ³1962); Dussel, *Church* pp. 90ff, 220ff; Latourette, *Expansion* V, pp. 68ff.

264. Mexico: Priest in the Fight for Independence

The fight for independence also divided the church. In general it can be said that the upper clergy and the bishops who came from Spain remained loyal to the mother country, while the lower clergy, mostly Creoles, Mestizos, and Indians, supported the struggle for independence. In Mexico the fight was led by priests like Miguel Hidalgo and José María Morelos. Hidalgo (document a) attempted to forge an alliance of Indians, Mestizos and Creoles against the Spaniards. In his peasant army, however, it was virtually only the Indians and Mestizos who fought in the name of the Virgin of Guadalupe. Similar to Túpac Amaru II's uprising in the Andes (cf. document 260); Hidalgo's struggle had the characteristics of a social revolution to which the Creole upper class could not be won over. This condemned the struggle to failure. Hidalgo was shot on July 27, 1811. His successor, Morelos, tried (document b) to keep the fight for independence from degenerating into an uprising of the colored against the whites, but could not secure the trust of the Creoles: he also failed. Mexico's independence only became possible when Catholic Creoles proclaimed independence under the leadership of Agustín de Iturbide on February 24, 1821, in part to protect the Catholic religion, for they felt threatened by the liberal and anticlerical turn that had occurred in the government of the mother country after the Spanish Revolution in 1820. Simón Bolívar (1783-1830), the liberator of South America, was, however, a liberal freemason who nonetheless recognized the advantage of religion especially during the Mexican fight for independence (document c).

a. On the Hidalgo Manifestos to the Americans (1810)

To ensure the happiness of the kingdom it is necessary to remove the mandate and power from the hands of Europeans; this is the whole purpose of our enterprise, for which we are authorized by the common voice of the nation and by the heartfelt sentiments of all Creoles. . . . Therefore in view of the sacred fire that burns in us and the justice of our cause, let the sons of the fatherland take heart, for the day of America's glory and public happiness has arrived. Rise up, noble American souls! . . . If you have human feelings, if you are horrified to see the blood of your brothers spilled . . . ; if you wish for public peace, your own security and that of your families and ranches, and the prosperity of this kingdom; if you desire that these movements not degenerate into the revolution that all Americans seek to avoid, which would cause confusion and bring in a foreigner to dominate us; in short, if you would be happy, then desert from the troops of the Europeans and come over to join us, let the people from across the sea defend themselves and you will see this over in a day with no harm to them or to you, and without a single person perishing. . . . Open your eyes: consider that the Europeans are trying to set Creoles against Creoles. . . . The safety and protection of our brothers is more important to us; the only thing we want is not to have to take up arms against them; a single drop of American blood matters more to us than victory in some battle, which we seek to avoid wherever possible, and which denies us the happiness to which we aspire.

b. Decree of José Maria Morelos (October 13, 1811)

I declare that our plan is only directed towards having political and military rule, which is in the hands of the Europeans, pass over to the Creoles who will best preserve the rights of Ferdinand VII [Spanish king in French captivity]. . . . Since the white people were the first representatives of the empire and initially took up arms to defend the natives of the towns and the rest of the colored inhabitants, joining forces with them, the white people should be the object of our gratitude because of this service and not of animosity which is beginning to spread against them. . . . Since it is not our plan to take action against the rich simply because they are rich, and even less against the rich Creoles, no one should dare to seize the possessions of someone, however rich he may be, since such action is opposed to every law and above all against divine law which forbids our stealing and appropriating somebody else's property against the will of the owner, indeed even coveting someone else's things in thought.

c. Mexico: Simón Bolívar and the Religion (1815)

Happily, the leaders of the Mexican independence movement have made use of this fanaticism to excellent purpose by proclaiming the famous Virgin of Guadalupe the Queen of the Patriots, invoking her name in all difficult situations and placing her image on their banners. As a result, political enthusiasms have been commingled with religion, thus producing an intense devotion to the sacred cause of liberty. The veneration of this image in Mexico is greater than the exaltation that the most sagacious prophet could inspire.

Source: (a) Ernesto de la Torre Villar, *La Constitución de Apatzingán y los creadores del Estado Mexicano* (Mexico City, 1964), p. 204; (b) *Historia documental de México,* vol. 2 (Mexico City, 1964), p. 55; (c) *Selected Writings of Bolivar,* compiled by Vicente Lecuna, volume I: 1810-1822 (New York, 1951), p. 121. — *Further Reading:* D. A. Brading (ed.), *Caudillo and Peasant in the Mexican Revolution* (Cambridge, 1980); idem, *Classic Republicanism and Creole Patriotism: Simon Bolivar (1783-1830) and the Spanish American Revolution* (Cambridge, 1983); H. M. Hamill, *The Hidalgo Revolt: Prelude to Mexican Independence* (Gainesville, 1966); L. E. Fisher, *The Background of the Revolution for Mexican Independence* (Boston, 1934); C. I. Archer (ed.), *The Birth of Modern Mexico, 1780-1824* (Wilmington, Del., 2003); H. J. Miller, *Padre Miguel Hidalgo: Father of Mexican Independence* (Edinburg, Tex., 2004); F. De Varona, *Miguel Hidalgo y Costilla: Father of Mexican Independence* (Brookfield, 1993); B. Scott, *The Grito of September Sixteenth: Biography of Padre Miguel Hidalgo, Father of Mexican Independence* (Ingleside, 1981); P. Rink, *Warrior Priests and Tyrant Kings: The Beginnings of Mexican Independence* (Garden City, 1976); C. Arango Zuluaga, *Crucifijos, sotanas y fusiles. La participación de la iglesia en las luchas armadas de los pueblos latinoamericanos* (Bogotá, 1991); E. de la Torre Villar, *Miguel Hidalgo. Libérateur du Méxique* (Mexico City, 1973); C. M. de Bustamante, *Tres estudios sobre Don José Maria Morelos y Pavón* (Mexico City, 1963); J. L. Romero, L. A. Romero (eds.), *Pensamiento político de la emancipación,* 2 vols. (Caracas, 1985); J. Lafaye, *Quetzalcóatl and Guadalupe:The Formation of Mexican National Consciousness, 1531-1813* (Chicago, 1976); Dussel, *Church,* pp. 90ff, 220ff; Borges, *Historia I,* pp. 815-834.

265. Demand for a Memorial for Las Casas (1813)

In the wake of the fight for independence, Las Casas' document "A Very Brief Account of the Devastation of the West Indies" was published several times. In this account he documented the atrocities that occurred during the first decades of the conquest and labeled the Spaniards — Las Casas meant by this the conquistadors and *encomenderos,* not missionaries and other good Spaniards — as tyrants and enemies of humanity. Creoles, such as Servando Teresa de Mier, a former Dominican (cf. document 262), wrote prefaces which were characterized by the dialectic: we (oppressed) Americans against you Spaniards (enemies of humanity). At the same time, Bolívar and the other liberators instrumentalized Las Casas' prophetic accusation against the early colonial period in order to justify the fight for independence. The Creoles neatly slipped into the Indians' role of victim, assuming their rights, too. Thus they regarded Las Casas, the "father of the Indians," as a kind of "patron saint" of America.

In short, if you are free at the end of this war, gratitude demands that the first monument erected by free hands should be dedicated to the celestial man who so valiantly struggled for the freedom of the earliest Americans against the fury of the conquest, our tireless advocate, our true apostle, the perfect model of evangelical charity who is worthy to be placed on altars for the devotion of everyone in the universe, except for some Spaniards. Casas, whom they persecuted for three hundred years, should find refuge among his children. Make your covenants and sing your songs of freedom around his statue: no more pleasant aroma can be offered to the tutelary spirit of the Americas, the Bishop of Cuzco and Chiapa, to earn us his blessings in both the Northern and Southern continents. His shadow will bring you the respect of all the nations, and no one will be able to say that the people of Casas are not virtuous. . . . I would put on it this inscription, as simple as the hero himself: "Foreigner! If you love virtue, stop here with reverence. This is CASAS, the father of the Indians."

Source: J. L. Romero, L. A. Romero (eds.), *Pensamiento político de la emancipación* (Caracas, 1985), vol. 2, p. 52. — *Further Reading:* M. Sievernich, "Die Brevisima als 'Fürstenspiegel,'" in: *Las Casas* (WA), pp. 2, 27-44; R. Tisnes, Una edición granadina de la "Brevísima relación de la destrucción de las Indias," in: CEHILA (ed.), *B. de Las Casas (1474-1974) e historia de la Iglesia en América Latina* (Barcelona, 1976), pp. 121-136; M. Delgado, "Die Jungfrau von Guadalupe, der Apostel Thomas und die kreolischen Emanzipationsbestrebungen in Mexiko um 1800," in: K. Koschorke (ed.), *Transkontinentale Beziehungen in der Geschichte des Außereuropäischen Christentums* (Wiesbaden, 2002), pp. 315-327; J. V. Lombardi, *The Political Ideology of Fray Servando Teresa de Mier, Propagandist for Independence* (Cuernavaca, 1968); *The Memoirs of Fray Servando Teresa de Mier* (New York, 1998); E. Marroquín, "Fray Servando Teresa de Mier," in: P. Richard (ed.), *Raíces de la teología latinoamericana* (San José, 1987), pp. 85-96; J. Lafaye, *Quetzalcóatl and Guadalupe: The Formation of Mexican National Consciousness, 1531-1813* (Chicago, 1976).

266. Colombia: Political Catechism (1814)

"Political" catechisms that were mostly written by members of the lower clergy were part of the propaganda battle in the shadow of the fight for independence. In a question-answer format, these catechisms presented independence to the common people as a just and sacred cause. In this catechism by the priest V. J. F. de Sotomayor the three main arguments justifying Spanish rule since the sixteenth century (papal donation, the conquest, and the evangelization) are refuted.

What titles have been presented to maintain this dependence [of America on Spain]? There are three: the pope's donation, the conquest, and the propagation of the Christian religion.

The pope's donation is not a legitimate title? No, because the vicar of Jesus Christ cannot give away what was never his, certainly not in his role as the pope or successor to St. Peter, who has no temporal authority or dominion. . . .

And the conquest is not a just reason to dominate America? The conquest is nothing but the right that comes from power over the weak. . . .

What should we say about the propagation of the Christian religion; can this be a title justifying dependence? It is harmful to the religion itself, to believe that it has been spread among us in order to subjugate us. . . .

From all that has been said in this lesson, it follows that this dependence does not have a legitimate basis in justice. . . . Therefore the declaration of our independence, and the war we are waging to preserve it, are just and holy.

Source: J. Fernández de Sotomayor, *Catecismo o instrucción popular* (Cartagena de Indias, 1814), pp. 7-29. — *Further Reading:* C. Arango Zuluaga, *Crucifijos, sotanas y fusiles. La participación de la iglesia en las luchas armadas de los pueblos latinoamericanos* (Bogotá, 1991); J. L. Romero, L. A. Romero (eds.), *Pensamiento político de la emancipación.* 2 vols. (Caracas, 1985); D. A. Brading, *The First America: The Spanish Monarchy, Creole Patriots and the Liberal State, 1492-1867* (Cambridge, 1991); Dussel, *Church,* pp. 81-105; Borges, *Historia* I, pp. 815-834; Latourette, *Expansion* V, pp. 68ff.

267. Simón Bolívar: On the Rights of the Indian (1825)

Independence also entailed the abolition of the Spanish protective laws for the Indians and a formal equality for them as citizens, as becomes apparent in this decree by Bolívar from July 4, 1825. The well-intended emancipation largely failed, and for two reasons. Firstly, the Indians were not used to their new status and knew little about the laws so that they became easy prey for the new local power elite; secondly, their cultural rights were no longer protected and they ran the risk of losing their identity. In the Creole republics and new states, the Indians quickly gained the reputation of being a population that inhibited progress and had to be modernized at all costs. The new secular religion was disseminated by means of laws and schools (its apostles were judges, mayors, and teachers) which, in many instances, took less account of the cultural identity of the Indians than the evangelization project of the colonial period. In the nineteenth century, rural Indians were systematically hunted down in some places, such as in the Argentinean pampas, much like in the American Wild West. It was only around 1900, in the wake of indigenism, that Creole intellectuals in countries with a large indigenous population discovered the Indian issue as a cultural question and held debates on the identity of these young countries.

1. No individual of the state may directly or indirectly require personal service from the Peruvian Indians, except as preceded by a free contract regarding the wage to be paid.

2. Departmental prefects, superintendents, governors and judges, ecclesiastical prelates, priests and their assistants, ranchers, and mine or factory owners are prohibited from employing Indians against their will in chores, draft labor *(faenas, mitas, söptimas y ponqueajes)*, and other types of common domestic service.

3. For public works of common benefit commissioned by the government, the Indians alone will not be drafted into service as is customarily done; all citizens must participate in proportion to their number and abilities. . . .

7. The Indians are not required to pay a higher fee for parish rights than the rates established at present or in the future.

8. Parish priests and their assistants may not negotiate these rights with the Indians, without the intervention of the superintendent or governor of the town.

Source: Decretos del Libertador, vol. 1, 1813-1825 (Caracas, 1961), pp. 407-408. — *Further Reading:* D. A. Brading, *Classic Republicanism and Creole Patriotism: Simón Bolívar (1783-1830) and the Spanish American Revolution* (Cambridge, 1983); M. Kossok, *Simón Bolívar und das historische Schicksal Spanisch-Amerikas* (Berlin, 1984).

B. ROME AND THE NEW COUNTRIES

268. Leo XII: Encyclical *Etsi Iam Diu* (September 24, 1824)

Rome also interfered during the course of Spanish America's fight for independence. Two papal encyclicals are of particular significance: Pius VII's *Etsi Longissimo* of January 30, 1816, and Leo XII's *Etsi Iam Diu* of September 24, 1824. In the first encyclical, the bishops are admonished "to advise the people emphatically to show befitting loyalty and the necessary obedience toward the Spanish monarch." It was issued after the Congress of Vienna in the spirit of the Restoration and without pressure from the Spanish government: as the French Revolution had been defeated in Europe, it was widely felt that the old order should also be restored in Spanish America. The second encyclical did not admonish the bishops to perform the same task, despite pressure from the Spanish government, but "merely" to make peace in the Latin American "civil war" and to praise the Spaniards "in Europe" loyal to the virtuous Catholic King Ferdinand VII (1808, 1814-1833).

But we are certainly honored that a matter of such gravity, under your influence and with God's help, will bring the happy and early results that We hope for if You devote yourself to explaining to your flock the august and distinguished qualities that mark our beloved son Fernando, the Catholic king of the Spains . . . and if with all due zeal you expound for the consideration of all, the illustrious and inaccessible merits of the Spaniards living in Europe who have entrusted their ever constant loyalty, and the sacrifice of their interests and their lives, to the honor and defense of the religion and of the legitimate power.

Source: P. de Leturia, *Relaciones entre la Santa Sede e Hispanoamérica 1493-1835* (Rome, 1959), vol. 2, p. 269. — *Further Reading:* ibid.; idem, "Der Heilige Stuhl und das spanische Patronat in Amerika," in: *HJ* 46 (1926), pp. 1-71; idem, *La acción diplomática de Bolívar ante Pío VII (1820-1823)* (Caracas, 1984); A. Gutiérrez, *La Iglesia que entendió el libertador Simón Bolívar* (Maracaibo, 1981); Dussel, *Church*, pp. 105-117; Borges, *Historia I*, pp. 815-834; Latourette, *Expansion V*, pp. 68ff.

269. A Report on the State of the Church (1825)

In the course of the fight for independence, many dioceses remained vacant since the bishops loyal to the king returned to Spain. The new governments frequently endeavored to take over the inheritance of the Spanish patronage. In 1821 the Chilean senate dispatched a procurator to Rome to negotiate two petitions. According to the first, Rome should send a Chilean as envoy, grant the Chilean head of state (General O'Higgins) the right of patronage, as it had once been granted to the Spanish kings, and make Santiago an archbishopric. The second petition requested an envoy, Chilean or not, the patronage, and the appointment of bishops for the vacant dioceses. Pius VII thereupon sent Giovanni Muzi as the apostolic vicar to Chile on July 3, 1823, with authority for the Plata region as well, accompanied by the young canon Giovanni M. Mastai, subsequently Pius IX. With respect to the solution of episcopal appointments in Chile and the Plata region, the Muzi mission failed, largely because he was rather undiplomatic. However, his mission was useful in other regards, such as securing the loyalty of these countries to Rome and writing valuable reports about their political and religious situations. Muzi sent the following report to Rome in August of 1825.

It is quite difficult to elect persons to promote to the episcopacy. Governments only promote the supporters of patriotism. In practice it is very rare for such people to be concerned with the good of the Church. The safest way would be to conduct and discuss the process in Rome, as has always been done, and also to gather information separately on the feelings and behavior of the candidates presented. A Papal Envoy empowered to conduct the process here would find himself in a difficult situation, perhaps even requiring deception.

Freedom of the press causes a great harm, from perverse books and writings, which the ordinary church leader cannot prevent. . . . Freedom of worship, whether imposed by law or as a given reality, not only offends the Catholic Religion but also insults the common sense of these peoples, who support the currently prevailing religion.

Religious orders are non-existent in many places. Where they still exist, the members are generally beyond all observation of the rule. They would have to relate directly to the General Father in Rome, or at least each order would need a Vicar General subordinate to the General in Rome. . . .

Ever since the advocates of independence gained power, the sacred missions established to convert the Indians or maintain them in the religion have been abandoned. All the Franciscan fathers, who were sent from Spain as missionaries and were exempt from the jurisdiction of the American provincials, have fled or have had to remain as prisoners. There is no thought of replacing them with other religious workers. Without government assistance and material support it is useless to think about sacred missions, at least about bringing in new missionaries.

These reflections can provide a basis for discussions and decisions to be taken in Rome if the representatives from America should come. Once the principles are established, it would be possible to consider sending one or more Papal Envoys to America to oversee the fulfillment of the decisions taken in Rome.

Source: P. de Leturia, M. Batllori (eds.), *La primera misión pontificia a Hispanoamérica 1823-1825. Relación oficial de Mons. Giovanni Muzi* (Vatican City, 1963), pp. 574-575. — *Further Reading:* ibid.; P. de Leturia, "Der Heilige Stuhl und das spanische Patronat in Amerika" in: *HJ* 46 (1926), pp. 1-71; Dussel, *Church*, pp. 105-117; Borges, *Historia I*, pp. 799-814; Latourette, *Expansion V*, pp. 68ff.

270. Ecuador: Concordat of September 26, 1862

After the initial recognition of the new republics by Pope Gregory XVI with the constitution *Sollicitudo Ecclesiarum* of August 5, 1831, the new republics and Rome slowly negotiated mutual recognition and amicable regulation of the open patronage issues and church affairs, culminating in concordats (Bolivia 1851, Guatemala and Costa Rica 1852, Haiti 1860, Nicaragua and Honduras 1861, El Salvador, Venezuela, and Ecuador 1862) signed by the Latin American expert Pius IX (cf. commentary to document 270). With these concordats the Catholic Church received a privileged status — sometimes, as in the following concordat with Ecuador, including the prohibition of all other faiths — as well as authority over education. Rome, on the other hand, granted the governments of the new republics some patronage rights such as the right to propose candidates for the vacant episcopal sees. At the same time, however, Rome took great pains to make sure that bishops and clerics were able to communicate freely with the Holy See, unlike the situation during the entire Spanish patronage period, when monarchical control over communication had seriously limited the *libertas ecclesiae.* In his letter of August 7, 1826, to Leo XII, Giustiniani, the first papal nuncio in Latin America, had recorded the following concerning the Spanish patronage which was still formally in existence then: "The laws of India are so unreasonable as to not allow the bishops to report to Rome about the dioceses without permission of the [Portuguese] high council of India. And in order to hinder any prelates wanting to defy this ban from fulfilling a so holy and indispensable duty, King Charles III ordered in a very harsh decree that even the powers given to the procurator for a visit *ad limina* must bear the *vidimus* of the council. [...] The obstacles put in the way of ecclesiastical authorities in America are enough to destroy all the principles of canon law and to introduce a type of Anglican supremacy in Spain" (Lecturia, The Holy See, 61). This is precisely what Rome wanted to avoid with respect to the new republics.

1. The Catholic, Apostolic, Roman Religion will continue to be the only Religion of the Republic of Ecuador, and will always be preserved with all the rights and prerogatives that are due it under the law of God and the Canonical dispositions. Therefore no other dissident cult, nor any association condemned by the Church, may ever be permitted. ....

3. The instruction of youth in the Universities, Colleges, faculties, public and private schools will conform in all things to the doctrine of the Catholic Religion. To this end the Bishops will have the exclusive right to designate documents for teaching, both in the Ecclesiastical sciences and in moral and religious instruction. ....

5. Because by Divine right the Roman Pontiff has the primacy of honor and jurisdiction in the Universal Church, the Bishops, Clergy and Faithful will have freedom of communication with the Holy See. Therefore no secular authority may obstruct the full and free exercise of such communication, requiring the Bishops, Clergy and people to go through the Government to appeal to the Roman See for their needs, or subjecting its Bulls, Briefs or Decrees to the *exequatur* of the Government. ....

12. In virtue of the right of patronage that the Sovereign Pontiff grants to the President of Ecuador, the latter may nominate to Archdioceses and Dioceses, Priests who are worthy in terms of the Holy Canons. To this end, immediately upon the vacancy of an Episcopal Throne, the Archbishop will ask the other Bishops for their votes to supply the vacancy; if the Archbishop's place is vacant, the most senior Bishop will collect the votes and present a list of at least three candidates to the President, who will select one of these and propose him to the Sovereign Pontiff, so that he may confer Canonical institution according to the rule prescribed by the Holy Canons. In the event that the Bishops' nomination is not made within six months, for any reason, the President of Ecuador may do it himself; and if he does not do it within three months, the selection reverts to the Holy See, as he himself [the President of Ecuador] has requested.

Source: F. J. Hernáez (ed.), *Colección de bulas breves y otros documentos relativos a la Iglesia de América y Filipinas, Brussels 1879* (Vaduz, [R]1964), vol. 2, pp. 629-633. — *Further Reading:* P. de Leturia, "Der Heilige Stuhl und das spanische Patronat in Amerika," in: *HJ* 46 (1926), pp. 1-71; idem, *Relaciones entre la Santa Sede e Hispanoamérica 1493-1835*, vol. 2 (Rome, 1959); J. Tobar Donoso, *La Iglesia Ecuatoriana en el Siglo XIX*, 2 vols. (Quito, 1934-1935); idem, "El primer

Concordato Ecuatoriano" in: *Monografías Históricas* (Quito, 1938), pp. 256-310; Dussel, *Church*, pp. 105-117; Borges, *Historia I*, pp. 815-834; Latourette, *Expansion V*, pp. 68ff.

271. Surrounding Vatican I (1869-1870)

Whereas the Spanish patronage could forbid the bishops of Spanish America from participating in the Council of Trent in the sixteenth century, unobstructed direct communication with Rome (cf. document 270) was written down in the new national concordats. For this reason most of the Latin American bishops, specifically 52, took part in Vatican I. The Council experience contributed considerably to tying Latin American Catholicism to Rome. Another contributing factor was the founding of the Latin American Pius College in Rome by Pius IX in 1858 to train a clerical elite that was theologically better qualified and more loyal to Rome. The Latin American bishops belonged to the party of those who thought the Pope was infallible, although it was only during the Council itself that many of them arrived at this conviction. Two pastoral letters of the Chilean bishop, José Hipólito Salas, serve as an example of the shift from a general recognition of the Pope's jurisdictional primacy to the explicit acceptance of infallibility.

From a Pastoral Letter dated August 5, 1869:

[The Pope is] the first in faith, the first in love; the first among all the Apostles; the first when it was necessary to fill the vacancy left by Judas the traitor; the first to confirm faith in a miracle; the first in converting the Jews; the first in receiving the Gentiles; the first in all places, in Jerusalem, in Antioch, and finally in Rome.

From a Pastoral Letter dated September 29, 1870:

[The Pope is] the Vicar of Christ, the successor to St. Peter, the indestructible rock, the foundation of the Church, against whom the gates of hell shall not prevail, the Pope, Prince of the whole Catholic episcopacy, the center of Catholic unity, Father and Teacher of all Christians, the Supreme Chief of the Kingdom of God on earth, the Pope is the mouth of the Church, *os Ecclesiae*, the infallible Doctor and Teacher of the truth, the Great Priest, greater than Melchisedek and Aaron, who blesses the city and the World so that the city and the World will never be submerged or perish.

Source: J. Villegas, "El Concilio Vaticano I y la Iglesia en América Latina," in: Pontificia Commissio pro America Latina (ed.), *Los últimos cien años de la evangelización en América Latina* (Vatican City, 2000), pp. 1434-1436. — *Further Reading:* Villegas, ibid.; Dussel, *Church*, pp. 105ff; Borges, *Historia I*, pp. 815-834.

C. Popular Religion and the State
of the Church and the Missions

272. Indian Religiosity in the Andes (1801)

Alexander von Humboldt's expedition to America lasted five years (from July 16, 1799, to August 3, 1804) and took him to Venezuela, Cuba, New Granada, Quito, Peru, Mexico, Cuba again, and the United States. He published the scholarly results of his "Journey to the Equinoctial Regions of the New Continent" over the next three decades in thirty-four French-language volumes. Humboldt also left behind a total of nine handwritten travel journals in which he recorded his impressions of the land and people during his America trip. In these journals there are interesting observations about Latin American popular piety around 1800 which he could make at close range since many of his hosts were priests. The document describes a folk festival in the Andes where Indian and Iberian customs blend harmoniously since the Indians play the same instruments (drum and pipe) heard at Spanish village festivals and perform a dance introduced by the missionaries to honor the Blessed Sacrament. Humboldt, however, sees this as proof that the Indians had simply exchanged their "idols" for Christian ones.

We spent the feast of St. Francis in the new village of la Ascensión, as one calls a few houses on a high pass. In a shed, the church, a young boyish priest performed all the acts which one does in St. Peter's in Rome. Lumps of clay were the candlesticks of the altar. Opposite the altar a table was placed over which a straw roof hung. That represented the choir stall. The strangest thing of all, however, was the Indian dance during the Mass. The Capitán de los Indios was decked out like a harlequin, a helmet of linen festooned with seventeen glass necklaces and a train of ribbons. His straight hair flew Medusan-like around his shoulders. There were countless rosaries around his neck. He wore a short woman's skirt down to his knees and was barefoot, but had leather around his calves festooned with countless bells. He carried a staff in his hand. He had two companions with similar bells whose finery, however, due to the meagerness of their dress, was much less ostentatious. The priest greeted the Indians at the door of the church, and they waved their staffs in front of the priest and danced a kind of ballet in front of the altar to the beat of a drum and a pipe. One Indian played both instruments at the same time. The movement of the feet was very simple, a step to the beat to make the bells ring from which a sound arose almost like a bolero with castanets. The movement of the arms, the waving of the staffs, and the running about in all directions were all the more intricate, and all this with immense gravity and an expression full of pretension. With the beginning of the Mass, the dance ceased, but how amazed we were when the Indian music resounded once again at Communion, just when the priest was holding up the chalice and the host. The masked men danced around the priest in a bacchanalian manner for more than a quarter of an hour — a dance at the most serious moment of the Christian sacrifice. After the ballet the priest concluded the celebration of the Eucharist, asked for *Zuecos,* and then the procession began. As if in a frenzy the Indians danced a kind of chain through the course of the procession, waving the staffs in front of the Christian idols. I have made a drawing of the whole scene.

Source: A. von Humboldt, *Die Wiederentdeckung der Neuen Welt,* ed. P. Kanut Schäfer (Munich, 1992), pp. 261-262. — *Further Reading:* J. Meier, "Die Kirche in Spanisch-Amerika um 1800 nach den Reiseschilderungen Alexanders von Humboldt," in: *CrSt* 17 (1996), pp. 485-516; W. Greive (ed.), *Alexander von Humboldt* (Loccum, 1993); M. Z. Thomas, *Alexander von Humboldt: Scientist, Explorer, Adventurer* (Pantheon, 1960); G. Helferich, *Humboldt's Cosmos: Alexander von Humboldt and the Latin American Journey That Changed the Way We See the World* (New York, 2004).

273. Ecuador: On the Decadence of the Clergy in Quito (1805)

Francisco José de Caldas (1768-1816), an enlightened Creole from New Granada, took part in José Celestino Mutis' botanical expedition and was also in touch with Alexander von Humboldt. Like Humboldt, he left behind scholarly works and descriptions of his journeys. Here Caldas mercilessly describes the moral decadence of religious life and of the clergy in Quito at the time of the struggle for independence. He finds the poor level of education and the lack of interest in the natural sciences especially grave.

None of them live in common, having. . . . The common funds, those devout sacrifices of the people for the benefit of worship and customs, are to be found in the hands of the Prelates. . . . The Provincial, arbiter of the wealth of his brethren, appropriates whatever he wants. . . . This explains the unlimited aspiration to the Provincialate and other lucrative offices. . . . It explains the greed, the expenditures, the disorders and the complete corruption that we observe in almost all the members of these Bodies.

Teaching is at the same level as behavior. Observance and teaching go hand in hand. . . . I heard one of them describe the astronomical laws of Kepler as a fable. . . . Need I refer to the monstrosities I have so often witnessed?

They have two schools for the education of the youth. The first, named after St. Fernando, is in the charge of the Dominican Fathers. What can we expect of teachers trained in the way we have just indicated? The delirium of Aristotle; the fatuities of the school upheld with all imaginable zeal and obstinacy; an unlimited addition to the writing of St. Thomas; a lack of rigor in work and discipline; long periods dedicated to idleness and rest; great attention to adornment, are the wheels on which this machine rolls. Can it educate citizens? . . .

A prodigious number of doctors of all ages, classes and conditions, gathered under a Rector whom they themselves elect, comprises the University of Quito. Except for a small number of those who, dissatisfied with the knowledge of the schools in their country, have quietly educated themselves, the rest are doctors only in name. The unlimited condescension of the examiners leads the youth to aspire to a title that is awarded without requiring knowledge. There is no evidence in the annals of this Body of a single failure among the incalculable number of doctorates granted. Might Quito be the uniquely privileged exception to the common proverb: *Non omnes doctores?*

Source: F. J. de Caldas, *Un peregrino de las ciencias* (Madrid, 1992), pp. 343-345. — *Further Reading:* W. Krauss, *Die Aufklärung in Spanien, Portugal und Lateinamerika* (Munich, 1973); B. Lavalle (ed.), *L'Amérique espagnole à l'époque des Lumières* (Paris, 1987); M. Pérez González, *Caldas y la Expedición Botánica* (Bogotá, 1984); Dussel, *Church*, pp. 81ff.

274. Uruguay: Report on a Former Reduction (1825)

On his way back to Rome, Giovanni Muzi, the first papal nuncio to Latin America (cf. commentary to document 271), recorded his impressions — apologetically colored — of a former reduction near Montevideo, showing that the Franciscans had carried on the work of the Jesuits. It was only when many missionaries had returned to Spain following independence that the Indians of the former reductions were left to their own devices for many decades.

I have seen one of those Indian villages that were built by the Jesuits and later destroyed by the Portuguese; but now that the Portuguese are the lords of the province inhabited by the Indians, they are trying to gather them into villages. One of these villages has been established in the Oriental Province of Montevideo; one must admire the way these Indians have kept all the sacred customs they learned from the Jesuits. The whole tribe makes up one reduction, which has its church and a chaplain, a Franciscan father. The reduction consists of compounds with several families each. Each compound has its own chapel, where all the families go to pray in the morning and afternoon. During the mass I saw that there is music with singing and instruments. Everything is the way it was done in the time of the Jesuits. When they didn't have their own chaplain, the chief led a mass without communion, with songs. So we can see that the good done by the Jesuits goes on permanently. It is incredible how much the number of these Indians has decreased since the suppression of the Jesuits. From 141,000 in the year 1767, there are now only 5,000. So we see that religion edifies, and philosophy destroys.

Source: P. de Leturia, M. Batllori (eds.), *La primera misión pontificia a Hispanoamérica 1823-1825* (Città del Vaticano, 1963), p. 519. — *Further Reading:* ibid.; P. de Leturia, "Der Heilige Stuhl und das spanische Patronat in Amerika," in: *HJ* 46 (1926), pp. 1-71; Dussel, *Church,* pp. 351-362; Delgado, *Gott,* pp. 292-295.

275. Cuba: Catholicism and the Religion of African-Americans (ca. 1880)

Esteban Montejo, who had escaped from slavery, told his life story in 1963 at the age of 104. This story was translated into many languages, and in 1971 it was set to music in German *(El Cimarrón)*. It was a very personal account. The value of the source lies precisely in the way a simple man from the masses sees things. In the following document, Montejo gives us his view of Catholicism and of the African religions of Cuba at the end of the nineteenth century.

In this country Catholicism always seems to get mixed up with magic somewhere along the way. This is a fact. There is no such thing as a Catholic pure and simple. The rich people were Catholics, but they also paid heed to witchcraft from time to time. [. . .] Lots of people here tell you they are Catholic and Apostolic. I don't believe a word of it! Here almost everyone has their little missal and their stick. No person is one thing pure and simple in this country, because all the religions have got mixed together. The African brought his, which is the stronger one, and the Spaniard brought his, which isn't so strong, but you should respect them all. That is my way of thinking.

The African religions are more entertaining because you dance, sing, amuse yourself, fight. There is the *maní* dance, the stick game, and *quimbumbia*. At sunset the various groups got together to play *quimbumbia*, which was like witchcraft, and they almost always used drums as in the stick game. *Quimbumbia* was a Congolese thing. At one time two teams of magic-men used to compete with each other. First they planted a plantain-tree in the middle of a circle drawn on the ground, and then each magic-man cast a spell on the plantain-tree to make it grow fruit. They would pass in front of it, kneel, squirt two or three mouthfuls of alcohol over it, and the first one to make it grow fruit was the winner. The winner could eat the bananas or share them out among his team, if he liked.

Source: The Autobiography of a Runaway Slave Esteban Montejo, ed. by M. Barnet (London, Basingstoke, 1993), pp. 161-162. — *Further Reading:* R. Gray, *Black Christians and White Missionaries* (New Haven, 1990); J. Meier, "Der Überlebenskampf der Negersklaven," in: W. Dreier (ed.), *Entdeckung, Eroberung, Befreiung* (Würzburg, 1993), pp. 66-81; M. Teipel, *Die Versklavung der Schwarzen* (Münster, 1999); CEHILA (ed.), *Escravidão negra e História da Igreja na américa Latina e no Caribe* (Petrópolis, 1987); Dussel, *Church,* pp. 363-374.

D. Protestantism

The movement for independence in the Spanish and Portuguese colonies led to the formation of nation states from 1808 to 1825. They were concerned with political liberalization, secularization and economic liberalization, followed by the creation of a national identity and the ending of the colonial state church. However, the size of the population adhering to Catholicism was important and guaranteed the cohesion of the newly emerging society. Nevertheless, from that time on the spread of Protestantism became possible. The first Protestants were residents — foreign merchants and sailors — who were in Latin America temporarily and practiced the religion of their country of origin in foreign congregations (document 276a). In legal terms, exercising the Protestant faith was limited to the private sphere, since only Catholicism was recognized by the State (document 276b). Some Protestant immigrants from Europe established their own congregations primarily to maintain their allegiance to their homeland (document 277). Independent Bible distributors were primarily interested in spreading the gospel (document 278). Somewhat later, the Anglo-Saxon missionary movement began, which led to the founding of denominational congregations within the formerly Catholic population (document 279). German missionaries of the Moravian Church turned to the Indian population in Nicaragua, founding a Protestant church of Moravian confession on the Atlantic coast in the mid-nineteenth century (document 280). Despite their early expansion, Protestantism in Latin American society remained marginal in the nineteenth century (document 281), its workers finding the process of securing their recognition and importance long and arduous.

276. English Overseas Congregation in Rio de Janeiro (1819ff)

A trade contract between Portugal and England on February 19, 1810, allowed Protestant English subjects to practice their religion in Brazil for the first time, resulting in the first Protestant community in the country being founded in Rio de Janeiro. Their chapel, built in 1819, was the first Anglican — perhaps even the first Protestant — church on Latin American soil. The English minister, Robert Walsh, reports on the English Anglicans in Rio de Janeiro.

a. The First Anglican Chapel in South America (1819)

The edifice stands on the Rua des Barbonos, and is distinguished as being the first ever erected [Anglican chapel] in South America. Before it was built [in 1819], [Anglican] divine service was only performed occasionally on board of [British] ships, in the bay, of which the English on shore used to avail themselves. But in the year 1810, by one of the articles of the treaty then made by Lord Strangford, with the Brazilian government, it was stipulated, that the British should be permitted to build a church for divine service, provided it was erected, not as a public edifice, but as a private house, and did not use bells. [. . .]

The bishop of Rio [José Caetano da Silva Coutinho] eagerly supported the cause. He is not only a tolerant and liberal man, but a man of excellent good sense and knowledge of the world. He advocated the cause, in a characteristic manner, with the prejudiced few who opposed it. "The English," said he, "have really no religion; but they are a proud and obstinate people. If you oppose them, they will persist, and make it an affair of infinite importance; but if you concede to their wishes, the chapel will be built, and nobody will ever go near it." . . .

b. Legal Status of Protestants (1824)

Brazil had won independence from Portugal on September 7, 1822. The constitution of the new monarchy under Dom Pedro I of March 24, 1824, conceded to the Protestants the exercise of their religious freedom for the first time. Similar to what occurred in Brazil, religious freedom as well as the primacy of the Catholic Church was granted in the constitutions of the newly constituted states in the rest of Latin America.

Article V. The Roman Apostolic Catholic religion will continue to be the religion of the Empire. All other religions will be permitted, with their domestic or private worship, in houses destined for this purpose, but under no circumstances outside the temple.

Source: (a) R. Walsh, *Notices of Brazil in 1828 and 1829* (London, 1830), pp. 1, 322-324; (b) D. A. Reily, *História documental do Protestantismo no Brasil* (São Paulo, 1993), p. 40. — *Further Reading:* (a) McManners, *Illustrated History,* pp. 420-425; Latourette, *Expansion V,* p. 105; Prien, *Geschichte,* pp. 748-753; Bastian, *Protestantismus,* pp. 111-114; C. J. Hahn, "Evangelical Worship in Brazil: Its Origins and Development" (Theol. Diss. Edinburgh, 1970 [unpublished]); T. Bruneau, *The Political Transformation of the Brazilian Catholic Church* (London, 1974), pp. 11-37; (b) E. Willems, *Followers of the New Faith* (Nashville, 1967), pp. 57-59; Bastian, *Protestantismus,* pp. 103-109; Dussel, *Church,* pp. 318ff; Prien, *Geschichte,* pp. 401-511; A. G. Mendonça, "A History of Christianity in Brazil," in: *IRM* 85 (1996), pp. 367-388.

277. Brazil: Problems of a German Immigrant Congregation (1833)

Protestants emigrated predominantly from Germany to Brazil during the first half of the nineteenth century. The first group came from Kirnbecherbach (in the German state of Hessen) and arrived together with their pastor, Friedrich Sauerbronn, in Rio de Janeiro on January 13, 1824. Together with a Swiss family, the German colonists founded the first German-speaking Protestant community in Latin America in Nova Friburgo in May 1824. The Protestant settlers in the imperial colony of Nova Friburgo were under the protection of the Brazilian government. In a letter, Pastor Sauerbronn turned directly to the Monarch Dom Pedro II and pointed to the desperate situation in which he and the other colonists found themselves.

[. . .] Lured through extraordinary promises of the Brazilian emperor's agent . . . Kretzschmar, I left the best parish in the most beautiful area of Germany, and came immediately with 334 of my fellow believers to Brazil. On January 13, 1824 after a long, dangerous and burdensome journey, we arrived in Armação [harbor in Rio de Janeiro]. There we had to wait for 3 months, and then we were sent to the New Freyburg colony, where finally after many complaints, my salary of 400 *Milreis* was approved, hardly a third of what I would have had in Germany. This salary was rightly paid to me until the departure of Your Majesty the Emperor Don Pedro I. After this time, I got only half. . . . Most of the dear colonists have moved from the local colony and gone partly to the capital and partly into other areas of Brazil. My situation becomes more grievous every day as I am without the most basic necessities, and in the morning, I often do not know how I shall get the most essential foods for me and my entire family. Shortly, if the fastest aid is not granted me, despair will be my lot. [. . .]

Source: F. Hepp (ed.), "A imigração alemã em Nova Friburgo" (Nova Friburgo, 1987, unpublished). — *Further Reading:* Bastian, *Protestantismus*, pp. 114-121; H.-J. Prien, *Evangelische Kirchwerdung in Brasilien* (Gütersloh, 1989), pp. 27-58, 68f; Prien, *Geschichte*, pp. 753-767; W. R. Read, *New Patterns of Church Growth in Brazil* (Grand Rapids, 1965), pp. 196-200; J. M. Bonino, *Faces of Latin American Protestantism* (Grand Rapids, 1997), pp. 79-106; E. Willems, "Immigrants and Their Assimilation in Brazil," in: T. Lynn Smith et al. (eds.), *Brazil, Portrait of Half a Continent* (Westport, Conn., 1972), pp. 209-225; Latourette, *Expansion V*, pp. 106f.

278. Private Initiatives for the Distribution of Bibles (1826)

Even before British and American Bible societies sent their official representatives to Latin America, individual laymen distributed Bibles to the people with great commitment. This was greeted enthusiastically by local liberal political groups since it corresponded to their idea of enlightenment and progress. The British merchant, S. R. McKay, reports to John Jackson of the British and Foreign Bible Society (BFBS) about his experiences in Rio de Janeiro in a letter from May 22, 1826.

In July of 1824, captain Tanner of Devonshire, left a package for his friend, Mr. Peter Gilfillan containing twenty Bibles and one hundred Testaments, . . . and everything was left with me. I took care of everything according to my best judgment: most of it I sold, and the other part was distributed for free. A little before Mr. [Edmund] Pink left the city, he also gave me a package of two hundred Testaments that were to the care of my dear friend Fowke do H. M. S.

Blanche. In accord with the request of this gentleman, I am distributing the Testaments — selling or giving them away. [. . .]

In my experience, I have discovered that the Testament does not have the same demand as the [complete] Bible. . . . The only reason that I can attribute to this fact is that those who have any desire to own the Scriptures prefer to have the whole Bible rather than just a part of it. I have seen among the people a great eagerness to have the Bible, but I think that in most cases this is born not out of love of its blessed contents, but rather out of curiosity to know that which was for so long hidden from their eyes. One can hope that while they satisfy their curiosity, influence will accompany the examination of the divine oracles, conviction will become in this way firm and the knowledge of divine things so begun and increased that they may be made wise for eternal life. In any case, whatever the motive that moves them, seeing a demand for the Scriptures is hopeful circumstance and as long as this disposition is evident, I am willing to fulfill it as extensively as the circumstances permit. . . .

Source: D. A. Reily, *História documental do Protestantismo no Brasil* (São Paulo, 1993), p. 75. — *Further Reading:* Bastian, *Protestantismus,* p. 109; Prien, *Geschichte,* pp. 742-747; Latourette, *Expansion V,* pp. 109f.

279. Brazil: Anglo-Saxon Missionary Protestantism (1862)

The first missionary of the North-American Presbyterian Church to Brazil was Ashbel Green Simonton (1833-1867) from West Hannover, Pennsylvania. After a born-again experience and theological study, he dedicated himself to Brazil. On May 19, 1861, Simonton celebrated his first worship service in Rio de Janeiro, which led to many conversions. The first (re-)baptism of the converted, among whom there was one Brazilian, took place on January 12, 1862. The day is remembered as the founding date of the Presbyterian Church in Brazil.

Sunday, the 12th [of January 1862], we celebrated the Lord's Supper, receiving Henry E. Milford and Cardoso Camilo de Jesus by profession of faith. In this way, we organized ourselves as the Church of Jesus Christ in Brazil. It was a moment of joy and satisfaction. Much earlier than my little faith had expected, God offered us the first fruits of the mission. [. . .] Communion was directed by Mr. [Francis Joseph Christopher] Schneider and myself in English and Portuguese. Upon his request and according to what we thought best, after much study and a certain hesitation, Mr. Cardoso was baptized. He took an examination that satisfied Mr. Schneider and me completely, without leaving any doubt in our minds about the sincerity of his conversion. Thanks be to God for the confirmation of our weak faith, for we see that we did not preach the Gospel in vain.

Source: M. A. Rizzo (ed.), *Simonton. Inspirações de uma existência* (São Paulo, 1962), p. 82, quoted in: D. A. Reily, *História documental do Protestantismo no Brasil* (São Paulo, 1993), p. 118. — *Further Reading:* Bastian, *Protestantismus,* pp. 130-146; Prien, *Geschichte,* pp. 825-843; C. J. Hahn, "Evangelical Worship in Brazil" (Theol. Diss. Edinburgh, 1970 [unpubl.]); W. R. Read, *New Patterns of Church Growth in Brazil* (Grand Rapids, 1965), pp. 45-83; J. M. Bonino, *Faces of Latin American Protestantism* (Grand Rapids, 1997), pp. 27-39; Latourette, *Expansion V,* p. 122.

280. Nicaragua: Native American Moravian Indian Communities (1849)

Moravian German missionaries arrived from Jamaica on the east coast of Nicaragua in 1849 in the Mosquitia region, which was at the time under British influence and later formed an autonomous reservation between 1860 and 1894. The Moravian missionaries turned their attention first to the mixed population of Creoles in urban areas. After 1855 they also worked among the Misquito, Suma and Rama Native American tribes. Their learning of the Native American languages and intensive evangelistic work led to the success of their mission, as did the training of Indian congregational helpers and pastors. Thus Protestant models became part of Native American culture and contributed to their renewal, the result being an ethnic Protestantism on Nicaragua's Atlantic coast in today's Zelaya Province. The missionary, Heinrich Ziock, reports about a debate with the inhabitants of a village in the north of Mosquitia.

But also spiritual conversations were held, and the Natives like to use our get-togethers to seek clarity concerning the application of specific "Christian laws" as they call God's word. During these which they hold among themselves. In the end, after all the pros and cons have been discussed, the missionary is asked to make the final decision over the debated question. Therefore, I must carefully follow each discussion point in order to give a final judgment. In this manner, they kept me up in *Sandyhay* until midnight once, while I, dead tired from my trip, yearned for my hammock. [. . .]

The third topic of discussion was the question of holy Sundays. I certainly don't want to go into this issue here, but just mention, that the Indians in this regard have very strict opinions and only allow that the most important work be performed. In Quamvatla, for example, it so happened that a woman of the *Wita* [chieftain] was condemned to long and hard labor because on Sunday morning she had sewn on a loose shirt button for her husband. — If the Indians are traveling, however, or if they are working at a job, they sometimes get into a situation where, in their opinion, they must profane the Day of our Lord. Once a man accused himself of this sin because he had eaten beef that was known to have been slaughtered on Sunday. He initially would not eat anything; however, after fasting the whole day, he was so hungry that in the evening he could not resist the temptation any longer.

Source: H. Ziock, Moskitiküste. "Bericht Br. Ziocks von seiner 2. Missionsreise vom 17-20 April 1891," in: *Missionsblatt der Brüdergemeinde* 55 (1891), pp. 365-379, 368, 370f; also published in: E. von Oertzen et al. (eds.), *The Nicaraguan Mosquitia in Historical Documents 1844-1927* (Berlin, 1990), pp. 225, 227. — *Further Reading:* L. Rossbach, ". . . die armen wilden Indianer mit dem Evangelium bekannt machen," in: K. Meschkat u.a. (eds.), *Mosquitia* (Hamburg, 1987), pp. 65-98; idem, "Indian Life through the Eyes of Moravian Missionaries," in: von Oertzen et al. (eds.), ibid., pp. 41-59; Latourette, *Expansion V*, pp. 104f; Barrett, *WCE I*, pp. 543-546.

281. Mexico: Civil Status of Protestants (1843)

Despite religious tolerance for Protestants, their position in society remained marginal. Inter-confessional marriages were rejected by both the Catholic clergy and the upper class, though occasionally sanctioned after humiliating procedures. An example is the report of a German Protestant merchant, Adolf Riensch, who lived in Mexico for eleven years and married a Catholic woman.

Only when Haas promised to become Catholic, did the elderly gentleman [the bride's father] give his consent. [. . .] The poor young lover was treated badly by the Catholic priests. He first had to take lessons on the duties and rules of the Catholic church from the *Cura* [priest], he had to knock on the closed church door, dressed in penitent garments, and while standing outside, answer the question given from inside: "A poor lost sinner who asks to be accepted into the arms of the only true religion" and so on. Then came further formalities that ended with the testimony of parents and relations. [. . .] However, it took weeks — an agonizing time for the new Catholic — before all difficulties were taken away and the document received that allowed for the marriage union. [. . .] Before this formality took place, poor Haas had to walk in the streets with a candle in solemn procession and had to present a general confession as well as give his solemn promise to fulfill all duties that the Church stipulates for married couples.

Source: A. Riensch, "Erinnerungen aus meinem Leben während der Jahre 1830-1858" (Hamburg, 1960), p. 81, quoted in: Bastian, *Protestantismus*, pp. 114f. — *Further Reading:* ibid., pp. 121-130; Latourette, *Expansion V*, pp. 75-77; K. Latourette, *Christianity in a Revolutionary Age.* Vol. 3 (London, 1961), pp. 303-310; Dussel, *Church*, pp. 318-322; Barrett, *WCE I*, pp. 494-500.

IV. LATIN AMERICA 1890-1945

A. Catholicism Becomes More Roman and European

282. The Latin American Plenary Council of 1899 in Rome

With his letter of December 25, 1898, Leo XIII called the first Latin American Plenary Council in Rome. In this document he stated that, since the four-hundredth anniversary of the discovery of America (1892), he had concentrated intensely on the question of how to guard the interests of the Latin race *(sic)* to which more than half of the New World belonged. He thought it best to invite all the bishops of the new states to a council. He left it up to them to choose the place. For practical reasons most of them opted for Rome. The Pope was happy to agree since he saw in this, among other things, proof of their love for the Holy See. The Council dealt with questions of faith, cult, church discipline and order, interaction with non-Catholics, whom the Council still called "heretics," and lastly with pastoral care or missionary work. The Council was opened with pomp and circumstance on May 28, 1899, and ended on July 9, 1899. The selection below documents the state of awareness of the Catholic Church with respect to ecumenical affairs (a) and missionary work among the pagans (c) as well as the important role that the Catholic universities in Latin America (b) and the Latin American College founded by Pius IX in Rome (d) should play in the renewal of Catholicism. Most of the bishops who participated in the Plenary Council had already graduated from this college.

a. Relations with Non-Catholics

Let our faithful be advised that it is in no way permitted to celebrate with heretics any religious act in which they participate by faith, nor may they have communion in sacred things; and that it is absolutely forbidden to attend the sermons preached in the heretics' meetings, or their worship services, as if they were participating in them. Those who in this way join the heretics, as well as those who receive them, direct them, and defend them, will incur excommunication *latae sententiae*, which is specifically reserved to the Roman Pontiff.

b. The Establishment of Catholic Universities

It is to be desired that every republic or district in Latin America have a truly Catholic University which would serve as a center of sciences, literature, and the good arts. Although this cannot be done immediately in all places, the way should at least be prepared and the means arranged for achieving it.

c. Missions among the Indians

It is the grave duty of the ecclesiastical as well as civil authority to seek to carry civilization to the tribes that remain faithless, by means of evangelical preaching. . . . Neither Bishops nor priests, knowing that there are still unconverted Indians in the territory under their jurisdiction, can assume that they have fulfilled their pastoral duties if, concerning themselves only with the faithful, they do not strive to bring these others out of the darkness of faithlessness and call them to Christ. . . . Since experience shows that the greatest obstacle to the propagation of the faith among the faithless is ignorance of the Indian languages, care must be taken that the priests charged with converting them, or who have parishes in or near territory inhabited by the faithless, learn the language of the local tribe. . . . Wherefore the Apostolic See has desired, recommended and ordered nothing so frequently and so widely as that the Missionaries learn quickly, and come to master, the languages of the peoples that they are charged with evangelizing.

d. Commendation of the "Pius Latin American Seminary" in Rome

For the spiritual benefit of all Latin America, we strongly commend the Pius Latin American Seminary in Rome, in which so many and illustrious evangelical preachers and priests have been educated in the Capital of the Christian World and under the eyes of the Roman Pontiffs, and in which many worthy followers are now being educated. We therefore instruct the Bishops of all our Provinces to protect and promote it, and we declare that only students who enjoy good health and are endowed with outstanding talent and manly spirit should be sent there.

Source: (a) Pontifica Comisión para América Latina, *Acta et decreta concilii plenarii Americae Latinae in urbe celebrati anno domini MDCCCXCIX* (Vatican City, 1999) (A facsimile of the first edition 1906), p. 96; (b) ibid., pp. 394-395; (c) ibid., pp. 435-437; (d) ibid., p. 419. — *Further Reading:* Pontificia Commissio pro America Latina (ed.), *Los últimos cien años de la evangelización en América Latina* (Città del Vaticano, 2000); L. Medina Ascensio, *Historia del Colegio Pío Latinoamericano* (Roma, 1858-1978, Mexico City, 1979); F. Morando, "Il primo Concilio Plenario Latinoamericano" (unpublished thesis) (Rome, 1981); Dussel, *Church,* pp. 129ff; R. Azzi e.a. (eds.), *Theologiegeschichte der Dritten Welt. Lateinamerika* (Munich, 1993), pp. 220-230; Latourette, *Expansion V,* pp. 68ff.

283. Brazil: Immigration from Non-Iberian Europe

The constant stream of immigrants during the latter half of the nineteenth and the early part of the twentieth century contributed to the diversification and modification of Brazilian Catholicism. Those Germans, Italians and Poles who had Catholic roots in their homeland brought their specific forms of Catholicism with them. They often established language-based congregations that were ministered to by clergy from their homeland. An "immigrant Catholicism" that chose its clergy from among the immigrant descendants was dominant in the south and some regions of central Brazil. Document a reflects the situation of the "Igreja da Glória" congregation in Juiz de Fora (Minas Gerais, Brazil). German immigrants who had lived there since 1856 found their way to this congregation and were initially served by the Brazilian priests from the main church. After the arrival of Dutch Redemptorists, the congregation yearned for and achieved independence as a parish in 1894. The following document comes from the notes of a Dutch missionary in 1893. In document b Joáo Becker (Archbishop of Porto Alegre), a Brazilian bishop of German ancestry, emphasized the right of German immigrants to receive pastoral care in their mother tongue. This is a principle that the Catholic Church stresses with regard to contemporary pastoral care for migrant workers in central Europe (guest worker generation). This has also led to the creation of "foreign missions," similar to those in the USA and Germany, held in the mother tongue of the immigrants.

a. Development of Parish of Catholic Immigrants (1893)

Juiz-de-Fora is a very extensive parish with about 30,000 souls. The city itself, twenty years ago a small place without importance, has now developed considerably with almost 20,000 inhabitants and is growing more and more. In the parish there are many French and Polish but primarily Italian and German immigrants. Within the urban perimeters, there are three churches: the Mother church with the vicar forane, Dr. Café, the *Dos Passos* Church with two priests, and the German church. Besides these, at a distance of two or three leagues from the city, one can find the chapels of *Grama, São Pedro, Santana,* etc. In general, the people are quiet, although religious indifference is widespread. Before our arrival, 80 percent did not go to mass on Sundays or attend religious festivals and even worse were the number who attended Easter. Very many lived or live in illicit unions and most die without the sacraments.

Briefly, we would like to note that the situation of almost all the parishes of this diocese is the same if not worse, even though the Mariana diocese enjoys the privilege of having been governed (from 1844 to 1875) by the Holy Bishop Dom Vicoso and is considered to be the best organized in Brazil. From this we can have an idea of the religious and moral level of this poor land.

b. On the Right of German-Speaking Catholics to Preserve Their Culture (1912)

The German-Brazilian Catholics should and must preserve their distinctiveness, their language and literature, and their customs and good traditions in toto. And if it became necessary, I would guarantee this since the loss of such cultural values would be a great pity.

Source: (a) "Congregatio Sanctissimi Redemptoris, Crônica da Nossa Casa em Juiz de Fora sob o título de N.ª Sr.ª da Glória (1894-1923)," in: Centro da Memória da Igreja de Juiz de Fora: Arquivo. Seminário Arquidiocesano Santo Antônio, Juiz de Fora — MG. Signatur: Isaho V.I.39, pp. 13f; (b) P. F. Diel, *Ein katholisches Volk, aber eine Herde ohne Hirte* (St. Augustin, 2001), p. 61. — *Further Reading:* F. Weber, *Gewagte Inkulturation* (Mainz, 1996); L. van den Hoogen, "The Romanization of the Brazilian Church," in: A. Droogers et al. (eds.), *Popular Power in Latin American Religions* (Saarbrücken, Fort Lauderdale, 1991), pp. 128-152; E. Willems, "Immigrants and Their Assimilation in Brazil," in: T. Lynn Smith et al. (eds.), *Brazil, Portrait of Half a Continent* (Westport, Conn., 1972), pp. 209-225; Latourette, *Expansion V*, pp. 85f. 98-101; Dussel, *Church*, pp. 129-137, 195f; Latourette, *Expansion V*, pp. 68ff.

284. Brazil: Problems with Popular Piety

Here a German missionary expresses his problems with Brazilian popular piety which, in his eyes, should frequently be equated with superstition. In contrast, Polish and Italian Catholics had fewer problems with this.

As a result of inadequate religious education superstition is getting out of control. God is taken into consideration less than the saints. On the other hand, the Holy Spirit and the Sacred Heart of Jesus enjoy particular veneration, not, however, as God, but because they are "holy." Every Brazilian has a family altar on which numerous saints *(santos)* are placed. Whoever among them proves to be the most helpful gets the place of honor; but if this saint is hard of hearing, then he or she is placed in the corner. If the saint still does not give up his or her hard-heartedness, then he or she must feel the anger of the people and is placed outside in the rain as a punishment.

Source: P. F. Diel, *Ein katholisches Volk, aber eine Herde ohne Hirte* (St. Augustin, 2001), p. 343. — *Further Reading:* F. Weber, *Gewagte Inkulturation* (Mainz, 1996); J. Meier, ". . . dem zerfallenden und dem Verderben zueilenden Katholizismus Brasiliens Hülfe bringen," in: *ZMR 77* (1993), pp. 3-24; A. Droogers et al. (eds.), *Popular Power in Latin American Religions* (Saarbrücken: Fort Lauderdale, 1991), pp. 128-152; T. Lynn Smith et al. (eds.), *Brazil, Portrait of Half a Continent* (Westport, Conn., 1972); Dussel, *Church*, pp. 129-137, 195f; Latourette, *Expansion V*, pp. 68ff.

B. Confessional Pluralization

285. Protestant Emigrant Cubans in the USA (1880)

Many Cuban immigrants became Protestant in the United States of America, joining Spanish-speaking churches such as the Iglesia de Santiago Apóstol in New York in 1866, as well as other Cuban Protestant congregations primarily in Key West. Their members were known for their strong patriotism during the time of the Cuban struggle for independence from 1868 to 1898, after which a portion returned to an independent Cuba. There the Protestants built cells, spreading the new faith. Joaquín de Palma, probably the first Protestant Cuban pastor, writes in 1880 about the beginnings of congregations in exile in the USA.

The few Cubans who built the "Santiago" Church [in New York] were pioneers to the conversion of the Latin Race of the Americas to the purity of the Protestant belief. This was also the first organized church where the prayer book [i.e., the Anglican Common Book of Prayer] was read in the Spanish language. We can claim that the "Santiago" Mission . . . can be considered as the mother church of [Cuban] Protestantism, not only because of its historical uniqueness, but also because of the influence that it had. [. . .] Several of the original members of the Episcopal congregation founded in Key West were previously members of the "Santiago" congregation. Exactly while this was the first Episcopal Church in which the Spanish language was used, so I have the honor of being the first Cuban — almost 10 years ago — to be ordained for the Ministry.

Source: T. Tschuy, *Hundert Jahre Kubanischer Protestantismus (1968-1961)* (Frankfurt a. M., 1978), pp. 71f. — *Further Reading:* G. Castellanos, *Misión a Cuba y motivos de Cayo Hueso* (La Habana, 1944); M. A. Ramos, *Panorama del protestantismo en Cuba* (San José, 1986), pp. 91-106; Latourette, *Expansion V,* 124; K. Latourette, *Christianity in a Revolutionary Age,* vol. 3 (London, 1961), pp. 316f.

286. Brazil: Beginnings of the Pentecostal Movement (1911)

Two Swedish Baptists, Daniel Berg (1885-1963) and Gunnar Vingren (1879-1933), immigrated to the USA in 1902 and 1903, and affiliated themselves to the emerging Pentecostal movement. Berg belonged to William Durham's Church in Chicago, and Vingren studied at Charles Parham's Bible School in Topeka, Kansas. Together they arrived at the end of 1910 in Belém, Pará, in northeast Brazil, and worked in the Baptist congregation there. Due to differing views on the work of the Holy Spirit, Berg and Vingren, together with another eighteen Baptists, were expelled from the congregation — probably on June 13, 1911. From then on, they celebrated their own worship services. This was the beginning of the independent Pentecostal movement in Brazil and the founding of further

Pentecostal congregations (Assembleias de Deus). Daniel Berg reports about the separation of the communities in the following document.

One evening the local [Baptist] preacher appeared in our simple premises. When he opened the door, a wave of song and prayers struck him. We got up and invited him to take part in our improvised Service. He refused and declared that it was now time to make a decision. He said that a short time before he had discovered that people had dared to engage in a discussion of doctrine, something that had never happened before. He accused us of sowing doubt and unrest and of being separatists.

Gunnar Vingren got up and declared that we did not desire any division. On the contrary, we wanted unity among everyone. If only everyone had the experience of the baptism of the Spirit, we would never be divided. On the contrary, we would then be more than brothers, like a family.

The local preacher spoke again. The discussion was open. He said that the Bible did indeed speak about the baptism of the Spirit and also said that Jesus healed the sick. But that was in *those* days. He said that it would be absurd if educated people of our time believed that such things could happen today. We had to be realistic — he continued — and not waste time with dreams and false prophecies. Nowadays we had knowledge to know what to do with it. 'If you do not mend your ways and recognize your error, it is my duty to inform all the Baptist congregations and to warn them about your false doctrine.' [. . .]

Hoping for an expression in his support, the preacher let his eyes sweep round the room. In vain. He turned to me and brother Vingren and said, 'I have come to a decision. From now on you may not meet here any longer. Look for another place. After what has happened here we no longer want you.' Then he turned to the small group of people and asked, 'How many of you are in agreement with the false teaching?' Eighteen people resolutely raised their hands. They knew that that meant their expulsion from the [Baptist] church.

Source: H. McKennie Goodpasture (ed.), *Cross and Sword* (Maryknoll, 1989), pp. 195f — *Further Reading:* W. J. Hollenweger, *Enthusiastisches Christentum* (Wuppertal, Zürich, 1969), pp. 79-88; idem, "Evangelism and Brazilian Pentecostal," in: *Ecumenical Review* 20 (1968), pp. 163-170; W. Read, *New Patterns of Church Growth in Brazil* (Grand Rapids, 1965), pp. 117-143; Prien, *Geschichte,* pp. 857-875; Bastian, *Protestantismus,* pp. 201-203; E. Willems, *Followers of the New Faith* (Nashville, 1967), pp. 118-122; J. M. Bonino, *Faces of Latin American Protestantism* (Grand Rapids, 1997), pp. 53-78.

287. Panama Congress 1916: Beginnings of an Inter-Protestant Network

Contrary to the conclusions of the World Missionary Conference in Edinburgh in 1910 (cf. document 70), North American missionaries saw Catholic Latin America as being only superficially Christianized and therefore a valid Protestant missionary field. In 1916, in the middle of World War I, a congress on "Christian Work in Latin America" was held in Panama. The goal of the conference — which was dominated by North American associations — was the coordinated organization of mission work in Latin America. A gesture towards ecumenicism was attempted by inviting Catholic observers, but none chose to appear. Contrary to the Latin American Plenary Council of 1899 in Rome (cf. document 282) and similar to Edinburgh in 1910, situational analysis and structured criticism were the concerns. At the same time the growing nationalism of Latin American societies was particularly emphasized and identified as a stimulus for the establishment of independent churches and the organization of national and pan-continental cooperation.

National ideals as a unifying motif:

Any survey of the forces making for unity in Latin America would not be complete without taking into account the strong nationalistic spirit of these countries. That this feeling; will be active in the evangelical Churches in the future is inevitable [. . .]

1. The strong nationalistic feeling among the churches

Probably in no other country except Japan have the missionaries encountered so strong a nationalistic feeling as in some Latin-American lands. It is one appeal that can always be counted on everywhere to bring a sympathetic response. It would seem that the countries in which it has shown itself most strongly in connection with the evangelical Churches are Brazil, Chile, Porto Rico and Mexico. If well trained leaders are gradually developed and put in control, it may fairly be expected that larger advances will be made and that a stronger Church will develop, even though for a time schismatic tendencies might show themselves during the period of immature church consciousness. In fact, a desire to secure eventually a national Church to which all the evangelical Christians shall belong is discernible in parts of Latin America, just as it is in China, though less organized.

[. . .]

Another confirmation of this underlying desire among the Latin Americans for national evangelical Churches is found in Mexico. A movement of independence from foreigners and missionary support was begun by preachers who had been previously employed by mission Boards, some of them from the United States, but most of them Mexicans. They refused to have anything to do with mission Boards, identifying them with a foreign invasion. They appealed particularly to the patriotism of the people, and naturally to their prejudices. At one time in the Mexican churches in San Antonio, Texas, there was such a strong movement that the denominational churches were practically depopulated, and all the Mexicans came together in an immense *"Iglesia Evangelica Independiente."* This movement grew very rapidly for a while. The pastors received no stated salary. It was largely wrecked on the financial rock, though there are still some strong congregations existing and doing good work. While it seemed to the missionaries that the whole movement was selfish, yet its great temporary success showed the strong appeal nationalism makes and the tendency among all the people to unite in a national Church which refuses to recognize the differences which exist in the United States.

Source: Committee on Cooperation in Latin America (ed.), *Christian Work in Latin America.* Vol. III (New York, 1917), pp. 65ff. — *Further Reading:* Bastian, *Protestantismus,* pp. 162-170; Prien, *Geschichte,* pp. 794-800, 914-924; Latourette, *Expansion VII,* pp. 172-185; H. P. Beach, *An Outline and Interpretation of the CCWLA* (New York, 1916); J. M. Bonino, *Faces of Latin American Protestantism* (Grand Rapids, 1997), pp. 1-25; Dussel, *Church,* pp. 332-335.

288. Beginnings of an Afro-Brazilian Religion: Umbanda (1939)

Umbanda is a genuine Brazilian religion that comprises all levels of society. Umbanda combines elements of (white) Spiritism in the tradition of Alan Kardec, (black) Afro-Brazilian cults (Candomble, Macumba), Indian religiosity, as well as Christianity. Central to the religion is the belief in a world of spiritual beings: deities, mythical figures, as well as the souls of the deceased. The latter become incarnate in initiated mediums in séance events, thereby making communication with the real world of humans possible. The practice of the Umbanda religion began under the cover of Spiritism, and it was legally allowed for the first time in 1934. Zélio de Moraes, who maintained the first place of worship, also set up seven more so-called Umbanda places (terreiros) in Rio de Janeiro between 1930 and 1937. The new religion was established definitively with their merger into a federation of the "União Espírita da Umbanda do Brasil" in 1939. The founding myth that has been passed down describes how the seventeen-year-old Zélio de Moraes allegedly took part in a spiritual sitting on November 15, 1908, and became the decisive protagonist for the formation of the Umbanda religion.

Zélio was invited to participate in the [Spiritist session] . . . [and he was] taken [there] by strange force against his will. [. . .] This attitude caused an enormous commotion among those present, primarily because, at the same time this happened, surprising manifestations of *caboclos* [spirits of indigenous] and *pretos-velhos* [Afro-brazilian spirits] occurred. The director of the session considered all of that to be absurd and warned them harshly, citing "their spiritual backwardness" and inviting them to leave. [. . .]

Again a strange force overtook the young Zélio and through him a spirit said: "Why did you repel the presence of the cited spirits, you were not even dignified enough to hear their messages. Could it be because of your social origins and color?" From this admonition from the Entity who was with the medium Zélio there arose great confusion [. . .].

Still in trance, the medium Zélio responded, "If you want a name, than have it be this: I am the *Caboclo das Sete Encruzilhadas* [Caboclo of the Seven Crossings], because for me there will be no closed paths." The seer interrupted the Entity saying that he identified him as a caboclo but that he saw in him traces of priestly clothes. The Entity responded then: "What you see in me, are traces of an earlier existence. I was priest and my name was Gabriel Malagrida. Accused of witchcraft, I was sacrificed in the fires of the Inquisition in Lisbon, in the year 1761. But in my last physical existence, God gave me the privilege to be born as a Brazilian caboclo."

And still using the medium, he announced the type of mission that brought him to Astral: to establish the basis for a ceremony, in which all of the spirits of *caboclos* and *pretos-velhos* could perform the determinations of the Spiritual Plan, and that on the next day [November 16, 1908] he would descend to the residence of the medium at 8 o'clock in the evening and would found a Temple where there would be equality for all, whether living [incarnated] or dead [unincarnated]. [. . .]

Source: D. F. Trindade, *Umbanda e sua história* (São Paulo, 1991), pp. 59-61. — *Further Reading:* R. Bastide, *The African Religions of Brasil* (Baltimore etc., 1978), pp. 304-342; D. Brown, *Umbanda* (Ann Arbor, 1986); R. Ortiz, *A morte branca do feitiçeiro negro* (Petrópolis, 1978); G. Huizer, "Religious Penetration and Power Struggle in Latin America," in: A. Droogers et al. (eds.), *Popular Power in Latin American Religions* (Saarbrücken, Fort Lauderdale, 1991), pp. 26-54; H. Lindsay, "Pretos Velhos in Brazil," in: V. G. Burnett (ed.), *On Earth as It Is in Heaven* (Wilmington, Del., 2000), pp. 107-132. H.-A. Johnson, "Umbanda: A Modern Brazilian Religion," in: D. J. Hesselgrave (ed.), *Dynamic Religious Movements* (Grand Rapids, 1978), pp. 247-269.

289. Brazil: German Immigrants and the Third Reich (1934)

Protestant immigrants of German extraction in Brazil were partly enthused about the emergence of the National Socialist movement in Germany. On the other hand, they often regarded nationalism as a matter of cultural tradition *(Volkstum)*. In any case, the inner struggles of the German Protestants also had an impact on Brazil. The National Socialist pastors in Brazil organized themselves into the movement of "German Christians of Brazil" and appointed Erich Knäpper as their regional leader on December 31, 1933. Knäpper expressed their aims in a communiqué to the secretary of the Lutheran Synod, Ferdinand Schlünzen. It is likely that the presidents of the other three synods of German congregations received the same communiqué.

I humbly would like to inform the Evangelical Lutheran Synod of Santa Catarina, Paraná and other states that I have been nominated on December 31, 1933 as Director of the "German Christians" for Brazil. As a result of the [German] *Reichskirche* [dominated by the "German Christians"] and also of the four Synods here, which remain in a much too loose relationship, our main concern should be to create a unity that can face the State as one Church. In Rio Grande do Sul, the National Socialist Pastorate, which includes two thirds of all pastors as party supporters, has been organized for a long time and has formed a section within the Party. All party members are also German Christians. The task of the NS-Pastorate is large, since for example, it concerns itself with maintaining the synods as well as the foreign pastors. It is possible to extend the NS-Pastorate throughout Brazil. It would be best if a Trustee were nominated for the area of these Synods. I await your reply to this letter. Heil Hitler — Knäpper.

Source: M. Dreher, *Kirche und Deutschtum in der Entwicklung der Evangelischen Kirche Lutherischen Bekenntnisses in Brasilien* (Göttingen, 1978), p. 123. — *Further Reading:* ibid., pp. 119-148; H.-J. Prien, *Evangelische Kirchwerdung in Brasilien* (Gütersloh, 1989), pp. 436-461; H.-J. Prien (ed.), *Das Evangelium im Abendland und in der Neuen Welt* (Frankfurt, 2000), pp. 572-603.

C. Faces of Latin American Catholicism

290. Brazil: Antônio Conselheiro and His Movement "Os canudos"

At the end of the nineteenth century, the layman Antônio Vicente Mendes Maciel (1830-1897), called "Conselheiro" (advisor), traveled through the Brazilian *Sertão*, or the hinterland, as an ascetic and itinerant preacher. He soon acquired an excellent reputation among the simple peasants (document a), who revered him as a prophet. His unorthodox conduct aroused mistrust among the clergy and with the bishop, so much so that the latter forbade him to preach in parishes (document b), not least of all because Conselheiro preached a strict morality and a more all-embracing view of Christianity. After the fall of Emperor Dom Pedro II in 1889 and the proclamation of a republic with the progress-oriented motto "Ordem e progresso" (Order and Progress), Brazil was to be brought into line with the spirit of the times. This meant separation of the Catholic Church from the State, introduction of religious freedom and civil marriage, and abolition of the aristocracy. Conselheiro condemned the new times as the work of the devil and propagated messianic prophesies about the return of the legendary King Dom Sabastião (d. 1578, Sebastianism) in order to restore his Catholic empire and put an end to the godless republic. Many simple people followed Conselheiro on his way into the Brazilian hinterland in order to find the promised land there and to create a messianic contra-society. Between 1896 and 1897 the army waged the so-called "War of the Canudos" against them. Conselheiro died on September 22, 1897. Today he is one of the most researched personalities of Brazilian history.

a. The Beginnings of Conselheiro during the Monarchy (1877)

An individual who calls himself António Conselheiro has appeared in the northern region of the Sertão. He holds great influence over the spirit of the popular classes and uses his strange appearance and ascetic customs to impose himself on their ignorance and naïvete. He has let his beard and hair grow, he wears a cotton tunic, and he eats very little. He looks almost like a mummy. Accompanied by two disciples, he spends the day reciting the rosary, singing litanies, preaching and giving advice to the multitudes that follow him; he does this wherever the priests permit it; in the disguise of religious sentiments he gathers the people and leads his flock. He seems to be intelligent, but not an educated man.

b. Conselheiro's Preaching Prohibited by the Archbishop of Bahia (1882)

Having been informed that in the central parishes of this archdiocese an individual named António Conselheiro is preaching, to the people who gather to hear him, superstitious doctrines and an excessively rigid morality that perturbs their consciences and greatly weakens the authority of the priests, we order Your Reverence not to consent to such abuses in your parish, but rather to inform all the faithful that We definitively forbid them to meet to hear such speeches. For the holy mission of instructing the people belongs only to the ministers of the religion and is the exclusive competence of the Catholic Church. A layperson, whoever he is, even an educated and virtuous person, has no authority to do so.

c. Conselheiro's Prophecies against the Republic (1889)

In truth I tell you that while some nations quarrel among themselves, Brazil with Brazil, England with England, Prussia with Prussia, Don Sebastião will rise out of the waves with all his army. Ever since the creation of the world he has suffered under a spell along with all his army, which he has called to a state of war. And when the spell was cast he sheathed his sword, securing it in the stone and saying: "Farewell world, you will endure perhaps a thousand years or more, but in no case as many as two thousand." That day he will come out with his army and will slay with the sword all who have played a part in the Republic. The end of the war will take place at the Holy House of Rome and the blood will reach to the High Assembly.

Source: (a) Euclydes da Cunha, *Les terres de Canudos* (Rio de Janeiro, 1947), p. 117; (b) ibid., pp. 122-123; (c) ibid., p. 121. — *Further Reading:* E. Hoornaert, *The Memory of the Christian People*

(Tunbridge Wells, 1988); idem, *Os anjos de Canudos. Uma revisao histórica* (Petrópolis, 1998); idem, Antônio Conselheiro, "Negociador do sagrado," in: S. Branão (ed.), *História das Religiões no Brasil* (Recife, 2001), pp. 39-77; CEHILA (ed.), *Antônio Conselheiro e a tragédia de Canudos* (São Paulo, 1986); A. Q. de França, *Antônio Conselheiro e a Guerra de Canudos* (Fortaleza, 2002); C. R. B. Graham, *A Brazilian Mystic: Being the Life and Miracles of Antonio Conselheiro* (William Heinemann, 1920); Alexandre H. Otten, *"Só Deus é grande"* (São Paulo, 1990); M. I. Pereira de Queiroz, *O Messianismo no Brasil e no Mundo* (São Paulo, 1991); D. Bartelt, *Nation gegen Hinterland. Der Krieg von Canudos in Brasilien. Ein diskursives Ereignis (1874-1903)* (Stuttgart, 2004).

291. Mexico: The "Cristiada" (1926-1929)

The anti-church measures of the 1917 constitution (nationalization of all churches, abolition of the right of the clergy to vote, restricted admission of clerics to one priest per 15,000 inhabitants, and much more) were toughened by P. E. Calles through his addition of thirty-three articles that were nailed to all church doors and which took effect on July 31, 1926 (among others, the expulsion of all foreign priests, imprisonment of many other priests, and suppression of Catholic lay organizations). The bishops excommunicated anyone who collaborated in the implementation of the new laws. In addition they forbade the priests to celebrate public Catholic worship in the churches under such circumstances; the churches were still supposed to remain open to the faithful. The bishops also recommended the development of types of catacomb churches. In conclusion they approved the *Cristiada,* the public uprising of the peasant Catholic population (the so-called *Cristeros*), who fought against the government in the name of the figure of Christ the King. Pope Pius XI decried the anti-Christian laws of the Mexican government in the encyclical *Iniquis Affictisque* of November 18, 1926, and expressed his admiration for the *Cristeros.* The fiercest phase of the conflict, with numerous victims on both sides, ended in 1929 with the resignation of Calles and the arrangement of a *modus vivendi* between the government and the episcopacy. The tensions persisted, however, until 1941 when Avila Camacho introduced a policy of respect for the religious feelings of the Mexican people. In document a the Jesuit Miguel Pro (1891-1927) tells, not without humor, about his work as a covert pastor in Mexico City and relates how he outwitted the secret police. Pro was later arrested, charged with participating in the murder of President Alvaro Obregón, and shot without due process on November 23, 1927. Shortly thereafter he was regarded as a martyr; he was beatified in 1988. In document b, the *Cristero* Francisco Campos relates the reasons why the peasants participated in the *Cristiada.*

a. Pastoral Care after the Prohibition of the Catholic Cult

I once wanted to distribute Holy Communion in a house of the Eucharistic stations; it was six o'clock in the morning. Suddenly a servant came running in with the terrifying message: *"Los Técnicos"* (our code for the police). Everyone turned pale, and there was confusion all round! I urged: "Just keep calm! Put away your Communion veils, spread yourselves out over the individual rooms, and don't make too much noise!"

On this day I wore a cap and a light-gray business suit which was already somewhat threadbare and discolored in some spots. In addition I lit a cigarette and puffed huge clouds of smoke. I had the Blessed Sacrament hidden on my chest. This is how I waited for the intruders. "A forbidden cult is being held here!" they shouted at me. I responded: "You must be joking!" "No we aren't, sir, a public ritual act was being performed here."

"Gentlemen, stop serving up such nonsense to me!"

"We saw the priest come in here!"

"You don't say, you jokers! Shall we bet half a glass of the 'water of life' that no priest is here?"

"We have orders to carry out a house search. Come with us!" . . .

No priest was found, of course, and the clever *Técnicos* had to content themselves with posting a lookout in front of the door. I said goodbye to them there with the words: "If I didn't have a date with a lady I would gladly stay with you until you have apprehended the impudent priest who dares to make such a fool of the commendable vigilance of such a laudable police force."

b. On the Causes of the People's Uprising of 1926-1929

On July 31, 1926, some men sent our Lord God away from their churches, from their altars, from Catholic homes, but other men brought him back again; these men did not see that the government had many soldiers, many arms, a lot of money to make war on them; they didn't see that, but what they saw was the need to defend their God, their Religion, the Holy Church their Mother; that is what they saw. Those men were not afraid to leave their homes, their parents, their children, their wives and everything they had; they went to the battlefields in search of our Lord God. The valleys, the mountains, the woods, the hills are witness that those men talked to the Lord our God with the Holy Name of Viva Christ the King, Viva the Holy Virgin of Guadalupe, Viva Mexico. These same places are witness that those men drenched the earth with their blood, and if that wasn't enough, they gave their very lives to bring our Lord God back again. And when our Lord God saw that these men were truly seeking him, he came back to their churches, to their altars, to Catholic homes, as we are seeing now, and he charged today's youth that if it should happen again, they must never forget the example set by our forefathers.

Source: (a) A. Dragon, *Opfertod in Mexiko* (Saarbrücken, 1933), pp. 123-125; (b) A. Azkue, *La Cristiada* (Barcelona, 2000), pp. 42-43. — *Further Reading:* A. Dragon, *Blessed Miguel Pro SJ: Martyr of Christ the King* (Anand, India, 1993); J. A. Meyer, *The Cristero Rebellion* (Cambridge,

1976); D. C. Bailey, ¡Viva Cristo Rey! The Cristero Rebellion and the Church-State Conflict in Mexico (Austin, 1974); P. A. Schell, Church and State Education in Revolutionary Mexico City (Tucson, 2003); J. Tuck, The Holy War in Los Altos: A Regional Analysis of Mexico's Cristero Rebellion (Tucson, 1982); M. Butler, Popular Piety and Political Identity in Mexico's Cristero Rebellion, Michoacán 1927-29 (Oxford, 2004); J. A. Foley, Colima, Mexico and the Cristero Rebellion (Chicago, 1979); W. Parsons, Mexican Martyrdom (New York, 1936); M. Sievernich, "Märtyrer im mexikanischen Kirchenkampf," in: GuL 61 (1988), pp. 285-302; P. C. Stanchina, Das Verhältnis von Staat und Kirche in Mexiko seit der Revolution von 1910/17 bis heute (Munich, 1978); H. W. Tobler, Die mexikanische Revolution (Frankfurt, 1984); Dussel, Church, pp. 222ff.

292. Peru: Conflict between the Supporters of the Indigenous and the Supporters of the Hispanics

The question of whether the Indians had really become Christians occupied intellectuals from the indigenous and Hispanic camps during the 1920s and 1930s. They reached conflicting decisions on this matter. José Carlos Mariátegui (1894-1930), the father of Latin American Marxism, regards the grandiose liturgy of Baroque Catholicism, which was enthusiastically received by the Indians, as the missionaries' decisive means of persuasion, but also, at the same time, as the reason for the superficial conversion of the Indians (document a). The Catholic and Hispanic author Victor Andrés Belaúnde (1883-1966), a contemporary and dialectical opponent of Mariátegui, assesses this situation differently (document b). He admits that the magnificent Catholic religious services did indeed contribute to the spread of the new religion; but this new religion has definitely touched and changed the souls of the Indians, as one can see in their reaction to affliction and in their veneration of Mary.

a. José Carlos Mariátegui: The Evangelization of the Indian (1928)

Catholicism, with its sumptuous mass and its sorrowful devotion, was perhaps the only religion able to attract a population that could not easily rise to a spiritual, abstract religion. It was also aided by its astonishing ability to accommodate to any historical epoch or setting. The work of absorbing old myths and appropriating pagan dates, which had begun many centuries earlier in the west, was continued in Peru. Lake Titicaca, apparently the birthplace of the Inca theocracy, is the site of the most famous shrine of the Virgin [cf. document 248]. The intelligent and scholarly writer Emilio Romero has interesting comments on the substitution of Catholic rites and images for Inca gods: "The Indians thrilled with emotion before the majesty of the Catholic ceremony. They saw the image of the sun in the shimmering brocade of the chasuble and cope and they saw the violet tones of the rainbow woven into the fine silk threads of the rochet. Perhaps they saw the quipus symbolized in the purple tassels of the abbot and the knotted cords of the Franciscan friar" [. . .]. The external trappings of Catholicism captivated the Indian, who accepted conversion and the cate-chism with the same ease and lack of comprehension. For a people who had never differentiated between the spiritual and temporal, political control incor-porated ecclesiastic control. The missionaries did not instill a faith; they in-stilled a system of worship and a liturgy, wisely adapting them to Indian cus-toms. Native paganism subsisted under Catholic worship.

b. Victor Andrés Belaúnde: Reply to J. C. Mariátegui (1931)

One can understand why Mariátegui, seeing only the liturgy and not the spirit of Catholicism, should argue that the missionary effort did not transform the religious soul of the Indian and that Catholic worship was simply juxtaposed on primitive fetishism. Today it is difficult to judge the results of the missionary action, preserved under unfavorable conditions by the secular Church in the Colony and in the Republic. On the other hand a religion of such profound, complex and mysterious spirituality as Catholicism would be almost impossi-ble to preserve among the masses. Even in advanced countries and educated so-cieties, reversions to superstition coexist with Catholic idealism. We should not be surprised by such commingling; in the Indian masses it only shows a fatal human weakness. Underneath it, on the other hand, are undeniable signs of the penetration of the Catholic spirit among the Indian masses. I should point out the two main ones: their collective reaction to pain, which in the Indian is not expressed in cool resignation but in prayer and hopefulness; and the breadth and intensity of the cult of Mary. These two facts are inseparable. . . .

One should not speak of the religious psychology of the Indian without an in-depth study of the history and present life of the sanctuaries, especially those of Copacabana and Guadalupe [see documents 242 and 248]. The Marian cult, brought by the Spaniards, has emerged in new incarnations or modalities as a natural flowering in American soil. The legends, facts or fiction — it no longer matters which — are purely Indian; they were initiated and revealed by Indians. As in the Middle Ages, the Marian cult is the cult of the people's soul. . . . There is a new link between the dominant and the dominated races; Indians, mestizos and whites all claim this common maternity.

Source: (a) J. C. Mariátegui, *Seven Interpretative Essays on Peruvian Reality* (Austin, London, 1974), pp. 134-135; (b) V. A. Belaúnde, *Obras completas,* vol. 3 (Lima, 1987), pp. 77-86. — *Further Reading:* Delgado, *Abschied,* pp. 323-330; idem, *Gott,* pp. 321-340; idem, "Missionstheologische und anthropologische Gemeinsamkeiten und Unterschiede zwischen Katholiken und Protestanten im Entdeckungszeitalter," in: *ZMR* 87 (2003), pp. 93-111; M. Sarkisyanz, *Temblor en los Andes. Profetas del resurgimiento indio en el Perú* (Quito, Rome, 1992); M. M. Marzal, *The In-dian Face of God in Latin America* (Maryknoll, 1996); idem, *La transformación religiosa peruana*

(Lima, 1983); idem, *El sincretismo iberoamericano* (Lima, 1985); P. Morandé, *Synkretismus und offizielles Christentum in Lateinamerika* (München, 1992); B. C. Hedrick, *Religious Syncretism in Spanish America* (Greeley, 1967); M. Greenfield, A. Droogers (eds.), *Reinventing Religions: Syncretism and Transformation in Africa and the Americas* (Oxford, 2001); G. Kruip, *Kirche und Gesellschaft im Prozeß ethisch-historischer Selbstverständigung* (Münster, 1996).

293. Brazil: Black African Popular Piety (1941)

Stefan Zweig, the Austrian author who immigrated to Brazil in 1938, where he and his wife committed suicide together in 1942, describes here Afro-Brazilian popular piety in the city of Salvador Bahia. The account gives an impression of the emotional character of this popular piety as well as of its intensity and its ardent nature which can culminate in ecstasy and cast a spell over the European observer. Zweig also regards the magnificent liturgy as an asset of Catholicism.

I asked the friendly priest who took me round if Bahia were still, as it once had been, the city of piety. With an almost imperceptible smile, he answered: "Yes, the people here are pious, but pious in their own way." [. . .]The negroes [. . .] have been for centuries the most faithful, eager, and passionate followers of the Church — with this difference, that their piousness has also inwardly a different shade of colour. [. . .] What really attracts them towards Catholicism is its splendour, its mysticism, its colour, the exuberance of its ritual, and even Anchieta [one of the first Jesuit-missionaries in Brazil, †1591], four hundred years ago, reported that what achieves the best results of conversion is music. To this good-natured race, with its senses so easily excited, religion today is still inseparably connected with festivity, joy and show. Every procession, every Mass, makes them thoroughly happy. The result is that Bahia is famous for its religious festivals. [. . .] So one does not have to be particularly fortunate to witness a festival in Bahia. I was, however, lucky enough to be on the spot for one of the most impressive, the annual celebration of Bomfim, the city's saint. This Bomfim, non-existent on the calendar, has in Bahia his own church, about an hour and a half from the city, with a beautiful view from the top of a hill. For a whole week it is the centre of all manner of celebration. [. . .] But the real, the unforgettable ceremony of this week is the *lavagem de Bomfim* — the cleaning of the church. The history of this custom, practised nowhere else, is typical of Bahia. The church of Bomfim was originally a Negro church; and it seems that at one time the priest told the congregation that it was a proper thing to do to clean and wash the floor of the church thoroughly the day before the anniversary. The black Christians accepted the order willingly. [. . .] But in keeping with their naive, childish mentality, this cleaning of the Church developed (as with all Negro religious activities) into a festival. They made competition out of the sweeping and polishing, as though it were their own sins they were endeavouring to wash away. Hundreds, thousands came from far and near, their number increasing every year. And suddenly the custom grew into a popular fete — one so wild and ecstatic that the clergy were scandalized and put an end to it all. But the people, determined to have their own holiday, compelled the return of the *lavagem de Bomfim*. Today it is a festival for the whole town, and one of the most impressive I have ever witnessed.

Source: S. Zweig, *Brazil: Land of the Future.* Trans. Andrew St. James (London, 1942), pp. 260-263. — *Further Reading:* R. Bastide, *Les Religions Africaines au Brésil* (Paris, 1960), pp. 265-281, 306-396; V. Berkenbrock, *Die Erfahrung der Orixás* (Bonn, 1995); H. Figge, *Geisterkult, Besessenheit und Magie in der Umbanda-Religion Brasiliens* (Freiburg, Munich, 1973); F. Rehbein, *Heil im Christentum und in afro-brasilianischen Kulten* (Bonn, 1989); J. Baumgartner (ed.), *Wiederentdeckung der Volksreligiosität* (Regensburg, 1979); B. C. Hedrick, *Religious Syncretism in Spanish America* (Greeley, 1967); M. Greenfield, A. Droogers (eds.), *Reinventing Religions: Syncretism and Transformation in Africa and the Americas* (Oxford, 2001); G. S. Wilmore, *Black Religion and Black Radicalism: An Interpretation of the Religious History of Afro-American People* (Maryknoll, 1983); L. E. Barrett, *Soul-force: African Heritage in Afro-American Religion* (Garden City, 1974); G. R. Jackson, *Afro-American Religion and Church and Race Relations* (Bloomington, 1969); J. L. Matory, *Black Atlantic Religion: Tradition, Transnationalism, and Matriarchy in the Afro-Brazilian Candomblé* (Princeton, 2005); F. D. Goodman, *Trance, Healing, and Hallucination: Three Field Studies in Religious Experience* (Huntington, 1982); D. DeG. Brown, *Umbanda: Religion and Politics in Urban Brazil* (New York, 1994); V. de Osa, *Umbanda. Brazil's Old and New Spiritism* (Bognor Regis, 1984); A. J. Langguth, *Macumba: White and Black Magic in Brazil* (New York, 1975).

D. THE EMERGENCE OF THE SOCIAL QUESTION

294. Gabriela Mistral: For a Social Christianity (1925)

It took some time for Leo XIII's encyclical *Rerum Novarum* (1891) on social issues to be received in Latin America. Social awareness first had to be awakened in Creole Catholicism after independence. Chile was a trailblazer here. Involved lay people and intellectuals, such as the poet Gabriela Mistral (1889-1957, recipient of the Nobel Prize for Literature in 1945), also made a contribution. An entirely undogmatic piety shows through in Mistral's work in connection with a tendency toward a mystical, Franciscan Christianity. She clear-sightedly discerned the alienation between the working masses and the church and called for a social Christianity she saw modeled in examples in Catholic Belgium and in Germany. Later on the social awakening would lead to the establishment of Catholic Action in the various Latin American countries as an expression of the "new Christianity."

In Latin America at present we have the sorry spectacle of an absolute divorce between the popular masses and religion, or rather, between democracy and

Christianity. . . . What I have seen is this: our Christianity, unlike the Anglo-Saxon version, has <u>divorced itself from the social sphere</u>, has treated it disdainfully at least, and has paralyzed or killed off any sense of justice; then others began to feel a sense of justice and claimed it for themselves. . . . The working people have been abandoned to their fate, to a truly <u>medieval servitude,</u> and that has caused this divorce between religion and human justice. Agitators have come to them, saying that Christianity is a kind of "siren song," intended to suppress their claims for justice; leaders have assured them that the search for the kingdom of heaven is incompatible with the creation of an earthly kingdom, that is, economic well-being. . . . Unworthy shepherds have told them that the two cannot go together, and the people have chosen to follow whoever gave them bread and a roof for their children. We cannot afford to lose so many souls, because no matter how much ours are worth, God will not forgive us for abandoning the multitudes who make up most of the world. Catholicism must win back what it has lost through negligence or selfishness. . . . Catholic Belgium is implementing a great program to benefit its workers and peasants, which puts those of us who have seen it to shame; Catholics in Germany are also doing something heroic, which in our countries would be seen as an alarming radicalism. We must prepare to do something similar, even if it means losing many of the privileges that we disingenuously describe as rights.

Source: (a) G. Mistral, *Escritos políticos* (Mexico City, 1994), pp. 272-275. — *Further Reading:* L. Vargas Saavedra (ed.), *Prosa religiosa de Gabriela Mistral* (Santiago, 1978); C. Taylor (ed.), *Sensibilidad religiosa de Gabriela Mistral* (Madrid, 1975); L. Fiol-Matta, *Authority and Women's Writing: Sor Juana Inés de la Cruz, Gabriela Mistral and Rigoberta Menchu* (New Haven, Conn., 1995); M. Arce de Vázquez, *Gabriela Mistral: The Poet and Her Work* (New York, 1964).

295. A. Hurtado: On the Social Condition and the Church in Latin America (1947)

The Jesuit Alberto Hurtado (1901-1952) established important social programs in Chile, such as the "Hogar de Cristo," championed the implementation of Catholic social teaching in word and deed, and exerted great influence on Catholic Action and on Chile's Catholic trade union movement. He was beatified in 1994. During a private audience with Pope Pius XII on October 8, 1947, he was able to present a memorandum in French on the social, religious, and political situation in Latin America and, above all, in Chile. The following excerpts have been taken from this document. The memorandum stands out due to its frank language, astute analysis of the situation, and the naming of the weaknesses found in Latin American Catholicism, but also because of its constructive suggestions for solving the problems as well as its ability to learn from Protestantism.

Latin America is facing a decisive moment in its history; its countries are subjected to a very rapid process of industrialization, resulting from the investment of foreign capital, especially from the United States. Our cities emerge every day, deprived of religious services and subjected to all the influences of moral destruction and Marxist propaganda. Europe looks upon Latin America as an easy escape for its excess population. These emigrants are part of the source of revolutionary social ferment. The Church lacks the means to confront these movements. To speak only of the clergy: there are only 22,000 priests, counting both secular and regular, for 130,000 baptized members. . . . The gravest danger in my opinion is that we are unaware of the danger. People believe we are still in the midst of profoundly Catholic countries; they think the social agitation is caused only by Russian gold and that Protestant propaganda is the effect of American dollars alone. The priests, even the bishops, do not seem to notice the enormous tragedy that will take us by surprise. . . .

Catholic social attitudes seem to be focused more on stopping the advance of communism than on reversing the proletarization of the masses. There has been no effort to put into practice the teachings of the encyclicals, and the doctrines themselves have been taught with extraordinary "prudence" in order not to alienate the ruling classes. The working masses are rising without us, and they know it. The youth of Catholic Action have taken some social positions, but they have been criticized by several bishops and have therefore come under suspicion of sympathizing with communism. . . .

It seems to me that the gravest problem is a loss of confidence in the hierarchy on the part of many of the faithful. In general the hierarchy is blamed for failing to understand the social moment in which we live, and it is not seen as serving the proletariat because of its excessive commitment to the wealthy classes.

Communism is an extremely grave danger, but there is a tendency to combat it mostly with negative means, favoring the formation of attack groups which may lead to a bloody and useless struggle. On the other hand there is a fear of taking steps toward the teaching of doctrine and social action.

The Protestant campaign has been strong and successful. It is not so much the fruit of North American gold as of a thirst for God. Wherever there is a lack of priests, the Protestants go from house to house preaching the Gospel and practicing charity.

In order to reach the people better, I think it necessary to facilitate attendance at Mass in worker neighborhoods. Otherwise the masses will be left out of touch with the Church. It is also necessary to call on the laity, and show trust in them, to carry out social action.

Source: A. Magnet, *El Padre Hurtado* (Santiago, 1977), pp. 303-304, 307. — *Further Reading:* A. Hurtado, *¿Es Chile un país católico?* (Santiago, 1992); M. Sievernich, "Anwalt der Armen in

Chile," in: *GuL* 67 (1994), 28-52; J. A. Castellón Covarrubias, *Identificarse con Jesucristo sirviéndolo en su misión* (Rome, 1996); K. A. Gilfeather, *Alberto Hurtado, S.J.: A Man after God's Own Heart* (Anand, India, 1995); J. Dear, *You Will Be My Witnesses: Saints, Prophets, and Martyrs* (Maryknoll, 2006).

V. LATIN AMERICA 1945-1990

A. THE PATH TO A NEW LATIN AMERICAN CHRISTIANITY

296. Integration of Protestant Churches (CELA), 1949

The first Latin American Protestant conference (Conferencia evangélica latinoamericana, CELA I) took place in Buenos Aires in 1949. It was initiated entirely by Latin Americans and united fifty-six delegates from fifteen countries. In their plan of action, the participants called for strengthened social engagement in numerous areas. In addition, they called for a national (rather than denominational) orientation of church work — an indicator of the awakening of a Latin American Protestant consciousness. In this sense it appealed to Protestant immigrant churches, whose identity was often bound to the culture and language of their members.

In view of the important work that the foreign speaking Protestant churches have undertaken in order to preserve the religious and cultural values of their respective communities, we acknowledge their pioneer work in spreading the Gospel among the newly founded societies [of Latin America in the 19th and 20th centuries]. At the same time, we fraternally invite these churches not to limit their action to conserving their traditional values, but rather to guide the new generations, who are less and less held by the faith and the language of their parents, to a personal devotion to Christ so that they identify themselves with their Latin-American countries as true Protestant citizens. For this reason, we earnestly recommend that you try to combine what you do in your own languages with vigorous work in the national language [Spanish and Portuguese] with the vision of retaining the youth.

Source: El cristianismo evangélico en la América Latina (Buenos Aires, 1949), p. 54. — *Further Reading:* Bastian, *Protestantismus,* pp. 203-210; Prien, *Geschichte,* pp. 924-926; J. M. Bonino, *Faces of Latin American Protestantism* (Grand Rapids, 1997), pp. 1-25, 40-51; G. Cook, "The Genesis and Practise of Protestant Base Communities in Latin America," in: G. Cook (ed.), *New Face of the Church in Latin America* (Maryknoll, 1994), pp. 150-156; P. Freston, "Church Growth, Parachurch Agencies, and Politics," in: G. Cook (ed.), ibid., pp. 226-244; Dussel, *Church,* pp. 335-339.

297. The Formation of CELAM in 1955

The first general conference of the Latin American episcopate took place in Rio de Janeiro in July/August 1955. It was convened by Pope Pius XII. The Latin American bishops were meeting again for the first time since the Plenary Council of 1899 (cf. document 282), this time, however, not in Rome, but in Latin America. The synod was one of the most important pre-conciliar events for Latin American Catholicism. The document adopted there shaped pastoral work up to the Second Vatican Council. A response to the new challenges, namely to social issues and the "Protestant campaigns," was outlined, albeit often in a pre-ecumenical spirit. Moreover, the bishops gathered in Rio requested the creation of a permanent Latin American bishops conference from the Holy See (Consejo Episcopal Latinoamericano: CELAM) with special tasks that are named in the following document. The Latin American general conferences of bishops which have been organized by CELAM (1968 Medellín, 1979 Puebla, 1992 Santo Domingo) have not only shaped Latin American Catholicism in a decisive way, but have also been noted and received by the world church (cf. documents 303 and 305).

The General Assembly of Latin American Bishops has unanimously approved and respectfully submits to the Holy Apostolic See, a request for the creation of a Latin American Episcopal Council based on the following:

1) The Latin American Episcopal Council will be composed of Representatives of the National Episcopal Conferences in Latin America, with one Representative to be designated by each Episcopal Conference.
2) The functions of the Council will be:
   a) to study matters of concern to the Church in Latin America;
   b) to coordinate activities;
   c) to promote and assist in Catholic Works;
   d) to prepare for new Assemblies of Latin American Bishops, when they are summoned by the Holy See.
3) The Council will meet once a year.

Source: Documento de Rio de Janeiro (Lima, 1991), p. 56. — *Further Reading:* CELAM (ed.), *Bodas de plata, 1955-1980* (Bogotá, 1980); CELAM (ed.), *Elementos para su historia, 1955-1980* (Bogotá, 1982); H. J. Mohr (ed.), *Entstehung und Arbeitsweise des Lateinamerikanischen Bischofsrates* (Essen, 1980); Dussel, *Church*, pp. 150-153.

298. Argentina: Call for a Strong Christian State (1953)

Argentinean President Juan Perón's government (1946-1955) was characterized by the principles of political sovereignty, national economical development, and social justice. Perón was supported by the unions and large sectors of the population. He created the political system of "Peronism" with his populistic yet authoritarian style. Perón saw himself as an active Christian whose anti-liberal politics conformed with the demands of the conservative Catholic clergy. In a speech given on the occasion of the seventh convention of the Argentine Catholic Action ACA (Acción Católica Argentina) in the Archdiocese of Rosario, Cardinal Caggiano discussed the relation of Catholicism to Perón's social politics.

We will not remain in the churches or in the sacristies: fulfilling our duty there, we will go out and take the light of Christ to all places. [. . .] Just like the Church the Catholic Action does not seek to direct the unions or direct political parties. But rather it seeks to Christianize men to be good unionists and good Catholic citizens that do not betray the faith in the voting booth, voting for those without God or for the defenders of the lay school, for those in favor of divorce, for those that preach the separation of Church and State. We will not remain in the Church, we will go out, because we have the right to support and defend social justice and more humane and Christian salaries for our brothers, the workers. . . .

Source: L. M. Caimari, *Perón y la Iglesia Católica* (Buenos Aires, 1995), p. 305. — *Further Reading:* Prien, *Geschichte*, pp. 584-592; Dussel, *Church*, pp. 139-152, 160; A. Ivereigh, *Catholicism and Politics in Argentina, 1810-1960* (New York, 1995), pp. 143-174; M. A. Burdick, *For God and Fatherland: Religion and Politics in Argentina* (Albany, 1995), pp. 45-109; Latourette, *Expansion VII*, 169f; McManners, *Illustrated History*, pp. 440-442; Barrett, *WCE I*, pp. 71-76.

299. Cuba: Church and Revolution (1960)

A group of insurgents led by Fidel Castro was able to topple the military dictatorship of Fulgencio Batista in 1959. The new government launched a revolutionary process, which included the reallocation of land ownership, the expansion of state's social networks and intensified industrialization. At first the reforms were welcomed by the Catholic Church. The growing alliance with the Soviet Union and the Marxist model of society, however, increasingly led to discomfort with the hierarchy. In a pastoral letter, the Cuban episcopacy discusses the Cuban model on August 7, 1960.

The Church was certainly pleased when it became known a year ago that land reform would be installed. This land reform would allow a hundred thousand farmers to become property owners of the land they worked, after just compensation was made to the original landowners. [With] full hope and joy [we] also heard news of the big industrialization projects, through which the government would develop new production sources that could help solve the difficult problem of unemployment, without destroying private industry.

The church saw also with satisfaction that the government attempted in every manner to lower the cost of living and to raise the income of the poorest class; and it was very content with the increase in the number of schools and hospitals [. . .]

In the last months, the Cuban government has had close economic, cultural and diplomatic relations with the most important Communist countries, primarily with the Soviet Union. From the pastoral point of view, we would have nothing to say about the strictly economic character of these relations. What worries us deeply, however, is the fact that on these occasions the press, public employees, union leaders and even some high-up government officials have repeatedly and warmly praised . . . the style of life of these people. [. . .]

This causes us great concern, because Catholicism and communism have two fundamentally different concepts of human beings and of the world, which can never be reconciled.

Source: H.-J. Prien, *Lateinamerika: Gesellschaft, Kirche, Theologie* (Göttingen, 1981), 1, pp. 282-285. — *Further Reading:* Prien, *Geschichte 1006-1026*; R. Gómez Treto, *The Church and Socialism in Cuba* (Maryknoll, 1988), pp. 19-36; J. McManners (ed.), *The Oxford Illustrated History of Christianity* (Oxford/New York, 1992), pp. 442-446; Dussel, *Church*, pp. 153-165, 419-425; J. M. Kirk, *Between God and the Party* (Tampa, 1989), pp. 65-90; M. E. Crahan, "Cuba," in: P. E. Sigmund (ed.), *Religious Freedom and Evangelization in Latin America* (Maryknoll, 1999), pp. 87-112; J. Eagleton (ed.), *Christians and Socialism* (Maryknoll, 1975), pp. 136-140; Barrett, *WCE I*, pp. 225-229.

300. Brazil: Catholics on the Side of the Military Dictatorship (1964)

During the 1960s, military dictatorships came to power in a number of Latin American countries. In many cases they were greeted positively by the Catholic Church, who saw them as a controlling factor against feared communist infiltration. This was also the case in Brazil, where General Castelo Branco led a coup d'etat against the government of the reform-oriented social democrat João Goulart on April 1, 1964. Influential conservative Catholics had already demonstrated against President Goulart on March 19, 1964, with a "March of the Family with God for Freedom:" On April 4, 1964, the group published a manifesto entitled "Brazil Has Decided for Freedom."

Brazil chose freedom. An unavoidable option was imposed on our people: subjection to atheist communism or independence within the most authentic Christian traditions.

Brazil marched with God for freedom. [. . .] The people of the largest Catholic church in the world know the truth of divine revelation: in faithfulness to their evangelical vocation they carried on: "So if the Son sets you free, you will be free indeed" (Jn 8:36). The impartial observer can only see in the "Miracle of

April" [the coup d'etat] an unique act of divine providence. It is the first time in the entire world that communism was so rapidly defeated, without firing a shot, without the sacrifice of one single life. This lesson is an incentive for those people who are being dominated by the most degrading tyrants.

Those without God and against God were defeated by those that invoked divine protection. When women grasped their rosaries, men grasped their arms. The Mother of the Brazilians [the Holy Virgin of Immaculate Conception] defended her children.

Source: F. L. Lopes S.J., "O Brasil escolheu a liberdade," in: *O Estado de S. Paulo 4.4.1964,* quoted in: F. Grandini et al. (eds.), *As relações Igreja — Estado no Brasil.* Vol. 1: *Durante o governo do Marechal Castelo Branco 1964-1967* (São Paulo, 1986), pp. 25f. — *Further Reading:* Dussel, *Church,* pp. 197-199; S. Mainwaring, *The Catholic Church and Politics in Brazil* (Stanford, 1986), pp. 79-84; K. Serbin, *Secret Dialogues: Church-State Relations, Torture and Social Justice in Authoritarian Brazil* (Pittsburgh, 1990).

B. The Second Vatican Council and Its Reception

301. A Latin American Bishop at the Council

The contribution of Latin American bishops to Vatican II was, apart from a few exceptions, rather humble. This may have to do with the fact that they and Latin American Catholicism were not in general prepared for the Council's major themes (dialogue with the world today, ecumenism, greater lay participation in the structures and mission of the church, new theological insights). The Chilean Bishop Manuel Larraín (d. 1966), then president of CELAM, and the Brazilian Bishop Hélder Câmara (d. 1999), then vice-president of CELAM, were among the exceptions. Both spoke out in the condocument of the prophetic task of the church and the church of the poor. The following document is an excerpt from Larraín's speech on the prophetic task of the people of God which he gave on October 23, 1963, during the discussion of the proposed document for the Dogmatic Constitution on the Church, *Lumen Gentium* (cf. also document 98).

Let me now add a word about the prophetic function of the People of God. The prophetic function of the people of God means that everyone has a serious obligation to preach and witness. The people of God is "witness" or "martyr" to the mystery of Christ among men, by their actions and their whole life. We can rightly apply to the whole people of God what the evangelist said of John the Baptist: "He himself was not the light, but he came to testify to the light" (Jn 1:8). . . . Along with preaching, this mission of the Church also requires us to witness through an evangelical way of life. As St. Cyprian wrote: "we Christians do not speak of great things, we live them." The evangelical way of life must be clearly and constantly visible in unfeigned poverty, in loving chastity, in free obedience, in prayer and fasting, in persecutions, in charity.

Source: M. Larraín, *Escritos completos,* vol. 1: *La Iglesia en su vida íntima* (Santiago de Chile, 1988), pp. 89-91. — *Further Reading:* J. O. Beozzo (ed.), *Cristianismo e Iglesias de América Latina en vísperas del Vaticano II* (San José, 1992); G. Gutiérrez, "Die Kirche und die Armen in lateinamerikanischer Sicht," in: H.-J. Pottmeyer et al. (eds.), *Die Rezeption des Zweiten Vatikanischen Konzils* (Düsseldorf, 1986), pp. 221-247; J. Gremillion (ed.), *The Church and Culture since Vatican II: The Experience of North and Latin America* (Notre Dame, Ind., 1985); G. Alberigo, J. A. Komonchak (eds.), *History of Vatican II,* 4 vols. (Maryknoll/Leuven, 1995-2003); Dussel, *Church,* pp. 153ff.

302. Revolution and Violence

In Latin America the reception of the Second Vatican Council went hand in hand with dramatic social changes. In general it was thought that a radical change in society was necessary in order to form a more democratic, more just, and economically more independent Latin America. Even Christian democrats, like the Venezuelan Rafael Caldera, voiced support in 1962 for a "revolution in freedom." They were referring here to a third way for reshaping the continent which would distance itself from the military dictatorships on the right and from communism on the left. Only the means which were to lead to the transformation of Latin America were controversial. The spectrum ranged from peaceful reforms to the violent social revolution which was supposed to make a new beginning possible. Cuba's example and Che Guevara's attempt to export revolution to South America (his "Call for a Revolt of the Third World" from the autumn of 1966 is legendary) were received enthusiastically by certain segments of the clergy. These priests, for example the Colombian Camilo Torres (1929-1966), who had studied sociology at the University of Louvain, considered the revolutionary path to be an unavoidable "Christian duty" at this historic moment in Latin America (document a). They were sharply condemned by the bishops for their stance. In his encyclical *Populorum Progressio* of May 26, 1967 (document b), Pope Paul VI was not just content with condemning revolutionary violence and emphasizing the doctrine of the right to resist dictatorship under certain circumstances, but also dealt with the problems of the so-called Third World in general and of Latin America in particular. The Pope was aware that the issues of justice and peace in the human family, which had been touched upon in *Gaudium et Spes,* had to be discussed in greater detail. Though expressing understanding for the justified concerns of the Third World in the face of appalling injustice, the message of the encyclical is quite clear: just development and education, not social revolution, will secure world peace in the long run. The encyclical had the effect of a trumpet blast in Latin America. It was accepted faithfully, but was also intensified to some extent in the "Message of the Bishops of the Third World" issued on August 15, 1967. Among those who signed this document were nine Brazilian bishops under the spiritual leadership of Hélder Câmara.

a. The Way of Camilo Torres (1965)

Message to Christians [. . .]

The revolution can be a peaceful one if the minorities refrain from violent resistence. Revolution is, therefore, the way to obtain a government that will feed the hungry, clothe the naked, and teach the unschooled. Revolution will produce a government that carries out works of charity, of love for one's fellows — not for only a few but for the majority of our fellow men. This is why the revolution is not only permissible but obligatory for those Christians who see it as the only effective and far-reaching way to make the love of all people a reality. It is true that 'there exists no authority except from God' (Romans xiii, 1). But St Thomas teaches that it is the people who concretely have the right to authority.

When the existing authority is against the people, it is not legitimate, and we call it a tyranny. We Christians can and must fight against tyranny. The present government is tyrannical because it receives the support of only 20 per cent of the voters and because its decisions emanate from the privileged minorities. [. . .]

I have given up the duties and privileges of the clergy, but I have not ceased to be a priest. I believe that I have given myself to the revolution out of love for my fellow man. I have ceased to say Mass to practise love for my fellow man in the temporal, economic, and social spheres. When my fellow man has nothing against me, when he has carried out the revolution, then I will return to offering Mass, God permitting. [. . .] After the revolution we Colombians will be aware that we are establishing a system oriented towards the love of our neighbour. The struggle is long; let us begin now.

[. . .]

Message to Communists [. . .]

I believe that the Communist party consists of truly revolutionary elements, and hence I cannot be an anti-Communist either as a Columbian, a sociologist, a Christian, or a priest.

As a Colombian I am not an anti-Communist because anti-Communism hounds nonconformists among my compatriots regardless of whether they are Communists or not. Most of them are simply poor people. As a sociologist I am not an anti-Communist because the Communist theses concerning the fight against poverty, hunger, illiteracy, lack of shelter, and absence of public services offer effective scientific solutions to these problems. As a Christian I am not an anti-Communist because I believe that anti-Communism implies condemnation of everything that Communists stand for. As a priest I am not an anti-Communist because among the Communists themselves, whether they know it or not, there may be many true Christians. If they are of good faith, they are entitled to receive Holy Communion. And if they receive Holy Communion and if they love their neighbour, they will be saved. My duty as a priest, although I no longer practise the rites of the church, is to bring people nearer to God, and the best way to do this is to try to make people serve their neighbour according to the dictates of their conscience. I do not seek to proselytize my Communist brethren and induce them to accept the dogma and the rites of the church. What I strive for is that people should act according to their conscience, that they should sincerely search for the truth, and that they should truly love their fellow men.

b. From the Encyclical Populorum progressio (1967)

The injustice of certain situations cries out for God's attention. Lacking the bare necessities of life, whole nations are under the thumb of others; they cannot act on their own initiative; they cannot exercise personal responsibility; they cannot work toward a higher degree of cultural refinement or a greater participation in social and public life. They are sorely tempted to redress these insults to their human nature by violent means. Everyone knows, however, that revolutionary uprisings — except where there is manifest, longstanding tyranny which would do great damage to fundamental personal rights and dangerous harm to the common good of the country — engender new injustices, introduce new inequities and bring new disasters. The evil situation that exists, and it surely is evil, may not be dealt with in such a way that an even worse situation results. We want to be clearly understood on this point: The present state of affairs must be confronted boldly, and its concomitant injustices must be challenged and overcome. Continuing development calls for bold innovations that will work profound changes. The critical state of affairs must be corrected for the better without delay. Everyone must lend a ready hand to this task, particularly those who can do most by reason of their education, their office, or their authority. They should set a good example by contributing part of their own goods, as several of our brother bishops have done [. . .]

When we fight poverty and oppose the unfair conditions of the present, we are not just promoting human well-being; we are also furthering man's spiritual and moral development, and hence we are benefiting the whole human race. For peace is not simply the absence of warfare, based on a precarious balance of power; it is fashioned by efforts directed day after day toward the establishment of the ordered universe willed by God, with a more perfect form of justice among men.

Source: (a) J. Gerassi (ed.), *Revolutionary Priest: The Complete Writings and Messages of Camilo Torres* (Harmondsworth, 1973), pp. 374-376; (b) *Populorum progressio* no. 30-32 and 76-77. —

Further Reading: (a) J. Álvarez García, C. Restrepo Calle (ed.), *Camilo Torres, Priest and Revolutionary: The Document of His Political Programme and of His Messages to the Colombian People* (London, Sidney, 1968); Camilo Torres, *A Biography of the Priest-Guerrillero* (New York, 1975); J. Watson, *Camilo Torres* (Bognor Regis, 1981); A. W. Bradstock, *A Christian Contribution to Revolutionary Praxis: An Examination of the Significance of Religious Belief for the Political Philosophies of Gerrard Winstanley and Camilo Torres* (Canterbury, 1989); G. Guzmán Campos, *Camilo Torres* (New York, 1969); E. Stehle, *Der Weg der Gewalt. Camilo Torres* (Aschaffenburg, 1975); G. Adler (ed.), *Revolutionäres Lateinamerika* (Paderborn, 1970); R. McAfee Brown, *Von der gerechten Revolution* (Stuttgart, 1982); (b) A. Antweiler, *Fortschritt und Entwicklungshilfe* (Altenberge, 1983); R. Antoncich, J. M. Munárriz, *Die Soziallehre der Kirche* (Düsseldorf, 1988); P. Hünermann, J. C. Scannone (eds.), *Lateinamerika und die katholische Soziallehre* (Mainz, 1993); G. Kruip, *Entwicklung oder Befreiung?* (Saarbrücken, 1988); *"Populorum progressio" to the Third World: Conclusions of the Symposium on Intermediate Technology in Rural, Family and Community Development, Rome, 11 to 16 October 1968* (Rome, 1968); R. A. Markus, *Another Note on Pope Paul VI's encyclical "Populorum progressio"* (Oxford, 1968); Dussel, *Church*, pp. 153-165.

303. Second General Conference of the Episcopate in Medellín (1968)

The Second General Conference of the Latin American episcopate, now arranged by CELAM (cf. document 297), had the theme "The Church in the Present-Day Transformation of Latin America in Light of the Council," which had been suggested by Bishop Manuel Larraín (d. 1966). After a long period of preparation, the conference took place from August 24 to September 6, 1968, in the Colombian city of Medellín and in a socially unsettled Latin America. As the Medellín conference was approaching, Bishop Hélder Câmara demanded a structural revolution for Latin America in Paris on April 25, 1968. In many speeches and lectures by theologians what came to be known as "liberation theology" began to emerge. In general one can say that the bishops in Medellín — following the pastoral character of the Second Vatican Council, but in a selective as well as creative recourse to its documents — endeavored to ground their statements theologically and defined the church's task in light of Latin American problems. In a language not free from pathos, document a demonstrates the awareness and the ecumenical spirit of the bishops, but also their advocacy of the three-step method "See-Judge-Act" borrowed from the Young Christian Workers and of the holistic development postulated in *Populorum Progressio*. Document b again advocates — not without the influence of Paulo Freire — liberating education and training as a path to holistic development. Finally, document c justifies the preferential option for the poor which should be regarded as Latin America's greatest theological contribution to the world church.

a. Consciousness of the Historical Moment and an Ecumenical Spirit

As Christians, we believe that this stage in Latin American history is intimately linked to the History of Salvation.

As Pastors, with a shared responsibility, we commit ourselves to the life of all our peoples in the anguished search for adequate solutions to their many problems. Our mission is to contribute to the integral promotion of the people and communities of the continent.

We believe we are in a new historical era. It requires clear vision, lucid diagnosis, and solidary action.

[. . .]

We call on all people of good will to collaborate in truth, justice, love and freedom with this task of transforming our peoples, at the dawn of a new era.

Our call is addressed especially to the Churches and Christian communities that share with us one faith in the Lord Jesus. During this Conference, our brethren in these Christian confessions have been participating in our tasks and our hopes. Together with them, we shall witness to this spirit of collaboration.

b. Liberating Education as an Answer to Our Needs

Our reflection on this panorama leads us to propose a vision of education that is more in line with the integral development we support for our continent. We would call it "liberating education;" that is, education that sees the learner as the subject of his own development. Education is in fact the key way of liberating peoples from all enslavement and raising them "from less human to more human conditions," bearing in mind that human beings are responsible and the "principal actor in their success or failure."

To that end, education at all levels must become creative, for it must anticipate the new type of society that we seek in Latin America; it must base its efforts on the personalization of the coming generations, deepening their awareness of their human dignity, favoring their free self-determination and promoting their sense of community.

It must be open to dialogue, in order to enrich itself with the values which youth are sensing and discovering to be valid for the future, and thus promoting understanding among young people and between them and adults. This will offer the young people "the best examples and teachings of their parents and teachers, and the formation of tomorrow's society."

Education should also affirm local and national characteristics with sincere appreciation, and integrate them in the pluralistic unity of the continent and the world. Finally, it should prepare the new generations for the perennial and organic change that development entails.

This is the liberating education that Latin America needs in order to redeem itself from unjust enslavement, and above all from our own selfishness. This is the education that our integral development demands.

c. Option for the Poor

Within the condocument of the poverty and even of the wretchedness in which the great majority of the Latin American people live, we, bishops, priests and religious, have the necessities of life and a certain security while the poor lack that which is indispensable and struggle between anguish and uncertainty. And incidents are not lacking in which the poor feel that their bishops, or pastors and religious, do not really identify themselves with them, with their problems and afflictions, that they do not always support those that work with them or plead their cause. [. . .]

Because of the foregoing we wish the Latin American Church to be the evangelizer of the poor and one with them, a witness to the value of the riches of the Kingdom, and the humble servant of all our people. Its pastors and the other members of the People of God have to correlate their life and words, their attitudes and actions to the demands of the Gospel and the necessities of the men of Latin America.

The Lord's distinct commandment to "evangelize the poor" ought to bring us to a distribution of resources and apostolic personnel that effectively gives preference to the poorest and most needy sectors and to those segregated for any cause whatsoever, animating and accelerating the initiatives and studies that or already being made with that goal in mind.

Source: (a) "Die Kirche Lateinamerikas." Dokumente der II. und III. Generalversammlung des Latein-amerikanischen Episkopats in Medellín und Puebla (Bonn o.J. [1985]), pp. 15, 17f; (b) ibid., p. 50; (c) ibid., pp. 115-117. — Further Reading: The Church in the Present-Day Transformation of Latin America in the Light of the Council. Second General Conference of Latin American Bishops, Bogotá, 24 August, Medellin, 26 August–6 September, Colombia, 1968 (Bogotá, 1970-1973); J. Thomas, Liberation: Towards a Theology for the Church in the World. According to the Second General Conference of Latin American Bishops at Medellin, 1968 (Rome, 1972); J. Sobrino, "El Vaticano II y la Iglesia en América Latina," in: C. Floristán, J. J. Tamayo (eds.), El Vaticano II, veinte años después (Madrid, 1985), pp. 105-134; G. Gutiérrez, "Die Kirche und die Armen in lateinamerikanischer Sicht," in: H.-J. Pottmeyer et al. (eds.), Die Rezeption des Zweiten Vatikanischen Konzils (Düsseldorf, 1986), pp. 221-247; S. Galilea, "Lateinamerika in den Konferenzen von Medellín und Puebla," in: ibid., pp. 85-103; J. O. Beozzo, "Das II. Vaticanum und der kulturelle Wandel in Lateinamerika," in: P. Hünermann (ed.), Das II. Vatikanum. Christlicher Glaube im Horizont globaler Modernisierung (Paderborn, 1998), pp. 165-204; M. Delgado, "Kritische Anmerkungen zur selektiven Rezeption des II. Vatikanums in Lateinamerika," in: ibid., pp. 205-209; NZM 45 (3/1989: "Bekehrung einer Kirche: 30 Jahre Medellín"); J. O. Beozzo, "Das Zweite Vatikanische Konzil und die Kirche in Lateinamerika," in: K. Koschorke (ed.), Transkontinentale Beziehungen in der Geschichte des Außereuropäischen Christentums (Wiesbaden, 2002), pp. 219-242; G. Alberigo, J. A. Komonchak (eds.), History of Vatican II, 4 vols. (Maryknoll/Leuven, 1995-2003); Dussel, Church, pp. 153-165, 391ff.

304. Characteristics of Liberation Theology

In the wake of Medellín, what is known as liberation theology emerged as a theological movement and reflection oriented to condocument and action. It sought to be a new type of theology (document a) which does not give precedence to metaphysical understanding or the paradigm of faith and reason, but to social change and the paradigm of faith and justice, for which the three-step methodology of See-Judge-Act is important. Corresponding to the revolutionary climate in which the post-conciliar theological awakening of Latin America occurred, most liberation theologians did not advocate development, but social revolution (document b). They justified this by reverting to the dependence theory that was widespread in the 1960s as well as to categories and sections of Marxist social analysis. From the very beginning, liberation theology was rooted in a spiritual experience (document c) in which, following the Council (*Lumen Gentium* 8) and the judgment passage of Jesus (Matt. 25), the concrete poor person is perceived as a sacrament of the encounter with God. It also developed a new method of biblical interpretation which is practiced above all in base communities and essentially consists in correlating the Bible with social reality. Based on Paulo Freire's pedagogy of the oppressed, it aims at making the poor and the laity aware of their situation and encouraging them as hearers of the Word to speak so that they might evangelize themselves and us (document d). This form of biblical exegesis led to a new catechetical method; among its first mature fruits was the adult catechism "Vamos caminando" of the Peruvian diocese Cajamarca (document e). This catechism stands out due to its clear concentration on the Gospels and on the witness to Jesus' praxis with a special recourse to Exodus and the prophetic-messianic tradition. The catechetical experiment of Cajamarca, which had been controversial from the start, was put into question more and more after Bishop José Dammert Bellido's retirement in 1992. This led to controversy within the church. Many Latin American Christians paid for their commitment to the poor and to justice with their life, dying as martyrs. The most prominent among these is Oscar Romero, Bishop of San Salvador, who was shot at the altar during the Consecration on March 24, 1980. Document f witnesses to his theological view of the political dimensions of faith and of the option for the poor.

a. Gustavo Gutiérrez: A New Way to Do Theology

It is for all these reasons that the theology of liberation offers us not so much a new theme for reflection as a *new way* to do theology. Theology as critical reflection on historical praxis is a liberating theology, a theology of the liberating transformation of the history of mankind and also therefore that part of mankind — gathered into *ecclesia* — which openly confesses Christ. This is a theology which does not stop with reflecting on the world. But rather tries to be part of the process through which the world is transformed. It is a theology which is open — in the protest against trampled human dignity, in the struggle against the plunder of the vast majority of people, in liberating love, and in the building of a new, just, and fraternal society — to the gift of the Kingdom of God.

b. Gustavo Gutiérrez: Not Development, but Social Revolution

Much has been said in recent times about development. Poor countries competed for the help of the rich countries. There were even attempts to create a certain development mystique. Support for development was intense in Latin America in the 50s, producing high expectations. But since the supporters of development did not attack the roots of the evil, they failed and caused instead confusion and frustration.

One of the most important reasons for this turn of events is that development — approached from an economic and modernizing point of view — has been frequently promoted by international organizations closely linked to groups and governments which control the world economy. The changes encouraged were to be achieved within the formal structure of the existing institutions without challenging them. Great care was exercised, therefore, not to attack the interests of large international economic powers nor those of their natural allies, the ruling domestic interest groups. Furthermore, the so-called changes were often nothing more than new and underhanded ways of increasing the power of strong economic groups.

Developmentalism thus came to be synonymous with *reformism* and modernization, that is to say, synonymous with timid measures, really ineffective in the long run and counterproductive to achieving a real transformation. The poor countries are becoming ever more clearly aware that their underdevelopment is only the by-product of the development of other countries, because of the kind of relationship which exists between the rich and the poor countries. Moreover, they are realizing that their own development will come about only with a struggle to break the domination of the rich countries. [. . .] Only a radical break from the status quo, that is, a profound transformation of the private property system, access to power of the exploited class, and a social revolution that would break this dependence would allow for the change to a new society, a socialist society — or at least allow that such a society might be possible.

c. Hélder Câmara: The Spirituality of Liberation Theology

Put your ear to the ground
and listen,
hurried, worried footsteps,
bitterness, rebellion.
Hope
Hasn't yet begun.
Listen again.
Put out feelers.

The Lord is there.
He is far less likely
to abandon us
in hardship
than in times of ease.

d. Bible Interpretation of the Base Community of Solentiname (1973)

[From the interpretation of Luke 4:16-30] one of the women says: "What he read in the book of that prophet is prophecy of liberation. And it's a teaching that a lot of Christians haven't learned yet, because we can be in a church singing day and night tra-la-la-la, and it doesn't matter to us that are so many prisoners and that we're surrounded by injustice, with so many afflicted hearts, so many people without education who are like blind people, so much unfairness in the country, so many women whose eyes are filled with tears every day. And if they take somebody else prisoner, what do we lose? 'Maybe he did something,' they say, and that's the end of the story."

e. "Vamos Caminando," A Peruvian Catechism (1977)

What we are going to think about now is something that happened a very long time ago, about eight centuries before Jesus Christ.

The country of Israel was very rich. But the riches were in the hands of very few people, and the number of poor people was increasing dramatically. Those who had wealth and power made a mockery of the rights of the poor and humble. Meanwhile the worship of God continued, supported by the rich; the priests were on the side of the *status quo*, and were keeping very quiet about the injustice and exploitation. Until God called Amos, a poor shepherd, to be his prophet and announce his truth.

This is how Amos spoke: "Hear these words, you fools, who trample righteousness underfoot, who oppress the weak and rob them of their grain. You grind good men down, take bribes and prevent the poor from getting what is their right. But let justice roll down like waters, and righteousness like an ever-flowing stream" (after Amos 5:7-24).

And the shepherd Amos had quarrels with civil authorities as well as with priests.

Talking points:

We are living in times similar to those of Amos. Could you point out some of the similarities? Are there nowadays any shepherds or farm-workers whom you know, who raise their voices to protest against injustice? [. . .] And we — what are we doing?

f. Oscar Romero: The Political Dimension of the Faith

As a Church we are not political experts, nor do we wish to manage the mechanisms of politics. But if we are to uphold faith in a God of life and to follow Jesus, in truth and not only in words, it is necessary and urgent that we be engaged in the socio-political world where the life and death of the majorities are at stake. . . .

The Church will go on supporting the specifics of one political project or another, depending on how it affects the poor. We believe that this is the way to uphold the Church's identity and its very transcendence. That is, to be engaged in the socio-political process of our time, to judge it from the viewpoint of the poor, and to energize any liberation movements that lead to justice for the majorities and peace for the majorities. We believe that this is the way to uphold the transcendence and identity of the Church, because it is in this way that we uphold faith in God. The ancient Christians said: "Gloria Dei, vivens pauper" (the glory of God is the poor person who lives). We believe that the transcendence of the Gospel enables us to judge the true meaning of life for the poor; and we also believe that by taking sides with the poor and trying to give them life, we will understand the eternal truth of the Gospel.

Source: (a) Gustavo Gutiérrez, A Theology of Liberation: History, Politics and Salvation (Maryknoll, 1973), p. 15; (b) ibid., pp. 26-27; (c) Helder Camara, The Desert Is Fertile (London, 1974), pp. 29f; (d) E. Cardenal, The Gospel in Solentiname (Maryknoll, 1976), pp. 128-129; (e) Vamos Caminando: A Peruvian Catechism. Pastoral Team of Bambamarca (Maryknoll, 1985), pp. 128-129; (f) La voz de los sin voz. La palabra viva de Monseñor Romero (San Salvador, [6]2001), pp. 191-193. — Further Reading: (a) and (b) NHThG[2] 5, 147-158 (K. Füssel), StL[7] 5, pp. 457-460 (M. Sievernich), LThK[3] 2, pp. 130-137 (G. Collet/Th. Hausmanninger/G. Gutiérrez/N. Mette), RGG[4] 1, pp. 1207-1210 (W. Altmann/D. Mourkojannis); Dussel, Church, pp. 391-402; L. Boff, C. Boff, Introducing Liberation Theology (Maryknoll, NY, 1987); M. H. Ellis, O. Maduro (eds.), The Future of Liberation Theology: Essays in Honor of Gustavo Gutiérrez (Maryknoll, 1989); M. H. Ellis, O. Maduro (eds.), Expanding the View: Gustavo Gutiérrez and the Future of Liberation Theology (Maryknoll, 1990); R. M. Brown, Gustavo Gutiérrez: An Introduction to Liberation Theology (Maryknoll, 1990); Gustavo Gutiérrez, Essential Writings (Maryknoll, 1996); R. C. Larivee, The Relationship between Spirituality and Morality in the Writings of Gustavo Gutierrez (Chicago, 1998); H. Goldstein, Kleines Lexikon zur Theologie der Befreiung (Düsseldorf, 1991); I. Ellacuria, J. Sobrino (eds.), Mysterium Liberationis: Fundamental Concepts of Liberation Theology (Maryknoll, 1993); A. Müller, A. Tausch, P. M. Zulehner, Global Capitalism, Liberation Theology, and the Social Sciences: An Analysis of the Contradictions of Modernity at the Turn of the Millennium (Huntington, N.Y., 2000); I. Petrella (ed.), Latin American Liberation Theology: The Next Generation (Maryknoll, 2005); A. T. Hennelly (ed.), Liberation Theology: A Documentary History (Maryknoll, 1990); C. Cadorette (ed.), Liberation Theology: An Introductory Reader (Maryknoll, 1992); P. Berryman, Liberation Theology: Essential Facts about the Revolutionary Movement in Latin America and Beyond (Philadelphia, 1987); P. E. Sigmund, Liberation Theology: An Historical Evaluation (Washington, D.C., 1986); (c) M. Ph. D. Hall, The Impossible Dream: The Spiritu-

ality of Dom Helder Camara (Belfast, 1979); *The Gospel with Dom Helder Camara* (London, 1986); U. Eigenmann, *Politische Praxis des Glaubens* (Freiburg, Switzerland, 1984); J. de Broucker (ed.), *Die Bekehrungen eines Bischofs* (Wuppertal, 1978); J. Toulat, *Helder Camara* (Munich, 1990); E. Bonnin (ed.), *Spiritualität und Befreiung in Lateinamerika* (Wuppertal, 1984); G. Gutiérrez, *We Drink from Our Own Wells: The Spiritual Journey of a People* (Maryknoll, 2003); (d) J. J. Lyons, *Ernesto Cardenal: The Poetics of Love and Revolution* (London, 1980); L. Boff, *Die Neuentdeckung der Kirche* (Mainz, 1980); Th. Schmeller, *Das Recht der Anderen* (Münster, 1994); C. Mesters, *Vom Leben zur Bibel — von der Bibel zum Leben*, 2 vols. (Mainz, Munich, 1983); M. Manzanera, *Lateinamerikanische kirchliche Basisgemeinschaften* (München, 1988); F. Weber, *Gewagte Inkulturation* (Mainz, 1996); (e) E. Klinger, W. Knecht, O. Fuchs (eds.), *Die globale Verantwortung* (Würzburg, 2001); R. Estela, C. Trabert, J. de Roubaix, *El camino que se hace al andar* (Lima, 1992); (f) *The Violence of Love: The Pastoral Wisdom of Archbishop Oscar Romero* (Fount, 1989); H. M. Eaton, *Authority and the Role of Archbishop Oscar A. Romero in the Struggle for Liberation of the Salvadoran People* (San Salvador, 1994); J. R. Brockman, *The Word Remains: A Life of Oscar Romero* (Maryknoll, 1982); idem, *Oscar Romero: Bishop and Martyr* (London, 1982); M. Dennis, *Oscar Romero: Reflections on His Life and Writings* (Maryknoll, 2000); M. López-Vigil, *Oscar Romero: Memories in Mosaic* (London, 2000); J. Delgado, *Oscar Arnulfo Romero* (Madrid, 1986); G. Collet, J. Rechsteiner (eds.), *Vergessen heißt verraten* (Wuppertal, 1990); L. Weckel, *Um des Lebens willen* (Mainz, 1998).

305. Third General Conference of the Episcopate in Puebla (1979)

The Third General Conference of the Latin American episcopate in Puebla (January 1–February 13, 1979) occurred under a new Pope and in the shadow of the conflict over liberation theology (cf. document 304). The task in Puebla was, on the one hand, to preserve the continuity with Medellín and, on the other hand, to turn to new themes which had hitherto been neglected and concerned the reception of the Council. Among these were ecclesiological, Christological, and missiological issues. Subsequent to the issuance of *Evangelii Nuntiandi* (December 8, 1975), Puebla discussed the topic "Church and Culture" and the evangelization of the Ibero-American cultures and tackled the problem of autochthonous and minority cultures (the Indian native population, Afro-Americans) more thoroughly than Medellín. In the shadow of liberation theology's discovery of popular piety as an expression of the wisdom of the people, Puebla dealt with it intensely (document a), viewing popular piety in principle as positive, but not therefore forgetting to draw attention to its dangers, which means that it represents an important task with respect to evangelization. In continuity with Medellín, Puebla reinforced the preferential option for the poor (document b).

a. The Popular Piety

The religion of the Latin American people is an expression of the Catholic faith. It is a people's Catholicism. [. . .]

At its core the religiosity of the people is a storehouse of values that offers the answers of Christian wisdom to the great questions of life. The Catholic wisdom of the common people is capable of fashioning a vital synthesis. [. . .]

We can point to the following items as positive elements of the people's piety: the trinitarian presence evident in devotions and iconography: a sense of God the Father's providence; Christ celebrated in the mystery of his Incarnation (the Nativity, the child Jesus), in his crucifixion, in the Eucharist, and in the devotion to the Sacred Heart. Love for Mary. [. . .] She is venerated as the Immaculate Mother of God and of human beings, and as the Queen of our individual countries as well as of the whole continent. Other positive features are: veneration of the saints as protectors; remembrance of the dead; an awareness of personal dignity and of solidary solidarity of brotherhood; awareness of sin and the need to expiate it; the ability to express the faith in a total idiom that goes beyond all sorts of rationalism (chant, images, gesture, color, and dance); faith situated in time (feasts) and in various places (sanctuaries and shrines); a feel for pilgrimage as a symbol of human and Christian existence [. . .].

The negative aspects that we can point to are varied in origin. Some are of an ancestral type: superstition, magic, fatalism, idolatrous worship of power, fetishism, and ritualism. Some are due to distortions of catechesis: static archaism, misinformation and ignorance, syncretistic reinterpretation, and reduction of the faith to a mere contract with God. Some negative aspects are threats to the faith today: secularism as broadcasted by the media of social communication; consumptionism; sects; oriental and agnostic religions; ideological, economic, social, and political types of manipulation; various secularized forms of political messianism; and uprooting and urban proletarianization as the result of cultural change. We can state that many of these phenomena are real obstacles to evangelization.

b. Affirmation of the Preferential Option for the Poor

With renewed hope in the vivifying power of the Spirit, we are going to take up once again the position of the Second General Conference of the Latin American episcopate in Medellin, with adopting a clear and prophetic option expressing preference for, and solidarity with, the poor. [. . .] We affirm the need for conversion on the part of the whole Church to a preferential option for the poor, an option aimed at their integral liberation.

The vast majority of our fellow humans continue to live in a situation of poverty and even wretchedness that has grown more acute. [. . .]

We see that national episcopates and many segments of lay people, religious men and women, and priests have made their commitment to the poor a deeper and more realistic one. This witness, nascent but real, led the Latin

American Church to denounce the grave injustices stemming from mechanisms of oppression.

The poor, too, have been encouraged by the Church. They have begun to organize themselves to live their faith in an integral way, and hence to reclaim their rights.

The Church's prophetic denunciations and its concrete commitments to the poor have in not a few instances brought down persecution and oppression of various kinds upon it. The poor themselves have been the first victims of this oppression.

Source: (a) J. Eagleson, Ph. Scharper (eds.), *Puebla and Beyond: Documentation and Commentary* (Maryknoll, 1979), pp. 184-186 (No. 444, 448, 454, 456); (b) idem, pp. 264 (No. 1134, 1135, 1136, 1137, 1138). — *Further Reading:* A. López Trujillo, *De Medellín a Puebla* (Madrid, 1980); E. Dussel, *De Medellín a Puebla* (Mexico City, 1979); B. Schlegelberger, J. Sayer (eds.), *Von Medellín nach Puebla* (Düsseldorf, 1980); H. Schöpfer (ed.), *Kontinent der Hoffnung* (Munich, Mainz, 1979); S. Galilea, "Lateinamerika in den Konferenzen von Medellín und Puebla," in: H.-J. Pottmeyer et al. (eds.), *Die Rezeption des Zweiten Vatikanischen Konzils* (Düsseldorf, 1986), pp. 85-103; G. Gutiérrez, *The Power of the Poor in History* (Maryknoll, 1983); L. Boff, "Puebla aus der Sicht der unterdrückten Lateinamerikas," in: *ZMR* 64 (1980), pp. 161-191; P. E. Arns, "Was hat Puebla für die Kirche in Lateinamerika gebracht?" in: *Herder Korrespondenz* 33 (1979), pp. 235-241; H.-J. Prien, "Puebla," in: idem (ed.), *Lateinamerika: Gesellschaft, Kirche, Theologie* (Göttingen, 1981), vol. 2, pp. 61-208; G. Sánchez, *Religiosidad popular y opción por los pobres* (Mexico City, 1988); J. Marins, "Praxis de los Padres de América Latina." Los Documentos de las Conferencias Episcopales de Medellín a Puebla (Bogotá, 1978); K. Rahner e.a. (eds.), *Volksreligion — Religion des Volkes* (Stuttgart u.a., 1979); Dussel, *Church*, pp. 165-184.

C. The Conflict on the Theology of Liberation

306. Nicaragua: The Sandinista Revolution (1979)

With the Sandinista Revolution a Latin American country was ruled by a revolutionary movement for the first time in July of 1979. The movement had many Christians, priests, and theologians in its ranks who had been formed by liberation theology. The revolution's success was celebrated enthusiastically by these people and by the friends of liberation theology throughout the world, but also by the bishops of Nicaragua, for example by the Bishop of Managua, Obando y Bravo, who justified the revolution as a legitimate uprising against a dictatorship as defined by *Populorum Progressio* (cf. document 302). For many it appeared as though the messianic reign of truth and freedom and of justice and peace had found a home on earth in the land of volcanoes. Out of this close relationship between the Sandinista movement and liberation theology there soon developed a special form of political theology which intensified the controversy over the Marxist character of some of liberation theology's tendencies. Among these tendencies were such phenomena as the church of the masses promoted by the government and often understood as a class church, as well as attempts to reformulate the Our Father and the Creed according to revolutionary doctrine. Some of these attempts, such as the following document, are quite interesting in a theological sense, while others represent a clumsy politicization of faith. The more the Sandinista movement became a (political) church in this way, the more the Nicaraguan bishops and Rome distanced themselves from it.

"Our Father" of Nicaragua

Our Father, you also live in this our land, Nicaragua. We will seek you and meet you here — in our daily endeavour to rebuild our fatherland to the benefit of all. *Hallowed be your name* by our unity. Hallowed be your name by our solidarity with the most needy, by our untiring efforts for justice and peace. *Your kingdom come.* It shall come soon to the hungry, to the crying, to those who long for your justice, to those who have waited for a life in human dignity for centuries. Give us hope that we do not become tired to proclaim it and to fight for it — despite so many conflicts, threats and shortcomings. Give us a clear view that we see the horizon in this hour of our history and recognise in which way your kingdom comes to us. *Your will be done,* as in heaven so on earth. Your will, that we call only you Father and live together as sisters and brothers, shall be fulfilled in Nicaragua, too. Your will shall also happen in the church of Nicaragua, which has her unity in Jesus, your son and our Lord, the good shepherd, who brings the fold together, in a church of the poor, which Jesus blessed and which he entrusted the gospel, in a church, in which we shall be a heart and a soul under the guidance of Jesus' spirit and in which we shall have everything together. [. . .]

Source: D. Sölle, H. Goldstein (eds.), *Dank sei Gott und der Revolution* (Reinbek bei Hamburg, 1984), pp. 5-9. — *Further Reading:* T. Borges Martínez, *Die Revolution kämpft gegen die Theologie des Todes* (Freiburg, 1984); G. Heinen, *Mit Christus und der Revolution* (Stuttgart, 1995); R. Aragón, E. Löschke, *Die Kirche der Armen in Nicaragua* (Frankfurt, 1996); P. Casaldáliga, *Kampf und Prophetie* (Mödling, 1990); L. Zambrano, *Entstehung und theologisches Verständnis der "Kirche des Volkes" (Iglesia Popular) in Lateinamerika* (Frankfurt u.a., 1982); D. Ormrod, *Nicaragua: The Theology and Political Economy of Liberation* (Canterbury, 1988); A. Bradstock, *Saints and Sandinistas: The Catholic Church in Nicaragua and Its Response to the Revolution* (London, 1987); L. N. O'Shaughnessy, *The Church and Revolution in Nicaragua* (Athens, 1986); T. Cabestreros, *Ministers of God, Ministers of the People* (Maryknoll, 1986); G. Girardi, *Faith and Revolution in Nicaragua* (Maryknoll, 1986); D. C. Hodges, *Intellectual Foundation of the Nicaraguan Revolution* (Austin, Tex., 1986); Dussel, *Church,* pp. 427-434.

307. Ernesto Cardenal: Cuba as a Reference Model

The priest and poet Ernesto Cardenal, Secretary of Education and Cultural Affairs in the first Sandinista government, was among those who saw a liberation-theological variant of the Cuban reference model in the Sandinista movement and equated the new socialistic human being with the Christian human being.

The new human being is the person without egotism, the person in solidarity with others who lives for his or her neighbor, who lives to serve his or her neighbor. This is the person of a socialistic society in which a person no longer exploits another person, in which the value of a person is no longer judged according to what he or she takes away from another, but according to what he or she gives another. In Cuba the children are raised in the spirit of Che Guevara, that is in the spirit of love of one's neighbor. And I believe that one already sees this type of new human being very clearly in the Cuban youth. . . . The new human being in Cuba is the same new human being the New Testament talks about, the new Christian person.

Source: E. Cardenal, *Die Stunde Null* (Wuppertal, ²1980), p. 25. — *Further Reading:* J. J. Lyons, *Ernesto Cardenal: The Poetics of Love and Revolution* (London, 1980); E. Cardenal, *Chrétiens du Nicaragua* (Paris, 1980); T. Cabestrero (ed.), *Priester für Frieden und Revolution* (Wuppertal, 1983); G. Heinen, *Mit Christus und der Revolution* (Stuttgart, 1995); F. Betto, *Nachtgespräche mit Fidel* (Freiburg, 1986); B. Kern, *Theologie im Horizont des Marxismus* (Mainz, 1992); M. Sievernich, "Von der Utopie zur Ethik," in: *ThPh* 71 (1996), pp. 33-46; D. Ormrod, *Nicaragua: The Theology and Political Economy of Liberation* (Canterbury, 1988); A. Bradstock, *Saints and Sandinistas: The Catholic Church in Nicaragua and Its Response to the Revolution* (London, 1987); L. N. O'Shaughnessy, *The Church and Revolution in Nicaragua* (Athens, 1986); T. Cabestreros, *Ministers of God, Ministers of the People* (Maryknoll, 1986); G. Girardi, *Faith and Revolution in Nicaragua* (Maryknoll, 1986); D. C. Hodges, *Intellectual Foundation of the Nicaraguan Revolution* (Austin, Tex., 1986); Dussel, *Church*, pp. 427-434.

308. Instruction of the Congregation for the Doctrine of the Faith on August 6, 1984

Ever since the rise of liberation theology there has been a process of reception as well as criticism on the part of the magisterium. The documents from Medellín and Puebla, the Second Roman Synod of Bishops (1971), and *Evangelii Nuntiandi* include lines of thought from liberation theology. While the International Theological Commission of the Roman Congregation for the Doctrine the of the Faith warned against reductionisms in 1977, it still judged liberation theology's approach to be, all in all, well-intentioned and balanced. Sharp criticism first occurred in the shadow of the Sandinista revolution and of the excessive hopes it had awakened among many liberation theologians. In the mid-

1980's the Roman Congregation for the Doctrine of the Faith devoted two instructions to liberation theology. In the first, *Libertatis Nuntius* (1984), the basic concern of liberation theology is, in fact, evaluated positively, but the thrust of this Roman instruction consists in warning against deviations and dangers and in condemning ideas taken from Marxism that could lead to a political messianism. This first instruction generated a lively debate worldwide. The second instruction (*Libertatus Conscientia*, 1986), however, theologically justifies the liberating character of Christianity and emphasizes that the church's main task was of an educational and evangelizing nature.

But the "theologies of liberation," which reserve credit for restoring to a place of honor the great documents of the prophets and of the Gospel in defense of the poor, go on to a disastrous confusion between the 'poor' of the Scripture and the 'proletariat' of Marx. In this way they pervert the Christian meaning of the poor, and they transform the fight for the rights of the poor into a class fight within the ideological perspective of the class struggle. For them the 'Church of the poor' signifies the Church of the class which has become aware of the requirements of the revolutionary struggle as a step toward liberation and which celebrates this liberation in its liturgy.

A further remark regarding the expression, 'Church of the People', will not be out of place here. From the pastoral point of view, this expression might mean the favored recipients of evangelization to whom, because of their condition, the Church extends her pastoral love first of all. One might also refer to the Church as people of God, that is, people of the New Covenant established in Christ.

But the "theologies of liberation" of which we are speaking, mean by 'Church of the People' a Church of the class, a Church of the oppressed people whom it is necessary to "conscientize" in the light of the organized struggle for freedom. For some, the people, thus understood, even become the object of faith. [. . .]

The new 'hermeneutic' inherent in the "theologies of liberation" leads to an essentially 'political' re-reading of the Scriptures. Thus, a major importance is given to the Exodus event inasmuch as it is a liberation from political servitude. Likewise, a political reading of the "Magnificat" is proposed. The mistake here is not in bringing attention to a political dimension of the readings of Scripture, but in making of this one dimension the principal or exclusive component. This leads to a reductionist reading of the Bible.

Likewise, one places oneself within the perspective of a temporal messianism, which is one of the most radical of the expressions of secularization of the Kingdom of God and of its absorption into the immanence of human history.

In giving such priority to the political dimension, one is led to deny the 'radical newness' of the New Testament and above all to misunderstand the per-

son of Our Lord Jesus Christ, true God and true man, and thus the specific
character of the salvation he gave us, that is above all liberation from sin, which
is the source of all evils.

Moreover in setting aside the authoritative interpretation of the Church,
denounced as classist, one is at the same time departing from tradition. In that
way, one is robbed of an essential theological criterion of interpretation, and in
the vacuum thus created, one welcomes the most radical theses of rationalist
exegesis. Without a critical eye, one returns to the opposition of the "Jesus of
history" versus the "Jesus of faith."

*Source: Sacred Congregation for the Doctrine of the Faith, Instruction on Certain Aspects of the
"Theology of Liberation" (Libertatis nuntius; London, 1984). — Further Reading: J. L. Segundo,
Theology and the Church: A Response to Cardinal Ratzinger and the Whole Church (San Fran-
cisco, 1987); Liberation Theology and the Vatican Document (Quezon City, 1984); H. J. Venetz,
H. Vorgrimler (eds.), Das Lehramt der Kirche und der Schrei der Armen (Freiburg, 1985); J. B.
Metz (ed.), Die Theologie der Befreiung: Hoffnung oder Gefahr für die Kirche? (Düsseldorf, 1986);
J. Ratzinger, Politik und Erlösung (Opladen, 1986); R. Hoffmann (ed.), Gottesreich und Revolu-
tion (Münster, 1987); N. Greinacher, Konflikt um die Theologie der Befreiung (Zürich, 1985); H.-J.
Prien (ed.), "Lateinamerika. Gesellschaft, Kirche," Theologie, vol. 2: Der Streit um die Theologie
der Befreiung (Göttingen, 1981); Dussel, Church, pp. 398ff, 447ff.*

309. From the Encyclical *Sollicitudo rei socialis* (1987)

As has already been mentioned, liberation theology was not only criticized by the
magisterium, but also welcomed. The following excerpt from *Sollicitudo Rei Socialis*
(1987) may serve as an example of the latter. The encyclical was published twenty years
after *Populorum Progressio* (cf. document 302b) and came after the two instructions on
liberation theology of 1984 and 1986. The encyclical discusses central theological concerns of liberation theology, such as the preferential option for the poor and speech
about the structures of sin, and emphasizes at the same time that development and liberation belong together.

It will not be superfluous therefore to reexamine and further clarify in this light
the characteristic themes and guidelines dealt with by the Magisterium in recent years.

Here I would like to indicate one of them: the option or love of preference
for the poor. This is an option, or a special form of primacy in the exercise of
Christian charity, to which the whole tradition of the Church bears witness. It
affects the life of each Christian inasmuch as he or she seeks to imitate the life
of Christ, but it applies equally to our social responsibilities and hence to our
manner of living, and to the logical decisions to be made concerning the ownership and use of goods. [. . .]

It is fitting to add that the aspiration to freedom from all forms of slavery affecting the individual and society is something noble and legitimate. This in fact is the purpose of development, or rather liberation and development, taking into account the intimate connection between the two. [. . .] The principal obstacle to be overcome on the way to authentic liberation is sin and the structures produced by sin as it multiplies and spreads.

Source: The Logic of Solidarity: Commentaries on Pope John Paul II's Encyclical "On Social Concern," edited by G. Baum and R. Ellsberg, with the complete document of the encyclical (Maryknoll, 1989), no. 42 and 46 (pp. 46, 50f). — Further Reading: Aspiring to Freedom: Commentaries on John Paul II's Encyclical "The Social Concerns of the Church," by P. L. Berger et al.; edited by K. A. Myers, with the complete document of the encyclical (Grand Rapids, 1988); P. Hünermann, J. C. Scannone (eds.), Lateinamerika und die katholische Soziallehre, 3 vols. (Mainz, 1993); R. Antoncich, Christians in the Face of Injustice: A Latin American Reading of Catholic Social Teaching (Quezon City, 1987); R. Prantner (ed.), Die Sozialenzyklika Papst Johannes Paul II. "Sollicitudo rei socialis" im Widerstreit der Meinungen (Wien, 1989); J. Schasching (ed.), In Sorge um Entwicklung und Frieden (Wien, 1988); G. Kruip, Entwicklung oder Befreiung? (Saarbrücken, 1988).

D. Developments of Protestantism

310. Nicaragua: Indian Protestant Churches (1982)

The Sandinista ascension to power in 1979 was at first welcomed by the Protestant Native Americans on the Atlantic coast. Due to their cultural distinctness and their relatively independent position in the country, the Indians came more and more into conflict with the centrally organized Sandinista government. Some of the Indian Church members joined the Contra-rebels. The leadership of the Moravian Church (Iglesio Moraba), which had always been the most important social influence in the region, took a predominantly intermediary stance. The Bishop of the Moravian Church of Nicaragua, John F. Wilson gave the following explanation in February 1982:

[. . .] We propose that we search with all of our brothers and sisters to find the best way to deal together with the plans for economic and social development of the coast. We ask the authorities to keep us informed about these plans and to discuss them with the people, the state security officials and government members. We offer our cooperation in promoting understanding for the situation on the Atlantic coast and in contributing to the reduction of inadequacies and errors, that do not come from bad intentions, but rather from ignorance about this part of the country. If they work together, the Nicaraguan churches can take on the important function of mediator and show the world the true picture of our people's lives, countering distortions, slander, and economic, political and even military threats.

The small Moravian church from Nicaragua calls on the Christians of the world and primarily our brothers and sisters in the United States to maintain direct information channels open. We ask them not to let themselves be manipulated by certain interests, which pretend to defend our rights and those of the native people, but which actually were never concerned with our fate or with our human rights.

The Moravian church, that consists mostly of natives, calls on the indigenous people of the world to enter in solidarity with us and to help us build a new society, which could be the beginning of liberation for the remaining indigenous people from North and South America.

Source: "Konstruktiv bei der Konfliktlösung. Die Herrnhuter Brüdergemeinde und die Umsiedlung der Miskito-Indianer," in: *Junge Kirche* 43 (1982), pp. 558-563, 563. — *Further Reading:* K. Meschkat et al. (eds.), *Mosquitia* (Hamburg, 1987), pp. 255-276, 277-304; R. Reyes/J. K. Wilson, *Ráfaga: The Life Story of a Nicaraguan Miskito Comandante* (London, 1992); H.-J. Prien, *Das Evangelium im Abendland und in der Neuen Welt* (Frankfurt, 2000), pp. 537-572; C. A. Robertson, *The Moravians, the Miskitu, and the Sandinistas on Nicaragua's Atlantic Coast, 1979-1990* (Bethlehem, 1998).

311. Rubem Alves: A Protestant Liberation Theologian

Liberation theology is a genuinely Latin American response to the challenge of dependence, violence and military dictatorships on the continent. A first systematic articulation of liberation theology came from the Brazilian Presbyterian, Rubem Alves, whose dissertation, completed in 1968, was published in English in 1969 *(Towards a Theology of Human Hope)*. It was published in Spanish in 1970 *(Religión: Opio o instrumento de liberación)*. In the preface to the later Brazilian edition, he recalls his personal experiences from 1964 as he returned to Brazil. Military repression was the catalyst for his work on liberation theology.

I returned to Brazil. I began to learn to live with fear. Before, it was only imagination. Now, [it's present] in that man who examined my passport and compared it with a list of names. And there I waited, hanging over the abyss, pretending to be tranquil . . . until the passport was returned to me. On the road from the airport to my house, in the car of a friend, the validations begin: "Look, Rubem, a document was sent to the Supreme Council accusing six pastors, and you are one of them. And the story is going around that you were reported to the ID-IV [sector of the military], of Juiz de Fora." [. . .]

There were more than forty accusations: that we preached that Jesus had sexual relations with a prostitute, that we were delighted when our children wrote phrases of hate against the Americans on powdered milk cans donated by them (those were the years of the "Food for Peace" program), that we were subversives with funds from the Soviet Union. The good thing about the document was exactly in its virulence: not even the most obtuse person could believe that we were guilty of so many crimes. But the tragedy was precisely this: that people of the church, brothers and sisters, pastors and presbyters . . . were so ready to denounce us. [. . .]

It was then that the United Presbyterian Church — USA, together with the president of the Princeton theological seminary, invited me to do my doctorate. [. . .]

At the beginning, this book was to be an ecclesiology. Translated into a language that all understood: an exercise in utopia, the marks of a community that does not exist anywhere (it is invisible) and that for this reason is everywhere (it is catholic, universal), a horizon of desire, something that still has not been born. [. . .]

It became something different: a meditation on the possibility of liberation. And so I gave it the title "Towards a theology of liberation." This was in 1968.

Source: R. Alves, Introduction to *Sobre Deuses e caquis* (Da esperança, Campinas, 1987), pp. 29, 30, 36, 39. — *Further Reading:* Bastian, *Protestantismus*, pp. 223-241; Prien, *Geschichte*, pp. 1026-1041; R. Alves, *A Theology of Human Hope* (Washington etc., 1969); idem, "Protestantism in Latin America," in: *Ecumenical Review* 22 (1970), pp. 1-15; idem, *Protestantism and Repression: A Brazilian Case Study* (London, 1985); Dussel, *Church*, pp. 392-394; D. Kirkpatrick (ed.), *Faith Born in the Struggle for Life* (Grand Rapids, 1988).

312. Neo-Pentecostal Movements (since 1980)

Since the end of the 1970s, many neo-Pentecostal and charismatic groups arose and contributed to the quick growth of Protestantism throughout Latin America. They often began as traditional Pentecostal groups, yet they turned more and more to the middle and upper classes of society. Neo-Pentecostal movements are usually organized around a strong leader and are known for their basic authoritarian concept. They oppose any type of theological or political liberalism and incorporate an eschatology, according to which Christians are to fight a spiritual war. This is supposed to introduce the kingdom of God into the present society. In a sermon given in the Honduran church "Vida Abundante" in 1989, José Collado presents the gospel of prosperity as a concept opposed to solidarity with the poor, which is at the center of liberation theology. Personal prosperity is to be understood as a sign of God's kingdom (a). Harold Caballeros, pastor of the church El Shaddai, which he founded in 1983, propagates in a sermon a religious-nationalistic model for Guatemalan society achieved through individual conduct and the dominance of Christianity in the country. A significant fact is that Serrano Elías, a member of the El Shaddai church, became president of Guatemala from 1991 to 1993 (b).

a. Honduras: "Vida Abundante" (1989)

Enough with the Gospel of Suffering! The Gospel of Joy should start to fill each life, each home and each place in the world. Because Jesus announces a message of great joy. The Gospel of Joy. The angels sang the gospel of joy with Jesus' birth, and we announce this gospel everywhere today. [. . .]

Christians all over the world were given the gospel of false humility. I say it once again: Christians everywhere have been taught a gospel of false humility. Humility was interpreted as detached from its actual meaning and condocument. Humility does not mean poverty, in any way. A rich person can be humble, and a poor person can be humble. Humility is not poverty. [. . .]

Open your Bibles and read for yourselves, convince yourselves: Loved ones, I want you to do well in just *some* things. (Congregation: No!) In all things! It is about prosperity in all areas. You shall prosper in *all* areas. Which are they? In all! All things are all things! (Shouts: Amen, amen, hallelujah) Everything means everything. What is everything? Your shoes, your laundry, your clothes, your cabinet, your bedroom, your dining room, your little house, your car, your work, your studies, your hen, your cow [. . .], All prosper in God (Shouts: Hallelujah; applause).

b. Guatemala: The El Shaddai Church (1990)

[. . .] If the situation in Guatemala is the way it is, it is not the fault of the government: it is the fault of [us Christians as] the body of Christ, who is not praying, clamoring, making prayers, pleas, supplications before the throne of God, praying for the kings and for those that are in eminence [cf. 1 Peter 2:13], so that Guatemala lives quietly and restfully. [. . .] This [present] generation has the fate of the entire nation in its hands. The fate of Guatemala is in the hands of the Christian Church today. This Christian Church that is found in Guatemala at this time has . . . the key to its destiny, to the future of our nation, of our children, grandchildren, etc. [. . .] God has given to us our nation. [. . .] Because God has a plan for Guatemala. God wants to liberate this nation and this land, but He wants to use you and me. Each one of us will be responsible before the throne of God if we let the opportunity that God is giving us escape. . . .

Source: (a) K. Braungart, *Heiliger Geist und politische Herrschaft bei den Neopfingstlern in Honduras* (Frankfurt a. M., 1995), Appendix 3, pp. VI-VII, XII; (b) P. Sánchiz Ochoa, *Evangelismo y poder. Guatemala ante el nuevo milenio* (Sevilla, 1998), pp. 137-138. — *Further Reading:* Bastian, *Protestantismus*, pp. 258-260; K.-W. Westmeier, *Protestant Pentecostalism in Latin America* (Madison, 1999); B. Boudewijnse et al. (eds.), *More than Opium* (Lanham, London, 1988); E. Willems, *Followers of the New Faith* (Nashville, 1967); McManners, *Illustrated History*, pp. 448-451; (a) Barrett, *WCE I*, pp. 349-353; (b) E. Wilson, "Guatemalan Pentecostals: Something of

Their Own," in: E. L. Cleary (ed.), *Power, Politics and Pentecostals in Latin America* (Boulder, 1997), pp. 139-162; V. Garrard-Burnett, *Protestantism in Guatemala* (Austin, 1998); V. Melander, *The Hour of God?* (Uppsala, 1999); Barrett, *WCE I*, pp. 326-330.

E. Awakening and Multiplicity

313. Charismatic Catholicism (1977)

The charismatic movement was not limited to Protestant groups, but was also to be found within the Catholic Church in the 1970s. Thus, the "Catholic charismatic renewal movement" is recorded as being very popular in Brazil among the laity, priests and members of religious orders. At the behest of the Brazilian conference of bishops, CNBB, a study about the movement was completed in 1977, which includes many testimonials by its members about their "new life in Christ." One layman, who led a prayer group for just under three years, expresses his opinions about the Catholic Charismatic movement.

Likewise, the 'Charismatic Renewal' has been awakening in the [Catholic] Church a very great desire for the reading of the Holy Scripture, bringing them to rediscover the value of prayer (Luke 21:36) and to participate more consciously in the Sacraments. [. . .]

I would like to emphasize that charismatic prayer is not alienation. With the advent of Vatican II, various movements in the Church and an excessive concern with action arose! Paradoxically this activism without prayer generally failed. It is that the two things complement each other: prayer and action. Therefore note: By participating in Prayer Groups people are transforming and witnessing with concrete gestures of faith. Prayer brings us to witness that Jesus Christ is Lord, through living example, I consider to be the most eloquent way to preach the Gospel. [. . .] Even so, at each weekly meeting [of our charismatic group] there are innumerous testimonies of the marvelous gestures of action and faith, because as Jesus said "Do not light a lamp to hide it under a table!" (Mt 5:15).

Source: P. R. de Oliveira et al., *Renovação carismática católica* (Petrópolis, 1978), 137-139. — *Further Reading:* B. Boudewijnse, "The Development of the Charismatic Movement within the Catholic Church of Curaçao," in: A. Droogers et al. (eds.), *Popular Power in Latin American Religions* (Saarbrücken etc., 1991), pp. 175-195; M. das Dores Campos Machado, "Family, Sexuality, and Family Planning . . . in Rio de Janeiro," in: B. Boudewijnse et al. (eds.), *More than Opium* (London, 1988), pp. 169-202; M. de Theije, "Charismatic Renewal and Base Communities," in: B. Boudewijnse et al. (eds.), ibid., pp. 225-248; R. J. Bord/E. Faulkner, *The Catholic Charismatics* (University Park, 1983); M. B. McGuire, *Pentecostal Catholics* (Philadelphia, 1982); M. de Theije, "CEBs and Catholic Charismatics in Brazil," in: C. Smith et al. (eds.), *Latin American Religion in Motion* (New York, 1999), pp. 111-124; D. Lehmann, "Dissidence and Conformism in Religious Movements," in: *'Movements' in the Church* (London, 2003), pp. 122-138.

314. Recognition of Religious Pluralism (1985)

Semi-official contact between representatives of the Afro-Brazilian cults and the Catholic episcopate occurred for the first time during the 1980s. An example is presented by the exchange of letters between the Archbishop of Salvador (Brazil), Minister Avelar Brandão Vilela, and the leader of the "Worship Site of the White House" of Candomblé. Candomblé is a religion that arose in Brazil, in which many aspects of West-African Yorùbá culture are found. The "Worship Site of the White House" (Yorùbá: *Ilê Axé Iyá Nassô Oká*) in Salvador/Bahia is one of the oldest and most important centers of Candomblé. When a new priestess (Portuguese: *mãe-de-santo;* Yorùbá: *ialorixá*) was appointed, the worship site leader, Antônio Agnelo Pereira, notified the Archbishop about this and received the following answer:

Antonio Agnelo Pereira,
[I wish you] Peace!
I would like to thank you for communicating to me that Altamira Cecilia dos Santos, Oxum mi Tominwá [name in Yoruba], was chosen for the position of Ialorixá [Priestess] of Ilê Axé Iyá Nassô Oká [Name in Yoruba], of the 'White House' worship place. Thank you for your attention. God is the Eternal Father, as Jesus Christ, is our Divine Savior! May he reign in all hearts!

+Avelar, Cardeal B. Villa
Salvador March 24, 1985

Source: Arquivo da Sociedade Beneficente e Recreativa São Jorge do Engenho Velho, quoted in: O. Serra, *Águas do Rei* (Petrópolis, 1995), 256f. — *Further Reading:* R. Bastide, *The African Religions of Brazil* (Baltimore/London, 1978), pp. 191-201; A. Droogers, "Brazilian Minimal Religiosity," in: G. Banck et al. (eds.), *Social Change in Contemporary Brazil* (Amsterdam, 1988), pp. 165-176; L. Silverstein, "The Celebration of Our Lord of the Good End . . . in Bahia," in: D. Hess et al. (eds.), *The Brazilian Puzzle* (New York, 1995), pp. 134-151; R. Motta, "The Churchifying of Candomble: Priests . . . in Brazil," in: P. B. Clarke (ed.), *New Trends and Developments in African Religions* (Westport, Conn., 1998), pp. 45-57; P. B. Clarke, "Accounting for Recent Anti-syncretist Trends in Candomble-Catholic Relation," in: P. B. Clarke (ed.), ibid., 17-35; Mae M. St. de Azevedo-Santos, "A Call to the People of Orisha," in: D. Kortright (ed.), *African Creative Expressions of the Divine* (Washington, D.C., 1991), pp. 99-104; McManners, *Illustrated History,* pp. 453f.

315. An Ethnic Liturgy: The "Missa dos Quilombos" (1980)

After the Second Vatican Council, many liberation theologians found the Roman liturgy stereotypical and colonial, since it did not respond to the spiritual aspirations of the Afro-Indian/Latin American people. The result of this was the creation of many new liturgies based on Latin American music traditions (so-called ethnic liturgies). The *Missa dos Quilombos* by Milton Nascimento, Pedro Casaldáliga and Pedro Tierra reflects the history of the slaves and the current situation of blacks in Brazil. The Mass combines these in an act of inculturation with the liberating message of the gospel. A prayer addresses the tri-une God:

In name of God, may all People be made of tenderness and dust.
In name of the Father, may all flesh
Black and white, be made
Red in blood.
In name of the Son, Jesus our brother,
Who was born brown
Of the race of Abraham.
In name of the Holy Spirit,
Banner of song
Of the black carnivalesque
In name of the True God
Who loved us first
Without division.
In name of the Three
Who are only one God
Who was, is and will be.
In name of the People who await
In the Grace of Faith
For the voice of Xango [African god],
For the Quilombo [communities of runaway slaves] — the Passover
    that will set us free [. . .]

Source: M. Nascimento/P. Casaldáliga/P. Tierra, Missa dos Qilombos (LP: EMI-Odeon) (Rio de Janeiro, 1982); — *Further Reading:* W. D. Dinges, "Ritual Conflict as Social Conflict: Liturgical Reform in the Roman Catholic Church," in: *Sociological Analysis* 48 (1987), pp. 138-157; E. Hoornaert, Art. "Liturgie," in: idem (ed.), *Kleines Lexikon zur Theologie der Befreiung* (Düsseldorf, 1991), pp. 139-141; Dussel, *Church,* pp. 186f.

316. Debates Surrounding the 500-Year Celebration

There are many different tendencies to be observed in the debates on the occasion of the 500-year celebration of the discovery of America. Three of them are documented here. The liberation theologians (document a) distance themselves from the colonial mission-ary activity and discover Native Americans, Afro-Americans and women as special groups of the oppressed which should lead to new forms of liberation theology. The Na-tive Americans (document b) acquire a new self-consciousness and demand recognition of their territorial claims by the state and the church as well as respect for their cultures and religions. Finally, the Pope (document c), who was well aware that the conquest and evangelization of Latin America was a historical process with both light and dark sides, asks Native Americans and Afro-Americans to forgive everyone who did them wrong, gives them words of encouragement and promises them the solidarity and support of the Catholic Church.

a. A Letter to Third World Theologians (June 6, 1986)

We thank God for his work of salvation among the indigenous peoples, apart from the intervention of western Christians. We also salute the ways in which these indigenous and African American peoples have organized their faith and wisdom, and we consider it necessary to continue doing theology on that basis. The advances of the Theology of Liberation are beyond question, especially its rootedness in the struggles and hopes of the most westernized oppressed sectors. But we frankly see a need for us and for you to seriously orient our reflection toward the indigenous and African American peoples and toward women, whose struggle and wisdom are always present in Latin American history. These are priority tasks in our action and reflection.

b. Manifesto of the Indigenous Peoples (1986)

We the indigenous people, representing thirty nationalities in fifteen countries of Latin America, meeting on the occasion of the Second Ecumenical Consultation on Latin American Indigenous Pastoral Practice, in Quito, Ecuador, from June 30 to July 6, 1986, in view of the approaching celebrations of the 500th anniversary of the so-called discovery and the presumed first evangelization of Latin America . . . address the following demands:

1. To national states:

a) An end to integrationist and assimilationist policies and to the folkloric exploitation of our cultures.

b) Juridical recognition for our fundamental right of ownership of the territorial spaces that have always and by right belonged to us, in order to overcome the divisions caused by the artificial creation of national frontiers, ignoring the reality of the indigenous nations.

c) Recognition and respect for our right of communal ownership of the natural resources, surface and subsurface, pertaining to our territorial spaces. It is our fundamental demand that governments not sell these resources to national or international companies.

d) Respect for and recognition of our self-governed organizations and finally our own systems of government, a fundamental element of our self-determination.

e) To permit us to organize and implement our own educational system for the recovery and development of our cultural values, conducive to the affirmation of our identity.

2. To the churches:

a) An end to evangelization and pastoral practice allied to the dominant system, which is genocidal and ethnocidal toward the indigenous peoples and other oppressed sectors of the surrounding society.

b) To practice an authentic evangelization of accompaniment, dialogue and respect toward our struggles, beliefs and religious practices.

c) Unity among the churches in support of an ecumenical pastoral practice and against the penetration of divisive, culturally destructive religious sects and agencies.

c. Message of John Paul II (October 13, 1992)

From the message to the indigenous peoples:

The message that I send to you today on American soil in commemoration of five hundred years of the Gospel's presence among you, is intended as a call to hope and forgiveness. In the prayer that Jesus Christ taught us, we say: "Our father . . . and forgive us our trespasses, as we also forgive those who trespass against us." Jesus has "Words of eternal life" (John 6:68); he knows "what is in everyone" (John 2:25). In the name of Jesus Christ, as a pastor of the Church I beg you to forgive all who have been unjust toward you; to forgive all who during those five hundred years have caused you and your ancestors pain. . . . The Church which has accompanied you during those five hundred years will do everything in its power to ensure that the descendants of the ancient peoples of America will achieve their rightful place in society and in the ecclesial community.

From the message to African Americans:

Everyone knows well the injustice committed against those black populations of the African continent which were violently torn away from their lands, cultures and traditions and brought to America as slaves. . . . Therefore in this commemoration of the Quincentennial I exhort you to defend your identity, to be aware of your dignity and make it fruitful.

Source: (a) *Aporte de los pueblos indígenas de América Latina a la teología cristiana* (Quito, 1986), pp. 88-90; (b) ibid., pp. 85-87; (c) *Neue Evangelisierung, Förderung des Menschen, Christliche Kultur* (Bonn, 1992), pp. 192f, 195. — *Further Reading:* L. Accattoli (ed.), *When a Pope Asks Forgiveness: The Mea Culpa's of John Paul II* (New York, 1998); L. Boff, V. Elizondo, *1492-1992: The Voice of the Victims* (London/Philadelphia, 1990); *1492-1992: Commemorating 500 Years of Indigenous Resistance, A Community Reader* (Santa Cruz, Calif., 1992); P. Rottländer (ed.), *Blick zurück nach vorn* (Bonn, 1992); E. Kräutler, *500 Jahre Lateinamerika — kein Grund zum Feiern* (Wien, 1992); H. Waldenfels (ed.), *500 Jahre Lateinamerika* (Bonn, 1993); G. Müller-Fahrenholz (ed.), *Christentum in Lateinamerika* (Regensburg, 1992); W. Dreier et al. (eds.), *Entdeckung, Eroberung, Befreiung* (Würzburg, 1993); M. Sievernich, D. Spelthahn (eds.), *Fünfhundert Jahre Evangelisierung Lateinamerikas* (Frankfurt, 1995).

317. Ecumenism and Liberation (1989)

The base communities in Latin America played an important role not only on the local level, but also on the regional and denominational level by increasingly forming networks which transcended these boundaries. The seventh "Inter-ecclesial Meeting of Church Base Communities" took place from July 10-14, 1989, in Duque de Caxias, Brazil. In addition to the 1,800 delegates from various base communities in Brazil and other Latin American countries, almost two hundred representatives of twelve Protestant, Anglican and Orthodox churches also attended the meeting. The closing document, which was addressed to the "brothers and sisters of the people of God in Latin America," makes the ecumenical focus of the base communities clear.

At the end of the [second] day a big demonstration in the central plaza of Duque de Caxias took place. More than ten thousand people celebrated an ecumenical church service. [. . .]

Our base communities can feel in their own skin what the first Christians in their communities experienced of joy, togetherness and duty. [. . .]

The communities encourage people to join together and to carry out the task of liberation, which Jesus did for the poor of his time. As signs of their maturity, they request that the bishops commit themselves more strongly to a new society. [. . .] In [the base communities] the gifts of the Holy Spirit manifest themselves and make evident the multiplicity and the variety of the ministries that should promote people's lives and make solidarity tangible. So they emphasize the general priesthood of all believers, and they recognize the importance of the laity.

Gradually, also Indians and Blacks found their place, their identity and their task in the communities. Here, also women experience dignity and worth, [. . .]. The clearest sign of God's kingdom that has shaped our meeting the most persistently was the concern for Ecumenism. [. . .] Without Ecumenism, it is impossible to do the work that Jesus Christ has entrusted to us. When all that believe in him live in unity, this will be proof of the unity that shall prevail between men and women of all people on the earth according to God's will.

[. . .] Together the people in the base communities are engaged in the most ecumenical human task, in which one can only think: of working for Liberation and struggling for Liberation.

Source: "Brasilien . . . Brief des Siebten Interekklesialen Treffen Kirchlicher Basisgemeinden," in: *Weltkirche* 6 (1989), 194f. — *Further Reading:* T. C. Bruneau, "Brazil: The Catholic Church and Basic Christian Communities," in: D. Levine (ed.), *Religion and Political Conflict in Latin America* (London, 1986), pp. 106-123; A. Droogers, "Brazilian Minimal Religiosity," in: G. Banck et al. (eds.), *Social Change in Contemporary Brazil* (Amsterdam, 1988), pp. 165-176; G. Huizer, "'Power and Vital Force' in Popular Religion," in: A. Droogers et al. (eds.), *Popular Power in Latin American Religions* (Saarbrücken/Fort Lauderdale, 1991), pp. 276-312; J. Comblin, "Brazil: Base Communities in the Northeast," in: G. Cook (ed.), *New Face of the Church in Latin America* (Maryknoll, 1994), pp. 202-225; P. Richard, "Challenges to Liberation Theology in the Decade of the Nineties," in: G. Cook (ed.), ibid., pp. 245-258; D. Kirkpatrick (ed.), *Faith Born in the Struggle for Life* (Grand Rapids, 1988), pp. 265-324.

Acknowledgments

The editors and publisher gratefully acknowledge permission received to reprint the following material:

Document 2: Eberhard Schmitt, *Dokumente zur Geschichte der europäischen Expansion*. Reprinted by permission of Eberhard Schmitt.

Document 9: S. Neill, *A History of Christianity in India*. Reprinted by permission of Cambridge University Press.

Document 14: J. N. Schumacher, *Readings in Philippine Church History*. Reprinted by permission of the Loyola School of Theology.

Document 20: M. K. Kuriakose, *History of Christianity in India*. Reprinted by permission of the Society for Promoting Christian Knowledge.

Document 21: J. N. Schumacher, *Readings in Philippine Church History*. Reprinted by permission of the Loyola School of Theology.

Document 22: S. Neill, *A History of Christianity in India*. Reprinted by permission of Cambridge University Press.

Document 24: M. H. Reinstra, *Jesuit Letters from China 1583-1584*. Reprinted by permission of the University of Minnesota Press.

Document 25: M. K. Kuriakose, *History of Christianity in India*. Reprinted by permission of the Society for Promoting Christian Knowledge.

Document 28: Eberhard Schmitt, *Dokumente zur Geschichte der europäischen Expansion*. Reprinted by permission of Eberhard Schmitt.

Document 45: M. K. Kuriakose, *History of Christianity in India*. Reprinted by permission of the Society for Promoting Christian Knowledge.

Document 53: Notto Thelle, *Buddhism and Christianity in Japan*. Reprinted by permission of the University of Hawaii.

Document 56: O. Cary, *A History of Christianity in Japan*. Reprinted by permission.

Document 57: P. Tuck, *French Catholic Missionaries*. Reprinted by permission of Liverpool University Press.

Document 59: O. Cary, *A History of Christianity in Japan*. Reprinted by permission.

Document 73: M. K. Kuriakose, *History of Christianity in India*. Reprinted by permission of the Society for Promoting Christian Knowledge.

Document 78: A. Dohi et al., *Theologiegeschichte der Dritten Welt*. Reprinted by permission of Gütersloher Verlagshaus.

Document 84: Proceedings of the 18th General Assembly of the National Christian Council in Japan (Nov. 26-27, 1940). Reprinted by permission of Rev. Toshimasa Yamamoto.

Document 87: M. K. Kuriakose, *History of Christianity in India*. Reprinted by permission of the Society for Promoting Christian Knowledge.

Document 89: Nihon Kirisuto Kyodan (ed.), *Collection of Sources on the History of the Nihon Kirisuto* Kyodan (Jap.). Vol. III. Reprinted by permission.

Document 90: Evangelisches Missionswerk (ed.), *China und seine Christen*. Reprinted by permission of Evangelisches Missionswerk.

Document 95: Evangelisches Missionswerk (ed.), *China und seine Christen*. Reprinted by permission of Evangelisches Missionswerk.

Document 104: D. Johnston, *The Missing Dimension of Statecraft*. Reprinted by permission of Oxford University Press.

Document 106: Bong Rin Ro, *The Bible and Theology in Asian Contexts*. Reprinted by permission of the Asia Theological Association.

Document 109: E. A. Bufge, *The Queen of Sheba*. Reprinted by permission of Oxford University Press.

Document 110: S. Uhlig and G. Buehring, *Damian de Gois Schrift über Glauben und Sitten der Aethiopier*. Reprinted by permission of Harrassowitz Verlag.

Document 112: D. Buschiner and W. Spiewok (eds.), *Das große Abenteuer der Entdeckung der Welt im Mittelalter* (Greifswald, 1995). Reprinted by permission of Reineke Verlag.

Document 115: B. Davidson, *The African Past*. Reprinted by permission of Penguin Books.

Document 116: S. P. Freeman-Grenville, *The East African Coast*. Reprinted by permission of Clarendon Press.

Document 121: Eberhard Schmitt, *Dokumente zur Geschichte der europäischen Expansion*. Reprinted by permission of Eberhard Schmitt.

Document 122: B. Davidson, *The African Past*. Reprinted by permission of Penguin Books.

Document 123: S. Uhlig/G. Buehring, *Damian de Gois Schrift über Glauben und Sitten der Aethiopier.* Reprinted by permission of Harrassowitz Verlag.

Document 125: Hiob Ludolf, *Commentarius ad suam Historiam Aethiopicam,* translated by E. Ullendorff, "The Confessio Fidei of King Claudius of Ethiopia," *Journal of Semitic Studies* 32/1 (1987), pp. 159-176. Reprinted by permission of the *Journal of Semitic Studies.*

Document 130: Reprinted by permission of Waveland Press, Inc., from P. Curtin, *Africa Remembered: Narratives by West Africans from the Era of the Slave Trade,* Waveland Press, Inc., 1967 (reissued 1997). All rights reserved.

Document 140: Adam Jones, *Sources for West African History.* Reprinted by permission of Steiner, Wiesbaden.

Document 141: D. Kpobi, *Mission in Chains.* Reprinted by permission of Uitgeverij Boekencentrum.

Document 143: M. Craton, *Slavery, Abolition and Emancipation.* Reprinted by permission of Pearson Education.

Document 144: M. Craton, *Slavery, Abolition and Emancipation.* Reprinted by permission of Pearson Education.

Document 148: Lamin Sanneh, *Abolitionists Abroad: American Blacks and the Making of Modern West Africa.* Reprinted by permission of the author.

Document 150: Reprinted by permission of Waveland Press, Inc., from P. Curtin, *Africa Remembered: Narratives by West Africans from the Era of the Slave Trade,* Waveland Press, Inc., 1967 (reissued 1997). All rights reserved.

Document 164: *Mind of Buganda: Documents of the Modern History of an African Kingdom,* by D. A. Low, 1971 D. A. Low. Published by the University of California Press. Reprinted by permission.

Document 167: Werner Raupp, *Mission in Quellentexten.* Reprinted by permission of Erlanger Verlag für Mission und Oekumene.

Document 168a: Werner Raupp, *Mission in Quellentexten.* Reprinted by permission of Erlanger Verlag für Mission und Oekumene.

Document 168b: H. W. Debrunner, *Schweizer im kolonialen Afrika* (Basel, 1991). Reprinted by permission of the Basler Afrika Bibliographien.

Document 172: Irving Hexham and S. G. Oosthuizen, *The Story of Isaiah Shembe,* Volume 3. Reprinted by permission of Edwin Mellen Press.

Document 175: J. Iliffe, *A Modern History of Tanganyika.* Reprinted by permission of Cambridge University Press.

Document 197: E. Utuk, *Visions of Authenticity.* Reprinted by permission of the All Africa Council of Churches.

Document 200: E. Utuk, *Visions of Authenticity.* Reprinted by permission of the All Africa Council of Churches.

Document 206: Lamin Sanneh, "Pluralism and Christian Commitment," *Theology Today* 45/1 (April 1988). Reprinted by permission of the author.

Document 207: K. Dickson, *Theology in Africa*. Reprinted by permission of Orbis Books.

Document 209: Steve Biko, "Black Consciousness and the Quest for a True Humanity," in *The Challenge of Black Theology in South Africa*, ed. Basil Moore (Atlanta: John Knox, 1973). Reprinted by permission of Hurst Publishers.

Document 210: Manas Buthelezi, "An African Theology or a Black Theology," in *The Challenge of Black Theology in South Africa*, ed. Basil Moore (Atlanta: John Knox, 1973). Reprinted by permission of Hurst Publishers.

Document 213a, d: Charles Villa-Vicencio, *Between Christ and Caesar: Classic and Contemporary Texts on Church and State* (Cape Town: David Philip, 1986). Reprinted by permission of the author.

Document 213b: John W. De Gruchy and Charles Villa-Vicencio, *Apartheid Is a Heresy* (Cape Town: David Philip, 1983). Reprinted by permission of the authors.

Document 247: Chilam Balam, "Eleven Ahau," Verses 1645-1694, *Heaven born Merida and Its Destiny: The Book of Chilam Balam of Chumayel*. Reprinted by permission of the University of Texas Press.

Document 249: Christopher Wentworth Dilke, *Letter to a King: A Picture-History of the Inca Civilisation by Huamán Poma (Don Felipe Huamán Poma de Ayala* (London, 1978). Reprinted by permission of HarperCollins-UK and Taylor & Francis.

Document 258: C. G. A. Oldendoorp, *Geschichte der Mission der evangelischen Brüder auf den caraibischen Inseln st. Thomas, S. Croix and S. Jan*. Reprinted by permission of Georg Olms Verlag.

Document 259: R. Konetzke, *Lateinamerika seit 1492*. Reprinted by permission of Ernst Klett Verlag.

Document 276: D. A. Reily, *História documental do Protestantismo no Brasil* (São Paulo). Reprinted by permission.

Document 279: D. A. Reily, *História documental do Protestantismo no Brasil* (São Paulo). Reprinted by permission.

Document 312: K. Braungart, *Heiliger Geist und politische Herrschaft bei den Neopfingstlern in Honduras* (Frankfurt a. M., 1995). Reprinted by permission of Vervuert Verlagsgesellschaft.

Index

(Number and letter refer to the **documents**, not to the pages.)

II. Persons/Groups of People